On Track

Englisch für Gymnasien

5

von:
Friedrich Frenzel
Jon Hird
Claudia Maria Hugo
Heather Jones
Marc Proulx
Patricia Wedler
Story von Marcus Sedgwick mit
 Illustrationen von Pete Williamson
Graphic novel von Marcus Sedgwick
 mit Illustrationen von Steve
 Buccellato
herausgegeben von:
Helga Holtkamp

Unter Mitarbeit von: Stacy Bentz, Udo Diekmann, Christine House

Beratung durch: Margot Adami (Paderborn), Alexa Bradbury (Paderborn), Charlott Falkenhagen (Jena), Ulrike Handke (Berlin), Carolin Ihle (Stuttgart), Janina Klösters (Essen), Jürgen Kurtz (Dortmund), Juliane Lobischer (Berlin), Martina Stange (Bielefeld)

Illustrationen: Karen Donnelly, Pete Williamson (Story)
Karten: Franz-Josef Domke, Hannover

westermann GRUPPE

© 2022 Westermann Bildungsmedien Verlag GmbH, Georg-Westermann-Allee 66, 38104 Braunschweig
www.westermann.de

Das Werk und seine Teile sind urheberrechtlich geschützt. Jede Nutzung in anderen als den gesetzlich zugelassenen bzw. vertraglich zugestandenen Fällen bedarf der vorherigen schriftlichen Einwilligung des Verlages.
Nähere Informationen zur vertraglich gestatteten Anzahl von Kopien finden Sie auf www.schulbuchkopie.de.

Für Verweise (Links) auf Internet-Adressen gilt folgender Haftungshinweis: Trotz sorgfältiger inhaltlicher Kontrolle wird die Haftung für die Inhalte der externen Seiten ausgeschlossen. Für den Inhalt dieser externen Seiten sind ausschließlich deren Betreiber verantwortlich. Sollten Sie daher auf kostenpflichtige, illegale oder anstößige Inhalte treffen, so bedauern wir dies ausdrücklich und bitten Sie, uns umgehend per E-Mail davon in Kenntnis zu setzen, damit beim Nachdruck der Verweis gelöscht wird.

Druck A[1] / Jahr 2022
Alle Drucke der Serie A sind im Unterricht parallel verwendbar.

Umschlaggestaltung: Detlef Möller, Paderborn
Cover vorne: © Wim Wiskerke/Alamy Stock Photo. Sydney Opera House with Sydney Harbor Bridge
Cover hinten: © Andrew Michael/Alamy Stock Photo. Surf school on Main beach, Byron Bay, NSW, Australia
Druck und Bindung: Westermann Druck GmbH, Georg-Westermann-Allee 66, 38104 Braunschweig

ISBN 978-3-14-**040325**-2

How to use this book

On Track 5 starts with a *Welcome* double-page spread. Then there are three regular workshops and one extra workshop. Every regular workshop has the same three parts. Parts one and two teach you new things, and part three helps you practise what you've learned. The activities and exercises have numbers and letters. Sometimes they have symbols, too.

Here is an explanation of the symbols:

Symbols in *On Track 5*

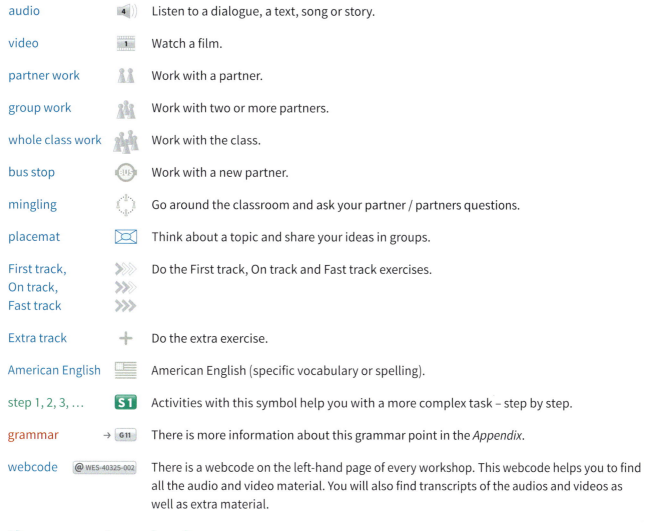

audio		Listen to a dialogue, a text, song or story.
video		Watch a film.
partner work		Work with a partner.
group work		Work with two or more partners.
whole class work		Work with the class.
bus stop		Work with a new partner.
mingling		Go around the classroom and ask your partner / partners questions.
placemat		Think about a topic and share your ideas in groups.
First track, On track, Fast track		Do the First track, On track and Fast track exercises.
Extra track		Do the extra exercise.
American English		American English (specific vocabulary or spelling).
step 1, 2, 3, …		Activities with this symbol help you with a more complex task – step by step.
grammar		There is more information about this grammar point in the *Appendix*.
webcode		There is a webcode on the left-hand page of every workshop. This webcode helps you to find all the audio and video material. You will also find transcripts of the audios and videos as well as extra material.

How to use the webcodes

A webcode is like a small website. All the *On Track* audio and video material that you need for class or homework is here: www.westermann.de/webcodes. There is also extra material. You can listen and watch online or download everything. Type in the code for the workshops (**WES-40325-001**) without the @ and click "Aufrufen" and you will find the page for *Workshop 1*. There are webcodes in your workbook, too.

These are the webcodes in *On Track 5*:

Welcome: WES-40325-000   Workshop 2: WES-40325-002   Workshop 4: WES-40325-004
Workshop 1: WES-40325-001   Workshop 3: WES-40325-003

Contents

Page	Workshop and topic	Communication
10	**Welcome to *On Track 5* English around the world**	
12	**Workshop 1 Aussies and Kiwis**	

PART 1

14	**Jason's choice**	Read and listen to a text.
	Talking about conflicts and decisions	Do research.
16	**Practice: Impressions of Australia**	Guess the meaning of unknown words.
18	**A new life Down Under**	Read, understand and make notes on historical information.
	Talking about Australian history	
20	**Practice: First Nations**	Show your understanding of an audio text and video.
		Interpret a song.
22	**Method coach: Understand new words and phrases**	
23	**Workshop task: Understand texts on a new topic**	

PART 2

24	**Discovering Australia**	Read and understand an informative text.
	Talking about Australian heritage	List advantages and disadvantages.
26	**Practice: Climate reality**	Write a short blogpost and an article.
		Give a presentation.
28	**A New Zealand visit**	Describe pictures.
	Talking about New Zealand	Write a comment.
30	**Practice: Land of the Long White Cloud**	Plan a trip.
		Do research.
		Listen to an interview.
		Read a text from a website.
		Write a blogpost.
32	**Method coach: Prepare to write an informative text**	
33	**Workshop task: Write an informative text**	

PART 3

34	**Mediation**	Bernhard Holtermann: Ein Leben mit vielen Kapiteln
36	**First track** (language help)	
38	**Reading**	Midnight Oil, *First Nation*; Aaradhna, *Brown Girl*
40	**My review** (progress check)	
43	**My practice pages** (individual practice)	
46	**Cudweed's crush: ONE** (Reading for fun)	

| 50 | **Workshop 2 Routes to your future** | |

PART 1

52	**New Directions**	Discuss future plans.
	Talking about what to do after school	Write a short text.
54	**Practice: A work opportunity**	Listen to a podcast.
		Discuss a topic with a partner.
		Give feedback.

Contents

Vocabulary	Grammar	Skills focus	
		Video 1: English – a global language	
		Video 2: Facts about Australia	
making decisions, conflicts, Australia	Present perfect and present perfect progressive (revision) (G 1) Indefinite article after *such, quite, half* (G 2)	Video 3: Slip, Slop, Slap, Seek, Slide Reading: Melbourne is the place!	
historic events, important historic figures and documents	Past perfect and past perfect progressive (revision) (G 3)	Viewing: Video 4: Sorry Day Video 5: Song	
sights, tourism, climate change	Passive (G 4 – G 8)	Speaking: Giving a presentation	
trips, Maori culture	Reported speech in statements, questions, requests and orders (revision) (G 9) Changes to adverbs of time and place in reported speech (G 10)	Writing: A blog	
		Video 6 – 8: At a careers fair	
jobs, work, career, plans	Gerunds and infinitives (revision) (G 11) Expressing the future (revision) (G 12) Future progressive (G 13)	Speaking: This is me	

five 5

Page	Workshop and topic	Communication
	PART 1	
56	**Applying for a job**	Read and understand a text from a website.
	Talking about applications and interviews	Give advice and feedback.
58	**Practice: Presenting your best self**	Write a CV and a cover letter.
60	**Method coach: Identify communication strategies**	
61	**Workshop task: Communicate effectively in an interview**	
	PART 2	
62	**The changing world of work**	Describe photos.
	Talking about the world of jobs	Summarize an online text.
64	**Practice: The wealth divide**	Write a short text.
		Listen to an interview.
		Give a presentation.
		Write a short article.
66	**An internship abroad**	Summarize a review.
	Talking about working abroad	Watch a video.
68	**Practice: Closing the gender gap**	Read an argumentative article.
		Edit a text.
		Present a business idea.
70	**Method coach: Practise workplace communication**	
71	**Workshop task: Role-play an induction**	
	PART 3	
72	**Mediation**	Work camps
74	**First track** (language help)	
76	**Reading**	Ben Ockrent, *Hacktivists*
78	**My review** (progress check)	
81	**My practice pages** (individual practice)	
84	**Cudweed's crush: TWO** (Reading for fun)	

88 Workshop 3   Who am I? Who are we?

PART 1

90	**We are family**	Read and understand an article.
	Talking about family life	Talk about changes in family life.
92	**Practice: The new normal**	Discuss cultural heritage.
		Identify different gender roles.
		Watch a video.
		Complete a summary.
94	**True friends**	Read and understand an article.
	Talking about friendship and love	Identify different types of behaviour.
96	**Practice: Is it love?**	Read an online article.
		Watch a video.
		Write a comment.
98	**Method coach: Understanding diagrams (1)**	
99	**Workshop task: Describing diagrams (1)**	

Contents

Vocabulary	Grammar	Skills focus
applications, interview, CV, work placement	Modal verbs (revision) (G 14) Modal substitutes (G 15)	Writing: A CV and a cover letter
		Video 9: Amir practises a job interview Video 10: Amir has a job interview
working life, social issues, charity	*make*, *let*, *allow* (G 16) *have something done* (G 17) *used to* / *didn't use to* / *would* (G 18)	Listening: Volunteer stories
internship, working abroad, entrepreneurship, gender and work	Participle constructions (G 19)	Video 11: Travelling the world Reading: An argumentative article
families, gender, teenage life	Defining and non-defining relative clauses (revision) (G 20) Participle constructions replacing relative clauses (G 21) *be used to* / *get used to* + noun / *-ing* (G 22)	Speaking: Giving advice Video 12: My genderation
teenage problems, love, friendship, relationships	Emphatic *do* / *does* / *did* (G 23) Emphatic pronouns with *-self* / *-selves* (G 24)	Viewing: Video 13: Love has no labels

seven 7

Page	Workshop and topic	Communication
100	**Youth crime and the law**
Talking about teenage problems	Read a text about legal rights.
Do a role-play.
102	**Practice: Healthy living?**	Describe photos.
Skim and summarize a text.
Write a summary.
Write a blogpost.
Present survey results.
104	**Advertising and Generation Z**
Talking about blogging and advertising	Read and understand a blogpost.
Do a mini-survey / questionnaire.
106	**Practice: Digital communication**	Listen to a podcast.
Discuss the meaning of abbreviations.
Watch a video of an advertisement.
Write a summary.
Do research and give a talk.
108	Method coach: Understanding diagrams (2)	
109	Workshop task: Describing diagrams (2)	
110	**Mediation**	Cybermobbing an der Schule /
Cyberbullying is a real problem in today's society
112	**First track** (language help)	
114	**Reading**	Karen McManus, *One of us is lying*
116	**My review** (progress check)	
119	**My practice pages** (individual practice)	
122	**Cudweed's crush: THREE** (Reading for fun)	

PART 2

PART 3

Page	Topic
126	**Workshop 4 Graphic novel –** *A Glimpse of the Death Saint*
126	Before and while-reading tasks
128	The novel
138	After-reading tasks
140	**Extra pages**
140	Feedback and peer editing
142	Skills and stragies
145	Literary analysis
146	Poetry

148	**Appendix**		
148	Grammatical terms	274	Dictionary: German – English
150	Grammar	310	Dictionary: Names
172	Irregular verbs	312	Acknowledgements
174	Vocabulary	314	Medienbildung
228	Dictionary: English – German	315	Classroom phrases

Vocabulary	Grammar	Skills focus
the law, crime, health, diet food	*If*-sentences type 2 and 3 (revision) (G 25) *If*-sentences mixed conditionals (G 26)	Writing: Write a summary
advertising, online / internet language, cyberbullying	Using *It* … and *What* … for emphasis (G 27) Using inversion to make a text more formal (G 28)	Reading: Choosing sides Video 14: A powerful message

Welcome to *On Track 5*
English around the world

1 English is spoken around the world, but where exactly? The flags below show some of the many countries where English plays an important role. Can you name them? Is it a first language, an official or a second language in these countries?

CULTURE CORNER

A first language is your native language – the one you learn from birth. A second language is one you learn to speak to communicate with native speakers of that language. An official language is used by a country's or state's government for official purposes.

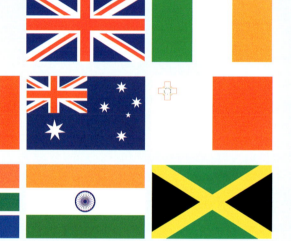

2 **a** English is a first language in Canada and Australia. Read and listen to what these young Canadians and Australians say about the language or languages they speak. Compare and discuss the similarities and differences.

b What's your first language? Do you speak any other languages? If so, which ones? How useful do you think it is to speak more than one language? Explain your answer.

My first language is French. In Quebec we have our own way of speaking it. I use English a lot, but my best friends are French Canadian. It's cool having two languages.

Camille

I speak Mandarin at home. It's good to have that connection with my roots. I feel totally Australian, though. English is what I speak with my friends – I even dream in English.

Amy

We live on a First Nations reserve, but speak English at home. I know some Squamish, our native language. My Granny is one of the last who can speak it. It's sad, but that's how it is in Canada.

Louis

 3 Why are you learning English? Why is it so important? Discuss these questions and create a flyer. Have a look at the example:

Here are five BIG reasons why learning English can improve your life.
- *It's the official language of 53 countries.*
- *It's one of the most widely spoken languages in the world.*
- *…*

 4 **a VIDEO TRACK:** Watch this video. What reasons for learning English does it mention that you hadn't thought of?

I never say I'm Greek Australian – only when asked about my family background. I've only ever really spoken English. When we went to Greece, I was glad that a lot of people there speak English.

Nick

 b Talk about everyday situations in your life in which you find it helpful to understand English. Do you think you will use it more in your own future work or studies? If so, how?

I wish I knew my people's language better. English is almost all I know. It's a big part of my Australian identity. But it's also part of the culture that tried to destroy us Aboriginals. That makes me sad.

Katrina

I don't think about language much. My parents learned English at school, so they were OK when they came to Canada. They speak Hindi on the phone sometimes. My favourite language is music!

Sanjay

Workshop 1
Aussies and Kiwis

@ WES-40325-001

 Do this mini quiz to see how much you already know about Australia.

1. Who were the first Australians?
   A Maoris
   B Aboriginal people and Torres Strait Islanders
   C Indians

The State Barrier Fence (the rabbit proof fence), Western Australia

Aboriginal culture show at Tjapukai Cultural Centre, Queensland

2. Who gave Australia its name?
   A The Aboriginal people
   B The British
   C The Dutch

3. What is Australia's nickname? And do you know why it is called this?
   A Down Under
   B Down South
   C Deep Down

4. What is Australia?
   A A continent
   B A country
   C A continent, a country and an island

Kakadu National Park, Northern Territory

5. How big is Australia?
   A 12 times bigger than Germany
   B 16 times bigger than Germany
   C 22 times bigger than Germany

6. The population of Germany is about 80 million and of Australia …
   A about 26 million.
   B about 50 million.
   C about 75 million.

7. There are more kangaroos than people in Australia.
   A True
   B False

12 twelve

Aboriginal rock painting of the Rainbow Serpent, Kakadu National Park

Christmas on Bondi Beach, Sydney, New South Wales

8 What is the capital of Australia?
 A Sydney
 B Melbourne
 C Canberra

9 The interior of Australia is mainly desert and bush. What is its name?
 A The Territory
 B The Outback
 C The Billabong

10 The flight time from Brisbane to Christchurch, New Zealand, is …
 A about 4 hours.
 B about 6 hours.
 C about 10 hours.

2 **VIDEO TRACK:** Watch the video to check your answers. You will find out more facts about this amazing country, so watch the video again and then make three questions for another pair.

YOUR TRACK

After this workshop you will be able to:
- use persuasive language.
- talk about Australia then and now.
- discuss climate change in Australia.
- describe your travel experiences in a blog.
- research and write a text about New Zealand. (Workshop task)

Auckland is New Zealand's biggest city.

thirteen 13

@ WES-40325-001

Jason's choice

1 The big news

a Jason Turner is a student at Bayview High School in Melbourne. He plays on the school rugby team with his friend Ricky Bates. Read the first two parts of the story and do the tasks.

1 Explain how the rugby team feels and why.
2 Describe the choice that Jason faces.

b Say whether these statements are true or false. Correct the false statements.

1 The boys are both excited by the news.
2 After rugby practice, Jasons's feelings change.
3 Jason's mum wants to pay for the trip.
4 Jason's dad understands Jason's dilemma.

2 Sharing with a friend

a Before you listen to the third part, look at the heading and picture. Speculate what will happen.

b Listen and do the tasks.

1 Describe what happens.
2 Compare and contrast how Jason and Ricky communicate with Eleni.
3 Explain which adjectives in the box best describe Eleni's reaction to the news.

> shocked ■ disappointed ■ excited ■
> angry ■ happy ■ supportive

[1] In the late afternoon sun the players were breathing hard and sweating as they gathered around Coach Hansen.
'Nice workout, guys,' he said. 'Now we've got half an hour for planning and organization. First, I've got some big news.'
Jason and Ricky exchanged puzzled looks.
'Papanui High School in Christchurch has invited us to play in their rugby tournament at the end of the school term,' he announced. 'Who wants to go to New Zealand?'
There was silence, then the whole team jumped and cheered. The noise echoed across the playing field and around the school campus.
'We're going to play against the Kiwis!' Jason said, giving Ricky a high five.
'Yeah, and we're going to *beat* them!' Ricky shouted.
When the coach announced the tournament dates, Jason's smile slowly disappeared. As they walked from the field, the others talked and laughed while Jason was quiet.

3 Good friends

a Look at these sentences:

*You boys **have had** such a good season so far.
Yeah, we**'ve been playing** really well.*

Why is the present perfect progressive used in the second sentence but not in the first?

> • We usually use the present perfect with state verbs like *have*, *know* or *want*.
> *The coach **has** always **wanted** to take the team to New Zealand.*
> • We use the present perfect progressive with action verbs like *go*, *play*, *run* or *try*.
> *He's **been trying** to organize a trip like this for a while.*

Words and phrases

godmother	a person who promises to be responsible for a child
mate	friend
supportive	giving help to sb.

At dinner Jason shared the news with his parents.
'That's brilliant, Jason!' his dad said. 'You boys have had such a good season so far. I'm not surprised.'
'Yeah, we've been playing really well,' Jason agreed.
5 'Christchurch, New Zealand? That's quite a trip,' his mum said. 'Who's going to pay for it?'
'The school sports fund will pay for the plane tickets,' Jason said. 'And we'll be able to stay with families of students from Papanui High School.'
10 'You don't look very enthusiastic,' his dad said. 'Is there a problem?'
Jason sighed. 'It's the same weekend when Nick's parents invited me to go to Sydney with them. It's Nick's and Eleni's sixteenth birthday.'
15 'Eleni?' his dad said.
'Nick's twin sister,' Jason's mum explained.
'Ah, yes. Jason, I know Nick is your mate, but the team need you,' his dad said.
'I think Jason needs to decide for himself what's more
20 important,' his mum said. Jason looked at his plate. 'But first you should eat up your dinner,' she added.

b Complete with the present perfect or the present perfect progressive. Sometimes both are possible.

1 Jason _____ (*know*) Ricky since year 2.
2 They _____ (*play*) rugby since they were 10.
3 Jason and Nick Kourakis _____ (*be*) friends for a long time, too.
4 Jason _____ (*work*) part-time at the Kourakis' Greek deli for the past year.

▶▶▶ page 36

CULTURE CORNER

A sporting nation
Sport is a big part of Australia's national identity. Australian athletes do well in international competitions in many sports including swimming, tennis, cricket, rugby, basketball, netball and football (or soccer). One of Australia's biggest and fastest-growing professional sports is its own Australian rules football. Team sports are extremely popular with young people. Many schools have teams that are active in inter-school competitions, and a lot of people play sports in local clubs.

Two of the most important sports in Australia: netball and cricket

Workshop 1

→ Workbook, pages 8/9

4 Playing to win

a Jason's mum says: *That's **quite a** trip*. Find examples in the story with *such* and *half*.

b These quotes are from an article about Jason's rugby team. Complete them with the word in brackets and *a* or *an*.

1 The boys' team are lucky to have | great coach. *(such)*
2 The girls' team have also had | good season. *(quite)*
3 The coach tells his players to drink | litre of water during practice. *(half)*
4 It's | great idea to go to New Zealand, but of course it will be | expensive trip. *(such, quite)*

5 So far and so close

a Jason gets a call that changes everything. Listen and complete the sentences.

1 Auntie Koula is ...
2 Eleni and Nick have to put off their birthday celebrations because ...
3 Jason and Eleni agree to ...

b Listen again and do the tasks.

1 Explain what the rugby team have been getting ready for.
2 Outline why Ricky is so excited about the tournament.
3 Describe what Jason has been looking forward to.
4 Explain what Eleni's news mean for Jason.

6 YOUR TURN: A sporting expert

a Look at the sports in the 'Culture corner'. Choose a sport and do some research. Then prepare a two-minute talk.

b Find a partner with another sport. Give your talks and ask each other questions.

Grammar and structures

Present perfect and present perfect progressive (revision) → G1
Eleni **hasn't known** about Aunt Koula's illness for very long.
They **have been playing** rugby since they were ten.

Indefinite article after *such, quite, half* → G2
It was **such a** shock.

Practice: Impressions of Australia

1 **GET STARTED!** The word 'selfie' originates from Australia. They love to add 'ie' or 'y' to words to make them informal. Guess what these words mean.

> Aussie ▪ brekkie ▪ footy ▪ lappy ▪ prezzie

2 **VIDEO TRACK: Slip, slop, slap, seek, slide.** Watch the video and find another word like this.

3 **No worries!**

a Here are some more examples of Australian English. Guess or find out what they mean.

> ace ▪ arvo ▪ barbie ▪ mozzie ▪ roo ▪ sickie ▪ swimmers ▪ ta ▪ tucker

b Use some of the words in **3a** to write a dialogue. Then share your dialogue in class.

4 **Ace!** Complete part of an interview with the present perfect or present perfect progressive.

Q. Coach Hansen, you **1** (*coach*) the boys' rugby team for eight years. What's good about the job and what **2** (*change*)?
A. I **3** (*always have*) the full support of the school. The parents **4** (*give*) me a lot of support, too. The inter-school competition in Melbourne **5** (*get*) better and better, so that **6** (*be*) a positive change.
Q. Why do you think the boys' team **7** (*be*) so successful this year?
A. We've got an ace team with players like Ricky Bates and Jason Turner, who **8** (*play*) rugby for over five years. Also, we **9** (*try out*) different game plans and I think we **10** (*find out*) what works.

5 **School of the air**

a Ricky is listening to an interview with Conny, a teenager from a remote area of New South Wales. Look at the pictures at the bottom of the page and speculate about her school life.

b Now listen and compare. Complete the sentences with the correct answers.

1 Conny doesn't go to a normal school because …
2 After breakfast, Conny turns on the computer and waits for …
3 After her daily lesson, Conny …
4 Sometimes she gets help from …
5 All the learning materials are paid for by …
6 Twice a year Conny goes to a …
7 Mini-school lasts … and deals with …

6 **Quite a challenge**

a Ricky talks to his dad, who comes from the same area as Conny. Rewrite their conversation using the words in brackets.

R. Is it really a long way to the next town? (1) (*such*)
D. Yes. When I was a kid, it took us a day to get there from our cattle station. (2) (*half*)
R. Wow! But School of the Air must be a hard way to learn. (3) (*such*)
D. Not really. When I look back, I had an easy childhood. (4) (*quite*)
R. But it must be a challenge with no teacher to explain things. (5) (*quite*)
D. It was, but just think: it takes you an hour to get to school. My desk was just a metre from my bed! (6) (*half, half*)

b In groups, discuss Ricky's last comment and your experience with online learning. What are the advantages and disadvantages?

A
B
C
D

Workshop 1

→ Workbook, pages 10 – 12

7 WORDPOWER: Phrasal verbs. Check out these phrasal verbs. Use them in the correct form to complete the text below.

> clean up ■ come out ■ go ahead ■
> look at ■ set down ■ sit down ■
> turn on ■ walk in

Jason was ▢1 at the deli when Ricky ▢2 . 'I wanted to see what a Greek deli is like,' he said. Mr Kourakis ▢3 of the kitchen. '▢4 ,' he said to Ricky, pointing to a chair. He ▢5 the stereo and played some Bouzouki music. Then he ▢6 a plate in front of Ricky with Baklava on it. First Ricky ▢7 it but didn't touch it. '▢8 , try it!' Mr Kourakis said.
Finally Ricky tried a piece. He smiled. 'Welcome to Greece!' Mr Kourakis said.

 page 36

8 READING FOCUS: Melbourne is the place! Read an article in the online magazine *Exchange International*. Then do the tasks.

1 Decide who the article is written for and what the writer's aim is. Give examples of language she uses to achieve this aim. Include the line numbers.

2 Look at the TIP box. Find and discuss examples of these techniques in the article.

> **TIP**
>
> **Useful techniques to persuade readers**
> - **Anecdotes** (short, personal stories) have an emotional effect.
> - **Comparisons** show that you are balanced and honest.
> - **Strongly positive or negative words** make the reader feel the same.
> - **Personal pronouns** like 'I', 'you' or 'we' speak directly to the individual.
> - **Direct questions** get the reader's interest.

Melbourne is the place!
By Emily Chan

Three months ago, I applied for a student exchange in Australia. My agency matched me with a host family in Melbourne. I didn't know a lot about the place. People compared it with that other big city, Sydney. They said Melbourne wasn't as warm and sunny, not as scenic, and
5 everybody there was crazy about Australian rules football. I arrived here wondering if I had made the right decision.
Now, three months later, I know I did because I've fallen in love with this city. My host family and my school have both been great. I've also made some good friends. But there are
10 heaps of other reasons to love Melbourne, too.
The narrow 'laneways' in the city centre are a good place to start. Do you like cool cafés, amazing street art and buskers playing great music? If so, then you'll enjoy Centre Place and Hosier Lane. What about colourful outdoor markets? I
15 love Queen Victoria Market – it's an awesome place for shopping, yummy street food and just hanging out. Getting around in the city centre is really easy, too: you can ride the trams for free, or do what lots of people do – cycle! Cycling is my favourite way of exploring the city's back streets and hitting the beach at St Kilda. The list of cool and cheap things that you can do here goes on and on.
20 Oh, and Australian rules football? It's totally exciting!
Sydney will always be a lovely place, but Melbourne has won my heart. Come check it out and this awesome city will win your heart, too.

A new life Down Under

1 History of modern Australia

a How much do you know about modern Australia and its history? True or false?

1. The first settlers in Australia were the British.
2. The Australian government has always welcomed immigrants from around the world.
3. Modern Australia is ethnically very diverse.

b Skim the text to check your answers.

2 Reading between the lines. Read the text again carefully and discuss the questions.

1. What can you guess about the way of life of Aboriginal peoples before the colonists arrived?
2. Why do you think the £10 ticket was so popular with British people in 1945?
3. What do you think made the Australian government end the White Australia policy?
4. What different reasons do you think draw immigrants to Australia today?

A new life Down Under

1787 The First Fleet
On 26 January 1788 eleven British ships with about 1000 people sailed into Port Jackson, today's Sydney Harbour. Most on board were prisoners about to start life in a penal colony. Up to 1782, Britain had been sending its
5 convicts to America. But, after the War of Independence, America refused to take any more, so convicts were sent to New South Wales. Other explorers had already discovered the new land, but this became the first European settlement in Australia.
These first settlers thought no one owned the land because they saw no
10 buildings or roads, crops or farm animals as in England. So the British government claimed the land for themselves. They ignored the rights of the Aboriginal people who had been living there for at least 60,000 years before they arrived.

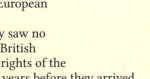

1850 Gold Rush
When gold was discovered in New South Wales in 1850, thousands of
15 immigrants arrived, hoping to make their fortunes. By the end of the 19th century, Australia had become the world's largest gold producer. The immigrants brought new skills and professions and helped to change the convict colonies into more modern cities.

1901 White Australia
20 The arrival of so many non-European immigrants had made the British angry. They believed the immigrants threatened their jobs and Australia's British culture. In 1901, the six colonies of Australia united to form a Federation. The new government passed a law to make non-white immigration more difficult.

1945 Ten pound ticket to a new life
25 World War 2 had led to a shortage of workers in Australia. The government wanted more white Britons to immigrate, so they offered cheap travel – adults only had to pay £10 for the fare and were promised a better life with job opportunities. By the end of the first year alone, 400,000 Britons had applied to go.

Words and phrases

to **claim** sth. (for yourself)	to say sth. is yours
convict	a person who has been found guilty of a crime
federation	a country consisting of a group of individual states
penal	connected with or used for punishment, especially by law
to **threaten**	to be likely to harm or destroy sth.

1966 – 1970s Becoming Australians
In 1966, the Australian government ended the White Australia policy. They encouraged skilled non-British migrants to immigrate. By the 1970s, Australia had changed enormously.

Modern times
Today Australia is one of the world's most ethnically diverse nations. Nearly a quarter of residents were born in other countries. The majority now come from China, India, Africa, the Philippines and the Middle East. However, Australia is still the number one destination for British migrants. Today's friendly society and outdoor lifestyle are very different from the harsh reality that the first migrants experienced.

3 Before and after

a Read the box and look at these sentences. Then find more examples in the text.

*Other explorers **had already discovered** the new land **by the time** the British **arrived**. Aboriginal people **had been living** in Australia for years **before** the Europeans **arrived**.*

- We use the past perfect to show one action happened before another in the past, often with time expressions, e.g. *by (date), when, already*.
- We use the past perfect progressive (often with *for*) to focus on the length of an earlier action.

b Based on information from the text, why …

1 was the first European settlement in Australia a penal colony?
   Before America became independent, …
2 did the convict colonies change and become modern cities?
   During the Gold Rush, …
3 did the government introduce the Immigration Restriction Act?
   The British population …
4 did the Australian government encourage more immigrants to come in 1945?
   World War 2 …
5 did so many British people emigrate to Australia after World War 2?
   The Australian government …

▶▶ page 36

4 A life-changing decision

a The Smith family from England have booked a holiday home next to the Turners, who've invited them to a barbecue. Listen to the first part of the story and do these tasks.

1 Explain the decision the Smiths have to make and what they have to think about.
2 Describe how Keira and Fred Smith feel and say why. Summarize their key reasons.

b What do we learn about Jason's grandparents in the second part? Complete the sentences. Then, with a partner, add more details.

1 They went to Australia in …
2 They travelled by …
3 They went because …
4 After five years in Australia, … But then …

5 YOUR TURN: Going to Australia

a Think: Would you be interested in going to Australia or another English-speaking country for a year? Why (not)? Make a list of pros and cons.

b Pair: Compare your answers with a partner.

c Share: Walk around and share your ideas with others. Find someone who agrees with you.

Grammar and structures

Past perfect and past perfect progressive (revision) → G3

Other European explorers **had already discovered** the new land **by the time** the British **arrived**.
Aboriginal people **had been living** in Australia for thousands of years **before** the Europeans **arrived**.

Practice: First Nations

1 **GET STARTED!** Read this acrostic poem about Australia and then write your own poem to show what you have learned so far. You can use the first line below or your own ideas.

Australia

A very beautiful country
U nderneath the rest of the world
S un and sandy beaches
T heme parks and great holiday locations
R ivers, lakes and oceans
A place to call my home
L ovely weather, for every season
I t's a wonderful island
A boriginal native land

An amazing country and continent
U …
…

2 **The story of the Rainbow Serpent**

a Read the story below and put the verbs into the correct tense.

 page 36

b Listen to what the old men said about the Rainbow Serpent. Explain who the Serpent was, what he had done and what he might do again.

3 **The settlers have come to stay.** Read about the impact of the settlers on the lives of the Aboriginal peoples. Sum up the main points and discuss why they behaved as they did.

The settlers have come to stay
Before the British colonizers arrived in Australia, over 500 Aboriginal nations inhabited the
5 continent. They lived in small communities and took care of their own traditional country. Their land gave them their identity and connected them to
10 their ancestors. The men hunted large animals and the women gathered fruit, root vegetables and berries or nuts. The whole community was responsible for looking after the children, educating them and passing on the traditions of the clan. The arrival of the European settlers had a terrible impact on
15 the indigenous Aboriginal peoples. The early settlers took over more and more of their lands for settlements and farming, then hunted them down and killed them when they tried to fight back. Huge numbers died as a result of colonial brutality. The lives of those who did not die and the lives of
20 future generations changed forever.

From the late 1800s, up to 100,000 Aboriginal children were removed from their families. The authorities put them in government institutions or with white families, where they were often badly treated. The aim was to cut them off from
25 their own culture and raise them to become 'white'. The policy did not end until 1969. These children became known as the Stolen Generations.

Australian governments and white Australians have only recently begun to accept that Aboriginal Australians have
30 suffered injustices as a result of unfair laws and policies.

The Rainbow Serpent
An Aboriginal tale from Australia
Australian aboriginal myths, also known as dreamtime stories, are traditionally told by the indigenous people of Australia. In one story, a group of Aboriginals __1__ (hunt) in the outback. After they __2__ (hunt) for many hours, they __3__ (decide) to
5 stop and rest. They __4__ (sit) around, telling stories by the fire when one of them __5__ (look up). On the horizon was a beautiful multi-coloured rainbow. The Aborigines __6__ (think) that it was a serpent that __7__ (move) from one waterhole to another and they were frightened.
10 They were grateful that he __8__ (not come) too near their own waterhole.
One young man wanted to know more about the Rainbow Serpent so when he __9__ (return) home, he
15 asked the old men of his tribe why the hunters __10__ (be) scared of the Rainbow Serpent when they were out hunting.

Words and phrases

heritage	features belonging to the culture of a particular society
indigenous	people who are the original inhabitants of a region
mistreatment	an unfair way of behaving towards a person an animal
to **suffer from sth.**	to have a bad / difficult experience

Workshop 1

→ Workbook, pages 15–17

4 WORDPOWER: Prefixes and suffixes

a Word building patterns help you understand new words and expand your vocabulary. Complete the examples in the box with words from **3**. Be careful of spelling changes.

> **Prefixes** change the meaning of a word:
> *un-* or *in-* = not, *fair* → **un***fair*, *justice* → **1**
> *dis-* or *mis-* = negative meanings, *understand* → **mis***understand*
> **Suffixes** form a new word or word class:
> noun to adjective: *culture* → **2** ; *colony* → **3**
> adjective to noun: *brutal* → *brutality* verb to noun: *arrive* → **4** ; *govern* → **5**

b You're going to watch a video of Australian Prime Minister Kevin Rudd's Apology to Australia's Indigenous Peoples which he gave in 2008. You will hear these words in the video. Try to work out the meaning using word formation.

> **mis**treatment ■ **suffer**ing ■ **loss** ■
> **remov**al ■ in**dignity** ■ **heal**ing

5 VIEWING FOCUS: Sorry Day

a Before you watch, what do you think Rudd apologized for? Write down your ideas, then watch. Did he mention them? What does Rudd say about the future?

b Look at the TIP box, then watch again. Analyse:
- how effective Rudd's speech was and why.
- why its impact on the audience was so strong.

> **TIP**
> Useful techniques to persuade listeners
> • Keep the message simple.
> • Use repetition to get the message across.
> • Show you really believe in what you're saying.
> • Show you want to change the audience's lives.
> • Use emotional language.

c Your teacher will give you the transcript. Find examples to illustrate the points in the TIP box.

6 Promises not kept.
Read about the situation in Australia today. Discuss why Aboriginal people, especially young people, feel let down.

> **FACTS AND FIGURES**
> Kevin Rudd promised to 'close the gap' between white and Aboriginal Australians. But statistics show that Aboriginal people
> • still live 10 to 17 years less than white Australians and
> • are more likely to die of preventable diseases.
> Aboriginal youths
> • have the highest suicide rate in the world due to mental health issues and
> • are arrested for minor offences – making too much noise or swearing – 26 times more than their non-indigenous peers.
> Many young Aboriginal people feel they've lost their cultural identity. One way to keep their language and culture alive is through music.

7 VIDEO TRACK: Song

a Watch and listen to a song about the importance of knowing and celebrating your cultural heritage. How does it make you feel?

What we can do
Who are you? Know where you're from,
know where you're going.
Who are you? Connection to your culture
will get you through it.
My identity – you can't take it.
My connection – you can't break it.
My foundation – you can't shake it.
Look at this future we created.

b Find out what 'Ngunnawal' written on the girl's hand means.

Method coach: Understand new words and phrases

S1 Identify main ideas. Before you start reading a text, first look at the title and pictures to get a general idea of what the text is about. Do this for the text below and discuss your ideas.

S2 Work out the meaning of new words and phrases. Read the text carefully. First look at the **blue** words. Then read the TIP box and work out what they mean.

> **TIP**
>
> **How to work out the meaning of new words**
> First decide if you need to know the meaning of the new word to understand the text. If you do, then follow these tips.
> - Is the word similar to a German or an international word?
> - Can you guess the meaning from the words before / after it? Or does the text give an explanation (often inside commas)?
> - Do you already know part of the word or another form of the word?

Before and after

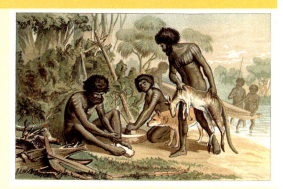

Australia's first peoples were hunter-gatherers who lived in small family groups and were **semi-nomadic**, systematically moving from place to place following the changes of the seasons. Each group lived in a
5 defined **territory** with its own **distinct** history and culture. Although the hunter-gatherers didn't develop an **agrarian**, or farming, society, they managed the land and wild animals in various ways to make sure they had **predictable** supplies of food
10 and water.

When the British arrived in 1788, about 770,000 Aboriginal people were living in Australia, with **approximately** 260 different language groups and 500 **dialects**. How did colonization **impact** these communities? The most immediate **consequence** was a wave of epidemic diseases such as smallpox, influenza and measles. These diseases killed many indigenous people because they had no
15 **resistance** to them.

Many also died in **random** killings or organized **massacres**. Massacres often took the form of mass shootings or driving groups of people off **cliffs**. As a result, there was a drastic **decline** in the Aboriginal population. By 1900, it was estimated that only about 117,000 indigenous people were still living in Australia.

S3 Use dictionaries to find the meaning of new words and phrases

a Discuss these questions.
- How often do you use a dictionary? If not very often, why not?
- Do you use a printed dictionary or an online dictionary? Monolingual or bilingual? What are the benefits of each?
- What can you use a dictionary for? Make a list of your ideas and compare in class.

b Now look at the **red** words and use a dictionary to find the right meaning in this context.

c You probably don't know the words *smallpox, influenza* and *measles*. Why is it not necessary to check the meaning in a dictionary?

d When you're using a dictionary, how can you avoid the problems in the cartoon?

"He's been in here all day just looking for trouble."

Workshop 1

→ Workbook, page 18

Workshop task: Understand texts on a new topic

S1 **Identify main ideas**

a Look at the title and the pictures. What do you think the text is about?

b Read the text and match the photos to the correct paragraphs.

Outback threatened by non-native species

Although much of Australia's **interior**, the outback, is **arid** desert, it isn't empty of life. If you camp out in the outback, you'll hear the **howls** of dingoes, or wild dogs, **echoing** across the landscape. Dingoes were **introduced** into Australia around 4,000 years ago, and today they are both loved and **loathed**. They attack
5 sheep and have caused the **decline** of many native species. **In spite of** this, it's exciting to see them **roam around** wild in Australia.

However, they are not the only non-native species that have become serious **pests**, causing enormous ecological **damage** to Australia. You'll also **come across** the world's largest herd of **feral** camels. Introduced from Arabia and India for
10 transport and work in the outback, they were **released** into the wild when they were no longer needed with the **advent** of powered engines. Other **invasive** species include foxes and rabbits, brought from Europe in the 19th century for sport hunting. They had few **predators**, so their populations **exploded**. Control **measures** have reduced their numbers, but they remain a big problem.

A

B

C

S2 **Work out the meaning of words and phrases.** Use the tips on page 22 to help you work out the meanings of the **blue** words. Then match the correct words to these definitions. What words in the text helped you guess?

1 an insect or an animal that destroys plants, etc.
2 sounding again and again
3 the sound a wild dog makes
4 to get bigger very quickly
5 the centre of a country
6 to bring an animal, a plant or disease to a country for the first time
7 bad effects

S3 **Use dictionaries to check the meaning of new words and phrases.** Now look at the words in **red**. Can you work out their meanings? Use a dictionary to check your guesses, or to find the correct meaning in the context. Compare your findings with a partner.

S4 **Use different kinds of dictionaries**

a In groups of three, read the last paragraph of the text. Note down any words or phrases you don't understand. Look at the tips on page 22 again and work out as many meanings as you can.

b Now each use a different method to check the rest of the list: (1) a monolingual dictionary, (2) a bilingual dictionary and (3) an online dictionary. When you have finished, compare your results.

15 Australia's prolonged drought is now driving large groups of camels out of the desert onto farms and into towns. In their desperate search for water, the camels demolish fences and foul critical watering holes, polluting the water and making it undrinkable. In an effort to defend farm properties, hundreds of camels are culled a day, leaving thousands of dead animals to rot. The culls are controversial. There is little agreement on a long-term solution.

twenty-three 23

Discovering Australia

1 Famous sites

a Look at the title, photos and introduction and discuss what you think the texts will be about. Then one of you reads text A and the other one text B. Make notes under these headings:

- Location
- Importance to Aboriginal people
- Creation legend

b Outline what you have learned to each other. Then decide which place you would most like to visit and why.

Sacred sites of Australia

Aboriginal and Torres Strait Islander nations have their own Creation or Dreamtime legends which have been passed down by the Elders from generation to generation. The whole continent is covered with sacred sites that are extremely important in Aboriginal tradition and folklore. Find out about two of them.

A Uluru (was once called Ayers Rock)

Uluru is one of the most sacred sites in Aboriginal folklore. It's a large rock formation located close to the exact centre of Australia, and has been designated a UNESCO World Heritage Site.

The rock resumed its original name in 1985 when the land was given back to the local people, the Anangu, by the Australian Government. They now own the Kata Tjuta National Park, of which Uluru is part. The Anangu had long wanted the site to be returned to them. According to their leaders, this is how we can make sure the place is looked after properly for everyone. Ancient Aboriginal paintings, which tell the story of the Dreaming, can be seen in caves in the rock.

Legend of Uluru according to the Anangu

Two tribes of ancient spirits were invited to a feast but they did not come. Their hosts were bitterly insulted. There was a great battle and many were killed. Uluru rose up to show that the land was deeply saddened by the bloodshed.

B Great Barrier Reef

The Great Barrier Reef is absolutely enormous. The size of about 70 million football fields, it is the only living thing on our planet that can be seen from space. It stretches 2,300 kilometres along the coast of Queensland and is home to a huge variety of marine creatures, including fish, seabirds, whales, dolphins and sharks. Fishing has been practised here for thousands of years by Aboriginal and Torres Strait Islanders, who are the traditional owners of the Great Barrier Reef region. Tourism is very important but it is carefully controlled to limit damage to the reef.

Legend according to Yindingi clan

This story tells of two brothers who went out fishing and were ordered by Bhiral, the Creator, not to hunt one particular kind of fish. One of the brothers disobeyed and speared the fish. Bhiral was extremely angry, so he threw lava and hot rocks down from the sky. The lava made the sea rise and when the lava had cooled, it formed what is now the Great Barrier Reef. The story is very similar to what scientists believe really happened.

2 What's most important?

Read the information in the box on page 25. Find more examples of passive sentences in the texts about Uluru and the Great Barrier Reef. Then decide why the passive was used. Choose from this list.

- The person or thing doing the action is not known or not important.
- To avoid using vague subjects like *someone, people, they*.
- The focus of the sentence is on the action, not the doer.

Words and phrases

folklore	the traditions and stories of a country or community		
reef	a long line of rocks or sand near the surface of the sea	variety	several different sorts of the same things

Workshop 1

→ Workbook, pages 19/20

3 Sacred sites

a Use the information below and write about Uluru and tourism. Use the passive.

Uluru is a very popular tourist destination. Busloads of tourists | bring in | every day | tour companies.
Busloads of tourists are brought in every day by tour companies.

1 Many visitors | expect | be allowed | climb the rock.
2 However, tourists | ban from | climb the sacred site | since 2019 because it is unacceptable to the Aboriginal owners.
3 Alternative activities | develop | for tourists since the ban. For example, walking tours | offer | around the base of Uluru with experienced guides.
4 The Anangu do not want | tourism | ban because it is one of their only sources of income.
5 They think they | should | give | a bigger share of the profits from tourism.
6 They hope that in future local people | offer | more and better jobs.

» page 37

b Choose **one** of these sacred sites each. Do some online research and write about the site, its history and the Dreamtime legends. Exchange your texts and compare the stories.

- Wolfe Creek Crater
- The Three Sisters

- We form the passive with a form of *be* and the past participle of the main verb.
  *Uluru **has been designated** a UNESCO World Heritage Site.*
- When a verb is followed by a **preposition**, this stays in the same position in the passive.
  *Creation legends **have been passed down** by the Elders.*
- If a verb has two objects (e.g. *give, offer, promise, show*), the passive can begin with either the **direct** or **indirect** object.
  *The land **was given back to** the local people.*
  OR *The local people **were given back** the land.*
- We use the **passive infinitive** after modal verbs (*must, have to*, etc.), and after verbs like *expect, hope, like, need, want*.
  *Ancient Aboriginal paintings **can be seen** in caves in the rock.*
  *They had long **wanted** the site **to be returned** to them.*

4 YOUR TURN: For and against

a Tourism has advantages and disadvantages. Brainstorm arguments for and against tourism.

For	Against
brings money for the local community	

» page 37

b Share your ideas. Then discuss: Should tourism be banned completely in some places?

In my opinion, …

On the one hand, … on the other hand, …

Grammar and structures

Passive – all tenses (revision) → G4
Passive with verb + preposition → G5
We can make sure the place **is looked after**.
Passive: verbs with two objects → G6
The land **was given back to** the local people.

Passive infinitive (with *to*) after *want*, *expect*, etc. → G7
The Anangu had long **wanted** the title deeds **to be returned**.
Passive infinitive (without *to*) after modal verbs → G8
Ancient Aboriginal paintings **can be seen** in caves in the rock.

Practice: Climate reality

1 **GET STARTED!** Look at the photos. What natural disasters do they show? Match the captions to the photos. How are these disasters connected to climate change and global warming?

1 Coral bleaching on the Great Barrier Reef caused by rising sea temperatures
2 Deadly bush fire driven by strong winds in New South Wales
3 Red kangaroo killed by drought in the outback

2 **Climate change in Australia**

a Complete the article about how Australia has been affected by climate change. Use the passive.

b Then read the article again and outline the main effects in your own words. What examples does the writer give to illustrate these effects?

3 **Standing up for the future**

a Jason's schoolmate Ricky is very concerned about climate change, so he and his friends are taking part in a demonstration. A radio journalist interviews them. Before you listen, check the meaning of these words.

> carbon dioxide ■ coal mine ■
> destroy forest and bush land ■
> droughts ■ floods ■
> fossil fuels ■ fracking ■
> global warming ■ hurricanes ■
> natural disasters ■
> renewable energy

The climate reality

Australia **is known** (*know*) for its stunning scenery, its fabulous beaches, and unique wildlife. Many animals such as koala bears, kangaroos, wombats __1__ (*can + only find*) in Australia. However, climate change scientists are warning that Australia is especially
5 at risk from the climate crisis. This is the climate reality:

Heat and drought
Australia is already a very hot and dry country and it's expected to get a lot hotter and drier if no action __2__ (*take*) on climate change. In 2018, temperatures in Sydney soared to over
10 47 degrees. Heatwaves are much more common and more severe than they have ever been. More heat means more droughts.

Bushfires / Wildfires
Drought creates the perfect conditions for bushfires. Bushfires are becoming much more frequent and more extreme. In 2018, there
15 were nearly 200 fires in Queensland. Conditions like these __3__ (*never see*) before in its history.

Farming
As Australia's climate changes, every type of farmer __4__ (*affect*). The climate crisis is making life extremely difficult for farmers.
20 Much of the country's food __5__ (*produce*) in Queensland. According to one farmer, 'Food security __6__ (*endanger*) by climate change, there's no doubt about that.'

The ocean and the Great Barrier Reef
Our oceans are becoming much warmer and more acidic. The
25 Great Barrier Reef __7__ (*hit*) incredibly hard by both factors. It __8__ (*build*) over many millions of years by tiny animals called polyps. But these are dying due to the rise in sea temperatures, and the future of the reef is in doubt.

Australia has a lot to lose. The causes of climate change need
30 __9__ (*tackle*) urgently.

WHO CAN CHANGE THIS? YOU!
JOIN THE CLIMATE FIGHT AND TAKE ACTION.

Words and phrases

carbon dioxide	a gas produced by people and animals
extinction	when a species of animals no longer exists
global warming	the increase in temperature of the earth's atmosphere
heatwave	period of unusually hot weather
renewable	sth. that can be replaced naturally such as energy produced from wind or water

Workshop 1

→ Workbook, pages 21 – 23

b Complete with words from **a**.

1 ▓▓ is one of the causes of severe weather conditions, for example ▓▓, which are long very dry periods with no rain.
2 ▓▓ are violent storms with very strong winds. They are often followed by heavy rainfall which can result in ▓▓ .
3 Coal and gas are both examples of ▓▓ . When they are burned, they produce large amounts of ▓▓ .
4 Solar power is a form of ▓▓ .
5 ▓▓ is a technology to get natural gas or oil from underground rocks. Some people think it can cause earthquakes.

c Read the interviewer's questions, then listen and take notes. Compare, then listen again and complete your notes.

1 Why are you all here, taking part in this demonstration?
2 Can you tell our listeners about Seed Mob – what is it?
3 Why is the land so important to Aboriginal people?
4 What do you think are the main causes of climate change here?
5 Isn't the government doing anything?
6 How does climate change affect Aboriginal people?
7 What do you want the government to do?
8 How hopeful are you?

d Think about climate issues and protest movements in Germany. How similar or different are they to those in Australia?

e Write a blogpost describing a protest movement you know about.

4 In the news

a Read the headline and the photo caption. What words are missing? Why are headlines and captions often written like this?

Unique Australian wildlife faced with extinction

Koala mother and Joey on a bulldozed log pile in Queensland

Threat to biodiversity worsened by climate change and habitat loss

b Use the notes to write an article. Use the passive when necessary.

- wildlife increasingly affected by climate change, not just humans
- over last ten years astonishing 50% of animal species in Australia wiped out
- koalas, kangaroos, reptiles, insects and many plants endangered by more frequent heatwaves and droughts
- 3 million hectares of trees could be lost in next 15 years
- 45 million animals killed each year from logging and land-clearing
- millions injured or killed in bushfires
- if nothing done, many species unique to Australia face extinction

c Find a partner and exchange your articles. Has your partner used the passive correctly? Suggest corrections or improvements if necessary.

5 SPEAKING FOCUS: Giving a presentation

a Choose one aspect of climate change for a presentation about how it affects Australia. Include the following and / or your own ideas.
- what the problem is, its causes and effects
- how to prevent the situation getting worse
- what young people are doing

b Give your presentation to the class.

twenty-seven 27

A New Zealand visit

1 **Away from home**

a Paige is in year 9 at Papanui High School in Christchurch, New Zealand. She lives with her Aunt Christine and Uncle Tai. Describe the pictures, then listen and add more details.

b Listen again and do the tasks.

1. Explain why Paige lives with her aunt and uncle.
2. Say how Paige and her uncle react to Aunt Christine's suggestion.
3. Describe two things that their guests learn during dinner.

2 **News from Christchurch.** Look at the box. Then read what Paige said to Jason. Back in Australia, Jason told his parents about it. Finish his sentences.

1. I like Papanui more than my old school.
   She told me …
2. Our girls' team beat an Aussie team recently.
   She mentioned that …
3. We're planning to play them here next season.
   She said …
4. We didn't play well yesterday.
   She added that …
5. Tai has helped me a lot with my game.
   She said …
6. If you have time tomorrow, he'll help you.
   She suggested that …

>>> page 37

- In reported speech, the **tense** moves back one step in time. And **pronouns** change.
  '**I'm** fine.' → He said (that) **he was** fine.
- **Adverbs** of time and place also change.
  'I spoke to an architect **yesterday**, so you can have a bigger room **here**.' → He mentioned that he'd spoken to an architect **the day before**, so I could have a bigger room **there**.

CULTURE CORNER

Aussies and Kiwis – a special relationship
Relations between Australia and New Zealand have often been compared to those between siblings or cousins.
Even though the countries share common experiences like fighting side-by-side in two World Wars, they don't always get along. They have different personalities and sometimes serious political differences. They also have a huge sporting rivalry – mainly in cricket, rugby and netball, and they like joking about each other.
However, when they are out in the big world, they often team together, and when they describe their relationship, they speak of the respect and trust they feel for each other.

  Words and phrases

rivalry	a situation when people, countries, etc. compete for the same thing
sibling	a brother or sister
to **tip over**	to turn over in water
white water	river water that looks white because it is moving fast over rocks

Workshop 1

→ Workbook, pages 24/25

3 South Island adventure

a Look at Jason's blog. What do you find most interesting about each post?

b Think of a good heading for each post. Share your ideas.

 jasonturner
4 October

♥ 💬 Liked by **elenikourakis**, **judithturner** and **7 others**

This is my NZ blog! Today after rugby practice, one of the guys asked us if we wanted to go to Christchurch Adventure Park. It's in the Port Hills. Amazing views! Then we rode the zipline. It's the longest in NZ – over 1 km. It's fast and scary. I asked one of the guys to take this photo of me. 👍👍👍

 jasonturner
5 October

♥ 💬 ✈ Liked by **elenikourakis**, **judithturner** and **6 others**

Today we visited Ko Tane, a living museum which shows how the Maori lived before the Europeans came. We did the hongi greeting (nose to nose!) and watched a welcoming dance. Tai was such a great guide. We asked him what the Maori words meant and he explained them. The best part was the hangi, a big meal cooked on hot rocks in the ground.

 jasonturner
7 October

♥ 💬 ✈ Liked by **elenikourakis**, **judithturner** and **7 others**

The day after losing our game (23 – 22 ☹) Coach Hansen organized a river rafting trip for us. 👍 The river was near the mountains where the Lord of the Rings trilogy was filmed! We practised paddling in the quiet part of the river, then we got to the white water. Our guide, Nina, told us to paddle and not to panic. We nearly tipped over once. At the end we swam in the river in our wetsuits. Awesome!

 c Choose one post and write a comment. Use the same informal style (e.g. emojis, etc.).

- To report *yes/no* questions we use *if* or *whether* and invert **subject** and **verb**.
  '**Do you want** to go to Christchurch Adventure Park?'
  → One of the guys asked us **if we wanted** to go to Christchurch Adventure Park.
- We report *wh*-questions like this:
  What **do the Maori words mean**?
  → We asked **what the Maori words meant**.
- For orders and requests we use the infinitive with (not) to.
  Paddle and **don't panic**.
  → Nina told us **to paddle** and **not to panic**.

4 An awesome trip.
Look at the box. How did Jason report what Tai, Nina and Paige said?

Please show respect for Maori culture. Don't walk or swim in sacred areas.
Tai

Have you been river rafting before?
Nina

When are you going to visit us again?
Paige

5 YOUR TURN: A trip to Christchurch

a You and your partner are touring New Zealand and have two days in Christchurch. What will you do there? Form groups of four – **Pair A** and **Pair B**. Each pair should look at Jasons's posts and do some more research about Christchurch. With your partner, discuss and agree on a plan.

b First **Pair A** presents their plan to **Pair B**. Then swap roles. Discuss the two plans and decide what you want to do in a group.

Grammar and structures

Reported speech in statements, questions, requests and orders (revision) → G9
Ricky **said** that he **wanted** to visit again.   They **asked** us **if** we **had enjoyed** the sightseeing.   I **asked** them **where** the high school **was**.
We **asked** Paige **to take** some photos.   Coach Hansen **told** us **to focus** on the game.

Changes to adverbs of time and place in reported speech → G10
They told us we could come **the following day**.   Paige said that she had been **there** once before.

twenty-nine 29

Practice: Land of the Long White Cloud

1 GET STARTED! Write notes on a placemat about things that you find interesting, unusual or attractive about New Zealand. Discuss your notes. Then list your group's top five things in the middle of your placemat. Present and compare your results in class.

2 Two islands make a nation. Read the text, then do these tasks.

1. Look at the map showing New Zealand. Find out which island the places are located on.
2. What do you learn about each place from the short programme description?

3 More than a game

a Paige listens to a radio interview with a film-maker. Write a statement to sum up what he says.

b Listen again and complete these questions, requests and statements.

1. Why don't we see …?
2. It's about our relationship to the game and how …
3. Please explain what …
4. The game was brought here in the late 19th century when …
5. Why did rugby become …?
6. Our team showed the world that this small island nation could …
7. Do the younger generations still …?
8. It's still very big, with team and league competition on …

c Tai comes home from work and Paige tells him about the interview. How does she report what is said in **b**?

> She asked why we …

> He said it was …

Two Islands Make a Nation
Starting Wednesday, April 19 at 9 pm

Amanda Nguyen and Shane Alcott visit our neighbours across the Tasman Sea to find out what makes New Zealand's North Island and South Island – distinctive, what challenges they face, and what they contribute to this unique island nation. The six weekly segments are:

- Part 1 **Auckland and Wellington** – why these cities matter and what makes each special
- Part 2 **Queenstown** – why this little town has become a tourist hot spot and how it began
- Part 3 **Rotorua** – the town's natural wonders and its cultural significance
- Part 4 **Christchurch** – the city's regional importance and the challenges it has faced
- Part 5 **Coromandel Peninsula** – what makes this area such a magnet for visitors
- Part 6 **Milford Sound** – a national treasure, its biological diversity and how it is being protected

Words and phrases

anthem	a song that has special importance for a country
distinctive	having a quality that makes sb./sth. different
ethnic	belonging to a group of people that share a cultural tradition
ritual	a series of actions that are always performed in the same way

Workshop 1

→ Workbook, pages 26–28

4 The Maori influence

a Ricky has found a tourist website with information about Maori culture. Scan it for answers to these questions.

1. Why is Maori culture protected by law?
2. What's 'hello' in the Maori language?
3. What does *whanau* mean?
4. What's 'essential' for New Zealanders?

Maori culture

To understand New Zealand culture, it's important to understand the Maori influence. As New Zealand's second-largest ethnic group, Maori make up 16.6 per cent of the country's population. They are the indigenous people of New
5 Zealand and their rights, culture and language have been protected by law since New Zealand became a country in 1840. The government has not always respected those rights, but relations between Maori and *Pakeha* (the Maori term for New Zealanders of European descent) have improved over time.

10 Today Maori culture is embraced everywhere in New Zealand. In everyday conversation, *kia ora* is a typical way of greeting or thanking somebody; when people talk about *Aotearoa* ('Land of the Long White Cloud') they mean New Zealand; and when a Kiwi asks about your *whanau*, he or she means your family.
15 Official signs are in both Maori and English. At an official event, the audience always sings the New Zealand national anthem first in the Maori language, *Te Reo* Maori, then in English. The national rugby team, the All Blacks, famously perform the haka before each game, and variations of this traditional Maori dance
20 are performed at events all over the country.

Many believe that the Maori cultural influence is one reason for the success of New Zealand's multicultural society. A survey reported that New Zealanders of every ethnic group see Maori culture as an 'essential' part of their way of life.

New Zealand Prime Minister Jacinda Ardern exchanging a hongi – the traditional Maori greeting.

The All Blacks rugby team performing the haka

b List some of the similarities and differences between Maoris and Australian Aboriginals.

5 WORDPOWER: Collective nouns.
How many collective nouns can you find in the text in **4**? List them. Then find at least two more collective nouns.

> A collective noun is a singular noun, such as *herd* or *committee*, that refers to a group of people or animals. It is followed by a plural or singular verb.
> *The committe meet / meets every month.*

6 WRITING FOCUS: A blog

a Look at Jason's blog again in **3** on page 29. Discuss the questions, then write your own blog about a trip you went on.
- Where and how often do blogs appear?
- What kinds of topics can they cover?
- Who is a blogger's audience?
- How are they structured?
- What is a typical style of a blog (e.g. formal / informal, conversational, instructive, etc.)?

b GALLERY WALK: Display your blogposts. Write your feedback on sticky notes. What do you like about each blog? How well do the structure and writing style fit the topic?

Method coach: Prepare to write an informative text

S1 **Researching a topic and evaluating notes**

a Your class has to research and write about New Zealand for your international website. Your article should include facts about the history, geography, people and wildlife. Decide which information in these notes are most useful and interesting.

> **TIP**
> When doing research:
> - Use more than one source.
> - Don't cut and paste. Use your own words.
> - Bookmark sources for easy reference.

- consists of two main islands — North Island and South Island
- 9th longest coastline in the world
- 600 smaller islands - largest = Rakiura island, also called Stewart Island
- first settled by the Maori people around 1300 — around 16% of population today
- first country to give women the vote in 1893
- unemployment 4%
- no snakes!

b Do your own online research and make notes. Look at the quiz questions on pages 12–13 for ideas about the kind of information to include.

S2 **Making a plan**

a Your text should have three main parts. Match the parts to their function.

- main body
- introduction
- conclusion

- summarizes key points or comments on the topic
- introduces the topic / purpose of the text
- provides the necessary information

b Organize the notes in **S1** into a logical sequence of paragraphs. Remember, the main body can be more than one paragraph.

S3 **Using an appropriate style.** Look at the TIP box. Then evaluate the extracts from another student's text. Say whether the style is appropriate or not, and why.

> **TIP**
> When writing an informative text:
> - Choose the right style to suit your topic and audience, formal or informal, serious or chatty.
> - Use a variety of sentence lengths and types, simple and complex.
> - Include interesting facts to engage the reader.

> What do you know about New Zealand? Can you find it on a map? Do you know which hemisphere it's in? Not sure? If you want to find out the coolest facts about this amazing country, read on!

> As it is so remote, New Zealand has some very unusual wildlife that cannot be found anywhere else in the world. Nearly all the land animals are birds. Many of them lost the ability to fly as they had no predators.

Workshop 1

→ Workbook, page 29

@ WES-40325-001

Workshop task: Write an informative text

S1 **Decide on a topic.** Look at the photos and tasks. Choose one of the topics to write about.

A

Write an informative article about High School exchange programmes for German students in Australia or New Zealand.

Divide your article into sections with headings to help the reader identify the key information. Headings could be typical questions which you give the answer to. Include this information:
- Reasons for going on a school exchange to Australia or New Zealand
- Organizations that arrange exchanges, what programmes they offer, their requirements (e.g. age, language level)
- What to expect at your High School – courses, after-school activities
- Benefits of staying with a host family
- Free time opportunities
- How to apply

B

Write an informative report about climate change in New Zealand. Choose a good title, e.g. *Climate change reality in NZ* or *No time to lose.*

Paragraph 1: Introduce the topic – concerns about climate change
Paragraph 2/3: Explain the main problems, causes and effects
Paragraph 3/4: Explain what's being done (by protesters / by the government)
Paragraph 4/5: Conclusion – say what's likely to happen in the future

TIP
- Use a chatty, personal style. Address your reader directly.
- Use adjectives like *great, exciting,* etc. to make your article more interesting and persuasive.

TIP
- Include key facts.
- Write in a neutral and factual style.
- Don't include your personal opinion.

S2 **Research your topic.** Look at the tips on page 32 and make notes. Then make a plan and order your notes.

S3 **Write and edit your text.** Use a dictionary to help you improve your text and check it for mistakes.

TIP

What's in a dictionary?
- the right meaning of a word (monolingual and bilingual dictionaries often give more than one meaning, so choose the right one for the context)
- the correct spelling of a word
- grammatical information (e.g. part of speech, plural forms, which preposition to use, verb patterns, etc.)
- synonyms

S4 **Evaluate your texts**

 a Form groups of three or four. Take turns explaining which topic you chose, and how you researched your topic.

 b Exchange your written products. Read them and give each other feedback. Did your classmates follow the guidelines in the TIP box?

Mediation

1 Bernhard Holtermann

a Your class is working on an article for your international website about Germans that emigrated to Australia. You focus on Bernhard Holtermann. Use the information below to write about his work, interests and ambitions. Include your own opinion about him as well.

Bernhard Holtermann: Ein Leben mit vielen Kapiteln

Von André Leslie

[…] Christoph Heins neues Buch *Australien 1872: Wie ein Deutscher sein Glück fand und Fotogeschichte schrieb* erzählt die Geschichte von Bernhard Holtermanns Leben und zeigt bisher
5 unveröffentlichte Fotos aus jener Zeit. Hein sprach mit André Leslie, dem Online-Editor des Goethe-Instituts Australien, über Holtermann und die Entstehung des Buchs.

Nachdem er mit Anfang 20 aus Hamburg nach
10 *Australien kam, scheint sich Bernhard Holtermann an zahlreichen Aspekten der australischen Gesellschaft aktiv beteiligt zu haben. Würden Sie ihn als Multitalent bezeichnen?*

Ja, er war sehr vielschichtig. […] Ich denke,
15 Holtermann wusste immer, wie er sich mit dem, was er tat, einen Vorteil verschaffen konnte, aber das ist in Ordnung, denn er tat wirklich viel zum Wohl der Allgemeinheit. […] Er wurde gewählter Politiker, setzte sich auf dieselbe Art, wie wir das
20 heute tun könnten, für Einwanderung ein und hatte sehr fortschrittliche Ansichten. In den 1880er Jahren spendete er einen Teil seines Vermögens für den Bau einer Brücke, die später die Sydney Harbour Bridge wurde. Ja, er achtete auf seinen
25 eigenen Vorteil, aber er hatte auch immer die Allgemeinheit im Sinn. Ich denke, das kann man heute mit Bestimmtheit sagen.

In Australien und insbesondere in Deutschland scheint es, als seien Holtermanns Leistungen etwas
30 *in Vergessenheit geraten. Würden Sie das auch so sehen?*

Ich sehe das absolut so. In Australien haben wir die Leute im Holtermann Museum in Gulgong und die in der Provinzstadt Hill End in New South Wales, die
35 noch in diesem Geist leben. Es gibt zudem ein paar neue, jüngere australische Künstler*innen, die mit den Fotos in der Holtermann Collection arbeiten.

[…] In Deutschland ist Holtermann überhaupt nicht bekannt. So stieß ich beispielsweise in einem
40 Hamburger Museum auf ein Fotoalbum mit Bildern, die wahrscheinlich Bayliss für Holtermann machte. Sie hatten das Album zwar, aber niemand wusste wirklich, was es war oder wie es dorthin gelangt war. […]

45 *Fotos scheinen für Holtermann sehr wichtig gewesen zu sein. Trotz der vielen verschiedenen Dinge, die er in seinem Leben machte, hat man den Eindruck, dass seine wahre Leidenschaft der Fotografie galt.*

Ich denke, das ist richtig. Holtermann scheint sehr
50 an neuer Technologie interessiert gewesen zu sein, er war Unternehmer. Er wollte die Nachricht davon, wie weit die Kolonie Australien damals entwickelt war, in die ganze Welt hinaustragen – und tat das auch buchstäblich. Australien war nicht mehr nur
55 ein Ort für ehemalige Gefangene. Der beste Weg, das zu zeigen, war damals über Fotos. Fotografie war für ihn das richtige Instrument, um von Australien zu erzählen, und das tat er auch. Er gründete zudem ein Pharmaunternehmen und war
60 im Import-Export der neuesten Maschinen tätig. Holtermann hatte immer einen guten Riecher für jede Chance, sich stärker zu profilieren. Er wurde berühmt, aber er wurde dadurch berühmt, dass er Australien dankte und der Welt zeigte, wie
65 fortschrittlich das Land in den 1870er und 1880er Jahren war.
Er und der berühmte australische Fotograf Beaufoy Merlin, der ebenfalls stets auf der Suche nach den neuesten Trends war, hatten eine großartige
70 Partnerschaft. Die beiden arbeiteten gut zusammen, sie waren Geistesverwandte.

Holtermann freundete sich immer mit Leuten mit Fähigkeiten an, die er gerade brauchte. In dieser Hinsicht war er sehr clever.

75 *Was, glauben Sie, können wir heute von Bernhard Holtermann lernen?*

Niemand kann sich heutzutage sein ganzes Leben lang auf nur einen Beruf verlassen, es heißt, man müsse bereit sein, alle fünf Jahre etwas anderes zu 80 machen. Holtermann wäre das perfekte Beispiel dafür. Er war alles Mögliche, und er war im wahrsten Sinne des Wortes ein Brückenbauer zwischen Europa und Australien. Er war ein Mann mit vielen Talenten und sehr mutig. Er wusste nie, ob er finanziellen 85 Erfolg haben oder verarmt sterben würde. Er verließ Europa per Schiff, als er 20 Jahre alt war, ohne jede Ahnung, ob er es nach Australien schaffen würde, und er sprach 90 damals kein Wort Englisch. Er stürzte sich da einfach hinein. Sein berühmter Goldfund ist ein gutes Beispiel. Sein 95 Geschäftspartner Louis Beyers war nicht in Hill End, als das Gold ausgegraben wurde, und Holtermann schlief, als seine Leute es fanden. 100 Aber es war immer als Holtermann Nugget bekannt. Das ist nicht ganz richtig. Sie hätten es zumindest Holtermann Beyers Nugget nennen sollen. […]

www.goethe.de

b You tell your mother about the article on Bernhard Holtermann. She wants to know if he is still famous today and you tell her about the Holtermann museum in Gulgong. You found some online reviews and explain what visitors think of the museum.

Community museums rule! ★★★★★
This small museum is an inspiration. I was impressed by the community working together to save two heritage buildings in order to house the Holtermann Collection of photographs and showcase Gulgong during the 1870s Gold Rush. Really well displayed and engaging content and brilliant staff. Really important stop if you visit this heritage town.
December 2021

The Holterman Gulgong museum is first class. ★★★★★
This museum is well thought out with great touchscreens if you want to dive deeper into Gold Rush life. Merlin and Baylis, the photographers hired by Holtermann, were masters of wet plate photography. The clarity of the enlarged photographs is superb giving a great panorama of the gold fields. Well worth a visit.
January 2022

Excellent discovery! ★★★★☆
What history. It's all here and brilliantly presented. Almost too much to take in. Just immerse yourself in this snapshot of history in the goldfields, and then delve into photos of Sydney and Melbourne in the horse-drawn era.
January 2022

**This UNESCO listed collection comes to life.
Enter the door!** ★★★★☆
What an amazing collection, and the presentation is stunning. Love that this significant historical collection is so accessible. And also so relevant – standing in Gulgong – it feels like you are back in history.
January 2022

Photography exhibition ★★★☆☆
An interesting photography museum primarily focused on the gold rush period. Rather small selection but great photos. Even our kids enjoyed them!
February 2022

First track

3 **b** Complete the sentences with the correct verb forms. Sometimes both are possible.
p.15

1. Jason **has known / has been knowing** Ricky since year 2.
2. They **have played / have been playing** rugby since they were 10.
3. Jason and Nick Kourakis **have been / have been being** friends for a long time, too.
4. Jason **has worked / has been working** part-time at the Kourakis' Greek deli for the past year.

7 **b** Complete the text with these phrasal verbs.
p.17

> was cleaning up ■ came out ■
> go ahead ■ looked at ■ set down ■
> sit down ■ turned on ■ walked in

Jason ⬚1 at the deli when Ricky ⬚2 .
'I wanted to see what a Greek deli is like,' he said. Mr Kourakis ⬚3 of the kitchen.
'⬚4 ,' he said to Ricky, pointing to a chair. He ⬚5 the stereo and played some Bouzouki music. Then he ⬚6 a plate in front of Ricky with Baklava on it. First Ricky ⬚7 it but didn't touch it.
'⬚8 , try it!' Mr Kourakis said.
Finally Ricky tried a piece. He smiled.
'Welcome to Greece!' Mr Kourakis said.

3 **b** Complete the answers with the past perfect or past perfect progressive.
p.19

1. Why was the first European settlement in Australia a penal colony?
   Before America became independent, Britain ⬚ (*send*) its convicts there, but after Independence America didn't want to take any more.
2. Why did the convict colonies change and become modern cities?
   During the Gold Rush, many immigrants ⬚ (*bring*) new skills.
3. Why did the government introduce the Immigration Restriction Act?
   The British population ⬚ (*become*) angry because so many non-European immigrants ⬚ (*arrive*) from countries like China.
4. Why did the Australian government encourage more immigrants to come in 1945?
   World War 2 ⬚ (*lead*) to labour shortages.
5. Why did so many British people emigrate to Australia after World War 2?
   The Australian government ⬚ (*promise*) them a better life with lots of job opportunities.

2 **a** Complete the story with the correct forms.
p.20

The Rainbow Serpent
An Aboriginal tale from Australia
Australian aboriginal myths, also known as dreamtime stories, are traditionally told by the indigenous people of Australia. In one story, a group of Aboriginals **hunted / were hunting** (1) in the outback. After they **had hunted / had been hunting** (2) for
5 many hours, they **decided / had decided** (3) to stop and rest. They **sat / were sitting** (4) around, telling stories by the fire when one of them **looked up / had looked up** (5). On the horizon was a beautiful multi-coloured rainbow. The Aborigines **thought / were thinking** (6) that it was a Serpent that **moved / was moving** (7) from one waterhole to another and they were frightened. They were grateful that he **didn't come / wasn't coming** (8) too near their own waterhole.
15 One young man wanted to know more about the Rainbow Serpent so when he **returned / was returning** (9) home, he asked the old men of his tribe why the hunters **were / had been** (10)
20 scared of the Rainbow Serpent when they were out hunting.

Workshop 1
FIRST TRACK

3 **a** Use the information below and write about Uluru and tourism. Use the passive.
p.25

Uluru is a very popular tourist destination. Busloads of tourists | bring in | every day | tour companies. (simple present passive)

Busloads of tourists are brought in every day by tour companies

1 Many visitors | expect | be allowed | climb the rock. (passive infinitive)
2 However, tourists | ban from | climb the sacred site | since 2019 because it is unacceptable to the Aboriginal owners. (present perfect passive)
3 Alternative activities | develop | for tourists since the ban. (present perfect passive) For example, walking tours | offer | around the base of Uluru with experienced guides. (simple present passive)
4 The Anangu do not want | tourism | ban because it is one of their only sources of income. (passive infinitive)
5 They think they | should | give | a bigger share of the profits from tourism. (modal passive)
6 They hope that in future local people | offer | more and better jobs. (future passive)

---

4 **a** Tourism can have advantages and disadvantages. Read the arguments for and against tourism. Can you think of more? Which arguments are more important in your opinion?
p.25

For	Against
brings money for the local community	local community often receives only a small share of the money
creates jobs for local people	jobs are often badly paid
money from tourism can be used to protect the local environment	local environment can be damaged (e.g. Great Barrier Reef) tourists drop litter, cause pollution when they travel
keeps local culture and traditions alive, e.g. tourists enjoy traditional shows	tourists don't always respect local culture and traditions (e.g. Uluru)
...	...

2 Read what Paige said to Jason. When he returned to Australia, Jason told his parents about their conversation. Choose the correct forms to complete his sentences.
p.28

1 I like Papanui more than my old school.
   She told me she **liked/had liked** Papanui more than her old school.
2 Our girls' team beat an Aussie team recently.
   She mentioned that their girls' team **have beaten/had beaten** an Aussie team recently.
3 We're planning to play them here next season.
   She said they **were planning/planned** to play them **here/there** next season.
4 We didn't play well yesterday.
   She added that they **hadn't played/haven't played** well **yesterday/the day before**.
5 Tai has helped me a lot with my game.
   She said Tai **has helped/had helped** her a lot with her game.
6 If you have time tomorrow, he'll help you.
   She suggested that if I **had/would have** time **the following day/tomorrow**, he **helped/would help** me.

Reading

1 The narrator of the song writes from the perspective of the First Nation people. Read the text and summarize what is being said about his/her people (4–5 sentences).

2 a The vocabulary below will help you understand and talk about the text. Explain what the words mean in the context of the song.

b Find three more words you think are important to discuss the content of the song. Give reasons for your choice.

3 a Describe the treatment of the natives in Australia by the white settlers.

 b Work on these tasks related to the song in small groups.

1. Discuss how the actions of the white men may have been justified and how they were perceived by the natives. Take notes and weigh up the positive and negative points.
2. Explain the idea of a 'nation within a nation'. What are they still waiting for?
3. Evaluate the four closing lines. Describe which view of the future the narrator has. Give reasons for your choice.

4 a Listen to the song. Comment on the music and how it supports the message.

b With a partner, talk about the emotions you felt while you were listening.

Midnight Oil, *First Nation* (2020)

First nation, first nation
First to deserve an explanation
First nation, first nation
Last to receive an invitation
5 First nation, first nation
When we gonna start the conversation?
When we gonna start the celebration?
When we gonna end the exploitation?
When we gonna say the word invasion?
10 Out loud, we're waiting
Still waiting, nation within the nation
Still waiting, nation within a nation

Earth black the church lacked the first fact
80 thou turned demon days and a dirt nap[1]
15 Generate the trauma that made a kid rage[2]
Now the ment' capat[3] be filled with all that
Fall back
Why my cousin commit?
Why my uncle locked up?
20 Why my aunty forget, how to put a glass cup down?
Fighting the fit
We done been[4] brainwashed into fighting the temptay[5]
Fought Armageddon and I be out the next day
Of course I'm a get 'em[6] till the spirit run empty[7]
25 My corpse full of venom outcome of the invade
How dare you try to put me up in grave

Strong vision, tradition
No ticket, no admission
No government indecision
30 No token[8] recognition
First nation, so ancient

Let's sit down and talk about appropriation
Let's sit down and talk about compensation
Let's sit down and talk about reconciliation
35 Out loud, we're waiting
Still waiting, nation within a nation
Still waiting, nation within a nation

Nation, nation within a nation
Nation, nation within a nation
40 Nation, nation within a nation

When will the light switch?
24/7 in the crisis
White noise killed black thoughts I sense
There's a shift, it'll come by the night's end
45 When will the light switch?
24/7 in the crisis
White noise killed black thoughts I sense
There's a shift, see the ship sink like this

---

[1] **dirt nap** (*sl.*) death (literally 'sleeping in the dirt') – [2] **to rage** *toben, wüten* – [3] **ment' capat** = mental capability = head/mind – [4] **we done been** (*sl.*) we have been – [5] **temptay** = temptation – [6] **I'm a get 'em** (*sl.*) I'm going to get them – [7] **to run empty** = to run on empty, losing enthusiasm or motivation (like a vehicle with low fuel) – [8] **token** *Geste*

Workshop 1
READING

Aaradhna, *Brown Girl* (2016)

I'm more than the colour of my skin
I'm a girl that likes to sing
All I know is what's within
Not just a brown girl in the ring[1]

5 Go to school and learn their ways
Told how to think and what to say
While my mother says to pray
I pray for better days

God, please help them see
10 They ain't no different from me
Not above, not beneath
Teach them equality

I'm not just a brown girl in the ring
I'm a girl that likes to sing
15 I'm not just a brown girl in the ring
I'm a girl that likes to sing

I'm more than what they think of me
More than the colour tones that they see
More than urban, R&B[2], more than a slang[3] that I speak

20 Close your eyes, don't say your word
Don't speak about what you seen or heard
Let's pretend that it's OK
Just the way the devil likes to play

Look in my eyes, look in my eyes
25 I can't lie, I can't lie
All these years of my life
I'm judged from the outside

I'm not just a brown girl in the ring
I'm a girl that likes to sing
30 I'm not just a brown girl in the ring
I'm a girl that likes to sing

And if you don't know by now
Time will show you what I'm talking 'bout
Said if you don't know by now
35 Time will show you what I'm talking 'bout
I'm talking 'bout

I'm not just a brown girl in the ring
I'm a girl that likes to sing
I'm not just a brown girl in the ring
40 I'm a girl that likes to sing

© Jeffrey Scott Productions LLC/Vincent John Music/Kobalt Music Publishing/Printrechte Hal Leonard Europe GmbH

5 a Listen, then do the tasks.
1 For the singer it is important to be 'more than …'. Find all the relevant lines and explain what they mean. Speculate which perspective for the future she develops.
2 In your own words, analyse her attitude towards education.

b Check the exact meaning of these words. Discuss to what extent they have a similar or a different meaning. Explain your choices.
- prejudice
- stereotype
- discrimination
- bullying

c Find examples of the words in **b** from real life, from your personal experience or from the news.

d Do some biographical research on the singer, prepare and then give a two-minute talk.

6 Imagine you have just had a lesson on the German constitution. Your English teacher asks you to explain Article 3 to an exchange student.

The law says …
Relevant examples are …
In my opinion, …

---

[1] **in the ring** (*idiom.*) referring to ring games that children play, in which one child is singled out and 'in the ring', surrounded by the other children –
[2] **R&B** = Rhythm and Blues, a music genre typically including elements of blues and African American folk music and marked by a strong beat –
[3] **slang** = informal language register, can be used in a regional or social sense, showing your origin and belonging to a region or affiliation to a group

My review

What can I do?

Look at these sentences about Workshop 1. Are the sentences true for you? Choose the right symbol for each sentence.

1 I can use persuasive language.
2 I can talk about Australia then and now.
3 I can discuss climate change in Australia.
4 I can describe my travel experiences in a blog.

> ⋙ = 'I'm great at this!'
> ⋙ = 'I'm good at this.'
> ⋙ = 'I'm OK at this.'

What do I know?

1 About persuasive language

a Replace the underlined words with words from the box to make the email more persuasive. Sometimes there is more than one possibility.

> ages ■ amazing ■ awesome ■
> blazing ■ heaps of ■ loads of ■ rather ■
> simply ■ uniquely ■ yummy

I've been in Melbourne for just over a week now, although it feels like longer (1). The first few days were a bit (2) strange, but now I just (3) can't get enough of the place! There are so many (4) things to do and see and so many good (5) places to go. One of my favourite things is going out to eat as there are lots of (6) really good restaurants with good (7) food. Weekends here are great (8). Every Sunday, my host family do something that is typically (9) Australian. They have a 'barbie' in the yard. Of course, I have to be careful of the hot (10) sun so I don't get sunburnt. ☺

■ / 10

Persuasive language, pp. 16–17

b Complete the phrasal verbs with the correct preposition or adverb.

I soon found ▨1▨ that the Sunday barbecue is a ritual for many Aussies. So, as you can imagine, I was really looking forward ▨2▨ my first Sunday here. A friend invited me to her uncle's – we picked ▨3▨ some desserts on our way over to his place and got there mid-afternoon.

Soon after we arrived, the grill was lit and the whole family gathered ▨4▨ . Everything had been prepared in advance, the steaks, sausages and the seafood. And, of course, there were loads of yummy salads. When the meat started sizzling, the neighbours came over with the drinks. There was lots of chatting and laughter, and a bit later the host turned ▨5▨ some music. The adults sat ▨6▨ to eat, but the kids played games and ate when they were hungry. The older kids looked ▨7▨ the younger ones and so their parents could relax. Of course, the children were excited about the promise of ice cream, but the rule was no desserts before they'd eaten ▨8▨ .
Although most people had to work the next day, no one rushed ▨9▨ early, so it was dark by the time everyone had cleaned ▨10▨ and the neighbours had left. All in all, a great day!

■ / 10

Phrasal verbs, pp. 16–17

Workshop 1

→ Workbook, page 32

2 **About Australian history.** Complete the text with the correct form of the verbs in brackets.

Robert O'Hara Burke and William Wills **1** (*be*) the first Europeans to successfully cross Australia from south to north. By the time they **2** (*begin*) their famous journey in 1860, the two men **3** (*live*) in Australia for seven years, but they **4** (*not take part in*) an expedition before. Burke was appointed as the leader and Wills, who **5** (*initially join*) the expedition party as third in command, was promoted to deputy leader.

By the time they **6** (*reach*) Cooper Creek on December 16, 1860, the men **7** (*travel*) for nearly four months. Burke **8** (*not be*) happy with the slow progress, so he travelled on with a smaller group and **9** (*leave*) the rest of the party there. Although Burke and his small group reached the Bay of Carpentaria quite quickly, they **10** (*not have*) enough food and water, and by the time they **11** (*get back*) to Cooper Creek one of the men, Charles Gray, **12** (*already die*). Unfortunately, when Burke, Wills and John King **13** (*return*) to Cooper Creek the remaining men **14** (*already leave*). Somehow, King managed to stay alive, but when he was finally rescued both Burke and Wills **15** (*also die*).

/ 15

Past perfect and past perfect progressive → G3 ; pp. 18–19

3 **About the climate.** Complete the talk with the correct passive form of the verbs in brackets.

Today I'm going to talk about climate change in Australia and the effect this is having on our unique wildlife. In the last ten years, around 50% of the animals **1** (*wipe out*). If we carry on like this, many animals that **2** (*can + only find*) in Australia face extinction. Reports about heatwaves, droughts and wildfires **3** (*show*) regularly on TV, so what is causing this extreme weather? One big problem is deforestation. Since the first European settlers arrived, more than half of the trees **4** (*cut down*). The problem **5** (*should not + ignore*) any longer. We have to do something. The effect of logging and other destructive practices **6** (*have to + make clear*) to the wider public. Experts say that around 45 million animals **7** (*kill*) each year because of logging! Action **8** (*must + take*) to tackle it soon. If nothing **9** (*do*), not only will temperatures increase, but some of our most iconic animals such as koalas and even our kangaroos **10** (*lose*). Is this what we want?

/ 10

Passives, → G4 – G8 ; pp. 24–25
Climate vocabulary, pp. 26–27

forty-one 41

4 About a travel experience

a Complete the first part of Paige's blogpost. Use each of the reporting verbs from the box once.

> asked ■ described ■ explained ■ said ■ told ■ wanted to know

Last week a school rugby team from Australia came to play against our school team. While they were here, my Uncle Tai took them out for a bit of an adventure and he ⟨1⟩ me if I wanted to go with them. We went to most of the usual sights and did some white-water rafting. One of the boys, Jason, ⟨2⟩ me he thought the whole experience was awesome and he ⟨3⟩ if I'd ever been to another country. I ⟨4⟩ my trip to Brighton the year before and ⟨5⟩ how I knew the family I stayed with there. He ⟨6⟩ that, in his opinion, it is really important to get to know other countries and cultures.

b Now complete the second part of the blogpost with information from the speech bubbles.

For example, friends of mine are with their family in Greece this week.

When we meet up next month, we'll be able to swap stories about Greece and New Zealand.

I think once they hear about my wonderful trip, they'll want to visit New Zealand as they've never been here.

He gave the example of friends of his who ⟨7⟩ with their family in Greece ⟨8⟩. He said that when they ⟨9⟩ ⟨10⟩, they ⟨11⟩ swap stories about Greece and New Zealand. He also thought once they ⟨12⟩ about his wonderful trip, they ⟨13⟩ to visit New Zealand as they ⟨14⟩ ⟨15⟩.

■ / 15

Reported speech → G9 – G10 ; pp. 28–29

■ / 60

What's my score?

Check your answers to the review (Workbook, p. 32). What are your scores for each section?

> **What was your total score?**
> ≫ score 46–60
> ≫ score 26–45
> ≫ score 0–25

Do you want to change your answers to the 'What can I do?' statements on page 40?
Look at the tasks on pages 43–45: ≫, ≫ and ≫. Choose the tasks to help you.

Workshop 1
MY PRACTICE PAGES

My practice pages

Using persuasive language

1 **I wish you were here!** Add words and phrases from the box to make these sentences more persuasive. Sometimes there is more than one possibility.

> absolutely ■ again and again ■ every inch of ■ fantastic ■ just ■ lively ■ simply ■ truly ■ way

1 I ▢ believe you'd enjoy being here in Melbourne.
2 This is an ▢ amazing city! You have to see it for yourself. I ▢ cannot get enough of it.
3 And there's one great place I return to ▢ – Hosier Lane.
4 Wherever I look there are paintings in a mixture of ▢ colours, covering ▢ the buildings.
5 This lane is ▢ better than any gallery.
6 Imagine ▢ how much fun we could have together in this ▢ city!

2 **Persuade me!** Read the blogpost. Rewrite it so it's more persuasive. Use some of the adjectives and adverbs from the box. There is more than one possible answer.

> amazing ■ especially ■ extremely ■ good ■ great ■ heaps of ■ interesting ■ really ■ simply ■ very

I have a new hobby – kite-surfing. It's a bit like surfing, except you use the wind to help you move. Sometimes you can go quickly and it can be dangerous if the wind is strong. Last week I went out on the sea for the first time. It was fun. I've had many lessons, but you aren't allowed out on your own straight away because it's too risky.

3 **You really should …** Write an email to a friend and try to persuade them to do one of these activities.
- read a particular book
- watch a particular movie
- take up a new sport / hobby

Talking about Australia then and now

4 **Australia's first prime minister.** Complete the text with the correct alternatives.

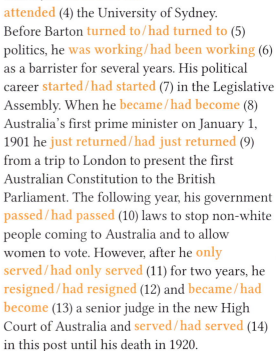

When Edmund Barton **was / had been** (1) born in 1849, his parents, originally from Great Britain, **already were / had already been** (2) in Australia for over twenty years. Barton was raised in Sydney and after he **completed / had completed** (3) school, he **attended / had attended** (4) the University of Sydney. Before Barton **turned to / had turned to** (5) politics, he **was working / had been working** (6) as a barrister for several years. His political career **started / had started** (7) in the Legislative Assembly. When he **became / had become** (8) Australia's first prime minister on January 1, 1901 he **just returned / had just returned** (9) from a trip to London to present the first Australian Constitution to the British Parliament. The following year, his government **passed / had passed** (10) laws to stop non-white people coming to Australia and to allow women to vote. However, after he **only served / had only served** (11) for two years, he **resigned / had resigned** (12) and **became / had become** (13) a senior judge in the new High Court of Australia and **served / had served** (14) in this post until his death in 1920.

forty-three 43

5 A famous Aboriginal. Complete the conversation with the correct form of the verbs in brackets.

Jack Hi, Bruce. What are you reading?
Bruce It's a book about Eddie Koiki Mabo.
Jack Who's he?
Bruce He **1** (be) a famous Aboriginal who **2** (fight) for his people's land rights.
Jack Interesting. So what have you learned?
Bruce He was born in the Torres Islands off the north coast of Australia, but in 1959 he **3** (move) to Queensland. He **4** (live) there for 13 years when he tried to return to Murray Island. He **5** (hope) to visit his father, but the government wouldn't let Eddie go because he **6** (not live) on the island for so long that they said he was a non-Islander.
Jack Wow! That sounds terrible.
Bruce Yes, just six weeks later, he **7** (receive) a message telling him his father **8** (die). Then he **9** (spend) the rest of his life trying to get equality for Aboriginal people in Australia.
Jack And what happened?
Bruce The Native Title Act was passed by the Australian Parliament in 1993. It said the land belonged to the Aborigines.
Jack Eddie Mabo must have been happy.
Bruce Sadly, he **10** (die) the year before.

6 The Crocodile Man. Use the facts about Steve Irwin to write a short biography. Think about the order of the information so you can use a mixture of simple past and past perfect.

- Born: Melbourne, 1962.
- Died: September 2006. Killed by stingray while diving.
- Spent childhood at parents' wildlife park.
- Learned to handle crocodiles and was given a snake as a present on his sixth birthday.
- Started filming a TV show *The Crocodile Hunter* in 1992.
- The US cable network *Animal Planet* bought the rights to the TV show in 1996.
- In 2001 appeared in the film *Dr Dolittle 2* with Eddie Murphy.
- Was famous as a wildlife educator and for his catchphrase *Crikey*!

Talking about the causes and effects of climate change

7 The Great Barrier Reef. Complete the leaflet with the words from the box.

> has been posted ■ has been set up ■
> is going to be held ■ is not taken ■
> is thought ■ is threatened ■ is visited ■
> was declared ■ will be shown

The Great Barrier Reef is one of nature's wonders. It **1** that more than 1,500 species of fish live in the reef and it **2** a World Heritage site in 1981. Every year it **3** by around two million tourists. Unfortunately, its very existence **4** by a number of issues connected to climate change. If action **5** soon, it will be too late! A campaign **6** to help save the reef for future generations. A march **7** next Saturday. Information about the march **8** on different social media platforms, so join us and help us save the Great Barrier Reef. The march **9** to audiences around the world to highlight the threat climate change poses.

8 Climate policy. Complete the short article with the correct passive form of the verbs in brackets.

Yesterday new laws **1** (discuss) by MPs in the Australian parliament. If they **2** (pass), a powerful message **3** (send) to businesses and companies to change their practices. Thousands of hectares of forest **4** (destroy) in the wildfires last year and many animals **5** (kill). In the future, hundreds of volunteers **6** (ask) to help when there are wildfires. They **7** (give) training by firefighters to help them prepare. A petition **8** (already organize) to highlight the seriousness of the current situation. An increase in the number of weather-related events **9** (record) in the past ten years. Climate experts claim these **10** (cause) by the use of fossil fuels or at least made worse. Large amounts of coal **11** (export) by mining companies, so some people worry that the industry **12** (damage) by the new laws.

Workshop 1
MY PRACTICE PAGES

9 **A climate protest.** Imagine you attended a demonstration about climate change. Write a short report for your school magazine about the protest. Include the ideas below. Say:
- where the demonstration was held.
- who made speeches.
- what happened (e.g. if anyone was arrested).

Remember to use the passive voice in your report.

Talking about travel experiences

10 **What did Jason say?** Choose the correct alternative to complete what Jason told his friends when he got back to Australia.

1. Ricky admitted that he just couldn't believe we'd lost the match **yesterday / the day before**.
2. The coach **told / said** us he was proud of us and asked us if we **wanted / did want** to do a rafting trip.
3. Of course we **said / told** yes, but we still felt disappointed and promised we **will win / would win** the game **next / the following month**.
4. We had a great guide on our rafting tour – Nina. We asked her **what we had to do / what did we have to do**.
5. She told us **paddle / to paddle** hard and **don't panic / not to panic**.
6. Afterwards everyone agreed that it **was / had been** awesome and that **this / that** trip had helped us forget the disappointment **the day before / yesterday**.

11 **Three conversations.** Report these three conversations. Use as many different reporting verbs as you can.

1 Jason and Tai

Tai, what do these Maori words mean?

It's a traditional greeting.

I … Tai … and he …

2 Coach Hansen and Ricky

Boys, you played well. Don't worry about losing – you can't win all the games.

You're right, but I'm still disappointed.

Coach Hansen …
I … that …, but …

3 Jason and Paige

So, tell me, what did you enjoy most?

I just can't say, Paige. The whole trip has been awesome.

Paige …
I …

12 **My blog.** Think of a recent trip or holiday you have had. Write a short blogpost about your experiences. Use the information below to help you. Say:
- where you went.
- what you did.
- what you enjoyed most.
- who you spoke to and what you said to each other.

Marcus Sedgwick

Cudweed's crush

ONE

I am a raven. I think I've told you *that* before?
I like being a raven. If I haven't told you that before, then I apologize. I want to make this clear: I like being a raven. In fact, I love it! One of the main reasons that I love being a raven is that I do not have to get out of bed in the morning. I get up when I feel like it, and *not before*. On the other hand, you humans, you're always having to set an alarm clock, and rush off to school, or go to work, or something like that. I don't really understand why you do these things. Someone once told me that it's important to go to school to learn things, and that you have to go to work to earn money. But, from a raven's point of view, both of these things are overrated[1]. Ravens don't go to school, and we certainly don't go to work, and we get along just fine.

Now, why am I telling you all this? I'm telling you this because I do not like getting up in the morning, and as I said, I only get up when I feel like it. And if it happens that I feel like it at three o'clock in the afternoon, then that is when I get up. And finally, I am telling you this, because if I *do* get woken up early in the morning, and I haven't had enough sleep, then I become a Very Grumpy Raven. Indeed.

And that is just what happened last Tuesday morning.

I was sleeping the morning away, in one of my favourite places – the barrel[2] of an old cannon in a long corridor upstairs in the castle. I was having a really excellent dream about dead frogs. You know, when you see a frog on the road? A dead one? And it's totally flat, because it has been run over by a car? Well, ravens love a dead frog of this kind. They have a strange salty flavour[3], which is delicious, even if you do get a hint of[4] rubber along with it. In my dream there were hundreds of dead frogs on a nice empty road, and the sun was shining, which is wonderful because it warms up the frog nicely. And then, all of a sudden, Cudweed was standing on the road in my dream, shouting.

He was shouting, 'No, I won't! And you can't make me!'

I looked up from my tasty dead frog and I watched Cudweed shouting. He wasn't shouting at me, but as I looked at him, a strange thing happened: he slowly turned into a frog.

It was a bit weird. Then I realized that I was in a dream, and woke up. I could still hear shouting, and I was really, really grumpy.

The noise was coming from downstairs, and I could hear the shouting all the way upstairs.

Now, I admit, I was in a *very* bad mood, and I flopped out of the barrel of the cannon and decided to go and peck the head of the first person I met. And peck hard.

I flew along the corridor, turned the corner[5], headed for the stairs, and shot down them faster than an elephant on ice skates. I arrived in the dining room, the scene of all the noise, and who was the first person I saw? Cudweed!

So did I start pecking his head?
No, I did not.
Why?

Because the look on his face stopped me in my tracks. If I thought I was angry, it was nothing compared with the mood Cudweed was in.

---

[1] **overrated** überbewertet; überschätzt – [2] **barrel** Kanonenrohr – [3] **flavour** Geschmack; Aroma – [4] **a hint of** ein Hauch von – [5] **to turn a corner** um die Ecke biegen

READING FOR FUN

His face was bright red, and there was steam coming out of his ears. (This last part is not actually true but it seemed to me that he was so angry that it was entirely possible his brain was boiling in his skull and was about to shoot out of his head.)

And he was shouting, 'No! I won't', over and over again.

There was one strange thing. One *other* strange thing, I mean. His trousers were slowly falling down. He was so angry, he hadn't noticed, but he made quite a sight as he kept shouting and we all got a good look at his underpants, which were, I was happy to see, the ones I chose for his last birthday, the ones with little ravens on them.

The rest of the family were staring at him, and the only one saying anything back was Minty.

'But you can't just stop like that,' she was saying. 'It's not right!'

I had no idea what was going on, so I landed on Solstice's shoulder to watch.

'Oh, good morning, Edgar,' she said. 'You're up early.'

'Grawk,' was all I had to say to that. And can you blame me? It was only ten o'clock! In the morning! Solstice ignored my rude word and nodded at her little brother.

'He's a vegan,' she whispered.

I stared at Cudweed.

I stared at him hard. But he didn't *look* any different. But Solstice was telling me he was a vegan, so I looked again, harder, and this time, I realized something.

I didn't know what 'vegan' meant.

I pecked Solstice's ear and said, 'Arrk?'

And then she told me what 'vegan' means.

At first, I couldn't believe it. So I pecked her again and said, 'Kork?'

'Yes,' she said. 'He won't eat meat anymore. And not only meat, he won't eat anything that has come from an animal, and he won't eat anything that means an animal has been hurt making it, and he won't wear anything that's made from an animal either. Like his leather belt.'

So that explained the thing about his trousers, at least. His belt was lying on the floor and I assumed he had thrown it there, since then, his trousers had been going South[6].

'I refuse!' Cudweed cried, pointing one finger at the ceiling dramatically.

Minty was also not keeping calm.

'But I have just bought *four hundred* of your favourite hamburgers to put in the freezer! You can't just stop!'

'But I can!' shouted Cudweed. 'And I have! So there!'

'Well, couldn't you stop in a week or so?' asked Minty. 'Once you've eaten all the hamburgers?'

'No!'

'Well, what am I going to do with all these hamburgers?' screamed Minty, and I thought her head might fall off, she was so angry.

---

[6] **to go South** *here*: herunterrutschen

'I will bury⁷ them in the back garden and we can all say sorry to the poor cows!'

With that, Cudweed tried to walk away, but the effect was ruined because he still did not know that his trousers were around his ankles. He fell flat on his face, said a rude word, got up, pulled his trousers up, and then stomped⁸ off to his room.

'Well, well,' said Solstice.

'Ark,' I agreed. Because what else could you say?

I was so confused by the whole thing that I couldn't get back to sleep. As the morning passed, I thought about being vegan … And I didn't like it. I didn't like it one little bit.

Now, as it happens, Solstice is already a vegetarian. She has been since she was a little girl. One day, when she was six, she told her parents she didn't want to eat animals anymore. She explained why.

'Edgar is a bird,' she said, 'and birds are animals. So that means Edgar is an animal. And if Edgar is an animal then I don't want to eat animals anymore. Because Edgar is my friend.'

It was very good logic, not bad at all for a six-year-old. I didn't like being called an animal, because you know, I'm a raven, and ravens are kind of special. And while I understood that it was very sweet of Solstice not to want to eat me, I didn't agree that that was the right way to behave. I mean, ravens *need* meat. We just do. I am in favour of people not eating *me*. And I am in favour of not eating *ravens in general*, but that's where I disagreed with Solstice. I think it's okay to eat *some* sorts of animals, and not others.

Anyway, from that day on Solstice was vegetarian. But now, here was Cudweed, a boy who has eaten more cows in a year than some small countries do, saying he was a vegan.

It was lunchtime.

Cudweed appeared. He was no longer angry, but he was still a little embarrassed by the thing with his trousers. He was the last to sit down at the dining table, and when he did, I saw that he had replaced his belt with a piece of string⁹.

'What's for lunch?' he said, suspiciously.

Minty looked at him. She looked hopeful.

'Have you changed your mind yet, dear?' she asked.

'About what?'

'About being a vegan. I've made some nice meatballs and – '

'No!' he said. 'It's only been two hours. I have not changed my mind! I will eat salad!'

So he did, and this was very strange, too, because Cudweed is a boy who never eats salad unless his parents pay him to eat it. (They sometimes do, to make sure he is getting fresh vegetables.)

⁷ **to bury sth.** etw. vergraben – ⁸ **to stomp** stapfen; stampfen – ⁹ **string** Schnur

So he ate a huge plateful of salad and as he did he simultaneously[10] stared at everyone and smiled at them, too. All while eating. It was a rather unpleasant sight, but when he was done, he got up from the table and made the following announcement.

'I shall be in my room. I shall be writing letters to various supermarkets and restaurants to inform them of their unethical behaviour towards animals. You will each be receiving a similar letter from me at dinner time. Until then, goodbye!'

And this time he stomped off with much more success than the first time, until the string in his belt broke, his trousers fell down and he fell flat on his face again.

It was later that afternoon that Solstice and I made our big discovery. Something was not right about this sudden change in Cudweed. If there is one thing you can be sure of about Cudweed, it is that he is *predictable*[11]. He likes the same things to happen on the same day at the same time. And one thing that he particularly likes is that his food is predictable, that it arrives when it's supposed to arrive. And that there are dead animals in it.

I agree with him about these last two points. Nothing is more stressful to me than a meal that arrives late, and then only contains *broccoli*. It's unbearable.

Strange. Cudweed's behaviour, I mean.

It seemed that Solstice was thinking the same thing, because just as I was trying (and failing) to fly at the height of Cudweed's keyhole, I heard her voice behind me.

'Edgar!' she said. 'Are you spying on Cudweed?'

'Urk,' I said, dropping to the floor.

'Good idea!' she said, and then she knelt and looked through Cudweed's keyhole, while I sat on her head and listened.

'I can't see anything,' she whispered, 'but I think he has someone in there with him. I think … it's a girl!'

'A girl!' I thought. 'Whatever next?!'

But we had to be sure, so I flew out of the nearest window, circled around the castle walls, and came to rest outside Cudweed's window.

He didn't see me. As far as I could see he was alone in his room, but I saw that he was staring at his computer screen. He was talking to a girl. He was gazing[12] at her, his head was resting in his hands, and they were chatting away. I swear that a bomb could have gone off in his wastepaper basket, and he wouldn't have noticed.

There was only one explanation: Cudweed was in love!

---

[10] **simultaneously** gleichzeitig – [11] **predictable** vorhersehbar, durchschaubar – [12] **to gaze at sb.** jmd. anstarren

Workshop 2
Routes to your future

@ WES-40325-002

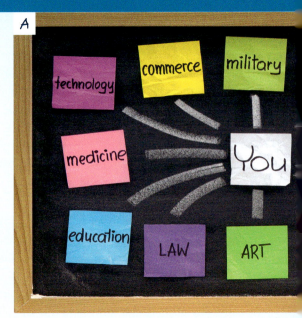

1. Have you thought about what you want to do when you leave school? Look at the stickers on the board (A) and check the words you don't know in a dictionary. What would you write on the empty stickers?

2. A careers fair is a good place to find out what career options are available and help you identify different routes into employment. Describe what you can see on the signpost (B). What routes does it show and what do you know about them?

3. **a** Look at the box (C) and check you know all the words and phrases and the German equivalents.

C

Career options
- to take GCSE / A-level exams
- to get good grades / exam results
- to apply for / to do an apprenticeship / an internship / a degree course
- to study for vocational qualifications
- to learn practical skills
- to get academic qualifications / a degree in …
- to spend a year abroad
- to graduate (from university)

Career Paths

D

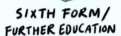

SIXTH FORM/ FURTHER EDUCATION

DEGREE/ DEGREE APPRENTICESHIP

APPRENTICESHIP

6 b VIDEO TRACK: Sammy, Emily and Lucas are at a careers fair. First read their career goals. Then look at the infographic (D) and watch the first video to see what advice Sammy gets.

Sammy, 17

"I'm studying languages and I'd like a career where I can use them."

Emily, 15

"My goal is to work with animals. I want to find out what my options are after I've taken my GCSEs."

"I'm interested in a career in engineering. I want to get some advice about what to do after A-levels."

Lucas, 18

c VIDEO TRACK: The advisor gives Sammy a takeaway showing a possible career path for him. Watch the interviews with Emily and Lucas and complete their takeaways. At the end of each video, compare your ideas with the advisor's.

4 Discuss the advantages as well as disadvantages of each route on the signpost in **2**.

"One of the disadvantages of going to university is that you might have to leave home."

"For me, that would be an advantage!"

YOUR TRACK

After this workshop you will be able to:
- discuss your hopes and plans after finishing school.
- write your CV and a letter of application for a job.
- compare working life today with the past.
- talk about volunteering and social issues.
- use communication strategies in a job interview. (Workshop task)

CULTURE CORNER

GSCE (General Certificate of Secondary Education) exams are taken in up to 12 subjects by students aged 15–16 in the UK. A minimum of five GSCEs is required by most sixth form colleges – where students study for their A-level (Advanced Level) exams. Most students take these two-year courses in three subjects. A-levels are a requirement for most British universities.

New Directions

1 **What's next?** *New Directions*, a career website, has asked students to share their hopes and plans when they leave school. Read what four students say and complete the sentences in your own words.

1. Amir is interested in ..., so his uncle recommends ...
2. Daniela plans ... before she starts ...
3. Ben doesn't want ..., so he's going to try ...
4. Sisi and her friend hope ...

> - Some verbs are always followed by a gerund, while others are followed by a *to*-infinitive.
> - Some verbs (*like, hate, start*, etc.) can be followed by a gerund or an infinitive with no change in meaning.
> - The verbs *remember, forget, stop* and *try* can be followed by either a gerund or an infinitive but the meaning changes.

| Home | Further education | Undergraduate | Alternatives | **Careers** |

NEW DIRECTIONS ▶ What are your hopes and plans after you finish school?

Amir, 16, from London, England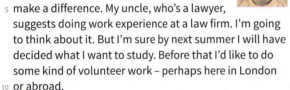
I want to go to university. In my student activist group, we focus on social issues like discrimination. I can see how lawyers can
5 make a difference. My uncle, who's a lawyer, suggests doing work experience at a law firm. I'm going to think about it. But I'm sure by next summer I will have decided what I want to study. Before that I'd like to do some kind of volunteer work – perhaps here in London
10 or abroad.

Daniela, 18, from Berlin, Germany
Next spring I take my final exams. After that I want to study medicine. You need really good grades, but based on my work so far, I'll be
15 OK. But first my best friend and I are going to Australia for the summer. Then I'll be able to start my studies in Berlin. Medical students usually do an internship in a hospital. I'd like to do mine in the UK or Ireland.

Ben, 18, from Cardiff, Wales
I'd like to find a computing job. My parents think I should go to university, but you don't need a degree to start in computing. In March I have an interview for a job as an apprentice software developer. Next week, I'm meeting 25
my cousin who's been with the company for four years. He's sure I'll get an offer. The apprenticeship starts in September. I'll have finished my A-levels by then.

Sisi, 17, from Manchester, England
A friend and I like buying vintage clothes, making changes to them and then selling 30
them at markets. We want to turn this into an online business. We're going to apply to a start-up incubator for help. They offer start-up money. It's a three-month programme. By the time we finish, we'll have written a business plan, and then we'll see 35
what happens.

2 **Choices, choices**

 a Choose the idea you like the most. Walk around the class and find someone who has made the same choice. Compare your reasons.

> *I'd like to start my own business like Sisi – not with clothes, but ...*

 b Talk about someone with a positive story after leaving school. It can be someone you follow on social media or someone you know personally.

 c Write a description for *New Directions* of the route that the person you discussed in **b** took and where it has led him or her.

21) **Words and phrases**

apprentice	a young person who works for sb. to learn particular skills
au pair	a young person who lives with a family in a foreign country
developer	a person who creates sth.
firm	a business or company

Workshop 2

→ Workbook, pages 33/34

3 A bright future

a Look at the sentences in the box. Then read about the students' hopes and plans again and find more examples of these future forms.

> When we talk about the future, we use different tenses to express different things.
> 1 *I'm going to think about* it. (plan)
> 2 *Based on my work so far, I'll be* OK. (prediction)
> 3 *My best friend and I are going to Australia for the summer.* (arrangement)
> 4 *The apprenticeship starts in July.* (timetable)
> 5 *By next summer, I will have decided* what to do. (action finished before a future time)

b Make more sentences about the future.

1 Amir: My final exams | start next spring. I | finish by the end of May.
2 Daniela: I | check out flights soon. My dad thinks booking now | be cheaper.
3 Ben: I | have my interview in four weeks. My cousin | help me prepare.
4 Sisi: My friend | do a design course next month. That | be a big help.

 page 74

4 A future au pair

a Now read about Lauren's plans. What do you think she will have to do as an au pair?

> **Lauren, 17, from Dublin, Ireland**
> Next year my friends will be studying or doing an apprenticeship. I'm not ready for that yet. I'd like to take a gap year to get some ideas about what I really want to do. As soon as my exams are over, I'll be applying for an au pair job. Hopefully by September I'll be working somewhere in the US.

b Look at this sentence from Lauren's statement: *Next year my friends will be studying or doing an apprenticeship.*
Read the information in the box. Find more examples of the future progressive in Lauren's statement and explain why they are in this tense.

> • We form the future progressive with will + 1 + 2 .
> • We use it for a planned action in the future that will be happening ...
> – over a period of time: *during the holidays, for the whole semester.*
> – at a certain time: *after lunch, at 5.30.*
> – when something else happens: *when the course finishes.*

c Complete Lauren's plans, then match each one with the rules above.

1 The au pair agency _____ (contact) the applicants during the next few weeks.
2 Maybe I _____ (live) somewhere warm and sunny this winter.
3 I hope that my employers _____ (wait) at the airport when I arrive.
4 I _____ (blog) once a week to share my experiences.

5 YOUR TURN: The next step.
Make a double circle. The inner-circle partner asks about the outer-circle partner's hopes and plans after finishing school. Examples:

What ...? / Where ...? / How long ...? / How are you going to pay for it? / What will you do if ...? / What are you afraid of most?

After two minutes, move to the next partner and change roles.

Grammar and structures

Gerunds and infinitives (revision) → G11
Many young people **enjoy travelling** and **want to volunteer** abroad.

Expressing the future (revision) → G12
She**'ll probably go** to business school.
I'm going to take some time off and travel.
My interview **is** in July.
We**'re visiting** a careers fair next week.
He **will have made up** his mind by then.

Future progressive → G13
During the summer, they**'ll be inviting** the applicants for interviews.

Practice: A work opportunity

1 **GET STARTED!**

 a In year 9, many students do work experience to help them think about where they might like to work later. Where would you like to do this and why?

 b Talk about who might be able to help you find a work placement.

2 **Job advertisements**

a Look at this job advert from a UK employment website. Which of the students from page 52 could be interested in the advert? Explain why.

Work experience placement

Putney Legal Advice Centre, London

Putney Legal Advice Centre is pleased to offer an unpaid work experience placement to a candidate
5   between 15 and 19 years old who shows an interest in one of the careers we offer.

This is a great opportunity to learn about the work of a legal professional and about how a legal advice centre protects the rights of people who cannot afford a
10   lawyer. We can also help you explore career options in the legal profession.

We offer three weeks of work experience at our London office.

Apply in writing to liz.hunt@putneylegal.co.uk.

---

b Answer the questions.

1 What kind of work opportunity is being offered?
2 What advantages are described?
3 How long does the work last?
4 How much does it pay?

3 **Get it right**

a Amir has just got a message from his uncle. Read it and explain the difference between the **highlighted** structures.

> Did you **remember to check out** the links I sent you? I've just had another idea. Do you **remember meeting** Saira at my birthday party? She's also a lawyer and she may be able to help. You can contact her on …

b Complete Amir's answer with the verbs from the box in the correct form. There are two you don't need.

> contact ■ look after ■ look at ■ make ■ save ■ talk ■ text ■ write

> Don't worry, I didn't forget **1** the links. One ad was really interesting, so in the middle of my homework I stopped **2** an application. Stupid me – I didn't remember **3** my essay, so now I've got to start again! Thanks for Saira's number. Sure, I remember **4** to her. I'll try **5** her tomorrow. I must stop **6** now otherwise I'll never finish my homework!

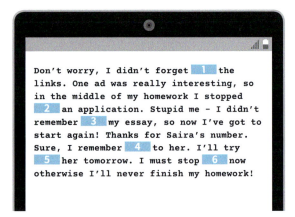

>>> page 74

Words and phrases

department   a section of a large organization
publisher   a company that prepares and prints books, magazines, etc. and makes them available to the public

Workshop 2

→ Workbook, pages 35–37

4 **It's a small world!** Amir follows his uncle's advice and contacts Saira. Complete their exchange with the correct form of the verbs in brackets.

S. Morning Amir. Sure, I __1__ (*help*) you if I can. My husband's oldest friend, Neil, is a lawyer at Putney Legal. We __2__ (*meet*) the Saturday after next to celebrate the men's birthdays and the fact that on that day they __3__ (*know*) each other for 35 years. (Their mothers gave birth on the same day in the same hospital!)

A. Amazing! I __4__ (*see*) my uncle over the weekend to work on my CV, so by the time you all meet, Putney Legal __5__ (*receive*) my application.

S. Fine. I __6__ (*give*) Neil a ring to tell him that your application __7__ (*come*) next week. Then, he __8__ (*read*) it by the time I see him. OK?

>>> page 74

5 **Work. Explore. Grow.**

a Why do you think many school leavers take a gap year? Discuss and note down your ideas.

b Now listen to a *New Directions* podcast. Are any ideas you didn't think of mentioned?

c Look at 1–6, then listen again. Are the statements true or false? Correct the false statements.

1 Lucy is planning to go to university in September.
2 She will be working while she's in the US.
3 By March, she will have returned from her trip.
4 In spring, Simon will be volunteering in Greece again in an environmental project.
5 By the end of the project, several Greek islands will have benefitted from the volunteers' work.
6 Simon will be applying for jobs when he gets back from Greece.

d Compare their motivations for taking a gap year. How are they similar and different?

6 **SPEAKING FOCUS: This is me**

a Copy the table and make notes about yourself. The words and phrases in the box can help you.

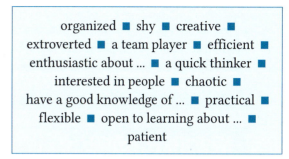

What am I like?	(Choose three adjectives to describe yourself.)
My strengths	(What are you good at?)
My weaknesses	(What aren't you so good at?)

b Tell your partner about yourself and get feedback. What have you overlooked? How could you describe some aspects better? Then find a new partner and do the same again.

c Write a short text about yourself using your notes and feedback. Don't include your name.

d **GALLERY WALK:** Put up your texts in class. You'll probably recognize your partners' texts, but who do the other texts describe? Give feedback.

fifty-five 55

Applying for a job

1 Tips for teenagers

a Amir is looking at the *New Directions* website for information about job applications. Read the text and decide where the missing sub headings go.

> Conclude with a call to action. ■ Explain why you're the right person. ■ Include the essentials. ■ Know your options. ■ Show who you are. ■ Talk about relevant skills.

NEW DIRECTIONS ▶ The application process – Tips for teenagers

The written application

For students or school leavers with little experience, applying for work is always a challenge. Whether it's work experience, a training programme or an actual job, you'll have to apply in writing. This means an up-to-date Curriculum Vitae or CV and a cover letter. How do you get the most from your CV and cover letter?

A winning CV

Be clear and brief. Your CV should have a clear format and structure. It should also be detailed but not too long. Normally, for teens with little or no work experience, one page is enough.

1 In some countries, you don't have to give personal details that could be used to discriminate against you because of your race, nationality, gender or a disability. In the UK, you are not obliged to add a headshot photo. Similarly, your date of birth is also optional. However, in some European countries you are supposed to include this information. Check what is expected in the country where you are applying.

2 Employers are interested in your education, work experience and skills. These details must be in your CV.

3 You can show more of your personality by listing hobbies and interests. If you have awards or other achievements, you should highlight them.

An effective cover letter

A cover letter can help you sell the skills and knowledge that you have. To make your cover letter effective:

- *Introduce yourself clearly.* Explain who you are, the position you are applying for, and how you found out about the opportunity.
- **4** Give a real-life example that shows why you are right for the job.
- **5** Identify the skills you've gained in part-time jobs, activities and sports. Explain how you'll be able to use them.
- **6** You need to leave a strong final impression, so invite the employer to contact you.

b Read the text again and answer the questions.

1 Why doesn't a CV always have to include a photo?
2 When is it an advantage to list your hobbies in your CV?
3 How can a cover letter be useful?
4 What's a good way to end a cover letter?

2 Getting it right

  a How many modal verbs can you think of? Make a list, then complete the rules in the box.

> We often use modal substitutes to talk about the past and future.
> - *be able to* is the substitute for **1**.
>   Say how you **were able to** use your skills.
> - *have to* is the substitute for **2**.
>   I **will have to** apply in writing.
> - We use *should* to talk about the present and future. To talk about the past we use *should have* + **3**.
>   She **should have listed** her hobbies.

 Words and phrases

cover letter   a written document attached to your job application

Workshop 2

→ Workbook, pages 38/39

b Amir is thinking about his first application. Complete his thoughts.

1. My cousin Salma said she ▁▁ (must) include a headshot with her last application. I wonder if I ▁▁ (must) send one.
2. I hope I ▁▁ (can) speak much better French after my course in Paris next month. If not, I ▁▁ (not can) add French to my CV.
3. When I spoke to Uncle Nasir, I ▁▁ (should) asked him which skills are important.

3 In other words. Look at these ways of expressing *should* and *must* in English. Find the German equivalents for the **highlighted** phrases.

1. In the UK, you **are not obliged to** include a headshot photo.
2. In some European countries, you **are supposed to** include this information.
3. If you have awards or other achievements, you **ought to** highlight them here.
4. You **need to** leave a strong final impression.

4 WORDPOWER: Sentence adverbs. Read the information below. Then complete the sentences with the adverbs from the box.

> A sentence adverb shows a person's attidude towards the content of a sentence.
> *Theoretically, I could begin next week.*

> Additionally ■ Fortunately ■
> Ideally ■ Naturally ■ Normally

1. I have a lot of camping experience. ▁▁ , I am an enthusiastic rock climber.
2. ▁▁ , I have visited Glasgow several times, so I know the city well.
3. ▁▁ , I don't include a video CV with my job applications, but this is a special case.
4. ▁▁ , I would like to begin in July, but of course I could start sooner if necessary.
5. ▁▁ , I will send my exam results as soon as I receive them.

5 The job interview: Dos and don'ts

a Listen to part 1 of a *New Directions* podcast about job interviews and do the tasks.

1. Explain why Rose focuses on the most basic dos and don'ts.
2. Give examples of how you should 'do your homework'.
3. Describe how you ought to dress for an interview.
4. Explain why Rose says 'Don't feel obliged to act overly cheerful'.

b What specific advice is given? Listen to part 2 and match the sentence beginnings and endings.

1. You shouldn't …   a prepare a couple of questions to ask.
2. If I were you, I'd …   b arrive about ten minutes early.
3. You ought to …   c turn off your phone before you sit down?
4. Why don't you …   d practise too much.
5. You should …   e only ask about the salary if they offer you the position.

6 YOUR TURN: Good advice. Practise giving each other advice. First, individually, think of a difficult situation or decision you have to make. You can use the ideas in the box or your own. Then take turns to describe your challenge and ask for advice. Remember to use the expressions for giving advice from **5b**.

> You're late for a job interview. ■ You've lost your mobile. ■ You forgot to do some important homework. ■
> You forgot a good friend's birthday. ■ Two friends want you to go with them to a US summer camp.

Grammar and structures

Modal verbs (revision) → G14
Modal substitutes → G15
With her CV, I think she**'ll be able to** get an apprenticeship.
He **had to** do an interview with the manager.
You **ought to** prepare some questions to ask the interviewer.

@ WES-40325-002

Practice: Presenting your best self

1 **GET STARTED!** Writing a CV is about presenting yourself in the most positive way possible. What strengths, interests and skills do you have that employers might be interested in? Look back at **6** on page 55. Name two and explain how they might be useful in a job.

2 **Amir's CV.** Amir is applying for the work experience placement on page 54. Read his CV and do the tasks.

1 Name the school achievements Amir lists.
2 Explain his most recent work experience.
3 Describe any volunteer experience.
4 Say which languages he speaks fluently.
5 Explain what 'French B1' means.
6 Name two of Amir's interests.

CURRICULUM VITAE

Personal information
Address   7 Grantley St, London E1 4BN
Mobile   +44 7146549876
Email   a.shah@mail.co.uk
Date of birth   5 April 20..

Profile   As a member of a student activist group which focuses on social issues, I have realized how important it is for everyone to have access to legal advice. My aim is to gain some practical experience in this field before studying law at university.

Education
September 20.. – present   Langdon Park Sixth Form, London E14 0RZ
                           Studying for A-levels in English, Sociology, Law.
20.. – 20..   Swanlea School, London E1 5DJ
                           Completed 11 GCSEs including English (7), Maths (6+).

Work experience
January – June 20..   Part-time typist and transcriber
                           Fuse Universal, Tower Hamlets, London
                           Helped transcribe listening materials for learning software.
August 20..   Volunteer, RSPCA (animal rescue shelter)
                           Looked after rescued dogs and cats.
October 20.. – June 20..   Writer, school newspaper club
                           Wrote about social, political and sport topics.

Personal skills
Mother tongues   English, Bengali
Other language(s)   French B1
Computer skills   Competent in most office programs
Driving licence   B
Interest & hobbies Active in school clubs (student newspaper, community activism). Interested in politics and culture. Played on school football team.

3 **Amir's career route.** Amir's uncle is giving him advice about becoming a legal aid lawyer. Choose the right verbs to complete what he says.

I think you're making a good choice, Amir, but you'll **be able to / have to** (1) work hard as a legal aid lawyer. The government is **forced to / supposed to** (2) give legal aid to people who can't afford it, but there is so little government support that lawyers are **able to / obliged to** (3) compete for the jobs. But there are opportunities for legal aid lawyers. I think you **should / shouldn't** (4) follow the standard career route, which includes university and legal training. If you don't do a law degree, then you'll **need to / be able to** (5) complete a post-graduate diploma in law. Get real-world work experience. I **should have / ought to** (6) done this. Volunteer for a non-profit organization – that way you'll **need to / be able to** (7) learn about giving advice and solving problems.

Workshop 2

→ Workbook, pages 40–42

4 A formal letter. Amir wrote a cover letter (A) to include with his CV. His uncle helped correct and improve it (B). Note down the differences and discuss why B is better. Then talk about your conclusions in class.

5 WRITING FOCUS: A CV and a cover letter

a Choose one of the jobs advertised below and write a CV and cover letter.

Summer sales assistant

At Mack's, a leader in fashion clothing, we are looking for a motivated, young sales assistant to join our Berlin sales team from mid-July to late August. You will assist our customers while also keeping our store tidy and helping in the stockroom. You should have good English skills and be able to communicate well with customers of all ages and backgrounds. Please apply online at: www.macksrecruitment.co.uk.

Assistant gardener

Do you love the outdoors? Are you able to work both alone and in a small team? You will help look after the lawns, trees and hedges on the large, beautiful property of the Piedmont Park Hotel. This full-time position for the month of August is suitable for a hard-working student with good communication skills. Experience in lawn and garden care is helpful but not necessary. We offer a competitive salary, meals and accommodation.
Apply in writing to:
dan.simms@piedmont-park-hotel.com.

b GALLERY WALK: Put up all your job applications. Walk around and give each other feedback.

A

Liz Hunt
Putney Legal Advice Centre
129 Putney High St
London SW 15

London, 20 November 20..

Dear Liz

my name is Amir Shah and I'm a 17-year-old student at Langdon Park Sixth Form in London. I'd like to apply for the work placement at your law firm. I think I'm the right person for this placement because I've already done my GCSEs and now I'm doing my A-levels in English, Sociology and Law. I'm not sure if I want to study law or not, so I'm applying for this job. I'm in a student activist group that deals with lots of social issues. I also write for the school newspaper. I speak English and Bengali. I have some work experience as a part-time typist and transcriber and as a volunteer for the RSPCA. I think I'm a good candidate for this work placement.

I hope you'll offer me the job.

Best
Amir

B

7 Grantley St
London E1 4BN

Liz Hunt
Putney Legal Advice Centre
129 Putney High St
London SW 15

20 November 20..

Application for work placement

Dear Liz Hunt

My name is Amir Shah and I'm a 17-year-old student at Langdon Park Sixth Form in London. I would like to apply for the work placement at your law firm which you advertised on 19 November on *youngjobs.co.uk*.

I think I am the right person for this placement because I feel strongly about standing up for people's rights. In my free time, I am involved in student work in this area and would like to do similar work as a career. I am interested in learning about the work that your lawyers do at Putney Legal Advice Centre.

At school, I am a member of an activist group that deals with social issues like discrimination. I also write for the school newspaper. I speak English and Bengali and already have some work experience. In my opinion, these activities, together with my computer skills, make me an ideal candidate for this work placement.

Thank you for considering my application. I look forward to hearing from you soon and scheduling an interview.

Kind regards

Amir Shah

Method coach: Identify communication strategies

S1 **Optimize communication.** You are going to listen to extracts from two job interviews. The two candidates Sunita and Ron are interviewing for the same apprenticeship. First look at the TIP box, then listen. Which of the strategies do the speakers use?

> **TIP**
> **How to communicate effectively in an interview**
> Here are some common strategies:
> 1 Speak clearly and use plain language.
> 2 If you haven't heard what was said, ask the speaker to repeat it.
> 3 If you don't understand a question, ask for clarification.
> 4 Rephrase a statement in your own words to confirm understanding.

S2 **Avoid misunderstanding.** Listen to Sunita and Ron again and complete the phrases.

Communication strategies

Asking for repetition
Could you 1 that, please?
Sorry, I didn't 2 that last part.

Asking for clarification
Sorry. What do you 3 by …?
I'm not 4 what you mean.

Rephrasing
Sorry, let me 5 .
In other 6 , …

Confirming understanding
I 7 .
I understand.
Right.

Making time to think
Let me 8 – well …
So, …
…, you know …

S3 **Role-play: Make yourself understood**

 a Choose your roles from the cards on the right. Use at least two communication strategies from **S2**. Then do your role-play. You can start like this:

A Hi (B's name), I'm (name).
B Hi.
A Thanks for coming. So, you'd like to be our DJ?
B …

b Find a new partner and swap roles.

A
You are in a student group that is organizing a school dance. Your group is looking for a DJ and you've heard that Student B works as a part-time DJ. You've asked him / her to come for an interview.

You want to find out:
- if he / she has experience
- the kind of music he / she plays
- equipment
- his / her favourite music
- his / her fees
- …
- …

B
You have turned your music hobby into a part-time job as a DJ. A student group in your school is organizing a dance and they have heard about you. Student A has asked you to come for an interview.

Your partner wants to know:
- how long you've done the job
- the music you play
- about your equipment
- your favourite music
- the fees you charge
- …
- …

Workshop 2

→ Workbook, page 43

Workshop task: Communicate effectively in an interview

S1 Prepare to evaluate an interview. Copy this interview evaluation sheet. Discuss further evaluation points based on the strategies on page 60 and the TIP box. Add them to your evaluation sheet.

	very good	OK	needs work
1 The candidate speaks clearly.	???	???	???
2 He looks confident and calm.	???	???	???
3 He asks for repetition when he hasn't heard what was said.	???	???	???

TIP

Non-verbal strategies in an interview – dos and don'ts
- Look confident and calm.
- Don't slump in your chair.
- Don't cross your arms.
- Make eye contact.
- Don't forget to smile.

S2 VIDEO TRACK: Evaluate Amir's interviews

9 a Amir has an interview at Putney Legal Advice. Watch him practising with his uncle and make notes on your evaluation sheet.

10 b Watch his real interview at Putney Legal and do the same.

c Compare the two interviews using the notes on your evaluation sheet. How does Amir improve?

S3 Role-play: Do your own interview

a In groups of three, take turns as a candidate interviewing for a job, an interviewer and an observer. You can choose one of the jobs in **5** on page 59 or the one below. First look at the instructions. Decide on the roles and take a few minutes to prepare. If possible, make a video of each interview.

Theme Park Work Experience Programme

Awesome Adventure Parks
You will experience every aspect of our theme park operation. One day you will take bookings
5 for holidays or sell theme park tickets, and the next day help to operate a ride and serve guests their lunch.
Our work experience placement is a fantastic way to learn what it is like to work in our
10 different departments. You will get practical training to expand your skills and a certificate at the end of your placement.
Are you interested in a career in the leisure industry? Then apply now.

The candidate: Look at the job advert. You have applied for this placement and will be interviewed. Think about how to answer these questions:

1 Why do you want this work experience placement?
2 What skills would you like to learn?
3 Why do you think you're a perfect candidate?
4 What questions do you have?

The interviewer: Your interview should look something like this.

1 Greet the candidate.
2 Ask three or four questions (see above).
3 You can ask follow-up questions, too. (e.g. *Can you give me an example? What do you mean?*)
4 Conclude the interview.

The observer: Use the evaluation sheet from **S1** to assess how effectively the candidate communicated.

b Use your observer's notes to give each other feedback. Watch the videos of each interview. Discuss who communicated most effectively and why.

The changing world of work

1 New ways of working. 'Generation Z' – those born between 1997 and 2012 – face a world of work that is very different from that of their parents or grandparents. What do the photos show about changes in working life?

2 A job for life?

a Read the text from an online forum and summarize the main points. Include this information:
- how the world of work has changed
- what the 'gig economy' is

b Discuss the advantages and the disadvantages of the gig economy. Make notes on these points: *holiday pay, security, social interaction, workers' rights, working conditions*. Then compare as a class.

3 Rules and regulations. Complete the sentences from the text. Then answer the questions in the box.

1. People have more things ▭ than ever before.
2. New technology has made us ▭ our work-life balance.
3. The gig economy allows you ▭ your own work schedule.
4. Specialized apps let you ▭ when and where you want to work.

The changing world of work

The world is forever changing and new developments create new challenges and chances – also in the world of work. A recent example is the Corona pandemic and, as in any crisis situation, there were
5 winners and losers. One of the winners was delivery services – nowadays people have more things delivered than ever before.

By blurring the boundaries between the workplace and home, new technology has made us reassess our work-life balance and how best to manage it. Right up until the 1980s, most workers expected to stay
10 with the same company for life, and there was a clear division between work and free time. Today a job for life is no longer the norm. 'Job hopping' – changing jobs frequently – is much more common, especially among younger people. Also, many companies now prefer to hire independent contractors for short-term work instead of taking
15 on permanent employees. So, people are only paid for the 'gigs' they do. Gig work can range from well-paid consultants to on-demand drivers. The gig economy has its advantages – it allows you to plan your own work schedule and be more independent, but it requires you to be more organized and flexible. You could, of course, choose to
20 have the best of both worlds – take on a job with regular hours and do a few part-time gigs on the side to top up your income. Specialized apps let you choose when and where you want to work.

However, these developments don't mean it is no longer necessary to think carefully about what you want to do after school. There nothing
25 has changed – even if 'a job for life' is a thing of the past, work is still an important part of many people's lives, so you need to choose a career path that fits your skills and interests. It's never too early to start planning. A first step towards checking out what's right for you could be the work placement you do in year 9 or 10.

- Which verbs are followed by:
  – object + *to*-infinitive?
  – object + infinitive without *to*?
  – object + past participle?
- How are these structures expressed in German?

Words and phrases

boundary	a real or imagined line that marks the limits of sth. or sb. and separates it from other things/places
commute	to travel between your place of work and your home
freelancer	sb. who works independently
gig	a single professional engagement, usually of short duration

Workshop 2

→ Workbook, pages 44/45

4 Work experience. Complete these comments by ninth graders after their work experience. Put the verbs in the correct form and, if necessary, add an object and *to*. Where do you think the students worked?

They *made me watch* (*make/watch*) a wisdom tooth operation – awful!

That's at a hospital because the person watched an operation.

No, it can't be. It says 'tooth operation'. It must be at a dentist's.

1 The boss promised he wouldn't ▭ (*make/watch*) an animal being put to sleep.
2 I did my work experience with a friend. They ▭ (*allow/decide*) which group we wanted to work in – with the under three-year-olds or the older kids.
3 They asked me to help the elderly residents with their tablets. Modern communication ▭ (*let/stay*) in touch with their families who can't visit them regularly.
4 I didn't enjoy it much. The woman I worked with had an easy life. She ▭ (*make/clean*) the bathrooms while she tidied the bedrooms.

≫ page 74

5 The way it was

 a For a school history project, Ben from Cardiff asked his grandmother to record herself talking about working life in the past. Listen. In what order does she talk about these topics?

  a main industries
  b technology in the office
  c gender pay gap
  d new ways of working
  e length of the working day

 b Listen again. Are these sentences true or false? Correct the false sentences. What does Ben's grandmother say about the situation today?

1 The manufacturing industry used to be the biggest employer.
2 Women used to be paid the same as men.
3 People would communicate face-to-face or by landline.
4 The workplace didn't use to be so stressful.
5 In the past, workers would travel to their workplace every day.

c Look at the box. Then complete the sentences below with *used to* or *didn't use to* and compare with today.

> • With *used to* + infinitive we talk about something in the past that is no longer true.
> This industry **used to be** the biggest employer.
> • We form the negative with *didn't use to* + infinitive.
> There **didn't use to be** so many short-ups.

1 People ▭ type or handwrite letters.
2 Women ▭ wear trousers or jeans to work.
3 You ▭ be allowed to smoke at work.
4 There ▭ be so many freelancers.

> **TIP**
> We can use *would* or *used to* + infinitive to describe repeated actions in the past.
> He **would commute**/**used to commute** to work.

6 YOUR TURN: Then and now

a Write about your life as a child and now. Include one sentence that isn't true.

We used to live in Ukraine. When I was a kid, I used to have long hair, but now it's short and spiky. I used to play tennis, but now I hate it.

 b Read out your paragraphs. The others guess which sentence isn't true.

Grammar and structures

make, let, allow → G16
No one can **make you do** anything you don't want to do.
A freelance career **lets you set** your own hours.
The gig economy **allows you to plan** your own work schedule.

have something done → G17
Many people **have groceries delivered** to their home.
used to/didn't use to/would → G18
Working life **used to be** very different.

Practice: The wealth divide

1 GET STARTED! Describe the picture and the message behind it.

2 Life as a Royal

a Discuss the heading of the article below.

| NEWS | CALENDAR | CONTACTS | BLOG | GALLERY |

LIFE AS A ROYAL – HEAVEN OR HELL?

Some people complain that the British Royal Family costs the tax-payer too much. They lead a life of privilege and luxury, so why not make them pay their way?

As a matter of fact, some royals work very hard – they use their status to fight poverty and injustice both at home and abroad. They support hundreds of charities, including ones that help the homeless and children at risk. A
5 royal patron allows a charity to gain important publicity. They also attend thousands of official events a year. Their work lets them fly around the world, but life is not all fun and games. Members of the Royal Family are expected to follow some strict royal rules and protocol, such as no bright nail varnish, no jeans in the presence of the monarch and no low-cut dresses or short skirts! Military uniforms at weddings and funerals, yes, but shorts in the summer? No way! Here are a few more rules – are they outdated or is there a reason for them?

10 • The Royal Family are not allowed to express political opinions or vote.
   • Protocol doesn't let them show affection in public.
   • They shouldn't have their photo taken with a member of the public, so no selfies.
   • They must ask for the monarch's permission before proposing marriage.
   • Royals must have an all-black outfit packed when they travel.
15 • Protocol doesn't allow royal heirs to travel together.

b Match the sentence halves to complete the royal rules. Then discuss possible reasons for them.

1 The Royal Family aren't allowed   a to wear nail varnish.
2 Protocol doesn't allow heirs to the throne b to express political opinions.
3 Members of the Royal Family aren't supposed c to show affection in public.
4 Royals are required   d to marry without the permission of the monarch.
5 Royal women aren't permitted   e to wear clothes that don't show too much of the body.
6 Royals aren't allowed   f to travel together.

3 Life today

a How does Generation Z feel about their lives and giving money to charity? An organization did some research. Listen, which issues are mentioned?

b Summarize what has changed according to the young people, and how are they helping.

climate change
the poor and disadvantaged
high tuition fees
unemployment
gig economy
knife crime
mental health
cyber-mobbing

Words and phrases

| privilege | a special advantage that a person has |
| unemployed | without a job |

Workshop 2

→ Workbook, pages 46–48

4 Making a difference

a Read the printed version of the interview. You can access it on the webcode. Then rewrite the underlined sentences in the interview with *used to / didn't use to* or *would*.

Yet the proportion of young people donating money to charities <u>was much greater in the past</u>. → *used to be much greater*

b How would you answer the questions?

5 LISTENING FOCUS: Volunteer stories

a Two of the young people interviewed in **4** spoke at *Helping Hands*, an annual event for young people interested in charity work. Listen and decide if these statements are true or false.

1. None of Nikki's classmates live in poverty.
2. You don't have to pay for your school lunch if you're from a poor family.
3. If you don't get enough to eat regularly, you can become ill.
4. It is hard for young people to find jobs after school.
5. Duncan uses social media to help these kids.
6. Duncan believes carrying a knife protects kids from violence.

b Now read the questions, listen again and take notes. Discuss your answers with a partner.
- What issue is each person concerned about?
- Why / How did they decide to get involved?
- What are the causes and effects of the issue?
- What actions are they taking to help?

page 75

> **TIP**
>
> **Reasons, causes and effects**
> Listen for signal words that introduce reasons, causes and effects.
>
> | Reasons / Causes | Effects |
> |---|---|
> | One / Another reason is … | …, so … |
> | On top of that … | As a result (of that) … |
> | That's why … | That means … |
> | Due to (+ noun) | That leads to … |

6 WORDPOWER: Adjectives used as nouns

a Complete with phrases from the box.

> Some adjectives can be used as nouns with the article *the*, e.g.: *the rich, the poor, the disadvantaged, the young, the old/elderly, the jobless, the unemployed, the deaf, the blind.*

1.  are privileged and they should help ▁▁▁.
2. The government isn't doing enough to help ▁▁▁ find jobs.
3. ▁▁▁ are passionate about helping others and making a difference.
4. The best way to care for ▁▁▁ is to keep in regular touch with them.

b Say if you agree with the statements and why.

7 Social action project

a Your class wants to set up a class charity group to campaign about a social issue. Discuss these questions and note down your ideas.

1. What social problems exist in your area? Which issue are you all interested in?
2. What can you do to help? How will you make it happen? Plan your campaign.
3. How will you get the word out there?

b Prepare a two-minute presentation for the class. The class votes for their favourite project.

c Write an article for your school's international website on the problems in your area and how you want to help.

An internship abroad

1 **Daniela in Ireland.** Daniela (see page 52) did an internship in Ireland, arranged by an Irish organization. Skim the review she wrote for their website. Summarize how she benefitted from the intern programme and why she recommends it.

Medical internship in Dublin, Ireland with InternIreland

Daniela
Age 19, Germany

I came across InternIreland while researching internships abroad. This agency, based in Dublin, helps young people find an ideal placement and provides support before, during and after their time in Ireland. No previous experience is required, but you have to be over 18 to apply for an internship. After filling in an online application, I was invited to a 30-minute video interview which I passed with no problems.
5   InternIreland then set up an eight-week medical internship for me. Not having any experience of living abroad, I was grateful for the information pack sent by the agency which answered all my questions and contained a lot of useful tips. If asked, I would recommend InternIreland to anyone wishing to gain pre-university experience.

Before arriving, I had contact with the other interns living in my house, so I knew I wouldn't be far from the
10   city centre. Being so central, I was able to walk everywhere and so I got to know Dublin really well. All the interns lived and worked independently – although the team at InternIreland was always there if needed. Wanting to get as much experience as possible, I didn't mind having to work at weekends. I shadowed a doctor at one of Dublin's top hospitals. She explained everything to me and let me watch her both in clinic and in surgery. Having already done their first year at university, the students at the hospital gave
15   me some useful insights.
My internship helped me to gain practical work experience while also allowing me to get to know Dublin and Ireland. Never having been to Ireland before, I used my free time to do and see as much as I could. Dublin itself is an amazing city with a great cultural offer and the Irish countryside is truly beautiful.

2 **Daniela's review (I)**

a Read these sentences from Daniela's first draft. Find the equivalent sentences in the first section of the review and explain how they are different.

1. I came across InternIreland while I was researching internships abroad.
2. After I had filled in an online application, I was invited to a 30-minute video interview.
3. As I didn't have any experience of living abroad, I was grateful for the information pack.
4. I would recommend InternIreland to anyone who wishes to gain pre-university experience.

Words and phrases

insight	understanding what sth. is like
intern	sb. who is getting practical experience in a job
to shadow	to follow sb. closely at work to see what they are doing

b Look at the box and decide which sentences in **a** match which explanation. Then find more examples in the second section of the review.

- The present participle is the *-ing* form of the verb. We often use participle clauses in written English if two actions are done by the same person.
- We use a present participle:
  a to shorten an active relative clause
  b with *before*, *after* or *since*
  c with *while* or *when*
  d instead of *because*, *as* or *so*

3 Daniela's review (II)

a Read some more sentences from Daniela's first draft. How are the equivalent sentences in the first section of the review different?

1 This agency, which is based in Dublin, helps young people find an ideal placement.
2 I was grateful for the information pack which was sent by the agency.
3 If I was asked, I would recommend InternIreland.

b Look at the box and decide which sentences in **a** match which explanation. Then find more examples in the second section of the review.

- The past participle is the 3rd form of the verb.
- We use a past participle:
  a to shorten a passive relative clause
  b to shorten a clause with *if*

TIP

The present perfect participle (*having* + the past participle) is used to show that one action came before another and caused the second one.
As the students had already done their first year at university, … → *Having already done their first year at university, the students …*

4 **Improving your writing skills.** Use participle clauses to improve Daniela's draft summary.

After I spent eight wonderful weeks in Ireland, I can thoroughly recommend doing an internship there. Before you apply for such a placement, it is important to think carefully about everything. You are not paid while you work as an intern and it is expensive to live abroad. However, in my opinion, it is definitely worth it. When I look back on my time there, I can genuinely say that it gave me more confidence in my career choice and my abilities. If I was given the chance, I would definitely return.

>>> page 75

5 **VIDEO TRACK: Travelling the world**

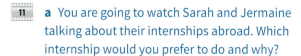

a You are going to watch Sarah and Jermaine talking about their internships abroad. Which internship would you prefer to do and why?

b Watch again. Each of you focus on one person and listen for the answers to these questions.

1 Why did they decide to do an internship?
2 Where did they choose to do it and why?
3 What exciting things did they do and see?
4 Did they face any challenges?
5 How do they rate their experience?

6 **YOUR TURN: Planning ahead**

a What would you like to do after school?

Do you want to do an internship abroad?
YES → Where do you want to work and why?
NO → What are your plans after school?
What do you hope to gain from this experience?

 b Share your plans and ideas with your group.

Grammar and structures

Participle constructions → G19
Before arriving, I received lots of information.
Wanting to get hospital experience, I shadowed a doctor.
This agency helps anyone **wishing** to gain pre-university experience.

Having spent eight wonderful weeks there, I can thoroughly recommend …
I was grateful for the information pack **sent** by the agency.

Practice: Closing the gender gap

1 **GET STARTED!** Look at the photos and describe the jobs they show. Think about the world of work 50 years ago. What has changed?

A
B
C
D
E

2 **READING FOCUS: An argumentative article**

a Skim the article by reading the first and last paragraphs and the first sentence of the middle paragraphs. Decide what the writer's purpose was and think of a good title for the article.

b Read the text and identify these points. Say which ideas you agree/disagree with, and why.
- the reasons some people give for the gender gap in STEM jobs
- the reasons that the writer gives
- the solutions that the writer suggests
- the writer's view of the future

> **TIP**
>
> **Linking words**
> Look for words that the writer uses to
> - link ideas to show cause and effect (e.g. *so, which/that is why*)
> - introduce contrasting opinions (e.g. *Although, However, By contrast, whereas*)
> - add information (e.g. *Furthermore, Another point*)
> - indicate his/her personal view (e.g. *Fortunately*)
>
> This makes it easier to understand the writer's message in an argumentative article.

Women and men still tend to work in different types of jobs. Although girls perform as well as boys in maths and science at school, statistics show that fewer girls consider taking up a
5 professional career in STEM (science, technology, engineering and mathematics). The gender gap is especially wide in information and communication technologies. So why is this?
Some people argue it's because men and women
10 think differently and have different career goals. It is often claimed that girls aren't logical, so they can't do maths or science. They are more interested in helping people, which is why they prefer careers in healthcare, social work or education. By contrast, they say, boys are more 15 interested in jobs that involve machines, construction, or software development.
However, the real reason is gender stereotyping. Upbringing and education have a lot to do with career choices. Parents may discourage girls from 20

34)) **Words and phrases**

to discourage sb. (from doing sth.) to try to stop sb. from doing sth.
empower to give sb. the power to do sth.
stereotype a fixed idea people have of a person or a thing
to tend to to be more likely to do sth.

pursuing STEM careers because they see them as 'male'. At school, girls may be made to feel they can't be good at maths or science. Furthermore, school career services tend to guide girls towards 'female' careers, whereas boys are encouraged to go into 'male' jobs.

How can more girls be encouraged into STEM? One way is to point out that boys have to work just as hard as girls to be good at maths and science. Another strategy is to provide positive role models – women who have been successful engineers, scientists or software designers. Point out as well that scientists and engineers can solve problems that help people in their everyday lives. Once girls know how rewarding STEM careers can be, there will be more women in those fields. Fortunately, stereotypes change with time; 60 years ago, no one could have imagined that Germany, Europe's largest economy, would be run by a woman. Today, an ever-increasing number of scientists and engineers around the world are women. So the future looks bright.

3 WORDPOWER: Phrasal verbs

a Read Nancy's post. Replace the **highlighted** verbs with phrasal verbs from the box. There is one you don't need.

| come up with ■ get round ■ |
| go into ■ point out ■ |
| take up ■ think about |

I would like a career in engineering so I **am considering** (1) applying for an engineering apprenticeship after I leave school. My parents aren't very happy about it. When they say that engineering careers are just for boys, I **explain** (2) that there are lots of famous women engineers! And girls are just as good as boys at **finding** (3) ideas and solutions to problems! But they really want me to become a teacher. Did anyone here have to convince their parents to let them **pursue** (4) a STEM career? What do I do if they continue to say no? Any ideas how to **persuade** (5) my parents?

b How would you answer Nancy's questions?

4 Ireland's Best Young Entrepreneurs (IBYE).
Read about the IBYE competition. Then edit the texts about two past finalists to make them shorter and more formal. Use participle constructions.

Ireland's Best Young Entrepreneurs Competition

Are you a young entrepreneur with an outstanding and innovative business? Then the IBYE Competition is for you. There's a €2 million Investment Fund and personal business support to help you develop your business idea. Send your application to …

WENDY OKE – TEACHKLOUD
Wendy gained a first-class degree and PhD in Early Childhood Learning and wanted to put her knowledge into practice. She is passionate about child development and she wants every child to receive a high-quality education in order to reach their full potential. Based on this, she created TeachKloud. This cloud-based platform allows teachers who are burnt out from their huge workloads and mountains of paperwork to work smart and improve the quality of their teaching.

DARRAGH LUCEY – YOONI
Every year millions of students go to college, but up to 60 % of them drop out because they have chosen the wrong course. Darragh saw the drop-out problem first-hand while he was taking his Electrical & Electronical Engineering degree at university, and he wanted to help. The Yooni platform, which was developed by Darragh and his friend Nathan, uses AI algorithms to empower school-leavers to choose the right course.

  page 75

5 YOUR CHOICE: A great business idea.
Choose task A or B, then write a short description or give a mini presentation.

A Research another young entrepreneur, e.g.:
Gabi Cox, founder of Chroma Stationery
Maciek Kacprzyk, founder of Wonky drinks
Orla Stafford, founder of Izmoo Gelateria

B Think of your own business idea for a product or service.

Method coach: Practise workplace communication

S1 **Paraphrasing.** Paraphrasing is a useful communication strategy when you don't know the word for something. Look at the examples and match them to the TIP box.

1 I think this is a good, erm, chance to do something. – Yes, it is a good opportunity.
2 It's cold here. Where's the switch to make it warmer? – The thermostat is over there.
3 What's it called when a new employee is shown around the workplace? – That's an induction.

A forklift? What's that?

You know, that small electric vehicle that can lift heavy boxes and things.

S2 **Follow Amir on his first day at work**

a It's the first day of Amir's work experience at the legal advice centre. Listen to his induction. Put A – G in the order they are shown to Amir.

A kitchen
B Amir's desk
C shopping rota
D open-plan areas
E supply room
F conference room
G breakout areas

> **TIP**
> **How to explain something if you don't know the word**
> - Use vocabulary that you already know.
>   *It's a thing you use to put two holes in a piece of paper. Oh, you mean a hole punch.*
> - Describe the concept. Explain who uses it, why it's used, or where.
>   *What's that thing where you can get a drink of water? That's a water dispenser.*
> - Use a synonym.
>   *Jack has been dismissed. – Sorry? – He's been fired.*

b Look at hese communication strategies. Then read the phrases below and decide which of the four categories they belong to.

Communication strategies

1 Paraphrasing
What do you call the thing that …?
What's it called when you …?
It's a thing for …

2 Asking for repetition
Pardon? What was the question?
Sorry, what was that?

3 Asking for clarification
Sorry, what do you mean by …?
Sorry, what's that?
Does that mean that …?

4 Rephrasing
What I mean is …
To put it another way, …

- Sorry, what did you say?
- Have I got it right that …?
- What you're saying is …
- Could you say that again, please?

- What I wanted to know is …
- It's sort / kind of like a …
- It's a thing you can use to …
- Sorry, I didn't get that.

Workshop 2

→ Workbook, page 54

Workshop task: Role-play an induction

S1 **Expand your communication strategies.** Before you listen to the second part of Amir's induction, take turns describing these objects and concepts using the non-verbal strategies in the TIP box.

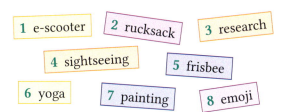

> **TIP**
>
> **Non-verbal strategies**
> Showing or demonstrating something can be more effective than describing it. You can:
> 1 point or use a gesture
> 2 demonstrate an action or a sound
> 3 draw a simple picture

S2 **Identify verbal strategies**

a Listen to the second part of Amir's induction. Which of the items in the list does he learn about and in which order?
- fire escapes
- toilets
- legal pads
- hole punch
- fire extinguisher
- supply room
- printer
- first aid kit

b Listen again. What strategies is Amir using when he is not quite sure what Jackie is talking about. Compare your answers in class.

> **TIP**
>
> **Verbal communication strategies**
>
> - **Paraphrasing using statements and questions.**
>   *It's a thing for … -ing. / It's a thing that you use to … / It's sort / kind of like a …*
>   *What do you call the thing that you use to …? What's it called when you …?*
> - **Asking for repetition**
>   *Sorry, what was that? / I'm sorry, what did you say?*
> - **Asking for clarification**
>   *Does that mean that …? / Have I got it right that …?*
> - **Rephrasing**
>   *What I mean is … / To put it another way, … / What you're saying is …*

S3 **Role-play: School induction**

a A British exchange student is being shown around your school. Choose your roles, then begin your tour of the school. Add as many different rooms, places and objects as you like.

> **Student A**
> You want to show **Student B**, an English exchange student, some of the rooms, places and objects listed below. He or she doesn't speak German yet, and you don't know the English names of these things in your school (even if in reality you do). Choose five items from the list and add two of your own to show **Student B**:
> - Sekretariat
> - Serverraum
> - Hausmeisterraum
> - Kollegstufenraum
> - Mensa, Cafeteria
> - Soziale Arbeit
> - Aufenthaltsraum für Schüler/innen
> - Raum der Schulleitung
> - Fachraum Chemie
> - großer Mehrzweckraum

> **Student B**
> You are trying to learn German, so you want to find out the names of different places and things in your school – more than just the ones **Student A** explained to you. You can show them to **Student A** or you can paraphrase with questions like:
> - *What do you call the place where you / the students …?*
> - *What's the thing that you use to …?*

b Student A, find somebody from another pair who was **Student B**. Swap roles and do the role-play again.

Mediation

1 Work camps

a You would like to take part in a work camp together with your English friend Mason. Tell him in an email what work camps are, why taking part in one is a good idea, and which kind of work camp you would prefer and why. You should also tell him why you would like to stay in Germany or choose another country. Write about 120 words.

🔍   NEWS   CALENDAR   CONTACTS   BLOG   GALLERY

[…] DIE IDEE

Bei einem internationalen Workcamp leben junge Menschen aus verschiedenen Ländern für zwei bis drei Wochen zusammen und arbeiten dabei für ein gemeinsames und gemeinnütziges Ziel. Ohne Bezahlung, dafür aber mit viel Engagement unterstützen sie soziale, kulturelle, denkmalpflegerische oder
5 ökologische Projekte. Durch die Kooperation mit Partnerorganisationen auf der ganzen Welt können die Freiwilligen auswählen, welches Land, welches Thema und welches Projekt sie am meisten interessiert. Neben der Projektarbeit verbringen die internationalen Gruppen auch ihren Alltag zusammen, planen Ausflüge in die Umgebung, kochen gemeinsam und organisieren ihre Freizeitaktivitäten. Das bringt Menschen mit verschiedenen Lebensstilen und kulturellen Hintergründen zusammen – eine wertvolle
10 Erfahrung für alle Beteiligten.
Internationale Workcamps unterstützen durch tatkräftige Hilfe gemeinnützige Projekte. Sie fördern Respekt und Offenheit, tragen zum Abbau von Vorurteilen bei und leisten so einen Beitrag zum friedlichen Zusammenleben.

WORKCAMPS IN DEUTSCHLAND

15 In Deutschland finden jedes Jahr mehr als 350 internationale Workcamps statt, an denen junge Menschen aus dem In- und Ausland teilnehmen. […]
Die Vermittlung in ein Camp in Deutschland kostet zwischen 40 und 100 Euro, Unterkunft und Verpflegung sind in der Regel frei.
Die Gruppen sind international zusammengesetzt, in der Regel wird Englisch gesprochen. […]
20 Gleichzeitig lernst du durch deine Gruppe andere Länder und Kulturen kennen, ohne dafür ins Ausland reisen zu müssen.

WORKCAMPS IM AUSLAND

Unsere Workcamp-Organisationen vermitteln jedes Jahr junge Freiwillige aus Deutschland in mehr als 2.000 internationale Workcamps in über 100 Ländern.
25 Ein internationales Workcamp im Ausland ist eine einzigartige Möglichkeit:
- ganz besondere Erfahrungen in einem anderen Land zu sammeln, […]
- Fremdsprachenkenntnisse auszuprobieren,
- sich für ein sinnvolles Projekt zu engagieren […]

Die Vermittlung in ein Workcamp im Ausland kostet zwischen 60 und 160 Euro. Anmelden kannst du
30 dich über eine Workcamp-Organisation in Deutschland. Von dieser erhältst du alle wichtigen Informationen zum Projekt, zur Reiseplanung und Vorbereitung sowie zur Unterkunft. […]
Die meisten Workcamps finden während der Sommermonate statt. In welchen Projekten aktuell Freiwillige gesucht werden, was für die Bewerbung notwendig ist und wie du dich auf einen Workcamp-Einsatz vorbereiten kannst, das kannst du auf den Websites der jeweiligen Workcamp-Organisationen
35 nachlesen. Oder du rufst einfach direkt mal an und fragst nach!
www.workcamps.org

Workshop 2

→ Workbook, pages 55/56

b Mason likes your idea and has done some research about work camps. He has found Xiao's report, which he sent you. While you're reading it, your mother comes into your room and asks you questions. She wants to know
- what project Xiao worked on and what her tasks were,
- if Xiao thought the job was OK,
- what she thought about the other participants and
- if a project like this is something you would like to do as well.

Answer her questions.

Starting the journey

[…] I departed from Beijing Capital International Airport and took a direct flight to Frankfurt Airport in Germany. After a subway and a train ride, I
5 finally arrived at the destination of this trip, Rothenfels. This quiet and beautiful town is surrounded by a rich forest, and the purpose of my visit has a lot to do with the forest: our mission at the volunteer camp is "Help to maintain the
10 forest".

Exploring the forest as an international volunteer was a novelty to me. I walked among the trees and saw the mist filling the air like a white veil. The trees stood quietly under the blue sky, with their arms open to the sun. But the most important thing for me was to learn how to protect the forest. At first, we
15 mainly learned how to clear the roads in the forest. We used hoes, iron brooms, shovels and other tools, none of which were easy to use. Although the forest staff was patient and demonstrated how it's done,

it still felt very laborious without experience. The average temperature in the forest was only 20 degrees but everyone was sweating. However,
20 when I saw the nearby residents smiling at us and giving us a thumbs-up, I felt it was all worth it. The meaning of volunteer work lies in service and dedication.

In the next few days, we tried to cut down trees
25 […] and build "hotels" for insects. I benefited a lot from each activity, and I felt the close integration between humans and nature. Many people stereotype and claim that all human activities will destroy nature, which is also a kind of prejudice, because humans' proper participation can also protect nature, which is a win-win for humans
30 and nature.

Apart from volunteer activities, I also got to know new friends from different countries in the camp. The 16 of us were from 11 different countries, ranging in age from 16 to 26 years old. When we had free time, we went to the supermarket, swam and even visited other cities on weekends. Thank you very much for this volunteer activity, which enabled me to gain precious friendships.

35 **Conclusion**

After just two weeks of volunteer activities, I have a deeper understanding of volunteer work. Thanks to every volunteer in this event, we all made great efforts to make the forest better and made a small but profound contribution to the green of the earth.

www.archiv.ijgd.de

First track

3 **b** Make more sentences about the future. The information in brackets will help you.
p. 53

1 Amir: My final exams | start next spring. *(timetable)*
I | finish by the end of May. *(action finished before a future time)*

2 Daniela: I | check out flights to soon. *(plan)*
My dad thinks booking now | be cheaper. *(prediction)*

3 Ben: I | have my interview in four weeks. *(timetable)*
My cousin | help me prepare. *(plan)*

4 Sisi: My friend | do a design course next month. *(arrangement)*
That | be a big help. *(prediction)*

3 **b** Complete Amir's answer with the correct forms.
p. 54

Don't worry, I didn't forget **looking at/ to look at** (1) the links. One ad was really interesting, so in the middle of my homework, I stopped **writing/to write** (2) an application. Stupid me - I didn't remember **saving/to save** (3) my essay, so now I've got to start again! Thanks for Saira's number. Sure, I remember **talking/to talk** (4) to her. I'll try **contacting/to contact** (5) her tomorrow. I must stop **texting/to text** (6) now otherwise I'll never finish my homework!

4 Amir follows his uncle's advice and contacts Saira. Choose the best future form to complete their exchange.
p. 55

S. Morning Amir. Sure, **I'll help/I'll have helped** (1) you if I can. My husband's oldest friend, Neil, is a lawyer at Putney Legal. **We're meeting/We'll have met** (2) the Saturday after next to celebrate the men's birthdays and the fact that on that day they **will be knowing/will have known** (3) each other for 35 years. (Their mothers gave birth on the same day in the same hospital!)

A. Amazing! **I'll be seeing/I'll have seen** (4) my uncle over the weekend to work on my CV, so by the time you all meet, Putney Legal **will be receiving/will have received** (5) my application.

S. Fine. **I will give/I will have given** (6) Neil a ring to tell him that your application **will be coming/will have come** (7) next week. Then, **he'll be reading/he'll have read** (8) it by the time I see him. OK?

4 Complete these comments by ninth graders after their work experience. Use *make*, *let* or *allow* in the correct form. Decide where they worked.
p. 63

They *made* me watch a wisdom tooth operation – awful!

That's at a hospital because the person watched an operation.

No, it can't be. It says 'tooth operation'. It must be at a dentist's.

1 The boss promised me that he wouldn't ▬ me watch an animal being put to sleep.
2 I did my work experience with a friend. They ▬ us to decide which group we wanted to work in – with the under three-year-olds or the older kids.
3 They asked me to help the elderly residents with their tablets. Modern communication ▬ them stay in touch with their families who can't visit them regularly.
4 I didn't enjoy it. The woman I worked with had an easy life. She ▬ me clean the bathrooms while she tidied the bedrooms.

Workshop 2
FIRST TRACK

5 **b** Listen again and complete the missing information about Nikki and Duncan. Then read the questions and discuss your answers with a partner.

p. 65

- What issue is each person concerned about?
- Why / How did they decide to get involved?

- What are the causes and effects of the issue?
- What actions are they taking to help?

Nikki Harris
- volunteers at local …
- worried about …
- decided to help because some classmates …
Causes
- families can't afford to buy …
- kids don't have enough …
Effects
- health problems, e.g. …
- can't concentrate on lessons – don't do well …
- can't get …
Action
- planning to start …

Duncan
- worried about …
- joined team of volunteers to …
Causes
- youth clubs …
Effects
- teenagers …
- difficult for teenagers to …
- this leads to …
- kids carry knives because …
Action
- actions to raise awareness: …
- ways to get young people off the street: …

4 Choose the correct participle clauses to complete Daniela's draft summary.

p. 67

Spending / Having spent (1) eight wonderful weeks in Ireland, I can thoroughly recommend doing an internship there. Before **applying / applied** (2) for such a placement, it is important to think carefully about everything. You are not paid while you work as an intern and it is expensive to live abroad. However, in my opinion, it is definitely worth it. **Looking / Looked** (3) back on my time there, I can genuinely say that it gave me more confidence in my career choice and my abilities. **Giving / Given** (4) the chance, I would definitely return.

4 Read about two past finalists. Replace the underlined clauses with participles to make them shorter and more formal. You will need to make other small changes, too, as in the example.

p. 69

Having gained a first-class degree and PhD in Early Childhood Learning, Wendy wanted …

Wendy Oke – TEACHKLOUD
Wendy gained a first-class degree and PhD in Early Childhood Learning and wanted to put her knowledge into practice. She is passionate about
5 child development and she wants every child to receive a high-quality education in order to reach their full potential. Based on this, she created TeachKloud. This cloud-based platform allows teachers who are burnt out from their huge
10 workloads and mountains of paperwork to work smart and improve the quality of their teaching.

Darragh Lucey – YOONI
Every year millions of students go to college, but up to 60% of them drop out because they have chosen the wrong course. Darragh saw the drop-
5 out problem first-hand while he was taking his Electrical & Electronical Engineering degree at university, and he wanted to help. The Yooni platform, which was developed by Darragh and his friend Nathan, uses AI algorithms to empower
10 school-leavers to choose the right course.

Reading

Ben Ockrent, *Hacktivists* (2015)

Ben Ockrent is an award-winning writer and director for theatre, film, television and radio. Some of the UK's leading
5 actors have worked with him and he has had his work produced and broadcast all over the world.

In a recent interview he spoke
10 about his motivation:

Finally, what is your main motivation when writing a play? Is it simply to entertain the audience, or do you also want to encourage them to think?

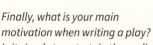
Ben Ockrent and his wife, the British actress Jemima Rooper

15 It depends on the project, but ultimately both. Though there's an arrogance in assuming that you have any new insights that will challenge the audience to question what they really think. Entertainment is what it is. It's not a lecture. I want people to have a good time and to leave thinking … I don't
20 know what else we should aspire more to in life than just enjoying an experience with other people. To be able to live in a culture where we can access that and to do a job where I can at least aspire to be a part of that experience for other people, that's the inspiration or the dream.

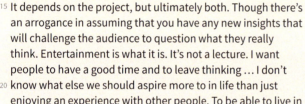

'It's Impossible,' said Pride.
'It's Risky,' said Experience.
'It's Pointless,' said Reason.
If you really are a Hacker, then Give it a try.

1 **a** Describe the illustration and say what effect it has on you. Include at least five adjectives modified by an adverb, e.g. 'fairly frightening'.

b Now analyse the text in the illustration. Who is talking and what is the message? Do you agree? Consider the stylistic device of personification in this context.

Scene Two

Music cuts and throwies[1] are extinguished simultaneously[2] to lights up on Archie and Beth facing each other adversarially[3]. Eloise enters, followed by Mark, Steve and Cath. The atmosphere is tense …
5

BETH (*Understatement*). Well, that was embarrassing.
ARCHIE. It's his house. He was free to decide who he lets in.
BETH. But not to humiliate[4] me. 10
ARCHIE. He didn't humiliate you.
ELOISE. He made you get down on your knees in front of the entire party and beg you to let us in.
ARCHIE. He was just having a laugh. So what? 15
That's fine.
ELOISE. And did you find it funny?
ARCHIE. Yeah, maybe I did, actually.
ELOISE. You're lying.
ARCHIE. Alright then, no, I didn't find it 20
'funny', exactly –
CATH. Then why did you do it?
Hugs enters, followed by Jenny, Tania, Nisha, Seb, Pez and Drew.
HUGS. It's all over YouTube. 25
STEVE. What is?
NISHA. Archie on his knees in front of everyone at the party. Someone filmed it from a window.
MARK. We should make it stop now before it's 30
trending[5].
ARCHIE. Take it down and we make it look like Daniel Cooper's got to us[6]. Don't give him the satisfaction. (*To Hugs and Beth*) You were right. We weren't invited. I accept that. But 35
you know what? I don't care. We're better than him. We're better than all of them.
BETH. Then maybe it's about time they found out.
HUGS. How? 40
BETH. By teaching this Daniel Cooper a lesson.
ARCHIE. Now, hang on a minute –
BETH. We agreed. If he didn't let us in, we'd start putting this place – all of your talents – to real use. You can't go back on that. 45
HUGS (*To Archie*). Mate, a deal's a deal.

---

[1] **throwie** a form of LED light art used for creating non-destructive graffiti and light displays – [2] **simultaneous** at the same time – [3] **adversarially** facing each other like enemies – [4] **to humiliate** to show no respect and embarrass sb., especially in the presence of other people – [5] **to trend** to go viral on the internet – [6] **to get to sb.** (*coll.*) to make sb. feel upset and angry

ARCHIE. We said we'd turn this into a real hackerspace. We never said anything about teaching anyone a lesson.
50 BETH. I'm sorry, but can anyone remind me why the Headmaster let you have this place?
PEZ. Because she wants us to become the next tech giants?
BETH. Sorry, tech what?
55 ELOISE. Giants.
BETH. Oh, giants! Because that's what geeks[7] can be these days. (*To Mark*) Can't they, Mogul?
MARK. Potentially.
60 BETH. So long as what?
MARK. They know what they're doing.
BETH. Pez, you said you could take down that video.
TANIA. They've made it into a song. Used a
65 re-mix of that Madcon[8] song 'Beggin'.
DREW. Quite catchy, actually.
NISHA. (*Glancing at her phone*) Uh-oh.
MARK. What?
NISHA. Someone's posted it on Twitter.
70 PEZ. What's the hashtag?
NISHA. (*Reading her phone*) HashtagMassive BellEnd.
HUGS. Amazing.
ARCHIE. But I can't have been down on my
75 knees for more than ten seconds!
JENNY. They're fairly liberal with the slow-mo.
CATH. And the rewinds[9].
TANIA. And the freeze-frames[10].
ARCHIE. But why would they do that?
80 HUGS. Coz it's funny?
NISHA. It's not funny, Hugs. It's mean.
PEZ. I could probably hack into the YouTube account and take down the video if you want?
85 STEVE. Do it.
ARCHIE. No. Leave it up. I don't care.
STEVE. Mate, it's probably not even been seen by that many people yet.
DREW. (*Reading his phone*) Twenty-three
90 thousand, four hundred and nineteen … twenty … twenty-one …

Ben Ockrent, *Hacktivist*, Hrsg. Andreas Galle. Ditzngen: Reclam, 2020

[7] **geek** (*coll.*) a computer nerd who is an expert on the one hand but doesn't know how to behave socially on the other hand – [8] **Madcon** a Norwegian musical duo, playing hip hop, dance pop and rap; one of their songs is called "Beggin'" with the line "I'm beggin' on my knees" in it – [9] **rewind** backward movement – [10] **freeze-frame** picture in a standstill

c Read some more lines from scene 2. Discuss Hugs' and Beth's attitude towards the issue of hacking. Is it positive or negative, moderate or extreme …?

ARCHIE. Alright, then what is the point?
HUGS. Freedom.
BETH. … That's what hacking is. It's breaking down barriers. Overcoming limitations.

2 a Plays are intended to be performed on stage. Get together in a group and imagine you're on a stage. Do a role-play and read the text aloud.

b Sum up the scene in three to five sentences and outline the overall topic of the conversation.

3 Now read the excerpt again and do the tasks.

1 Examine the various attitudes towards what has happened to Archie.
2 Describe the atmosphere and tone of their meeting.
3 Characterize Beth and Archie and define their roles in the play.
4 Cyberbullying has become quite common these days. Examine the way it is practised here, the reasons for it and its effects.

4 The setting in the *Hacktivists* is described as a 'hackerspace' in a Portacabin on the school grounds where the students of the computer club meet at lunchtime. Use your imagination and design the interior. You can either draw a picture or describe it.

TIP

Setting and stage directions
Instructions for the setting and stage directions give information about how the actors have to move, behave or what tone their voices should have, etc. They are special to the genre of drama and are usually given by the author.

My review

What can I do?

Look at these sentences about Workshop 2. Are the sentences true for you? Choose the right symbol for each sentence.

1 I can discuss my hopes and plans after finishing school.
2 I can write my CV and a letter of application for a job.
3 I can compare working life today with the past.
4 I can talk about volunteering and social issues.

>>> = 'I'm great at this!'
>>> = 'I'm good at this.'
>>> = 'I'm OK at this.'

What do I know?

1 About making plans

a Complete the email below with words and expressions connected to working and studying after school.

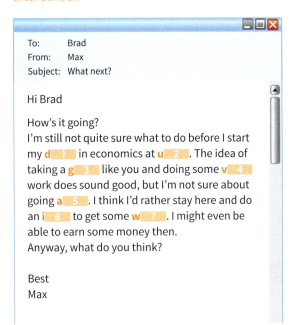

To: Brad
From: Max
Subject: What next?

Hi Brad

How's it going?
I'm still not quite sure what to do before I start my d⬚1⬚ in economics at u⬚2⬚. The idea of taking a g⬚3⬚ like you and doing some v⬚4⬚ work does sound good, but I'm not sure about going a⬚5⬚. I think I'd rather stay here and do an i⬚6⬚ to get some w⬚7⬚. I might even be able to earn some money then.
Anyway, what do you think?

Best
Max

■ / 7

b Complete the conversation with the correct future forms of the verbs in brackets.

Jenny So, have you decided what you want to do after you finish school?
Max The only thing which is clear is that this time next month I ⬚1⬚ (*relax*) on a beach in Spain! Then, after the holiday I ⬚2⬚ (*need*) to make some decisions.
Jenny Sure. What are the choices?
Max Well, my cousin is working in Malawi at the moment.
Jenny Wow! That sounds exciting. What's he doing there?

Max He's working on a solar project. The plan is that by the end of May the organization ⬚3⬚ (*install*) more than 5,000 solar panels in the country.
Jenny ⬚4⬚ (*he / stay*) there?
Max No, he ⬚5⬚ (*come back*) in June. He ⬚6⬚ (*study*) engineering at university from September.
Jenny So, ⬚7⬚ (*you / think*) of joining him and working on the same project?
Max That's one option, but I'm not sure yet.

■ / 7

Work and study-related vocabulary, pp. 52–53
Future tenses → G12 – G13 ; pp. 52–53

Workshop 2

→ Workbook, page 57

2 **About applications.** Complete Emily's cover letter with the words from the box. There are two words you don't need.

> additionally ■ advertised ■ application ■ apply ■ basically ■ considering ■ hear ■ hearing ■ ideally ■ naturally ■ passionate ■ regards ■ volunteer ■ wishes

14 Grange Road
Horsham RH12 1AE
Surrey

Croxley Stables
Horsham RH12 4PX
Surrey

24 May 20..

1 for apprenticeship

Dear Martin Bishop

I am 16 years old and a student at Thornton Lane Sixth Form College in Surrey. I wish to **2** for the apprenticeship which you **3** on 22 May on the website youngjobs.co.uk.

I think I am the right person for this apprenticeship because I feel **4** about riding and horses. I **5** at weekends and during the holidays at a local riding school. I've been doing this for six months now and love it. **6** , I would like a career working with horses.

At the riding school I have had a range of jobs. **7** , these include working in the stables and looking after the horses. **8** , I also help take riding classes for young children. **9** , I think this experience will help me with the apprenticeship.

Thank you for **10** my application. I look forward to **11** from you soon and scheduling an interview.

Kind **12**
Emily Sullivan

■ / 12

Job applications, pp. 54 – 55
Sentence adverbs, pp. 56 – 57

3 **About then and now.** Read the text about Adam Jameson, then rewrite the underlined sentence parts with *used to* and *didn't use to*.

> My name's Adam Jameson and I work as a freelance journalist. I started working in the 'gig' economy just over five years ago. Before that, <u>I worked for a local newspaper</u> (1). I would get up at around six in the morning and commute to work on a very crowded train. Then I spent most of the day in a big office full of people, <u>so I didn't find it easy to concentrate</u> (2). Now I work from a small room in my house, which is wonderful! I guess the one advantage of being employed was that <u>weekends were free</u> (3). However, there were lots of disadvantages. First of all, I was told what stories to cover. At the beginning, <u>the boss gave me all the boring local assignments</u> (4), which wasn't much fun. Then after a couple of years, the work improved, but that meant I often had to work at lunchtime, <u>so I didn't get a proper break</u> (5). It was very stressful, but at least <u>I didn't worry about money</u> (6), as of course I was always paid at the end of the month. Anyway, there's no going back now. <u>Small newspapers like the one I worked for</u> (7) are finding it hard nowadays. Of course, some of the bigger national papers are also struggling. So many people <u>who bought a newspaper</u> (8) now read the news on their phone or tablet. Freelance journalism is definitely the future.

■ / 8

used to, didn't use to → G18 ; pp. 62 – 63

4 About volunteering and social issues

a Two students have written articles for a website about volunteering and social issues. Rewrite the underlined parts of the first article using participles. You may have to make other, small changes.

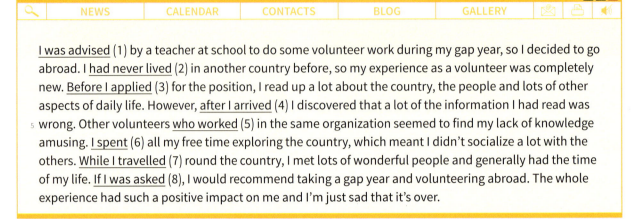

I was advised (1) by a teacher at school to do some volunteer work during my gap year, so I decided to go abroad. I had never lived (2) in another country before, so my experience as a volunteer was completely new. Before I applied (3) for the position, I read up a lot about the country, the people and lots of other aspects of daily life. However, after I arrived (4) I discovered that a lot of the information I had read was wrong. Other volunteers who worked (5) in the same organization seemed to find my lack of knowledge amusing. I spent (6) all my free time exploring the country, which meant I didn't socialize a lot with the others. While I travelled (7) round the country, I met lots of wonderful people and generally had the time of my life. If I was asked (8), I would recommend taking a gap year and volunteering abroad. The whole experience had such a positive impact on me and I'm just sad that it's over.

/ 8

b Complete the second article with the words from the box.

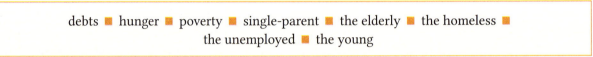

debts ■ hunger ■ poverty ■ single-parent ■ the elderly ■ the homeless ■ the unemployed ■ the young

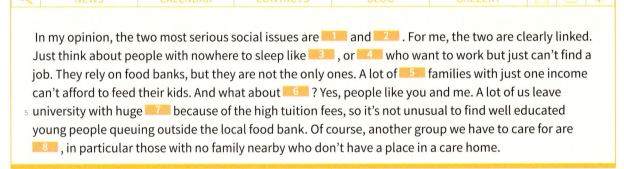

In my opinion, the two most serious social issues are ⬛1⬛ and ⬛2⬛. For me, the two are clearly linked. Just think about people with nowhere to sleep like ⬛3⬛, or ⬛4⬛ who want to work but just can't find a job. They rely on food banks, but they are not the only ones. A lot of ⬛5⬛ families with just one income can't afford to feed their kids. And what about ⬛6⬛? Yes, people like you and me. A lot of us leave university with huge ⬛7⬛ because of the high tuition fees, so it's not unusual to find well educated young people queuing outside the local food bank. Of course, another group we have to care for are ⬛8⬛, in particular those with no family nearby who don't have a place in a care home.

/ 8

Social issues, pp. 64 – 65
Participle constructions → G19 , G21 ; pp. 66 – 67

/ 50

What's my score?

Check your answers to the review (Workbook, p. 57). What are your scores for each section?

What was your total score?
- ⟫⟫⟫ score 36 – 50
- ⟫⟫ score 16 – 35
- ⟫ score 0 – 15

Do you want to change your answers to the 'What can I do?' statements on page 78?
Look at the tasks on pages 81 – 83: ⟫, ⟫⟫ and ⟫⟫⟫. Choose the tasks to help you.

My practice pages

Workshop 2 — MY PRACTICE PAGES

WES-40325-002

Talking about hopes and plans after finishing school

1 After school. Choose the best alternatives to complete what people say about the future.

1. After I take my exams, I hope **I am going to find / I will find** a good job.
2. Next week **I am starting / I'll have started** a course at a college.
3. I'm not sure what to do after school, but **I'll decide / I'm deciding** soon.
4. **I'll be working / I'll have worked** as a volunteer during the holidays.
5. **I will probably get / I am probably going to get** a job at my dad's company.
6. My new job **starts / will start** next week.
7. **I am going to take / I take** a gap year before university.
8. By the time my gap year ends, **I am going to visit / I will have visited** five countries.

2 Future talk. Complete the short conversations. Use the prompts and the correct future forms.

1. **A:** When will we know the exams results?
   B: We | let you know | next week.
2. **A:** What do you plan to do after you finish school?
   B: I | study | university. I've got a place at LSE in London.
3. **A:** When are you going on holiday?
   B: At the beginning of July. I | finish | my exams | by then.
4. **A:** What will happen if you don't get good grades?
   B: I | consider | my options when I know my grades.
5. **A:** Are you starting your internship tomorrow?
   B: No, my internship | not start | until next week.
6. **A:** Do you know what you want to study?
   B: Yes, I | take a business course. I want to work in finance.

3 Your hopes and plans. Complete the sentences for yourself.

1. I'm going to …
2. During my holidays, I …
3. I hope …
4. By the time …
5. Next year …
6. After finishing school …
7. I'm sure …
8. By the time I'm 25 …

Writing application letters for a job

4 Tim's application. Choose the best alternatives to complete the cover letter.

> 33 Solihull Street
> Birmingham
> B1 1BA
>
> Henry Swanson
> TRT Engineering
> Birmingham
> B1 1DA
>
> 4 April 20..
>
> Application for work placement
>
> **Dear / Hi** (1) Henry Swanson
>
> **I'm / I am** (2) 17 years old and a student at City Sixth Form College in Birmingham. I am applying for the work placement in your **ad / advertisement** (3) on the website youngjobs.co.uk. **I am definitely / I think I am** (4) the right person for this work placement because I **will / would like to** (5) become an engineer. **I am doing / I do** (6) A-levels in maths and science at college and I have always been interested in mechanical things. I believe that this work placement would give me the opportunity to learn more. **Could you tell / Tell** (7) me more about the job?
>
> Thank you for **considering / liking** (8) my application. I look forward to **hearing / hear** (9) from you soon.
>
> **Kind regards / Best** (10)
> Tim Mattinson

5 **Getting it right.** Read Aesha's cover letter. Rewrite it so that she might get a job interview.

> Hi there
>
> I'm a 17-year-old student in Cambridge. I saw your ad for an au pair on the website gapyearjobs.com and thought 'Wow – that's a perfect job for me'. I think I'm the best person for the job as I
> 5 have two younger twin sisters. I often look after them in the evening. We usually watch TV and eat popcorn. It's great! Of course, my parents don't pay me, which is a bit annoying. I plan to go to university next year, but first I want to travel and earn some money. I'm good with kids, oh and I passed my driving
> 10 test first time – you can tell I'm good at everything I do. Anyway, I hope you like my application and will get in touch with me. It would be awesome to come to the USA. Before I forget, what's the pay?
>
> All the best
> 15 Aesha

6 **Your turn.** Write a cover letter for this advert.

Wanted – Waiter

An exciting opportunity has come up in a small family-run café. We are looking for an enthusiastic young person for the summer (five or six days a week) and possibly continuing after the vacation. No previous experience necessary. Good hourly rate plus tips.

Apply to: Marvin Green, Manager, email: mgreen@greens.

Comparing working life today and in the past

7 **The world of work**

a Write sentences using *used to / didn't use to*.

1 My dad | work | office | now | work | home.
2 People | have 'job for life' | now work | 'gig' economy.
3 People | not write emails.
4 My mum | take train to work | now | cycle.
5 My dad | wear a suit and tie | every day. | Now | only | if | have a meeting with clients.
6 My dad | get paid a fixed salary | now | get a bonus | depending on sales.
7 People | go out for lunch | now | eat at desks.
8 Work meetings | be online. | Now | most meetings | be virtual.

b Look at the pairs of sentences. Is the meaning of the two sentences the same or different?

1 a Starting a new job is often a challenge.
  b When you start a new job, it is often challenging.
2 a After completing my application, I had to wait two weeks for feedback.
  b After I completed my application, I had to wait two weeks for feedback.
3 a Wanting to make a good impression, I arrived early on my first day.
  b I made a good impression on my first day because I arrived early.
4 a My colleagues, knowing I was nervous, were really helpful and supportive.
  b My colleagues, who knew I was nervous, were really helpful and supportive.
5 a If offered the job, I'd be happy.
  b Being offered the job made me happy.
6 a While working for a children's charity, I decided to study psychology.
  b Having worked for a children's charity, I decided to study psychology.

8 **Changes**

a Use the prompts to write sentences about how work has changed using *used to* and *didn't use to*.

1 office desk | typewriter | dial phone
2 laptop | mobile phone
3 meetings | meeting room | face-to-face
4 online | virtual
5 male boss | gender roles
6 female boss | mixed team

b Rewrite the underlined parts with participles. You may need to make other, small changes.

1 <u>I applied</u> for ten jobs and I was hopeful I'd be offered at least one.
2 <u>As I didn't want</u> to work at weekends, I turned down a job at the local factory.
3 <u>Before I started</u> my first job, I asked my parents for some advice.
4 My car broke down on my way to work, <u>which caused</u> me to be late.
5 <u>As I knew</u> what to do, I didn't need to have any training.
6 <u>I felt</u> tired after my first day at work, so I took a nap. School was much easier!

Workshop 2
MY PRACTICE PAGES

9 How life changes

a Write an article for your school magazine about how work has changed in the last 50 years. Use these ideas and your own: where people worked, pay, work conditions, times, roles of men and women, job security, types of jobs.

b Complete with an appropriate participle.

1. _____ school, I began my internship on 1 September.
2. _____ in an office before, it was a completely new experience for me.
3. _____ to make a good first impression, I arrived early.
4. _____ the summer holidays in Greece, meant I was relaxed and ready for a new challenge.
5. The boss, _____ I was inexperienced, gave me some really good advice.
6. If _____ , I'd say my first day was a success.

Talking about social issues

10 Homeless! Complete the text with the words from the box.

> Although ■ As a result ■ gig economy ■ health problems ■ On top of that ■ One reason for this ■ poverty ■ the homeless ■ well paid

A lot of charities in the UK are dedicated to helping __1__ . Many offer food and somewhere to sleep. __2__ is that rough sleeping, when you are sleeping on the street, can lead to serious __3__ . Why are there so many homeless people in a country like the UK? Around 22% of people are living in __4__ ! __5__ unemployment is very low, many jobs are in the __6__ . __7__ many of these jobs aren't very __8__ . That's why experts say that lots of people are just one payday away from becoming homeless. __9__ , some charities focus on trying to keep people in their homes before they end up on the street.

11 Cause and effect. Put the words in 1–6 in the correct order. Then match them to a–f. Note: the complete sentences can start with 1–6 or a–f.

1. become | why | homeless | people | one reason
2. he | a result | pay | as | rent | his | can't | so | .
3. high | houses | due to | the | of | cost
4. many | closed down | have | youth clubs | because | .
5. often | children | don't | breakfast | have | in the morning.
6. jobs | why | poorly paid | have | which is | they | often | .

a ... because they come from poor homes.
b Mike lost his job, ...
c There is nowhere for young people to go after school ...
d ... is because they are unemployed.
e Women often stay at home to look after children, ...
f ..., many young people still live at home after leaving school.

12 Our class charity group.
Your class has decided to set up a class charity group. Write an email to a friend to explain your plans. Include the following points:

- What problem does your charity focus on?
- Why is this an important issue for you?
- What reasons are there for the issue?
- What are the effects?
- How will your charity be able to help?

TWO

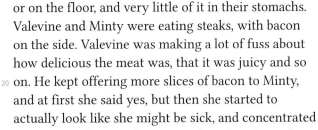

It was dinnertime.
'Ask Cudweed why he's become a vegan, mother,' said Solstice to Minty.
It was the first thing anyone had said in twenty minutes. Solstice was eating a toasted peanut butter and jelly sandwich. The twins were eating spaghetti with a cheese sauce. I say 'eating', but most of it was in their hair or on the floor, and very little of it in their stomachs. Valevine and Minty were eating steaks, with bacon on the side. Valevine was making a lot of fuss about how delicious the meat was, that it was juicy and so on. He kept offering more slices of bacon to Minty, and at first she said yes, but then she started to actually look like she might be sick, and concentrated on a piece of lettuce that was on her plate instead. So Valevine helped himself to the rest of the bacon and then grabbed the rest of the twins' cheese sauce and poured that all over his steak and bacon. He kept looking at Cudweed, and I finally realized that he was trying to get him to give up the idea of being a vegan, and eat something that came from an animal.

But Cudweed took no notice. He kept chewing away on a bowl of salad that seemed to stay the same size, no matter how much he ate. (That's one of the things I have noticed about salad; no one ever finishes it.) He didn't look once at his father, or his mother, and he especially didn't look at their plates of food, not even when Valevine picked his plate up and began licking it clean. This was very strange indeed, because he has a set of rules about how to behave at the dinner table. He's always talking to the children about their behaviour. If *they* had licked their plates, they would have been in big trouble.

Now, if Valevine's food wasn't having any effect on Cudweed, it certainly was having a big effect on *me*.

Another of Valevine's rules at the dinner table is one I really don't like: No Ravens Allowed. I don't like this rule at all, or understand it. As a result, I usually stay away while the others are eating, but the smell of all this lovely bacon was too much, and I had flown into the dining room, secretly.

I was sitting on a chandelier high above the dining table, watching what was going on, and waiting for a chance to grab a piece of bacon or a forkful[1] of steak. Now Valevine had finished eating approximately half a cow, and I was disappointed. But I was still hopeful about Minty's plate, because it looked like she was about to give up. I just had to wait for my chance. And then Solstice said, 'So, Mother, why don't you ask Cudweed *why* he's suddenly become a vegan?'

Minty stared at her daughter for a moment, then realized that this was actually a very good idea.
'Well, Cudweed?' asked Minty. 'What do you have to say for yourself?'
Cudweed was chewing away at his salad, then he shrugged, swallowed[2], and said very calmly, 'Eating meat is unethical.'
'What's that?' cried Valevine. 'Unethical? You don't even know what that means!'
Cudweed put down his fork.
'Unethical: not morally[3] correct,' he said, sounding like a talking dictionary, 'lacking moral principles, in this case inflicting[4] unnecessary cruelty and death upon sentient[5] creatures.'

---

[1] **a forkful** eine Gabel voll – [2] **to swallow** hinunterschlucken – [3] **morally** moralisch – [4] **to inflict** zufügen – [5] **sentient** empfindsam

Valevine's mouth fell open.
Solstice's did, too.

'But I told you that it was *unethical* to eat animals years ago!' she yelled. 'And all you said was "but I really like bacon"! So what's changed?'

'Yes, dear,' said Minty, trying to be understanding, 'what's changed?'

Cudweed opened his mouth to speak, but his sister was too quick!

'I'll tell you what's changed,' she said. She was getting a little bit upset now, and she pointed a finger straight at her brother. 'He's in LOVE!'

She said it like it was a really bad thing. And she wasn't finished.

'He's in love with a GIRL!'

Cudweed glared[6] at his sister and I moved to a different chandelier, one that was directly above Minty's plate. I had a feeling that my chance was coming.

'So what?' cried Cudweed.

'In love?' cried Minty. 'Is this true? You didn't tell us!'

'Why should I?' Cudweed asked, looking mad. 'Do I have to tell you everything?'

'Yes!' cried Minty. 'Well, no, but ... this girl, she's made you become a vegan, has she?'

'She hasn't *made* me do anything!' Cudweed shouted, and stood up. He was on the verge[7] of storming out of the room again and I only hoped for his sake that he had fixed the problem of a belt by now. I took a good look, and as far as I could see, he had wound some Sellotape[8] across the top of his trousers. Clever, I thought. Not bad at all.

'Well,' asked Solstice, 'is *she* a vegan?'

Cudweed glared at his sister.

'Yes,' he said, eventually, 'but all she did was tell me about certain things. Things about how we treat animals so badly, in farms and so on. And now I know it is only right to be a vegan.'

'But I told you all that! And you just kept moaning about sausages!'

'I do not moan,' said Cudweed, moaning. 'Now, if you'll excuse me, I have to go and call Joanna.'

'Oooh, "Joanna", is it?' said Solstice, and I was surprised, because she suddenly started acting very childishly. Even for a child. 'Oooh, Cudweed loves Joanna, Cudweed loves Joanna.'

And I love bacon, I thought, and if I am not mistaken[9], I am about to get some. Hee hee.

I hopped to the back of Minty's chair, and with everything that was going on, no one paid me any attention at all.

'Now see here, young man,' said Valevine, doing his best impression of being an angry parent. 'You will leave the table when I say so! And not before!'

'Really?' said Cudweed.

'You've already spent all day talking to her,' said Solstice. 'Why do you need to talk to her again?'

'Because I want to,' said Cudweed.

That started Solstice again.

'Cudweed loves Joanna,' she sang, 'Cudweed loves Joanna.'

'So what?' asked Cudweed. 'Just because you don't have a boyfriend!'

Uh-oh. That did it.

I should explain that Solstice had just broken up with her boyfriend Douglas, about three weeks before this. She was still feeling sensitive about it, poor thing. And she burst into tears.

Then Valevine started shouting at Cudweed; Cudweed turned and ran out of the room, the Sellotape snapped and his trousers fell down; Minty ran over to put her arms around Solstice; and I jumped onto Minty's plate and stole three enormous slices of bacon.

'That bird is so irritating!' shouted Valevine, but I was gone. Like a jet plane, out of the dining room, and upstairs, and into the cannon where no one would be able to stop me eating the bacon, not even with a very long pole.

---

[6] **to glare at sb.** jmd. zornig anstarren – [7] **to be on the verge of** kurz vor etw. sein – [8] **Sellotape** Klebestreifen – [9] **to be mistaken** sich irren

It was quiet after dinner time. I snoozed in my cannon for a while, fat and happy after my success with the bacon. But it does make you thirsty, and I decided to pay a visit to the kitchen to see if I could find some water to drink. There is usually a pile of pots and pans in the kitchen sink with some washing-up water left in, and I was in luck! There was a huge soup pan, left soaking in the sink, half full of water.

I was standing on the edge and taking a sip of water flavoured with pea soup, when I heard someone come in behind me.

It was Valevine. He was in his pyjamas and dressing gown, so I guessed it was late. He was not angry at me for drinking from the sink, which he usually would have been. He was holding two huge white pills in one hand, and an empty glass in the other. 'Ah, hello, bird,' he said. 'I'm sorry for shouting at you earlier.'

'Awwk,' I said. I wasn't angry with him; I knew that everyone had been upset at dinner time.

'Funny thing about that son of mine,' he said. And he shook his head.

'Kark,' I agreed.

'Love!' he shouted, suddenly. 'The boy is in love. And when we are in love, well …' I knew what he meant.

Maybe drinking cold pea flavoured water from the sink had done something to my brain, but I suddenly felt a little romantic myself. You know, I was in love once. Well, maybe more than once, but the most important time I fell in love was when I met Mrs Edgar. I mean, that wasn't her name when I met her. Her real name was Eulalia Lillibella, but that was hard for everyone to remember, and even harder to say, and when we got married, everyone just called her Mrs Edgar instead. It sounds sexist[10] now, but times were different then. Anyway, I loved Mrs Edgar from the day I met her to the day she fell out of a tree and the dogs ate her. Sigh.

Poor Mrs Edgar, I thought, poor, poor Eulalia, and a single fat tear rolled down my beak, and fell into the soup pan, with a loud plop!

That woke us both up, Lord Valevine and me, I mean, and he turned on the tap[11] and filled his glass of water. He showed me the large white pills in his hand.

'I have terrible stomach ache,' he said, 'I can't think why.'

But I knew why. Stupid human. He had eaten too much meat, and, I had to admit, that Cudweed and his girlfriend had a point – eating too much meat isn't good for you.

I went to sleep. It was very late by now, and maybe because I had already had a little nap after dinner, or maybe because I had eaten too much bacon before bedtime, I had trouble falling asleep.

---

[10] **sexist** sexistisch – [11] **tap** Wasserhahn

When I finally did, I had terrible dreams. In my
235 dreams, I was being chased all around the
countryside by a giant sheep that had Cudweed's
face. The sheep-that-was-Cudweed was crying out,
'I'm going to eat you! All of you! Even your beak!'
and as hard as I tried, I couldn't get away from him.
240 Then he turned into a giant cheese, a Swiss one, I
think, because he was full of holes. He started
breaking large lumps[12] off himself and eating them.
As he was doing that, it began raining broccoli from
the sky, and then in the next moment, the whole
245 family was there, and everyone was sitting around a
dining table on the hillside. They were all holding
knives and forks and had serviettes tucked under
their chins. I was sitting in the middle of the table,
and they were staring at me, grinning. Then I saw
250 that I was sitting on a serving plate, and then I woke
up squawking like a parrot with a problem.

If that nightmare wasn't bad enough, things got
worse on Wednesday morning. I woke up very late,
and I flew around trying to find someone to annoy.
255 Finally, I found Solstice. She was in her room, and
because I felt stupid for not looking there first, I
decided to peck her ears.
'Don't Edgar,' she said, but she wasn't mad. In fact,
she seemed sad, really sad.
260 'Kork?' I asked.
'I don't understand,' she said. 'I told Cudweed all
about how bad it is to eat animals, and he took no
notice[13]. And now this stupid girl tells him and
suddenly ... bam! He's a vegan!'
265 'Rurk,' I pointed out.
'I know!' she said. 'But I thought he loved me, too!
I'm his big sister!'
'Ork,' I added.
'Well, anyway,' said Solstice. 'We're going to find out
270 what she's like. She's coming here. Cudweed has
invited her to come and meet everyone. Tomorrow.'
'Arrrk?' I said.
'Yes, Edgar, "arrk".'
We stared out of her window for a while, and I
275 suppose we were both thinking about Cudweed. It
seemed that young Cudweed was growing up.
'Hey Edgar,' said Solstice suddenly. 'Do you want to
hear a joke? It's very, very funny.'
'Rork,' I said, though I didn't much feel like a joke.
280 'How do you know if someone is vegan?' she asked.
'Ark,' I said, because I had no idea.
'They tell you!' she said. Then she started laughing
and didn't stop.

---

[12] **lump** Brocken; Klumpen – [13] **to take notice** etw. wahrnehmen

Workshop 3
Who am I? Who are we?

A

1 Read the quotes and look at the photos. Identify one theme they have in common.

> No matter our religion, where we were born, what colour our skin, or what language we speak, we are equal members of this great country.
> Justin Trudeau, Canadian Prime Minister

> Diversity is the mix. Inclusion is making the mix work.
> Andrés Tapia, US employment executive and author

B

> What a dull and pointless life it would be if everyone was the same.
> Angelina Jolie, American actor

> A lot of different flowers make a bouquet.
> Islamic proverb

C

D

When everyone is included, everyone wins.
Jesse Jackson, political activist and Baptist minister

My parents are immigrants who moved to Canada in the '60s. [...] I am an example of the opportunity that exists here. But we cannot deny that racism exists here, too.
Charles Officer, Canadian film director and actor

2 a Listen to four Canadians talking about diversity. Compare their views. How are they similar or different?

b How have you experienced diversity? How important is it? Give examples and reasons for your answers.

3 a How do people express their identity? Make a mind map.

b Talk about how important individual identity is for you. Give examples.

YOUR TRACK

After this Workshop you will be able to:
- talk and write about family life and gender identity today.
- comment on friendships and relationships.
- discuss the best ways of dealing with youth crime.
- understand and talk about advertising for Generation Z.
- understand, describe and analyse graphs and charts. (Workshop task)

We are family

1 Modern families

a Think about your own family. How have family structures changed over the last few generations? Then read the introduction to the article below to see if it confirms your ideas.

b Read what Sadie and Mac say about their families and do the tasks.

1. Describe what kind of family Sadie and Mac each has.
2. Explain the difficulties each of them has experienced.
3. Outline what they feel is the best thing about their families.

Families have changed!

Families are becoming increasingly diverse in Canada and around the world. The traditional nuclear family that consists of two married parents and their children is no longer the standard.

Up to half of marriages end in divorce, and many people get married again. This creates the blended family, which means the children have to get used to living in a new unit. Single-parent families, which can be a single mum or dad plus kids, are increasingly common.

Same-sex marriage, which was legalized in Canada in 2005, has led to even more family diversity. Another example of change is the census published in 2021. It contains two separate questions which focus on gender, one asking about 'sex at birth' and one for gender. This allows for individuals to be included who don't identify as male or female.

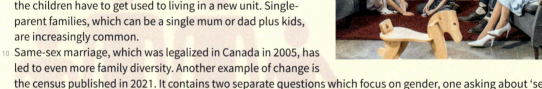

> I was twelve when my mom and dad divorced. My two older brothers went to live with my dad, and me and my sister Kristen, who's actually my twin, lived with my mom. We were both upset about Mom and Dad splitting up. But Dad made very clear that we're still part of his family no matter what happens. Mom would always tell us the good parts of having two families like, 'You'll get two Christmas presents', which of course is true and I was really happy. On weekends we'd go to my dad's house. When my friends came over, they'd ask, 'Why don't you live here?' and I'd just tell them about exactly what I just said and they'd be understanding, they'd just be like, 'Oh, okay'.
> Sadie, 16

> Most people would probably think my family is a bit irregular, because I have two moms, as in gay moms. But to me, my family's just normal. We do things that every other family does. It's a very easy-going family, not very uptight, but the best thing is that it's loving. A harder thing about being part of my family is the fact that I experienced teasing and bullying at school in the past. No one wanted to play with me because they were afraid they'd be bullied like me. Kids who came over would sometimes ask, 'Where's your dad?', and I'd have to explain. But my family has taught me to be accepting of everyone, no matter what race, skin colour, gender or really anything.
> Mac, 15

Words and phrases

blended	combined or mixed
divorce	the legal ending of a mariage
uptight	strict, not very relaxed

Workshop 3

→ Workbook, pages 58/59

2 Giving information

a Read the box. Find more examples in the text.

> - Defining relative clauses give important information about a person or thing.
>   *The traditional nuclear family that consists of two married parents and their children is no longer the standard.*
> - Non-defining relative clauses add extra information, separated from the rest of the sentence by commas.
>   *Same-sex marriage, which was legalized in Canada in 2005, has led to even more family diversity.*
> - A relative clause can be shortened using a participle.
>   *The traditional nuclear family consisting of two married parents …*
>   *Same-sex marriage, legalized in Canada …*

b Rewrite the descriptions of different family structures using ideas in the box above.

A Extended family
The extended family consists of cousins, aunts or uncles and grandparents who live together and who help to raise the children and carry out household duties. Children who are brought up
5 in such families often have a very close relationship to relatives other than their parents.

B Grandparent family
Growing numbers of children live with a grandparent or grandparents. The grandparents may be raising their grandchildren for various reasons.

C Mixed unions
Mixed unions involve couples of different national or ethnic origins. Mixed unions are growing in number in Canada.

3 Family stories

a Listen to a podcast about Canadian families and write one sentence which sums it up.

b Listen again and answer these questions.

1. What difficulties do immigrants to Canada often face, according to the presenter?
2. Where is Valerie's grandmother originally from? Why did she come to Canada?
3. What problems did Valerie's grandmother have?
4. How does Valerie feel about her cultural heritage and identity?
5. What does Mike tell us about his family background?
6. How does he feel about his cultural heritage and identity?

» page 112

> **TIP**
>
> *be used to / get used to (doing) something*
> - The verb phrase *be used to* means being familiar with something.
>   *She wasn't used to living alone.*
> - The verb phrase *get used to* describes the process of becoming familiar with something.
>   *It was hard for her to get used to the cold.*

c Discuss what people moving to Germany may not be used to and need to get used to.

4 YOUR TURN: Family matters

a List phrases to show you are listening to somebody.

> Active listening phrases
> Go on! Tell me more.
> …

b Choose a topic related to families. Take turns to speak about it for at least a minute. When you are listening, use phrases from your list.

c Write a paragraph about your topic.

Grammar and structures

Defining and non-defining relative clauses (revision) → G20
Participle constructions replacing relative clauses → G21
The traditional nuclear family **consisting of** two married parents and their children is no longer standard.

be used to / get used to + noun / -ing → G22
Children in blended families have to **get used to living** in a new unit.

WES-40325-003

Practice: The new normal

1 **GET STARTED!** Here are some causes of conflict between teens and their parents and siblings. Add at least three more. Which ones cause the most arguments in your family?

> smartphone use ■ chores ■ curfews ■ personal appearance ■ privacy

2 **Can we just get along?**

 Three teens talk about family conflicts. They are all given some expert advice. Listen to Gabriel first and answer the questions. Then do the same for Emily and Nicole.

1. What's the reason for Gabriel's conflict with his mother?
2. Which expressions in the TIP box does he use to describe his feelings?
3. Would you give the same or different advice?

> **TIP**
>
> **Describing feelings**
> I (just) get (really) upset / annoyed / frustrated / angry …
> It's so annoying / frustrating …
> I wouldn't mind if …, but …
>
> **Advice on ways to deal with conflict**
> - Don't just jump in and interrupt. Stop and listen.
> - Look at it from the other person's point of view.
> - Compromise – try to reach an agreement that works for everyone.
> - Agree to disagree.

3 **SPEAKING FOCUS: Giving advice**

a Choose one of the reasons for conflicts from **1**. Take turns to ask for and give advice. Use phrases and ideas from the TIP box in **2**.

b Find a new partner and share your problem again. Which advice did you find most helpful?

c Conduct a poll or an online survey to find which issues are most common. Present your results.

4 **WORDPOWER: Collocations.** Make a list of words and collocations with the word 'gender'. Add to your list after reading the texts on the next page.

> genderless
> gender-neutral name
> encourage gender bias
> …

5 **Challenging gender stereotypes.** Look at the cartoon. What gender expectations and roles are being challenged? Then read the texts on page 93 and identify:
- typical gender stereotypes for boys and girls,
- how gender roles are learned and reinforced,
- how / why things are changing today,
- what Canadian parents are doing to raise gender-neutral kids.

 Words and phrases

to **conform** to sth.   to behave in a traditional way
to **reinforce**   to give support to an idea and make it stronger

Workshop 3

→ Workbook, pages 60–62

Parents raise their children gender-neutral

We used to raise girls and boys based on gender stereotypes. We believed that being a boy or a girl dictated who you were and what you could do. But ideas about gender identity have changed. More and more parents in Canada are raising their kids to be more gender-neutral. They choose clothes and toys that don't reinforce stereotypes. Some don't even tell their children what gender they are. They want to give them the freedom to choose their own identity when they are old enough.

Gender expectations

Research shows that children start to understand gender expectations as young as four. They develop ideas by watching and copying how people around them behave. Parents or carers who want to raise gender-neutral children should model what they want their kids to believe by making sure household chores aren't gendered – mom cleans the house, dad mows the grass; mom looks after the baby, dad goes out to work. This can help kids understand that gender doesn't determine what tasks they do.

Gender-neutral names never more popular

According to a Canadian newspaper, the last two decades have seen a big increase in gender-neutral baby names in Canada – Avery, Riley and Parker are currently the most popular choices. Parents who don't want their children to conform to stereotypical expectations – 'boys climb trees and girls play with dolls' – are giving their children a unisex or genderless name. This could be helpful later when applying for jobs, as gender bias still exists in the world of work.

 6 **Gender stereotypes at home.** In your group, discuss how
- your home life encourages / doesn't encourage gender bias,
- to create a gender-neutral home life.

Present your ideas to the class.

CULTURE CORNER

LGBTQIA refers to lesbian, gay, bisexual, transgender, queer (anyone who doesn't identify as heterosexual or 'straight'), intersex (people who have sex organs or hormones that don't match their gender) and asexual (people who are not interested in sex).

7 **VIDEO TRACK: My genderation**

 a Before you watch a video about 14-years-old Tayler, say what you think the title refers to.

b Add the information below in the correct places to complete this summary of Tayler's story. Use relative clauses and commas if necessary.

Tayler likes skateboarding, drawing and playing on his video console.

> Tayler is a 14-year-old trans boy from Wales, *who likes skateboarding, drawing and playing on his video console.* Tayler wanted to make the transition to become a boy. He is currently on hormone-blocker medication. He was helped by Fox Fisher from Stonewall, an organization which supports LGBTQ people. He gave a talk at Tayler's school and told the other kids about him. Tayler felt relieved after Fox's visit. His mum was surprised when Tayler first told her that he felt like a boy trapped in a girl's body. She remembered how she had tried to make Tayler wear dresses. Finally, she accepted him for who he is and now she feels very proud of him.

1. He realized that he wasn't supposed to be a girl when he was 10 or 11.
2. This prevents puberty from starting.
3. Tayler had been worried about telling everyone himself.
4. His mum didn't think she had forced gender roles on him.
5. This had made him angry because he'd only wanted to wear trousers.

 page 112

 8 **The new normal.** Now you've done all the tasks, discuss and explain the title of this double page.

True friends

1 **Peer pressure.** Think of two or three situations in which teenagers can feel influenced or pressured by their peers to do something. Talk about when this pressure is harmless or even positive and when it is harmful.

2 **To act or not to act?** Read an article in *TeenTime*, a Canadian magazine, about two teens' experiences with peer pressure and do the tasks below.

Romy

Before we moved from Montreal to Vancouver, I'd never thought about my accent myself, but the kids at my new school started
5 teasing me about how I talked. They weren't mean about it, but I did get the message. I was the new, exotic kid. I didn't want to stick out, so I started to talk
10 more and more like them. Maybe it was a silly reaction, but it did make my life easier.
One of the first friends I made in Vancouver was Grace. She was so nice to me, and funny, too. Grace liked doing risky stuff, like riding the buses and
15 trains without a ticket. I knew it was dumb, but I did it a few times with her anyway. We didn't get caught ourselves, but a kid from our school did. His parents had to pay 170 dollars. After that I told Grace never again. She called me a wimp, but I stuck to my
20 decision. I said 'Maybe I'm a wimp, but I'd rather do the right thing and feel good about it.' She didn't say anything. I wasn't expecting her to behave any differently herself, but guess what? Now Grace always rides with a ticket.

Mark

At school a lot of kids dress alike, so we do influence each other. But that's nothing compared to what happened recently. There's a girl at school
5 who's socially a bit awkward. Some friends of mine were making fun of her, talking and laughing about her behind her back. They wanted me to join in. The girl was in one
10 of my classes and I saw her crying. She was really hurt. She's not even a bad person – she's just different. Then they continued it on social media. My sister Carla saw it and got really angry with me. I didn't understand – I hadn't done anything. 'That's
15 the problem!' she said. My friends were behaving badly and I was allowing it to happen. The next day I told them what they were doing wasn't cool. I also talked to the girl myself and tried to comfort her. One friend felt bad and stopped, but the others
20 didn't. Finally, I told a teacher about them. Now they don't talk to me anymore – they say I'm a snitch – but I don't care. My sister says she's proud of me.

1 Describe examples of both positive and negative peer pressure in Romy's and Mark's stories.
2 Analyse how they both resisted pressure from their friends and how their friends reacted.
3 Explain what you think of the choices that Romy and Mark made. Discuss your views in class.

Words and phrases

awkward	moving or behaving in a way that is not natural or relaxed
snitch *(infml.)*	a person who tells others when sb. does sth. wrong
theft	the crime of stealing sth. from a person or place
wimp *(infml.)*	a weak person who is afraid to do sth. difficult

Workshop 3

→ Workbook, pages 63/64

3 Stress your message

 a How do the writers stress their messages in the sentences below? Complete the information in the box, then find more examples in the texts.

*I'd never thought about my accent **myself**.*
*We **do** influence each other.*

> - We use emphatic pronouns, like , to stress a noun or a pronoun.
> - We add the verb to a positive statement to stress the verb.

b How can Romy add more emphasis to these sentences using the correct form of the verb *do*? Where would you add them to her story?

1 My accent wasn't very strong, but it probably sounded quite unusual to my new classmates.
2 She has a wild side to her personality, but I like that about her.
3 Grace said, 'You never take risks' and I said, 'I take risks sometimes'.
4 I said, 'Hey you didn't buy a ticket.' She said, 'I bought one. It's in my pocket.'

→ page 112

c Mark wants to add these ideas. Rewrite them using some of the emphatic pronouns from the box. Where would you add them to his story?

> myself ■ yourself ■ himself ■ herself ■
> itself ■ ourselves ■ yourselves ■
> themselves

1 They couldn't see it, but it was clear that they were being really mean.
2 Carla said, 'They're not going to stop. You have to stop them.'
3 I hadn't realized it, but Carla was right.
4 We notice when other people do something dumb, but not always when we do it.

→ page 112

4 That's what friends are for

 a THINK: Listen to three dialogues. Decide if the behaviour in each is OK or not. Make notes.

b PAIR: Compare your answers from **a**. Note down a good heading for each dialogue.

c SHARE: Talk about your ideas in class. Vote on the best heading for each dialogue.

 5 YOUR TURN: Friendship. Make a double circle. Discuss the first quote with the person opposite you for one minute. Is the statement true in your experience? Then discuss the next quote with a new partner and so on.

> Friends ask how you are and then wait to hear the answer.

> A fair-weather friend is fun, but what happens when it rains?

> The only way to have a friend is to be one.

> One friend can change your whole life.

> One loyal friend is worth more than a thousand fake ones.

> In the end, we will remember not the words of our enemies, but the silence of our friends.

Grammar and structures

Emphatic *do/does/did* → G23
He **did** help me.

Emphatic pronouns with *-self/-selves* → G24
I knew **myself** that it was wrong.

Practice: Is it love?

1 GET STARTED! Look at these two ideas and then find a way to illustrate what love or friendship means to you.

F ight for you
R espect you
I nclude you
E ncourage you
N eed you
D eserve you
S tand by you

2 True love

a Look at the heading of this article and the photo. How would you answer the questions? Now read on.

IS TEENAGE LOVE REAL? AND CAN IT LAST?

Nicki Ferris, counsellor

A lot of adults don't believe that teen relationships can be meaningful and lasting. Maybe those adults never experienced real teen love themselves. Some teenage relationships simply don't last, but not because the feelings weren't real or deep. What's true for adults is true for teens, too: some, not all, love is real. True love depends on the individuals and whether they can develop their feelings for each other further.

5 When you're attracted to another person for the first time, it's usually a physical attraction. There's an excitement and energy, but it doesn't go any deeper than this. This is what it means to have a crush on someone. This is lust, not love. Love goes much deeper than physical attraction. It's when you really care about the other person.

Ask yourself this: Are you dating someone because you want to find your life
10 partner? Or are you just having a good time? The answer might help you understand whether your love is real and if it's a serious relationship. True love means your feelings don't change when things get tough.

Can teen love last? Sure. Just look at all the high school sweethearts who are still together decades later. But when you're a teenager, love does come with
15 big challenges. You're still growing and finding yourselves. Two young people either have to be very mature at the beginning of their relationship, or they need to be willing to discover themselves and grow within the relationship.

b Which four statements paraphrase in the correct order what Nicki Ferris is saying?

1 Having a crush on someone and being in love are not the same thing.
2 For teenagers, lasting love is hard.
3 Lust is necessary before you can find love.
4 It's good to understand why you want to date someone.
5 Dating is usually a sign of real love.
6 Real love is not just something for adults.

▶▶ page 112

Words and phrases

attract	to make sb. interested in sth.
lust	a strong feeling of sexual attraction
mature	behaving like an adult
nosebleed	when blood comes out of a person's nose

Workshop 3

→ Workbook, pages 65–67

> **TIP**
>
> We often use verbs like *hear*, *see*, *watch*, *notice* and *feel* followed by an object and a present participle.
> *I saw him **looking** at me.*
> *He heard me **talking** to her.*

3 How we met

a People often meet in strange ways. Read the TIP box, then complete the story with the correct form of the verbs in the box.

> look ■ make ■ move ■ sit ■ smile ■
> stand ■ try ■ walk

I remember when Wayne and I first met. I can see him ⬚1 there in a
5 chair in the school secretary's office with something white sticking out of his nose. I'd just come from the dentist and I needed permission to return to class. Out of the corner
10 of his eye, he noticed me ⬚2 there. I smiled and felt my lips ⬚3 in weird ways. It was embarrassing so I turned away, but I could feel him ⬚4 at me. When I spoke to the secretary, she heard me ⬚5 strange noises and stopped
15 me. 'It's OK, sweetheart,' she said. I probably sounded like a Neanderthal, but she understood. She handed me a permission note and I turned to leave. He watched me ⬚6 towards the door. 'Dentist?' he asked. I covered
20 my mouth. 'I knew it,' he said. I was curious. I tried to say 'What about you?', but it didn't sound quite right. I noticed him ⬚7 . 'Wabodowboo?' he teased. When he saw me ⬚8 not to laugh, he had to laugh himself. I
25 pointed to the white stuff in his nose. 'It's a tissue. I had a nosebleed,' he said, shrugging his shoulders. 'It happens.' We've been dating ever since.

 b Think of someone you are good friends with. How did you meet? Discuss your stories, then tell the class the most interesting one in your group.

4 Talking about relationships.

TeenTime invited some young people to discuss their views on dating and relationships. Complete their comments by adding emphasis with a form of the verb *do* or an emphatic pronoun with *-self/-selves*.

1 I don't know what it's like because I've never been in a relationship ⬚ .
2 I ⬚ want to find a serious partner, but until then I'll keep dating.
3 My girlfriend told me I didn't care about her, but it isn't true. I ⬚ care.
4 My friend Tarek was too scared to ask someone out ⬚ , so I had to ask for him.
5 You're right. We ⬚ depend too much on texting.
6 Our friends can't believe we're still going out. We can't believe it ⬚ .

5 VIEWING FOCUS: Love has no labels

a Watch this short video. What is it that keeps your attention?

b Read the questions in the TIP box. Then watch again and make notes to describe what the video shows.

> **TIP**
>
> Think about these questions when you watch a video. This will help you describe it and the idea behind it.
> • What is the mood of the video?
> • How does the music affect your reaction?
> • How do the people in the video influence you?
> • What is the central message?
> • Who do you think made the video and why?

c Look at these comments on the video, then write your own posts.

> "I love my sister." This is my favourite part. Makes me smile everytime. ☺

> Amazing video, great message!

> This video gives me hope for the world.

Method coach: Understanding diagrams (1)

S1 **Understanding the information.** Look at the line graph and the bar chart. How does each diagram present the information? Choose one diagram each and complete the description.

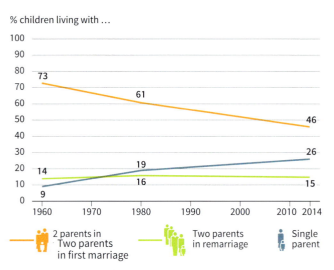

% children living with …

Source: Pew Research Center, 2015

The graph gives information about changes in family life in the USA.

In 1960, 73% of all children were living in a family with two parents in their first marriage. By ⟨1⟩, the number of children living in this type of family had declined to 61%. By 2014, the figure had fallen to less than ⟨2⟩ (46%). By contrast, there has been a really dramatic rise in the percentage of children living with single parents. In 2014, ⟨3⟩ of children were living with one parent. The share of children living in a remarriage stood at ⟨4⟩, a small ⟨5⟩ from 14% in 1960.

We can conclude that the make-up of US family life changed considerably between 1960 and 2014.

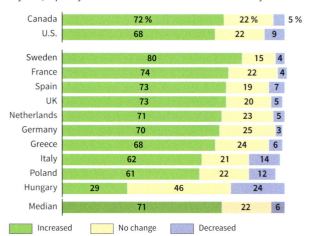

% of people in 12 different countries who say over the past 20 years, equality between men and women in our country has …

Source: Pew Research Center, 2020

The chart compares the views of people in 12 countries on gender equality.

It shows that a majority of people in all but ⟨1⟩ of the countries surveyed believe that gender equality has increased over the past few years. The countries with the ⟨2⟩ percentage holding this view are Sweden and France. In Sweden ⟨3⟩ of people say it has increased, compared with a tiny minority who say it has declined. In contrast, fewer than a ⟨4⟩ of Hungarians believe it has increased. ⟨5⟩ say it has not changed and ⟨6⟩ even say it has decreased.

To sum up, most countries surveyed believe there has been an increase in gender equality over the last 20 years.

S2 **Explaining the information.** Take turns to explain the information. First make a list of useful expressions to check or confirm understanding. Use these if you would like your partner to repeat or clarify something.

TIP

Describing the diagram
The chart shows / gives information about / compares …

Describing change
By (date), the figure had fallen / increased to / levelled off / reached a peak.
There has been a (dramatic / slight) rise / fall in (the number / percentage of) …

Comparing data
The majority / A minority of people think that …
Less / More / Fewer than (00)% / a half / a third think …
In contrast, …

Concluding
Overall, / In conclusion …

Workshop 3

→ Workbook, page 68

Workshop task: Describing diagrams (1)

S1 **Complete a description**

a Skim the text in the yellow box. Explain what aspect of changing gender roles it describes.

"I'M RIGHT HERE. FOCUSED!"

b Complete it with the words from the box. Mind the tenses!

> (to) decline ■ increase ■
> less than ■ (to) level off ■
> more than ■ (to) reach ■
> (to) rise ■ (to) stand at ■ third

> The graph shows the ⬛1 in the number of mothers in the US labor force since 1975. It compares the percentage of working mothers with children under 3, 6 and 18.
>
> As we can see, in 1975, ⬛2 half of mothers with children younger than 18 were in employment. Only 40 % of those with children under 6 and about a ⬛3 of those with children younger than 3 years old were working outside of the home.
>
> However, those numbers ⬛4 dramatically. By 2000, 73 % of all mothers were in the labor force. Since 2000, participation rates of mothers ⬛5 and more or less ⬛6 a peak. Labor force participation today ⬛7 70 % among all mothers of children younger than 18, and 64 % of mothers with preschool-aged children.
>
> In conclusion, we can see that the participation of mothers in the labor force has greatly increased since 1975. Although it ⬛8 since 2000, it is far ⬛9 it was four decades ago.

S2 **How to organize a description**

a Outline what information each paragraph gives.

b What words and phrases are used to link the paragraphs?

[1] % of mothers who are in the labor force with children …

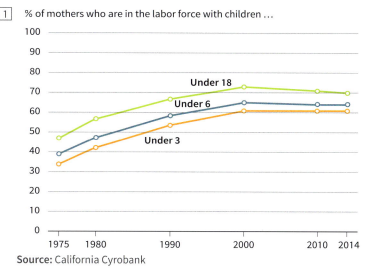

Source: California Cyrobank

S3 **Write a description**

a Describe the information in the bar chart. Look at the TIP box on page 98 for help.
- Introduction: Say what information the chart shows. What is the survey based on?
- Paragraph 2: Describe the highest statistics.
- Paragraph 3: Describe the lower statistics and those that show no change.
- Conclusion: Summarize what can be seen from the survey.

b Exchange descriptions and edit each other's texts. Then make any changes necessary to your description.

[2] % who say over the past 20 years …

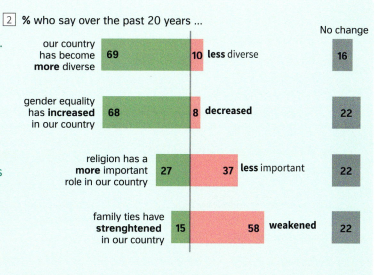

Source: Office for National Statistics, UK 2020

Youth crime and the law

1 Foolish mistakes. Many young people do things – some of which are actually crimes – to impress others or because they're bored. What examples can you think of?

2 Exploring the law

a Read the information about the Canadian Youth Criminal Justice Act. List the specialist vocabulary and check new words in a dictionary.

b Do these tasks using some of the vocabulary from **a**.

1 Explain the main aims of the law.
2 Outline the measures that can be taken to achieve these aims.

Legal rights for youth

The Youth Criminal Justice Act (YCJA) guarantees the rights of young offenders aged 12 to 17. The main aims of the law are to:
- prevent future crimes by tackling the reasons for the offence,
- help offenders become responsible members of their communities,
- ensure offenders understand the effect of their actions and make amends,
- keep youth out of jail and only use custody for the most serious crimes.

How can the law hold youth offenders accountable?
Before going to court:
For a first or non-serious offence, the police or Crown prosecutor may:
- give a warning – this is up to the police,
- refer the youth to a community program or agency for counselling,
- require the youth to apologize to the victim/s, pay compensation or do community service to repair the harm done.

If arrested and found guilty in court:
Sentencing options apart from custody include: a fine, compensation to the victim, community service, probation or a combination of these.
The judge must consider the circumstances of the case and decide on a fair sentence based on the seriousness of the offence, the impact on the victim, if the offender has a criminal record or shows remorse. There are also special programs for Aboriginal youth.

3 Jake's story. Read about a Canadian teenager. What sentencing option(s) would you choose if you were the judge? Discuss these questions before coming to a group decision.

1 Is Jake's offence serious enough to justify sending him to jail?
2 What are the drawbacks of a jail sentence?
3 What are the advantages and disadvantages of community service?
4 What other alternatives could you consider?

Jake's Story

I'm 16 years old. I did something stupid and now I'm really in trouble. It all started out as fun. Some friends and I were hanging out and drinking beer one night. I don't have a driver's licence, but somehow I got the idea of borrowing my sister's car and going for a joyride. I knew she often kept her car keys on the fridge. If they hadn't been there that night, this would never have happened.
Anyway, I got the keys and the car. Me and my buddies were drinking and cruising along when it happened. I guess I'm not a great driver yet and the road was icy. I accidentally went up over a curb and drove into a group of students. Two of them were taken to hospital. I guess if the road hadn't been icy, I wouldn't have lost control of the car.
The police and ambulance showed up and I was arrested. I was charged with drunk driving and aggravated assault. What a mess for me and my family. If I was over 18, I would definitely go to jail.

Words and phrases

counselling	professional advice about a problem
to **hold sb. accountable**	to make sb. feel responsible for their actions
to **make amends**	to do sth. good to show you are sorry about sth. you have done
probation	alternative to prison, offenders have to report to the police

4 Hopes and regrets

a Read what Jake said. Which sentence refers to the past? Which to the future?

1 If the road **hadn't been** icy, I **wouldn't have lost** control of the car.
2 If I **was** over 18, I **would** definitely **go** to jail.

- We use *if*-sentences type 2 to talk about situations now or in the future that are impossible or unlikely to happen.
  If-clause (condition)   Main clause (result)
  If + simple past   would/wouldn't + infinitive

- We use *if*-sentences type 3 to talk about something in the past that didn't happen.
  If-clause (condition)   Main clause (result)
  If + past perfect   would/wouldn't have + past participle

- If the *if*-clause comes first, we separate the clauses with a comma.

b Read the statements made by some of the people involved in the incident. Write *if*-sentences type 3. Who made each statement?

The police arrested me because I behaved so stupidly.
If I **hadn't behaved** so stupidly, the police **wouldn't have arrested** me. (Jake)

1 We were drunk and that's why we took Jake's sister's car.
2 Jake took my car because he knew where I keep the keys.
3 I'd stopped on the corner to make a call, so I wasn't with the others when they were hit.
4 The accident happened near the hospital, which is why we got there so quickly.
5 Another officer was off sick, which is why I was on duty that evening.

 page 113

5 Then and now

a Read Jake's statement, then complete the box.

If I **hadn't been** so stupid, I **wouldn't be** in court now.

- We can mix a past/present event with a past/present result.
  If-clause   Main clause
  If + past perfect would/wouldn't + infinitive

b Rewrite what Jake's mother said.

1 Jake went for a joyride with his friends. Now he has to go to court.
   If Jake …
2 Jake was drunk. Two students are in hospital now.
3 Jake took Emma's car without asking, which is why I'm so angry.
4 Two people were injured – I feel so ashamed.

page 113

6 At court.
Listen and note down what the Crown counsel and Defence counsel recommend. Who do you agree with and why?

7 YOUR TURN: You are the judge.
Read the case below and role-play the court scene. Check the options of the YCJA on page 100.
- Crown counsel and Defence counsel, prepare your recommendations to the judge.
- Judge, list your options.

Joe, 16, and his friend Kyle, 15, broke into a house while the family were away. When the neighbours were at work, they went into the backyard and broke a window with a stone. They stole money and some valuable rings. Joe had been on probation for theft before. This was Kyle's first offence.

Grammar and structures

If-sentences type 2 and 3 (revision) → G25
If Jake **was** older, he **would have to** go to jail.
If Jake **hadn't taken** his sister's car, the accident **wouldn't have happened**.

If-sentences mixed conditionals → G26
If Jake **hadn't been** so stupid, he **wouldn't be** in court now.

Practice: Healthy living?

1 **GET STARTED!** Look at the photos. What issues do they illustrate linked to body image? How much do looks or physical appearance matter in today's society? Comment on the statement: *'Your looks don't define you, it's the beauty inside that does.'*

A

B

C

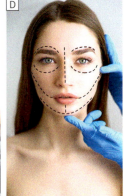
D

2 **How to avoid the dangers**

a Read the introduction to the article from a website that offers advice to teens. Then skim the rest and answer the questions.

1 What is the article about?
2 What is the writer's purpose?

b Read the article again carefully and make notes, using your own words.

1 What are the best ways to achieve and maintain a healthy weight?
2 What are the dangers of strength training for teens?
3 How can teens develop their physical fitness safely?

Teen Healthline

Body image: Avoiding the dangers
Teens often have an ideal body image that isn't realistic. There's so much pressure to be perfect and conform to the standards we see in the media. Many teens go on
5 crash diets or take pills to be super-thin like their celebrity idols. Boys often use supplements to help them bulk up and look like their superheroes. But extreme dieting and fitness supplements are bad for your health. Here are some tips on how to stay in shape AND healthy.

10 **Dieting: Don't overdo it!**
It's good to stay at a weight that's normal for your height – but it's dangerous to overdo it and go to extremes trying to get super-model thin. The best way to achieve and maintain a healthy weight is to do
15 regular exercise and follow a healthy eating plan. Experts recommend teens do 60 minutes of physical activity every day, such as jogging or dancing. Eat lean meats, fruit, vegetables, whole grains, and healthy
20 fats. Avoid junk foods – they are full of bad fat and salt. Soda drinks contain large amounts of sugar and caffeine, so cut them out, too.

Body-building: It's not worth the risk!
25 It's good to do regular exercise, but strength training can be dangerous if you don't practise it correctly or do too much. If you're under 16, your body is still developing. If you lift too much weight or lift weights incorrectly, you could injure yourself. Instead, build up your strength and
30 fitness safely by following these simple tips. Check out your local gym and sign up for a class to learn the correct techniques. Steer clear of fitness supplements, including steroids as they can raise the risk of heart disease or liver damage.
35 Eat a well-balanced diet. Don't count your calories, load up on protein, or cut out carbohydrates – this can slow down your growth and development.

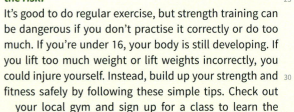

Words and phrases

supplement a thing that is added to sth. else to improve it

Workshop 3

→ Workbook, pages 71 – 73

3 WRITING FOCUS: Write a summary

a Write a summary of the article with your notes from **2b**.

> **TIP**
>
> When you write a summary:
> - state the topic in your introductory sentence(s). Include the author, date and source if known.
> - include only the main ideas and key points.

 b Swap and correct each other's summaries.

4 My self-image. Complete what these people say about their health and body image.

1 If I _____ (*not decide*) to avoid fast food when I was a teenager, I _____ (*be*) overweight now.
2 If social media _____ (*not be invented*), my life _____ (*be*) easier.
3 If Dan _____ (*spend*) time with his friends, he _____ (*not be able to*) train every day.
4 If my dad _____ (*not make*) such a fuss, I _____ (*continue*) taking supplements.

5 Eat less meat!

a Kevin wants to convince his classmates to become vegetarians or vegans. Listen to his talk. What five results does he describe?

b Listen again and note down the facts and figures Kevin gives to support his argument.

1 There are _____ vegetarians in Canada and nearly _____ vegans.
2 Livestock produce over _____ per cent of all greenhouse gas emissions.
3 Around _____ per cent of deforestation in the Amazon is due to cattle ranching.
4 The proportion of farm animals raised on factory farms is _____ in _____ .
5 Around _____ per cent of the antibiotics used in the US are given to farm animals.

≫ page 113

c Write a blogpost about what would happen if we all stopped eating meat. Use some ideas from Kevin's talk and your own.

6 Teen food attitudes

a Read the results of a survey into teen food attitudes in the USA. Discuss if anything surprises you.

TEEN FOOD ATTITUDES Survey
- Teens snack 2 – 3 times per day.
- Top 5 snack foods for teens:
  1 chips, 2 fruit, 3 pizza, 4 frozen snacks, 5 yogurt.
- The favorite meal among teens is dinner.
- More than 90% of teens enjoy sitting down to a family meal.
- Parents are teens no. 1 source of food knowledge.
- 30% of the grocery bill is driven by teens.
- 52% of teens say meals served by their parents don't always suit their tastes or dietary lifestyle.
- 28% of teens are interested in changing food preferences. Of those, most are interested in
  – low-carb 38%, – low-fat 35%, – vegetarian / vegan 32%.
- Three times a week is the average number of times that teens help parents out in the kitchen.

b In your group, conduct a Teen Food Attitudes survey with ideas from **a** and your own.

c Write at least eight questions and note down the results in a table. Then present your results to the class.

Questions	Name	Name	Name	Name
How often do you snack daily?				
…				

one hundred and three **103**

Advertising and Generation Z

1 **Ads and us.** Sam is a Canadian teen who writes about media topics. Read his blogpost and do the tasks.

1. Describe the decision Sam made when he started blogging and why he took it.
2. List the different kinds of advertising he mentions.
3. Describe how Sam as a user reacts to these different kinds of advertising.
4. Explain why, in his view, teens react differently to advertising by vloggers.

| BLOG | ABOUT ME | GUEST BLOGGERS | COOL STUFF | ARCHIVE |

Media Geek

Ads and us
by Sam

You rarely see a website with no advertising. But mine's different. I don't sell advertising space because I want my blog to be all about the content.

Advertising is everywhere. Need some statistics? The average
5 teenager sees 400 – 600 ads daily. In the US, companies spend $1.6 billion every year on marketing to teens. Businesses know that Generation Z makes up a quarter of the population. As a market segment, we're worth between $44 and $150 billion a year. So, if they want to sell their product or service, they have to get our attention.

10 As 'digital natives' we socialize, shop and entertain ourselves online, and as users and consumers we're pretty savvy. I know I'm going to get blasted with ads every time I check my social media feeds, but I haven't once clicked or tapped on one of those ads.

Of course, advertisers use lots of tricks to get onto our screens and into our heads. Think about the paid content at the bottom of news sites, etc. – they look like serious articles with attention-grabbing headlines.

15 The video ads slipped in between the content we watch on video-sharing sites can be more interesting. I click past most of them, but if the music is cool or the ad speaks to me personally, I'll watch it and even share it with friends. This doesn't mean that we then go out and buy the product. What it means is that we enjoy clever content, even if it's advertising. Ads have to be original, creative and personalized to get our attention.

20 Some advertising is harder to separate from real content. When a film or TV show character is drinking a popular brand of cola or wearing stylish sneakers with a logo, this is called 'product placement'. So, when you see or hear about a brand or product on social media or anywhere online, it's probably sponsored. The vloggers we know and love are often sponsored, too, but they're a special case. Sure, we know that brands pay them to influence our buying choices, but we still watch and listen to them because we trust
25 that they won't sell a product they don't believe in. Also, they're open about it and say they're getting paid. It's casual and personalized, and that makes it more authentic. The best vloggers don't really want to sell us anything. It's the advertisers who want our money.

Take my advertising mini-survey and leave a comment!

 Words and phrases

authentic	known to be real, true and accurate
banner ad	an advert that is placed on a webpage and that links to a website
geek	a person of high intelligence who typically doesn't fit into popular social groups
savvy *(infml.)*	having practical knowledge or understanding about sth.

Workshop 3

→ Workbook, pages 74/75

2 The thing about ads

a Explain what advertisers need to do, according to Sam, to get the attention of teenagers. Do you agree with him? What gets your attention?

b Think of other ways that advertisers try to influence you online. Make a list with a partner. Compare and discuss your lists in class.

c Write a comment to post under Sam's blog.

3 Making your point

a Sam changed two sentences from his first draft to make his opinions clearer. Look at the examples, then complete the explanations in the box.

Draft: It means that we enjoy clever content, even if it's advertising.
Blog: **What** *it means* **is** *that we enjoy clever content, even if it's advertising.*

Draft: The advertisers want our money.
Blog: **It's** *the advertisers* **who** *want our money.*

> - To make a point clearer, we add the words ⬚1 … ⬚2 / *are* or *was / were*.
> - To emphasize the subject or object, we put it between ⬚3 and ⬚4 or *which / that*.

b In his first draft, Sam wanted to emphasize the underlined information. Rewrite the sentences starting with the word in brackets.

Those ads blocking the content <u>are so annoying</u>. (What …)
What *is so annoying* **are** *those ads blocking the content.*

1 <u>All the paid content I saw on other sites</u> made me go ad-free. (It …)
2 <u>The video ads</u> really get into your head. (It …)
3 <u>Teenagers like</u> ads that feel authentic. (What …)
4 <u>Influencers are good at</u> introducing you to cool stuff. (What …)

4 Getting the right feel

a Parts of Sam's first draft were too formal. How did he change them in his blog?

Rarely do you see a website with no advertising. Not once have I clicked on one of those ads.

> We can emphasize *hardly ever, rarely, not once, never, only later* and *in no way* by putting them at the beginning of the sentence. The position of the **subject** and **auxiliary** – which you might have to add – changes.
>
> *I* **am** *not saying all advertising is bad.*
> *In no way* **am** *I saying all advertising is bad.*
>
> *I* **rarely** *take any notice of banner ads.*
> *Rarely* **do** *I take any notice of banner ads.*

b How can Sam change the underlined parts of a school assignment to make them more formal? Use the words in brackets.

1 <u>You hardly ever see</u> websites with no advertising. *(Hardly ever do)*
2 At first, I thought about selling advertising space, but <u>later I realized</u> how important it is to focus on the content. *(only later did)*
3 <u>I didn't intend</u> to spoil my website with ads just to make a few dollars. *(In no way did)*
4 <u>I didn't regret</u> my decision. *(Not once did)*

5 YOUR TURN: What makes a good ad?

a Use these ideas and your own to write four questions to ask someone about ads.

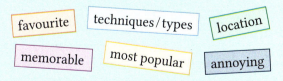

favourite   techniques / types   location
memorable   most popular   annoying

b Use your questions to interview a partner.

c Compare your answers and draw conclusions.

Grammar and structures

Using *It …* **and** *What …* **for emphasis** → G27
It's all the advertising which annoys me.
What annoys me is all the advertising.

Using inversion to make a text more formal → G28
Not once have I sold advertising space.

one hundred and five   **105**

Practice: Digital communication

1 **GET STARTED!** Discuss how digitalization has changed the way we communicate.

2 **Writing in the internet age.** Listen to a podcast about how the internet has influenced the way we write. Then do these tasks.

1. Discuss if the changes described in the podcast also apply to other languages.
2. Find examples of differences between your grandparents' language and yours.

3 **WORDPOWER: Abbreviations in texting**

a One of the changes which has been brought about by digitalization is creative texting and the use of abbreviations. Look at the boxes. Match the texting abbreviations with their meaning.

> 1 CUL ■ 2 HBD ■ 3 BTW ■ 4 THX ■
> 5 ILY ■ 6 NP ■ 7 IMO ■ 8 GR8 ■ 9 BRB

> **A** by the way ■ **B** in my opinion ■
> **C** great ■ **D** Happy Birthday ■ **E** see you later ■ **F** I love you ■ **G** thanks ■
> **H** no problem ■ **I** be right back

b Which words do these abbreviations sound like? Write the word for each.

| 1 4 | 3 C | 5 O | 7 U |
| 2 B | 4 I | 6 R | 8 Y |

c Read this exchange between two friends and discuss the meaning of the abbreviations.

> Hi! How RU? Want 2 C a film together? 2moro at my plc?

> SRY, but 2moro I have lots 2 do. THX, anyway. BTW, RU free L8TR 2day? I have time 4 a coffee.

> GR8! I'll wait 4 U at the usual plc at 3. Don't B l8.

> NP. CU then.

4 **A mini-survey.** First answer Sam' questionnaire alone, then compare your answers in a group.

Advertising and you

Hey guys, let's compare our advertising experiences. Just answer this questionnaire and I'll post the results in a few weeks. Thanks! Sam

1 Where do you notice advertising the most when you're online?
☐ social media feeds ☐ websites and blogs
☐ video sharing portals ☐ shows and films

2 Which of these ad types attract your attention the most? Rank them from 1 (= most) to 6 (= least).
☐ banners ☐ pop-ups ☐ paid content
☐ video ads ☐ product placement
☐ influencers

3 How often do you open online ads?
☐ at least once a day ☐ 1 – 2 times a week
☐ once every two weeks ☐ very seldom
☐ never

4 How much influence do online ads have on what you buy?
☐ none at all ☐ not very much ☐ some
☐ a lot

5 **Attitudes to advertising.** Sam is drafting a blogpost with the results of his advertising survey. He wants to emphasize the underlined sentences. Use his notes in the margin to rewrite them.

The number of you who answered the questionnaire surprised me. (1) There were 8,681 respondents – that's awesome! Your answers sometimes surprised me, too. (2)	What … did
Let's start with #1: A lot of you say you notice advertising the most on social media feeds, but many more of you have a different experience: websites and blogs have the most advertising. (3)	It's …
Your answers to #2 were more unexpected. I thought most of you would say that influencers got your attention most (4), but no: video ads really grab your attention. (5) For question #3 I asked how often you click or tap on online ads. Surprise again! Most of you say '1 – 2 times a week'. (6) Maybe those ads are more effective than I thought. The most popular answer to #4 was no shock: online ads don't have very much influence on what you buy. Our friends influence us most. (7) I hope you had fun with this mini-survey – I sure did!	did it's … What … It's …

▶▶▶ page 113

6 **READING FOCUS: Choosing sides**

a Look at this public service message. Describe what you see. What issue does the ad address?

> When it comes to cyberbullying, we all have to choose sides.
>
> ### Whose side are you on?
>
>
>
> - One in three young people say they've been a victim of cyberbullying.
> - 66% say they've witnessed other people join in when someone was cyberbullied.
> - 21% say they've also joined in.
> - 80% say they have defended the victim. 25% have done so frequently.
>
> **DON'T BE THE BAD GUY. BE THE HERO.**
>
> Source: www.enough.org

b A public service message has a different aim than a commercial advertisement, but both use similar strategies to get the reader's attention. Read the information in the TIP box. Identify as many of the elements as you can in the ad.

> **TIP**
>
> Basic elements of public service advertisements
> - a headline or slogan to catch the reader's attention
> - the body, or the ad text
> - artwork – a photo, illustration or graphic
> - a call to action, e.g. 'Talk to your …' or 'Go to our website at …'
> - contact information including the name and web address of the organization

c Analyse how the text and picture work together to create a powerful message. What is the role and effect of the heading? What about the text under it? How is the picture important?

7 **VIDEO TRACK: A powerful message.** Watch the public-service advert 'Are your words doing damage?'. Discuss the main message. Compare this advertisement with the print advert in **6**. What are the strengths and weaknesses of each?

8 **YOUR CHOICE: Cyberbullying**

a Your school plans to post the video 'Are your words doing damage?' on its international website to highlight just how serious the consequences of bullying can be. Choose task A or task B.

A Write a summary explaining what the video shows and why you think it is effective.

B Research the background to the video and give a short talk.

b Find another video about cyberbullying on the net which impresses you and present it to the class. Explain why you feel it is effective.

Method coach: Understanding diagrams (2)

S1 Understanding the information. Choose one diagram each and complete the short description and analysis of the information shown.

1 The pie chart gives us information about ▢1 in the US.
It is based on a sample of ▢2 in ▢3. A tiny minority of teenagers ▢4. Five times as many ▢5 as ▢6. Just over a quarter ▢7. The vast majority, almost ▢8, stated that ▢9.
Overall, we can see that bullying is ▢10.

2 The line graph compares ▢1 by ▢2 in England and Wales in a period between ▢3.
The number of young people who received sentences was ▢4 in each age group at the beginning of this period. In 2010, just over ▢5 10–14-year-olds were sentenced. The figure for 15-year-olds (20,000) was about a ▢6 lower. The number in the other two age groups was between ▢7 and ▢8.
Overall, this 10-year period saw a steady ▢9 in the number of convicted young people for each age group. The largest drop was for the number of ▢10-year-olds, from over 30,000 to 5,000.

3 The bar chart shows which factors motivate teenagers to ▢1.
While film stars are the ▢2 for both genders, they are more important for boys ▢3.
The next most important factor for both boys and girls is ▢4, but they ▢5 girls more than boys. Both genders agree, however, that print ads are the ▢6 motivating. This is followed by ▢7 and ▢8 for boys.
In conclusion, there is not a ▢9 difference in what motivates boys and girls to do physical exercise. However, almost ▢10 girls as boys list reading as an important factor.

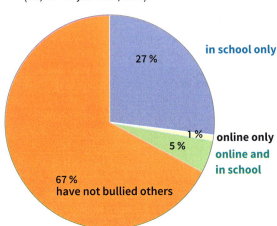

1 Bullied others in school and online (US, 12–17-year-olds, 2016)
- 27 % in school only
- 1 % online only
- 5 % online and in school
- 67 % have not bullied others

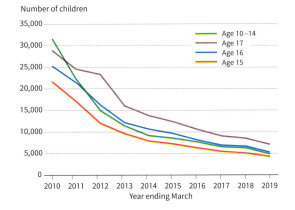

2 Number of children receiving a sentence by age (England and Wales)

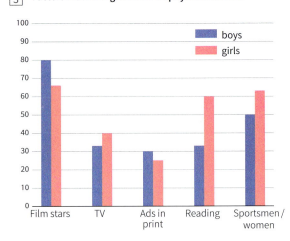

3 Factors motivating teens to do physical exercise

Sources: (1) Cyberbullying Research Center, US 2016; (2) Ministry of Justice, UK 2020; (3) Journal of Clinical Nutrition and Dietetics, India 2018

S2 Discuss the data. Think about the reasons behind the trends. Discuss and compare what you know about the same topics in Germany.

Workshop 3

→ Workbook, page 79

Workshop task: Describing diagrams (2)

S1 **Choose a diagram.** With a partner, discuss the two diagrams below and choose one to describe. Refer to the TIP on page 98 for useful language and look at the descriptions on page 108.

S2 **Write a description.** Organize your description into the following parts:
- Introduction: say what the diagram shows / is about
- Main body: explain and describe the key points
- Conclusion: summarize the main point(s) expressed in the diagram

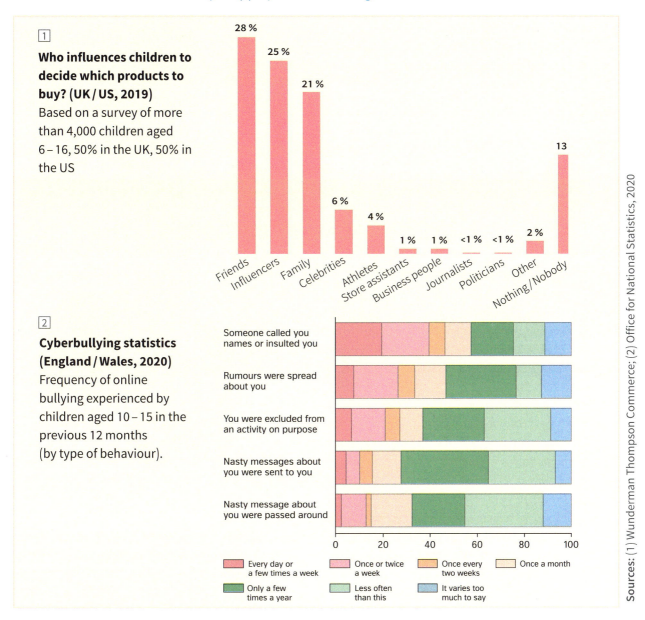

1 Who influences children to decide which products to buy? (UK / US, 2019)
Based on a survey of more than 4,000 children aged 6–16, 50% in the UK, 50% in the US

2 Cyberbullying statistics (England / Wales, 2020)
Frequency of online bullying experienced by children aged 10–15 in the previous 12 months (by type of behaviour).

Sources: (1) Wunderman Thompson Commerce; (2) Office for National Statistics, 2020

S3 **Finalize your description.** Swap texts with a pair who looked at the other diagram. Look at the TIP box, then give each other feedback. Correct and finalize your original text.

TIP
When you edit a text, check the following:
- structure
- language
- content
- spelling

Mediation

1 **Bullying in school.** Sally, your friend from England, is being bullied in school. She wrote an email to you asking for help and advice. You researched the topic and found an article online. Use the information in the article and answer Sally's email. Tell her what she can do, what you would do if you were in her position and what her parents can do.

Hi!
How are you? I feel really bad because all my classmates hate me. You know that my brother Steve is autistic. For me, this isn't a big deal. But my classmates say that he's a freak. I know Steve's special – he for example knows the phone numbers of everyone in our village. But why's that bad? He just loves numbers. It's no big deal.
Last week, Steve and I were walking around the village and he pointed at all the numbers – you know, car number plates and house numbers. We laughed a lot and I was happy for him when he found another number. Cory and Mandy, two girls in my class, saw us and made fun of us. They even filmed us and put the video in our class chat group. Now all my classmates say that I'm a freak, too. Whenever they see me, they point at me and laugh. I don't want to go to school any more. I don't know what to do …

XXX
Sally

Cybermobbing an der Schule [...]

[...] Schüler werden zu Tätern

Mobbing ist [...] ein bekanntes Problem. Durch die neuen Medien verlagert es sich aktuell aus der realen Welt in die fiktive, wo die beleidigenden
5 Handlungen eine grenzenlose Reichweite mit weitgreifenden Folgen haben. Das Opfer wird somit nicht nur innerhalb der Klasse, auf dem Pausenhof oder Schulweg bloßgestellt. Das Internet bietet dem Täter zudem die Option anonym zu bleiben.
10 Dadurch wird die Hemmschwelle geringer und Cybermobbing unter Schülern zu einem großen Problem. Trotz der Anonymität weiß das Opfer aber meistens, wer der Täter ist. [...]

Wie wird typischerweise im Netz gemobbt?

- Gerüchte verbreiten: Unwahrheiten über
15 Soziale Medien und Messenger-Services kommunizieren
- Schikane: in Chats, via E-Mail, SMS oder in sozialen Netzwerken wiederholt verletzende Nachrichten verschicken
20 - Bloßstellung: Geheimnisse und andere im Vertrauen weitergegebene Informationen an einen großen Personenkreis verraten
- Ausschließen oder Ignorieren: Opfer aus Chats, Nachrichten-Gruppen und sozialen Aktivitäten im Internet ausschließen [...]

Was können Betroffene tun?

Cybermobbing sollten betroffene Schüler keineswegs verschweigen, sondern sich anderen anvertrauen. Das können ihre Eltern, Freunde oder Lehrer sein. Die Schule ist in jedem Fall von den Beleidigungen oder Drohungen im Internet zu informieren. Das können Sie als Mutter oder Vater zum Beispiel im Rahmen einer Lehrersprechstunde oder am Elternsprechtag tun. Schüler können sich dafür an einen Vertrauenslehrer wenden. Auch bei Mobbing-Experten wie Beratungsstellen und Psychologen finden Betroffene Hilfe und Unterstützung. Cybermobbing ist grundsätzlich kein dummer Kinderscherz, sondern kann eine Straftat nach sich ziehen. [...]

Weitere Tipps für Maßnahmen gegen Cybermobbing und die Prävention:

- Eltern sollten sich umfassend mit dem Problem auseinandersetzen. Da es ein junges Phänomen ist, wissen viele nicht genau darüber Bescheid oder haben davon noch nie etwas gehört.
- Mütter und Väter sollten ihren Kindern klare Regeln für den Umgang mit Smartphones, Tablets und PCs sowie dem Internet aufstellen.
- Beleidigungen, Belästigungen und weitere Formen des Mobbings im Internet sind zu dokumentieren. Sie dienen als Beweismittel, um die Täter zur Rechenschaft ziehen zu können.
- Wenden Sie sich an die Betreiber sozialer Netzwerke mit der Bitte, die verleumderischen Beiträge und Nachrichten umgehend zu löschen. Melden Sie den Täter außerdem, so dass sein Profil gelöscht werden kann.
- In der Schule sollte grundsätzlich ein Handyverbot während des Unterrichts ausgesprochen werden. Das Filmen sollte auf dem Schulgelände verboten sein.
- Teil des Unterrichts sollte der umsichtige und sinnvolle Umgang mit den neuen Medien sein. [...]
- Vorträge oder Workshops an der Schule durch Polizeibeamte sind empfehlenswert. [...]

www.schulranzen.net

2 Cyberbullying in the UK. You told your parents about Sally's problem. They ask you if cyberbullying is a big problem in the UK. You did some research on the topic and present your findings to your parents.

Cyberbullying is a real problem in today's society

- Overall, 36.5% of people feel they have been cyberbullied in their lifetime, and 17.4% have reported it has happened at some point in the last 30 days.
- These numbers are more than double what they were in 2007, and both represent an increase from 2018–2019, suggesting we are heading in the wrong direction when it comes to stopping cyberbullying.
- 87% of young people have seen cyberbullying occurring online.

Cyberbullying Research Centre, 2019

First track

3b Listen again and complete the sentences.
p.91
1. Immigrants have to get used to …
2. Valerie's grandmother came to Canada from Guyana in order to …
3. She missed her family and she didn't like …
4. Valerie is … that she learned about her culture from her family. Her favourite family tradition is …
5. Mike's grandmother was born in … . Her parents wanted her to have … in Canada. His father was born in …
6. Mike doesn't know much about his … He's confused about his …

7b Add the extra information below to complete
p.93 the summary of Tayler's story.

> Tayler is a 14-year-old trans boy from Wales, *who likes skateboarding, drawing and playing on his video console*. Tayler, **1**, decided he wanted to make the
> 5 transition to become a boy. He is currently on hormone-blocker medication **2** . He was helped by Fox Fisher from Stonewall, an organization which supports LGBTQ people. He gave a talk at Tayler's school
> 10 and told the other kids about him. Tayler, **3** , felt very relieved after Fox's visit. His mum, **4** , was surprised when Tayler first told her that he felt like a boy trapped in a girl's body. Tayler reminded
> 15 her that she had tried to make him wear dresses, **5** . Finally, she accepted him for who he is and she feels very proud of him.

Tayler likes skateboarding, drawing and playing on his video console.

a He realized that he wasn't supposed to be a girl when he was 10 or 11.
b This prevents puberty from starting.
c Tayler had been worried about telling everyone himself.
d His mum didn't think she had forced gender roles on him.
e This had made him angry because he'd only wanted to wear trousers.

3b Romy is rewriting her article. How can she add
p.95 more emphasis to these sentences? Complete them with the correct form of the verb *do*.

1. My accent wasn't very strong, but it probably ▓▓ sound quite unusual to my new classmates.
2. She ▓▓ have a wild side to her personality I like that about her.
3. Grace said, 'You never take risks' and I said, 'Yes, I ▓▓ take risks sometimes'.
4. I said, 'Hey you didn't buy a ticket.' She said, 'I ▓▓ buy one. It's in my pocket'.

3c Mark decides to include these ideas in his
p.95 article. Complete his statements using some of the emphatic pronouns from the box. Where would you add them to his story?

> myself ■ yourself ■ himself ■ herself ■ itself ■ ourselves ■ yourselves ■ themselves

1. They couldn't see it ▓▓ , but it was clear that they were being really mean.
2. Carla said, 'They're not going to stop. You have to stop them ▓▓ .'
3. I hadn't realized it ▓▓ , but Carla was right.
4. We notice when other people do something dumb, but not always when we do it ▓▓ .

2b Choose four statements from 1–6 that
p.96 correctly paraphrase what Nicki Ferris is saying.

1. Real love is not just something for adults.
2. Lust is necessary before you can find love.
3. Having a crush on someone and being in love are not the same thing.
4. Dating is usually a sign of real love.
5. It's good to understand why you want to date someone.
6. For teenagers, lasting love is hard.

Workshop 3
FIRST TRACK

4 **b** Read the statements made by some of the people involved in the incident. Complete the *if*-sentences type 3. Who made each statement?

p. 101

The police arrested me because I behaved so stupidly.
If **I hadn't behaved** (not behave) so stupidly, the police **wouldn't have arrested** (not arrest) me.

1. We were drunk and that's why we took Jake's sister's car.
   If we _____ (not be) drunk, we _____ (not take) Jake's sister's car.
2. Jake took my car because he knew where I keep the keys.
   If Jake _____ (not know) where I keep the keys, he _____ (not take) my car.
3. I'd stopped on the corner to make a call, so I wasn't with the others when they were hit.
   If I _____ (not stop) on the corner to make a call, I _____ (be) with the others when they were hit.
4. The accident happened near the hospital, which is why we got there so quickly.
   If the accident _____ (not happen) near the hospital, we _____ (not get) there so quickly.
5. Another officer was off sick, which is why I was on duty that evening.
   If another officer _____ (not be) off sick, I _____ (not be) on duty that evening.

5 **b** Jake's mother is telling her sister what happened. Rewrite what she said.

p. 101

1. Jake went for a joyride with his friends. Now he has to go to court.
   If Jake _____ (not go) for a joyride with his friends, he _____ (not have to) go to court now.
2. Jake was drunk. Now two students are in hospital.
   If Jake _____ (not be) drunk, two students _____ (not be) in hospital now.
3. Jake took Emma's car without asking, which is why I'm so angry.
   If Jake _____ (not take) Emma's car without asking, I _____ (not be) so angry.
4. Two people were injured – I feel so ashamed.
   If two people _____ (not be) injured, I _____ (not feel) so ashamed.

5 **b** Listen again and choose the correct figures from the box to complete the facts Kevin uses to support his argument.

p. 103

| 1 ■ 2 ■ 2.3 ■ 3 ■ 14 ■ 70 ■ 70 |

1. There are _____ million vegetarians in Canada and nearly _____ million vegans.
2. Livestock produce over _____ per cent of all greenhouse gas emissions.
3. Around _____ per cent of deforestation in the Amazon is due to cattle ranching.
4. The proportion of farm animals raised on factory farms is _____ in _____ .
5. Around _____ per cent of the antibiotics used in the US are given to farm animals.

5 Sam is drafting a blogpost with the results of his mini-survey. He wants to emphasize the underlined sentences. Use his notes below to rewrite them.

p. 107

1. What really surprised me …
2. Your answers did
3. it's websites and blogs …
4. I did …
5. it's video ads …
6. What most of you say …
7. It's our friends …

The number of you who answered the questionnaire surprised me. (1) There were 8,681 respondents – that's awesome! Your answers sometimes surprised me, too. (2)
⁵ Let's start with #1: A lot of you say you notice advertising the most on social media feeds, but many more of you have a different experience: websites and blogs have the most advertising. (3) Your answers to #2 were more unexpected. I thought
¹⁰ most of you would say that influencers got your attention most (4), but no: video ads really grab your attention. (5)
For question #3 I asked how often you click or tap on online ads. Surprise again! Most of you say '1 – 2
¹⁵ times a week'. (6) Maybe those ads are more effective than I thought.
The most popular answer to #4 was no shock: online ads don't have very much influence on what you buy. Our friends influence us most. (7)
²⁰ I hope you had fun with this mini-survey – I sure did!

Reading

Karen McManus, *One of us is lying* (2019), Chapter Twenty

Four teenagers at Bay View High try to find out how their schoolmate Simon could be murdered while they were all together in detention. Now prime suspects, the secrets each of them has been hiding are slowly revealed. One of the four is Cooper. As events unfold, he has to face the consequences of deceiving others as well as himself.

Tuesday, October 16, 5:45 p.m.
'Pass the milk, would you, Cooperstown[1]?' Pop[1] jerks his chin at me during dinner, his eyes drifting toward the muted television in our living room, where college
5 football scores scroll along the bottom of the screen. 'So what'd you do with your night off?' [...] I hand over the carton and picture myself answering his question honestly. Hung out with Kris, the guy I'm in love with. Yeah, Pop, I said guy. No, Pop, I'm not
10 kidding. He's a premed[2] freshman at UCSD who does modeling on the side. Total catch[3]. You'd like him. And then Pop's head explodes. That's how it always ends in my imagination. 'Just drove around for a while,' I say instead. I'm not ashamed of Kris. I'm not. But it's
15 complicated. Thing is, I didn't realize I could feel that way about a guy till I met him. I mean, yeah, I suspected. Since I was eleven or so. But I buried those thoughts as far down as I could because I'm a Southern jock[4] shooting for an MLB[5] career and that's not how
20 we're supposed to be wired. I really did believe that for most of my life.
I've always had a girlfriend. But it was never hard to hold off[6] till marriage like I was raised. I only recently understood that was more of an excuse than a deeply
25 held moral belief. I've been lying to Keely for months, but I did tell her the truth about Kris. I met him through baseball, although he doesn't play. He's friends with another guy I made the exhibition rounds with, who invited us both to his birthday party. And he
30 is German. I just left out the part about being in love with him. I can't admit that to anybody yet. That it's not a phase, or experimentation, or distraction from pressure. Nonny[7] was right. My stomach does flips when Kris calls or texts me. Every single time. And
35 when I'm with him I feel like a real person, not the robot Keely called me: programmed to perform as expected. But Cooper-and-Kris only exists in the bubble of his apartment. Moving it anyplace else scares the hell out of me. For one thing, it's hard enough
40 making it in baseball when you're a regular guy. The number of openly gay players who are part of a major league team stands at exactly one. And he's still in the minors. For another thing: Pop. My whole brain seizes[8]
45 when I imagine his reaction. He's the kind of good old boy who calls gay people 'fags'[9] and thinks we spend all our time hitting on straight[10] guys. The one time we saw a news story about the gay baseball player, he snorted in disgust and said, 'Normal guys shouldn't
50 have to deal with that crap in the locker room.'
If I tell him about Kris and me, seventeen years of being the perfect son would be gone in an instant. He'd never look at me the same. The way he's looking at me now, even though I'm a murder suspect who's
55 been accused of using steroids[11]. That he can handle. 'Testing tomorrow,' he reminds me. I have to get tested for steroids every damn week now. In the meantime I keep pitching[12], and no, my fastball hasn't gotten any slower. Because I haven't been lying. I didn't cheat. I
60 strategically improved. It was Pop's idea. He wanted me to hold back a little in junior year, not give my all, so there'd be more excitement around me during showcase season[13]. And there was. People like Josh Langley noticed me. But now, of course, it looks
65 suspicious. Thanks, Pop. At least he feels guilty about it. I was sure, when the police got ready to show me the unpublished *About That* posts[14] last month, that I was going to read something about Kris and me. I'd barely known Simon, only talked with him one-on-one
70 a few times. But anytime I got near him, I'd worry about him learning my secret.
Last spring at junior prom he'd been drunk off his ass, and when I ran into him in the bathroom he flung an arm around me and pulled me so close I practically
75 had a panic attack. I was sure that Simon – who'd never had a girlfriend as far as I knew – realized I was gay and was putting the moves on me[15]. I freaked out so bad, I had Vanessa disinvite him to her after-prom party. [...] I let it stand even after I saw Simon hitting
80 on Keely later with the kind of intensity you can't fake. I hadn't let myself think about that since Simon died; how the last time I'd talked to him, I acted like a jerk because I couldn't deal with who I was. And the worst part is, even after all this – I still can't.
85
Karen McManus, *One of us is lying* (English edition), Kindle, pp. 229–231

Workshop 3
READING

1 a Summarize the conversation at dinner time in three to five sentences.

b Describe the atmosphere. Speculate about Cooper's and his father's feelings.

c Examine the constellation of characters (family, friends, classmates) you read about in the excerpt. Make a mind map with Cooper in the centre and arrange the characters according to their closeness to the protagonist. Differentiate between emotional and physical distance.

d Collect the information you get from the text about Cooper's character and write a short characterization about him. Quote from the text in order to justify your statements. Make sure that you include descriptive adjectives.

e Analyse the relationship between father and son. Compare it to your understanding of a healthy parent-child relationship.

Literary terms

- **Narrator:** the person who tells the story in a book or play (NOT the author!)
- **Plot:** the sequence of events that forms and unifies the main story of a novel, play or film
- **Point of view:** the perspective from which a story is told. The point of view of a first-person narrator like Cooper in this excerpt allows the reader to see through the narrator's eyes, to hear and listen through his ears, to read the thoughts in his mind …
- **Protagonist:** the main or most important character in a story of a book, play or film
- **Setting:** the time when and place where the events in a book or film happen

---

2 a With a partner, discuss the problems of coming out in today's society.

b Comment on one of the following statements:

> The truth may hurt for a little while, but a lie hurts forever.

> Better to be slapped with the truth than kissed with a lie.

> Three things cannot be long hidden: the Sun, the Moon, and the Truth.

3 Cooper's thoughts are written in the form of an interior monologue. He verbalizes all of his jumbled thoughts. Imagine yourself at a decisive point in your life. It might be happy or sad, something difficult you are afraid of or something you are looking forward to. Look at the text again and write down an interior monologue of your own in a similar style. Write 150 – 200 words.

- **Step 1:** Collect adjectives that express your feelings.
- **Step 2:** Think of verbs that express what you might / could do or don't dare to do.
- **Step 3:** Then, think of three people that could get involved in your life at this point and describe their potential reactions to your situation.
- **Step 4:** Write the monologue.

> **Interior monologue** is the technical literary term for a character's train of thought and is usually found in a novel. For the reader it is like looking into a character's mind, gaining insights into the ideas and feelings in real time. The character's inner voice is speaking (self-talk) and often internal secrets are revealed.

---

[1] **Cooperstown / Pop** nicknames for Cooper and Cooper's father (from 'poppa' = dad) – [2] **premed freshman at USCD** Kris is a first-year-student at the University of California, San Diego. – [3] **catch** (*infml.*) a desirable person to start a relationship with ('a good catch') – [4] **jock** (AE, *infml.*) a student who practises a lot of sport but is less interested in or talented for an academic career – [5] **MLB** Major League Baseball, the American baseball league – [6] **to hold off** to delay sth., *here:* not to have sex before marriage – [7] **Nonny** = Grandma – [8] **my brain seizes** my brain stops working – [9] **fag** (AE, *slang*) taboo word for a homosexual man – [10] **straight** heterosexual – [11] **steroids** substances that should make your muscles grow and get stronger – [12] **to pitch** to throw the ball (in baseball) – [13] **showcase season** talent scouting: young players are keen to present their talents in order to be recruited for a well-reputed professional league club – [14] **About That** posts *About That* is a gossip app that Simon, one of the students at school, has been running, feeding it with ugly news and revealing secrets about his classmates until his death – [15] **to put the moves on sb.** to try and develop a (sexual) relationship with sb. you have a crush on

My review

What can I do?

Look at these sentences about Workshop 3. Are the sentences true for you? Choose the right symbol for each sentence.

1 I can talk and write about family life and gender identity today.
2 I can comment on friendships and relationships.
3 I can discuss the best ways of dealing with youth crime.
4 I can understand and talk about advertising for Generation Z.

>>> = 'I'm great at this!'
>> = 'I'm good at this.'
> = 'I'm OK at this.'

What do I know?

1 About families

a Complete this text with the family words from the box and *be used to / get used to* + the *-ing* form of the verbs in brackets.

> blended ■ divorced ■ extended ■
> mixed union ■ same-sex ■ traditional

I'm Sam from Vancouver in Canada. It's a really diverse city. Take my family, for example. Mom is Chinese and Dad is from a first nations tribe, so a **1** family. For the first ten years of my life, I **2** (*be*) part of a **3** family: mom, dad and two kids, but then my parents got **4** . My mom and sister and I moved into a little flat. It was hard to **5** (*live*) in such a small place, but we managed. At first, my sister and I really missed Dad, but now it seems normal and we **6** (*pack*) a bag twice a month for a weekend with him. Then Mom met her new partner – Cathy, so I had to **7** (*have*) two moms! In fact, **8** couples are not so unusual nowadays and living in a **9** family is fun! I also have a big **10** family on my Chinese mom's side, so I think I'm lucky with everything.

■ / 10

b Sam wrote about his family for the school magazine. Improve parts of his article by using relative clauses to combine the sentences in 1–3 and participles to shorten sentences 4–6.

1 I love Vancouver. Vancouver was recently ranked the third most 'livable place in the world'.
2 My family consists of my mom and dad, my younger sister and my mom's new partner Cathy. My family is known as a blended family.
3 My mom still has some family members in China. She came here with her parents when she was four.
4 My parents are mixed union. Mixed union is a term which describes a couple of different national or ethnic origin.
5 Mom and Dad got divorced, which forced them to sell our family home.
6 We are a great example of family diversity in Canada, which proves that the traditional nuclear family is no longer the only acceptable family form.

■ / 6

Family vocabulary, pp. 90–91
be used to / get used to → G22 ; pp. 90–91
Relative clauses → G20 , G21 ; pp. 90–91

Workshop 3

→ Workbook, page 82

@ WES-40325-003

2 About making your point!

a Complete the conversation with emphatic pronouns with -self / -selves.

Jess Mom, were you like me as a teenager?
Mom Yes. I made decisions about what I wanted to do [1] when I was your age. I did things that made my life [2] easier.
Jess Easier? How?
Mom Well, teenagers [3] don't always think. They often act to impress others. I didn't behave badly, but my best friend and I hung around with one girl who was often in trouble [4]. She was so popular and we wanted her to like us, but luckily we never got caught [5].
Jess So, what happened?
Mom My dad knew that girl and other kids were a bad influence and that he couldn't do anything about it [6], so we moved.
Jess So that's why you moved?
Mom Yes, I guess my behaviour [7] really worried Mom and Dad. As it was clear I wouldn't give up my friends, they decided to do something about it [8].
Jess But moving, that's drastic!
Mom I know and at the time I was really angry, but now I have a teenage daughter [9], I understand them. So just remember that you [10] are responsible for your life.

■ / 10

b Rewrite these sentences with emphatic do / does / did.

1 I made a mistake.
2 She understands how important it is.
3 You don't remember, but I told you.
4 Most parents worry about their children.
5 They knew they were in trouble.
6 I regret what happened,.
7 Sam feels he's often misunderstood.
8 You promised to help me.

■ / 8

Emphatic do / does / did → G23 ; pp. 94–95
Emphatic pronouns with -self / -selves → G24 ;
pp. 94–95

3 About crime and punishment

a Use the prompts to complete these conditional sentences.

1 If I hadn't been caught, I | not be in trouble now.
2 If I'd been found guilty in court, I | have a criminal record.
3 If I hadn't hung around with those other guys, I | not get into trouble.
4 If I hadn't wanted to impress my friends, I | not commit the offence.
5 If I had been an adult, I | be in even more trouble than I am.
6 If I had been sent to jail, my mom | be devastated.
7 If I hadn't stolen something, I | not be in court now.
8 If the law hadn't changed in 2012, the judge | send me to jail last week.
9 What | you do if one of your friends dared you to steal something?
10 How would you react if one of your friends | suggest doing something illegal?

■ / 10

b Read the stories and complete the sentences.

1 I wanted to impress my best friend so I stole a T-shirt. I got caught and now I have to do thirty hours of community service.
  a If I hadn't wanted …
  b If I hadn't been caught, …
2 Mary's mum offered her extra lessons to help prepare for her exams, but she didn't take them. Unfortunately, she failed all her exams and now she has to retake the year.
  a If Mary had taken …
  b If Mary had passed …
3 Tom's dad told him not to play football in the garden. He did and broke a window. He had to pay £50 for a new one.
  a If Tom had listened …
  b If Tom hadn't broken …

■ / 6

If-sentences type 2 & 3 and mixed conditionals → G25 , G26 ; pp. 100–101

one hundred and seventeen **117**

4 About advertising tricks. Here are some responses to the survey on advertising to Generation Z. Rewrite the sentences using the new sentence beginnings.

1. The pop-up ads really annoy me, especially when you're in the middle of watching something.
   It's ...
2. I find it unacceptable when hidden adverts target young children.
   What ...
3. I think this kind of sneaky advertising should be banned.
   It's ...
4. It's really worrying that these ads are often personalized with my name! How do advertisers get hold of details like that?
   What's ...
5. It's really annoying that so many online ads are just not relevant – they are badly targeted.
   What's ...
6. Later I realized that what I'd seen was in fact an ad. It was so cleverly integrated that I'd mistakenly thought it was part of the programme.
   Only later did ...
7. An advertiser has never asked if I'd like to see the pop-up ads.
   Never has ...
8. You rarely see a TV programme or a movie without product placement somewhere.
   Rarely do ...
9. I didn't realize how much I was influenced by pop-up adverts.
   Not once did ...
10. I don't blame influencers who are paid for advertising certain products. After all, they need to earn a living.
    In no way do ...

 / 10

Using *It...* and *What...* for emphasis → G27 ; pp. 104–105
Using inversion to make a text more formal → G28 ; pp. 104–105

 / 60

What's my score?

Check your answers to the review (Workbook, p. 82) What are your scores?

What was your total score?
- score 51–60
- score 36–50
- score 0–35

Do you want to change your answers on p. 116? Look at the tasks on pages 119–121: ⟫⟫, ⟫⟫ and ⟫⟫. Choose the tasks to help you.

Workshop 3
MY PRACTICE PAGES

My practice pages

Talking about family life and gender today

1 Family life

a Choose the correct alternatives to complete the sentences.

1 Jake's parents got **divorced / extended** when he was twelve. He now lives with his dad.
2 When Jake moved in with his dad, he had to **be used to / get used to** helping at home.
3 Carter's mom is African-American and his father is from a First Nations tribe so they are a **mixed union / same-sex** couple.
4 In Canada, same-sex relationships have been legal since 1969, so now people **are used to / get used to** seeing same-sex couples.
5 When Rachel's mother remarried, her new husband had two children. They all live together as **a blended / an extended** family.
6 When Rachel moved in with her step-family she **didn't get used to / wasn't used to** sharing a bedroom.
7 In a recent survey in Canada, 67% of families are still **extended / traditional** with mum, dad and one or more kids.
8 Did you find it difficult **being used to / getting used to** living with your step-father and his family?

b Add *who* or *which* and commas if necessary.

1 Family structures have changed in recent years ___ means we have more diversity.
2 Today many people ___ get divorced remarry at a later date.
3 A single parent ___ can be a mother or father often has to take on both roles.
4 Same-sex marriage ___ can be two female or two male partners has been possible in Canada since 2005.
5 In some countries, it is common for several generations to live together ___ means grandparents also play an important role in bringing up the children.
6 Children ___ grow up in an extended family often have close contact to their grandparents.

2 Megan & Pete

a Complete the conversation with family words and *be used to / get used to* + the *-ing* form of the verbs in brackets.

M. So, how's the new situation, Pete?
P. I'm okay. I think I ☐1 (*deal*) with everything now.
M. It's always difficult to ☐2 (*live*) with new people.
P. I guess so. I've ☐3 (*visit*) my dad at weekends …
M. Yes, it's always tough when your parents get d☐4 . Everything changes.
P. What about you?
M. Well my sister's getting married next week. It's all a bit strange.
P. In what way?
M. Well, she's in a s☐5 relationship …
P. And?
M. I took quite a long time for my mom and dad to ☐6 (*see*) Amy with another woman, and I'm not sure how they took the news of the wedding.
P. Surely it's not unusual nowadays?
M. Not at all. But it's a bit more complicated than that.
P. How?
M. Well, her partner is originally from China …
P. Right – so they're a mixed u☐7 couple.
M. Yep, and she also has two children …
P. What? She was married before?
M. Yes, so it'll be a b☐8 family as well.
P. That does sound complicated, but as long as she's happy.
M. That's exactly what I told our parents.

b Improve these sentences by using relative clauses to combine the two sentences in 1–3 and participles to shorten sentences 4–6.

1. Pete's parents still get on well with each other. Pete's parents got divorced two years ago.
2. Last year, his mother married a man with two sons. This means Pete now has two step-brothers.
3. Pete is now relatively happy with the new situation. He really missed his dad at the beginning.
4. Amy, who understood that her parents might be upset, first introduced her new partner as a friend.
5. Amy's mom, who is more tolerant than her father, soon accepted her new partner and welcomed her to the family.
6. Amy's future wife has two children, which means Amy will soon be part of a blended family.

3 **My family.** Write a short article about changes in your family that you are now used to or had to get used to. If you like, be creative! If possible, use relative clauses and/or participles.

Talking about friendships and relationships

4 **It's stronger.** Complete the sentences by adding emphasis with either *do/does/did* or an emphatic pronoun with *-self/-selves*.

1. Sam really ▭ need the support of his friends when he was in trouble.
2. My behaviour was unacceptable. I realize that ▭ now.
3. They stopped ▭ from doing anything stupid before they got caught.
4. Teenagers ▭ behave badly, but they often don't realize what they are doing.
5. I couldn't see ▭ how much my friends were missing me.
6. She ▭ try to tell you, but you wouldn't listen.
7. He really upset her. He ▭ understand that now.
8. Being motivated to do well is an important factor ▭ .

5 **Making it stronger.** Each sentence can take an emphatic *do* or a pronoun with *-self/-selves*. Rewrite them adding the emphasis in the correct place.

1. It's true that friends influence each other.
2. We didn't know it, but our friendship was very strong.
3. I thought you wouldn't mind, but I understand why you're angry.
4. She didn't realize it, but her friends often copied what she did.
5. It's not something I've thought about.
6. I didn't think my friend could cope with the task, but in the end he didn't need my help.
7. Most teenagers copy the behaviour of their friends.
8. I wanted to ask a girl out from my class, but I was just too shy.

6 **How do friends behave?** Think of a situation where you didn't behave well. Write what happened. Use emphatic *do/does/did* or pronouns with *-self/-selves* to make your statements stronger.

Talking about youth crime

7 **Criminal acts.** Match (1–8) with (a–h) to make sentences connected to youth crime.

1. Young people wouldn't commit crimes
2. If my friends hadn't broken the law,
3. I wouldn't have taken the items from the shop
4. If politicians wanted to stop young people committing crimes,
5. Perhaps the judge would have been more understanding
6. If they hadn't changed the law,
7. The police wouldn't have stopped me
8. If I'd had a driving licence,

a. they would provide youth centres to keep them off the street.
b. if I'd had enough money to pay for them.
c. our jails would be full of teenagers.
d. if they had enough interesting things to do.
e. the police wouldn't have arrested me.
f. if I hadn't driven through a red light.
g. they wouldn't be in trouble now.
h. if I had said sorry for what I'd done.

Workshop 3
MY PRACTICE PAGES

8 Shoplifting. Read Lara's story, then choose verbs from the box to complete the sentences. There is one form you don't need.

Dad and I live alone – Mum left two years ago. One day when I was 15, I was in town with some girls from school. They all bought new T-shirts, but I had no money. 'Just take one,' suggested Emily, the most popular girl in class. 'Go on – I dare you.' So I did. It was so easy. That was the start of my 'shoplifting career'. The more I stole, the more I wanted. There's only one big clothes store in town, so I always went there. Just before my 16th birthday, I needed a new dress for my party, but I was caught. Dad was so angry. The shop owner is an old school friend of his and he agreed not to tell the police. But now I have to work in his storeroom every Saturday for the next six months and repay everything.

| had ■ had been ■ hadn't been ■ had had ■ was ■ |
| were ■ would be ■ would have ■ wouldn't have |

1 If Dad ▬ a better paid job, I would get more pocket money.
2 If I ▬ stronger, I wouldn't have accepted Emily's dare.
3 I wouldn't have stolen the dress if I ▬ the money to buy it.
4 I ▬ real problems now if the shop owner had called the police.
5 I ▬ an unpaid Saturday job now if I ▬ so stupid.
6 I often think that life ▬ easier Mum and Dad ▬ still together.

9 Oh no! Write *if*-sentences abot Henry's story.

Last night, when I met my friends in the park, they were already drinking. I'm not used to alcohol, so I quickly became drunk. Then one of the boys suggested we spray some graffiti on the café by the lake in the park. When it
5 was my turn, I was so focused on what I was doing that I didn't hear the warning. By the time I realized that my friends had run off, the police were really close. I decided to escape by jumping into the lake, but I fell over on the pier. The police arrested me and phoned my dad. He was
10 really angry and grounded me for two weeks. I also have to pay the €150 fine I was given for the graffiti.

If I hadn't met my friends at the park, …

Talking about advertising + Gen Z

10 You're the target! Put the words in order to make sentences.

1 worrying | I | really | What | find | are | personalized ads | .
2 websites | which | It's | really | with | annoy me | those | banner ads | .
3 shocking | the amount | is | advertising | What's | spent on | of money | .
4 programmes | that | in the middle | I | find | annoying | It's | of | the advert breaks | .
5 a free website | doesn't | Rarely | which | find | do | you | ads | have | .
6 pop-up ads | because | anything | have | Never | bought | I | of | .

11 Make your point! Rewrite with the words in brackets and by making other small changes, too.

1 Many young people trust influencer advertising. *(It's …)*
2 I really do not like adverts which target children. *(It's …)*
3 People often buy things they really don't need. That amazes me. *(What …)*
4 I don't think all ads are bad. *(In no way do …)*
5 I only realized later just how much I'd spent on things I didn't need. *(Only later did …)*
6 The average person rarely notices ads on the internet. *(Rarely does …)*

12 Adverts and you. Use the prompts to write six sentences about the impact of advertising on you.

It's …
What …
Rarely …
Not once …
Only later …
In no way …

THREE

Joanna came to lunch on Thursday. Looking back, I think it might have been better if she had not been invited to a meal, not at first. Things were difficult right from the start.

In order to make his girlfriend happy, Cudweed had demanded that the lunch was 100% vegan. He had spent the whole morning in the kitchen, looking at the lists of ingredients in sauces and salad dressings and anything else that had a label on it. At one point, I even saw him holding up a cabbage and staring at it hard. He was still staring at it when Solstice walked by.

'Why are you staring at that cabbage?' she asked. Cudweed looked worried.

'Cabbages are vegan, right?' he asked.

'Of course cabbages are vegan!' she replied.

'Well, you never know,' said Cudweed.

'Yes, you do. Cabbages are vegan, it's very simple.' Cudweed sighed.

'I thought it was simple, but it isn't,' he said. 'I thought honey would be okay, but Joanna says it isn't. People seem to argue about all sorts of details.' Solstice ignored him.

'I see you've solved the problem of your trousers,' she said, looking at his belt. Cudweed had replaced the Sellotape with a cord[1] from one of Minty's dressing gowns. It was a rather nice red colour, and I thought it looked quite stylish, but then Solstice said, 'You know that's made of silk[2], don't you?'

Cudweed looked even more worried.

'It is …?' he said, 'And silk …?'

'Isn't vegan!' said Solstice. 'It's made by little worms. Silkworms! If you are going to be an ethical vegan, you can't wear silk!'

'A what?' asked Cudweed.

'A dietary[3] vegan only avoids animal foods, an *ethical* vegan avoids *all* animal products. I thought you would know that.'

'I told you it wasn't simple!' cried Cudweed and ran off to find something to replace the silk with.

At lunch time, Joanna arrived. I was fascinated to see what she looked like, and so I snuck up[4] onto the chandelier in the dining room again.

She didn't *look* vegan. I mean, you couldn't have guessed just by looking at her. She didn't have horns[5], or stripes[6], or anything. In fact, she was quite pretty, and I could see why young Cudweed had fallen in love. I started to wonder if I was wrong about vegans. Maybe they're not so different from anyone else. They just don't eat animals.

No one was speaking very much. Valevine was in a terrible mood, from being forced to eat nothing but tomatoes and avocados. Solstice was sulking. Cudweed was very nervous. But Minty tried to make conversation.

'So, Joanna,' she said, 'how did you two meet?'

'On the internet, Mrs Otherhand,' she said.

'Internet,' Cudweed added.

And that was the end of that conversation.

'So, er …' Minty tried again. 'Have you been vegan a long time?'

'All my life,' she said. 'My parents raised me as a vegan. I have never eaten an animal.'

'She's never eaten an animal,' added Cudweed.

'Never!' said Valevine, exploding. 'That's not possible!'

'I assure you it is possible, Mr Otherhand,' Joanna said.

'It is possible,' added Cudweed.

---

[1] **cord** Band – [2] **silk** Seide – [3] **dietary** Ernährungs-; diätisch – [4] **to sneak up to (snuck, snuck)** heranschleichen – [5] **horn** Horn – [6] **stripe** Streifen

'But, but ...' said Minty. 'It's not healthy, is it? I mean, it's one thing for adults to stop eating meat, but children need certain things.'

'Certain things?' asked Joanna.

'Certain things?' added Cudweed.

'Yes,' said Minty. 'Certain things ... to grow up ... right.'

Joanna put down her fork.

'All the vital[7] components necessary for the healthy development of a child can be obtained[8] from a vegan diet, given the addition of certain vitamins and proteins through dietary supplements[9].'

'... the addition of certain vitamins and proteins through dietary supplements,' added Cudweed.

I wasn't the only one who had noticed he was repeating everything Joanna said, and I wasn't the only one who was finding it annoying. Solstice was glaring at her little brother.

'Oh,' said Minty, 'I see. Well. That's nice. Chocolate cake anyone?'

'*Vegan* chocolate cake,' added Cudweed, seeing the look on Joanna's face. 'I made it myself. It's totally vegan. It has no eggs, or milk in it. Or flour, it's gluten free, too.'

'What does it have in it?' asked Valevine suspiciously.

'Chocolate, I suppose?'

He started to laugh at his joke until Cudweed said, 'No. Actually it doesn't have any chocolate in it. It has vegan chocolate instead.'

Valevine looked like he might faint, but Minty got the chocolate cake, and everyone had a slice. The room was filled with silence as everyone chewed the cake.

'Very ... very nice dear,' said Minty to Cudweed, looking like she might be sick. Solstice pushed her plate away, the cake half-finished. Valevine took one look at his and that was that. Only Joanna ate all of her slice of cake.

'Excellent,' she said. 'And doesn't it taste so *much nicer* knowing that no animals were harmed to make it?'

'No animals were harmed to make it,' added Cudweed. 'So much nicer, isn't it?'

'No,' said Valevine, 'it isn't.'

It looked as if Joanna might start arguing with Valevine. Cudweed saw it coming, and tried to do something.

'Why don't we go to my room, Joanna,' he said, 'and design some posters for veganism? Or something?'

Joanna was about to reply when something bad happened.

It's a little embarrassing for me to tell you what happened next. I am really very ashamed. It was a total accident, I swear, but well ... It's like this. I had eaten those three large slices of bacon. Then, the following day, I found that someone had left the fridge door open and there was a huge bowl of cheese sauce in there. Not all ravens like cheese sauce, but I do ... And then, when Cudweed was making his chocolate cake, he found out that he couldn't put normal chocolate in it, and he left the bars[10] of chocolate out of the cupboard. Three of them, and I ... Well, you can imagine.

So now, after three days of food like that, things were 'not right' in my poor old raven's stomach. In fact, as I sat on the chandelier, I suddenly felt something moving in my insides.

Ark! I thought. I need to excuse myself! I need to leave the room! I need to ...

But it was too late, and I released a small amount of raven poo. All over Joanna's head.

She screamed and looked up to see me, and then she screamed again.

'What is that?' she yelled. 'And what is this?' She added, wiping at her hair with her napkin.

'Edgar!' cried Minty, 'What are you doing in here?'

'That thing has a name?' cried Joanna.

Thing? I thought. Who is she calling a *thing*?

'That's Edgar,' said Solstice, angrily.

'And he is our raven.'

'You have a pet?' said Joanna.

No, I thought, I am not a pet, but I could see no one was interested in my opinion.

'You are keeping a living animal as a slave in your house? A prisoner? Unable to be free, as it would be in nature?'

---

[7] **vital** lebensnotwendig – [8] **to obtain** erhalten – [9] **supplement** Ergänzung – [10] **bar** Riegel

'... would be in nature?' added Cudweed, and I suddenly wanted to leave something on his head, too. 'Edgar is not our pet,' said Solstice. 'He lives here. With us. It's his choice.'

'Oh, really?' said Joanna. 'And he told you that, did he?'

'Did he?' asked Cudweed. Then he added, 'Actually, did he tell us that?'

'Not exactly,' said Solstice, 'but this is his home. He doesn't want to go anywhere else!'

Well, I do like a nice holiday every once in a while, I thought, and I told them so.

'Korrrrk!' I said, and Joanna stared at me.

'It's very ugly, isn't it?'

Well, that was that.

Solstice stood up and started shouting at Joanna, Valevine started shouting at Solstice not to shout, Minty put her head in her hands, and Cudweed stood up, grabbed Joanna's hand and pulled her away from the table.

He was flustered[11].

'I'll take you to my room and you can wash my hair,' he said.

Everyone stared at him.

'I mean, we can wash your hair,' he said to Joanna, correcting himself.

They started to walk off and then I saw that Cudweed's trousers were held up by an extremely long elastic band[12]. But not long enough. As he reached the stairs, the rubber band snapped, and down came his trousers again. I saw that he was still wearing the raven underpants, which was very sweet, but I made a note to tell him that if he was going to have a girlfriend, he might need to learn to change his underwear from time to time.

There was silence in the house for some time. Everyone had disappeared. Cudweed and Joanna had gone to his room and hadn't been seen since. I flapped around the castle, very bored, but also very angry at being called ugly. I was also still very embarrassed by what had happened at the dinner table. What I had done, I mean.

I decided to go for a long fly over the lake and back. It does me good to get out into nature when I am in a bad mood. I do it whenever I am feeling grumpy, or depressed, or worrying. I spend a lot of time in nature. Anyway, when I got back, I was feeling a little better, and as I flew along into the Small Hall, I saw Solstice sitting in an armchair reading a book.

'Oh, hello, Edgar,' she said, and I went to see what she was reading.

It was a book called 'A Young Person's Guide to Philosophy.'

'Kark?' I said.

'I'm trying to be a better person,' she said. 'I am reading about morals. And ethics; about how we know what the right thing to do is. Stuff like that.'

'Kark,' I said, because Solstice is the best person I know, and I didn't think she needed a book to help her be any better.

Then Cudweed appeared, and he wandered[13] over. He looked extremely miserable.

'Cudweed?' asked Solstice. 'Is everything okay?'

'Yes,' he said. Then, 'No. It isn't okay. It's very difficult. I totally love Joanna, but we have been arguing. I understand why it's a good idea. For example, did you know that the world would have enough food for everyone if everyone was even just a vegetarian? That there would be less global warming?'

Solstice rolled her eyes.

'Yes, I told you that about a million times!'

Cudweed wasn't listening.

'But it's so hard to be a vegan,' he said, 'Joanna says I can't even eat chocolate on my birthday, not the kind with milk in, which is my favourite. And right now, she's going through all my books, and I'm going to have to throw half of them away because the glue in the older ones is made from dead horses.'

'Ewww,' said Solstice, 'horse glue. Ugh.'

I thought that sounded rather tasty, but I decided it wasn't the right moment to say so.

'Cudweed,' said Solstice. 'Just because she's your girlfriend, it doesn't mean you have to do *everything* she says.'

Cudweed looked at his sister.

'But I'm afraid that if I don't, she won't go out with me anymore.'

'Well, you are going to have to make a decision,' said Solstice. 'Milk chocolate, or Joanna. She might even respect you more for standing up for yourself.'

And just then, Joanna appeared.

'Oh, there you are, Cudweed,' she said.

'Joanna, I have something to say –' began Cudweed, but Joanna interrupted him.

'Wait! I have something to tell you,' she said.

'Cudweed, I don't think we can go out anymore.'

'What??' cried Cudweed. 'Why not?'

---

[11] **flustered** durcheinander – [12] **elastic band** Gummiband – [13] **to wander** umherziehen; wandern

'Because we are not right for each other. And you are keeping an animal prisoner in your house.'

'Kork!' I said, and looked for somewhere I could sit right above her head.

'I ... oh,' said Cudweed. 'Oh.'

'Now, what was it you wanted to tell me?' asked Joanna.

'Oh,' said Cudweed. 'I was going to say I don't think I can be a vegan anymore. It's too hard for me.'

Joanna shrugged.

'It is difficult for some people. But if you believe in something, it's really quite easy. Anyway, you must do what you think is right.'

Cudweed looked very sad. Joanna said she was sorry and that she had enjoyed the cake, and then she left. And that was that.

Solstice and I spent the rest of the day trying to cheer Cudweed up.

'Chocolate?' suggested Solstice, and he smiled. 'Milk chocolate?'

'Okay,' he said, and we all went to the kitchen to see what we could find.

As he was eating the chocolate, Solstice chatted away.

'You know, I think it was very sweet of you to try to be a vegan for your girlfriend,' she said, 'but you don't have to change yourself to be liked, you know.'

'No?'

'No,' said Solstice. 'One day, you'll meet someone who likes you for who you are.'

'I will?'

'You will. And I will, too.'

She smiled at the idea.

'Now,' she said, 'how about we ask for sausages for you, for dinner?'

'Erm, actually,' said Cudweed. 'No.'

'No?' said Solstice.

'Krark?' I said.

'No,' said Cudweed. 'I have decided not to be a vegan, but I am going to be a vegetarian from now on.'

'You are?'

'I am,' said Cudweed.

'But why?'

Cudweed shrugged.

'Because I think it's the right thing to do. Veganism is a great idea, but even being vegetarian helps the planet a lot. It's healthier. But most of all I don't want to eat animals anymore.' And he tickled the feathers under my chin.

So that was that, how Cudweed became a vegetarian. And it's only been a week, but I think it suits him already. He's already lost a little weight, but he's using a belt again, so at least his trousers have stopped falling down.

A Glimpse of the Death Saint (Before and while-reading)

1 Famous graphic novels

a Read these descriptions of four famous graphic novels. Tell your group which one you would like to read and why. Did you make similar choices?

> **Watchmen by Alan Moore**
> This award-winning graphic novel has an exciting murder mystery plot and an amazing art style. The story features a cast of six superheroes who carry out brave deeds while struggling with personal problems and a lack of confidence.

> **The City of Ember by Jeanne DuPrau**
> Originally a dystopian novel that was later turned into a graphic novel, this is the story of two children who grow up in darkness in an underworld city. By following clues left by the builders of the city, they manage to escape.

> **Persepolis by Marjane Satrapi**
> This is the memoir of a young girl coming of age in Iran in a time of conflict, oppression and war. The simple black and white pictures tell a powerful and unforgettable story about home and public life. At times funny, it is also heart-breaking.

> **I am Alfonso Jones by Tony Medina**
> Young African American Alfonso Jones is shot and killed by police, but his spirit lives on in the afterlife, along with other victims of police shootings. Meanwhile Alfonso's family and friends fight for justice for him.

b What kinds of story are the graphic novels in **a**? What other types do you associate with graphic novels?

mystery, …

c Are you a fan of graphic novels? Why? / Why not?

2 The Death Saint

a Look at the title of the graphic novel. Explain what you think it means.

A 'glimpse' means …
I think people get a glimpse of the Death Saint when …

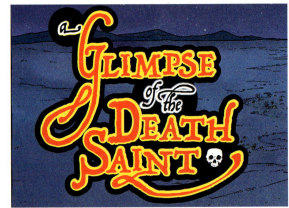

b Look at the picture of the Death Saint. Describe and analyse what further information you get from the picture. What gender do you think the Death Saint is? Is it good or evil? Explain the reasons for your ideas.

The picture shows …
I think the figure looks …
The figure is holding its hands like that because …
In my opinion, the Death Saint …
I would say people fear / respect / love / …

c Share your ideas from **a** and **b** with the class.

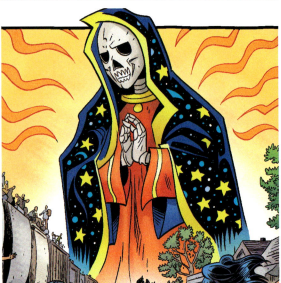

Workshop 4
BEFORE AND WHILE-READING TASKS

3 **The characters, setting and plot**

a Look at the illustrations on pages 128 – 129 of the graphic novel and make notes.
- **Student A:** Who are the characters on these pages?
- **Student B:** Where does the story take place (the setting) and what is happening (the plot)?

b Share your ideas from **a** with another pair. Discuss how you think the story continues. Together, write three questions you have about the story.

4 **Attitudes and feelings**

a Now read the first two pages of the graphic novel and check your ideas from **3**. Add more information to your notes.

b Describe the attitudes of the man from the water company, the reporter and the camera guys towards the group of people.
Use adjectives from the cloud and your own ideas. Explain why you get this impression.

c Explain why the girl doesn't want to give her name. Describe how you think she is feeling now.

5 **Were you right?** Read the rest of the story and check your ideas. Were your three questions answered in the story?

6 **The girl's story.** Write notes under these headings.
- where the girl was born
- living / economic situation of her family
- what happened to her father and brother
- what happened to her mother and why
- her journey to the border of 'El Norte' (the USA)
- her life at the border
- how she crossed the border

7 **After the interview.** What happened when the girl was talking to the reporter after the interview? Decide if these sentences are true or false, and correct the false sentences.

1 Immigration officials suddenly appeared.
2 They had weapons.
3 The immigrants were all adults.
4 The coyote disappeared.
5 Everyone crossed the border.
6 The girl crossed the border with another immigrant.

CULTURE CORNER

ICE is the USA's Immigration and Customs Enforcement. Its function is to prevent illegal immigration and border crime such as drug smuggling.

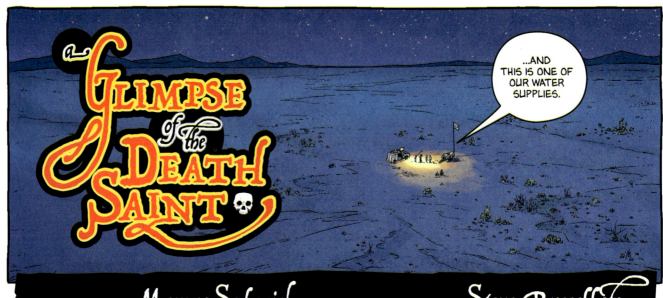

Workshop 4
THE NOVEL

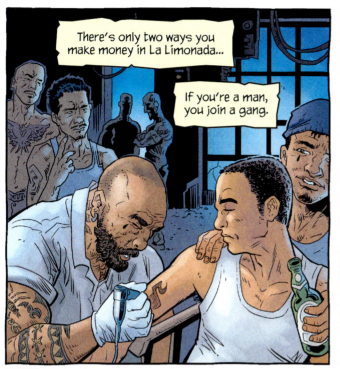

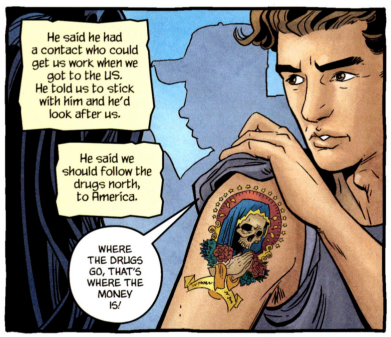

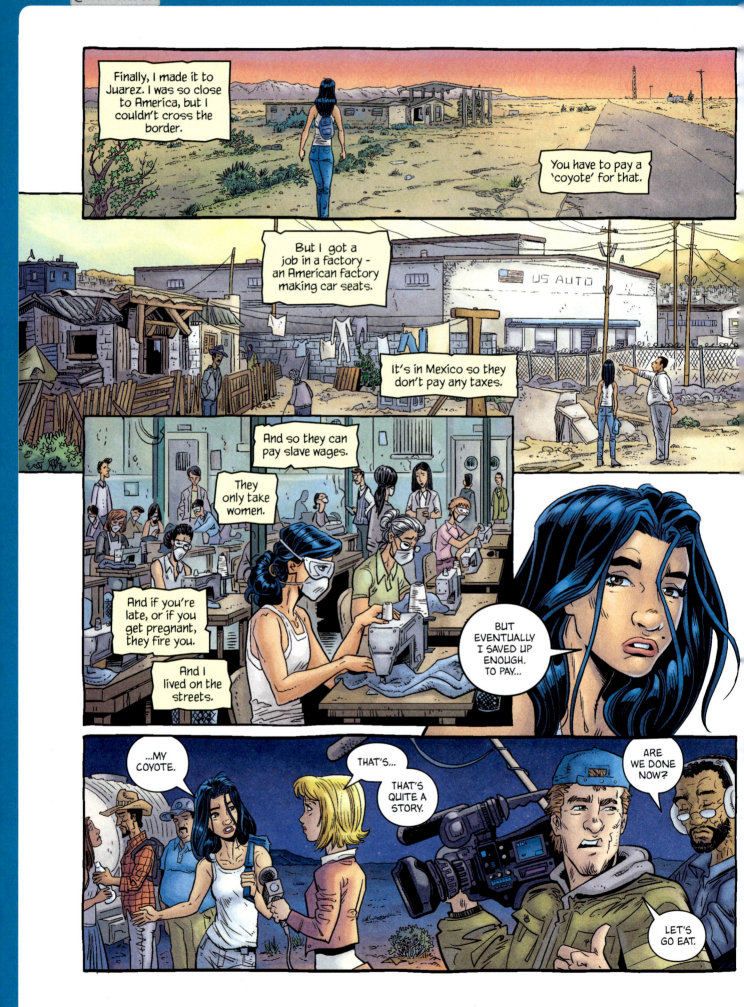

Workshop 4
THE NOVEL

A Glimpse of the Death Saint (After-reading)

1 **Your reaction and opinion**

a Tell a partner how you felt while reading the story and why. Give specific examples from the story which made you feel like that.

When I read ..., I felt ...
The part about ... made me feel ...
I really identified with / sympathized with ... when ...
To give another example, ...

b The girl crossed the border into the USA illegally, which is a crime. Analyse how the graphic novel makes us sympathize with the girl's story.

c What do you think about the issue of illegal immigration from Mexico into the USA? Discuss your opinions.

In my view, ...
On the one hand, ... on the other hand, ...
Although ...

2 **Attitudes.** Look back at **4b** on page 127 and the last two pages of the story. Explain how the attitudes of the reporter and the cameramen changed or didn't change after hearing the girl's story.

The reporter / cameraman asks / looks / says / wishes ...

3 **What does it mean?**

a Write a definition for the following names in the story. Explain why you think the thing or person has this name.

1 The Beast (pages 132 – 133)
2 a coyote (pages 136 – 137)

b Match these words with the correct explanations. There are two definitions you don't need.

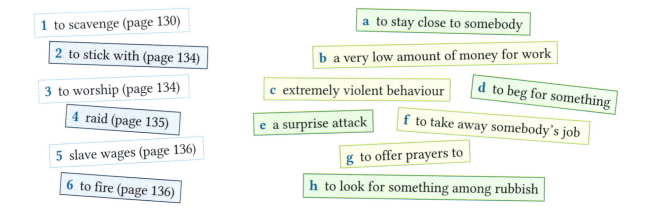

1 to scavenge (page 130)
2 to stick with (page 134)
3 to worship (page 134)
4 raid (page 135)
5 slave wages (page 136)
6 to fire (page 136)

a to stay close to somebody
b a very low amount of money for work
c extremely violent behaviour
d to beg for something
e a surprise attack
f to take away somebody's job
g to offer prayers to
h to look for something among rubbish

Workshop 4
AFTER-READING TASKS

4 An American factory in Mexico

a Read the description of the girl's work on page 136 again. Describe the working conditions there and why they can't be improved.

b When you buy a product such as jeans, trainers or electronic equipment, how can you be sure that it was made under conditions that did not harm the workers and the environment? Think about where it was made, specific brands, certified labels and logos, etc.

5 The reporter's article. Write the reporter's article for an online website. Make sure to include details about the girl's living conditions and working conditions at the border. Start like this:

It's shocking but it's true. Every day, immigrants from Central America risk their lives to cross the border into the USA. I spoke to one girl, let's call her …, who told me her thought-provoking story.

6 La Limonada

a La Limonada in Guatemala is the largest city slum in Central America. Do some research online and make notes about the following questions.
- How many people live there?
- When and why did people move there?
- What is it like to live there?

b Exchange information with the class.

7 YOUR CHOICE: What happened to the girl?
Choose one of these tasks below. Find another pair who has done the same task. Exchange and compare your texts.

A Continue the graphic novel. Make a page or two pages where you show what happened to the girl after the interview. Draw pictures and write speech bubbles. You can use a similar style or your own style.

B You are the girl many years later. You tell your children the story of how you crossed the border, why you did it and what you did afterwards. Make notes, then write your story.

8 Graphic novels as a genre

a Think: What are the characteristics of graphic novels and how are they different from text-based stories? Think about *A Glimpse of the Death Saint* and other graphic novels that you know. Use the ideas in the box to help you.

> character development ■ expression of feelings and attitudes ■ illustrations ■ text style ■ use of frames ■ who tells the story

b Pair: Exchange your ideas with a partner with examples from *A Glimpse of the Death Saint*.

c Share: Discuss ideas with the class. Agree on a definition of a graphic novel together.

9 A presentation of a graphic novel. Present a graphic novel you have read to your group. Talk about the characters and the story as well as the style of the illustrations and their effect.

Feedback and peer editing

1 Define the terms *feedback* and *peer editing* and reflect on the advantages and disadvantages of this process. Explain why it can be helpful. What is the message of the illustration regarding feedback?

Giving feedback: Dos and don'ts

Giving and accepting peer feedback can help you write good texts or give interesting presentations. Use the feedback you receive to reflect on your work and revise it. When you give feedback, pay attention to these rules:

- **Be polite:** Before you start, it is important to recall the 'Code of Conduct', i.e. don't be rude! Show respect and consideration for the writer's feelings. Only appropriate, clear and constructive comments are helpful.

- **Be balanced:** Point out the strengths as well as the weaknesses of the document / presentation / speech, etc. It is a good idea to follow a three-step approach:
  1. Complimenting (start with something positive that develops trust and encouragement)
  2. Suggesting (make a suggestion for something that could be improved)
  3. Correcting (tell the writer where he / she should correct aspects that are wrong)

- **Be constructive:** You can offer a solution or raise questions, but remember that your own opinion or point of view is not relevant. Of course, personal criticism should be avoided, i.e. your comments should not be biased.

- **Be precise:** Vague feedback like 'This should be more interesting' is not helpful at all. Instead, you should always be as clear and detailed as possible, for example: 'A description of the protagonist's outer appearance / character / behaviour could help the reader to imagine him / her better'.

2 Peer editing is a very useful form of feedback. It is often used with writing tasks. Students exchange drafts of material they have written and provide each other with suggestions for improvement. Peer editing can be used at any point in the writing process, at the concept or draft stage or for the almost finished product. Choose a text you have produced lately and give it to a partner, then discuss possible improvements.

Extra pages
FEEDBACK AND PEER EDITING

Feedback is a message that you send to somebody. It is always interactive and there are numerous ways of conveying the message. When giving feedback, non-verbal communication, e.g. body language or facial expression, is as important as explicitly verbal communication, like opinions, criticism or suggestions. Remember that criticism has to go beyond just giving a 'thumbs up or down' or using emoticons – it has to be constructive and clearly voiced. The phrases below may be helpful for giving feedback on a presentation or a written text.

Phrases for giving feedback

Starting and summing up
- What I really like(d) about your talk / presentation / essay / piece of writing is (was) that …
- Generally I like(d) the way you …, but in particular the way you …
- What I like(d) most about … is (was) …
- My favourite part is (was) …, because …

Expressing an opinion / Asking for an opinion
- From my point of view, …
- For me, … came across as …
- I'm worried because this may lead to / might result in …
- … is interesting / relevant / only partly true.
- Have you considered …?
- I had not seen … from that angle before, but what do you think about …?

Suggesting / Asking for ideas
- I think your pronunciation / intonation / body language / vocabulary / grammar … needs some improvement.
- Why don't you (use) …?
- I suggest that you add / leave out …
- It could make a big difference if you …
- It might be helpful if you always check … first / at the end.
- Have you got any ideas how I could do this differently in the future?
- How do you suggest improving on this next time?
- What could I do to …?
- How else could I …?
- Can you think of any alternatives …?

Talking about positive and negative points
- I thought … was very effective.
- … surprised me positively / fascinated me because …
- I was impressed by the fact that you …
- The logical structure of … is not evident …
- At several points, I recognized …
- Of course, it is important …, but …
- When you presented …, I noticed that …
- … annoyed me / made me angry because …

Asking for clarification
- When I listened to your talk / presentation, I didn't quite understand …
- When I read your essay / text, I could not place … in a meaningful context.

Linking arguments
- First of all / Second / Third …
- There are various reasons for …
- Moreover, … / Furthermore, … / In addition, …
- Although it is true that …, it would be wrong …
- Another point to mention / clarify / explain more clearly is …

Giving an example
- Let me give you an example of what I mean by …
- A good example is …
- Let me explain … with the help of an example.
- An example I can offer to illustrate …
- Take …, for instance, …

Mediation

1 **What is the difference between mediation and translation?** Mediation is transferring important information from one language to another. This information may be in English or German, in a spoken or a written text, for example an interview, an informative text, an infographic or a leaflet.

You don't have to mediate everything, only the facts the other person (the addressee) needs to do a certain task. This will be explained in the instructions. They will also tell you how you should mediate, for example in an email or an article. Look at the mediation on pages 34 and 35 and answer these questions. Then make notes and do the task.

- Do you have to mediate in English or in German?
- How is the information presented?
- Who is the addressee?
- Which information is important for the task?
- How should you present the facts you mediate?

2 **How do you deal with culture-specific words in a mediation?** A culture-specific word is one which you only find in one language or culture – often there is no direct translation, so you have to explain the word. Such a word may not even be important, for example if *Currywurst* occurs as an example of one of the many sausages Germans like in an article about German eating habits. If your mediation task is to explain the kind of food Germans eat, then you don't need to specifically mention *Currywurst*. But it is important if you are at an *Imbissbude* with a friend who doesn't speak German and *Currywurst* is on the menu. Look at this menu and decide which items you can translate and which you need to explain.

- Currywurst od. Schaschlik mit Pommes rot-weiß
- Schweinebraten mit Knödeln und Rotkohl
- Fischfrikadellen mit Kartoffelsalat
- Kartoffelpuffer mit Apfelmus
- Apfelsaft – Wasser – Bier – Schorle

3 **How formal or informal should your mediation be?**

a The kind of English, or register, you use depends on the situation and on the addressee. Is it a friend, your parents, a teacher, a future employer? What kind of English should you use? Match the expressions (1–3) with the situations (a–c).

1. informal chatty English (*Hi, gonna, wanna, gotta, ain't, cool, …*)
2. neutral, factual English (*Hello, going to, want to, have got to, isn't, interesting, …*)
3. formal English (*Dear Mr/Ms, going to, would like to, have to, is not, intriguing, …*)

a in written communication with somebody you don't know, e.g. a new employer or an official
b with a friend in spoken communication
c in spoken and written texts for almost any situation

b Look at the German article about work camps on page 72. Decide what kind of English you should use in your email. How would this change if you were writing to your head teacher to ask for permission to miss the last two weeks of school to go on a work camp? Decide who writes to the friend and who writes to the teacher. Write your emails and compare.

> **TIP**
>
> Make sure you understand the difference between a mediation and a text production task.
>
> **Text production**
> Be creative and express your own ideas or arguments.
>
> **Mediation**
> Listen or read carefully and transfer the important and relevant ideas from the original text(s).
> - Don't add arguments or facts that are not in the text(s).
> - Don't make comments.
> - Don't give your opinion.

Speaking

1 **Identify situations in which you need to speak English.** Sometimes you have time to prepare before you speak English and sometimes you don't. Look at the situations below and decide if they are spontaneous or not. Can you add more examples?
- **Monologue:** giving directions, giving a presentation, …
- **Dialogue:** asking for and giving information, talking on the phone to one speaker, …
- **Multilogue:** participating in a group discussion or an online meeting, …

2 Speak confidently in a presentation

a When you give a presentation, there are some dos and don'ts. With a partner, make a list.

b It's not easy to speak freely for more than one or two minutes. Prompt cards help you remember the main points. Look at this prompt card about toads. What is your first impression? Discuss how you could improve the card.

c A good presentation needs a clear structure with signposting language to guide the audience. Discuss what makes a good structure and come up with some useful phrases for each part.

d It is also important to engage your audience. How can you do this? Put the strategies in the box next to the examples.

> Ask rhetorical questions ■
> Encourage your listeners to ask questions ■
> Explain special terms ■
> Repeat important information or messages ■
> Use emphasis ■ Use question tags

1 This isn't a frog, is it?
2 What is unbelievable is the fact that …
3 Is it important to distinguish between frogs and toads? Yes, it is because …
4 Today there are 200 million toads in Australia. Yes, 200 million.
5 I'll be very happy to take questions at the end of my talk.
6 The cane toad has poisonous glands. These are small organs …

3 Useful expressions for a dialogue or discussion. When you speak to other people, it is not always possible to prepare beforehand. If you use some of these expressions, your English will sound more authentic. Can you add more?

- If you need to collect your thoughts before you speak: *Well, … / Let me think … / …*
- Sometimes you want other people to say something, too: *What about you? / And what is your opinion on …? / …*
- Or you would like to say something yourself: *Can I say something? / May I interrupt you for a second? / …*

4 Improve your speaking skills. Look at the ideas below. Which strategies do you already use? Which ones could be useful in the future? Use the language from **3** to discuss your opinions.

- Communicate with native speakers.
- Read English books, listen to English songs, or watch English films.
- Learn new words and phrases in their context: learn collocations, e. g. *give a presentation, hold a speech* or, if a word is followed by a preposition, learn it that way, e. g. *spend time on sth., be used to doing sth.*
- Work with the audios. Listen, stop and guess the next word, then listen and compare.

Language awareness

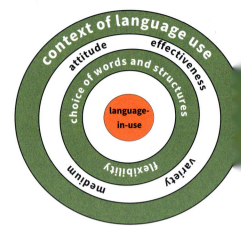

1 **What is language awareness?**

a Language awareness is a complex subject, but a basic understanding of it can help you to improve your English and make your learning more efficient. Look at these simplified definitions and decide which one(s) best describe(s) language awareness.

A understanding grammar rules and using them correctly
B deciding which new words and phrases you need to learn
C knowing when it is appropriate to use certain words and phrases

b Create your own language awareness target. Copy the illustration above and complete it for yourself, based on your learning goals as well as the situations and contexts in which you need English. Here are some ideas, but you can add your own, too: *correct structures, intonation, dialect, context, register, intercultural competence*.

2 **Misunderstandings.** Look at these pairs of sentences. What is the difference in meaning?

1 **a** Ben moved to the US for two years.
   b Ben moved to the US two years ago.

2 **a** I'm in Paris for five days.
   b I've been in Paris for five days.

3 **a** I'm looking for the kids in the park.
   b I'm looking after the kids in the park.

4 **a** Emily stopped taking photos.
   b Emily stopped to take some photos.

3 **Be aware of which words and phrases you need to understand and learn**

a In *On Track 5*, you have covered various topics. Each one has its own specialist vocabulary. Choose a topic which particularly interests you and note down words and phrases linked to that topic which you feel are important. You will need them in **4c**.

b If you chose the topic 'law' in **a**, you will probably understand the verb *prosecute* in sign A. If your 'knowledge of the world' is not enough to help you with the word *trespasser*, a dictionary will give you the meaning. Which words would you put in your vocabulary book to actively learn?

c To understand sign B and the 'joke', you first need to check the various meanings of 'bill' in a dictionary as the first meaning 'Rechnung' clearly doesn't fit here. But you need to know more than the dictionary can tell you, for example that 'Bill' can also be a name or that *-er* added to a verb often denotes a person (e.g. *teach > teacher*). Can you explain the handwritten message?

4 **Be aware of the appropriate register**

a Certain words are inappropriate in some situations. Who do you think is talking in this dialogue?
A Hi Tim! Got your sports stuff?
B F***, no! I dumped it all on my bed, then this morning was like, you know. My mum was like nagging me cos I was late and I just like forgot.
A I have an extra shirt. Wanna borrow it?
B Cool! Cheers mate.

b If Tim was talking to a teacher, how would the dialogue differ? Rewrite it in the correct register.

c Tim uses the word *like* three times in **a**. Why? Many young people overuse this word and aren't aware that they do so. Take turns to talk about the topic you chose in **3a**. Your partner should check if you use *like* and, if so, how often. Together, improve your talk if necessary.

Literary analysis

When analysing a literary text, you do not only pay attention to its form (a poem, a novel, a play, etc.) but also to stylistic devices. They are used to achieve a certain effect:
- to emphasize a certain aspect and make the text lively,
- to grab the reader's interest and make them think, to surprise them or to provoke a particuar response,
- to criticize a situation, a person, an idea or event.

Here are ten common devices often found in literary texts:

Literary devices: Definitions

- **alliteration:** repetition of a sound at the beginning of neighbouring words
- **climax:** highest point of tension in a storyline
- **irony:** saying the opposite of what you really mean
- **metaphor:** a figure of speech that directly compares one thing to another for rhetorical effect
- **parallelism:** deliberately using similar or identical words, phrases or structures in neighbouring lines, sentences or paragraphs (= repetition)
- **personification:** presenting ideas, objects or animals as human beings
- **register:** a particular type of language used in a specific situation or for a specific purpose
- **rhetorical question:** question to which no answer is expected because it is obvious
- **rhyme vs. free verse:** using words that repeat syllable sounds vs. poetry without a regular metre or rhyme
- **symbol:** an idea or image that stands for something abstract

The analysis of dramatic texts differs from that of novels or poems. A dramatic text is not just written to be read but is meant to be performed on a stage or in a theatre. It often contains a conflict between characters and encourages the audience to identify with them, so that they can participate in their experiences. There are two main types or genres of drama: tragedy (which usually has a sad ending, often leading to the death of one or more protagonists) and comedy (which usually has a happy ending). Usually, a play is made up of five acts and, like short stories, each one is centred around one important event. Below you will find some important keywords for analysing dramatic texts:

Dramatic texts: Keywords

- **act and scenes:** the formal structure of a play; each act usually consists of one or more scenes
- **dialogue:** a conversation between characters
- **monologue (= soliloquy):** a character revealing his / her thoughts and emotions, ideas, sorrows, fears to the audience
- **playwright:** the author of a play
- **properties ('props'):** items used by actors on stage
- **stage directions:** what the author wants the actors to do on stage, e.g. dance, a description of their outward appearance e.g. costumes, their voice, intonation, facial expression. They can also describe the scenery and the effects.
- **flat and round characters:** the characters act in a predictable way and do not develop in the course of actions (flat) or have a complex personality and undergo transformation (round)
- **inner and outer system of communication:** communication among the characters (inner) and communication between the playwright and the audience (outer)
- **dramatic irony:** a situation in which the audience knows something that the characters don't, for example, the words or actions of a character may have a special meaning for the audience that the characters are unaware of
- **reported action:** relevant background information about the characters, the setting or the plot that is provided by the actors for the audience
- **comic relief:** a means of including humorous elements in the plot, often to relieve tension. It can be an amusing scene or character, a comic remark or incident. They are often found in Shakespeare's tragedies.

Poetry

When talking about the particular way in which a poem can be understood, analysed and explained (= interpretation), you can approach it in different ways. Although there is no fixed approach and you should and will develop your own, the following procedure might be helpful for a successful and satisfying leap into the world of poetry.

And, of course, you can read the lyrics of a song like a poem. However, the music can add further meaning to the text and have an effect on the audience. Remember: poetry is always meant to be read or recited aloud so that the power of its words can be properly experienced and understood. So, start by reading out the poem and listening to how it sounds.

A 10-step poetry analysis

First steps

1. Try to express the impression that reading the poem has made on you and write down some keywords or phrases for the main idea you associate with the text.
2. Note words and phrases you remember word for word.
3. Is there a personal message for you in the text? Does it appeal to your senses? What can you hear, see, taste and feel?

Analysis

4. Check unknown words in order to understand their literal meaning as a basis for interpretation. It is important to be aware that words in poetry often convey images or metaphors, so sometimes the literal meaning is not what the writer intended to express.
5. Point out formal aspects, e.g. structure (stanza), rhyme scheme, …
6. Define stylistic devices, explain their function in the text and the effect on the reader.
7. Analyse figurative language and motifs.
8. Research the poet's personal background (biography) and find out any facts that might have influenced his or her way of seeing and writing about the world.

Summary

9. Sum up your results to write a critical evaluation of the poem in about 120 words.
10. Say the lines aloud again and try to memorize the first stanza and the last (or an adequate number of lines if there is no division into stanzas). If you want to, you can learn the complete poem by heart.

Information (1975)

By David Ignatow (American poet, 1914–1997)

This tree has two million and seventy-five thousand leaves. Perhaps I missed a leaf or two but I do feel triumphant at having persisted in counting by hand branch by branch and marked down on paper with pencil each total. Adding them up was a pleasure I could understand; I did something on my own that was not dependent on others, and to count leaves is not less meaningful than to count the stars, as
5 astronomers are always doing. They want the facts to be sure they have them all. It would help them to know whether the world is finite. I discovered one tree that is finite. I must try counting the hairs on my head, and you too. We could swap information.

© *Against the Evidence: Selected Poems 1934 – 1994* (1994)

I, Too (1925)

By Langston Hughes
(American poet and activist, 1902–1967)

I, too, sing America.
I am the darker brother.
They send me to eat in the kitchen
When company comes,
⁵ But I laugh,
And eat well,
And grow strong.

Tomorrow,
I'll be at the table
¹⁰ When company comes.
Nobody'll dare
Say to me,
'Eat in the kitchen,'
Then.

¹⁵ Besides,
They'll see how beautiful I am
And be ashamed

I, too, am America.

© *The Collected Works of Langston Hughes* (2001)

Trees (2005)

By Mark Haddon (British novelist and poet, *1962)

They stand in parks and graveyards and gardens.
Some of them are taller than department stores,
yet they do not draw attention to themselves.

You will be fitting a heated towel rail one day
⁵ and see, through the louvre window,
a shoal of olive-green fish changing direction
in the air that swims above the little gardens.

Or you will wake at your aunt's cottage,
your sleep broken by a coal train on the empty hill
¹⁰ as the oaks roar in the wind off the channel.

Your kindness to animals, your skill at the clarinet,
these are accidental things.
We lost this game a long way back.
Look at you. You're reading poetry.
¹⁵ Outside the spring air is thick
with the seeds of their children.

© Mark Haddon (2011)

The Journey (1986)

By Mary Oliver
(American poet, 1935–2019)

One day you finally knew
what you had to do, and began,
though the voices around you
kept shouting
⁵ their bad advice
though the whole house
began to tremble
and you felt the old tug
at your ankles.
¹⁰ 'Mend my life!'
each voice cried.

But you didn't stop.

You knew what you had to do,
though the wind pried
¹⁵ with its stiff fingers
at the very foundations,
though their melancholy
was terrible.

It was already late
²⁰ enough, and a wild night,
and the road full of fallen
branches and stones.

But little by little,
as you left their voices behind,
²⁵ the stars began to burn
through the sheets of clouds,
and there was a new voice
which you slowly
recognized as your own,
³⁰ that kept you company
as you strode deeper and deeper
into the world,
determined to do
the only thing you could do
³⁵ determined to save
the only life you could save.

© Mary Oliver

Appendix

Grammatical terms

> Here are some of the most important **grammatical terms** in English:

active	aktiv
adjective	Adjektiv
adverb	Adverb
adverb of frequency	Adverb der Häufigkeit
adverb of manner	Adverb der Art und Weise
adverb of place	Adverb des Ortes
adverb of time	Adverb der Zeit
article	Artikel
definite article	bestimmter Artikel
indefinite article	unbestimmter Artikel
aspect	Aspekt
auxiliary	Hilfsverb
clause	Teilsatz
adverbial clause	Adverbialsatz
comment clause	nicht notwendiger Relativsatz, der sich auf den gesamten Satz bezieht
contact clause	notwendiger Relativsatz ohne Relativpronomen
if-clause	Bedingungssatz; Konditionalis
main clause	Hauptsatz
relative clause	Relativsatz
defining relative clause	notwendiger Relativsatz
non-defining relative clause	nicht notwendiger Relativsatz
subordinate clause (of time)	Temporalsatz
comparative	Komparativ; Vergleichsform
conditional	Konditionalis; Konditionalsatz
conditional type I, II, III, mixed	
demonstrative determiner	Demonstrativbegleiter
future	Futur; Zukunft
future perfect	Futur II
future progressive	Verlaufsform des Futur
future with *going to*	Futur mit *going to*
future with *will*	Futur mit *will*
present progressive with future meaning	Verlaufsform des Präsens mit Zukunftsbezug
simple present with future meaning	einfache Form des Präsens mit Zukunftsbezug
gerund	Gerundium
imperative	Imperativ; Befehlsform
infinitive	Infinitiv; Grundform
to-infinitive	*to*-Infinitiv
modal	Modalverb
modal substitute	Ersatzform eines Modalverbs
negative	negativ; verneinend
noun	Substantiv; Nomen
countable noun	zählbares Substantiv
uncountable noun	nicht zählbares Substantiv

object
    direct object
    indirect object
	Objekt
	    direktes Objekt
	    indirektes Objekt

participle
    participle construction
    past participle
    perfect participle
    present participle
	Partizip
	    Partizipialkonstruktion
	    Partizip Perfekt
	    having + Partizip Perfekt
	    Partizip Präsens

passive
    by-agent
	Passiv
	    Handelnde(r) im Passivsatz

past
    simple past
    past progressive
	Präteritum; Vergangenheit
	    einfache Form der Vergangenheit
	    Verlaufsform der Vergangenheit

past perfect
    past perfect
    past perfect progressive
	Plusquamperfekt
	    einfache Form des Plusquamperfekts
	    Verlaufsform des Plusquamperfekts

plural	Plural; Mehrzahl
positive	positiv; bejaht
possessive 's	*s*-Genitiv
possessive determiner	Possessivbegleiter

preposition
    preposition of place
    preposition of time
	Präposition
	    Präposition des Ortes
	    Präposition der Zeit

present
    simple present
    present progressive
	Präsens; Gegenwart
	    einfache Form des Präsens
	    Verlaufsform des Präsens

present perfect
    present perfect
    present perfect progressive
	Perfekt
	    einfache Form des Perfekt
	    Verlaufsform des Perfekt

pronoun
    indefinite pronoun
    interrogative pronoun
    object pronoun
    personal pronoun
    possessive pronoun
    reciprocal pronoun
    reflexive pronoun
    relative pronoun
    subject pronoun
	Pronomen
	    Indefinitpronomen; unbestimmtes Pronomen
	    Interrogativpronomen; Fragepronomen
	    Objektpronomen
	    Personalpronomen
	    Possessivpronomen; besitzanzeigendes Pronomen
	    Reziprokpronomen
	    Reflexivpronomen
	    Relativpronomen
	    Subjektpronomen

prop word *one/ones*	Stützwort *one/ones*
quantifier	Numeral; Zahlwort

question
    question tag
	Frage
	    Frageanhängsel; Bestätigungsfrage

reported speech
    backshift
	indirekte Rede
	    Rücksetzung der Zeitform um eine Stufe

singular	Singular; Einzahl
statement	Aussagesatz
subject	Subjekt
superlative	Superlativ
tense	Zeitform

verb
    irregular verb
    regular verb
	Verb; Tätigkeitswort
	    unregelmäßiges Verb
	    regelmäßiges Verb

word order	Wortstellung

Grammar

Do you have questions about grammar? The **grammar appendix** explains all the grammar that you learn in this book.

G 1	Present perfect and present perfect progressive (revision)	WS 1
G 2	Indefinite article after *such*, *quite*, *half*	WS 1
G 3	Past perfect and past perfect progressive (revision)	WS 1
G 4	Passive – all tenses (revision)	WS 1
G 5	Passive with verb + preposition	WS 1
G 6	Passive: verbs with two objects	WS 1
G 7	Passive infinitive (with *to*) after *want*, *expect*, etc.	WS 1
G 8	Passive infinitive (without *to*) after modal verbs	WS 1
G 9	Reported speech in statements, questions, requests and orders (revision)	WS 1
G 10	Changes to adverbs of time and place in reported speech	WS 1
G 11	Gerunds and infinitives (revision)	WS 2
G 12	Expressing the future (revision)	WS 2
G 13	Future progressive	WS 2
G 14	Modal verbs (revision)	WS 2
G 15	Modal substitutes	WS 2
G 16	*make, let, allow*	WS 2
G 17	*have something done*	WS 2
G 18	*used to / didn't use to / would*	WS 2
G 19	Participle constructions	WS 2
G 20	Defining and non-defining relative clauses (revision)	WS 3
G 21	Participle constructions replacing relative clauses	WS 3
G 22	*be used to / get used to* + noun / *-ing*	WS 3
G 23	Emphatic *do / does / did*	WS 3
G 24	Emphatic pronouns with *-self / -selves*	WS 3
G 25	*If*-sentences type 2 and 3 (revision)	WS 3
G 26	*If*-sentences mixed conditionals	WS 3
G 27	Using *It …* and *What …* for emphasis	WS 3
G 28	Using inversion to make a text more formal	WS 3

G 1 Present perfect and present perfect progressive (revision)

Workshop 1, pages 14–15

We form the present perfect with *has / have* + past participle.

	has / have	past participle	
You boys	**have**	**had**	such a good season so far.
I	**'ve**	**been**	to Australia twice.
I	**haven't**	**been**	to New Zealand.
Jason	**has**	**known**	Ricky since primary school.
	Have you	**seen**	Bruce recently?

We form the present perfect progressive with *has / have been* + *-ing*.

	has / have been	*-ing*	
You boys	**have been**	**playing**	so well.
She	**has been**	**coaching**	the rugby team for ten years.
We	**haven't been**	**living**	here for long.
How long	**have** you **been**	**waiting**?	

The present perfect connects the past and the present. This is usually an action or a situation in the past which is connected with or has a consequence in the present. It can also be something that started in the past and continues in the present.

- We use the present perfect to emphasize the result. We also use it to express 'how much / many'.
  Our partner school in Christchurch **has invited** us to play in their rugby tournament.
  I**'ve tried** surfing many times, but I just can't do it.
  I**'ve been** to the outback several times.

- We use the present perfect progressive to emphasize the duration of an action.
  The coach **has been trying** to organize a trip like this for a while.
  I**'ve been working** in the café since April.
  We**'ve been training** hard all month.

State verbs (e.g. *have, know, understand*) do not usually have a progressive form, so we use the present perfect when we are expressing the duration of an action.
He**'s wanted** to take the team to play in New Zealand since he started coaching them.
Eleni **hasn't known** about Aunt Koula's illness for very long.
NOT ~~Eleni hasn't been knowing about Aunt Koula's illness for very long.~~

Examples I**'ve tried** to fix the computer, but I can't find the problem.
I'm exhausted. We**'ve been driving** all day.
How long **have** you **been living** in Perth?
How many and which Australian cities **have** you **visited**?
We**'ve known** each other since kindergarten.

Appendix

GRAMMAR

G 2 Indefinite article after *such*, *quite*, *half*

Workshop 1, pages 14–15

We use *such a / quite a / half a* + noun phrase. The noun phrase is often a noun on its own or an adjective + noun.
She's **such a** great teacher.
It was **quite a** long journey.
I drank **half a** litre of water.

Note that we use *such an / quite an / half an* before a vowel sound.
It was **such an** amazing day.
It's **quite an** old idea.
It takes **half an** hour.

G 3 Past perfect and past perfect progressive (revision)

Workshop 1, pages 18–19

We form the past perfect with *had* + past participle.

	had	past participle	
I	had	been	there twice already.
She	hadn't	seen	the film before.
	Had they	met	before?

We form the past perfect progressive with *had been* + *-ing*.

	had been	-ing	
We	had been	driving	for about an hour.
We	hadn't been	living	there for long.
How long	had you been	waiting?	

- We use the past perfect (often with *already*) to show that one action or situation happened before another event or before a specific time in the past. We often connect the two events with time expressions such as *by the time, before, when, after* and *until*. We also use *by* + time / date.
Other European explorers **had** already **discovered** the new land by the time the British arrived.
We went for a walk after we**'d eaten** lunch.
We**'d finished** the meeting by mid-morning.

- We use the past perfect progressive to focus on the length of the earlier action and to show that it was in progress before the second action started.
Aboriginal people **had been living** in Australia for thousands of years before the Europeans arrived.
They**'d been waiting** for ages by the time we arrived.

Examples
I got to the station two minutes after the train **had left**.
I **had** never **been** to Sydney until last month.
We**'d been walking** for miles before we stopped for a rest.

Appendix
GRAMMAR

G 4 Passive – all tenses (revision)
Workshop 1, pages 24–25

- We often use the passive when we do not mention who does the action. This is because we are more interested in what happens, or because the person who does the action is obvious, unknown or not important. The passive also means we can avoid using vague subjects like *someone*, *people* and *they*. The passive is often used in English when we use a construction with 'man' in German.
  The rugby world cup **is held** *every four years. It* **was** *first* **held** *in 1987.*
  Uluru **has been designated** *a UNESCO World Heritage Site.*

- However, we can use the passive with *by* to say who does the action. This is usually when we are giving new information about an existing topic. The passive enables us to put the existing information first and the new information second.
  New Zealand was first settled **by the Maori people** *as early as 1300 AD.*
  Busloads of tourists are brought here every day **by big tour companies**.

We use the passive in different tenses. We form the passive with *be* + past participle.

- Simple present (*am* / *is* / *are* + past participle)
  Rugby union **is played** *by two teams of 15 players.*
  Many different crops **are grown** *in Australia.*

- Simple past (*was* / *were* + past participle)
  The president **was elected** *for a second term of office.*
  The Olympics **were** *first* **held** *in Australia in 1956.*

- Present progressive (*am* / *is* / *are being* + past participle)
  The room **is being cleaned**.
  The election votes **are being counted**.

- Past progressive (*was* / *were being* + past participle)
  My computer **was being repaired**.
  The rooms **were being cleaned**.

- Present perfect (*has* / *have been* + past participle)
  The election result **has been announced**.
  Relations between Australia and New Zealand **have** *often* **been compared** *to those of cousins.*

- Past perfect (*had been* + past participle)
  The beach hut **had been cleaned** *when we got back.*

- We form a question by putting the subject after the auxiliary verb *be or* between the auxiliaries if there are two of them.
  When **was** *Parliament House* **built**?
  Has *the World Cup ever* **been held** *in Australia?*

Examples
Australia **was** *first* **named** *Terra Australis, which* **was** *later* **abbreviated** *to the current form.*
When **was** *Australia first* **settled** *by Europeans?*
Is *Australia Day* **celebrated** *on the same date each year?*
It **is believed** *that Australia* **has been inhabited** *for at least 40,000 years.*

G 5 Passive with verb + preposition

Workshop 1, pages 24–25

When a verb is followed by a preposition, the preposition stays in the same position in the passive.
Each nation has its own Creation legends which **have been passed down** by the Elders.
We can make sure the place **is looked after**.
At the hotel, all diets **are catered for**.

Examples

Their hotel room **was broken into**.
The meeting **has been called off**.
Today, most goods **are paid for** electronically.

G 6 Passive: verbs with two objects

Workshop 1, pages 24–25

Some active verbs have two objects. There are two possible structures. Note that the **direct object** (e.g. *the land, a story*) is usually a thing and the **indirect object** is usually a person (e.g. *the local people, the children*).
They gave *the local people the land* back.   Or   They gave *the land* back to *the local people*.
The teacher read *the children a story*.   Or   The teacher read *a story* to *the children*.
They saved *us four seats*.   Or   They saved *four seats* for *us*.

- When we use a verb with two objects in the passive, there are also two possible structures. When we begin with the **direct object**, we use the preposition *to* or *for* before the **indirect object**.
  The local people were given back *the land*.   Or   *The land* was given back to *the local people*.
  The children were read *a story*.   Or   *A story* was read to *the children*.
  We were saved *four seats*.   Or   *Four seats* were saved for *us*.

Verbs with two objects are: *award, buy, find, get, give, make, offer, promise, reserve, save, send, show*.

Examples

Tim Hogan **was awarded** man-of-the-match.
Man-of-the-match **was awarded** to Tim Hogan.
Has Jack **been sent** the contract?
Has the contract **been sent** to Jack?

G 7 Passive infinitive (with *to*) after *want, expect*, etc.

Workshop 1, pages 24–25

Some verbs (e.g. *arrange, ask, expect, hope, need, plan, try, want, would like*) are followed by the *to*-infinitive. When there is a passive meaning, these verbs are followed by the passive infinitive (with *to*) (e.g. *to be met, to be invited*).
We didn't expect **to be met** at the airport.
I hope **to be invited** to the opening ceremony.
The battery needs **to be charged** overnight.
They had long wanted the site **to be returned** to them.

Appendix

GRAMMAR

G 8 Passive infinitive (without *to*) after modal verbs

Workshop 1, pages 24–25

Modal verbs (e.g. *can, will, must*) are followed by the infinitive (without *to*). When there is passive meaning, modal verbs are followed by the passive infinitive (without *to*) (e.g. *be seen, be opened, be invited*).
Ancient Aboriginal paintings **can be seen** in caves in the rock.
Some form of ID **must be shown** when entering the building.
The museum **will be opened** by the Prime Minister.
The new website **might be launched** soon.

Examples

Tasmania **can be reached** by boat in about ten hours from Melbourne.
This email address **can't be used** for replies.
You **will be given** plenty of opportunity to visit galleries and exhibitions.
You **won't be contacted** unless you give us permission.
Tickets for this museum **must be booked** online.
The flight **might be delayed**.

G 9 Reported speech in statements, questions, requests and orders (revision)

Workshop 1, pages 28–29

Statements

- When reporting statements, we often use the past tense forms *said, told, mentioned, added, suggested*, etc. When we do this, we usually 'backshift' the tense (move the tense one step back in time) in the comment we are reporting. We also change the pronouns (I → he / she, you → me, we → they, etc.).

Present tense	→	Past tense
I'**m** from Darwin.		She said she **was** from Darwin.
We'**re having** a barbecue.		She mentioned they **were having** a barbecue.

Past tense / Present perfect	→	Past perfect
Steve **forgot** his phone.		She told me that Steve **had forgotten** his phone.
We'**ve** just **arrived**.		He said they'**d** just **arrived**.

Will	→	Would
I'**ll** call you later.		She said she'**d** call me later.

Can	→	Could
I **can't** find the address.		He told me he **couldn't** find the address.

Must	→	Had to
We **must** leave.		She said they **had to** leave.

- However, we sometimes use the past tense forms *said, told, mentioned,* etc. and do not change the tense. This is usually to show or make clear that something is still true, relevant or important.
  Sam **left** about an hour ago. → He mentioned that Sam **left** about an hour ago.
  I'**ll** be home in ten minutes. → She said she'**ll** be home in ten minutes.

one hundred and fifty-five **155**

Appendix

GRAMMAR

Questions
- When we report questions, we often use the past tense forms *asked, wanted to know, wondered, was wondering*, etc. We usually 'backshift' the tense in the question we are reporting.
  Where **are** they **going**? → She wanted to know where they **were going**.
  What **did** you **buy**? → He was wondering what I**'d bought**.

- However, we sometimes use the past tense forms *asked, wanted to know, was wondering*, etc. but do not change the tense. This is usually to show that something is still true, relevant or important.
  Where**'s** Jamie **going**? → She was wondering where Jamie**'s going**.

- To report a *yes / no* question (without a question word) we use *if* or *whether*.
  Are you a student? → He asked me **if** I was a student.
  Can you give me a surfing lesson? → Olga was wondering **whether** I could give her a surfing lesson.

Note that the word order is different from direct questions.
Where **does he live**? → She asked me where **he lived**.
NOT ~~She asked me where did he live~~.
When **are we leaving**? → He wanted to know when **we were leaving**.
NOT ~~He wanted to know when were we leaving~~.

Requests and orders
- We can report a request with verbs such as *asked* and *wanted* + object + *to*-infinitive.
  Could you repeat the question? → She asked **me to repeat** the question.
  Can you wait for me? → She wanted **us to wait** for her.

- We can report an order with *told* + object + (*not*) *to*-infinitive.
  You should apologize to them. → She told **me to apologize** to them.
  Don't be late again. → He told **me not to be** late again.

Reporting verbs in a present tense
- We sometimes use a reporting verb in a present tense (e.g. *He says ..., She tells me ..., She's asked ..., Dave's suggesting ...*). In this case, the reported information stays in the same tense as the original comment.
  It**'s** Jenna's birthday today. → Alice tells me it**'s** your birthday!
  We**'re going** to the beach. → Luke has just told me that they**'re going** to the beach.
  How long **has** she **lived** here? → She wants to know how long you**'ve lived** here.

- We can also report requests and orders with a verb in a present tense.
  Will you help me? → Gareth **wants** me to help him.
  Wait, please. → She**'s asked** us to wait.

Examples

He said he **was** from Wellington.
She said they **were going** to have a barbecue.
He asked me if I **was** OK.
Olga asked me if I **can give** her a surfing lesson.
He wanted to know where I **worked**.
Oliver wants me **to phone** him.
The receptionist asked us **to wait** a few minutes.
The teacher told the children **to be** quiet.
Oscar wants to know if you **can give** him a lift to the airport.
Magdalena tells me you**'re applying** for Australian citizenship.

G 10 Changes to adverbs of time and place in reported speech

Workshop 1, pages 28–29

When we are reporting, we sometimes need to change adverbs of time and place.
*I saw Anders **yesterday**.* → *She mentioned she'd seen Anders **the day before**.*
*I'll call you **next week**.* → *She said she'd call me **the following week**.*
*This is the first time I've been **here**.* → *He said it was the first time he'd been **there**.*

Common changes include:
yesterday → *the day before*
tomorrow → *the next day / the day after*
last weekend / week / month / year → *the weekend / week / month / year before*
next weekend / week / month / year → *the following weekend / week / month / year*
here → *there*

G 11 Gerunds and infinitives (revision)

Workshop 2, pages 52–53

Sometimes we use two verbs together. When one verb follows another verb, the second verb is usually a gerund (*-ing*) or a *to*-infinitive.

- We use the gerund (*-ing*) after certain verbs. These include: *admit, avoid, deny, don't mind, enjoy, feel like, finish, imagine, look forward to, mention, miss, practise, prefer, recommend, risk, suggest.*
  *Many young people **enjoy travelling** and want to volunteer abroad.*
  *Have you **finished reading** the article?*
  *He **suggests doing** work experience at a law firm.*

- We use the *to*-infinitive after certain verbs. These include: *arrange, choose, decide, expect, hope, intend, learn, manage, need, offer, plan, promise, want, would like.*
  *She's **decided to study** music at university.*
  *Many young people enjoy travelling and **want to volunteer** abroad.*
  *I'**d like to do** some kind of volunteer work.*

- Some verbs can be followed by the gerund or the *to*-infinitive with no or little difference in meaning. These include: *like, love, hate, prefer, start.*
  *I **hate getting up** early.   I really **hate to be** late.*
  *I **prefer doing** sport.   I **prefer to study** languages.*

Some verbs can be followed by a gerund or the *to*-infinitive but there is a difference in meaning. These include: *try, remember, forget, stop.*

- *Try*
  We use *try* + gerund when we do something to see what the results will be.
  *I **tried turning** the computer on and off, but the program still didn't work.*

  We use *try* + *to*-infinitive when we make an effort to achieve something.
  *I'm **trying to learn** Russian, but it's very difficult.*

- *Remember* and *forget*

  We use *remember / forget* + gerund to talk about memories.
  Do you **remember going** to school for the first time?
  I'll never **forget visiting** Prague. It's so beautiful.

  We use *remember / forget* + *to*-infinitive to say we do or don't do something.
  Did you **remember to email** Julia?
  Don't **forget to update** your CV!

- *Stop*

  We use *stop* + gerund to talk about something ending or stopping.
  I **stopped eating** meat when I was 16.

  We use *stop* + *to*-infinitive to express the reason or purpose.
  I was working, but I **stopped to check** the news for a while.

G 12 Expressing the future (revision)

Workshop 2, pages 52 – 53

Will for decisions and predictions
- We use *will* for spontaneous decisions. This includes offers, promises and requests.
  We've got a free hour or so. I think I**'ll do** some sightseeing.
  Are you ready to order? – Yes, I**'ll have** the vegetarian pizza, please.
  I**'ll help** you with the cooking if you like.

- We use *will* for predictions that are based on personal feeling or opinion.
  I am sure you**'ll have** a great time in Australia.
  Based on my work so far, I**'ll be** OK.
  They **won't win**. We're a much better team.

Be going to for future plans
- We use *be going to* for future plans and intentions.
  I**'m going to ask** for a pay rise.
  James **is going to book** his plane tickets at the weekend.
  Are you **going to apply for** the job?

Note that to avoid repeating *go*, we often omit *to go*.
We**'re going** (to go) shopping this evening.
My best friend and I **are going** (to go) to Australia for the summer.

Simple present with future meaning
- We use the simple present to talk about events in the future that are part of a fixed timetable, itinerary or programme.
  In March, I **have** an interview for a job. It**'s** on the 16th.
  The apprenticeship **starts** in September.
  The doors **open** at 6.30 and the show **starts** at 7.30.
  The flight **leaves** at 11.00. When **does** it **arrive** in Perth?

Appendix
GRAMMAR

Present progressive with future meaning
- We use the present progressive with a future time to talk about future arrangements.
  Next week, I**'m meeting** my cousin to talk things through.
  I**'m seeing** my friends tomorrow evening. We**'re going** for a pizza.
  Did you know that Michael**'s having** a party next Saturday?
  When **are** Chris and Jo **getting married**?

Future perfect
- We use the future perfect (*will have* + past participle) to talk about something already completed at a point in the future.
  The apprenticeship starts in September. I**'ll have finished** my A-levels by then.
  I'm sure we**'ll have arrived** by midnight.
  Will you **have had** dinner by 8.30?

- We can use the future perfect to talk about something not completed at a point in the future.
  I'm afraid I **won't have finished** my report by Friday.
  I **won't have had** time to do much research before the interview.

- We often use the future perfect with *by*.
  We'll have finished the meeting **by** 10.30.

G 13 Future progressive
Workshop 2, pages 52 – 53

- We form the future progressive with *will be* + *-ing*.
  We**'ll be travelling** all day.
  I**'ll be waiting** when you arrive.

- We use the future progressive for something in progress at a specific time in the future.
  Next year most of my friends **will be doing** a university course or an apprenticeship.
  Hopefully by September I**'ll be working** somewhere in the US or Canada.
  This time tomorrow, I**'ll be having** my interview.
  At 3 o'clock, we**'ll be driving** to the airport.

G 14 Modal verbs (revision)
Workshop 2, pages 56 – 57

The modal verbs are *can, could, must, might, may, would, will, shall* and *should*.
- A modal verb always has the same form. The ending never changes.
  She **can** speak English.

- We use an infinitive without *to* after a modal verb.
  I **will** help you.

- To form a question, we put the modal verb before the subject.
  Can you help me?

- To form a negative, we put *not* or *n't* after the modal verb.
  You **mustn't** do that.

Appendix

GRAMMAR

Can and *could*

We use *can* to talk about ability. We use it:
- to talk about general abilities and skills.
  Amir **can** use many computer programs.
  I **can** speak French and Spanish. But I **can't** speak Italian.

- to talk about ability at a particular time.
  I **can't** read this. The writing is too small.

The past tense of *can* is *could*.
I **could** speak some English when I was four years old.

We use *can* to talk about permission. We use it:
- to talk about rules and laws and permission given by an individual.
  You **can't** wear trainers at work. But you **can** wear jeans.
  You **can** leave when you have finished the report.

The past tense of *can* is *could*.
We **could** wear trainers at work in my last job.

We use *can* to talk about possibility.
We **can** have the meeting on Thursday or Friday.
A cover letter **can** help you sell your skills and knowledge.

May and *might*

We use *may* and *might* to say that something is possible or likely. *Might* is more common in informal contexts. The negative is *may not* and *might not*. We use them:
- to say what is possible or likely in the future.
  I **might** start looking for a new job.
  There **may** be a slight delay with your order.

- to say what we think is possible or likely in the present.
  This **might** be Nina's office. But I'm not sure.
  She didn't answer the phone. She **might not** be at home.

Must

We use *must* to talk about what is necessary or what is required. We use *must not* (or *mustn't*) to say that something is not allowed or forbidden.
Education and work experience details **must** be included in your CV.
You **mustn't** be late for your interview!

Should

We use *should* to make suggestions and give advice. The negative form is *shouldn't*.
Your CV **should** have a clear format and structure.
You **shouldn't** invent information in your CV.

The past tense of *should* is *should have* + past participle.
We're going to be late – we **should have left** earlier.

Will and *shall*

We use *will* in a number of ways. Note that *will* is often contracted to *'ll*. We use *will*:

- to express spontaneous decisions.
  I'll help you if you want me to.
  I think I'll take a short break.

- to express predictions or assumptions about the future, present or past.
  I'm hoping I'll finish the report by Friday.
  Hurry up! The taxi will be waiting.
  I think the meeting will have finished by now.

- to talk about facts we see as inevitable or certain.
  I'll be at work all day tomorrow.
  She'll be 21 in January.
  No hiring manager will be willing to consider your application.

We mainly use *shall* in the form of a question to make offers and suggestions. We use it in this way with *I* and *we*.
Shall *I help you?*
What time **shall** *we meet?*

G 15 Modal substitutes

Workshop 2, pages 56 – 57

Modal substitutes include: *be able to, have to, need to, be obliged to, ought to* and *be supposed to*.

Alternatives to *can* and *could*

- We use *be able to* as an alternative to *can* and *could*. This is usually in more formal contexts and with *will* and the present perfect.
  Some people **are able to** *speak several languages.*
  I'm not **able to** *fix the problem, I'm afraid.*
  Unfortunately, I **wasn't able to** *find his office.*
  With her CV, I think she'll **be able to** *get an apprenticeship.*
  I've been able to speak English since I was four.

- We can sometimes use *be allowed to* as an alternative to *can* and *could* to talk about permission.
  Are *you* **allowed to** *wear jeans at work?*
  I **was** *never* **allowed to** *stay up late on a school night.*

Appendix

GRAMMAR

Alternatives to *must*

- We use *need to* and *have to* as alternatives to *must*. When they are used in this way, there is usually little difference in meaning (e.g. *I **need to** prepare for my interview.* / *I **have to** prepare for my interview.* / *I **must** prepare for my interview.*).
  *You **need to** show some ID to get into the building.*
  *You **need to** leave by 5.30 at the latest.*
  *Do you **have to** wear a tie at work?*

- In more informal contexts, such as conversation, we can use *have got to*.
  *I**'ve got to** prepare for my interview.*
  *What time **have** we **got to** leave?*

- The past tenses are *needed to* and *had to*. We use *had to* as the past tense of *must*.
  *Sorry I'm late. I **needed to** stop at the shops on the way here.*
  *I **had to** stay at work later than usual today.*
  *He **had to** do an interview with the manager.*

- We use *don't need to* and *don't have to* to say that something isn't necessary.
  *We **don't need to** leave until midday.*
  *In some countries, you **don't have to** give personal details in your CV.*

- We use *be obliged to* as an alternative in more formal contexts. This is usually when the obligation is a rule or law.
  *You **are obliged to** report to the reception on arrival and when leaving the building.*
  *In the UK, you **are not obliged to** add a headshot photo.*

Alternatives to *should*

- We can sometimes use *ought to* as an alternative to *should* when we are making suggestions or giving advice.
  *If you have skills, awards or other achievements, you **ought to** highlight them here.*
  *You **ought to** wear a tie for the interview.*
  *I think we **ought to** leave now.*

- We use *be supposed to* as an alternative to *should* when we are expressing the correct thing to do.
  *Are we **supposed to** include our age in our CV?*
  *In some European countries you**'re supposed to** include this information.*

Examples *I **wasn't able to** get there in time, I'm afraid.*
*Will you **be able to** fix it, do you think?*
*I **might be able to** go on the visit, but I'm not sure.*
*I**'ve got to** finish this report.*
*What time **do** we **need to** leave?*
*I **had to** work late last night.*
*We **don't have to** go to the meeting. But you can if you want to.*
*The meeting **ought to** take about an hour.*

G 16 make, let, allow

Workshop 2, pages 62–63

Verb phrases with *make, let, allow* + object + infinitive can often be expressed with 'lassen' or 'veranlassen' in German.
The sudden noise **made him scream**. *(Das plötzliche Geräusch ließ ihn aufschreien.)*

- We use *make* + object + infinitive (without *to*).
  Technological advances have **made us reassess** our work-life balance.
  No one can **make you do** anything you don't want to do.

- We use *let* + object + infinitive (without *to*).
  Specialized apps **let you choose** when and where you want to work.
  A freelance career **lets you set** your own hours.

- We use *allow* + object + *to*-infinitive.
  The gig economy **allows you to plan** your own work schedule and be more independent.
  Freelancer platforms **allow you to bid** for jobs that match your skills.

G 17 have something done

Workshop 2, pages 62–63

- We use *have something done* to say that someone does something for us. This is usually when we have arranged it, often when it is some kind of service. The form is *have* + object + past participle.
  Many people **have groceries delivered** to their home.
  We **had the office decorated** last month.
  I'**m having my hair cut** tomorrow.

- We can also use *get something done*. This is generally in more informal contexts, such as a conversation.
  We **get the car serviced** every year.
  Where do you **get your hair cut**?

G 18 used to / didn't use to / would

Workshop 2, pages 62–63

Used to
We use *used to* + infinitive to talk about past actions or situations that no longer exist. This could be:
- past actions, habits and routines
  My dad **used to spend** an hour a day commuting to work.
  I **didn't use to drive** to work, but these days I usually do.
  Do you work in advertising? – No, but I **used to**.

- past states
  The manufacturing industry **used to be** the biggest employer.
  The workplace **didn't use to be** as stressful as today.
  There **used to be** a cinema here.

Note that there is no final 'd' in negatives and questions.
There **didn't use to be** so many service industries here.
What **did** people **use to do** before mobile phones?

Would
- We can also use *would* + infinitive to talk about past actions, habits and routines. *Would* is usually contracted to *'d* after pronouns.
  In the past, workers **would travel** to their workplace every day.
  Employees **would commute** to the office every day.
  In my old job, we**'d have** a meeting almost every day.

- We do not, however, use *would* to talk about past states.
  NOT ~~The manufacturing industry would be the biggest employer.~~

Examples
We **used to live** in Frankfurt.
I **used to cycle** to school every day.
There **used to be** a lovely park here.
Didn't there **use to be** an office here?
As a child, I**'d spend** hours playing computer games.
We**'d often stay up** all night when we were students.

G 19 Participle constructions

Workshop 2, pages 66 – 67

There are two main types of participle:

- the present participle (the *-ing* form of the verb)
  Before **arriving**, I received lots of information.
  Wanting to become a teacher, he volunteered at his local school.

- the past participle (the regular *-ed* form or an irregular form).
  If **asked**, I would do it again.
  I came across a fantastic organization, **run** by an Irish government agency.

We also use the perfect participle (e.g. *having done*).
Having spent eight wonderful weeks there, I can thoroughly recommend it.

To form the negative, we put *not* or *never* before the participle.
Not wanting to be late, they set off in plenty of time.
Never having been to Ireland before, I was determined to see as much as I could.

We can use present participle constructions:
- in clauses beginning with *before, after, while, since, when*, etc.
  Before arriving, I received lots of information. (= Before I arrived, I received lots of information.)
  I came across InternIreland **while researching internships abroad**.
  After filling in an online application, I was invited to a 30-minute video interview.
  She's worked here **since finishing university**.

- when we express the reason for an action:
  Feeling tired, he left work early. (= Because he felt tired, he left work early.)
  Wanting to get as much experience as possible, I didn't mind having to work some weekends.
  Not earning much at the factory, he took a second job working in a café.

Note that in the above present participle constructions, the subject of both clauses is the same person.

- in reduced relative clauses when we shorten a defining relative clause, for example:
  in progressive tenses when we remove the relative pronoun and *be* or in place of a relative pronoun + simple tense to express a fact, state or permanent situation.
  Who are the people **talking to Harry**? (= Who are the people who are talking to Harry?)
  I work in an office **overlooking the river**. (= I work in an office that overlooks the river.)

We can use perfect participle constructions when one event happens before another event. We use the perfect participle to emphasize that the first event is completed before the second or that there is a time interval between the two events.
Having finished all their exams, they organized a big party.
Having overslept, she was late for work.

Note that beginning a sentence with a participle clause is more common in more formal writing and literary contexts.

We can use past participle constructions:
- in reduced defining or non-defining relative clauses. We remove the relative pronoun and the verb *be* in passive structure.
  It's a local business, **run** by the same family for over 200 years. (= It's a local business, which has been run by the same family for over 200 years.)
  Have they found the money **stolen** from the office?
  Cars **parked** here will be removed.

- in shortened *if* clauses to give passive meaning. We can include *if* or leave out *if*.
  If **asked** about it, I'd say it was the prettiest place I've visited so far. (= If I was asked about it, …)
  Given the chance to take the exam again, I'd do it without hesitation. (= If I was given the chance, …)

Examples
After leaving university, he got a job in a bank.
Living alone, Fred always looked forward to the few visitors he had.
Having suddenly **quit** his job, he needed to look for something else.
Having passed all my exams, I felt quite pleased with myself.
Bags **left** unattended will be destroyed.
Given the chance, I'd love to live abroad for a year or two.

G 20 Defining and non-defining relative clauses (revision)

Workshop 3, pages 90–91

Relative pronouns
We use *who* for people and *which* for things. We can use *that* for both people and things. We use *whose* to show possession.

Defining relative clauses
A defining relative clause defines, identifies or gives necessary information about a person or thing.
A defining relative clause comes immediately after this person or thing. The relative clause begins with a relative pronoun.
The traditional nuclear family **that consists of two married parents and their children** *is no longer the standard.*
Kids **who came over** *would sometimes ask, 'Where's your dad?'*
Is this the book **which your parents gave you as a birthday gift?**
Mac and his family do things **that every other family does.**
This is my friend **whose paintings I showed you.**

Omission of the relative pronoun
A relative pronoun can be the subject or the object of a relative clause.

	relative pronoun / subject	verb	object	
There's the man	who	helped	us	yesterday.

	relative pronoun / object	subject	verb	
There's the man	who	we	helped	yesterday.

We can omit *who, which* or *that* when it is the object of the relative clause.
There's the man (who) we helped yesterday.
Is this the book (which) your parents gave you as a birthday gift?
Mac and his family do things (that) every other family does.
Is this the café (that) Luke mentioned the other day?
NOT ~~There's the man helped us yesterday.~~

Non-defining relative clauses
A non-defining relative clause gives extra non-essential information about a person or thing. The non-defining relative clause comes immediately after this person or thing and begins with *who* or *which,* but not *that*. We always separate a non-defining relative clause from the main clause with commas.
*Same-sex marriage***, which was legalized in Canada in 2005,** *has led to even more diversity.*
*Single-parent families***, which can be a single mum or a dad plus kids,** *are not unusual.*
*My two older brothers***, who I've always been very close to,** *went to live with my dad.*
*My best friend***, whose parents divorced when she was a baby,** *was brought up by her mum.*
*He was born in Avalon***, which is a small town near Los Angeles.**

Note that non-defining relative clauses are used more in writing and in more formal spoken contexts.

We can also use a non-defining relative clause beginning with *which* to comment on the whole of the previous clause.
I was at a party last weekend, **which was great fun***.*
The school became mixed-sex in the 1980s, **which was a major step forwards***.*
I missed the bus, **which was really annoying***.*

Note that non-defining relative clauses used to comment on the whole of the previous clause are quite common in spoken and more informal English.

Where and when
We can use the relative adverbs *where* and *when* in relative clauses. We use *where* to identify a place and *when* to identify a time.
The hotel **where we stayed** *is in the city centre.*
Thanksgiving is a day **when families and friends get together***.*
Carmel, **where we went the other week***, is one of my favourite places.*

Examples

The friend **who you met the other day** *is a lawyer.*
The couple **that live in the flat above us** *are very noisy.*
What's that game **we were playing** *last night?*
Mr Jones, **who also actually taught my mum***, is my maths teacher.*
Christmas is usually a time **when families come together***.*
Maria offered to help, **which was very kind of her***.*

G 21 Participle constructions replacing relative clauses

Workshop 3, pages 90 – 91

A relative clause can be shortened using a present or past participle.
- When the relative pronoun is followed by the verb *be*, we can usually omit both the relative pronoun and *be*.
  Who are the people **talking** *to Erica? (= Who are the people* **who are talking** *to Erica?)*
  Canada is a nation **composed** *mostly of immigrants. (= Canada is a nation* **which is composed** *mostly of immigrants.)*

- We can sometimes use a present participle in place of a relative pronoun and simple tense. This is when we express a fact, state or permanent situation.
  The traditional nuclear family **consisting of** *two married parents and their children is no longer the standard. (= The traditional nuclear family* **which consists** *of two married parents and their children is no longer the standard.)*
  The majority of people **living** *in Canada are originally from elsewhere. (= The majority of people* **who live** *in Canada are originally from elsewhere.)*

Examples

We stayed in a hotel **overlooking** *the main square.*
Bags **left** *unattended will be removed.*
The people **living** *next door are very friendly.*

Appendix

GRAMMAR

G 22 — be used to / get used to + noun / -ing

Workshop 3, pages 90–91

- The verb phrase *be used to* means being familiar with something.
  *I've lived here for a few years, so I'**m used to the weather**.*
  *Valerie's grandmother **wasn't used to living alone**.*
  *I'**m not used to driving on the right**. I'm from the UK.*

- The verb phrase *get used to* describes the process of becoming familiar with something.
  *Immigrants have to **get used to a new culture** and new customs.*
  *I'm finally **getting used to the Canadian way of life**.*
  *Children in blended families have to **get used to living in a new unit**.*

Note that *be / get used to* is followed by a noun or the *-ing* form of a verb.

Examples
*I'**m not used to speaking** English all day.*
*I didn't take me long to **get used to the Canadian accent**.*
***Are** you **getting used to the way of life** here?*

G 23 — Emphatic do / does / did

Workshop 3, pages 94–95

We can use a form of the auxiliary verb *do* (*do / does / did*) to give emphasis to a statement.
In speaking, we stress *do / does / did*. We use *do* in this way for two reasons:

- to emphasize our feelings or emotions
  *Maybe it was a silly reaction, but it **did** make my life easier.*
  *At school a lot of kids dress alike, so we **do** influence each other.*
  *Anna **does** have some great ideas, don't you think?*
  *I **do** like Mexican food, especially the spicier dishes.*

- to emphasize a contrast
  *We didn't get caught ourselves, but a kid from our school **did**.*
  *I don't do any sport, but I **do** like watching it on TV.*
  *He doesn't drive, but he **does** have a motorbike licence.*

Note that with tenses and forms that already have an auxiliary verb, in speaking we stress the auxiliary verb to express emphasis in a similar way.
*I **am** looking forward to the party next weekend.*
*We really **have** had a great time, thank you.*

Examples
*I **do** agree with you. Please believe me!*
*The new sports centre **does** have an amazing offer.*
*My friend didn't like it, but I **did** enjoy the film.*

Appendix
GRAMMAR

G 24 Emphatic pronouns with -self / -selves
Workshop 3, pages 94 – 95

The reflexive pronouns *myself, yourself, himself, herself, itself, ourselves, yourselves* and *themselves* can also be used for emphasis.

- We can use them after a verb to emphasize the person or thing that does the action.
  *I knew **myself** that it was wrong.*
  *We didn't get caught **ourselves**, but a kid from our school did.*
  *He admitted **himself** that it was wrong.*

- They can also occur directly after the subject or subject pronoun.
  *Alex **herself** invited me to the party.*
  *You **yourself** created the problem, I'm afraid.*

G 25 *If*-sentences type 2 and 3 (revision)
Workshop 3, pages 100 – 101

If-sentences type 2

- We use *if*-sentences type 2 to talk about things that are impossible or hypothetical in the present or unlikely to happen in the future.

- *If*-sentences type 2 have the form *if* + simple past, *would / wouldn't* + infinitive.
  *If I **was** over 18, I **would** definitely **go** to jail.*
  *If we **drove** less, there **wouldn't be** so much air pollution.*
  *If I **had** more money, **I'd buy** a new phone.*

Note that we often use *'d* instead of *would*, especially in speaking and informal writing.

- We do not use *would* in the *if*-clause.
  *If I **had** more time, I'd read more books.* NOT ~~If I would have more time, I'd read more books.~~

- We can usually swap the order of the two clauses. When the *if* clause is first, there is a comma between the clauses.
  *If I had more time**,** I'd read more books.   I'd read more books if I had more time.*

- We can usually use *If I was …* or *If I were …* . However, we normally use *If I were you, …* .
  *If I **was / were** richer, I'd get a new car.*
  ***If I were you**, I'd work a bit harder at school.*

Note that we can use *could* or *might* in an *if*-sentence type 2.
*If I had more money, I **could buy** a new phone.*
*If we drove less, there **might not be** so much air pollution.*

If-sentences type 3

- We use *if*-sentences type 3 to talk about something that didn't happen in the past. We talk about it in an imaginary or a hypothetical way.

- *If*-sentences type 3 have the form *if* + past perfect, *would / wouldn't have* + past participle.
  *If the road **hadn't been** icy, I **wouldn't have lost** control of the car.*
  *If Jake **hadn't taken** his sister's car, the accident **wouldn't have happened**.*
  *If you**'d got** up earlier, you **wouldn't have missed** the bus.*

Appendix
GRAMMAR

- We often use *'d* instead of *had* and *would*, especially in speaking and informal writing. We also often use *'ve* instead of *have*.
  If I'd had more money, I'd've got a taxi.

- We can usually swap the order of the two clauses. When the *if* clause is first, there is a comma between the clauses.
  If I'd had more money, I would've bought it.   I would've bought it if I'd had more money.

Note that we can use *could have* or *might have* in an *if*-sentence type 3.
If I hadn't been ill last week, I could have gone to the meeting.
If I'd worked harder, I might've got better grades in my exams.

Examples
If I had more time, I'd help you.
What would you do if you found a wallet in the street?
If I was richer, I'd buy a sports car and drive round Europe for a year!
If I'd had more time, I'd have been able to help you.
If we'd left earlier, we'd have missed the terrible traffic.

G 26 *If*-sentences mixed conditionals
Workshop 3, pages 100 – 101

We use a 'mixed' conditional to talk about a past event with a present consequence. To do this we combine a type 3-conditional (to refer to the past) with a type-2 conditional (to refer to the present).

If Jake hadn't been so stupid, he wouldn't be in court now.
If you'd listened to the advice, you wouldn't be in this mess now.
If you'd gone to bed earlier last night, you wouldn't be so tired now.
He'd be at university now if he hadn't failed his exams.

Note that we can use *might* in a mixed conditional sentence.
If you'd listened to the advice, you might not be in this mess now.

G 27 Using *It ...* and *What ...* for emphasis
Workshop 3, pages 104 – 105

We can use sentences beginning with *It ...* or *What ...* to give emphasis to what we are saying. This helps to focus attention on or 'spotlights' the important information.

Neutral sentence	→	Sentence with emphasis
I didn't delete the files.		*It wasn't me who deleted the files.*
All the advertising annoys me.		*What annoys me is all the advertising.*

The main forms are:
- *It is / was ... that / who / which ...*
  It's all the advertising which annoys me.
  It's the advertisers who want our money.
  It's the video ads that really catch your attention.
  It was Jenny who phoned, not Maria.

- *What ... is / are / was / were ...*
  *What it means **is** that we enjoy clever content, even if it's advertising.*
  *What is really annoying **are** those ads blocking the content.*
  *What we needed **was** a better internet connection.*
  *What we needed **were** more options to choose from.*

Examples

*It **was** clicking on the ad **that** caused the virus.*
*It **wasn't** Masha **who** phoned, it was Olga.*
***Was it** Professor Jones **who** retired last month?*
***What I** don't understand **is** why no one said anything to her.*
***What** annoys me **is** his lazy attitude.*

G 28 Using inversion to make a text more formal   Workshop 3, pages 104 – 105

In more formal contexts, we can sometimes start a sentence with a negative adverbial such as *Hardly ever ..., Rarely ..., Never ..., Not once ..., In no way ..., Only later, ...*, etc. We do this to give emphasis or for dramatic effect. Compare the following sentences:

Neutral sentence	→	Sentence with emphasis
You rarely see a website with no advertising.		**Rarely** do you see a website with no advertising.
I haven't once sold advertising space.		**Not once** have I sold advertising space.

Note that when we start a sentence with a negative adverbial, we change the word order: the **auxiliary verb** is before the **subject**. In the simple present, we add the auxiliary *do* or *does*; in the simple past *did*.

Rarely do you see a website with no advertising.   NOT ~~Rarely you see a website with no advertising.~~
Not once have I sold advertising space.   NOT ~~Not once I have sold advertising space.~~

Examples

*In no way **am** I saying all advertising is bad.*
*Rarely **do** I take any notice of banner ads.*
*Never before **have** I heard such stupidity.*
*Hardly ever **does** such an opportunity arise.*
*At no time **did** I say that.*
*Not once, **did he** apologize.*
*Only later, **did we** realize we'd made such a terrible mistake.*

Irregular verbs

infinitive	simple past	past participle	German
to be	was / were	been	sein
to beat	beat	beaten	schlagen
to become	became	become	werden
to begin	began	begun	beginnen, anfangen
to bet	bet	bet	wetten
to bite [baɪt]	bit [bɪt]	bitten ['bɪtn]	beißen
to blow	blew	blown	blasen
to break	broke	broken	brechen
to bring	brought	brought	bringen
to build	built	built	bauen
to burn	burnt / burned	burnt / burned	(ver)brennen
to buy	bought	bought	kaufen
to catch	caught	caught	fangen
to choose [u:]	chose [əʊ]	chosen [əʊ]	auswählen
to come	came	come	kommen
to cost	cost	cost	kosten
to cut	cut	cut	schneiden
to deal [di:l]	dealt [delt]	dealt [delt]	handeln
to dig	dug	dug	graben
to do	did	done [dʌn]	machen, tun
to draw	drew	drawn	zeichnen
to dream	dreamt / dreamed [dremt]	dreamt / dreamed [dremt]	träumen
to drink	drank	drunk	trinken
to drive	drove	driven	fahren
to eat	ate	eaten	essen
to fall	fell	fallen	fallen, stürzen
to feed [fi:d]	fed [fed]	fed [fed]	füttern

infinitive	simple past	past participle	German
to feel [fi:l]	felt [felt]	felt [felt]	(sich) fühlen, spüren
to fight	fought	fought	kämpfen
to find	found	found	finden
to fly	flew	flown	fliegen
to forget	forgot	forgotten	vergessen
to forgive	forgave	forgiven	vergeben
to freeze	froze	frozen	frieren
to get	got	got / gotten (AE)	bekommen, holen
to give	gave	given	geben, schenken
to go	went	gone	gehen, fahren
to grow	grew	grown	wachsen, anbauen
to hang	hung	hung	hängen
to have (got)	had	had	haben
to hear [ɪə]	heard [ɜ:]	heard [ɜ:]	hören
to hide [haɪd]	hid [hɪd]	hidden [hɪdn]	(sich) verstecken
to hit	hit	hit	schlagen
to hold	held	held	halten
to hurt	hurt	hurt	wehtun
to keep [ki:p]	kept [kept]	kept [kept]	(be)halten
to kneel [ni:l]	knelt [nelt]	knelt [nelt]	knien
to know [nəʊ]	knew [nju:]	known [nəʊn]	wissen, kennen
to lead [li:d]	led [led]	led [led]	führen
to learn	learnt / learned	learnt / learned	lernen
to leave	left	left	verlassen
to lend	lent	lent	leihen

Appendix

IRREGULAR VERBS

infinitive	simple past	past participle	German
to let	let	let	lassen
to lie	lay	lain	liegen
to light	lit / lighted	lit / lighted	anzünden, anmachen
to lose [uː]	lost [ɒ]	lost [ɒ]	verlieren
to make	made	made	machen, herstellen
to mean [iː]	meant [e]	meant [e]	bedeuten
to meet [miːt]	met [met]	met [met]	(sich) treffen, kennenlernen
to mow	mowed	mown / mowed	mähen
to pay	paid	paid	bezahlen
to put	put	put	stellen
to quit	quit	quit	aufhören
to read [iː]	read [e]	read [e]	lesen
to rebuild	rebuilt	rebuilt	wieder aufbauen
to rewrite	rewrote	rewritten	umschreiben
to ride	rode	ridden	fahren, reiten
to ring	rang	rung	klingeln, anrufen
to rise	rose	risen	ansteigen, (sich) erheben
to run	ran	run	laufen, rennen, leiten
to say	said	said	sagen
to see	saw	seen	sehen
to sell	sold	sold	verkaufen
to send	sent	sent	schicken
to set	set	set	setzen, stellen, legen
to shake	shook	shaken	schütteln
to shine	shone	shone	scheinen

infinitive	simple past	past participle	German
to shoot [ʃuːt]	shot [ʃɒt]	shot [ʃɒt]	schießen
to show	showed	shown / showed	zeigen
to sing	sang	sung	singen
to sink	sank	sunk	sinken
to sit	sat	sat	sitzen
to sleep [sliːp]	slept [slept]	slept [slept]	schlafen
to smell	smelt / smelled	smelt / smelled	riechen
to speak	spoke	spoken	sprechen
to spend	spent	spent	verbringen, ausgeben
to split	split	split	sich trennen
to spoil	spoilt	spoilt	verderben
to spread	spread	spread	(sich) ausbreiten
to stand	stood	stood	stehen
to steal	stole	stolen	stehlen
to stick	stuck	stuck	kleben
to sting	stung	stung	stechen
to swim	swam	swum	schwimmen
to take	took	taken	nehmen, dauern
to teach	taught	taught	unterrichten
to tell	told	told	sagen, erzählen
to think	thought	thought	denken, glauben
to throw	threw	thrown	werfen
to understand	understood	understood	verstehen
to wake up	woke up	woken up	aufwachen, aufwecken
to wear	wore	worn	tragen
to win	won [ʌ]	won	gewinnen
to write	wrote	written	schreiben

Appendix

VOCABULARY

Vocabulary

> **Here are all the words from the workshops. They are in the same order as in the workshop.**
>
> There is the page number and the activity.
>
> A ▢ at the side is for words from the listening text. A ▢ is for words from videos.
>
> Words in grey are important for one text. They are only in this text and you don't have to learn them.
>
> The phonetic transcription [ ] tells you how you say a word.
>
> Sometimes there are irregular forms (shut, shut, shut).
>
> The example sentence shows you how we use a word.
> = shows words with the same meaning
> ≠ shows words with the opposite meaning
> ⓘ shows words with the same meaning in French and Latin or it gives other interesting information about the word.
>
> When you work with the *Vocabulary*, cover the German, look at the English word and the example or picture and say the German word. You can also cover the German and the example sentences to practise the English.

page	exercise	Welcome Workshop		
11	4a	**realistically** [ˌriːəˈlɪstɪkli]	We can not realistically think that climate change will end on its own.	realistisch
		due to [djuː tə]	Coral reefs are dying due to the rise in sea temperature. = *because of*	wegen; aufgrund von
		trade [treɪd]	English has become the language of trade, so it's important in business. = *commerce*	Handel; Geschäft
		effort [ˈefət]	Is it really worth putting all that time and effort into learning English? ⓘ Fr. 'effort' (m.)	Anstrengung; Mühe
		to consider [kənˈsɪdə]	Let's consider how speaking English well can change your life. = *think about something* ⓘ Fr. 'considérer', Lat. 'considerare (considero)'	nachdenken über
		fluency [ˈfluːənsi]	Fluency in English can provide opportunities in the future.	Sprachbeherrschung
		foremost [ˈfɔːməʊst]	First and foremost, English opens new career opportunities. ≠ *last*	zuvorderst
		dominant [ˈdɒmɪnənt]	English is the dominant business language. = *most important*	wichtig; überwiegend
		necessity [nəˈsesəti]	To be able to participate in these courses will be a necessity. ≠ *extra*	Notwendigkeit
		workforce [ˈwɜːkfɔːs]	Women are almost half the workforce, but the gender pay gap hasn't changed much. = *labour pool*	Arbeitskräfte

174 one hundred and seventy-four

Appendix

VOCABULARY

page	exercise	**Welcome Workshop**		
		to **mandate** [ˈmændeɪt]	Some companies mandate English as the language in their offices around the world.	anordnen
		corporate [ˈkɔːpərət]	What is the corporate language in your office? = business	Korporations…; unternehmensweit
		marketplace [ˈmɑːkɪtpleɪs]	The importance of English in the international marketplace is obvious.	Markt
		to **understate** [ˌʌndəˈsteɪt]	You cannot understate the importance of an education. = downplay	unterbewerten; untertreiben
		to **frequent** [ˈfriːkwənt]	It is always easy to find English speakers, especially at hotels and in areas frequented by tourists.	aufsuchen
		moreover [mɔːrˈəʊvə]	Moreover, for a research study to get sufficient attention it should be published in English. = furthermore	außerdem
		exclusively [ɪkˈskluːsɪvli]	Many courses are taught exclusively in English. = completely	ausschließlich
		academic [ˌækəˈdemɪk]	Many of the top academic journals are published in English. ❗ Fr. 'académique'	akademisch
		journal [ˈdʒɜːnl]	Students and academics need strong English reading and writing skills as many top academic journals are published in English. = periodical	Journal; Fachzeitschrift
		publication [ˌpʌblɪˈkeɪʃn]	Academic publications are usually published in English.	Veröffentlichung
		sufficient [səˈfɪʃnt]	A university degree alone is not sufficient to practice law.	ausreichend; genug
		to **rely** [rɪˈlaɪ]	Many families don't have enough to eat and rely on food banks. ≠ disregard	sich verlassen auf
		to **subscribe** [səbˈskraɪb]	Please subscribe to the channel.	abonnieren
		icon [ˈaɪkɒn]	Press the bell icon for future videos.	Symbol; Ikone
page	exercise	**Workshop 1**		
12	1	**islander** [ˈaɪləndə]	Maori and Pacific Islanders have had a big influence on rugby in New Zealand. = somebody who lives on an island	Insulaner(in)
		kangaroo [ˌkæŋɡəˈruː]	There are more kangaroos than people in Australia.	Känguru
		fence [fens]	The State Barrier Fence is a rabbit proof fence in Australia.	Zaun

Appendix

VOCABULARY

page	exercise	Workshop 1		
		territory [ˈterətri]	There are tropical rainforests in the Northern Territory and snow-covered mountains along the East coast.	Gebiet
13		**serpent** [ˈsɜːpənt]	= snake	Schlange
		interior [ɪnˈtɪəriər]	The interior of Australia is mainly desert and bush. = exterior	Binnenland; das Innere
	2	**approximately** [əˈprɒksɪmətli]	They've been here for approximately 60,000 years. = roughly ≠ exactly	ungefähr; etwa
		to nickname [ˈnɪkneɪm]	Can you guess why Australia is nicknamed 'Down Under'?	Spitzname geben
		equator [ɪˈkweɪtər]	When it's winter in Europe, it's summer below the equator.	Äquator
		hemisphere [ˈhemɪsfɪər]	Australia is underneath the equator in the southern hemisphere.	Hemisphäre
		globe [gləʊb]	Can you find Australia on the globe?	Globus; Erdkugel
		remote [rɪˈməʊt]	Australia is really remote and because of this, it's got animals and plants that can't be found anywhere else in the world. ❗ Lat. 'removere (removeo, removi, remotum)' = to remove	entfernt; abgelegen
		load [ləʊd]	We have a large load of supplies to deliver to the building site.	Ladung
		platypus [ˈplætɪpəs]	Platypus live in the wild in Australia.	Schnabeltier
		koala [kəʊˈɑːlə]	Many animals such as koala bears, kangaroos and wombats can only be found in Australia.	Koala
		kookaburra [ˈkʊkəbʌrə]	The strange laughing bird is called a kookaburra.	Kookaburra; Lachender Hans
		creepy [ˈkriːpi]	Here is a really creepy fact: Australia is home to some of the deadliest animals on the planet.	gruselig
		to unite [juˈnaɪt]	The six independent colonies of Australia agreed to unite and form a single nation in 1901.	sich vereinigen
		pleasant [ˈpleznt]	They built their house in a place with a pleasant climate, which is not too hot and not too cold. ≠ unpleasant	angenehm
		downhill [ˌdaʊnˈhɪl]	Aussies love winter sports, especially downhill skiing, cross-country skiing and snowboarding.	bergab
	YT	**persuasive** [pəˈsweɪsɪv]	After this workshop you will be able to use persuasive language.	überzeugend

Appendix

VOCABULARY

page	exercise	Workshop 1		
14	1a	**workout** [ˈwɜːkaʊt]	That was a great workout, but now I need a shower.	Fitnesstraining
		to echo [ˈekəʊ]	The noise echoed across the playing field.	nachhallen; nachklingen
	2b	**mate** [meɪt]	It's my best mate's birthday, so I can't miss the party. = friend	Kumpel
		supportive [səˈpɔːtɪv]	My colleagues, knowing I was nervous, were really helpful and supportive. ≠ unsupportive	unterstützend
15	3b	**deli** [ˈdeli]	Jason has worked part-time at the Kourakis' Greek deli for the past year.	Feinkostladen
	4b	**litre** [ˈliːtə]	The coach tells his players to drink a litre of water during practice. ❗ AE = liter	Liter
	5a	**auntie** [ˈɑːnti]	My mother's sister is my Auntie Koula.	Tantchen
		godmother [ˈɡɒdmʌðər]	My godmother took care of me after my parents died.	Patentante
	CC	**sporting** [ˈspɔːtɪŋ]	Australia is a sporting nation because sport is a big part of Australians national identity.	sportlich; Sport…
16		**Aussie slang** **ace** [eɪs] klasse **arvo** [ˈɑːvəʊ] Nachmittag **bogey** [ˈbəʊɡi] Schwimmen **brekkie** [ˈbreki] Frühstück **chockers** [ˈtʃɒkəz] voll **footy** [ˈfʊti] Fußball **g'day** [ɡəˈdeɪ] guten Tag **lappy** [ˈlæpi] Laptop **mozzie** [ˈmɒzi] Mücke	**nana** [ˈnænə] Banane **pom** [pɒm] Brite / Britin **prezzie** [ˈprezi] Geschenk **roo** [ruː] Känguru **sunnies** [ˈsʌniz] Sonnenbrille **sickie** [ˈsɪki] Krankheitstag **tog** [tɒɡ] Sachen; Zeug **tucker** [ˈtʌkə] Essen	
		impression [ɪmˈpreʃn]	What is your impression of the graphic novel?	Eindruck
	1	**to originate** [əˈrɪdʒɪneɪt]	The word 'selfie' originates from Australia. = come from	entstehen
		informal [ɪnˈfɔːml]	We sit in a circle for informal meetings or brainstorming sessions. ≠ formal	informell
	2	**to slip on** [slɪp]	When you sit on the beach, slip on a shirt to protect you from the sun.	rasch anziehen
		to slop on [slɒp ɒn]	Slop on some sunscreen or you'll get a sunburn.	auftragen
		to slap on [slæp ɒn]	Slap on a hat when you go to the beach.	aufsetzen

Appendix

VOCABULARY

page	exercise	Workshop 1		
	5b	**to seek** [siːk]	If you get too hot, seek shade quickly.	suchen
		shade [ʃeɪd]	At noon it is best to get out of the sun and into the shade.	Schatten
		cattle [ˈkætl]	Raising animals like cattle produces more greenhouse gases than driving cars.	Rinder
		chore [tʃɔːr]	I feed the chickens and help my dad with the other morning chores.	Routinearbeit
		actively [ˈæktɪvli]	Which words would you put in your vocabulary book to actively learn? ≠ passively	aktiv
		electronic [ɪˌlekˈtrɒnɪk]	Our teacher demonstrated some problems on the electronic whiteboard.	elektronisch
17	TIP	**emotional** [ɪˈməʊʃənl]	Using techniques such as anecdotes can have an emotional effect. ⚠ Fr. 'émotionnel'	emotional
	8	**scenic** [ˈsiːnɪk]	They said Melbourne isn't as warm, sunny and scenic as other cities.	malerisch
		laneway [leɪnweɪ]	The narrow laneways in the city centre are a good place to start learning to drive. = small road	Sträßchen
		busker [ˈbʌskər]	Do you like cool cafés, amazing street art and buskers playing great music? = street musician	Straßenmusiker(in)
		market [ˈmɑːkɪt]	I love Queen Victoria Market – it's an awesome place for shopping.	Markt; Börse
		to hang out [hæŋ aʊt], **hung, hung** [hʌŋ, hʌŋ]	Some friends and I were hanging out and listening to music.	rumhängen; abhängen
18	1a	**ethnically** [ˈeθnɪkli]	Today Australia is one of the world's most ethnically diverse nations.	ethnisch
	1b	**to skim** [skɪm]	Skim the text to check your answers.	querlesen; überfliegen
		prisoner [ˈprɪznər]	Most of the people on the ships going to Australia at that time were prisoners.	Gefangene; Häftling
		penal [ˈpiːnl]	Most people on board were prisoners about to start life in a penal colony.	strafrechtlich
		convict [ˈkɒnvɪkt]	Before America became independent, Britain sent its convicts there.	Verurteilte(r)
		independence [ˌɪndɪˈpendəns]	After the War of Independence, America refused to take any more convicts from Britain. = liberty	Unabhängigkeit
		to claim [kleɪm]	It is often claimed that girls aren't logical, so they can't do maths or science. = allege	behaupten; beanspruchen

Appendix

VOCABULARY

page	exercise	Workshop 1		
		producer [prəˈdjuːsər]	By the end of the 19th century, Australia had become the world's largest gold producer.	Erzeuger; Hersteller
		profession [prəˈfeʃn]	The immigrants brought new skills and professions and changed the colonies into more modern cities.	Beruf; Profession
		to threaten [ˈθretn]	They believed the immigrants threatened their jobs and Australia's British culture.	gefährden
		federation [ˌfedəˈreɪʃn]	In 1901, the six colonies of Australia united to form a federation.	Bund
		shortage [ˈʃɔːtɪdʒ]	World War II led to a shortage of workers in Australia.	Mangel
		to immigrate [ˈɪmɪɡreɪt]	They encouraged skilled migrants to immigrate to Australia.	einwandern
		fare [feɪk]	Anyone who wanted to go only had to pay ten pounds for the fare by sea. = fee	Fahrpreis
19		**harsh** [hɑːʃ]	Today's friendly society is very different from the harsh reality that the first migrants experienced. = rough	rau
	3b	**to base on** [beɪs ɒn]	You need good grades, but based on your work so far, you'll be OK.	auf der Grundlage von; basierend auf
		restriction [rɪˈstrɪkʃn]	Why did the government introduce the Immigration Restriction Act?	Einschränkung
		act [ækt]	The Native Title Act was passed by the Australian Parliament in 1993. = law	Gesetz; Verordnung
	4a	**formal** [ˈfɔːml]	We're not so formal round here, Keira, I'm Judith and this is Adrian. ≠ informal ❗ Fr. 'formel, formelle'	förmlich; formell
		cosmopolitan [ˌkɒzməˈpɒlɪtən]	Shanghai is incredibly international and cosmopolitan and it's growing really fast. = worldly	kosmopolitisch; weltoffen
		vibrant [ˈvaɪbrənt]	The city on the ocean is diverse and vibrant. = colourful	dynamisch; lebhaft
		undecided [ˌʌndɪˈsaɪdɪd]	I'm undecided about moving, because I don't want to leave my friends or my school. ≠ certain	unentschieden; unentschlossen
	4b	**to head back** [hed bæk]	After a year back in London, they decided to head back to Australia. = return	gehen zurück; zurückkehren

Appendix

VOCABULARY

page	exercise	Workshop 1		
20	1	**acrostic** [əˈkrɒstɪk]	In an acrostic poem the first letter of each line spells out a specific word.	Akrostichon
	2a	**myth** [mɪθ]	All cultures have myths they tell about their peoples. = legend ❗ Fr. 'mythe' (m.)	Mythos; Legende
		dreamtime [ˈdriːmtaɪm]	Australian aboriginal myths, also known as dreamtime stories, are traditionally told by the indigenous people of Australia.	Traumzeit
		indigenous [ɪnˈdɪdʒənəs]	The arrival of the European settlers had a terrible impact on the indigenous Aboriginal peoples.	einheimisch
		horizon [həˈraɪzn]	On the horizon was a beautiful multi-coloured rainbow.	Horizont
		grateful [ˈɡreɪtfl]	I was grateful for the information pack sent by the agency which answered all my questions. ≠ thankless	dankbar
		waterhole [ˈwɔːtəhəʊl]	Thirsty animals came to the waterhole.	Wasserloch
		hunter [ˈhʌntə]	The hunters killed animals for food.	Jäger(in)
	2b	**earth** [ɜːθ]	People used to believe that the earth was flat.	Erde
		to wind [ˈwaɪnd], **wound, wound** [waʊnd, waʊnd]	As the Rainbow Serpent wound his way across the land, his body formed the mountains and the valleys where the rivers lived.	sich schlängeln; winden
		powerful [ˈpaʊəfl]	When you see a team of both white and black players doing the haka, it's a powerful symbol of unity. ≠ weak	mächtig; kräftig
		to crawl [krɔːl]	The Rainbow Serpent crawled into a waterhole and lay in the cool water. = to move slowly ≠ to race	krabbeln; kriechen
		rainstorm [ˈreɪnstɔːm]	The snake came out into the sun after the rainstorm had ended.	Regenschauer; Gewitter
		to disturb [dɪˈstɜːb]	He only came out after heavy rainstorms had disturbed his waterhole.	stören
	3	**to sum up** [sʌm ʌp]	Sum up your ideas in a critical evaluation of the poem. = summarize	zusammenfassen
		colonizer [ˈkɒlənaɪzər]	Before the British colonizers arrived in Australia, over 500 Aboriginal nations lived on the continent.	Ansiedler/in
		to inhabit [ɪnˈhæbɪt]	Over 500 Aboriginal nations inhabited the continent. = take up residence	bewohnen

Appendix

VOCABULARY

page	exercise	Workshop 1		
		to **educate** [ˈedʒukeɪt]	The whole community was responsible for looking after the children, educating them and passing on the traditions of the clan.	erziehen
		brutality [bruːˈtæləti]	Huge numbers died as a result of colonial brutality.	Brutalität
		to **suffer** [ˈsʌfə]	Homeless people suffer many stigmas in society. = endure	leiden
21	4a	to **misunderstand** [ˌmɪsʌndəˈstænd], **misunderstood, missunderstood** [ˌmɪsʌndəˈstʊd], [ˌmɪsʌndəˈstʊd]	He misunderstood my comments and is mad at me. ≠ understand	missverstehen
		brutal [ˈbruːtl]	Nature can be brutal, but humans can be, too. = viscious	brutal
	4b	**formation** [fɔːˈmeɪʃn]	It's a large rock formation located close to the exact centre of Australia.	Formation
		mistreatment [ˌmɪsˈtriːtmənt]	We reflect on their past mistreatment of indigenous peoples. ≠ kindness	Misshandlung
		loss [lɒs]	Habitat loss is a crisis for many animals in the wild. ≠ gain	Verlust
		removal [rɪˈmuːvl]	They apologized for the removal of Aboriginal and Torres Strait Islander children from their families.	Entfernung
		indignity [ɪnˈdɪgnəti]	We are sorry for the indignity and degradation inflicted on a proud people and a proud culture.	Demütigung
		healing [ˈhiːlɪŋ]	The apology should be received in the spirit in which it is offered as part of the healing of the nation.	Heilung
	5a	to **honour** [ˈɒnə]	Today we honour the indigenous peoples of this land, the oldest continuing cultures in human history. ❗ AE = honor	ehren
		to **reflect** [rɪˈflekt]	Use the feedback you receive to reflect on your work and revise it.	spiegeln
		in particular [ɪn pəˈtɪkjələr]	We reflect in particular on the mistreatment of those who were Stolen Generations.	insbesondere
		blemished [ˈblemɪʃd]	The mistreatment of the Stolen Generations is a blemished chapter in our national history. = flawed	fehlerhaft
		to **right** [raɪt]	The time has come to right the wrongs of the past and move forward with confidence into the future.	aufrichten

Appendix

VOCABULARY

page	exercise	Workshop 1		
		confidence [ˈkɒnfɪdəns]	My counsellor gave me more confidence in my abilities. ≠ doubt	Selbstvertrauen
		successive [səkˈsesɪv]	We apologize for the racist laws and policies of successive parliaments and governments.	aufeinanderfolgend; fortlaufend
		to **inflict** [ɪnˈflɪkt]	Mining practices inflict damage on poor communities. = impose	aufdrängen
		profound [prəˈfaʊnd]	The results of the discrimination are profound and cannot be denied.	profund; tief
		grief [griːf]	The policies inflicted suffering and grief on the Maori people.	Trauer
		fellow [ˈfeləʊ]	The Maori are our fellow Australians.	zur gleichen Gruppe gehörend; gleichartig
		degradation [ˌdegrəˈdeɪʃn]	For the indignity and degradation thus inflicted on a proud people and a proud culture, we say sorry.	Degradierung
		thus [ðʌs]	Regular exercise makes you healthier, thus making you happier. = thereby	dadurch; daher
		to **resolve** [rɪˈzɒlv]	For the future we take heart and resolve that this new page in history can now be written.	entscheiden
		to **acknowledge** [əkˈnɒlɪdʒ]	Acknowledging the past and laying claim to a future that embraces all Australians is important. = recognize	bestätigen; anerkennen
		to **embrace** [ɪmˈbreɪs]	They embraced and forgave one another.	umarmen
		on behalf of [ɒn bɪˈhɑːf əv]	On behalf of the government of Australia I offer an apology. = for	im Interesse von
		qualification [ˌkwɒlɪfɪˈkeɪʃn]	Having a National Vocational Qualification will help you get another job if you move on.	Qualifikation; Eignung
		opposition [ˌɒpəˈzɪʃn]	Both the ruling party and the opposition were in favour of the law.	Opposition; Gegner
		commonwealth [ˈkɒmənwelθ]	A commonwealth is a political relationship between countries.	Commonwealth
	5b	**effective** [ɪˈfektɪv]	An effective cover letter can help you sell your skills and knowledge. ≠ ineffective ❗ Fr. 'efficace'	wirksam
	5c	**transcript** [ˈtrænskrɪpt]	Read the transcript before listening to the podcast.	Abschrift; Niederschrift
	6	**statistic** [stəˈtɪstɪk]	Statistics show that Aboriginal people still live 10 to 17 years less than white Australians. ❗ Fr. 'statistique' (f.)	Statistik

Appendix

VOCABULARY

page	exercise	Workshop 1		
		preventable [prɪˈventəbl]	Statistics show that Aboriginal people are more likely to die of preventable diseases.	vermeidbar
		suicide [ˈsuːɪsaɪd]	Aboriginal youths have the highest suicide rate in the world.	Selbstmord
		to arrest [əˈrest]	Aboriginal youths are arrested more than white people. ❗ Fr. 'arrêter'	gefangen nehmen; verhaften
		minor [ˈmaɪnər]	Minorities are more likely to be arrested for minor offences. ≠ major	gering; klein
		offence [əˈfens]	The judge has to consider what sentence will prevent you from committing any further offences.	Straftat
		to swear [sweər]	My brother gets in trouble for swearing in school.	fluchen
		peer [pɪə]	Teenagers can feel influenced or pressured by their peers to drink alcohol.	Peer
	7a	**heritage** [ˈherɪtɪdʒ]	This is a song about the importance of cultural heritage.	Erbe; Tradition
		foundation [faʊnˈdeɪʃn]	The foundation of the house is solid.	Grundlage; Fundament
		underdog [ˈʌndədɒg]	I always end up being friends with the underdog.	Außenseiter(in); Underdog
		eagle [ˈiːgl]	We could see the eagle fly while we hiked in the mountains.	Adler
		fist [fɪst]	We fought with blood and fist so we can dance in the sun.	Faust
		mob [mɒb]	The Seed Mob is a group of my people who are standing up to protect our communities. = crowd	Meute
		kin [kɪn]	My kin come from the country plains. = family	Verwandtschaft; Familie
		plains [pleɪnz]	There are a lot of farms on our country plains. = Prairie	Prärie; Flachland
		elder [ˈeldə]	The elders have authority and make decisions.	Älteste(r)
		determination [dɪˌtɜːmɪˈneɪʃn]	We believe in self-determination, freedom and basic human rights. ❗ Fr. 'détermination' (f.)	Entschlossenheit
		beneath [bɪˈniːθ]	My kin fought with blood and fist so we can dance beneath the sun. ≠ on top	darunter
		invasion [ɪnˈveɪʒn]	Nothing good can come of the country's invasion of its neighbour.	Invasion; Eingriff
		legislation [ˌledʒɪsˈleɪʃn]	We must end racist government legislation across the nation.	Rechtsvorschriften

Appendix

VOCABULARY

page	exercise	Workshop 1		
		downward [ˈdaʊnwəd]	The western way of thinking has the world going downward. ≠ upward	abwärts; absteigend
		spiral [ˈspaɪrəl]	Wars and the pandemic – sometimes it feels like humans are on a downward spiral.	Spirale; Wendel
		vein [veɪn]	The blood of my ancestors is pumping through my veins.	Vene; Ader
		to bounce back [baʊns]	Our culture will bounce back from the social injustice of the past.	wieder auf die Beine kommen
		to dust off [dʌst ɒf]	If you drop something on the ground, pick it up and dust if off.	abwischen; abstauben
22	S2	**gatherer** [ˈgæðərər]	Australia's first peoples were hunter-gatherers who lived in small family groups.	Sammler(in)
		semi- [ˈsemi]	When you put 'semi' before a word, it means a part of something. = half-	halb-
		nomadic [nəʊˈmædɪk]	The hunter-gatherers lived in small family groups and were semi-nomadic. ≠ settled	nomadisch
		systematically [ˌsɪstəˈmætɪkli]	We systematically learn the grammar so that we can use complex sentences.	systematisch
		distinct [dɪˈstɪŋkt]	Each group lived in a defined territory with its own distinct history.	eindeutig; eigenständig
		agrarian [əˈgreərɪən]	The hunter-gatherers didn't develop an agrarian, or farming, society. ≠ rural	landwirtschaftlich
		various [ˈveərɪəs]	They managed land and wild animals in various ways to make sure they had enough supplies.	verschiedene
		predictable [prɪˈdɪktəbl]	I think most young people still want the stable, predictable hours and pay that a full-time, permanent job gives.	vorhersehbar
		dialect [ˈdaɪəlekt]	In 1788, there were 260 different language groups and 500 dialects.	Dialekt
		colonization [ˌkɒlənaɪˈzeɪʃn]	How did colonization impact indigenous communities?	Kolonialisierung
		immediate [ɪˈmiːdɪət]	The most immediate consequence was a wave of epidemic diseases.	unmittelbar; umgehend
		influenza [ˌɪnfluˈenzə]	There were epidemic diseases such as smallpox, influenza and measles.	Grippe; Influenza
		measles [ˈmiːzlz]	Epidemic diseases such as measles can still be a problem today.	Masern
		resistance [rɪˈzɪstəns]	These diseases killed many indigenous people because they had no resistance to them.	Widerstand; hier: Resistenz

Appendix

VOCABULARY

page	exercise	Workshop 1		
		random [ˈrændəm]	Many also died in random killings or organized massacres.	zufällig; willkürlich
		cliff [klɪf]	Massacres often took the form of mass shootings or driving groups of people off cliffs.	Klippe; Felsen
		drastic [ˈdræstɪk]	As a result, there was a drastic decrease in the Aboriginal population.	drastisch; extrem
		decline [dɪˈklaɪn]	There has been a decline in many native species. ≠ increase	Rückgang
		to **estimate** [ˈestɪmeɪt]	By 1900, it was estimated that only about 117,000 indigenous people were still living in Australia.	schätzen
	S3	**monolingual** [ˌmɒnəˈlɪŋgwəl]	Many English speakers are monolingual. ≠ multilingual	einsprachig
23	S1a	**species** [ˈspiːʃiːz]	They attack sheep and have caused the decline of many native species.	Spezies; Art
	S1b	**arid** [ˈærɪd]	Although much of the outback is arid desert, it isn't empty of life. = dry	dürr; trocken
		howl [haʊl]	The howls of wild dogs echo across the landscape.	Geheul
		dingo [ˈdɪŋgəʊ]	If you camp out in the outback, you'll hear the howls of dingoes, or wild dogs, echoing across the landscape.	Dingo
		to **loathe** [ləʊð]	Dingoes were introduced into Australia a long time ago, and today they are both loved and loathed. = hate ≠ love	nicht ausstehen können; hassen
		in spite of [ɪn spaɪt əv]	In spite of this, it's exciting to see them run around wild in Australia.	trotz
		to **roam around** [rəʊm əˈraʊnd]	People living in the country can let their dogs roam around free.	durchstromern; herumwandern
		ecological [ˌiːkəˈlɒdʒɪkl]	Enormous ecological damage was caused by fires.	ökologisch
		feral [ˈferəl]	You'll also come across the world's largest herd of feral camels.	wild
		camel [ˈkæml]	In desert countries, camels are used to ride on.	Kamel
		advent [ˈædvent]	The camels were no longer needed with the advent of powered engines.	Beginn; Einführung
		invasive [ɪnˈveɪsɪv]	Other invasive species include foxes and rabbits, brought from Europe in the 19th century.	invasiv
		predator [ˈpredətər]	When there aren't any predators, a species can grow uncontrolled.	Raubtier; Räuber

Appendix

VOCABULARY

page	exercise	Workshop 1		
		to **explode** [ɪkˈspləʊd]	They had few predators, so their populations exploded.	explodieren
	S3	**finding** [ˈfaɪndɪŋ]	Compare your findings about climate change with a partner. = result	Ergebnis; Erkenntnis
	S4	**prolonged** [prəˈlɒŋd]	The prolonged hot weather is bad for farmers and animals. = drawn-out	anhaltend; verlängert
		drought [draʊt]	Australia's prolonged drought drives camels out of the desert onto farms and into towns.	Dürre
		desperate [ˈdespərət]	The child was desperate for attention. ❗ Fr. 'désespéré, désespérée'	verzweifelt
		to **demolish** [dɪˈmɒlɪʃ]	Camels demolish fences on ranches in their search for water. ≠ build	abreißen
		critical [ˈkrɪtɪkl]	In the desert, it is critical to have enough water.	kritisch; wichtig
		watering hole [ˈwɔːtərɪŋ həʊl]	Watering holes are important to people and animals living on this arid land.	Wasserstelle
		to **pollute** [pəˈluːt]	Mining companies are polluting the environment.	verschmutzen; verseuchen
		undrinkable [ʌnˈdrɪŋkəbl]	The camels polluted the watering holes and made the water undrinkable.	untrinkbar
		property [ˈprɒpəti]	We built a fence around the property.	Eigentum; Immobilie
		to **cull** [kʌl]	In an effort to defend farm properties, hundreds of camels are culled a day. = extract	keulen; selektiv schlachten
		to **rot** [ˈrəʊtə]	The camels that are killed are left to rot.	verfaulen
		cull [kʌl]	The culls of camels are ordered by the government.	Schlachten; Keulen
		controversial [ˌkɒntrəˈvɜːʃl]	The activists discussed controversial topics regarding to social justice. ❗ Fr. 'controversé, controversée'	umstritten
24	1a	**location** [ləʊˈkeɪʃn]	We found a location that would make our wedding memorable. ❗ Lat. 'locus, -i' (m.) = place	Standort
		folklore [ˈfəʊklɔːr]	The continent is covered with sacred sites that are important in Aboriginal tradition and folklore.	Folklore
		located [ləʊˈkeɪtɪd]	Our office is located in the centre of the city.	gelegen
		to **designate** [ˈdezɪgneɪt]	Uluru has been designated a UNESCO World Heritage site.	ernennen; designieren

Appendix

VOCABULARY

page	exercise	Workshop 1		
		to **resume** [rɪˈzjuːm]	The rock resumed its original name in 1985 when the land was given back to the local people. = begin again	übernehmen; wieder annehmen
		according to [əˈkɔːdɪŋ tə]	According to this line graph, the problem affects a lot of teens. = in accordance with	nach; gemäß
		bitterly [ˈbɪtəli]	He was bitterly disappointed and cried.	bitterlich
		insulted [ˈɪnsʌltd]	Our hosts were bitterly insulted by his bad behaviour. ≠ complimented	beleidigt
		saddened [ˈsædnd]	I was deeply saddened when I heard he was dead.	betrübt
		bloodshed [ˈblʌdʃed]	When a lot of people are killed, we call it bloodshed.	Blutvergießen
		reef [riːf]	Tourism is very important but it is carefully controlled to limit damage to the reef.	Riff
		variety [vəˈraɪəti]	Use a variety of sentence lengths and types in your writing. = array	Vielfalt; Auswahl
		seabird [ˈsiːbɜːd]	The coast of Queensland is home to a huge variety of animals, including fish and seabirds.	Seevogel
		shark [ʃɑːk]	Shark attacks are not common but have increased in recent years.	Hai
		to **control** [kənˈtrəʊl]	Tourism is very important but it is carefully controlled to limit damage to the reef. = curb	kontrollieren; steuern
		to **disobey** [ˌdɪsəˈbeɪ]	Don't disobey your parents. ≠ obey	nicht gehorchen
		to **spear** [spɪər]	One of the brothers disobeyed and speared the fish anyway.	aufspießen
		lava [ˈlɑːvə]	Bhiral was angry, so he threw lava and hot rocks from the sky.	Lava
	2	**vague** [veɪg]	Be precise and avoid using vague subjects like someone, people or they.	unbestimmt; vage
25	3a	**busload** [ˈbʌsləʊd]	Busloads of tourists are brought in to see the site every day.	Busladung
		unacceptable [ˌʌnəkˈseptəbl]	I find it unacceptable when hidden adverts target young children. ≠ acceptable	inakzeptabel
26	1	**global warming** [ˈgləʊbl ˈwɔːmɪŋ]	How are these disasters connected to climate change and global warming?	Erderwärmung
		coral [ˈkɒrəl]	The reef's colourful coral was home to many fish.	Koralle

one hundred and eighty-seven **187**

Appendix

VOCABULARY

page	exercise	Workshop 1		
		bleaching [bliːtʃ]	Coral bleaching is caused by rising sea temperatures.	Entfärbung
	2a	**stunning** [ˈstʌnɪŋ]	Australia is known for its stunning beaches and diverse wildlife.	toll; atemberaubend
		wombat [ˈwɒmbæt]	Wombats have short tail and legs.	Wombat
		degree [dɪˈgriː]	We need to keep global warming below two degrees.	Grad
		heatwave [ˈhiːtweɪv]	Heatwaves are more common than they have ever been.	Hitzewelle
		severe [sɪˈvɪə]	Heatwaves are also more severe than ever. = strong	schwer; stark
		bushfire [ˈbʊʃfaɪər]	Drought creates the perfect conditions for bushfires.	Buschfeuer
		frequent [ˈfriːkwənt]	Bushfires are becoming much more frequent and more extreme. ≠ inconstant	häufig
		to endanger [ɪnˈdeɪndʒər]	According to one farmer, food security is endangered by climate change.	gefährden
		acidic [əˈsɪdɪk]	Our oceans are becoming much warmer and more acidic.	sauer
		factor [ˈfæktə]	The bar chart shows which factors motivate teenagers to shop online. ❗ Lat. 'factum, -i' (nt.) = fact	Faktor
		polyp [ˈpɒlɪp]	The coral reef is built over many millions of years by tiny animals called polyps.	Polyp
		urgently [ˈɜːdʒəntli]	The causes of climate change need tackling urgently.	dringend
	3a	**concerned** [kənˈsɜːnd]	We are very concerned about the future of the planet. = worried	besorgt
		carbon dioxide [ˌkɑːbəndaɪˈɒksaɪd]	Burning fossil fuels like coal and gas produces CO2, carbon dioxide. ❗ Fr. 'dioxyde de carbone' (m.)	Kohlendioxid
		fracking [ˈfrækɪŋ]	Fracking is bad for the environment and should be stopped.	Fracking
		hurricane [ˈhʌrɪkən]	Hurricanes are very destructive storms.	Hurrikan; Orkan
		renewable [rɪˈnjuːəbl]	We want them to encourage renewable energy sources, like the sun. = inexhaustible	erneuerbar
27	3b	**violent** [ˈvaɪələnt]	Violent storms with very strong winds are common here and cause a lot of damage.	gewalttätig

Appendix

VOCABULARY

page	exercise	Workshop 1		
		rainfall [ˈreɪnfɔːl]	*These storms are often followed by heavy rainfall which can result in floods.*	Regen; Niederschlag
		power [ˈpaʊə]	*Listen closely to the language of the poem so that you can understand the power of its words.*	Kraft; Macht
	3c	**hopeful** [ˈhəʊpfl]	*I applied for ten jobs and I was hopeful I'd be offered at least one.*	hoffnungsvoll
		movement [ˈmuːvmənt]	*Write a blogpost describing a protest movement you know about.*	Bewegung
		youth [juːθ]	*Youth clubs have been closing down everywhere because there isn't enough money for them.*	Jugend
		network [ˈnetwɜːk]	*We are a network of organizations that help homeless people.* = structure	Netzwerk
		exporter [ekˈspɔːtər]	*Australia is the world's biggest exporter of coal and gas.*	Exporteur(in)
		to frack [fræk]	*They're allowing the mining companies to frack huge parts of the Northern Territory.*	fracken
		wheat [wiːt]	*They clear the land to raise animals and grow wheat, that's why the droughts are getting worse.*	Weizen
		federal government [ˈfedərəl ˈɡʌvənmənt]	*We want the federal government to stop all new coal or gas projects.*	Bundesregierung
		bushland [ˈbʊʃlænd]	*We demand that the company stop destroying forest and bushland.*	Buschland
		tipping point [ˈtɪpɪŋ pɔɪnt]	*We've only got a few years before we reach the final tipping point.*	Kipppunkt; Trendwende
	4a	**extinction** [ɪkˈstɪŋkʃn]	*If we carry on like this, many animals only found here face extinction.*	Aussterben
		to bulldoze [ˈbʊldəʊz]	*The animals sat on top of the logs that were bulldozed.*	planieren
		pile [paɪl]	*That pile of logs used to be several trees where animals lived.*	Haufen; Stapel
		threat [θret]	*The threat to biodiversity in Australia is very high.* = danger	Gefahr
		to worsen [ˈwɜːsn]	*The threat to biodiversity has been worsened by climate change, which has lead to the loss of habitat.*	verschlechtern; verschlimmern
	4b	**increasingly** [ɪnˈkriːsɪŋli]	*Families are becoming increasingly diverse in Canada and around the world.* = more and more ≠ less	zunehmend
		human [ˈhjuːmən]	*Wildlife is increasingly affected by the climate change caused by humans.*	Mensch

one hundred and eighty-nine **189**

Appendix

VOCABULARY

page	exercise	Workshop 1		
		astonishing [əˈstɒnɪʃɪŋ]	Over the last ten years, an astonishing 50% of animal species in Australia have been wiped out. = amazing	erstaunlich
		hectare [ˈhekteər]	Thousands of hectares of forest were destroyed in the wildfires last year.	Hektar
28	1a	**weed** [wiːd]	I'm taking out all these weeds around the tomatoes.	Unkraut
		architect [ˈɑːkɪtekt]	I spoke to an architect about making changes to the house. ❗ Lat. 'architectus, -ti' (m.)	Architekt(in)
		slang [slæŋ]	Slang is a language that consists of words, phrases and grammar that are very informal.	Slang
	CC	**sibling** [ˈsɪblɪŋ]	Relations between Australia and New Zealand have often been compared to those between siblings or cousins.	Geschwister(kind); Bruder
		rivalry [ˈraɪvlri]	They have a huge sporting rivalry – mainly in cricket, rugby and netball.	Konkurrenz
29	3a	**greeting** [ˈɡriːtɪŋ]	The photo shows the prime minister exchanging a traditional Maori greeting.	Gruß
		trilogy [ˈtrɪlədʒi]	I am reading the third book in a trilogy.	Trilogie
		to tip over [tɪp ˈəʊvə]	We nearly tipped over in the canoe.	umkippen
	4	**to invert** [ɪnˈvɜːt]	To report yes/no questions use 'if' or 'whether' and invert the subject and verb.	umkehren; umstellen
	5a	**to tour** [tʊə]	We are touring New Zealand and will have two days in Christchurch.	besuchen; besichten
30	2	**distinctive** [dɪˈstɪŋktɪv]	The island's distinctive feature is it's beach.	unverwechselbar; ausgeprägt
		segment [ˈseɡmənt]	The text has six segments.	Segment; Abschnitt
		significance [sɪɡˈnɪfɪkəns]	The book details the town's natural wonders and its cultural significance.	Bedeutung; Wichtigkeit
		regional [ˈriːdʒənl]	Describe the city's regional importance. = territorial	regional
		biological [ˌbaɪəˈlɒdʒɪkl]	They explain the area's biological diversity and how it is being protected.	biologisch
	3a	**filmmaker** [ˈfɪlm meɪkə]	Documentary filmmaker Shaun Reed is here in the studio to talk about his new film.	Filmemacher(in)
		studio [ˈstjuːdiəʊ]	We are in the studio today to discuss his new film.	Studio
		beyond [bɪˈjɒnd]	That's Shaun Reed talking about his new film 'Beyond the Black'.	jenseits

Appendix

VOCABULARY

page	exercise	Workshop 1		
		phenomenon [fəˈnɒmɪnən]	The film looks at the rugby phenomenon in our country.	Phänomen
		isle [aɪl]	In 1905, New Zealand's first national rugby team toured the British Isles and France.	Eiland; kleine Insel
		intense [ɪnˈtens]	The film shows the intense rivalry between two schools prior to a game.	stark; ernsthaft
		college [ˈkɒlɪdʒ]	I study urban planning at college and when I've finished I want to apply to graduate schools. = university	Hochschule; Universität
		to **adopt** [əˈdɒpt]	The national team adopted a dance.	annehmen
		ritual [ˈrɪtʃuəl]	I soon found that the Sunday barbecue is a ritual for many Aussies. = practice	Ritual
		unity [ˈjuːnəti]	National holidays create unity among people.	Einheit
31	4a	**ethnic** [ˈeθnɪk]	New Zealanders of every ethnic group see Maori culture as an essential part of their way of life.	ethnisch
		descent [dɪˈsent]	The term Pakeha refers to New Zealanders of European descent.	Abstammung
		anthem [ˈænθəm]	At official events, audiences sing the New Zealand national anthem in the Maori language, then in English. = hymn	Nationalhymne; Hymne
		variation [ˌveəriˈeɪʃn]	Variations of the traditional Maori dance are performed at events all over the country.	Variante; Variation
		multicultural [ˌmʌltiˈkʌltʃərəl]	The Maori cultural influence is one reason for the success of New Zealand's multicultural society.	multikulturell
	5	**committee** [kəˈmɪti]	The committee meets every month to discuss the event. = board	Kommission; Komitee
	6	to **structure** [ˈstrʌktʃə]	How do you structure an acrostic poem?	strukturieren; aufbauen
		conversational [ˌkɒnvəˈseɪʃənl]	Think of some good conversational topics before the meeting.	Gesprächs...
		instructive [ɪnˈstrʌktɪv]	The instructive video showed the proper use of the first aid kit.	instruktiv; lehrreich
32	S1a	to **consist of** [kənˈsɪst əv]	The traditional family consisting of two married parents and their children is no longer the standard.	aus etw. bestehen
		coastline [ˈkəʊstlaɪn]	Australia has a lot of coastline.	Küstenlinie; Küste
	S2b	**logical** [ˈlɒdʒɪkl]	Organize your ideas into a logical order before writing your essay. ≠ illogical	logisch; folgerichtig

Appendix

VOCABULARY

page	exercise	Workshop 1		
	TIP	**complex** [ˈkɒmpleks]	I like novels with complex characters who transform in the story. ≠ simple	komplex
33	S1	**requirement** [rɪˈkwaɪəmənt]	Check what programmes they offer and their requirements before applying.	Voraussetzung
		concern [kənˈsɜːn]	Explain your concerns about climate change. = worry	Sorge; Bedenken
		protester [prəˈtestə]	What are the protesters doing to try to change things?	Demonstrant(in); Protestierer(in)
38	1	**narrator** [nəˈreɪtə]	The narrator is the person who tells the story.	Erzähler(in)
	2a	**appropriation** [əˌprəʊpriˈeɪʃn]	Let's talk about appropriation of another culture's traditions.	Aneignung
		to **brainwash** [ˈbreɪnwɒʃ]	People have been brainwashed into thinking that more money will make them happy.	einer Gehirnwäsche unterziehen
		compensation [ˌkɒmpenˈseɪʃn]	She asked for compensation for her job. = allowance	Entschädigung
		demon [ˈdiːmən]	The superheroes kept the demon from stealing the magic stone.	Dämon
		reconciliation [ˌrekənsɪliˈeɪʃn]	They achieved reconciliation with the enemy.	Versöhnung
		trauma [ˈtrɔːmə]	Aboriginal culture carries the trauma of the past.	Trauma
		venom [ˈvenəm]	Stay away from the poisonous snake, as its venom is dangerous.	Gift
	3a	**treatment** [ˈtriːtmənt]	He started treatment for his illness and already feels better.	Behandlung
	3b	to **justify** [ˈdʒʌstɪfaɪ]	It is difficult to justify the high level of social injustice in our society.	rechtfertigen
		to **perceive** [pəˈsiːv]	They were perceived to be simple to use but weren't.	empfinden; erkennen
	4a	**nap** [næp]	I felt tired after my first day at work, so I took a nap.	Nickerchen
		to **rage** [reɪdʒ]	What could generate the trauma that made a kid rage so badly?	wüten
		corpse [kɔːps]	The corpses lay in the field after the invasion.	Leiche
		outcome [ˈaʊtkʌm]	War never leads to a good outcome.	Ergebnis; Resultat
		grave [greɪv]	They dug graves for the corpses.	Grab
		admission [ədˈmɪʃn]	There is no admission to the concert without a ticket.	Eintritt
		indecision [ˌɪndɪˈsɪʒn]	Government indecision is making the climate crisis worse.	Unentschlossenheit

Appendix

VOCABULARY

page	exercise	Workshop 1		
		token [ˈtəʊkən]	Please accept this token of my thanks.	Zeichen; Geste
		recognition [ˌrekəgˈnɪʃn]	The gift is a token of recognition for your hard work.	Anerkennung
39	5a	**attitude** [ˈætɪtjuːd]	The way that someone dresses doesn't actually show their attitude about life.	Ansicht; Einstellung
		to pray [preɪ]	During the pandemic, I prayed for better days. ❗ Fr. 'prier'	beten
		equality [iˈkwɒləti]	We aren't a nation of grand cultural tolerance and equality.	Gleichberechtigung
		tone [təʊn]	I chose special colour tones for my painting.	Ton
		devil [ˈdevl]	Do you believe in the devil?	Teufel
	5b	**extent** [ɪkˈstent]	Discuss to what extent they agree on the issue.	Ausmaß
		prejudice [ˈpredʒədɪs]	My organization tries to reduce prejudice and racism through education.	Nachteil; Vorurteil
		stereotype [ˈsteriətaɪp]	It is time to forget old stereotypes, like that women should stay home.	Stereotype; Klischee
		discrimination [dɪˌskrɪmɪˈneɪʃn]	In my student activist group, we focus on social issues like discrimination.	Diskriminierung; Ausgrenzung
	5d	**biographical** [ˌbaɪəˈɡræfɪkl]	Do some biographical research on the singer.	biografisch
	6	**constitution** [ˌkɒnstɪˈtjuːʃn]	He presented the first Australian Constitution to the British Parliament. ❗ Fr. 'constitution' (f.)	Verfassung
40	1a	**blazing** [ˈbleɪzɪŋ]	The blazing sun can be very hot at the beach.	brennend
		sunburnt [ˈsʌnbɜːnt]	I have to be careful of the hot sun so I don't get sunburnt.	sonnenverbrannt
	1b	**grill** [ɡrɪl]	When we arrived, the grill was lit and the family gathered for dinner. = BBQ	Grill
		to light [laɪt]	The familiy lit the grill and gathered for dinner.	anzünden
		to sizzle [ˈsɪzl]	When the meat started sizzling, the neighbours came over.	knistern
		to clean [kliːn]	On the weekend my father cleans the apartment.	putzen; reinigen
41	2	**to appoint** [əˈpɔɪnt]	Burke was appointed as the leader. ≠ disallow	ernennen
		initially [ɪˈnɪʃəli]	He initially joined the expedition as third in command but was promoted. = observation	zunächst; anfangs

Appendix

VOCABULARY

page	exercise	**Workshop 1**		
		to **promote** [prəˈməʊt]	Once my boss left the company I was promoted to her position.	fördern
		deputy [ˈdepjuti]	When his boss was promoted he became the deputy leader.	stellvertretend
		remaining [rɪˈmeɪnɪŋ]	Unfortunately, by the time they arrived, the remaining men had already left.	restlich; übrig
		somehow [ˈsʌmhaʊ]	Somehow, King managed to stay alive by himself in the forest.	irgendwie
		to **rescue** [ˈreskjuː]	The animal shelter rescues dogs and cats.	retten
	3	**deforestation** [ˌdiːˌfɒrɪˈsteɪʃn]	Deforestation of the Amazon is a global problem.	Abholzung
		destructive [dɪˈstrʌktɪv]	We educate the public about the effect of logging and other destructive practices.	zerstörend; schädlich
43	1	**lively** [ˈlaɪvli]	This is a lively and vibrant place to live.	lebhaft
		truly [ˈtruːli]	Dublin is an amazing city with a great cultural offer and the Irish countryside is truly beautiful.	wirklich
	2	**kite-surfing** [kaɪt ˈsɜːfɪŋ]	I have a new hobby – kite-surfing.	Kitesurfen
	4	**university** [ˌjuːnɪˈvɜːsəti]	If you get good grades in your A-levels, you can go on to do a degree in engineering at university.	Universität; Hochschule
		barrister [ˈbærɪstər]	Before he turned to politics, he had been working as a barrister for several years. = lawyer	Rechtsanwalt; Rechtsanwältin
		to **resign** [rɪˈzaɪn]	After serving for two years, he resigned and became a senior judge in the new High Court of Australia.	zurücktreten
		court [kɔːt]	He was arrested and found guilty in court.	Gericht
44	6	**crocodile** [ˈkrɒkədaɪl]	Crocodiles can live in fresh or salt water.	Krokodil
		stingray [ˈstɪŋreɪ]	He was killed by a stingray while diving.	Stachelrochen
		cable [ˈkeɪbl]	The US cable network Animal Planet bought the rights to the TV show.	Kabel
		catchphrase [ˈkætʃfreɪz]	The TV actor was also famous for his catchphrase. = slogan	Schlagwort
	7	to **declare** [dɪˈkleə]	The Great Barrier Reef has been declared a World Heritage site.	ausrufen; verkünden
		existence [ɪɡˈzɪstəns]	Unfortunately, its very existence is in danger from tourism.	Existenz

Appendix

VOCABULARY

page	exercise	Workshop 1		
		to **pose a threat** [pəʊz ə θret]	Climate change poses a great threat to future generations.	eine Bedrohung darstellen
	8	**MP (Members of Parliament)** [ˌem ˈpiː]	New environmental laws were discussed by MPs in the Australian parliament.	Abgeordnete
		seriousness [ˈsɪəriəsnəs]	A petition was organized to highlight the seriousness of the situation. ≠ insincerity	Ernsthaftigkeit
		export [ɪkˈsplɪsɪtli]	Large amounts of coal are exported by Australian mining companies. ≠ import	exportieren
45	10	**disappointment** [ˌdɪsəˈpɔɪntmənt]	It was awesome and helped us forget the disappointment yesterday. = letdown	Enttäuschung

page	exercise	Workshop 2		
50	1	**commerce** [ˈkɒmɜːs]	I would like to have a job in commerce when I finish school. = trade	Handel; Kommerz
	2	**employment** [ɪmˈplɔɪmənt]	Look at this job advert from a UK employment website. ≠ unemployment	Beschäftigung; Arbeit
		signpost [ˈsaɪnpəʊst]	The signpost gives directions.	Wegweiser; Schild
		apprenticeship [əˈprentɪʃɪp]	Degree apprenticeships combine working for a company with studying part-time in university.	Lehrstelle; Ausbildung
		work placement [ˈwɜːk pleɪsmənt]	Were you doing an online search for work placements, or did someone tell you about this website?	Praktikum
	3a	**vocational** [vəʊˈkeɪʃənl]	I went to a vocational college not a university. = employment	beruflich
51	3c	**advisor** [ədˈvaɪzə]	The advisor gives Sammy a takeaway showing him a possible career path. = consultant	Berater(in)
		management [ˈmænɪdʒmənt]	I'm doing an apprenticeship in Horse Care and Management at a riding centre.	Management; Geschäftsführung
		NVQs (national vocational qualifications) [en viː kjuː]	He got his national vocational qualifications or NVQs at a local college.	nationale berufliche Abschlüsse
		permanent [ˈpɜːmənənt]	If you work hard, they might offer you a permanent job. ≠ temporary	permanent; dauerhaft
		to assess [əˈses]	They assess you on practical assignments plus your portfolio. = appraise	beurteilen

Appendix

VOCABULARY

page	exercise	Workshop 2		
		qualified [ˈkwɒlɪfaɪd]	She is a qualified nurse. ≠ unqualified	qualifiziert
		assessor [əˈsesər]	An assessor will watch you and ask you questions about your work. = controller	Gutacher(in)
		computing [kəmˈpjuːtɪŋ]	You don't need a degree to start in computing, you need to be good at programming.	Computing
52	1	**activist** [ˈæktɪvɪst]	The student activists focus on social issues like discrimination.	Aktivist(in)
		firm [fɜːm]	My uncle, who's a lawyer, suggests doing work experience at a law firm. = company	Firma; Kanzlei
		apprentice [əˈprentɪs]	In March, I have an interview for a job as an apprentice software developer. = trainee	Auszubildende(r); Lehrling
		developer [dɪˈveləpə]	I would like to work as a software developer.	Entwickler(in)
		vintage [ˈvɪntɪdʒ]	I like buying vintage clothes, making changes to them and then selling them at the markets.	alt; klassisch
		incubator [ˈɪŋkjubeɪtər]	We're going to apply to a start-up incubator for help.	Inkubator; Unterstützer von Start-ups
53	4a	**au pair** [ˌəʊ ˈpeər]	I worked as an au pair in France during my gap year.	Au-pair
	5	**inner** [ˈɪnər]	Try to listen to your inner voice when making decisions. ≠ outer	innerer
		outer [ˈaʊtər]	How would you describe the protagonist's outer appearance? ≠ inner	Außen...
54	2a	**unpaid** [ˌʌnˈpeɪd]	We are offering an unpaid work experience placement to a school leaver. ≠ paid	unbezahlt
	3b	**otherwise** [ˈʌðəwaɪz]	I must stop playing now, otherwise I'll never finish my homework.	sonst; ansonsten
55	5a	**school leaver** [ˈskuːl liːvər]	Each year over 200,000 school leavers in the UK choose to take a one-year break before starting university. = graduate	Schulabgänger(in)
	5b	**department** [dɪˈpɑːtmənt]	I work in the sales department of a big company.	Abteilung
		publisher [ˈpʌblɪʃə]	I worked in the marketing department of a book publisher.	Verleger(in)
	5c	**motivation** [ˌməʊtɪˈveɪʃn]	Compare the two students' motivations for taking a gap year. = catalyst	Motivation; Begründung

Appendix

VOCABULARY

page	exercise	Workshop 2		
	6a	**extroverted** [ˈekstrəvɜːtɪd]	She is extroverted and likes to be with friends all the time. ≠ introverted	extrovertiert
		chaotic [keɪˈɒtɪk]	The classroom was chaotic after the teacher left the room. ≠ ordered	chaotisch
	6b	**to overlook** [ˌəʊvəˈlʊk]	Read the passage again to see what you may have overlooked.	übersehen
56	1a	**actual** [ˈæktʃuəl]	Whether it's work experience or an actual job, you'll have to apply in writing. = real	richtig; wirklich
		Curriculum Vitae [kəˌrɪkjələm ˈviːtaɪ]	To apply for the job, you need an up-to-date Curriculum Vitae and a cover letter.	Lebenslauf; Vita
		winning [ˈwɪnɪŋ]	This award-winning graphic novel has an exciting mystery plot. ≠ losing	gewinnend
		brief [briːf]	A winning CV should be clear and brief. = concise	kurz
		format [ˈfɔːmæt]	Your CV should have a clear format and structure.	Format
		to discriminate [dɪˈskrɪmɪneɪt]	In some countries, you don't have to give details that could be used to discriminate against you. = disadvantage	unterschiedlich behandeln; diskriminieren
		obliged [əˈblaɪdʒd]	Don't feel obliged to act cheerful when interviewing for a job.	verpflichtet
		headshot [ˈhedʃɒt]	In the UK, you are not obliged to add a headshot to your CV.	Portraitfoto
57	3	**ought to** [ˈɔːt tə]	If you have awards or other achievements, you ought to highlight them in your CV. = should	sollte etw. tun
	4	**theoretically** [ˌθɪəˈretɪkli]	Theoretically, I could begin next week, but I have to organize care for my children first.	theoretisch
		fortunately [ˈfɔːtʃənətli]	Fortunately, stereotypes change with time. ≠ unfortunately	glücklicherweise
		ideally [aɪˈdiːəli]	Ideally, I'd finish the project before leaving this afternoon.	idealerweise
	5a	**overly** [ˈəʊvəli]	He did not feel overly disappointed to have missed the test. ≠ moderately	übermäßig

Appendix

VOCABULARY

page	exercise	Workshop 2		
		cheerful [ˈtʃɪəfl]	Don't feel obliged to act cheerful when you are tired. = happy	fröhlich
		formally [ˈfɔːməli]	If you're not sure, then you ought to dress more formally. ≠ informally	formell
		to **greet** [ɡriːt]	Greet the secretary or the receptionist and introduce yourself.	grüßen
		flowing [ˈfləʊɪŋ]	An interview that is flowing and smooth is good for both participants. ≠ slow	fließend
	5b	**salary** [ˈsæləri]	Only ask about the salary if they offer you the position. = pay	Gehalt; Lohn
		to **tempt** [tempt]	Close the door so you won't be tempted to look at it.	versuchen; locken
58	2	**sociology** [ˌsəʊsiˈɒlədʒi]	I'm doing my A-levels in English, Sociology and Law.	Soziologie
		typist [ˈtaɪpɪst]	My grandmother worked as a typist and taught me to use a typewriter.	Schreibkraft
		transcriber [trænˈskraɪbə]	I have some work experience as a part-time typist and transcriber.	Transkribierer(in)
		universal [ˌjuːnɪˈvɜːsl]	We all have different religions but we have universal love as well.	allgemein; universal
		to **transcribe** [trænˈskraɪb]	Please transcribe this audio file for me.	abschreiben; transkribieren
		competent [ˈkɒmpɪtənt]	I am competent in most office programs. = capable	fähig; kompetent
	3	**legal aid** [ˌliːɡl ˈeɪd]	Amir's uncle is giving him advice about becoming a legal aid lawyer.	Rechtshilfe
		diploma [dɪˈpləʊmə]	If you don't do a law degree, then you'll need to be able to complete a post-graduate diploma in law.	Diplom; Urkunde
59	4	to **schedule** [ˈʃedjuːl]	Let's schedule an interview for next week.	festlegen; vereinbaren
	5a	**motivated** [ˈməʊtɪveɪtɪd]	We are looking for motivated, young people to join our team.	motiviert
		to **assist** [əˈsɪst]	My job is to assist customers who come to the store. = help	unterstützen
		stockroom [ˈstɒkruːm]	The employees usually eat their lunch in the stockroom.	Lagerraum
		lawn [lɔːn]	My sister mows our lawn every Saturday.	Rasen
		hedge [hedʒ]	We look after the lawns, trees and hedges of this beautiful property.	Hecke

Appendix

VOCABULARY

page	exercise	Workshop 2		
60	S1	to **optimize** [ˈɒptɪmaɪz]	Optimize your communication skills learning new strategies. ≠ worsen	optimieren
		besides [bɪˈsaɪdz]	Besides the fact that I can study for it in my hometown, I think graphic design is the perfect job for me.	außerdem
		arty [ˈɑːti]	I've always been the arty type and like to go to museums.	gewollt künstlerisch
		to **design** [dɪˈzaɪn]	We've also designed T-shirts with our logo.	planen
		graphic [ˈɡræfɪk]	I like the challenge of working with digital texts and graphics.	Graphik
		visually [ˈvɪʒuəli]	I love designing things that are visually interesting and useful.	optisch; visuell
61	S1	**evaluation** [ɪˌvæljuˈeɪʃn]	I got a pay raise after my evaluation at work.	Bewertung
	TIP	**verbal** [ˈvɜːbl]	Find examples of non-verbal strategies Jackie uses when she's explaining things to Amir.	verbal; mündlich
	S2a	**disadvantaged** [ˌdɪsədˈvɑːntɪdʒd]	I'm very enthusiastic about helping disadvantaged people. ≠ advantaged	benachteiligt
	S2b	**basis** [ˈbeɪsɪs]	Check unknown words in order to understand their literal meaning as a basis for interpretation.	Grundlage; Basis
		humanitarian [hjuːˌmænɪˈteəriən]	Some of my friends have gone on to work in humanitarian law.	humanitär
		defence [dɪˈfens]	Some lawyers specialize in criminal defence.	Verteidigung
		pro bono [ˌprəʊ ˈbəʊnəʊ]	My law firm does work in criminal defence on a pro bono basis. = without compensation	ehrenamtlich; kostenlos
	S3a	**observer** [əbˈzɜːvə]	Take turns as a candidate interviewing for a job, an interviewer and an observer.	Beobachter(in)
		to **operate** [ˈɒpəreɪt]	At work I help to operate a ride and serve guests their lunch. ❗ Fr. 'opérer'	bedienen; operieren

Appendix

VOCABULARY

page	exercise	Workshop 2		
62		**The world of work**		
		applicant [ˈæplɪkənt]	Bewerber(in); Anmelder(in)	
		apprentice [əˈprentɪs]	Auszubildende(r); Lehrling	
		apprenticeship [əˈprentɪʃɪp]	Lehrstelle; Ausbildung	
		contractor [kənˈtræktə]	Auftragnehmer(in)	
		economy [ɪˈkɒnəmi]	Ökonomie; Wirtschaft	
		employee [ɪmˈplɔɪiː]	Angestellte(r)	
		employer [ɪmˈplɔɪə]	Arbeitgeber(in)	
		enterprise [ˈentəpraɪz]	Unternehmen	
		entrepreneur [ˌɒntrəprəˈnɜː]	Unternehmer(in)	
		freelance [ˈfriːlɑːns]	freiberuflich	
		freelancer [ˈfriːlɑːnsə]	Freiberufler(in)	
		gig economy [ɡɪɡ ɪˈkɒnəmi]	*In einer Gig-Economy gibt es keine festen Angestellten, die Arbeitskräfte werden für Einzelaufträge (Gigs) bezahlt.*	
		intern [ɪnˈtɜːn]	Praktikant(in); Volontär(in)	
		internship [ˈɪntɜːnʃɪp]	Praktikum	
		job hopping [dʒɒb ˈhɒpɪŋ]	wiederholter Stellenwechsel	
		letter of reference [ˌletə əv ˈrefrəns]	Referenzschreiben; Empfehlungsschreiben	
		menial [ˈmiːniəl]	untergeordnet; nieder	
		overtime [ˈəʊvətaɪm]	Überstunden	
		to quit [kwɪt], quit, quit	kündigen	
		salary [ˈsæləri]	Gehalt; Lohn	
		sector [ˈsektə]	Bereich	
		self-employed [ˌself ɪmˈplɔɪd]	selbstständig	
		to shadow sb. [ˈʃædəʊ]	bei jmdm. hospitieren	
		sideline [ˈsaɪdlaɪn]	Nebenberuf	
		start-up [ˈstɑːtʌp]	junges Unternehmen	
		traineeship [ˌtreɪˈniːʃɪp]	Praktikumsplatz	
		unemployed [ˌʌnɪmˈplɔɪd]	arbeitslos	
		unpaid [ˌʌnˈpeɪd]	unbezahlt	
		venture [ˈventʃə]	Unternehmen	
		vocational [vəʊˈkeɪʃənl]	beruflich	
		workforce [ˈwɜːkfɔːs]	Arbeitskräfte	
2a		forum [ˈfɔːrəm]	*Read the text from an online forum and summarize the main points.*	Forum
		gig [ɡɪɡ]	*The gig economy allows you to plan your own work schedule and be independent.* = job	Gig; Auftritt
		pandemic [pænˈdemɪk]	*I missed a lot of school during the Corona pandemic.*	Pandemie
		loser [ˈluːzər]	*There are winners and losers in all crisis situations.* ≠ winner	Verlierer(in)
		to deliver [dɪˈlɪvə]	*Nowadays people have more things delivered than ever before.* = transfer	liefern

Appendix

VOCABULARY

page	exercise	**Workshop 2**		
		to **blur** [blɜːr]	The picture was blurred and I couldn't see very much. ≠ clarify	verschwimmen
		boundary [ˈbaʊndri]	The boundary between work and home life is not so clear any more. = border	Grenze
		to **reassess** [ˌriːəˈses]	We have to reassess our work-life balance. = reevaluate	einschätzen
		division [dɪˈvɪʒn]	Right up until the 1980s, there was a clear division between work and free time. ≠ combination	Trennung; Teilung
		norm [nɔːm]	Working long hours seems to be the norm these days.	Regel; Standard
		job hopping [ˈdʒɒb hɒpɪŋ]	Job hopping is changing jobs frequently.	wiederholter Stellenwechsel
		contractor [kənˈtræktə]	Many companies hire independent contractors for short-term work.	Auftragnehmer(in)
		consultant [kənˈsʌltənt]	Gig work can range from well-paid consultants to on-demand drivers.	Berater(in)
		to **specialize** [ˈspeʃəlaɪz]	These specialized apps let freelancers choose when and where to work.	sich spezialisieren
	3	**regulation** [ˌregjuˈleɪʃn]	Be sure to read the rules and regulations before beginning. = rule	Vorschrift; Regulation
63	4	**wisdom tooth** [ˈwɪzdəm]	Humans have four wisdom teeth. ≠ ignorance	Weisheitszahn
		dentist [ˈdentɪst]	My tooth hurts, so I am going to the dentist.	Zahnarzt; Zahnärztin
	5a	**manufacturing** [ˌmænjuˈfæktʃərɪŋ]	Many jobs were seen as jobs for life, especially if you worked in manufacturing.	Produktion; Herstellung
		banking [ˈbæŋkɪŋ]	Most jobs are in service industries, like the health service, education, banking, financial services and tourism.	Banking; Bankwesen
		financial [faɪˈnænʃl]	We may not have the financial means to help, but by offering support we can make a real difference.	finanziell
		breadwinner [ˈbredwɪnə]	The man worked away from home and was the main breadwinner. = provider	Ernährer(in); Brotverdiener(in)
		housewife [ˈhaʊswaɪf] , **housewives** [ˈhaʊswaɪvz]	When I was growing up, my mum was a housewife. = homemaker	Hausfrau

Appendix

VOCABULARY

page	exercise	Workshop 2		
		tech-orientated [tekɔːrientɪd]	The workplace used to be a lot less tech-orientated in the 70s, for example, email didn't exist.	techorientiert
		remotely [rɪˈməʊtli]	With the internet, smart phones, and online file sharing, a lot of employees can work remotely.	aus der Ferne
		to commute [kəˈmjuːt]	In the past, employees would commute to work every day – now they can work anywhere.	pendeln
		self-employed [ˌself ɪmˈplɔɪd]	There are lots more self-employed people than there used to be. = freelance	selbständig
		stable [ˈsteɪbl]	Gig work doesn't give you a stable income like a permanent job does. = constant	stabil; sicher
	5c	**to handwrite** [ˈhændraɪt]	I like to handwrite letters I send to people.	mit der Hand schreiben
		freelancer [ˈfriːlɑːnsə]	The number of freelancers have increased in the past years.	Freiberufler(in)
	6	**spiky** [ˈspaɪki]	When I was a kid, I used to have long hair, but now it's short and spiky.	stachelig; spitz
64	2a	**heaven** [ˈhevn]	Do you believe there is a heaven? ≠ hell	Himmel
		hell [hel]	It was so hot, it was like hell. = heaven	Hölle
		tax-payer [ˈtækspeɪər]	Some people complain that the British Royal Family costs the tax-payer too much.	Steuerzahler(in)
		privilege [ˈprɪvəlɪdʒ]	I have lived a life of privilege and have never had a job.	Privileg; Recht
		luxury [ˈlʌkʃəri]	They lead a life in luxury, so why not make them pay their way. = opulence	Luxus
		royal [ˈrɔɪəl]	Royals must have an all-black outfit packed when they travel.	königlich
		patron [ˈpeɪtrən]	A royal patron is very helpful for a charity.	Schirmherr(in)
		publicity [pʌbˈlɪsəti]	Somebody famous gives a charity important publicity.	Publizität
		protocol [ˈprəʊtəkɒl]	Protocol doesn't allow heirs to the throne to express political opinions.	Protokoll
		nail [neɪl]	When he showed his hands, his nails were dirty.	Nagel; Fingernagel
		varnish [ˈvɑːnɪʃ]	She's got pink nail varnish.	Lack
		monarch [ˈmɒnək]	The monarch is the head of the royal family.	Monarch(in); Herrscher(in)

Appendix

VOCABULARY

page	exercise	Workshop 2		
		funeral [ˈfjuːnərəl]	Military uniforms are worn at weddings and funerals. ⚠ Lat. 'funus (-neris)' (n)	Beerdigung
		outdated [ˌaʊtˈdeɪtɪd]	The rules seem outdated, but there is good reason for them. ≠ current	veraltet
		affection [əˈfekʃn]	They never show affection in public. = care	Zuneigung
		to propose [prəˈpəʊz]	My mother's boyfriend proposed, so they will get married.	einen Heiratsantrag machen
		marriage [ˈmærɪdʒ]	They had a long and successful marriage. ⚠ Fr. 'mariage' (m.)	Ehe
		outfit [ˈaʊtfɪt]	Royals must have an all-black outfit packed when they travel. = clothes	Kleider; Outfit
		heir [eər]	Royal heirs are not allowed to travel together.	Erbe/Erbin
	2b	**throne** [θrəʊn]	Who is on the British throne right now? = the chair of a queen or king	Thron
		to permit [pəˈmɪt]	You aren't permitted to drink alcohol if you are underage. = allow ⚠ Lat. 'permittere (permitto, permisi, permissum)' = to permit; to allow	erlauben
	3a	**tuition** [tjuˈɪʃn]	We have to pay tuition fees at university. ⚠ used in the singular	Studiengebühr(en)
		aware [əˈweər]	Young people today are very socially aware. ≠ unaware	bewusst
		passionately [ˈpæʃənətli]	We feel passionately about fighting climate change and helping the poor.	leidenschaftlich
		proportion [prəˈpɔːʃn]	The proportion of young people donating money to charities was much greater in the past.	Anteil
		to struggle [ˈstrʌgl]	It's hard to give money to others when you're struggling to survive yourself.	sich anstrengen; sich bemühen
		loan [ləʊn]	As a university student you have to take out loans to help with living costs.	Darlehen; Leihgabe
		grant [grɑːnt]	Students get grants from the government to study. = scholarship	Förderung; Zuschuss

Appendix

VOCABULARY

page	exercise	Workshop 2		
		secure [sɪˈkjʊə]	In the past, people had secure jobs, but they don't anymore. = safe ≠ insecure ⓘ Lat. 'securitas, -atis' (f.) = security	sicher
		stability [stəˈbɪləti]	Some people find secure jobs with stability boring. ≠ instability	Stabilität
		awareness [əˈweənəs]	At my college we campaign to raise awareness about different social issues like food poverty. = understanding	Bewusstsein
		gang [gæŋ]	He became a member of a motorcycle gang when he was quite young.	Bande; Gang
65	5a	**annual** [ˈænjuəl]	This is an annual event for young people interested in charity work.	jährlich
		stigma [ˈstɪgmə]	There is a real stigma to having to go up for a free school meal, and that's embarrassing for children.	Stigma
		cold [kəʊld]	If you don't get enough sleep, you'll have colds all the time in winter.	Erkältung
		diabetes [ˌdaɪəˈbiːtiːz]	If you eat a lot of meat, you could get diabetes.	Diabetes
		to attack [əˈtæk]	Kids are often attacked with their own knife.	angreifen
		hashtag [ˈhæʃtæg]	We created a hashtag and went on social media to help raise awareness.	Hashtag
	6a	**jobless** [ˈdʒɒbləs]	Our organization helps the jobless find work. = unemployed	arbeitslos
		unemployed [ˌʌnɪmˈplɔɪd]	Families can be under a lot of pressure when one of the adults is unemployed. = jobless	arbeitslos
		deaf [def]	The deaf are often disadvantaged in our society. = without hearing	Gehörlose
		privileged [ˈprɪvəlɪdʒd]	We are privileged and should help people in need.	privilegiert
66	1	**intern** [ɪnˈtɜːn]	I shared a flat with other interns who were working with us.	Praktikant(in); Volontär(in)
		independently [ˌɪndɪˈpendəntli]	All the interns who came lived and worked independently.	selbstständig; unabhängig
		to shadow [ˈʃædəʊ]	I shadowed a doctor at one of Dublin's top hospitals.	auf Schritt und Tritt begleiten; beschatten
		clinic [ˈklɪnɪk]	She let me watch her working in the clinic.	Klinik
		surgery [ˈsɜːdʒəri]	She held a surgery three times a week.	Sprechstunde; Praxis

Appendix

VOCABULARY

page	exercise	Workshop 2		
		insight [ˈɪnsaɪt]	Having already done their first year at university, other students gave me some useful insights. = observation	Einsicht
67	2b	to shorten [ˈʃɔːtn]	Shorten your text by combining some of the sentences. = make shorter	kürzen; abkürzen
	4	thoroughly [ˈθʌrəli]	After I spent eight wonderful weeks in Ireland, I can thoroughly recommend doing an internship there. = really	völlig; durchaus
		genuinely [ˈdʒenjuːnli]	Looking back, I can genuinely say that my internship gave me more confidence. = really	echt
	5a	hype [haɪp]	I want to feel the energy, I want that hype.	Hype
		to appreciate [əˈpriːʃieɪt]	You guys better appreciate this great meal we made. ≠ be critical ❗ Fr. 'apprécier'	anerkennen; schätzen
		psychology [saɪˈkɒlədʒi]	While working for a children's charity, I decided to study psychology.	Psychologie
		transition [trænˈzɪʃn]	Internships are the best way of preparing for the transition from being a student to the workplace.	Wechsel; Übergang
		psychologist [saɪˈkɒlədʒɪst]	Understanding different cultures prepares me for a career as a psychologist or a non-profit worker.	Psychologe; Psychologin
		paragliding [ˈpærəɡlaɪdɪŋ]	I tried things like paragliding and shark cage diving – that was scary.	Gleitschirmfliegen
		skyline [ˈskaɪlaɪn]	The skyline with those high rises just looks amazing.	Skyline
		roommate [ˈruːmˌmeɪt]	After work and on weekends, I explored the city with my roommates. ❗ BE = flatmate	Mitbewohner(in)
68	2	argumentative [ˌɑːɡjuˈmentətɪv]	Try to understand the message in this argumentative article.	argumentativ
	TIP	whereas [ˌweərˈæz]	Boys chose technical careers whereas girls went more into arts and literature.	während
		furthermore [ˌfɜːðəˈmɔːr]	Furthermore, school career services tend to guide girls towards 'female' careers.	außerdem; weiterhin
		to indicate [ˈɪndɪkeɪt]	Which points indicate the author's personal view?	angeben; zeigen

Appendix

VOCABULARY

page	exercise	Workshop 2		
	2a	**STEM (science, technology, engineering, mathematics)** [stem]	Once girls know how rewarding STEM careers can be, there will be more women in those fields.	MINT (Mathematik, Informatik, Naturwissenschaft und Technik)
		to tend to [tend]	Children tend to learn better when they have a lot of time to play.	zu etw. neigen; zu etw. tendieren
		to stereotype [ˈsteriətaɪp]	Gender stereotyping leads to girls playing with dolls and boys playing with toy cars.	stereotypisieren
		upbringing [ˈʌpbrɪŋɪŋ]	Upbringing and education have a lot to do with career choices.	Erziehung
		to discourage [dɪsˈkʌrɪdʒ]	Parents may discourage girls from studying science or maths.	entmutigen
69	4	**entrepreneur** [ˌɒntrəprəˈnɜː]	With her job search platform, she won a prize for best young entrepreneur.	Unternehmer(in)
		finalist [ˈfaɪnəlɪst]	There were two finalists in the last round of the competition.	Finalist(in)
		PhD (Doctor of Philosophy) [ˌpiː eɪtʃ ˈdiː]	Wendy gained a first-class degree and PhD in Early Childhood Learning.	Doktortitel; Doktor der Philosophie
		potential [pəˈtenʃl]	She wants every child to receive a high-quality education in order to reach their full potential. = possibility	Potenzial
		workload [ˈwɜːkləʊd]	Many people feel that they have too big of a workload.	Arbeitsbelastung; Arbeitslast
		paperwork [ˈpeɪpəwɜːk]	Teachers are burned out from their huge workloads and mountains of paperwork.	Schreibarbeit
		electronical [ɪˌlekˈtrɒnɪkl]	He is taking his Electrical & Electronical Engineering degree.	elektronisch
		AI (artificial intelligence) [ˌeɪ ˈaɪ]	The platform's AI algorithms empower school-leavers to choose the right course.	künstliche Intelligenz
		algorithm [ˈælgərɪðəm]	They have developed an algorithm to make the computer process faster.	Algorithmus
		to empower [ɪmˈpaʊə]	They hope to empower school-leavers to choose the right course. ≠ deny	stärken; ermächtigen
	5	**founder** [ˈfaʊndər]	She is the founder of the very successful company.	Gründer(in)
		stationery [ˈsteɪʃənri]	The stationery company said people used more paper and pens during the pandemic.	Schreibwaren
		gelateria [ˌdʒeləˈtɪəriə]	I founded a gelateria and try not to eat too much of my product.	italienisches Eiscafé
70	S1	**forklift** [ˌfɔːklɪft]	A forklift is a small electric vehicle that can lift heavy boxes and things.	Gabelstapler
		thermostat [ˈθɜːməstæt]	Use the thermostat to turn up the heat.	Thermostat; Temperaturregler

Appendix

VOCABULARY

page	exercise	Workshop 2		
		induction [ɪnˈdʌkʃn]	I got an induction on my first day.	Einführung
	S2a	**hole punch** [həʊl pʌntʃ]	I need to use the hole punch before putting the papers away.	Locher
		dispenser [dɪˈspensə]	That's a water dispenser, if you are thirsty.	Spender
		to dismiss [dɪsˈmɪs]	Jack has been dismissed from his job. = let go	entlassen; wegschicken
		to fire [ˈfaɪə]	My boss fired me from my job. = make redundant	entlassen
		shopping rota [ˈʃɒpɪŋ ˈrəʊtə]	We have a shopping rota for tea, coffee and milk.	Einkaufsdienst
		breakout area [ˈbreɪkaʊt ˈeəriə]	You can eat your lunch in the breakout area.	Aufenthaltsraum
		workspace [ˈwɜːkspeɪs]	There're different workspaces you can use, some for working quietly and others for meetings.	Arbeitsbereich
		lanyard [ˈlænjɑːd]	The best way to carry your company ID with you is to clip it onto a lanyard.	Umhängeband; Kordel
		strip [strɪp]	You will get a strip round your neck with a plastic card.	Band; Streifen
		holder [ˈhəʊldər]	Your card is in a plastic holder.	Halter
		client [ˈklaɪənt]	Most of our clients are not very wealthy. = customer	Mandant(in); Kunde/Kundin
		microwave [ˈmaɪkrəweɪv]	The microwave is good for heating up food quickly.	Mikrowelle
		timer [ˈtaɪmər]	Select the function and set the timer for how long it should run.	Timer; Zeituhr
	S2b	**pardon** [ˈpɑːdn]	Pardon, may I ask the time?	Verzeihung; Entschuldigung
71	S1	**e-scooter** [ˈiːskuːtə]	In cities there are e-scooters for rent.	E-Roller
		yoga [ˈjəʊgə]	To relax I go to yoga class.	Yoga
		pad [pæd]	If you need an extra pad of paper, look in the supply room.	Notizblock
		extinguisher [ɪkˈstɪŋgwɪʃər]	The fire extinguisher is in the closet.	Löscher
		printer [ˈprɪntər]	My new printer came with toner cartridges.	Drucker
	S2a	**toner cartridge** [ˈtəʊnə ˈkɑːtrɪdʒ]	My printer seems to use a lot of toner cartridges.	Tonerkartusche
		to instruct [ɪnˈstrʌkt]	We were instructed on where the first aid kit is and how to use it. = teach	einweisen
		cabinet [ˈkæbɪnət]	In case of fire, the fire extinguishers are in that cabinet over there.	Schrank; Kabinett
	S3a	**to paraphrase** [ˈpærəfreɪz]	Which four statements paraphrase what Nicki Ferris is saying? = interpret	umschreiben

two hundred and seven **207**

Appendix

VOCABULARY

page	exercise	Workshop 2		
78	1a	**economics** [ˌiːkəˈnɒmɪks]	I'm not quite sure what to do before I start my degree in economics.	Wirtschaftswissenschaften
	1b	**panel** [ˈpænl]	We have installed more than 5,000 solar panels in the country.	Paneel; Platte
79	3	**freelance** [ˈfriːlɑːns]	My name's Adam Jameson and I work as a freelance journalist.	freiberuflich
		journalism [ˈdʒɜːnəlɪzəm]	I think that good reporting is really important, so journalism is definitely the future for me.	Journalismus
80	4a	**amusing** [əˈmjuːzɪŋ]	Other volunteers seem to find my lack of knowledge amusing. = funny	amüsant; lustig
81	2	**finance** [ˈfaɪnæns]	I want to work in finance once I finish my degree.	Finanzwirtschaft
	4	**mechanical** [məˈkænɪkl]	I am doing A-levels in maths and science at college since I have always been interested in mechanical things.	mechanisch
82	6	**hourly** [ˈaʊəli]	Working here you can make a good hourly rate plus tips.	stündlich; Stunden-
	7a	**bonus** [ˈbəʊnəs]	My dad will get a bonus that depends on sales.	Bonus
	7b	**colleague** [ˈkɒliːg]	My colleagues were really helpful and supportive.	Kollege; Kollegin; Mitarbeiter(in)
	8a	**typewriter** [ˈtaɪpraɪtə]	My grandmother wrote on a typewriter, not a computer.	Schreibmaschine
83	9b	**inexperienced** [ˌɪnɪkˈspɪəriənst]	I was inexperienced and needed someone to give me advice. ≠ experienced	unerfahren
	10	**dedicated** [ˈdedɪkeɪtɪd]	A lot of charities in the UK are dedicated to helping the homeless. = devoted	engagiert
		payday [ˈpeɪdeɪ]	That's why experts say that lots of people are just one payday away from becoming homeless.	Zahltag

page	exercise	Workshop 3		
88	1	**elsewhere** [ˌelsˈweər]	20% of Canadians were born elsewhere and immigrated to Canada.	woanders
		inclusion [ɪnˈkluːʒn]	Inclusion is making diversity in schools work. ≠ exclusion	Inklusion
		executive [ɪgˈzekjətɪv]	He is an executive at a large global company.	Führungskraft
		dull [dʌl]	What a dull and pointless life it would be if everyone was the same.	uninteressant; langweilig
		Islamic [ɪzˈlæmɪk]	My grandmother knows some beautiful Islamic poems.	islamisch

Appendix

VOCABULARY

page	exercise	Workshop 3		
89		proverb [ˈprɒvɜːb]	There is a lot to think about in old proverbs.	Sprichwort
		grand [ɡrænd]	This is the grand shopping street in our city. = impressive	grandios; großartig
		tolerance [ˈtɒlərəns]	My generation shows more tolerance to people who are not like us. ≠ intolerance	Toleranz
		to deny [dɪˈnaɪ]	We cannot deny that some people are treated differently because of race. ≠ admit	leugnen
		racism [ˈreɪsɪzəm]	But we cannot deny that racism exists today, as it did in the past.	Rassismus
	2a	gay [ɡeɪ]	My mother is gay and married to a woman.	schwul; *früher:* fröhlich
		discriminated [dɪˈskrɪmɪneɪt]	I've been discriminated against because of my disability.	benachteiligt
	3a	possession [pəˈzeʃn]	A sweater my grandma made for me is my favourite possession.	Besitz
	YT	to deal with [diːl wɪð], dealt, dealt [delt, delt]	Discuss the best ways of dealing with youth crime. = cope	umgehen
		graph [ɡrɑːf]	Describe and analyse the information from the line graph.	Graph; Diagramm
90	1a	blended [ˈblendɪd]	Two parents with different children form a blended family.	gemischt
		unit [ˈjuːnɪt]	My grandma, my mom and my brother are my entire family unit. ≠ part	Einheit
		sex [seks]	We usually speak about the female and the male sex.	Geschlecht; Sex
		to legalize [ˈliːɡəlaɪz]	Same-sex marriage, which was legalized in Canada in 2005, has led to even more family diversity.	legalisieren
		census [ˈsensəs]	The last census shows how much families have changed.	Bevölkerungszählung; Befragung
	1b	to divorce [dɪˈvɔːs]	My parents divorced when I was a kid.	sich scheiden lassen
		to split up [ˌsplɪtˈʌp], split, split	We were both upset about Mom and Dad splitting up.	sich trennen
		uptight [ˌʌpˈtaɪt]	It's a very easy-going family, not very uptight, and very loving. ≠ easy-going	verklemmt
		to bully [ˈbʊli]	No one wanted to play with me because they were afraid they'd be bullied like me. = intimidate	mobben
91	2a	to separate [ˈsepəreɪt]	His parents are separated, but he hopes they will get back together. ≠ attached	(sich) trennen

VOCABULARY

Workshop 3

page	exercise			
	2b	**extended** [ɪkˈstendɪd]	Children who grow up in an extended family often have close contact to their grandparents.	erweitert
		duty [ˈdjuːti]	We share household duties so that nobody has to do it all alone.	Pflicht
		union [ˈjuːniən]	Mixed unions involve couples of different ethnic or racial groups. = association	Union; Bund
	3a	**to emigrate** [ˈemɪgreɪt]	They wanted to give their daughter a better life, so they emigrated to Canada. ≠ immigrate	auswandern
		to colonize [ˈkɒlənaɪz]	Guyana was colonized by the British and the official language is English. = settle ❗ Fr. 'coloniser'	kolonisieren
		to descend from [dɪˈsend frəm]	His family are directly descended from African slaves.	von jmdm. abstammen
		to envy [ˈenvi]	When I was younger, I used to envy my friends' families a lot.	beneiden
	3b	**presenter** [prɪˈzentə]	According to the presenter, what difficulties do immigrants face?	Moderator(in)
92	2	**insane** [ɪnˈseɪn]	I always tidy my room up eventually – usually when it starts to drive me insane. = crazy	verrückt; wahnsinnig
		to blame [bleɪm]	If you don't do what your mother asks you to do, you can't blame her for getting angry. = accuse	jmdm. Vorwürfe machen
		hairstyle [ˈheəstaɪl]	When I was younger, I was interested in clothes and my hairstyle.	Frisur
	TIP	**frustrating** [frʌˈstreɪtɪŋ]	The situation is frustrating because I can't win.	frustrierend
		compromise [ˈkɒmprəmaɪz]	Try to reach a compromise, an agreement that works for everyone.	Kompromiss
	3c	**poll** [pəʊl]	Conduct a poll or an online survey to find which issues are most common. = survey	Umfrage
	4	**genderless** [ˈdʒendələs]	Many parents dress their children in genderless clothing.	geschlechtslos
		bias [ˈbaɪəs]	A lot of gender bias still exists in the world of work.	Voreingenommenheit
	5	**expectation** [ˌekspekˈteɪʃn]	We have great expectations for the future.	Erwartung
		to challenge [ˈtʃælɪndʒ]	What gender expectations and roles are being challenged?	herausfordern

Appendix

VOCABULARY

page	exercise	Workshop 3		
		to **reinforce** [ˌriːɪnˈfɔːs]	Consider how gender roles are learned and reinforced. = add to	verstärken; bekräftigen
93		to **dictate** [dɪkˈteɪt]	Did gender dictate who you are and what you can do?	bestimmen
		carer [ˈkeərər]	Parents or carers spend time helping their children with their school work.	Betreuer(in)
		gendered [ˈdʒendəd]	Chores aren't gendered in my family – dad cleans the house and mom mows the lawn.	geschlechtsspezifisch
		to **mow** [məʊ]	We need to mow the grass before it rains.	mähen
		to **determine** [dɪˈtɜːmɪn]	Gender doesn't determine what tasks people do. = decide	ausmachen; bestimmen
		decade [ˈdekeɪd]	These high school sweethearts were still together decades later.	Dekade; Jahrzehnt
		currently [ˈkʌrəntli]	He is currently on hormone-blocker medication.	derzeit; gerade
		to **conform** [kənˈfɔːm]	There's so much pressure to conform to the standards we see in the media.	anpassen
		stereotypical [ˌsteriəˈtɪpɪkl]	Many parents don't want their children to conform to stereotypical ideas about life.	stereotypisch
		unisex [ˈjuːnɪseks]	Many parents dress their children in unisex clothing.	Unisex-; nicht geschlechtsspezifisch
	CC	**lesbian** [ˈlezbiən]	Lesbian couples have more rights now than they did only a decade ago.	lesbisch
		bisexual [ˌbaɪˈsekʃuəl]	Bisexual people are attracted to men and women.	bisexuell
		transgender [trænzˈdʒendər]	Transgender people are fighting for their rights around the world.	transsexuell
		queer [kwɪər]	Anyone who doesn't identify as heterosexual or 'straight' is considered 'queer'.	schwul; queer
		heterosexual [ˌhetərəˈsekʃuəl]	Heterosexual people are referred to as 'straight'.	heterosexuell
		straight [streɪt]	Someone who is 'straight' is romantically interested in people of a different sex.	heterosexuell
		intersex [ˈɪntəseks]	Intersex people have sex organs or hormones that don't match their gender.	Intersex
		hormone [ˈhɔːməʊn]	Hormones are chemical substances that influence how the cells in your body function.	Hormon
		asexual [ˌeɪˈsekʃuəl]	Asexual people are not interested in sex.	asexuell

Appendix

VOCABULARY

page	exercise	Workshop 3		
	7a	**BMXing** [ˌbiː em ˈeksɪŋ]	I like skateboarding, BMXing and playing on my Xbox.	BMX-Rad fahren
		to muck around [mʌk əˈraʊnd]	I like mucking around with my friends after school.	Herumblödeln
		peace [piːs]	In the future I think I'd like to start in the peace service. ≠ war ❗ Fr. 'paix' (f.), Lat. 'pax, pacis' (f.)	Frieden
		armed [ɑːmd]	The man was armed when he stole the money.	bewaffnet
		blocker [blɒkər]	Hormone blockers stop the production of hormones.	Blocker
		to conceal [kənˈsiːl]	He is trying to conceal the note he's reading while the teacher is speaking. = hide	verbergen
		to trap [træp]	Tayler told her that he felt like a boy trapped in a girl's body.	fangen
		tomboy [ˈtɒmbɔɪ]	I thought that I just had a bit of a tomboy, a wild girl.	burschikoses Mädchen; Wildfang
		to disgust [dɪsˈgʌst]	My daughter is disgusted by meat.	ekeln; empören
	7b	**trans** [trænz]	Tayler is a 14-year-old trans boy from Wales.	trans…
		medication [ˌmedɪˈkeɪʃn]	He is currently on hormone-blocker medication.	Medikation
		puberty [ˈpjuːbəti]	The medication stops puberty from starting.	Pubertät
94	1	**pressured** [ˈpreʃəd]	Think of a few situations in which teenagers can feel pressured by their peers to do something.	unter Druck gesetzt
		harmless [ˈhɑːmləs]	Drinking even a little bit of alcohol is not harmless.	harmlos; unbedenklich
		theft [θeft]	He has been on probabtion before for theft.	Diebstahl
	2	**dumb** [dʌm]	We notice when other people do something dumb, but not always when we do it. = stupid	blöd; dumm
		wimp [wɪmp]	She called me a wimp, but I stuck to my decision not to do something dangerous.	Feigling; Schwachmat
		alike [əˈlaɪk]	At school a lot of kids dress alike, so we do influence each other.	ebenso
		awkward [ˈɔːkwəd]	There's a girl at school who's socially a bit awkward. ≠ artful	ungeschickt; unbeholfen

Appendix

VOCABULARY

page	exercise	Workshop 3		
		to **comfort** [ˈkʌmfət]	I also talked to the girl myself and tried to comfort her.	trösten
		snitch [snɪtʃ]	They say I'm a snitch because I told a teacher about their plan.	Verräter(in)
		to **resist** [rɪˈzɪst]	Analyse how they both resisted pressure from their friends.	widerstehen
95	3b	**emphasis** [ˈemfəsɪs]	How can she add more emphasis to these sentences?	Betonung
		risk [rɪsk]	If you never take risks, you never make mistakes. ⚠ Fr. 'risque' (m.)	Risiko; Gefahr
	4a	**sweaty** [ˈsweti]	You don't want to wear someone's sweaty old T-shirt.	verschwitzt
		sweetheart [ˈswiːtɑːt]	Thank you so much, you're a sweetheart!	Liebste(r); Liebes
		to **chill** [tʃɪl]	I was tired, so I went home and chilled. = relax	chillen; sich entspannen
		flea market [fliː ˈmɑːkɪt]	Leo and I went to the flea market and I found this cool denim jacket.	Flohmarkt; Trödelmarkt
		episode [ˈepɪsəʊd]	The last episode of your podcast was better.	Folge
	5	**loyal** [ˈlɔɪəl]	I am so happy to have a loyal friend since kindergarten. ≠ disloyal	treu
		fake [feɪk]	One loyal friend is worth more than a thousand fake ones.	falsch; unecht
96	2a	**meaningful** [ˈmiːnɪŋfl]	A lot of adults don't believe that teen relationships can be meaningful. ≠ insignificant	sinnvoll
		lust [lʌst]	There is a difference between love and lust.	Lust
		to **date** [deɪt]	I want to find a serious partner, but until then I'll keep dating.	mit jmdm. ausgehen
		mature [məˈtʃʊər]	These children look very mature for their age. ≠ immature	reif; mündig
97	3a	to **hand** [hænd]	She handed me the list of groceries we needed for dinner.	reichen
		tissue [ˈtɪʃuː]	Do you have any tissues? I have a cold.	Taschentuch
		nosebleed [ˈnəʊzbliːd]	He had a nosebleed and couldn't play in the game.	Nasenbluten
		to **shrug** [ʃrʌg]	She shrugged and went off.	Achseln zucken
	TIP	**mood** [muːd]	The mood of the song is very happy and makes me want to dance.	Stimmung

Appendix

VOCABULARY

page	exercise	Workshop 3		
98	S1	**remarriage** [ˌriːˈmærɪdʒ]	The percentage of children living in a remarriage has increased.	Wiederverheiratung
		to increase [ɪnˈkriːs]	The labor force has greatly increased since 1975. ≠ decrease	erhöhen
		to decrease [dɪˈkriːs]	Does gender equality increase or decrease in our country? = decline	fallen; zurückgehen
		to decline [dɪˈklaɪn]	A minority of people think that violence has declined. = decrease	verfallen
		dramatic [drəˈmætɪk]	The analysis of dramatic texts differs from that of novels or poems.	dramatisch
		considerably [kənˈsɪdərəbli]	After my mom got married again, our family life changed considerably.	deutlich; umfangreich
		to survey [ˈsɜːveɪ]	Most countries surveyed believe individual rights are important.	befragen
		minority [maɪˈnɒrəti]	Only a minority do not know anyone who has been bullied online. ≠ majority	Minderheit
	TIP	**to level off** [ˈlevl ɒf]	The chart shows that the number of deaths have levelled off recently.	einpendeln
		peak [piːk]	In 2000, sales reached a peak and we haven't sold as much since.	Gipfel; Spitzen…
		slight [slaɪt]	There has been a slight increase in the number of reported cases.	gering; leicht
99	S1a	**participation** [pɑːˌtɪsɪˈpeɪʃn]	Rates of participation of mothers in the work force continues to increase.	Beteiligung
		preschool [ˈpriːskuːl]	Children learn important social skills in preschool.	Kindergarten; Vorschule
	S3a	**to strengthen** [ˈstreŋkθn]	In the last decade, family ties have strengthened in our country. = become stronger ≠ weaken	stärker werden; stärker machen

Appendix

VOCABULARY

page	exercise			
100		**Workshop 3**		

The law

to **accuse** [əˈkjuːz]		beschuldigen; anklagen
aggravated assault [ˌægrəveɪtɪd əˈsɔːlt]		schwere Körperverletzung
amends [əˈmendz]		Wiedergutmachung; Schadensersatz
assault [əˈsɔːlt]		Angriff; Überfall
caution [ˈkɔːʃn]		Verwarnung; Warnung
to **charge (with)** [tʃɑːdʒ]		anklagen (wegen)
client [ˈklaɪənt]		Mandant(in); Kunde / Kundin
compensation [ˌkɒmpenˈseɪʃn]		Entschädigung
to **convict** [kənˈvɪkt]		verurteilen
conviction [kənˈvɪkʃn]		Verurteilung
counselling [ˈkaʊnsəlɪŋ]		Beratung
criminal record [ˌkrɪmɪnəl ˈrekɔːd]		Vorstrafenregister
custodial sentence [kʌˈstəʊdiəl ˈsentəns]		Freiheitsstrafe
custody [ˈkʌstədi]		Verwahrung; Schutz; Sorgerecht
defence [dɪˈfens]		Verteidigung
guard [ɡɑːd]		Sicherheitsbeamter(in); Wächter(in)
to **hold accountable** [həʊld əˈkaʊntəbl], **held, held** [həld, həld]		zur Rechenschaft ziehen
joyride [ˈdʒɔɪraɪd]		Spritztour (mit einem gestohlenen Auto)
justice [ˈdʒʌstɪs]		Justiz
to **legalize** [ˈliːɡəlaɪz]		legalisieren
offender [əˈfendə]		Täter(in)
offence [əˈfens]		Straftat
to **plead guilty** [pliːd ˈɡɪlti]		sich schuldig bekennen
probation [prəˈbeɪʃn]		Bewährung
prosecution [ˌprɒsɪˈkjuːʃn]		Staatsanwaltschaft
prosecutor [ˈprɒsɪkjuːtə]		Staatsanwalt / -anwältin
remorse [rɪˈmɔːs]		Reue
to **sentence** [ˈsentəns]		verurteilen
sentence [ˈsentəns]		Verurteilung; Strafe
supervision [ˌsuːpəˈvɪʒn]		Überwachung; Aufsicht
shoplifting [ˈʃɒplɪftɪŋ]		Ladendiebstahl
theft [θeft]		Diebstahl
tribunal [traɪˈbjuːnl]		Tribunal; Gericht
victim [ˈvɪktɪm]		Opfer

	1	**foolish** [ˈfuːlɪʃ]	We all made foolish mistakes when we were young.	unklug; blöd
		crime [kraɪm]	Many young people do things – some of which are actually crimes – to show off.	Verbrechen
		to **impress** [ɪmˈpres]	I wanted to impress my best friend so I stole a T-shirt.	beeindrucken
	2a	**specialist** [ˈspeʃəlɪst]	List the specialist vocabulary and check new words in a dictionary.	speziell
		to **guarantee** [ˌɡærənˈtiː]	The customer's rights are guaranteed.	garantieren
		offender [əˈfendə]	Some offenders were very young when they committed a crime.	Täter(in)

Appendix

VOCABULARY

page	exercise	Workshop 3		
		to make amends [meɪk əˈmendz], **made, made** [meɪd, meɪd]	How can we help offenders to make amends for their crimes?	Wiedergutmachung leisten; entschädigen
		jail [dʒeɪl]	Is Jake's offence serious enough to justify sending him to jail? = prison	Gefängnis
		custody [ˈkʌstədi]	Custody should only be used for the most serious crimes.	Verwahrung; Schutz
		to hold accountable [həʊld əˈkaʊntəbl], **held, held** [held, held]	How can the law hold youth offenders accountable?	zur Rechenschaft ziehen
		prosecutor [ˈprɒsɪkjuːtə]	The Crown prosecutor is a lawyer.	Staatsanwalt; Staatsanwältin
		counselling [ˈkaʊnsəlɪŋ]	For a non-serious offence, the offender may be sent to an agency for counselling.	Beratung
		guilty [ˈɡɪlti]	I was found guilty in court, so I have a criminal record.	schuldig
		sentencing [ˈsentənsɪŋ]	What sentencing would you choose for his crime if you were the judge?	Verurteilung
		probation [prəˈbeɪʃn]	He is on probation for theft.	Bewährung
		circumstance [ˈsɜːkəmstəns]	The judge must consider the circumstances of the case and decide on a fair sentence.	Umstand; Lage
		remorse [rɪˈmɔːs]	If you show remorse, the judge might not be too hard on you.	Reue
	3	**drawback** [ˈdrɔːbæk]	There are many drawbacks of a jail sentence.	Nachteil
		joyride [ˈdʒɔɪraɪd]	I don't have a driver's license, but I got the idea of going for a joyride.	Spritztour (mit einem gestohlenen Auto)
		to cruise [kruːz]	Me and my buddies were drinking and cruising along when it happened. = sail	cruisen; herumfahren
		icy [ˈaɪsi]	I'm not a great driver yet and the road was icy.	eisig
		curb [kɜːb]	I accidentally went up over a curb and drove into a group of students.	Bordstein
		to charge [tʃɑːdʒ]	The offender was charged with several crimes.	anklagen
		assault [əˈsɔːlt]	There was an assault on several people.	Angriff; Überfall
		aggravated assault [ˈæɡrəveɪtɪd əˈsɔːlt]	Aggravated assault is a serious crime.	schwere Körperverletzung
101	4b	**incident** [ˈɪnsɪdənt]	Read the statements made by some of the people involved in the incident.	Vorfall; Ereignis
	6	**counsel** [ˈkaʊnsl]	Check what the Crown counsel and Defence counsel recommended.	Anwalt; Anwältin

Appendix

VOCABULARY

page	exercise	Workshop 3		
		to plead [pliːd]	If there was a witness to your crime you have to plead guilty.	sich bekennen; plädieren
		province [ˈprɒvɪns]	In this province the legal drinking age is 19.	Provinz
		joyriding [ˈdʒɔɪraɪdɪŋ]	I promise I'll never do any drinking and joyriding again.	Spritztour (mit einem gestohlenen Auto)
		recommendation [ˌrekəmenˈdeɪʃn]	The Crown counsel prepared the recommendations to the judge. = suggestion	Empfehlung
		license [ˈlaɪsns]	He was drinking and driving without a license.	Führerschein
		custodial [kʌˈstəʊdiəl]	I recommend a short custodial sentence followed by probation.	vormundschaftlich
		supervision [ˌsuːpəˈvɪʒn]	The judge recommends probation with supervision.	Überwachung; Aufsicht
		to take into account [teɪk ˈɪntə əˈkaʊnt], took, taken [tʊk, teɪkn]	Your choice of career should take your interests and talents into account.	berücksichtigen; beachten
102	2a	idol [ˈaɪdl]	Many teens want to look like their celebrity idols.	Idol
		supplement [ˈsʌplɪmənt]	Taking supplements may be bad for your health.	Nahrungsergänzung
		to bulk up [bʌlk ʌp]	Some people use supplements to help them bulk up.	Masse zusetzen; hier: Muskeln aufbauen
		superhero [ˈsuːpəhɪərəʊ]	The story features a cast of six superheroes who carry out brave deeds.	Superheld
		dieting [ˈdaɪətɪŋ]	Extreme dieting and fitness supplements are bad for your health.	Schlankheitskuren; Diäten
		to overdo [ˌəʊvəˈduː], overdid, overdone [ˌəʊvəˈdɪd, ˌəʊvəˈdʌn]	Don't overdo studying and don't forget to take breaks.	übertreiben
		extreme [ɪkˈstriːm]	It's dangerous to go to extremes trying to get super-model thin.	Extrem
		whole grain [ˈhəʊl ɡreɪn]	Eat lean meats, fruit, vegetables, whole grains, and healthy fats.	Vollkorn
		junk food [ˈdʒʌŋk fuːd]	Avoid junk foods – they are full of bad fat and salt. ≠ health food	ungesundes Essen
		soda [ˈsəʊdə]	Soda drinks contain large amounts of sugar.	Limo; Sprudel
		caffeine [ˈkæfiːn]	Coffee and tea contain large amounts of caffeine.	Koffein
		incorrectly [ˌɪnkəˈrektli]	If you lift weights incorrectly, you could injure yourself. ≠ correctly	falsch; fehlerhaft
		steroid [ˈsterɔɪd]	Steroids can raise the risk of heart disease.	Steroid
		liver [ˈlɪvər]	The liver is an important organ.	Leber

two hundred and seventeen **217**

page	exercise	Workshop 3		
		calorie [ˈkæləri]	Don't count your calories or cut out carbohydrates – this can slow down your development.	Kalorie
		to **load up** [ləʊd ʌp]	Loading up on healthy foods will help you to do well in school.	aufladen
		carbohydrate [ˌkɑːbəʊˈhaɪdreɪt]	Children need carbohydrates in their diet.	Kohlenhydrat
		growth [grəʊθ]	Eat well for your body's growth and development.	Wachstum
103	TIP	**introductory** [ˌɪntrəˈdʌktəri]	State the topic of your essay in your introductory sentences. ≠ concluding	Anfangs.-; Einführungs-
	4	**overweight** [ˌəʊvəˈweɪt]	If I had not decided to avoid fast food when I was a teenager, I would be overweight now.	übergewichtig
	5a	**livestock** [ˈlaɪvstɒk]	Livestock produce over 14% of all greenhouse gas emissions.	Vieh; Viehbestand
		cattle ranching [ˈkætl ˈrɑːntʃɪŋ]	Around 70% of deforestation in the Amazon is due to cattle ranching.	Viehhaltung
		cruelty [ˈkruːəlti]	If we stopped eating meat, we would end this terrible cruelty to animals. ≠ kindness	Quälerei; Grausamkeit
		antibiotic [ˌæntibaɪˈɒtɪk]	We want to reduce antibiotic resistance, which is a big health problem.	antibiotisch
		factory-farmed [ˈfæktri fɑːmd]	Factory-farmed animals get diseases very easily because they live in dirty, crowded sheds.	in Farmen gezüchtet; in Massen gezüchtet
		bacteria [bækˈtɪəriə]	Farmers give them loads of antibiotics to fight bacteria and keep them alive.	Bakterie
		resistant [rɪˈzɪstənt]	After a while, some bacteria become resistant to antibiotics.	widerstandsfähig; resistent
	6a	**grocery** [ˈgrəʊsəri]	We spend thirty percent of our money on groceries.	Lebensmittel
		dietary [ˈdaɪətəri]	Many teens say meals at home don't suit their tastes or dietary lifestyle.	diätetisch
		carb [kɑːb]	Many people are interested in a low-carb diet to lose weight.	Kohlenhydrat
104	1	**geek** [giːk]	Kids call me a geek because I like to study and am good at science.	Geek; Spezialist(in)
		market segment [ˌmɑːkɪt ˌsegment]	As a market segment, we're worth between $44 and $150 billion a year.	Marktsegment
		digital native [ˈdɪdʒɪtl ˈneɪtɪv]	Digital natives have grown up with the internet.	Digital Native
		consumer [kənˈsjuːmər]	Most consumers buy also on the internet.	Verbraucher(in)

Appendix

VOCABULARY

page	exercise	Workshop 3		
		savvy [ˈsævi]	Teens today are savvy users of technology. = clever ≠ stupid	klug; schlau
		to blast [ˈblɑːst]	The company blasts my social media feeds with ads.	absprengen
		trick [trɪk]	Advertisers use lots of tricks to get onto our screens and into our heads.	Trick
		to click [klɪk]	I click past most ads as soon as I can.	klicken
		to personalize [ˈpɜːsənəlaɪz]	Ads have to be original, creative and personalized to get our attention.	personalisieren
		product placement [ˌprɒdʌkt ˈpleɪsmənt]	When a film or TV show character is wearing stylish sneakers with a logo, this is called 'product placement'.	Produktplatzierung
		casual [ˈkæʒuəl]	Our brand is casual and personalized, and that makes it more authentic. ≠ formal	locker; lässig
		authentic [ɔːˈθentɪk]	If you use these expressions, your English will sound authentic. ≠ false	authentisch; echt
105	3a	to emphasize [ˈemfəsaɪz]	Sam wanted to emphasize specific information.	betonen
	3b	influencer [ˈɪnfluənsə]	Influencers are good at introducing you to cool stuff.	Influencer(in)
	4a	banner ad [ˈbænə æd]	I rarely take any notice of banner ads on websites.	Werbebanner
	4b	to intend [ɪnˈtend]	I didn't intend to spoil my website with ads just to make a few dollars. = plan	beabsichtigen
106	1	digitalization [ˌdɪdʒɪtəlaɪˈzeɪʃn]	Discuss how digitalization has changed the way we communicate.	Digitalisierung
	2	to evolve [ɪˈvɒlv]	Like any living language, English is always evolving.	sich entwickeln
		evolution [ˌiːvəˈluːʃn]	English is changing and the internet has driven this evolution.	Evolution; Entwicklung
		linguist [ˈlɪŋgwɪst]	As linguist David Crystal says, 'The vast majority of English is exactly the same today as it was 20 years ago.'	Sprachwissenschaftler(in); Linguist(in)
		vast [vɑːst]	The vast majority of people in Australia speak English. = huge	enorm; groß
		abbreviation [əˌbriːviˈeɪʃn]	We use a lot of abbreviations when we text. ❗ Lat. 'brevis, -e' = short	Abkürzung
		dynamic [daɪˈnæmɪk]	The internet has added a new dynamic to our fast changing world.	Dynamik
	3b	corresponding [ˌkɒrəˈspɒndɪŋ]	Match the words with their corresponding abbreviations.	entsprechend
	4	portal [ˈpɔːtl]	I like to post videos of the cakes I make on a video sharing portal.	Portalseite

two hundred and nineteen **219**

Appendix

VOCABULARY

page	exercise	Workshop 3		
		seldom [ˈseldəm]	I seldom get ads for things that I would actually buy. = rarely ≠ often	selten
107	5	**to draft** [drɑːft]	Sam is drafting a blog post with the results of his advertising survey.	entwerfen
		margin [ˈmɑːdʒɪn]	Use the notes in the margin to rewrite the article.	Rand
		respondent [rɪˈspɒndənt]	The had a lot of respondents to the survey.	Befragte(r)
		unexpected [ˌʌnɪkˈspektɪd]	He was shocked because the answer had been unexpected.	unerwartet
		shock [ʃɒk]	Most teens do not find these statistics to be a shock. ❗ Fr. 'choc' (m.)	Überraschung
	6a	**to witness** [ˈwɪtnəs]	A lot of people witnessed the crime. = see	Zeuge einer Sache sein; beobachten
		to cyberbully [ˈsaɪbəbʊli]	I witnessed other people join in when someone was cyberbullied.	cybermobben
	TIP	**artwork** [ˈɑːtwɜːk]	My parents have a lot of artwork on their walls.	Artwork; Kunstwerk
108	S1	**analysis** [əˈnæləsɪs]	Choose one diagram and use the notes to write a short description and analysis of the information shown.	Analyse; Untersuchung
		to state [steɪt]	He stated that the company would have to close for two weeks.	erklären; festlegen
		to sentence [ˈsentəns]	Youth cannot be sentenced for crimes the same way as adults.	verurteilen
		to convict [kənˈvɪkt]	We saw an increase in the number of convicted young people.	verurteilen
		motivating [ˈməʊtɪveɪtɪŋ]	Factors motivating teens to do physical exercise include team sports and peer involvement. = encouraging	motivierend; anregend
		clinical [ˈklɪnɪkl]	I read the study in a clinical journal.	klinisch
		nutrition [njuˈtrɪʃn]	Young people are learning about their health and nutrition.	Ernährung
109	S2	**rumour** [ˈruːmər]	Rumours were spread about the family, which made it difficult for the children at school.	Gerücht
		to exclude [ɪkˈskluːd]	They excluded him from playing the game.	ausschließen
		to vary [ˈveəri]	The length of each essay varies, some are very short and others are long. ≠ to stay the same	variieren
	S3	**to finalize** [ˈfaɪnəlaɪz]	Correct and finalize your original text.	fertigstellen; abschließen
115	1c	**constellation** [ˌkɒnstəˈleɪʃn]	Examine the constellation of characters in the story.	Konstellation
		excerpt [ekˈsɜːpt]	Read the excerpt from the novel.	Ausschnitt; Auszug

Appendix

VOCABULARY

page	exercise	Workshop 3		
		closeness [ˈkləʊsnəs]	The author helps readers feel a closeness to her characters. = proximity	Nähe; Dichte
		protagonist [prəˈtægənɪst]	Describe the protagonist's outer appearance as well as you can.	Protagonist(in)
		to differentiate [ˌdɪfəˈrenʃieɪt]	Differentiate between the two birds.	unterscheiden
	1d	**characterization** [ˌkærəktəraɪˈzeɪʃn]	She disagreed with the negative characterization of him.	Charakterisierung
		descriptive [dɪˈskrɪptɪv]	When you write your story, include a lot of descriptive adjectives.	beschreibend
	1e	**literary** [ˈlɪtərəri]	When analysing a literary text, don't just pay attention to its form.	literarisch
		to unify [ˈjuːnɪfaɪ]	The plot is the sequence of events and unifies the main story of a novel.	vereinigen
	3	**monologue** [ˈmɒnəlɒg]	Interior monologue is the technical literary term for the thoughts in a character's mind.	Monolog
		decisive [dɪˈsaɪsɪv]	We are at a decisive moment for climate change.	entscheidend
		internal [ɪnˈtɜːnl]	Internal secrets about the company are published in the documents. = external	intern
		to reveal [rɪˈviːl]	The documents reveal internal secrets.	verraten
116	1b	**livable** [ˈlɪvəbl]	Vancouver was recently ranked the third most livable place in the world. = habitable	bewohnbar
		acceptable [əkˈseptəbl]	The nuclear family is no longer the only acceptable family form. ≠ inacceptable	akzeptabel
117	3	**punishment** [ˈpʌnɪʃmənt]	My punishment for coming home late was that I had to mow the lawn.	Strafe
	3a	**devastated** [ˈdevəsteɪtɪd]	When I was sent to jail, my mom was devastated.	am Boden zerstört; erschüttert
118	4	**response** [rɪˈspɒns]	Here are some responses to the survey on advertising.	Reaktion; Antwort
		sneaky [ˈsniːki]	Sneaky advertising like product placement should be banned.	heimtückisch; hinterhältig
		to target [ˈtɑːgɪt]	Many online ads are not relevant – they are badly targeted.	zielen auf
		integrated [ˈɪntɪgreɪtɪd]	Many functions are integrated in the basic application.	integriert
		mistakenly [mɪˈsteɪkənli]	It was cleverly integrated and I mistakenly thought it was part of the programme.	fälschlich; irrtümlicherweise
		inversion [ɪnˈvɜːʃn]	You can use inversion in texts to make them more formal.	Inversion
119	1b	**to remarry** [ˌriːˈmæri]	Her mother remarried two years after her divorce.	wieder heiraten

Appendix

VOCABULARY

page	exercise	Workshop 3		
120	2b	**relatively** [ˈrelətɪvli]	Pete is now relatively happy with the new situation. = comparably	relativ; ziemlich
	5	**to cope** [kəʊp]	I didn't think my friend could cope, but in the end she didn't need my help. = deal with	zurechtkommen
121	8	**shoplifting** [ˈʃɒplɪftɪŋ]	Shoplifting is a crime.	Ladendiebstahl
		storeroom [ˈstɔːruːm]	I work in the storeroom organizing the deliveries. = stockroom	Lagerraum; Abstellraum
		to repay [rɪˈpeɪ]	I'll work every Saturday for the next six months and repay everything.	vergüten; zurückzahlen
	9	**to spray** [spreɪ]	Then one of the boys suggested we spray the front wall of the school.	sprühen
		graffiti [grəˈfiːti]	I had to pay the €150 fine I was given for the graffiti I left on the building.	Graffiti
		pier [pɪər]	When you visit our city on the sea, you must take a walk on the pier.	Kai
		to ground [graʊnd]	My dad was angry and grounded me for two weeks.	Hausarrest erteilen
	11	**to amaze** [əˈmeɪz]	My family's history amazes me. = astonish	verwundern; erstaunen

page	exercise	Workshop 4		
126		**glimpse** [glɪmps]	I would love to get a glimpse of the book before it starts being sold.	flüchtiger Blick
	1a	**watchman** [ˈwɒtʃmən]	The watchman is in the bank all night to ensure the money stays safe.	Wächter
		deed [diːd]	The story features six superheroes carrying out brave deeds.	Tat
		ember [ˈembər]	Burning embers from a camp fire can cause a forest fire.	glühende Kohle
		dystopian [dɪsˈtəʊpiən]	The dystopian novel was later turned into a graphic novel. ≠ utopian	dystopisch
		darkness [ˈdɑːknəs]	It is the story of two kids who grow up in darkness in a strange city. ≠ lightness	Dunkelheit
		underworld [ˈʌndəwɜːld]	This is the story of two children who grow up in an underworld city.	Unterwelt
		memoir [ˈmemwɑː]	The book is a memoir of a young girl who was not allowed to go to school.	Memoiren; Erinnerung
		oppression [əˈpreʃn]	In many places in the world women and girls suffer oppression.	Unterdrückung
		unforgettable [ˌʌnfəˈgetəbl]	The black and white pictures tell an unforgettable story about home.	unvergesslich
		afterlife [ˈɑːftəlaɪf]	He was shot and killed by police, but his spirit lives on in the afterlife.	Leben nach dem Tod

Appendix

VOCABULARY

page	exercise	Workshop 4		
		meanwhile [ˈmiːnwaɪl]	Meanwhile Alfonso's family and friends fight for justice for him.	inzwischen; mittlerweile
	2b	**evil** [ˈiːvl]	Some stories are about good and evil.	Übel; Böse
127	7	**coyote** [kaɪˈəʊti]	A coyote is an animal in North America but also refers to someone who smuggles immigrants.	Kojote; hier: Schlepper(in)
	CC	**enforcement** [ɪnˈfɔːsmənt]	The ICE is the USA's Immigration and Customs Enforcement.	Vollstreckung
128		to **vandalize** [ˈvændəlaɪz]	Some of the new benches and picnic tables in the park were vandalized.	zerstören; verwüsten
130		to **scavenge** [ˈskævɪndʒ]	My brother scavenged in his own closet for things to sell.	nach etw. suchen
132		**beast** [biːst]	A lot of children are afraid of the beast in the story.	Tier; Bestie
134		**runaway** [ˈrʌnəweɪ]	Many runaways try to reach the border.	Ausreißer(in)
135		**raid** [reɪd]	There was a police raid that lead to arrests.	Razzia
138	1a	to **sympathize** [ˈsɪmpəθaɪz]	I sympathize with people who don't have a home or enough to eat.	mit jmdm. mitleiden; mitfühlen
	2	**cameraman** [ˈkæmrəmæn], **cameramen** [ˈkæmrəmən]	The team consists of reporters and cameramen.	Kameramann
	3b	to **beg** [beg]	There are children in the streets begging for food.	betteln
139	4b	**certified** [ˈsɜːtɪfaɪd]	Think about whether your food has a certified label that it's organic. = authorized	beglaubigt; anerkannt
	5	**thought-provoking** [ˈθɔːt prəvəʊkɪŋ]	I spoke to one girl, who told me her thought-provoking story.	zum Nachdenken anregend
140	1	**regarding** [rɪˈgɑːdɪŋ]	What is the message of the illustration regarding feedback?	bezüglich
		to **recall** [rɪˈkɔːl]	Do you recall how many people have called about the ad?	erinnern an
		code of conduct [kəʊd əv kənˈdʌkt]	Remember our school's code of conduct before giving feedback on someone else's work.	Verhaltensregeln
		consideration [kənˌsɪdəˈreɪʃn]	Show respect and consideration for the feelings of others.	Rücksicht
		constructive [kənˈstrʌktɪv]	Only appropriate, clear and constructive comments are helpful. ≠ unproductive	konstruktiv
		compliment [ˈkɒmplɪmənt]	It is good to be honest when you give someone a compliment. ≠ criticism ❗ Fr. 'compliment' (m.)	Kompliment
		encouragement [ɪnˈkʌrɪdʒmənt]	Complimenting someone's writing gives encouragement.	Aufmunterung

Appendix

VOCABULARY

page	exercise	Workshop 4		
		criticism [ˈkrɪtɪsɪzəm]	Criticism has to be constructive and clearly voiced. ❗ Fr. 'critique' (f.)	Kritik
		precise [prɪˈsaɪs]	Be precise and avoid giving vague feedback.	genau; konkret
141		**interactive** [ˌɪntərˈæktɪv]	Feedback should be interactive, not just one-way.	interaktiv
		numerous [ˈnjuːmərəs]	There are numerous ways of getting messages to customers. = a lot	zahlreich; viele
		to **convey** [kənˈveɪ]	There are numerous ways of conveying messages online.	vermitteln
		facial [ˈfeɪʃl]	Your facial expressions can show your feelings about something.	Gesichts...
		explicitly [ɪkˈsplɪsɪtli]	Body language is as important as explicitly verbal communication.	explizit
		emoticon [ɪˈməʊtɪkɒn]	Emoticons don't provide good and constructive criticism.	Emoticon
		angle [ˈæŋgl]	I had not seen the building from that angle before.	Blickwinkel
		evident [ˈevɪdənt]	You write well and it is evident that you're interested in your subject.	offensichtlich; klar
		in addition [ɪn əˈdɪʃn]	In addition, we volunteer because we care about our community.	außerdem
		for instance [fə ˈɪnstəns]	Bush fires cause a lot of problems, for instance they endanger animals. = for example	beispielsweise; zum Beispiel
143	1	**spontaneous** [spɒnˈteɪniəs]	Look at the situations and decide if they are spontaneous or not.	spontan
		multilogue [ˈmʌltɪlɒg]	An example of a multilogue is a group discussion or an online meeting.	Multilog
		to **participate** [pɑːˈtɪsɪpeɪt]	I am participating in an event for young entrepreneurs.	teilnehmen
	2c	**signposting** [ˈsaɪnpəʊstɪŋ]	Good signposting helps tourists to get around the city.	Beschilderung; Wegweisung
	2d	**rhetorical** [rɪˈtɒrɪkl]	Rhetorical questions can be effective in persuasive writing.	rhetorisch
		frog [frɒg]	This isn't a frog, it is a toad.	Frosch
		to **distinguish between** [dɪˈstɪŋgwɪʃ bɪˈtwiːn]	Is it important to distinguish between frogs and toads.	zwischen etw. unterscheiden
		cane toad [keɪn təʊd]	The cane toad lives in Australia.	Agakröte
		poisonous [ˈpɔɪzənəs]	There are no poisonous snakes on the island.	giftig
		gland [glænd]	The cane toad has poisonous glands.	Drüse
	3	**beforehand** [bɪˈfɔːhænd]	When you give a presentation you should prepare beforehand.	im Voraus
144	1a	**simplified** [ˈsɪmplɪfaɪ]	Which of these simplified definitions best describe language awareness?	vereinfacht

Appendix

VOCABULARY

page	exercise	Workshop 4		
	1b	**effectiveness** [ɪˈfektɪvnəs]	Read your essay to someone to help assess its effectiveness.	Wirksamkeit
		flexibility [ˌfleksəˈbɪləti]	My mother's work provides flexibility so that she can be home when we get back from school.	Flexibilität
		intercultural [ˌɪntəˈkʌltʃərəl]	The job requires a high level of intercultural knowledge.	interkulturell
		competence [ˈkɒmpɪtəns]	Intercultural competence is becoming increasingly important.	Kompetenz
	3a	**particularly** [pəˈtɪkjələli]	Choose a topic which particularly interests you.	besonders
	3b	**to prosecute** [ˈprɒsɪkjuːt]	They prosecute people who break the law.	bestrafen; verfolgen
		trespasser [ˈtrespəsər]	A trespasser is someone who is not allowed to come here.	Unbefugte(r)
		authorized [ˈɔːθəraɪzd]	The construction area is for authorized staff only.	autorisiert; berechtigt
		personnel [ˌpɜːsəˈnel]	Only authorized personnel may enter the construction area.	Personal; Mitarbeiter
	3c	**to denote** [dɪˈnəʊt]	The word 'family' no longer denotes two parents and children.	auf etw. hindeuten
		handwritten [ˌhændˈrɪtn]	Can you explain the handwritten message?	handschriftlich
		innocent [ˈɪnəsnt]	He is innocent of the crime. ≠ guilty	unschuldig
	4a	**inappropriate** [ˌɪnəˈprəʊpriət]	Be aware of the register; some words are inappropriate in these situations. ≠ appropriate	unpassend
		to dump [dʌmp]	I dumped everything onto my bed and then had to clean it up.	kippen
		to nag [næg]	My mum was nagging me because I got home late for dinner.	meckern; nörgeln
	4b	**to differ** [ˈdɪfər]	If Tim was talking to a teacher, how would the dialogue differ?	abweichen
145		**stylistic** [staɪˈlɪstɪk]	Stylistic devices have a function in the text and an effect on the reader.	stilistisch
		to provoke [prəˈvəʊk]	The text grabs the reader's interest and provokes a particular response.	verursachen; hervorrufen
		alliteration [əˌlɪtəˈreɪʃn]	Alliteration is a literary device used in poetry.	Alliteration
		climax [ˈklaɪmæks]	The climax is the highest point of tension in a storyline.	Höhepunkt
		irony [ˈaɪrəni]	The irony is that he wanted the toy so badly but now finds it's not fun to play with!	Ironie
		metaphor [ˈmetəfər]	Metaphor is a figure of speech that directly compares one thing to another for rhetorical effect.	Metapher

Appendix

VOCABULARY

page	exercise	Workshop 4		
		parallelism [ˈpærəlelɪzəm]	Parallelism is when you use similar or identical words.	Parallelismus
		deliberately [dɪˈlɪbərətli]	She ignored him deliberately.	absichtlich; bewusst
		identical [aɪˈdentɪkl]	The two paintings look identical, but they're different. = exact	identisch
		personification [pəˌsɒnɪfɪˈkeɪʃn]	Personification presents ideas, objects or animals as human beings.	Personifikation; Verkörperung
		abstract [ˈæbstrækt]	The museum has a lot of abstract paintings.	abstrakt
		tragedy [ˈtrædʒədi]	There are two main types or genres of drama: tragedy and comedy.	Tragödie
		comedy [ˈkɒmədi]	A comedy usually has a happy ending.	Komödie
		to centre around [ˈsentər əˈraʊnd]	Usually, a play is made up of five acts and each one is centred around an important event.	sich auf etw. beziehen; sich auf etw. konzentrieren
		soliloquy [səˈlɪləkwi]	In the soliloquy, she revealed her emotions to the audience.	Monolog; Soliloquium
		sorrow [ˈsɒrəʊ]	The characters actions show his sorrow about the events.	Trauer; Kummer
		playwright [ˈpleɪraɪt]	A playwright is the author of a play for the stage.	Dramatiker(in)
		outward [ˈaʊtwəd]	She showed no outward sign of happiness.	äußerlich; äußere (r, -s)
		to undergo [ˌʌndəˈgəʊ], **underwent, undergone** [ˌʌndəˈwent, ˌʌndəˈgɒːn]	The characters undergo changes in the course of the story.	durchmachen
		unaware [ˌʌnəˈweər]	Words may have a special meaning that the characters are unaware of.	in Unkenntnis; unwissend
		to provide [prəˈvaɪd]	Don't forget to provide relevant background information. 🔒 Lat. 'providere (provido, providi, provisum)'	zur Verfügung stellen; versorgen (mit)
		humorous [ˈhjuːmərəs]	The story was humorous and made me laugh.	humorvoll
		to relieve [rɪˈliːv]	He was relieved to have taken the test. ≠ aggravate	erleichtern; entlasten
		remark [rɪˈmɑːk]	A comic remark or incident can make a story memorable.	Bemerkung
146		**interpretation** [ɪnˌtɜːprəˈteɪʃn]	Check unknown words in order to understand their literal meaning as a basis for interpretation. = analysis	Interpretation
		procedure [prəˈsiːdʒə]	The following procedure might be helpful for improving your writing. 🔒 Fr. 'procédure' (f.)	Prozedur; Verfahren

Appendix

VOCABULARY

page	exercise	**Workshop 4**		
		satisfying [ˈsætɪsfaɪɪŋ]	I wish you a successful and satisfying leap into the world of poetry.	zufriedenstellend; befriedigend
		leap [liːp]	My course will help you take a satisfying leap into the world of poetry.	Sprung
		to **recite** [rɪˈsaɪt]	Remember: poetry is always meant to be read or recited aloud.	rezitieren; auswendig aufsagen
		literal [ˈlɪtərəl]	Poems often use images and the literal meaning of words can be less important.	wörtlich
		stanza [ˈstænzə]	Say the lines of the poem aloud and try to memorize the first stanza.	Stanze; Strophe
		scheme [skiːm]	Pay attention to the rhyme scheme when reading poetry.	Schema
		figurative [ˈfɪgərətɪv]	He uses a lot of figurative language and images in his texts.	figurativ
		motif [məʊˈtiːf]	Analyse figurative language and motifs in the text.	Motiv
		adequate [ˈædɪkwət]	We need an adequate number of players for the game. ≠ inadequate	ausreichend; angemessen

Dictionary: English – German

3
3D printing [ˌθriː ˈdiː prɪntɪŋ] 3D-Druck OT 1

A
a [eɪ] ein(e) OT 1
abbreviation [əˌbriːviˈeɪʃn] Abkürzung WS 3, 106
to **abduct** [æbˈdʌkt] entführen OT 4
ability [əˈbɪləti] Können; Fähigkeit OT 2
able: to be able to [biː ˈeɪbl tuː] können OT 2
aboard [əˈbɔːd] an Bord OT 4
about [əˈbaʊt] über; ungefähr; um ... herum OT 1
above [əˈbʌv] oben; oberhalb OT 3
abroad [əˈbrɔːd] im Ausland OT 4
to **abseil** [ˈæbseɪl] (sich) abseilen OT 2
absolute [ˈæbsəluːt] absolut OT 3
   absolutely [ˈæbsəluːtli] durchaus; total; wirklich; absolut OT 2
abstract [ˈæbstrækt] abstrakt WS 4, 145
abuse [əˈbjuːs] Missbrauch OT 4
academic [ˌækəˈdemɪk] akademisch WW, 11
accent [ˈæksənt] Akzent OT 1
to **accept** [əkˈsept] annehmen OT 3
acceptable [əkˈseptəbl] akzeptabel WS 3, 116
access [ˈækses] Zugriff; Zugang OT 4
to **access** [ˈækses] zugreifen auf OT 4
accessible [əkˈsesəbl] zugänglich; barrierefrei OT 2
accessory [əkˈsesəri] Zubehör OT 3
accident [ˈæksɪdənt] Unfall OT 1
   Accident and Emergency [ˈæksɪdənt ənd iˌmɜːdʒənsi] Notaufnahme OT 1
   by accident [baɪ ˈæksɪdənt] versehentlich OT 2
accidentally [ˌæksɪˈdentəli] zufällig; versehentlich OT 3
accommodation [əˌkɒməˈdeɪʃn] Unterkunft OT 2
accompanied [əˈkʌmpənid] begleitet OT 3
according to [əˈkɔːdɪŋ tə] gemäß; nach OT 3
accordion [əˈkɔːdiən] Akkordeon OT 2
accountable: to hold accountable [həʊld əˈkaʊntəbl] zur Rechenschaft ziehen WS 3, 100
accurate [ˈækjərət] genau; präzise OT 4

to **ache** [eɪk] schmerzen; wehtun OT 3
to **achieve** [əˈtʃiːv] erreichen; schaffen OT 4
achievement [əˈtʃiːvmənt] Leistung OT 2
acidic [əˈsɪdɪk] sauer WS 1, 26
to **acknowledge** [əkˈnɒlɪdʒ] bestätigen; anerkennen WS 1, 21
acoustic [əˈkuːstɪk] akustisch OT 2
acre [ˈeɪkə] Morgen OT 4
across [əˈkrɒs] auf der anderen Seite; hinüber OT 1
acrostic [əˈkrɒstɪk] Akrostichon WS 1, 20
act [ækt] Gesetz; Verordnung WS 1, 19
to **act** [ækt] (sich) verhalten; Theater spielen OT 1
   to **act out** [ækt aʊt] vorführen OT 1
action [ˈækʃn] Aktion OT 1
   in action [ɪn ˈækʃn] im Einsatz OT 2
to **activate** [ˈæktɪveɪt] aktivieren OT 4
active [ˈæktɪv] aktiv OT 4
activism [ˈæktɪvɪzəm] Aktivismus OT 4
activist [ˈæktɪvɪst] Aktivist(in) WS 2, 52
activity [ækˈtɪvəti] Aktivität OT 1
actor [ˈæktə] Schauspieler(in) OT 1
actual [ˈæktʃuəl] richtig; wirklich WS 2, 56
actually [ˈæktʃuəli] eigentlich; sogar; tatsächlich OT 2
AD (Anno Domini) [ˌeɪ ˈdiː] n. Chr.; unserer Zeitrechnung OT 2
ad [æd] Werbung OT 2
adaptable [əˈdæptəbl] anpassungsfähig OT 4
to **add** [æd] hinzufügen OT 1
addicted [əˈdɪktɪd] süchtig; abhängig OT 3
addition: in addition to [ɪn əˈdɪʃn tə] zusätzlich zu; neben OT 4
   in addition [ɪn əˈdɪʃn] außerdem WS 4, 141
address [əˈdres] Adresse OT 1
adequate [ˈædɪkwət] ausreichend; angemessen WS 4, 146
adjective [ˈædʒɪktɪv] Adjektiv OT 1
adjoining [əˈdʒɔɪnɪŋ] angrenzend OT 3
admission [ədˈmɪʃn] Eintritt WS 1, 38
to **admit** [ədˈmɪt] zugeben OT 4
to **adopt** [əˈdɒpt] annehmen WS 1, 30
adrenaline rush [əˈdrenəlɪn rʌʃ] Adrenalinstoß OT 1

adult [ˈædʌlt] Erwachsene(r) OT 1
advance [ədˈvɑːns] Fortschritt OT 4
advanced [ədˈvɑːnst] fortgeschritten OT 4
advantage [ədˈvɑːntɪdʒ] Vorteil OT 3
advent [ˈædvent] Beginn; Einführung WS 1, 23
adventure [ədˈventʃə] Abenteuer OT 1
adventurous [ədˈventʃərəs] abenteuerlustig OT 2
adverb [ˈædvɜːb] Adverb; Umstandswort OT 1
advert [ˈædvɜːt] Inserat OT 1
to **advertise** [ˈædvətaɪz] Werbung machen für OT 2
advertisement [ədˈvɜːtɪsmənt] Werbung OT 1
advertiser [ˈædvətaɪzə] Werbeagentur; Werber OT 3
advertising [ˈædvətaɪzɪŋ] Werbung OT 2
advice [ədˈvaɪs] Rat OT 1
to **advise** [ədˈvaɪz] raten OT 4
advisor [ədˈvaɪzə] Berater(in) WS 2, 51
to **affect** [əˈfekt] sich auswirken auf OT 3
affection [əˈfekʃn] Zuneigung WS 2, 64
to **afford** [əˈfɔːd] (sich) leisten OT 2
affordable [əˈfɔːdəbl] bezahlbar OT 4
afraid [əˈfreɪd] ängstlich OT 2
African [ˈæfrɪkən] afrikanisch OT 2
after [ˈɑːftə] nach OT 1
afterlife [ˈɑːftəlaɪf] Leben nach dem Tod WS 4, 126
afternoon [ˌɑːftəˈnuːn] Nachmittag OT 1
afterwards [ˈɑːftəwədz] danach; nachher OT 3
again [əˈgen] wieder OT 1
against [əˈgenst] gegen OT 1
age [eɪdʒ] Alter OT 1
aged [eɪdʒd] im Alter von OT 1
agency [ˈeɪdʒənsi] Agentur; Organisation OT 4
agenda [əˈdʒendə] Tagesordnung OT 3
aggressive [əˈgresɪv] aggressiv OT 3
agile [ˈædʒaɪl] beweglich OT 3
ago [əˈgəʊ] vor OT 1
agrarian [əˈgreəriən] landwirtschaftlich WS 1, 22
to **agree** [əˈgriː] (sich) einig sein; zustimmen OT 1

Appendix

VOCABULARY

agreement [əˈgriːmənt] Vereinbarung OT 3
agricultural [ˌægrɪˈkʌltʃərəl] landwirtschaftlich OT 4
agriculture [ˈægrɪkʌltʃə] Landwirtschaft OT 2
ahead [əˈhed] voraus OT 3
AI (artificial intelligence) [ˌeɪ ˈaɪ] künstliche Intelligenz WS 2, 69
aim [eɪm] Absicht; Ziel OT 4
to aim [eɪm] zielen; beabsichtigen OT 4
air [eə] Luft OT 1
airplane [ˈeəpleɪn] Flugzeug OT 4
airport [ˈeəpɔːt] Flughafen OT 1
alarm [əˈlɑːm] Wecker; Alarm OT 2
alarm clock [əˈlɑːm klɒk] Wecker OT 2
alarmed [əˈlɑːmd] beunruhigt OT 3
Alaskan [əˈlæskən] alaskisch OT 2
album [ˈælbəm] Album OT 3
alcohol [ˈælkəhɒl] Alkohol OT 3
alcoholic [ˌælkəˈhɒlɪk] alkoholisch OT 3
to alert [əˈlɜːt] alarmieren OT 2
algorithm [ˈælgərɪðəm] Algorithmus WS 2, 69
alien [ˈeɪliən] Außerirdische(r); Alien OT 2
alike [əˈlaɪk] ebenso WS 3, 94
alive [əˈlaɪv] lebendig OT 4
all [ɔːl] alles; alle OT 1
    all over [ˈɔːl əʊvə] überall OT 2
    all right [ˌɔːl ˈraɪt] gut; in Ordnung OT 1
    all set [ɔːl ˈset] bereit OT 2
allergic [əˈlɜːdʒɪk] allergisch OT 2
allergy [ˈælədʒi] Allergie OT 1
alliteration [əˌlɪtəˈreɪʃn] Alliteration WS 4, 145
to allow [əˈlaʊ] erlauben OT 3
allowance [əˈlaʊəns] Taschengeld OT 3
allowed [əˈlaʊd] erlaubt OT 3
    to be allowed to [biː əˈlaʊd tuː] dürfen; können OT 2
almost [ˈɔːlməʊst] fast OT 2
alone [əˈləʊn] allein OT 1
along [əˈlɒŋ] entlang OT 1
aloud [əˈlaʊd] laut; mit lauter Stimme OT 2
alpaca [ælˈpækə] Alpaka OT 2
alphabet [ˈælfəbet] Alphabet OT 1
alphabetical [ˌælfəˈbetɪkl] alphabetisch OT 2
already [ɔːlˈredi] schon; bereits OT 2
alright [ɔːlˈraɪt] in Ordnung OT 1
also [ˈɔːlsəʊ] auch OT 1
alternative [ɔːlˈtɜːnətɪv] Alternative OT 2

although [ɔːlˈðəʊ] obwohl OT 2
alumnus [əˈlʌmnaɪ] Absolvent; Ehemalige OT 4
always [ˈɔːlweɪz] immer OT 1
to amaze [əˈmeɪz] verwundern; erstaunen WS 3, 121
amazed [əˈmeɪzd] erstaunt; überrascht OT 3
amazing [əˈmeɪzɪŋ] erstaunlich OT 1
ambition [æmˈbɪʃn] Ziel; Ambition OT 4
ambitious [æmˈbɪʃəs] ehrgeizig OT 4
ambulance [ˈæmbjələns] Krankenwagen OT 1
amends: to make amends [meɪk əˈmendz] Wiedergutmachung leisten; entschädigen WS 3, 100
American [əˈmerɪkən] amerikanisch OT 1
among [əˈmʌŋ] unter; zwischen OT 3
amount [əˈmaʊnt] Menge OT 2
amphitheatre [ˈæmfɪθɪətə] Arena; Amphitheater OT 3
amplifier [ˈæmplɪfaɪə] Verstärker OT 2
amused [əˈmjuːzd] amüsiert OT 3
amusing [əˈmjuːzɪŋ] amüsant; lustig WS 2, 80
an [æn] ein(e) OT 1
to analyse [ˈænəlaɪz] analysieren OT 3
analysis [əˈnæləsɪs] Analyse; Untersuchung WS 3, 108
ancestor [ˈænsestə] Vorfahr(in) OT 3
to anchor [ˈæŋkə] ankern OT 4
ancient [ˈeɪnʃənt] antik; uralt OT 2
and [ənd] und OT 1
anecdote [ˈænɪkdəʊt] Anekdote OT 4
angel [ˈeɪndʒl] Engel OT 3
anger [ˈæŋgə] Ärger; Wut OT 3
angle [ˈæŋgl] Blickwinkel WS 4, 141
angry [ˈæŋgri] böse OT 1
    angrily [ˈæŋgrəli] ärgerlich; böse; zornig OT 2
animal [ˈænɪml] Tier OT 1
ankle [ˈæŋkl] Fußknöchel OT 1
to announce [əˈnaʊns] ansagen; bekannt geben OT 2
announcement [əˈnaʊnsmənt] Bekanntgabe; Ansage OT 2
to annoy [əˈnɔɪ] ärgern OT 3
annoyed [əˈnɔɪd] genervt OT 2
annoying [əˈnɔɪɪŋ] ärgerlich; nervig OT 2
annual [ˈænjuəl] jährlich WS 2, 65
another [əˈnʌðə] noch ein(e); ein(e) andere(r, -s) OT 1
answer [ˈɑːnsə] Antwort OT 1

to answer [ˈɑːnsə] antworten; beantworten OT 1
antenna [ænˈtenə] Antenne OT 1
anthem [ˈænθəm] Nationalhymne; Hymne WS 1, 31
antibiotic [ˌæntibaɪˈɒtɪk] antibiotisch WS 3, 103
antiseptic [ˌæntiˈseptɪk] antiseptisch; keimtötend OT 2
anxious [ˈæŋkʃəs] besorgt OT 2
any [ˈeni] irgendein(e) OT 1
anybody [ˈenibɒdi] irgendjemand OT 1
anymore [ˌeni ˈmɔː] mehr; länger; weiter OT 2
anyone [ˈeniwʌn] irgendjemand OT 2
anything [ˈeniθɪŋ] irgendetwas OT 1
anytime [ˈenitaɪm] jederzeit OT 3
anyway [ˈeniweɪ] trotzdem; sowieso; jedenfalls OT 1
anywhere [ˈeniweə] irgendwo OT 2
apart from [əˈpɑːt frəm] außer OT 3
apartment [əˈpɑːtmənt] Wohnung OT 1
to apologize [əˈpɒlədʒaɪz] (sich) entschuldigen OT 2
apology [əˈpɒlədʒi] Entschuldigung OT 2
app [æp] App OT 4
apparently [əˈpærəntli] anscheinend OT 4
appeal [əˈpiːl] Aufruf OT 2
to appear [əˈpɪə] erscheinen; scheinen; auftauchen OT 3
appearance [əˈpɪərəns] Aussehen OT 3
appetizing [ˈæpɪtaɪzɪŋ] appetitlich OT 3
to applaud [əˈplɔːd] applaudieren OT 2
applause [əˈplɔːz] Applaus OT 2
apple [ˈæpl] Apfel OT 1
appliance [əˈplaɪəns] Gerät; Haushaltsgerät OT 3
applicant [ˈæplɪkənt] Bewerber(in) OT 4
application [ˌæplɪˈkeɪʃn] Bewerbung; Antrag OT 4
to apply [əˈplaɪ] sich bewerben OT 3
to appoint [əˈpɔɪnt] ernennen WS 1, 41
to appreciate [əˈpriːʃieɪt] anerkennen; schätzen WS 2, 67
apprentice [əˈprentɪs] Auszubildende(r); Lehrling WS 2, 52
apprenticeship [əˈprentɪʃɪp] Lehrstelle; Ausbildung WS 2, 50
to approach [əˈprəʊtʃ] näher kommen; sich nähern OT 4
appropriate [əˈprəʊpriət] angemessen OT 4

Appendix

VOCABULARY

appropriately [əˈprəʊpriətli] passend; angemessen OT 3
appropriation [əˌprəʊpriˈeɪʃn] Aneignung **WS 1**, 38
to **approve** [əˈpruːv] genehmigen; zustimmen OT 3
approximately [əˈprɒksɪmətli] ungefähr; etwa **WS 1**, 13
April [ˈeɪprəl] April OT 1
aquatic [əˈkwætɪk] aquatisch; Wasser… OT 4
aqueduct [ˈækwɪdʌkt] Aquädukt OT 3
archaeologist [ˌɑːkiˈɒlədʒɪst] Archäologe / Archäologin OT 3
architect [ˈɑːkɪtekt] Architekt(in) **WS 1**, 28
architecture [ˈɑːkɪtektʃə] Architektur OT 2
to **archive** [ˈɑːkaɪv] archivieren OT 4
Arctic [ˈɑːktɪk] arktisch; Arktis OT 4
area [ˈeəriə] Gebiet; Gegend OT 1
arena [əˈriːnə] Arena OT 1
aeroplane [ˈeərəpleɪn] Flugzeug OT 4
to **argue** [ˈɑːgjuː] streiten; argumentieren OT 2
argument [ˈɑːgjumənt] Streit; Auseinandersetzung OT 1
argumentative [ˌɑːgjuˈmentətɪv] argumentativ **WS 2**, 68
arid [ˈærɪd] dürr; trocken **WS 1**, 23
arm [ɑːm] Arm OT 1
armchair [ˈɑːmtʃeə] Sessel OT 1
armed [ɑːmd] bewaffnet **WS 3**, 93
army [ˈɑːmi] Armee OT 3
around [əˈraʊnd] um OT 1
to **arrange** [əˈreɪndʒ] planen; vereinbaren OT 2
arrangement [əˈreɪndʒmənt] Regelung; Vereinbarung OT 3
to **arrest** [əˈrest] gefangen nehmen; verhaften **WS 1**, 21
arrival [əˈraɪvl] Ankunft OT 2
to **arrive** [əˈraɪv] ankommen OT 1
arrow [ˈærəʊ] Pfeil OT 3
art [ɑːt] Kunst OT 1
   fine art [ˌfaɪn ˈɑːt] Kunstwissenschaft OT 2
article [ˈɑːtɪkl] Artikel; Geschlechtswort OT 1
   definite article [ˈdefɪnət ˌɑːtɪkl] bestimmter Artikel OT 1
   indefinite article [ɪnˌdefɪnət ˈɑːtɪkl] unbestimmter Artikel OT 1
artificial intelligence [ˌɑːtɪfɪʃl ɪnˈtelɪdʒəns] künstliche Intelligenz OT 4

artificially [ˌɑːtɪˈfɪʃəli] künstlich OT 3
artist [ˈɑːtɪst] Künstler(in) OT 3
artwork [ˈɑːtwɜːk] Artwork; Kunstwerk **WS 3**, 107
arty [ˈɑːti] gewollt künstlerisch **WS 2**, 60
as [æz] als; wie OT 1
   as well [əz wel] auch OT 1
asexual [ˌeɪˈsekʃuəl] asexuell **WS 3**, 93
ashamed [əˈʃeɪmd] beschämt OT 3
ashore [əˈʃɔːr] an Land OT 4
Asian [ˈeɪʒn] asiatisch OT 4
to **ask** [ɑːsk] fragen OT 1
aspect [ˈæspekt] Aspekt OT 4
aspen [ˈæspən] Espe OT 2
assault [əˈsɔːlt] Angriff; Überfall **WS 3**, 100
   aggravated assault [ˈægrəveɪtɪd əˈsɔːlt] schwere Körperverletzung **WS 3**, 100
assembly [əˈsembli] Versammlung OT 1
assembly hall [əˈsembli ˌhɔːl] Aula OT 1
assertive [sʌlk] bestimmt OT 3
to **assess** [əˈses] beurteilen **WS 2**, 51
assessor [əˈsesər] Gutacher(in) **WS 2**, 51
assignment [əˈsaɪnmənt] Aufgabe OT 4
assimilation [əˌsɪməˈleɪʃn] Assimilation; Anpassung OT 4
to **assist** [əˈsɪst] unterstützen **WS 2**, 59
assistant [əˈsɪstənt] Assistent OT 1
to **associate** [əˈsəʊsieɪt] assoziieren OT 4
association [əˌsəʊʃiˈeɪʃn] Verein; Verband OT 2
asterisk [ˈæstərɪsk] Sternchen; Asterisk OT 4
astonishing [əˈstɒnɪʃɪŋ] erstaunlich **WS 1**, 27
   astonishingly [əˈstɒnɪʃɪŋli] erstaunlicherweise OT 3
astronaut [ˈæstrənɔːt] Astronaut(in) OT 4
astronomy [əˈstrɒnəmi] Astronomie OT 1
asylum seeker [əˈsaɪləm siːkə] Asylbewerber(in) OT 4
at [ət] an; in; bei OT 1
   at … o'clock [æt … əˈklɒk] um … Uhr OT 1
   at the moment [ət ðə ˈməʊmənt] momentan OT 2
athlete [ˈæθliːt] Sportler(in) OT 2
athletic [æθˈletɪk] athletisch; sportlich OT 4
athletics [æθˈletɪks] Leichtathletik; Sport OT 1

atmosphere [ˈætməsfɪə] Atmosphäre OT 3
to **attach** [əˈtætʃ] befestigen OT 4
to **attack** [əˈtæk] angreifen OT 3
attacking [əˈtækɪŋ] angreifend OT 3
attempt [əˈtempt] Versuch OT 2
to **attend** [əˈtend] besuchen OT 2
attendant [əˈtendənt] Aufseher(in); Diener(in) OT 3
attention [əˈtenʃn] Aufmerksamkeit OT 2
   to **pay attention** [ˌpeɪ əˈtenʃn] aufpassen OT 2
attic [ˈætɪk] Dachboden OT 3
attitude [ˈætɪtjuːd] Haltung; Einstellung; Ansicht OT 3
to **attract** [əˈtrækt] anziehen OT 4
attraction [əˈtrækʃn] Sehenswürdigkeit OT 2
attractive [əˈtræktɪv] anziehend; attraktiv; reizvoll OT 4
audience [ˈɔːdiəns] Publikum OT 2
audio diary [ˈɔːdiəʊ daɪəri] Audiotagebuch OT 2
audio file [ˈɔːdiəʊ faɪl] Audiodatei OT 2
August [ɔːˈɡʌst] August OT 1
aunt [ɑːnt] Tante OT 1
auntie [ˈɑːnti] Tantchen OT 2
au pair [ˌəʊ ˈpeər] Au-pair **WS 2**, 53
Austrian [ˈɒstriən] Österreicher(in) OT 4
authentic [ɔːˈθentɪk] authentisch; echt **WS 3**, 104
author [ˈɔːθə] Autor(in) OT 2
authority [ɔːˈθɒrəti] Behörde; Autorität OT 4
authorized [ˈɔːθəraɪzd] autorisiert; berechtigt **WS 4**, 144
to **automate** [ˈɔːtəmeɪt] automatisieren OT 4
automobile [ˈɔːtəməbiːl] Automobil OT 4
autonomous [ɔːˈtɒnəməs] unabhängig; autonom OT 4
autumn [ˈɔːtəm] Herbst OT 2
available [əˈveɪləbl] verfügbar; erhältlich OT 3
avatar [ˈævətɑː] Avatar OT 3
avenue [ˈævənjuː] Allee OT 1
average [ˈævərɪdʒ] durchschnittlich OT 4
to **avoid** [əˈvɔɪd] vermeiden OT 4
awake [əˈweɪk] wach OT 2
award [əˈwɔːd] Auszeichnung OT 2
   award-winning [əˈwɔːd wɪnɪŋ] preisgekrönt OT 4

Appendix
VOCABULARY

to **award** [əˈwɔːd] vergeben; verleihen OT 4
aware [əˈweər] bewusst WS 2, 64
awareness [əˈweənəs] Bewusstsein WS 2, 64
away [əˈweɪ] weg OT 1
awesome [ˈɔːsəm] toll; großartig OT 2
awful [ˈɔːfl] fürchterlich; schrecklich OT 1
awkward [ˈɔːkwəd] ungeschickt; unbeholfen WS 3, 94
axis [ˈæksɪs] Achse OT 4
aye [aɪ] ja OT 2

B
baby [ˈbeɪbi] Säugling; Baby OT 1
to **babysit** [ˈbeɪbisɪt] babysitten OT 4
babysitter [ˈbeɪbisɪtə] Babysitter OT 4
back [bæk] Rücken; zurück OT 1
backbone [ˈbækbəʊn] Rückgrat OT 2
background [ˈbækɡraʊnd] Hintergrund OT 3
backhand [ˈbækhænd] Rückhand OT 3
backpack [ˈbækpæk] Rucksack OT 2
to **backpack** [ˈbækpæk] mit dem Rucksack reisen OT 3
backup [ˈbækʌp] Backup; Unterstützung OT 4
backwards [ˈbækwədz] nach hinten; rückwärts OT 3
backyard [ˌbækˈjɑːd] Garten (hinterm Haus) OT 2
bacon [ˈbeɪkən] Speck; Bacon OT 1
bacteria [bækˈtɪəriə] Bakterie WS 3, 103
bad [bæd] schlecht OT 1
 badly [ˈbædli] schlecht OT 2
badge [bædʒ] Abzeichen OT 1
badminton [ˈbædmɪntən] Badminton OT 1
bag [bæɡ] Tüte; Tasche OT 1
bagel [ˈbeɪɡl] Bagel OT 1
baggage [ˈbæɡɪdʒ] Gepäck OT 2
baggage claim [ˈbæɡɪdʒ kleɪm] Gepäckausgabe OT 2
bagpipe [ˈbæɡpaɪp] Dudelsack OT 3
to **bake** [beɪk] backen OT 1
baker [ˈbeɪkə] Bäcker(in) OT 3
bakery [ˈbeɪkəri] Bäckerei OT 4
balance [ˈbæləns] Gleichgewicht OT 3
ball [bɔːl] Ball OT 1
ballpoint pen [ˈbɔːlpɔɪnt pen] Kugelschreiber OT 1
ballet [ˈbæleɪ] Ballett OT 3
balloon [bəˈluːn] Ballon OT 3
to **ban** [bæn] verbieten OT 3
banana [bəˈnɑːnə] Banane OT 1

band [bænd] Band OT 1
bandage [ˈbændɪdʒ] Verband OT 2
Bangladeshi [ˌbæŋɡləˈdeʃi] Bangladescher(in) OT 4
bank [bæŋk] Ufer; Bank OT 3
bank teller [bæŋk ˈtelə] Kassierer(in) OT 4
banking [ˈbæŋkɪŋ] Banking; Bankwesen WS 2, 63
banner ad [ˈbænə æd] Werbebanner WS 3, 105
bar [bɑː] Riegel; Bar OT 1
barbecued [ˈbɑːbɪkjuːd] gegrillt OT 4
barbecue [ˈbɑːbɪkjuː] Grillen OT 2
bargain [ˈbɑːɡən] Schnäppchen OT 4
to **bark** [bɑːk] bellen OT 2
barn [bɑːn] Scheune OT 2
barrier [ˈbæriə] Barriere OT 3
barrister [ˈbærɪstər] Rechtsanwalt /-anwältin WS 1, 43
base [beɪs] Basis OT 4
to **base on** [beɪs ɒn] auf etw. basieren OT 4
baseball [ˈbeɪsbɔːl] Baseball OT 1
basic [ˈbeɪsɪk] Grund-; grundsätzlich; einfach OT 4
basically [ˈbeɪsɪkli] im Grunde OT 3
basin [ˈbeɪsn] Becken OT 3
basis [ˈbeɪsɪs] Grundlage; Basis WS 2, 61
basket [ˈbɑːskɪt] Korb OT 3
basketball [ˈbɑːskɪtbɔːl] Basketball OT 1
bat [bæt] Fledermaus; Schläger OT 1
 long-eared bat [ˌlɒŋɪəd ˈbæt] Braunes Langohr OT 2
bath [bɑːθ] Badewanne; Bad OT 2
bathroom [ˈbɑːθruːm] Badezimmer OT 1
battery [ˈbætri] Batterie OT 2
battle [ˈbætl] Schlacht OT 1
Bavarian [bəˈveəriən] bayerisch OT 2
bay [beɪ] Bucht OT 1
to **be** [biː] sein OT 1
beach [biːtʃ] Strand OT 1
beam [biːm] Balken OT 3
bean [biːn] Bohne OT 1
 baked beans [ˌbeɪkt ˈbiːnz] weiße Bohnen in Tomatensoße OT 1
bear [beə] Bär OT 1
beast [biːst] Tier; Bestie WS 4, 132
beat [biːt] Takt OT 1
to **beat** [biːt] schlagen; besiegen OT 2
beautiful [ˈbjuːtɪfl] schön OT 1
beauty [ˈbjuːti] Schönheit OT 3
because [bɪˈkɒz] weil OT 1
to **become** [bɪˈkʌm] werden OT 2
bed [bed] Bett; Beet OT 1

bedbug [ˈbedbʌɡ] Bettwanze OT 1
bedroom [ˈbedruːm] Schlafzimmer OT 1
bee [biː] Biene OT 1
beef [biːf] Rindfleisch OT 2
 beef brisket [biːf ˈbrɪskɪt] Rinderbrust OT 4
beer [bɪə] Bier OT 3
beetroot [ˈbiːtruːt] Rote Bete OT 4
before [bɪˈfɔː] vor OT 1
beforehand [bɪˈfɔːhænd] im Voraus WS 4, 143
to **beg** [beɡ] betteln WS 4, 138
to **begin** [bɪˈɡɪn] anfangen OT 1
beginning [bɪˈɡɪnɪŋ] beginnend OT 1
behalf: on behalf of [ɒn bɪˈhɑːf əv] im Interesse von WS 1, 21
to **behave** [bɪˈheɪv] (sich) benehmen OT 2
behaviour [bɪˈheɪvjə] Benehmen OT 2
to **behead** [bɪˈhed] enthaupten OT 3
behind [bɪˈhaɪnd] hinter OT 1
belief [bɪˈliːf] Glaube OT 4
to **believe** [bɪˈliːv] glauben OT 2
bell [bel] Glocke OT 1
to **belong** [bɪˈlɒŋ] gehören OT 2
belongings [bɪˈlɒŋɪŋz] persönliche Sachen; Habe OT 3
below [bɪˈləʊ] unter OT 2
belt [belt] Gürtel OT 2
bench [bentʃ] Bank OT 3
beneath [bɪˈniːθ] darunter WS 1, 21
beneficial [ˌbenɪˈfɪʃl] nützlich OT 2
benefit [ˈbenɪfɪt] Vorteil; Nutzen OT 2
to **benefit** [ˈbenɪfɪt] guttun; profitieren OT 2
berry [ˈberi] Beere OT 4
beside [bɪˈsaɪd] neben OT 2
besides [bɪˈsaɪdz] außerdem WS 2, 60
best [best] beste(r, -s) OT 1
to **bet** [bet] wetten OT 1
between [bɪˈtwiːn] zwischen OT 1
beyond [bɪˈjɒnd] jenseits WS 1, 30
bias [ˈbaɪəs] Voreingenommenheit WS 3, 92
biased [ˈbaɪəst] parteiisch OT 4
bicycle [ˈbaɪsɪkəl] Fahrrad OT 2
big [bɪɡ] groß OT 1
bike [baɪk] Fahrrad OT 1
bike lane [ˈbaɪk leɪn] Radstreifen OT 4
to **bike** [baɪk] Rad fahren OT 3
 mountain biking [ˈmaʊntən baɪkɪŋ] Mountainbiken OT 2
bilingual [ˌbaɪˈlɪŋɡwəl] bilingual; zweisprachig OT 2
bill [bɪl] Rechnung OT 3
billion [ˈbɪljən] Milliarde OT 2

Appendix

VOCABULARY

bin [bɪn] Eimer; Behälter OT 2
bingo [ˈbɪŋgəʊ] Bingo OT 1
binoculars [bɪˈnɒkjələz] Fernglas OT 2
biodiversity [ˌbaɪəʊdaɪˈvɜːsəti] Artenvielfalt; Biodiversität OT 4
biographical [ˌbaɪəˈgræfɪkl] biografisch WS 1, 39
biography [baɪˈɒgrəfi] Biografie OT 4
biological [ˌbaɪəˈlɒdʒɪkl] biologisch WS 1, 30
biologist [baɪˈɒlədʒɪst] Biologe / Biologin OT 4
biology [baɪˈɒlədʒi] Biologie OT 2
bird [bɜːd] Vogel OT 1
birth [bɜːθ] Geburt OT 2
  date of birth [ˌdeɪt əv ˈbɜːθ] Geburtsdatum OT 2
birthday [ˈbɜːθdeɪ] Geburtstag OT 1
birthplace [ˈbɜːθpleɪs] Geburtsort OT 4
biscuit [ˈbɪskɪt] Keks OT 1
bisexual [ˌbaɪˈsekʃuəl] bisexuell WS 3, 93
bit [bɪt] Stück OT 1
bite [baɪt] Biss OT 2
bitterly [ˈbɪtəli] bitterlich WS 1, 24
black [blæk] schwarz OT 1
blackberry [ˈblækbəri] Brombeere OT 1
to blame [bleɪm] jmdm. Vorwürfe machen WS 3, 92
blank [blæŋk] leer OT 4
blanket [ˈblæŋkɪt] Decke OT 2
to blast [blɑːst] absprengen WS 3, 104
blazer [ˈbleɪzər] Blazer; Sportjacke OT 1
blazing [ˈbleɪzɪŋ] brennend WS 1, 40
bleaching [bliːtʃ] Entfärbung WS 1, 26
blemished [ˈblemɪʃd] fehlerhaft WS 1, 21
blended [ˈblendɪd] gemischt WS 3, 90
blind [blaɪnd] blind OT 2
blister [ˈblɪstə] Blase (Haut) OT 2
to block [blɒk] blockieren OT 3
blocker [ˈblɒkər] Blocker WS 3, 93
blog [blɒg] Blog OT 1
blogger [ˈblɒgə] Blogger(in) OT 3
blogpost [ˈblɒgpəʊst] Blogeintrag OT 4
blonde [blɒnd] blond OT 1
blood [blʌd] Blut OT 2
bloodshed [ˈblʌdʃed] Blutvergießen WS 1, 24
to blow [bləʊ] blasen; pfeifen; wehen OT 2
blubber [ˈblʌbə] Walspeck OT 2
blue [bluː] blau OT 1
bluebird [ˈbluːbɜːd] Hüttensänger OT 3
blues [bluːz] Blues OT 1
to blur [blɜːr] verschwimmen WS 2, 62

BMXing [ˌbiː em ˈeksɪŋ] BMX-Rad fahren WS 3, 93
board [bɔːd] Brett; Tafel OT 1
to board [bɔːd] an Bord gehen OT 4
boat [bəʊt] Boot OT 1
body [ˈbɒdi] Körper OT 1
to boil [bɔɪl] kochen OT 2
boiled [bɔɪld] gekocht OT 1
boiling [ˈbɔɪlɪŋ] kochend heiß OT 1
bold [bəʊld] mutig; fettgedruckt OT 1
bomb [bɒm] Bombe OT 3
bonded laborer [ˌbɒndɪd ˈleɪbərə] Schuldknecht; Zwangsarbeiter(in) OT 4
bone [bəʊn] Knochen OT 1
bong [bɒŋ] Klang (einer Glocke) OT 1
bonus [ˈbəʊnəs] Bonus WS 2, 82
book [bʊk] Buch OT 1
to book [bʊk] buchen OT 2
bookcase [ˈbʊkkeɪs] Bücherregal OT 1
booking [ˈbʊkɪŋ] Buchung OT 2
booking office [ˈbʊkɪŋ ˌɒfɪs] Fahrkartenschalter OT 2
booklet [ˈbʊklət] Broschüre OT 2
to bookmark [ˈbʊkmɑːk] markieren OT 4
boot [buːt] Stiefel OT 1
booth [buːð] Zelle OT 4
border [ˈbɔːdə] Grenze OT 3
bored [bɔːd] gelangweilt OT 1
boring [ˈbɔːrɪŋ] langweilig OT 1
born: to be born [bi ˈbɔːn] geboren sein OT 2
to borrow [ˈbɒrəʊ] leihen OT 2
boss [bɒs] Chef(in) OT 2
bossy [ˈbɒsi] herrisch OT 2
both [bəʊθ] beide OT 1
to bother [ˈbɒðə] stören OT 4
bottle [ˈbɒtl] Flasche OT 1
bottled [ˈbɒtld] abgefüllt OT 3
bottom [ˈbɒtəm] unterster Teil; Boden OT 1
to bounce back [baʊns] wieder auf die Beine kommen WS 1, 21
boundary [ˈbaʊndri] Grenze WS 2, 62
bouquet [buˈkeɪ] Strauß; Bouquet OT 3
bow [bəʊ] Bogen OT 2
bow-tie [ˌbəʊ ˈtaɪ] Fliege OT 2
bowl [bəʊl] Schüssel OT 1
box [bɒks] Kiste; Kästchen OT 1
boy [bɔɪ] Junge OT 1
boyband [ˈbɔɪbænd] Boygroup OT 2
bracket [ˈbrækɪt] Klammer OT 2
brain [breɪn] Gehirn OT 2
to brainstorm [ˈbreɪnstɔːm] brainstormen OT 2

to brainwash [ˈbreɪnwɒʃ] einer Gehirnwäsche unterziehen WS 1, 38
branch [brɑːntʃ] Ast OT 2
brand [brænd] Marke OT 4
brand-new [ˌbrænd ˈnjuː] brandneu OT 2
brave [breɪv] tapfer OT 1
Brazilian [brəˈzɪliən] brasilianisch OT 2
bread [bred] Brot OT 1
breadcrumbs [ˈbredkrʌmz] Brotkrumen; Paniermehl OT 3
breadwinner [ˈbredwɪnə] Ernährer(in); Brotverdiener(in) WS 2, 63
break [breɪk] Pause OT 1
to break [breɪk] brechen OT 1
breakfast [ˈbrekfəst] Frühstück OT 1
breakout area [ˈbreɪkaʊt ˈeəriə] Aufenthaltsraum WS 2, 70
breath [breθ] Atem(zug) OT 2
  out of breath [ˌaʊt əv ˈbreθ] außer Atem OT 2
to breathe [briːð] atmen OT 2
breathless [ˈbreθləs] atemlos OT 3
breathtaking [ˈbreθteɪkɪŋ] atemberaubend OT 3
breeze [briːz] Brise OT 3
bridge [brɪdʒ] Brücke OT 1
brief [briːf] kurz WS 2, 56
bright [braɪt] leuchtend OT 1
brill [brɪl] sehr gut OT 1
brilliant [ˈbrɪliənt] genial OT 1
to bring [brɪŋ] bringen OT 1
British [ˈbrɪtɪʃ] britisch OT 1
broccoli [ˈbrɒkəli] Broccoli OT 1
brochure [ˈbrəʊʃə] Broschüre OT 1
broken [ˈbrəʊkən] gebrochen OT 1
brother [ˈbrʌðə] Bruder OT 1
brown [braʊn] braun OT 1
browser [ˈbraʊzər] Browser OT 4
brush [brʌʃ] Bürste; Pinsel OT 2
to brush [brʌʃ] bürsten; putzen OT 4
brutal [ˈbruːtl] brutal WS 1, 21
brutality [bruːˈtæləti] Brutalität WS 1, 20
bubble [ˈbʌbl] Blase OT 1
buddy [ˈbʌdi] Kumpel OT 2
budgie [ˈbʌdʒi] Wellensittich OT 1
buffalo [ˈbʌfələʊ] Büffel OT 4
buffet [ˈbʌfeɪ] Buffet OT 3
buggy [ˈbʌgi] Pferdewagen; Kutsche OT 4
bughouse [ˈbʌghaʊs] Insektenhaus OT 1
to build [bɪld] bauen OT 1
builder [ˈbɪldə] Bauarbeiter(in) OT 2
building [ˈbɪldɪŋ] Gebäude OT 1

Appendix

VOCABULARY

bulb: LED bulb [ˌel iː ˈdiː bʌlb] LED Birne OT 3
to **bulk up** [bʌlk ʌp] Masse zusetzen; hier: Muskeln aufbauen **WS 3**, 102
to **bulldoze** [ˈbʊldəʊz] planieren **WS 1**, 27
bulletin board [ˈbʊlətɪn bɔːd] Anschlagtafel; Pinwand OT 4
to **bully** [ˈbʊli] mobben **WS 3**, 90
bully [ˈbʊli] Mobbingtäter(in) OT 2
bullying [ˈbʊliɪŋ] Mobbing OT 2
to **bump** [bʌmp] stoßen OT 2
    to **bump into** [ˈbʌmp ˌɪntə] anstoßen; mit jmdm. zusammenstoßen OT 2
bumpy [ˈbʌmpi] holprig; uneben OT 4
bungee jumping [ˈbʌndʒi dʒʌmpɪŋ] Bungee-Jumping OT 3
bunk bed [bʌŋk bed] Etagenbett; Stockbett OT 3
burger [ˈbɜːɡə] Hamburger OT 1
to **burn** [bɜːn] brennen OT 2
burrito [bʊˈriːtəʊ] Burrito OT 4
bus [bʌs] Bus OT 1
bus stop [ˈbʌs stɒp] Bushaltestelle OT 1
bush [bʊʃ] Busch OT 2
bushfire [ˈbʊʃfaɪə] Buschfeuer **WS 1**, 26
bushland [ˈbʊʃlænd] Buschland **WS 1**, 27
business [ˈbɪznəs] Geschäft(e) OT 3
businessman [ˈbɪznəsmæn] Unternehmer; Geschäftsmann OT 4
businesswoman [ˈbɪznəswʊmən] Unternehmerin; Geschäftsfrau OT 4
busker [ˈbʌskər] Straßenmusiker(in) **WS 1**, 17
busload [ˈbʌsləʊd] Busladung **WS 1**, 25
busy [ˈbɪzi] beschäftigt OT 1
but [bʌt] aber OT 1
butcher [ˈbʊtʃə] Fleischer; Metzger OT 4
butterfly [ˈbʌtəflaɪ] Schmetterling OT 2
button [ˈbʌtn] Knopf OT 1
to **buy** [baɪ] kaufen OT 1
buzzard [ˈbʌzəd] Bussard OT 2
by [faɪv] bei; neben; von OT 1
bye [baɪ] Tschüss! OT 1

C

cab [kæb] Taxi; Fahrerkabine; Führerhaus OT 4
cabbage [ˈkæbɪdʒ] Kohl OT 1
caber [ˈkeɪbə] Baumstamm OT 3
cabin [ˈkæbɪn] Kabine OT 2
cabinet [ˈkæbɪnət] Schrank; Kabinett **WS 2**, 71
cable [ˈkeɪbl] Kabel **WS 1**, 44
café [ˈkæfeɪ] Café OT 1
cafeteria [ˌkæfəˈtɪəriə] Cafeteria OT 2
caffeine [ˈkæfiːn] Koffein **WS 3**, 102
cage [keɪdʒ] Käfig OT 4
cake [keɪk] Kuchen OT 1
calendar [ˈkælɪndə] Kalender OT 1
call [kɔːl] Anruf OT 1
to **call** [kɔːl] anrufen; nennen OT 1
called [kɔːld] namens; mit dem Namen OT 1
caller [ˈkɔːlə] Anrufer(in) OT 2
calm [kɑːm] ruhig OT 2
    calmly [ˈkɑːmli] ruhig OT 3
calorie [ˈkæləri] Kalorie **WS 3**, 102
camel [ˈkæml] Kamel **WS 1**, 23
camera [ˈkæmərə] Fotoapparat; Kamera OT 1
cameraman [ˈkæmrəmæn] Kameramann **WS 4**, 138
camp [kæmp] Camp; Ferienlager OT 1
    summer camp [ˈsʌmə kæmp] Ferienlager OT 2
to **camp** [kæmp] zelten OT 1
    campaign [kæmˈpeɪn] Kampagne; Aktion OT 3
to **campaign** [kæmˈpeɪn] Kampagne OT 3
camper [ˈkæmpə] Camper(in) OT 2
camper van [ˈkæmpə væn] Wohnmobil OT 4
campfire [ˈkæmpfaɪə] Lagerfeuer OT 2
campground [ˈkæmpɡraʊnd] Zeltplatz OT 2
camping [ˈkæmpɪŋ] Camping; Zelten OT 1
campsite [ˈkæmpsaɪt] Zeltplatz; Campingplatz OT 1
campus [ˈkæmpəs] Campus OT 2
can [kæn] können OT 1; Dose OT 2
canal [kəˈnæl] Kanal OT 3
to **cancel** [ˈkænsl] absagen OT 4
cancer [ˈkænsə] Krebs OT 4
candidate [ˈkændɪdət] Kandidat(in) OT 4
candle [ˈkændl] Kerze OT 2
candlelight [ˈkændllaɪt] Kerzenlicht OT 4
candy [ˈkændi] Süßigkeit OT 4
cane toad [keɪn təʊd] Agakröte **WS 4**, 143
canned [kænd] Dosen... OT 2
canoe [kəˈnuː] Kanu OT 1
canoeing [kəˈnuːɪŋ] Kanufahren OT 1
canteen [kænˈtiːn] Kantine OT 1
canyon [ˈkænjən] Schlucht; Canyon OT 3
canyoning [ˈkænjənɪŋ] Canyoning OT 3
cap [kæp] Mütze OT 1
capable [ˈkeɪpəbl] fähig OT 4
capital [ˈkæpɪtl] Hauptstadt OT 1
capital letter [ˌkæpɪtl ˈletə] Großbuchstabe OT 1
capsule [ˈkæpsjuːl] Kapsel; Raumkapsel OT 4
captain [ˈkæptɪn] Spielführer(in); Kommandant(in) OT 4
caption [ˈkæpʃn] Bildunterschrift; Bildtext; Untertitel OT 1
to **capture** [ˈkæptʃə] einfangen; festnehmen OT 4
car [kɑː] Auto OT 1
caramel [ˈkærəmel] Karamelle OT 3
caravan [ˈkærəvæn] Wohnwagen OT 1
carb [kɑːb] Kohlenhydrat **WS 3**, 103
carbohydrate [ˌkɑːbəʊˈhaɪdreɪt] Kohlenhydrat **WS 3**, 102
carbon [ˈkɑːbən] Karbon OT 3
carbon dioxide [ˌkɑːbəndaɪˈɒksaɪd] Kohlendioxid **WS 1**, 26
card [kɑːd] Karte OT 1
to **care** [keə] besorgt sein OT 1
    to **care about** [ˈkeə əˌbaʊt] (sich) interessieren; gern haben OT 2
career [kəˈrɪə] Karriere OT 3
careful [ˈkeəfl] vorsichtig; sorgfältig OT 1
careless [ˈkeələs] sorglos OT 2
    carelessly [ˈkeələsli] unvorsichtig; leichtsinnig OT 2
carer [ˈkeərər] Betreuer(in) **WS 3**, 93
caretaker [ˈkeəteɪkə] Hausmeister(in) OT 1
cargo [ˈkɑːɡəʊ] Ladung OT 3
car park [ˈkɑː pɑːk] Parkplatz OT 1
carpet [ˈkɑːpɪt] Teppich OT 4
carriage [ˈkærɪdʒ] Wagen OT 1
carriage driving [ˈkærɪdʒ ˈdraɪvɪŋ] Kutschfahrten OT 2
carrier bag [ˈkæriə bæɡ] Tragetasche OT 2
carrot [ˈkærət] Karotte OT 1
to **carry** [ˈkæri] tragen OT 1
carsick [ˈkɑːsɪk] autokrank OT 2
carton [ˈkɑːtn] Karton OT 2
cartoon [kɑːˈtuːn] Zeichentrickfilm; Cartoon OT 4
to **carve** [kɑːv] schnitzen OT 2
case [keɪs] Tasche; Koffer OT 1
cash [kæʃ] Kleingeld; Bargeld OT 1
cash register [ˈkæʃ redʒɪstə] Kasse OT 2
cashier [kæˈʃɪə] Kassierer(in) OT 4
to **cast a spell** [kɑːst ə ˈspel] einen Zauber bewirken OT 1

Appendix

VOCABULARY

castle [ˈkɑːsl] Burg OT 1
casual [ˈkæʒuəl] locker; lässig WS 3, 104
cat [kæt] Katze OT 1
catastrophic [ˌkætəˈstrɒfɪk] katastrophal OT 4
to **catch** [kætʃ] fangen OT 1
catchphrase [ˈkætʃfreɪz] Schlagwort WS 1, 44
category [ˈkætəgəri] Kategorie OT 3
catering service [ˈkeɪtərɪŋ ˈsɜːvɪs] Verpflegungsservice OT 4
cathedral [kəˈθiːdrəl] Kathedrale OT 1
Catholic [ˈkæθlɪk] Katholik(in) OT 3
cattle [ˈkætl] Rinder WS 1, 16
cattle ranching [ˈkætl ˈrɑːntʃɪŋ] Viehhaltung WS 3, 103
cause [kɔːz] Grund; Anliegen OT 2
to **cause** [kɔːz] verursachen OT 2
cave [keɪv] Höhle OT 1
ceiling [ˈsiːlɪŋ] Decke OT 4
to **celebrate** [ˈselɪbreɪt] feiern OT 1
celebration [ˌselɪˈbreɪʃn] Feier OT 2
celebrity [səˈlebrəti] Prominente(r) OT 3
cell [sel] Zelle OT 1
cellar [ˈselə] Keller OT 4
cellist [ˈtʃelɪst] Cellist(in) OT 2
cello [ˈtʃeləʊ] Cello OT 2
cell phone [ˈsel fəʊn] Handy OT 2
census [ˈsensəs] Bevölkerungszählung; Befragung WS 3, 90
cent [sent] Cent OT 1
center [ˈsentə] Mitte; Zentrum OT 1
centigrade [ˈsentɪgreɪd] Celsius OT 4
centimetre (cm) [ˈsentɪmiːtə] Zentimeter OT 2
central [ˈsentrəl] Zentral- OT 1
centre [ˈsentə] Mitte; Zentrum OT 1
to **centre around** [ˈsentər əˈraʊnd] sich auf etw. beziehen; sich auf etw. konzentrieren WS 4, 145
century [ˈsentʃəri] Jahrhundert OT 2
cereal [ˈsɪərɪəl] Cornflakes; Frühstücksflocken OT 1
ceremonial [ˌserɪˈməʊnɪəl] zeremoniell; feierlich OT 3
ceremony [ˈserəməni] Feier OT 2
certain [ˈsɜːtn] sicher OT 3
certainly [ˈsɜːtnli] sicher; sicherlich OT 1
certificate [səˈtɪfɪkət] Zeugnis; Zertifikat OT 1
certified [ˈsɜːtɪfaɪd] beglaubigt; anerkannt WS 4, 139

chain [tʃeɪn] Kette OT 2
chair [tʃeə] Stuhl OT 1
to **challenge** [ˈtʃælɪndʒ] herausfordern WS 3, 92
challenge [ˈtʃælɪndʒ] Herausforderung OT 2
challenging [ˈtʃælɪndʒɪŋ] schwierig OT 4
chamber [ˈtʃeɪmbə] Kammer OT 2
chance [tʃɑːns] Zufall; Möglichkeit OT 2
change [tʃeɪndʒ] Wechselgeld; Änderung OT 1
to **change** [tʃeɪndʒ] ändern; wechseln OT 1
changing room [ˈtʃeɪndʒɪŋ ˌruːm] Umkleide OT 1
channel [ˈtʃænl] Programm OT 2
chaotic [keɪˈɒtɪk] chaotisch WS 2, 55
chapter [ˈtʃæptə] Kapitel OT 1
character [ˈkærəktə] Charakter OT 1
characteristic [ˌkærəktəˈrɪstɪk] charakteristisches Merkmal OT 2
characterization [ˌkærəktəraɪˈzeɪʃn] Charakterisierung WS 3, 115
charge: in charge [ɪn ˈtʃɑːdʒ] zuständig OT 1
to **be in charge of** [tʃɑːdʒ] für etw. verantwortlich sein OT 3
to **charge** [tʃɑːdʒ] aufladen OT 4; anklagen WS 3, 100
charity [ˈtʃærəti] Wohlfahrtsorganisation OT 2
charming [ˈtʃɑːmɪŋ] charmant OT 3
chart [tʃɑːt] Diagramm; Chart OT 4
 bar chart [ˈbɑː tʃɑːt] Balkendiagramm OT 4
 pie chart [ˈpaɪ tʃɑːt] Tortendiagramm; Kreisdiagramm OT 4
to **chase** [tʃeɪs] jagen OT 1
chat [tʃæt] Unterhaltung OT 1
to **chatter** [ˈtʃætə] plaudern OT 2
chatty [ˈtʃæti] gesprächig OT 3
cheap [tʃiːp] billig OT 2
to **check** [tʃek] überprüfen OT 1
checker [ˈtʃekə] Prüfer(in) OT 3
checkers [ˈtʃekəz] Damespiel OT 1
check-in desk [ˈtʃek ɪn desk] Abflugschalter OT 2
checklist [ˈtʃeklɪst] Checkliste OT 4
check-out [ˈtʃekaʊt] Kasse OT 4
cheeky [ˈtʃiːki] frech OT 1
to **cheer** [tʃɪə] jubeln OT 2
 cheer up [tʃɪə ʌp] Kopf hoch! OT 1
cheerful [ˈtʃɪəfl] fröhlich WS 2, 57

cheerleader [ˈtʃɪəliːdə] Cheerleader(in) OT 3
cheese [tʃiːz] Käse OT 1
chef [ʃef] Küchenchef(in); Koch / Köchin OT 1
chemical [ˈkemɪkl] Chemikalie OT 3
chemist [ˈkemɪst] Apotheker(in); Chemiker(in) OT 2
 chemist's shop [ˈkemɪsts ʃɒp] Apotheke OT 2
chess [tʃes] Schach OT 1
chessboard [ˈtʃesbɔːd] Schachbrett OT 1
chicken [ˈtʃɪkɪn] Huhn; Hähnchen OT 1
child [tʃaɪld] Kind OT 1
childhood [ˈtʃaɪldhʊd] Kindheit OT 3
chili [ˈtʃɪli] Chili OT 2
to **chill** [tʃɪl] chillen; sich entspannen WS 3, 95
 to **chill out** [tʃɪl aʊt] sich entspannen OT 4
Chinese [ˌtʃaɪˈniːz] chinesisch OT 1
chip [tʃɪp] Fritte OT 1
chocoholic [ˌtʃɒkəˈhɒlɪk] Schokoladensüchtige(r) OT 3
chocolate [ˈtʃɒklət] Schokolade OT 1
choice [tʃɔɪs] Wahl OT 1
choir [ˈkwaɪə] Chor OT 1
cholera [ˈkɒlərə] Cholera OT 4
to **choose** [tʃuːz] auswählen OT 1
to **chop** [tʃɒp] schneiden OT 3
chopped [tʃɒpt] gehackt OT 2
chopstick [ˈtʃɒpstɪk] Essstäbchen OT 1
chore [tʃɔːr] Hausarbeit OT 4; Routinearbeit WS 1, 16
chorizo [tʃəˈriːzəʊ] Chorizo OT 2
chowder [ˈtʃaʊdə] dickflüssige Fischsuppe OT 3
Christmas [ˈkrɪsməs] Weihnachten OT 1
Christmas market [ˈkrɪsməs ˈmɑːkɪt] Weihnachtsmarkt OT 2
church [tʃɜːtʃ] Kirche OT 1
cinema [ˈsɪnəmə] Kino OT 1
circle [ˈsɜːkl] Kreis OT 1
circuit [ˈsɜːkɪt] Schaltkreis OT 4
to **circulate** [ˈsɜːkjəleɪt] kursieren; zirkulieren OT 4
circumstance [ˈsɜːkəmstəns] Umstand; Lage WS 3, 100
citation [saɪˈteɪʃn] Anführung (einer Quelle) OT 2
to **cite** [saɪt] anführen; zitieren OT 2
citizen [ˈsɪtɪzn] Einwohner(in) OT 3
city [ˈsɪti] Stadt OT 1
 inner city [ˌɪnə ˈsɪti] Innenstadt OT 4

VOCABULARY

to **claim** [kleɪm] behaupten; beanspruchen **WS 1**, 18
clan [klæn] Klan OT 3
to **clap** [klæp] klatschen OT 1
clarification [ˌklærəfɪˈkeɪʃn] Abklärung OT 4
to **clarify** [ˈklærəfaɪ] etw. klären OT 4
clarinet [ˌklærəˈnet] Klarinette OT 2
to **clash** [klæʃ] klirren; nicht zusammenpassen OT 2
class [klɑːs] Unterricht; Klasse OT 1
classic [ˈklæsɪk] klassisch OT 2
classical [ˈklæsɪkl] klassisch OT 2
classmate [ˈklɑːsmeɪt] Klassenkamerad(in) OT 3
classroom [ˈklɑːsruːm] Klassenzimmer OT 1
clause [klɔːz] Satzteil OT 2
　relative clause [relətɪv ˈklɔːz] Relativsatz OT 2
clay [kleɪ] Ton OT 4
clean [kliːn] sauber OT 1
to **clean** [kliːn] putzen; reinigen **WS 1**, 40
cleaner [ˈkliːnə] Reinigungsmittel OT 3
cleaning wipe [ˈkliːnɪŋ waɪp] Reinigungstuch OT 2
to **clear** [klɪə] räumen OT 4
clear [klɪə] klar OT 2
　clearly [ˈklɪəli] deutlich OT 3
clever [ˈklevə] intelligent OT 1
to **click** [klɪk] klicken **WS 3**, 104
　to **click on** [klɪk] anklicken OT 3
client [ˈklaɪənt] Mandant(in); Kunde / Kundin **WS 2**, 70
cliff [klɪf] Klippe; Felsen **WS 1**, 22
climate [ˈklaɪmət] Klima OT 2
climax [ˈklaɪmæks] Höhepunkt **WS 4**, 145
to **climb** [klaɪm] klettern; steigen OT 1
climber [ˈklaɪmə] Kletterer(in) OT 2
climbing [ˈklaɪmɪŋ] Klettern; Bergsteigen OT 1
to **cling** [klɪŋ] (sich) an etw. klammern; an etw. festhalten OT 2
clinic [ˈklɪnɪk] Klinik **WS 2**, 66
clinical [ˈklɪnɪkl] klinisch **WS 3**, 108
clip [klɪp] Klammer; Ausschnitt; Clip OT 1
cloak [kləʊk] Umhang OT 1
clock [klɒk] Uhr OT 1
to **close** [kləʊz] schließen OT 1
close [kləʊz] nah / nahe OT 4
　closely [ˈkləʊsli] eng OT 3
closed [kləʊzd] geschlossen OT 1

closeness [ˈkləʊsnəs] Nähe; Dichte **WS 3**, 115
closet [ˈklɒzɪt] kleine Kammer; Wandschrank OT 2
close-up [ˈkləʊsʌp] Großaufnahme OT 4
cloth [klɒθ] Lappen OT 2
clothes [kləʊðz] Kleidung; Kleider OT 1
clothing [ˈkləʊðɪŋ] Kleidung OT 3
cloud [klaʊd] Wolke OT 1
cloudy [ˈklaʊdi] wolkig; bewölkt; trüb OT 4
clout [klaʊt] Einfluss OT 4
club [klʌb] Klub; Verein OT 1
clue [kluː] Hinweis OT 1
clumsy [ˈklʌmzi] ungeschickt OT 2
co-ed [ˌkəʊˈed] gemischtgeschlechtlich OT 2
co-educational [ˌkəʊedjəˈkeɪʃənl] gemischtgeschlechtlich OT 2
to **co-found** [kəʊfaʊnd] mitbegründen OT 4
coach [kəʊtʃ] Reisebus; Trainer(in) OT 1
coaching [ˈkəʊtʃɪŋ] Coaching OT 4
coal [kəʊl] Kohle OT 2
coast [kəʊst] Küste OT 1
coastal [ˈkəʊstl] Küsten... OT 1
coastguard [ˈkəʊstgɑːd] Küstenwache OT 2
coastline [ˈkəʊstlaɪn] Küstenlinie; Küste **WS 1**, 32
coat [kəʊt] Mantel OT 1
code [kəʊd] Verschlüsselung OT 1
　code of conduct [kəʊd əv kənˈdʌkt] Verhaltensregeln **WS 4**, 140
coffee [ˈkɒfi] Kaffee OT 1
coin [kɔɪn] Münze OT 1
cola [ˈkəʊlə] Cola OT 1
cold [kəʊld] kalt OT 1; Erkältung **WS 2**, 65
collar [ˈkɒlə] Halsband OT 2
colleague [ˈkɒliːg] Kollege(-in); Mitarbeiter(in) OT 4
to **collect** [kəˈlekt] sammeln OT 1
collection [kəˈlekʃn] Sammlung OT 2
college [ˈkɒlɪdʒ] Hochschule OT 2
colonial [kəˈləʊniəl] kolonial OT 4
colonist [ˈkɒlənɪst] Kolonist(in) OT 3
colonization [ˌkɒlənaɪˈzeɪʃn] Kolonialisierung **WS 1**, 22
to **colonize** [ˈkɒlənaɪz] kolonisieren **WS 3**, 91
colonizer [ˈkɒlənaɪzər] Ansiedler(in) **WS 1**, 20
colony [ˈkɒləni] Kolonie OT 4
colour [ˈkʌlə] Farbe OT 1

coloured [ˈkʌləd] farbig; bunt OT 1
colourful [ˈkʌləfl] farbenfroh OT 3
column [ˈkɒləm] Säule; Spalte OT 1
comb [kəʊm] Kamm OT 2
combination [ˌkɒmbɪˈneɪʃn] Kombination; Verbindung OT 3
to **combine** [kəmˈbaɪn] kombinieren; mischen OT 4
to **come** [kʌm] kommen OT 1
　to **come first / second / third** [kʌm ˈfɜːst / sekənd / θɜːd] den ersten / zweiten / dritten Platz belegen OT 2
　Come in! [kʌm ˈɪn] Herein! OT 2
comedy [ˈkɒmədi] Komödie **WS 4**, 145
to **comfort** [ˈkʌmfət] trösten **WS 3**, 94
comfortable [ˈkʌmftəbl] bequem OT 1
comfy [ˈkʌmfi] gemütlich OT 4
comic [ˈkɒmɪk] Comicheft OT 1
comma [ˈkɒmə] Komma OT 3
commander [kəˈmɑːndə] Kommandant(in) OT 4
commanding [kəˈmɑːndɪŋ] befehlshabend OT 2
to **commence** [kəˈmens] anfangen OT 4
comment [ˈkɒment] Kommentar OT 1
to **comment** [ˈkɒment] kommentieren OT 3
commerce [ˈkɒmɜːs] Handel; Kommerz **WS 2**, 50
commercial [kəˈmɜːʃl] kommerziell OT 4
to **commit** [kəˈmɪt] begehen OT 4
committee [kəˈmɪti] Ausschuss; Komitee OT 2
common [ˈkɒmən] normal; gewöhnlich OT 4
commonwealth [ˈkɒmənwelθ] Commonwealth **WS 1**, 21
to **communicate** [kəˈmjuːnɪkeɪt] kommunizieren; etw. vermitteln OT 4
community [kəˈmjuːnəti] Gemeinschaft OT 2
to **commute** [kəˈmjuːt] pendeln **WS 2**, 63
commuter [kəˈmjuːtə] Pendler(in) OT 2
commuter rail [kəˌmjuːtə ˈreɪl] Pendlerbahn OT 2
company [ˈkʌmpəni] Unternehmen OT 4
comparative [kəmˈpærətɪv] Komparativ OT 2
to **compare** [kəmˈpeə] vergleichen OT 1
comparison [kəmˈpærɪsn] Vergleich OT 2
compass [ˈkʌmpəs] Kompass OT 2

VOCABULARY

compensation [ˌkɒmpenˈseɪʃn] Entschädigung **WS 1**, 38
to compete [kəmˈpiːt] mit jmdm. / etw. konkurrieren OT 2
competence [ˈkɒmpɪtəns] Kompetenz **WS 4**, 144
competent [ˈkɒmpɪtənt] fähig; kompetent **WS 2**, 58
competition [ˌkɒmpəˈtɪʃn] Konkurrenz; Wettbewerb OT 1
competitive [kəmˈpetətɪv] konkurrenzorientiert OT 4
competitively [kəmˈpetətɪvli] konkurrierend; wetteifernd OT 4
competitor [kəmˈpetɪtə] Konkurrent(in); Mitbewerber(in) OT 4
to complain [kəmˈpleɪn] sich beschweren OT 3
complaint [kəmˈpleɪnt] Beschwerde OT 2
to complete [kəmˈpliːt] vervollständigen OT 1
completely [kəmˈpliːtli] ganz OT 2
complex [ˈkɒmpleks] komplex **WS 1**, 32
complicated [ˈkɒmplɪkeɪtɪd] kompliziert OT 2
compliment [ˈkɒmplɪmənt] Kompliment **WS 4**, 140
to compose [kəmˈpəʊz] komponieren OT 3
composer [kəmˈpəʊzə] Komponist(in) OT 2
compost [ˈkɒmpɒst] Kompost OT 3
composting [ˈkɒmpɒstɪŋ] Kompostierungs- OT 4
compromise [ˈkɒmprəmaɪz] Kompromiss **WS 3**, 92
computer [kəmˈpjuːtə] Computer; Rechner OT 1
computerized [kəmˈpjuːtəraɪzd] computerbasiert; computergesteuert OT 4
computer lab [kəmˈpjuːtə ˌlæb] Computerraum OT 2
computing [kəmˈpjuːtɪŋ] Computing **WS 2**, 51
con [kɒn] Nachteil OT 2
to conceal [kənˈsiːl] verbergen **WS 3**, 93
to concentrate [ˈkɒnsntreɪt] konzentrieren OT 3
concentration [ˌkɒnsnˈtreɪʃn] Konzentration OT 4
concept [ˈkɒnsept] Konzept; Begriff OT 4
concern [kənˈsɜːn] Sorge; Bedenken **WS 1**, 33

concerned [kənˈsɜːnd] besorgt **WS 1**, 26
concert [ˈkɒnsət] Konzert OT 1
to conclude [kənˈkluːd] schließen (aus etw.); beenden OT 4
conclusion [kənˈkluːʒn] Schluss OT 3
condition [kənˈdɪʃn] Bedingung OT 3
condor [ˈkɒndɔː] Kondor OT 3
to conduct [kənˈdʌkt] durchführen OT 3
conference [ˈkɒnfərəns] Konferenz OT 4
  video conferencing [ˈvɪdiəʊ ˈkɒnfərənsɪŋ] Videokonferenztechnik OT 4
  web conference [web ˈkɒnfərəns] Webkonferenz OT 4
confidence [ˈkɒnfɪdəns] Selbstvertrauen **WS 1**, 21
confident [ˈkɒnfɪdənt] selbstbewusst; zuversichtlich OT 2
  confidently [ˈkɒnfɪdəntli] selbstbewusst; zuversichtlich OT 2
to confirm [kənˈfɜːm] bestätigen OT 4
conflict [ˈkɒnflɪkt] Konflikt OT 2
to conform [kənˈfɔːm] anpassen **WS 3**, 93
confused [kənˈfjuːzd] verwirrt OT 2
confusing [kənˈfjuːzɪŋ] verwirrend OT 2
to congratulate [kənˈɡrætʃuleɪt] gratulieren OT 2
congratulations [kənˌɡrætʃuˈleɪʃnz] Glückwünsche OT 2
to connect [kəˈnekt] verbinden OT 2
connected [kəˈnektɪd] verbunden OT 1
connection [kəˈnekʃn] Verbindung OT 2
consequence [ˈkɒnsɪkwəns] Folge; Konsequenz OT 4
conservation [ˌkɒnsəˈveɪʃn] Schutz; Erhaltung OT 2
to consider [kənˈsɪdə] nachdenken über WW, 11
considerably [kənˈsɪdərəbli] deutlich; umfangreich **WS 3**, 98
consideration [kənˌsɪdəˈreɪʃn] Rücksicht **WS 4**, 140
to consist of [kənˈsɪst əv] aus etw. bestehen **WS 1**, 32
constellation [ˌkɒnstəˈleɪʃn] Konstellation **WS 3**, 115
constitution [ˌkɒnstɪˈtjuːʃn] Verfassung **WS 1**, 39
construction [kənˈstrʌkʃn] Bau OT 4
constructive [kənˈstrʌktɪv] konstruktiv **WS 4**, 140
consultant [kənˈsʌltənt] Berater(in) **WS 2**, 62
consumer [kənˈsjuːmər] Verbraucher(in) **WS 3**, 104

contact [ˈkɒntækt] Kontakt OT 1
  to be in contact with [bi ɪn ˈkɒntækt wɪð] in Kontakt mit jmdm. sein OT 2
to contain [kənˈteɪn] beinhalten; enthalten OT 3
container [kənˈteɪnə] Behälter; Container OT 2
contemporary [kənˈtemprəri] zeitgenössisch OT 3
content [ˈkɒntents] Inhalt OT 2
context [ˈkɒntekst] Kontext; Zusammenhang OT 4
continent [ˈkɒntɪnənt] Kontinent OT 3
to continue [kənˈtɪnjuː] andauern; weitermachen OT 1
contractor [kənˈtræktə] Auftragnehmer(in) **WS 2**, 62
contrast [ˈkɒntrɑːst] Gegenteil; Kontrast OT 3
contrasting [kənˈtrɑːstɪŋ] gegensätzlich OT 4
to contribute [kənˈtrɪbjuːt] mitwirken OT 4
contribution [ˌkɒntrɪˈbjuːʃn] Beitrag; Mitwirkung OT 4
control [kənˈtrəʊl] Kontrolle OT 3
to control [kənˈtrəʊl] kontrollieren OT 4
controversial [ˌkɒntrəˈvɜːʃl] umstritten **WS 1**, 23
convenience [kənˈviːniəns] Bequemlichkeit; zweckmäßiges Gerät OT 4
convenient [kənˈviːniənt] günstig; praktisch OT 4
convention [kənˈvenʃn] Kongress; Konvention OT 4
conversation [ˌkɒnvəˈseɪʃn] Gespräch OT 1
conversational [ˌkɒnvəˈseɪʃənl] Gesprächs... **WS 1**, 31
to convey [kənˈveɪ] vermitteln **WS 4**, 141
convict [ˈkɒnvɪkt] Verurteilte(r) **WS 1**, 18
to convict [kənˈvɪkt] verurteilen **WS 3**, 108
to convince [kənˈvɪns] überzeugen; überreden OT 4
to cook [kʊk] kochen OT 1
cooker [ˈkʊkə] Herd OT 3
cookie [ˈkʊki] Keks OT 3
cooking [ˈkʊkɪŋ] Kochen OT 1
to cool [kuːl] kühlen OT 3
cool [kuːl] kühl; cool OT 1
cooling [ˈkuːlɪŋ] Kühl... OT 3
coop [kuːp] Hühnerstall OT 4

Appendix

VOCABULARY

to **cope** [kəʊp] zurechtkommen **WS 3**, 120
copper [ˈkɒpə] Kupfer OT 1
to **copy** [ˈkɒpi] kopieren OT 1
coral [ˈkɒrəl] Koralle **WS 1**, 26
core [kɔː] Kern; Haupt… OT 4
corn [kɔːn] Mais OT 3
cornbread [ˈkɔːnbred] Maisbrot OT 4
corner [ˈkɔːnə] Ecke OT 1
corporate [ˈkɔːpərət] Korporations…; unternehmensweit **WW**, 11
corporation [ˌkɔːpəˈreɪʃn] Unternehmen OT 4
corpse [kɔːps] Leiche **WS 1**, 38
to **correct** [kəˈrekt] korrigieren OT 1
correct [kəˈrekt] richtig OT 1
correction [kəˈrekʃn] Korrektur OT 4
correspondence [ˌkɒrəˈspɒndəns] Schriftverkehr OT 4
corresponding [ˌkɒrəˈspɒndɪŋ] entsprechend **WS 3**, 106
corridor [ˈkɒrɪdɔː] Korridor OT 2
cosmopolitan [ˌkɒzməˈpɒlɪtən] kosmopolitisch; weltoffen **WS 1**, 19
cost [kɒst] Kosten OT 1
to **cost** [kɒst] kosten OT 1
costume [ˈkɒstjuːm] Kostüm OT 2
cottage [ˈkɒtɪdʒ] Häuschen OT 3
cotton [ˈkɒtn] Baumwolle OT 4
to **cough** [kɒf] husten OT 2
council [ˈkaʊnsl] Rat OT 3
counsel [ˈkaʊnsl] Anwalt / Anwältin **WS 3**, 101
counselling [ˈkaʊnsəlɪŋ] Beratung **WS 3**, 100
counsellor [ˈkaʊnsələ] Jugendbetreuer(in); Berater(in); psychologischer Betreuer OT 2
to **count** [kaʊnt] zählen OT 1
countable [ˈkaʊntəbl] zählbar OT 1
countdown [ˈkaʊntdaʊn] Countdown OT 4
counter [ˈkaʊntə] Theke OT 3
country [ˈkʌntri] Land OT 1
country dancing [ˌkʌntri ˈdɑːnsɪŋ] Volkstanz OT 1
countryside [ˈkʌntrisaɪd] Land OT 1
couple [ˈkʌpl] Paar OT 2
coupon [ˈkuːpɒn] Gutschein OT 2
course [kɔːs] Kurs; Gang OT 1
court [kɔːt] Hof; Platz OT 3; Gericht **WS 1**, 43
courtyard [ˈkɔːtjɑːd] Hof; Innenhof OT 3
cousin [ˈkʌzn] Cousin(e) OT 1
cover [ˈkʌvə] Abdeckung; Hülle OT 1
to **cover** [ˈkʌvə] abdecken OT 2

cow [kaʊ] Kuh OT 1
cowboy word [ˈkaʊbɔɪ wɜːd] Wort, das im Englischen und Deutschen gleich ist OT 2
coyote [kaɪˈəʊti] Kojote; hier: Schlepper(in) **WS 4**, 127
cozy [ˈkəʊzi] gemütlich OT 3
cracker [ˈkrækə] Cracker OT 3
cramp [kræmp] Krampf OT 2
cramped [kræmpt] beengt OT 3
cranberry [ˈkrænbəri] Cranberry; Moosbeere OT 4
crane [kreɪn] Kran OT 4
to **crash** [kræʃ] krachen OT 3
crate [kreɪt] Kiste OT 4
to **crawl** [krɔːl] krabbeln; kriechen **WS 1**, 20
crazy [ˈkreɪzi] verrückt OT 2
cream [kriːm] Sahne OT 1
to **create** [kriˈeɪt] schaffen; kreieren OT 2
creative [kriˈeɪtɪv] kreativ OT 2
creativity [ˌkriːeɪˈtɪvəti] Kreativität OT 4
creature [ˈkriːtʃə] Lebewesen; Wesen OT 4
credit card [ˈkredɪt kɑːd] Kreditkarte OT 1
creek [kriːk] Bach OT 3
creepy [ˈkriːpi] gruselig **WS 1**, 13
 creepy-crawly [ˌkriːpiˈkrɔːli] Krabbeltier OT 2
crescent [ˈkresnt] Sichel; sichelförmige Bauform OT 2
crew [kruː] Mannschaft; Personal OT 2
crewed [kruːd] bemannt OT 4
cricket [ˈkrɪkɪt] Kricket OT 1
crime [kraɪm] Verbrechen OT 4
criminal [ˈkrɪmɪnl] Kriminelle(r) OT 3
crisis [ˈkraɪsɪs] Krise OT 3
crisp [krɪsp] Chip OT 1
critical [ˈkrɪtɪkl] kritisch; wichtig **WS 1**, 23
criticism [ˈkrɪtɪsɪzəm] Kritik **WS 4**, 140
to **criticize** [ˈkrɪtɪsaɪz] kritisieren OT 3
crocodile [ˈkrɒkədaɪl] Krokodil **WS 1**, 44
crop [krɒp] Ernte; Getreide OT 4
to **cross** [krɒs] überqueren; kreuzen OT 1
 to **cross out** [krɒs aʊt] ausstreichen OT 1
cross-country [ˌkrɒs ˈkʌntri] querfeldein OT 2
crossly [ˈkrɒsli] mürrisch OT 3
crossroads [ˈkrɒsrəʊdz] Kreuzung OT 1
crowd [kraʊd] Menge; Menschenmenge OT 1

crowded [ˈkraʊdɪd] überfüllt OT 2
crown [kraʊn] Krone OT 1
to **crown** [kraʊn] krönen OT 1
cruelty [ˈkruːəlti] Quälerei; Grausamkeit **WS 3**, 103
cruise [kruːz] Kreuzfahrt OT 2
to **cruise** [kruːz] mit dem Boot fahren; herumfahren OT 3
to **have a crush on sb.** [həv ə krʌʃ ɒn] in jmdn. verknallt sein OT 4
crutch [krʌtʃ] Krücke OT 2
to **cry** [kraɪ] weinen OT 1
cuddly [ˈkʌdli] kuschelig; knuddelig OT 1
cue card [ˈkjuː kɑːd] Karteikarte OT 4
cuisine [kwɪˈziːn] Küche OT 3
cull [kʌl] Schlachten; Keulen **WS 1**, 23
to **cull** [kʌl] keulen; selektiv schlachten **WS 1**, 23
to **cultivate** [ˈkʌltɪveɪt] anbauen; bebauen OT 4
cultural [ˈkʌltʃərəl] kulturell OT 3
culture [ˈkʌltʃə] Kultur OT 1
cultured [ˈkʌltʃəd] gebildet; kultiviert OT 4
Cumbrian [ˈkʌmbriən] von / aus Cumbria OT 2
cup [kʌp] Tasse OT 1
cupboard [ˈkʌbəd] Schrank OT 1
cupola [ˈkjuːpələ] Kuppel OT 4
curb [kɜːb] Bordstein **WS 3**, 100
to **cure** [kjʊə] heilen OT 4
curfew [ˈkɜːfjuː] Ausgangssperre OT 3
curiosity [ˌkjʊəriˈɒsəti] Neugier OT 4
curious [ˈkjʊəriəs] neugierig; gespannt OT 4
curly [ˈkɜːli] gelockt OT 3
current [ˈkʌrənt] aktuell OT 4
 currently [ˈkʌrəntli] derzeit; gerade **WS 3**, 93
Curriculum Vitae [kəˌrɪkjələm ˈviːtaɪ] Lebenslauf; Vita **WS 2**, 56
curry [ˈkʌri] Currygericht OT 1
 curried [ˈkʌrid] mit Curry gewürzt OT 1
cursor [ˈkɜːsə] Mauszeiger OT 3
curtain [ˈkɜːtn] Vorhang OT 2
cushion [ˈkʊʃn] Kissen OT 1
custard [ˈkʌstəd] Vanillesoße OT 1
custodial [kʌˈstəʊdiəl] vormundschaftlich **WS 3**, 101
custody [ˈkʌstədi] Verwahrung; Schutz **WS 3**, 100
customer [ˈkʌstəmə] Kunde / Kundin OT 3
customs [ˈkʌstəmz] Zoll OT 2

VOCABULARY

to **cut** [kʌt] schneiden OT 2
cute [kju:t] niedlich OT 1
cutlery [ˈkʌtləri] Besteck OT 3
to **cyberbully** [ˈsaɪbəbʊli] cybermobben WS 3, 107
cyberbullying [ˈsaɪbəbʊliŋ] Cybermobbing OT 4
cyber security [ˈsaɪbə sɪˈkjʊərəti] Cybersicherheit; Netzsicherheit OT 4
to **cycle** [ˈsaɪkl] mit dem Fahrrad fahren OT 1
cyclist [ˈsaɪklɪst] Radfahrer(in) OT 3

D

dad [dæd] Papa OT 1
daily [ˈdeɪli] täglich OT 2
to **damage** [ˈdæmɪdʒ] beschädigen; schaden OT 2
dance [dɑːns] Tanz OT 1
to **dance** [dɑːns] tanzen OT 1
dancer [ˈdɑːnsə] Tänzer(in) OT 3
dancing [ˈdɑːnsɪŋ] Tanzen OT 1
danger [ˈdeɪndʒə] Gefahr OT 2
dangerous [ˈdeɪndʒərəs] gefährlich OT 1
to **dare** [deə] wagen; sich trauen OT 2
dark [dɑːk] dunkel OT 1
darkness [ˈdɑːknəs] Dunkelheit WS 4, 126
data [ˈdeɪtə] Daten OT 3
date [deɪt] Datum OT 2
to **date** [deɪt] mit jmdm. ausgehen WS 3, 96
daughter [ˈdɔːtə] Tochter OT 1
dawn [dɔːn] Morgendämmerung OT 4
day [deɪ] Tag OT 1
  day out [deɪ ˈaʊt] Tagesausflug OT 2
daytime [ˈdeɪtaɪm] Tageszeit OT 1
day trip [ˈdeɪ trɪp] Tagesausflug OT 2
dead [ded] tot OT 1
deaf [def] Gehörlose WS 2, 65
deal [diːl] Geschäft; Deal OT 4
to **deal with** [diːl wɪð] umgehen OT 2
dear [dɪə] liebe(r, -s) OT 1
death [deθ] Tod OT 2
  date of death [ˌdeɪt əv ˈdeθ] Todesdatum OT 2
debate [dɪˈbeɪt] Debatte OT 3
debating club [dɪˈbeɪtɪŋ klʌb] Debattierklub OT 4
debt [det] Schuld OT 4
decade [ˈdekeɪd] Dekade; Jahrzehnt WS 3, 93
December [dɪˈsembə] Dezember OT 1
to **decide** [dɪˈsaɪd] entscheiden OT 1
decision [dɪˈsɪʒn] Entscheidung OT 1

decisive [dɪˈsaɪsɪv] entscheidend WS 3, 115
declaration [ˌdekləˈreɪʃn] Erklärung OT 4
to **declare** [dɪˈkleə] ausrufen; verkünden OT 4
decline [dɪˈklaɪn] Rückgang WS 1, 22
to **decline** [dɪˈklaɪn] verfallen WS 3, 98
to **decorate** [ˈdekəreɪt] dekorieren; schmücken OT 4
decorator [ˈdekəreɪtə] Dekorateur(in) OT 3
to **decrease** [dɪˈkriːs] fallen; zurückgehen WS 3, 98
dedicated [ˈdedɪkeɪtɪd] engagiert WS 2, 83
deed [diːd] Tat WS 4, 126
deep [diːp] tief OT 1
default [dɪˈfɔːlt] Standard OT 3
defence [dɪˈfens] Verteidigung WS 2, 61
to **defend** [dɪˈfend] verteidigen OT 3
defender [dɪˈfendə] Verteidiger(in) OT 3
to **define** [dɪˈfaɪn] definieren; bestimmen OT 4
definite [ˈdefɪnət] eindeutig; bestimmt OT 1
definitely [ˈdefɪnətli] eindeutig; bestimmt; definitiv OT 1
definition [ˌdefɪˈnɪʃn] Definition OT 1
deforestation [ˌdiːˌfɒrɪˈsteɪʃn] Abholzung WS 1, 41
degradation [ˌdegrəˈdeɪʃn] Degradierung WS 1, 21
degree [dɪˈɡriː] Grad; Abschluss OT 4
dehydrated [ˌdiːhaɪˈdreɪtɪd] dehydriert OT 2
to **delegate** [ˈdelɪɡət] delegieren; beauftragen OT 4
to **delete** [dɪˈliːt] löschen OT 4
deli [ˈdeli] Feinkostladen WS 1, 15
deliberately [dɪˈlɪbərətli] absichtlich; bewusst WS 4, 145
delicacy [ˈdelɪkəsi] Delikatesse OT 3
delicious [dɪˈlɪʃəs] lecker OT 1
delighted [dɪˈlaɪtɪd] entzückt; erfreut OT 3
to **deliver** [dɪˈlɪvə] liefern OT 4
delivery [dɪˈlɪvəri] Ausführung; Lieferung OT 3
demand [dɪˈmɑːnd] Nachfrage OT 4
to **demand** [dɪˈmɑːnd] fordern; verlangen OT 4
democratic [ˌdeməˈkrætɪk] demokratisch OT 4
to **demolish** [dɪˈmɒlɪʃ] abreißen WS 1, 23

demon [ˈdiːmən] Dämon WS 1, 38
to **demonstrate** [ˈdemənstreɪt] vorführen; zeigen OT 4
demonstration [ˌdemənˈstreɪʃn] Demonstration OT 4
demonstrative [dɪˈmɒnstrətɪv] Demonstrativbegleiter OT 1
denim [ˈdenɪm] Denim; Jeansstoff OT 4
to **denote** [dɪˈnəʊt] auf etw. hindeuten WS 4, 144
density [ˈdensəti] Dichte OT 4
dentist [ˈdentɪst] Zahnarzt / -ärztin WS 2, 63
to **deny** [dɪˈnaɪ] leugnen WS 3, 89
department [dɪˈpɑːtmənt] Abteilung WS 2, 55
departure [dɪˈpɑːtʃə] Abfahrt; Abflug OT 2
departure gate [dɪˈpɑːtʃə ˌɡeɪt] Abfluggate OT 2
to **depend** [dɪˈpend] (sich) verlassen (auf); abhängen (von) OT 2
to **deport** [dɪˈpɔːt] ausweisen; deportieren OT 4
depressed [dɪˈprest] deprimiert OT 4
depressing [dɪˈpresɪŋ] deprimierend OT 4
depression [dɪˈpreʃn] Depression OT 4
deputy [ˈdepjuti] stellvertretend WS 1, 41
to **descend from** [dɪˈsend frəm] von jmdm. abstammen WS 3, 91
descendant [dɪˈsendənt] Nachkomme OT 4
descent [dɪˈsent] Abstammung WS 1, 31
to **describe** [dɪˈskraɪb] beschreiben OT 1
description [dɪˈskrɪpʃn] Beschreibung OT 2
descriptive [dɪˈskrɪptɪv] beschreibend WS 3, 115
desert [ˈdezət] Wüste OT 3
to **deserve** [dɪˈzɜːv] verdienen OT 2
to **design** [dɪˈzaɪn] entwerfen OT 3; planen WS 2, 60
design [dɪˈzaɪn] Entwurf; Design OT 1
to **designate** [ˈdezɪɡneɪt] ernennen; designieren WS 1, 24
designer [dɪˈzaɪnə] Designer(in) OT 3
desk [desk] Schreibtisch OT 1
desktop [ˈdesktɒp] Desktop; Benutzeroberfläche OT 4
desperate [ˈdespərət] verzweifelt WS 1, 23
  desperately [ˈdespərətli] verzweifelt OT 3
dessert [dɪˈzɜːt] Nachtisch OT 1

VOCABULARY

destination [ˌdestɪˈneɪʃn] Reiseziel OT 4
to **destroy** [dɪˈstrɔɪ] zerstören OT 2
destructive [dɪˈstrʌktɪv] zerstörend; schädlich WS 1, 41
detail [ˈdiːteɪl] Detail OT 2
detailed [ˈdiːteɪld] detailliert; genau OT 3
determination [dɪˌtɜːmɪˈneɪʃn] Entschlossenheit WS 1, 21
to **determine** [dɪˈtɜːmɪn] ausmachen; bestimmen WS 3, 93
determined [dɪˈtɜːmɪnd] entschlossen OT 3
determiner [dɪˈtɜːmɪnə] Bestimmungswort OT 1
detox [ˈdiːtɒks] Entzugsprogramm OT 2
deuce [djuːs] Einstand OT 3
devastated [ˈdevəsteɪtɪd] am Boden zerstört; erschüttert WS 3, 117
to **develop** [dɪˈveləp] entwickeln OT 2
developer [dɪˈveləpə] Entwickler(in) WS 2, 52
development [dɪˈveləpmənt] Entwicklung OT 4
device [dɪˈvaɪs] Gerät OT 3
devil [ˈdevl] Teufel WS 1, 39
diabetes [ˌdaɪəˈbiːtiːz] Diabetes WS 2, 65
to **diagnose** [ˈdaɪəgnəʊz] diagnostizieren OT 4
diagram [ˈdaɪəgræm] Schaubild; Diagramm OT 3
to **dial** [ˈdaɪəl] wählen OT 2
dialect [ˈdaɪəlekt] Dialekt WS 1, 22
dialogue [ˈdaɪəlɒg] Dialog OT 1
diary [ˈdaɪəri] Terminkalender; Tagebuch OT 1
to **dictate** [dɪkˈteɪt] bestimmen WS 3, 93
dictionary [ˈdɪkʃənri] Wörterbuch OT 1
to **die** [daɪ] sterben OT 1
diesel [ˈdiːzl] Diesel OT 3
diet [ˈdaɪət] Diät OT 3
dietary [ˈdaɪətəri] diätetisch WS 3, 103
dieting [ˈdaɪətɪŋ] Schlankheitskuren; Diäten WS 3, 102
to **differ** [ˈdɪfər] abweichen WS 4, 144
difference [ˈdɪfrəns] Unterschied OT 1
different [ˈdɪfrənt] unterschiedlich OT 1
to **differentiate** [ˌdɪfəˈrenʃieɪt] unterscheiden WS 3, 115
difficult [ˈdɪfɪkəlt] schwer; schwierig OT 1
difficulty [ˈdɪfɪkəlti] Schwierigkeit OT 4
to **dig** [dɪg] graben OT 1
digit [ˈdɪdʒɪt] Ziffer OT 2

digital [ˈdɪdʒɪtl] digital OT 3
digitalization [ˌdɪdʒɪtəlaɪˈzeɪʃn] Digitalisierung WS 3, 106
digital native [ˈdɪdʒɪtl ˈneɪtɪv] Digital Native WS 3, 104
dilemma [dɪˈlemə] Dilemma OT 4
dim [dɪm] trüb; schwach OT 4
dimension [daɪˈmenʃn] Abmessung OT 2
dingo [ˈdɪŋgəʊ] Dingo WS 1, 23
dining room [ˈdaɪnɪŋ ruːm] Esszimmer OT 1
dinner [ˈdɪnə] Abendessen OT 1
dinosaur [ˈdaɪnəsɔː] Dinosaurier OT 1
to **dip** [dɪp] tauchen OT 4
diploma [dɪˈpləʊmə] Diplom; Urkunde WS 2, 58
direct [dəˈrekt] direkt OT 3
direction [dəˈrekʃn] Anweisung; Richtung OT 3
director [dəˈrektə] Leiter(in) OT 4
dirt [dɜːt] Dreck; Schmutz OT 4
dirty [ˈdɜːti] schmutzig OT 1
disability [ˌdɪsəˈbɪləti] Behinderung OT 2
disadvantage [ˌdɪsədˈvɑːntɪdʒ] Nachteil OT 3
disadvantaged [ˌdɪsədˈvɑːntɪdʒd] benachteiligt WS 2, 61
to **disagree** [ˌdɪsəˈgriː] anderer Meinung sein OT 2
disagreement [ˌdɪsəˈgriːmənt] Meinungsverschiedenheit OT 2
to **disappear** [ˌdɪsəˈpɪə] verschwinden OT 3
disappointed [ˌdɪsəˈpɔɪntɪd] enttäuscht OT 2
disappointingly [ˌdɪsəˈpɔɪntɪŋli] enttäuschend OT 3
disappointment [ˌdɪsəˈpɔɪntmənt] Enttäuschung WS 1, 45
disaster [dɪˈzɑːstə] Katastrophe OT 2
disaster area [dɪˈzɑːstər eəriə] Katastrophengebiet OT 2
to **discourage** [dɪsˈkʌrɪdʒ] entmutigen WS 2, 68
to **discover** [dɪsˈkʌvə] entdecken OT 3
discovery [dɪsˈkʌvəri] Entdeckung OT 4
to **discriminate** [dɪˈskrɪmɪneɪt] unterschiedlich behandeln; diskriminieren WS 2, 56
discriminated [dɪˈskrɪmɪneɪt] benachteiligt WS 3, 89
discrimination [dɪˌskrɪmɪˈneɪʃn] Diskriminierung; Ausgrenzung WS 1, 39

to **discuss** [dɪˈskʌs] besprechen OT 1
discussion [dɪˈskʌʃn] Besprechung; Diskussion OT 1
disease [dɪˈziːz] Krankheit OT 2
to **disgust** [dɪsˈgʌst] ekeln; empören WS 3, 93
disgusting [dɪsˈgʌstɪŋ] ekelhaft OT 3
dish [dɪʃ] Gericht; Schale OT 2
   dishes [ˈdɪʃɪz] Geschirr OT 2
   to **do the dishes** [ˌduː ðə ˈdɪʃɪz] den Abwasch machen OT 2
dishwasher [ˈdɪʃwɔːʃər] Geschirrspülmaschine OT 4
to **dislike** [dɪsˈlaɪk] nicht mögen OT 3
to **dismiss** [dɪsˈmɪs] entlassen; wegschicken WS 2, 70
to **disobey** [ˌdɪsəˈbeɪ] nicht gehorchen WS 1, 24
disorganized [dɪsˈɔːgənaɪzd] chaotisch OT 2
dispenser [dɪˈspensə] Spender WS 2, 70
display [dɪˈspleɪ] Ausstellung OT 3
disrespectful [ˌdɪsrɪˈspektfl] respektlos OT 3
distance [ˈdɪstəns] Entfernung OT 2
distinct [dɪˈstɪŋkt] eindeutig; eigenständig WS 1, 22
distinctive [dɪˈstɪŋktɪv] unverwechselbar; ausgeprägt WS 1, 30
to **distinguish between** [dɪˈstɪŋgwɪʃ bɪˈtwiːn] zwischen etw. unterscheiden WS 4, 143
to **distribute** [dɪˈstrɪbjuːt] verteilen OT 4
district [ˈdɪstrɪkt] Bezirk; Gegend OT 1
to **disturb** [dɪˈstɜːb] stören WS 1, 20
ditto [ˈdɪtəʊ] ditto; ebenfalls OT 4
to **dive** [daɪv] tauchen OT 1
diving [ˈdaɪvɪŋ] Tauchen OT 1
diverse [daɪˈvɜːs] vielfältig; verschieden OT 4
diversity [daɪˈvɜːsəti] Vielfältigkeit OT 4
to **divide** [dɪˈvaɪd] teilen OT 2
divided [dɪˈvaɪdɪd] getrennt; unterteilt OT 2
division [dɪˈvɪʒn] Trennung; Teilung WS 2, 62
divorce [dɪˈvɔːs] Scheidung OT 3
to **divorce** [dɪˈvɔːs] sich scheiden (lassen) OT 3
to **do** [duː] tun; machen OT 1
   to **do sth. about sth.** [ˌduː sʌmˈθɪŋ əˌbaʊt sʌmˈθɪŋ] etw. gegen etw. tun OT 2
dockyard [ˈdɒkjɑːd] Werft OT 3
doctor [ˈdɒktə] Arzt / Ärztin OT 1

Appendix

VOCABULARY

document [ˈdɒkjumənt] Dokument OT 4
documentary [ˌdɒkjuˈmentri] Dokumentation OT 2
dog [dɔːg] Hund OT 1
  guide dog [ˈgaɪd dɒg] Blindenführhund OT 2
  hot dog [ˈhɒt dɒg] Hotdog OT 2
  service dog [ˈsɜːvɪs dɒg] Assistenzhund OT 2
dog mess [ˈdɒg mes] Hundedreck OT 2
doll [dɒl] Puppe OT 3
dollar [ˈdɒlə] Dollar OT 1
dolphin [ˈdɒlfɪn] Delfin OT 1
dominant [ˈdɒmɪnənt] wichtig; überwiegend WW, 11
to donate [dəʊˈneɪt] spenden OT 2
donation [dəʊˈneɪʃn] Spende OT 2
  to make a donation [ˌmeɪk ə dəʊˈneɪʃn] spenden OT 2
door [dɔː] Tür OT 1
doorbell [ˈdɔːbel] Klingel OT 2
doorstep [ˈdɔːstep] direkt vor Ort; quasi vor der Haustür OT 4
double [ˈdʌbl] doppelt; Doppel... OT 1
  double bass [ˌdʌbl ˈbeɪs] Kontrabass OT 2
doubles [ˈdʌblz] Doppel OT 3
doubt [daʊt] Zweifel OT 4
dough [dəʊ] Knete; Teig OT 2
doughnut [ˈdəʊnʌt] Krapfen OT 2
down [daʊn] hinunter OT 1
downhill [ˌdaʊnˈhɪl] bergab WS 1, 13
downside [ˈdaʊnsaɪd] Nachteil OT 3
to downsize [ˈdaʊnsaɪz] reduzieren; sich einschränken OT 3
downstairs [ˈdaʊnsteəz] unten; im unteren Stockwerk OT 1
downtown [ˌdaʊnˈtaʊn] Innenstadt OT 4
downward [ˈdaʊnwəd] abwärts; absteigend WS 1, 21
dozen [ˈdʌzn] Dutzend OT 4
draft [drɑːft] Entwurf OT 2
to draft [drɑːft] entwerfen WS 3, 107
dragon [ˈdrægən] Drache OT 1
to drain [dreɪn] abgießen OT 2
drained [dreɪnd] abgetropft OT 2
drama [ˈdrɑːmə] Drama OT 1
dramatic [drəˈmætɪk] dramatisch WS 3, 98
drastic [ˈdræstɪk] drastisch; extrem WS 1, 22
draughts [drɑːfts] Damespiel OT 1
to draw [drɔː] ziehen; zeichnen OT 1

drawback [ˈdrɔːbæk] Nachteil WS 3, 100
drawer [drɔː] Schublade OT 3
drawing [ˈdrɔːɪŋ] Zeichen; Zeichnung OT 1
dream [driːm] Traum OT 1
to dream [driːm] träumen OT 4
dreamer [ˈdriːmə] Träumer(-in) OT 2
dreamtime [ˈdriːmtaɪm] Traumzeit WS 1, 20
dress [dres] Kleid OT 3
dress code [ˈdres kəʊd] Kleiderordnung; Dresscode OT 4
to dress up [dres ʌp] (sich) verkleiden OT 2
to drill [drɪl] bohren OT 4
drink [drɪŋk] Getränk OT 1
to drink [drɪŋk] trinken OT 1
to drip [drɪp] tropfen OT 3
to drive [draɪv] fahren OT 1
driver [ˈdraɪvə] Fahrer(in) OT 1
driverless [ˈdraɪvələs] führerlos OT 4
driver's license [ˈdraɪvəz laɪsns] Führerschein; Fahrerlaubnis OT 4
driving licence [ˈdraɪvɪŋ laɪsns] Führerschein OT 2
drone [drəʊn] Drohne OT 3
to drop [drɒp] fallen lassen OT 1
drought [draʊt] Dürre WS 1, 23
to drown [draʊn] ertrinken OT 3
drug [drʌg] Droge OT 3
drugstore [ˈdrʌgstɔː] Apotheke; Drogerie OT 2
drums [drʌmz] Schlagzeug OT 1
dry [draɪ] trocken OT 2
duck [dʌk] Ente OT 2
due to [djuː tə] wegen; aufgrund von WW, 11
dull [dʌl] uninteressant; langweilig WS 3, 88
dumb [dʌm] blöd; dumm WS 3, 94
to dump [dʌmp] kippen WS 4, 144
dumpling [ˈdʌmplɪŋ] Kloß; Knödel OT 4
during [ˈdjʊərɪŋ] während OT 2
to dust off [ˌdʌst ˈɒf] abwischen; abstauben WS 1, 21
duty [ˈdjuːti] Pflicht WS 3, 91
duty free [ˌdjuːti ˈfriː] zollfrei OT 2
dweller [ˈdwelə] Bewohner OT 4
dye [daɪ] Färbemittel; Farbe OT 4
dynamic [daɪˈnæmɪk] Dynamik WS 3, 106
dystopian [dɪsˈtəʊpiən] dystopisch WS 4, 126

E

each [iːtʃ] jede(r,-s) OT 1
eager [ˈiːgə] eifrig OT 2
eagle [ˈiːgl] Adler OT 2
ear [ɪə] Ohr OT 1
early [ˈɜːli] früh OT 1
to earn [ɜːn] verdienen OT 3
earth [ɜːθ] Erde OT 2
earthquake [ˈɜːθkweɪk] Erdbeben OT 2
east [iːst] Ost- OT 1
Easter [ˈiːstə] Ostern OT 1
eastern [ˈiːstən] östlich OT 2
easy [ˈiːzi] einfach OT 1
  easily [ˈiːzəli] leicht OT 2
to eat [iːt] essen OT 1
to echo [ˈekəʊ] nachhallen; nachklingen WS 1, 14
eco-friendly [ˌiːkəʊ ˈfrendli] ökologisch OT 3
ecological [ˌiːkəˈlɒdʒɪkl] ökologisch WS 1, 23
e-commerce [ˈiː kɒmɜːs] E-Commerce; Internethandel OT 4
economic [ˌiːkəˈnɒmɪk] wirtschaftlich OT 4
economics [ˌiːkəˈnɒmɪks] Wirtschaftswissenschaften WS 2, 78
economy [ɪˈkɒnəmi] Wirtschaft; Ökonomie OT 3
ecotourism [ˈiːkəʊtʊərɪzəm] Ökotourismus OT 3
edge [edʒ] Rand OT 3
to edit [ˈedɪt] überarbeiten; redigieren OT 3
editor [ˈedɪtə] Redakteur(in); Herausgeber(in) OT 2
to educate [ˈedʒukeɪt] erziehen WS 1, 20
education [ˌedjʊˈkeɪʃn] Ausbildung OT 3
educational [ˌedʒuˈkeɪʃnl] Bildungs- OT 3
educator [ˈedʒukeɪtə] Pädagoge/Pädagogin OT 4
eel [iːl] Aal OT 4
effect [ɪˈfekt] Wirkung OT 3
effective [ɪˈfektɪv] wirksam WS 1, 21
  effectively [ɪˈfektɪvli] wirksam OT 4
effectiveness [ɪˈfektɪvnəs] Wirksamkeit WS 4, 144
efficient [ɪˈfɪʃnt] effizient OT 4
  efficiently [ɪˈfɪʃntli] effizient OT 3
effort [ˈefət] Anstrengung; Mühe WW, 11
egg [eg] Ei OT 1
eggplant [ˈegplɑːnt] Aubergine OT 2

Appendix
VOCABULARY

eight [eɪt] acht OT 1
eighteen [ˌeɪˈtiːn] achtzehn OT 1
eighty [ˈeɪti] achtzig OT 1
either [ˈaɪðə] auch nicht OT 1
elbow [ˈelbəʊ] Ellbogen OT 1
elder [ˈeldə] Älteste(r) WS 1, 21
elderly [ˈeldəli] älter OT 4
to **elect** [ɪˈlekt] wählen; auswählen OT 4
election [ɪˈlekʃn] Wahl OT 3
elective [ɪˈlektɪv] Auswahlfach OT 4
electric [ɪˈlektrɪk] elektrisch OT 1
electrical [ɪˈlektrɪkl] elektrisch OT 4
electricity [ɪˌlekˈtrɪsəti] Strom OT 2
electronic [ɪˌlekˈtrɒnɪk] elektronisch WS 1, 16
electronical [ɪˌlekˈtrɒnɪkl] elektronisch WS 2, 69
   electronically [ɪˌlekˈtrɒnɪkli] elektronisch OT 4
electronics [ɪˌlekˈtrɒnɪks] Elektronik OT 2
element [ˈelɪmənt] Bestandteil OT 2
elementary [ˌelɪˈmentri] Grund-; elementar OT 2
elementary school [ˌelɪˈmentri skuːl] Grundschule OT 2
elephant [ˈelɪfənt] Elefant OT 1
eleven [ɪˈlevn] elf OT 1
elite sports [eɪˈliːt spɔːts] Spitzensport OT 3
else [els] sonst noch OT 1
elsewhere [ˌelsˈweər] woanders WS 3, 88
email [ˈiːmeɪl] E-Mail OT 1
to **email** [ˈiːmeɪl] eine E-Mail schreiben OT 2
embarrassed [ɪmˈbærəst] verlegen; peinlich berührt OT 3
embarrassing [ɪmˈbærəsɪŋ] peinlich OT 2
ember [ˈembər] glühende Kohle WS 4, 126
to **embrace** [ɪmˈbreɪs] umarmen WS 1, 21
emergency [ɪˈmɜːdʒənsi] Notfall OT 1
emergency services [ɪˈmɜːdʒənsi ˌsɜːvɪsɪz] Rettungsdienste OT 2
emigrant [ˈemɪɡrənt] Auswanderer / Auswanderin OT 3
to **emigrate** [ˈemɪɡreɪt] auswandern OT 4
emission [ɪˈmɪʃn] Ausstoss; Emission OT 3
emoji [ɪˈməʊdʒi] Emoji OT 3

emoticon [ɪˈməʊtɪkɒn] Emoticon WS 4, 141
emotion [ɪˈməʊʃn] Gefühl OT 3
emotional [ɪˈməʊʃənl] emotional WS 1, 17
emphasis [ˈemfəsɪs] Betonung WS 3, 95
to **emphasize** [ˈemfəsaɪz] betonen WS 3, 105
employee [ɪmˈplɔɪiː] Angestellte(r) OT 4
employer [ɪmˈplɔɪə] Arbeitgeber(in) OT 3
employment [ɪmˈplɔɪmənt] Beschäftigung; Arbeit WS 2, 50
to **empower** [ɪmˈpaʊə] stärken; ermächtigen WS 2, 69
to **empty** [ˈempti] entleeren; leeren OT 4
empty [ˈempti] leer OT 1
to **encourage** [ɪnˈkʌrɪdʒ] ermutigen OT 2
encouragement [ɪnˈkʌrɪdʒmənt] Aufmunterung WS 4, 140
end [end] Ende OT 1
to **end** [end] enden OT 1
to **endanger** [ɪnˈdeɪndʒər] gefährden WS 1, 26
endangered [ɪnˈdeɪndʒəd] gefährdet OT 2
ending [ˈendɪŋ] Ende; Endung OT 2
endless [ˈendləs] endlos; unendlich OT 4
endzone [ˈendzəʊn] Endzone OT 3
enemy [ˈenəmi] Feind OT 1
energetic [ˌenəˈdʒetɪk] aktiv; energisch OT 2
energy [ˈenədʒi] Energie OT 2
to **enforce** [ɪnˈfɔːs] durchsetzen OT 4
enforcement [ɪnˈfɔːsmənt] Vollstreckung WS 4, 127
to **engage** [ɪnˈɡeɪdʒ] (sich) beschäftigen OT 4
engine [ˈendʒɪn] Motor; Lokomotive OT 2
engineer [ˌendʒɪˈnɪə] Ingenieur(in); Lokführer(in) OT 3
engineering [ˌendʒɪˈnɪərɪŋ] Ingenieurwesen OT 1
to **engrave** [ɪnˈɡreɪv] gravieren; eingravieren OT 4
to **enjoy** [ɪnˈdʒɔɪ] genießen OT 1
enjoyable [ɪnˈdʒɔɪəbl] angenehm OT 2
enormous [ɪˈnɔːməs] riesig OT 1
enough [ɪˈnʌf] genug OT 1
to **ensure** [ɪnˈʃʊə] sicherstellen OT 4
to **enter** [ˈentə] eintreten; eintragen OT 2

to **entertain** [ˌentəˈteɪn] unterhalten OT 4
entertainer [ˌentəˈteɪnə] Künstler(in); Unterhalter(in) OT 3
entertaining [ˌentəˈteɪnɪŋ] unterhaltsam; amüsant OT 3
entertainment [ˌentəˈteɪnmənt] Unterhaltung OT 3
enthusiastic [ɪnˌθjuːziˈæstɪk] begeistert OT 3
entire [ɪnˈtaɪə] ganze(r,-s) OT 3
entrance [ˈentrəns] Eingang OT 1
entrance hall [ˈentrəns ˌhɔːl] Eingangsbereich; Eingangshalle OT 1
entrepreneur [ˌɒntrəprəˈnɜː] Unternehmer(in) WS 2, 69
entry [ˈentri] Eintrag; Einsendung OT 2
envelope [ˈenvələʊp] Briefumschlag OT 2
environment [ɪnˈvaɪrənmənt] Umfeld; Umwelt OT 2
environmental [ɪnˌvaɪrənˈmentl] Umwelt-; ökologisch OT 2
   environmentally [ɪnˌvaɪrənˈmentəli] umwelt... OT 3
environmentalist [ɪnˌvaɪrənˈmentəlɪst] Umweltschützer(in) OT 3
to **envy** [ˈenvi] beneiden WS 3, 91
epidemic [ˌepɪˈdemɪk] Epidemie OT 4
episode [ˈepɪsəʊd] Folge WS 3, 95
equal [ˈiːkwəl] gleich; gleichberechtigt OT 4
equality [iˈkwɒləti] Gleichberechtigung WS 1, 39
equator [ɪˈkweɪtər] Äquator WS 1, 13
equipment [ɪˈkwɪpmənt] Ausrüstung OT 2
equivalent [ɪˈkwɪvələnt] entsprechend OT 4
era [ˈɪərə] Ära OT 4
to **eradicate** [ɪˈrædɪkeɪt] ausmerzen; ausrotten OT 4
to **escape** [ɪˈskeɪp] entkommen OT 2
e-scooter [ˈiːskuːtə] E-Roller WS 2, 71
escort [ˈeskɔːt] Begleiter(in) OT 3
especially [ɪˈspeʃəli] besonders OT 2
essay [ˈeseɪ] Aufsatz OT 2
essential [ɪˈsenʃl] wichtig; wesentlich OT 4
to **establish** [ɪˈstæblɪʃ] begründen OT 4
to **estimate** [ˈestɪmeɪt] schätzen WS 1, 22
ETA (estimated time of arrival) [ˈestɪmeɪtɪd taɪm əv əˈraɪvl] geschätzte Ankunftszeit OT 2

Appendix

VOCABULARY

etc. (et cetera) [ˌet ˈsetərə] und so weiter; usw. OT 1
eternal [ɪˈtɜ:nl] ewig OT 4
ethical [ˈeθɪkl] ethisch; moralisch vertretbar OT 3
ethnic [ˈeθnɪk] ethnisch WS 1, 31
   ethnically [ˈeθnɪkli] ethnisch WS 1, 18
etiquette [ˈetɪkət] Etikette OT 3
eureka moment [juˈri:kə ˈməʊmənt] Heureka-Erlebnis OT 4
European [ˌjʊərəˈpi:ən] Europäer(in) OT 3
to evaluate [ɪˈvæljueɪt] bewerten OT 4
evaluation [ɪˌvæljuˈeɪʃn] Bewertung WS 2, 61
even [ˈi:vn] sogar OT 1
evening [ˈi:vnɪŋ] Abend OT 1
evenly [ˈi:vnli] ausgeglichen OT 4
event [ɪˈvent] Ereignis OT 1
eventually [ɪˈventʃuəli] schließlich OT 3
ever [ˈevə] je OT 1
every [ˈevri] jede(r,-s) OT 1
everybody [ˈevrɪbɒdi] jeder; alle OT 1
everyday [ˈevrɪdeɪ] alltäglich OT 3
everyone [ˈevriwʌn] jeder OT 1
everything [ˈevriθɪŋ] alles OT 1
everywhere [ˈevriweə] überall OT 1
evident [ˈevɪdənt] offensichtlich; klar WS 4, 141
evil [ˈi:vl] Übel; Böse WS 4, 126
evolution [ˌi:vəˈlu:ʃn] Evolution; Entwicklung WS 3, 106
to evolve [ɪˈvɒlv] (sich) entwickeln OT 4
exact [ɪɡˈzækt] genau OT 2
to exaggerate [ɪɡˈzædʒəreɪt] übertreiben OT 4
exam [ɪɡˈzæm] Prüfung OT 1
example [ɪɡˈzɑ:mpl] Beispiel OT 1
excellent [ˈeksələnt] ausgezeichnet OT 3
except [ɪkˈsept] außer OT 2
excerpt [ekˈsɜ:pt] Ausschnitt; Auszug WS 3, 115
exchange [ɪksˈtʃeɪndʒ] Austausch OT 1
excited [ɪkˈsaɪtɪd] begeistert; aufgeregt OT 1
excitement [ɪkˈsaɪtmənt] Aufregung OT 3
exciting [ɪkˈsaɪtɪŋ] aufregend OT 1
to exclude [ɪkˈsklu:d] ausschließen WS 3, 109
exclusively [ɪkˈsklu:sɪvli] ausschließlich WW, 11
to excuse [ɪkˈskju:z] entschuldigen OT 1
to execute [ˈeksɪkju:t] töten lassen; exekutieren OT 3

executive [ɪɡˈzekjətɪv] Führungskraft WS 3, 88
exercise [ˈeksəsaɪz] körperliche Bewegung; Übung OT 1
exercise book [ˈeksəsaɪz bʊk] Übungsheft OT 1
exhausted [ɪɡˈzɔ:stɪd] erschöpft OT 2
exhibit [ɪɡˈzɪbɪt] Ausstellung OT 2
to exhibit [ɪɡˈzɪbɪt] ausstellen OT 2
exhibition [ˌeksɪˈbɪʃn] Ausstellung OT 1
to exist [ɪɡˈzɪst] existieren OT 3
existence [ɪɡˈzɪstəns] Existenz WS 1, 44
exit [ˈeksɪt] Ausgang; Abfahrt OT 2
exotic [ɪɡˈzɒtɪk] exotisch OT 2
to expand [ɪkˈspænd] erweitern; expandieren OT 4
expanding [ɪkˈspænd] erweiternd OT 2
to expect [ɪkˈspekt] erwarten OT 2
expectation [ˌekspekˈteɪʃn] Erwartung WS 3, 92
expedition [ˌekspəˈdɪʃn] Expedition OT 2
expensive [ɪkˈspensɪv] teuer OT 1
experience [ɪkˈspɪəriəns] Erfahrung OT 2
experienced [ɪkˈspɪəriənst] erfahren OT 3
experiment [ɪkˈsperɪmənt] Experiment OT 1
to experiment [ɪkˈsperɪmənt] experimentieren OT 4
expert [ˈekspɜ:t] Experte / Expertin OT 3
to explain [ɪkˈspleɪn] erklären OT 1
explanation [ˌekspləˈneɪʃn] Erklärung OT 1
explicitly [ɪkˈsplɪsɪtli] explizit WS 4, 141
to explode [ɪkˈspləʊd] explodieren WS 1, 23
to exploit [ɪkˈsplɔɪt] ausbeuten OT 3
exploitation [ˌeksplɔɪˈteɪʃn] Ausbeutung OT 4
to explore [ɪkˈsplɔ:] erforschen; erkunden OT 1
explorer [ɪkˈsplɔ:rə] Forscher(in) OT 3
export [ɪkˈsplɪsɪtli] exportieren WS 1, 44
exporter [ekˈspɔ:tər] Exporteur(in) WS 1, 27
to express [ɪkˈspres] ausdrücken OT 3
expression [ɪkˈspreʃn] Ausdruck OT 1
extended [ɪkˈstendɪd] erweitert WS 3, 91
extent [ɪkˈstent] Ausmaß WS 1, 39
extinct [ɪkˈstɪŋkt] ausgestorben OT 2
extinction [ɪkˈstɪŋkʃn] Aussterben WS 1, 27

extinguisher [ɪkˈstɪŋɡwɪʃər] Löscher WS 2, 71
extra [ˈekstrə] Extra... OT 1
extract [ɪkˈstrækt] Auszug OT 4
extreme [ɪkˈstri:m] extrem OT 3; Extrem WS 3, 102
   extremely [ɪkˈstri:mli] extrem OT 3
extroverted [ˈekstrəvɜ:tɪd] extrovertiert WS 2, 55
eye [aɪ] Auge OT 1
eyebrow [ˈaɪbraʊ] Augenbraue OT 4
eyelid [ˈaɪlɪd] Augenlid OT 2

F

fabulous [ˈfæbjələs] fabelhaft OT 2
face [feɪs] Gesicht OT 1
face paint [ˈfeɪs peɪnt] Schminke OT 2
to face [feɪs] begegnen OT 4
facial expression [ˈfeɪʃl ɪkspreʃn] Gesichtsausdruck OT 4
facility [fəˈsɪləti] Anlage OT 4
fact [fækt] Tatsache; Fakt OT 1
factor [ˈfæktə] Faktor WS 1, 26
factory [ˈfæktri] Fabrik OT 4
factory-farmed [ˈfæktri fɑ:md] in Farmen gezüchtet; in Massen gezüchtet WS 3, 103
factual [ˈfæktʃuəl] sachlich OT 4
to fade [feɪd] verwelken; verblassen OT 2
to fail [feɪl] scheitern OT 2
failure [ˈfeɪljə] Misserfolg OT 4
faint [feɪnt] schwindlig OT 2
to faint [feɪnt] ohnmächtig werden OT 2
fair [feə] gerecht OT 2; Jahrmarkt OT 4
fairground [ˈfeəɡraʊnd] Jahrmarkt OT 2
fairy [ˈfeəri] Fee OT 2
fairy tale [ˈfeəri ˌteɪl] Märchen OT 1
fake [feɪk] falsch; unecht WS 3, 95
to fall [fɔ:l] fallen; stürzen OT 1
   to fall apart [fɔ:l əˈpɑ:t] auseinanderfallen OT 4
   to fall asleep [fɔ:l əˈsli:p] einschlafen OT 2
   to fall over [fɔ:l ˈəʊvə] hinfallen; umfallen OT 2
falls [fɔ:ls] Wasserfall OT 1
false [fɔ:ls] falsch OT 1
   false friend [ˌfɔ:ls ˈfrend] falscher Freund; Übersetzungsfalle OT 2
fame [feɪm] Ruhm; Ruf OT 3
familiar [fəˈmɪliə] vertraut; bekannt OT 2
family [ˈfæməli] Familie OT 1
famine [ˈfæmɪn] Hungersnot OT 4

Appendix

VOCABULARY

famous [ˈfeɪməs] berühmt OT 1
fan [fæn] Fan OT 1
fancy [ˈfænsi] schick; einfallsreich OT 2
   fancy dress [ˌfænsi ˈdres] Kostüm- OT 2
fantastic [fænˈtæstɪk] fantastisch OT 1
fantasy [ˈfæntəsi] Fantasy; Fantasie OT 2
FAQ (frequently asked questions) [ˌef eɪ ˈkjuː] häufig gestellte Fragen OT 1
far [fɑː] weit OT 1
   far-off [ˈfɑː ɒf] fern OT 2
   so far [səʊ ˈfɑː] bisher OT 2
faraway [ˈfɑːrəweɪ] fern OT 4
fare [feɪk] Fahrpreis WS 1, 18
farm [fɑːm] Bauernhof OT 1
farmer [ˈfɑːmə] Bauer / Bäuerin OT 2
farmhand [ˈfɑːmhænd] Erntehelfer(in); Landarbeiter(in) OT 4
farmhouse [ˈfɑːmhaʊs] Bauernhaus OT 3
farming [ˈfɑːmɪŋ] Landwirtschaft OT 2
farmland [ˈfɑːmlænd] Ackerland OT 4
farmworker [fɑːmwɜːkə] Landarbeiter(in); Farmarbeiter(in) OT 4
fascinating [ˈfæsɪneɪtɪŋ] faszinierend OT 3
fascination [ˌfæsɪˈneɪʃn] Faszination OT 4
fashion [ˈfæʃn] Trend; Mode OT 1
fast [fɑːst] schnell OT 1
to fasten [ˈfɑːsn] anschließen; festmachen OT 1
fat [fæt] Fett OT 2
father [ˈfɑːðə] Vater OT 1
faucet [ˈfɔːsɪt] Wasserhahn OT 4
fault [fɔːlt] Fehler OT 2
faulty [ˈfɔːlti] defekt OT 2
favourite [ˈfeɪvərɪt] Lieblings... OT 1
fear [fɪə] Angst; Furcht OT 3
feast [fiːst] Fest; Festmahl OT 4
to feast [fiːst] feiern; schlemmen OT 4
feather [ˈfeðə] Feder OT 2
feature [ˈfiːtʃə] Sonderbeitrag; Eigenschaft; Merkmal OT 1
to feature [ˈfiːtʃə] aufweisen; präsentieren OT 4
February [ˈfebruəri] Februar OT 1
federal government [ˈfedərəl ˈɡʌvənmənt] Bundesregierung WS 1, 27
federation [ˌfedəˈreɪʃn] Bund WS 1, 18
fee [fiː] Gebühr OT 3
to feed [fiːd] füttern OT 2
feedback [ˈfiːdbæk] Feedback OT 1

feeding [ˈfiːdɪŋ] Füttern OT 2
to feel [fiːl] (sich) fühlen; anfassen OT 1
feeling [ˈfiːlɪŋ] Gefühl OT 2
fell [fel] Berg (in Nordengland) OT 2
fellow [ˈfeləʊ] zur gleichen Gruppe gehörend; gleichartig WS 1, 21
female [ˈfiːmeɪl] weiblich OT 2
fence [fens] Zaun WS 1, 12
feral [ˈferəl] wild WS 1, 23
ferris wheel [ˈferɪs wiːl] Riesenrad OT 4
ferry [ˈferi] Fähre OT 2
fertilizer [ˈfɜːtəlaɪzə] Dünger OT 3
festival [ˈfestɪvl] Festival; Festspiele; Fest OT 1
festivity [feˈstɪvəti] Festlichkeit OT 4
to fetch [fetʃ] holen; abholen OT 4
few [fjuː] wenige OT 1
fiction [ˈfɪkʃn] Fiktion; Romanliteratur OT 2
fictional [ˈfɪkʃənl] erfunden OT 2
field [fiːld] Feld OT 1
fieldwork [ˈfiːldwɜːk] Geländearbeit OT 4
fifteen [ˌfɪfˈtiːn] fünfzehn OT 1
fifth [fɪfθ] fünfte(r, -s) OT 1
fifty [ˈfɪfti] fünfzig OT 1
fight [faɪt] Kampf OT 1
to fight [faɪt] kämpfen OT 1
figurative [ˈfɪɡərətɪv] figurativ WS 4, 146
figure [ˈfɪɡə] Zahl; Figur OT 3
file [faɪl] Datei OT 3
to fill [fɪl] füllen OT 2
film [fɪlm] Film OT 1
film director [fɪlm dəˈrektə] Regisseur(in) OT 2
filmmaker [ˈfɪlm meɪkə] Filmemacher(in) WS 1, 30
filthy [ˈfɪlθi] dreckig OT 4
final [ˈfaɪnl] endgültig OT 1
finalist [ˈfaɪnəlɪst] Finalist(in) WS 2, 69
to finalize [ˈfaɪnəlaɪz] fertigstellen; abschließen WS 3, 109
finally [ˈfaɪnəli] schließlich OT 1
finance [ˈfaɪnæns] Finanzwirtschaft WS 2, 81
financial [faɪˈnænʃl] finanziell WS 2, 63
to find [faɪnd] finden OT 1
   to find out [ˈfaɪnd aʊt] herausfinden OT 1
finding [ˈfaɪndɪŋ] Ergebnis; Befund OT 4
fine [faɪn] gut; prima OT 1
finger [ˈfɪŋɡə] Finger OT 1
   fingers crossed [ˈfɪŋɡəz krɒst] Daumen gedrückt OT 1
fingernail [ˈfɪŋɡəneɪl] Fingernagel OT 2

to finish [ˈfɪnɪʃ] abschließen; aufhören OT 1
fire [ˈfaɪə] Feuer OT 2
to fire [ˈfaɪə] entlassen WS 2, 70
   fire station [ˈfaɪə steɪʃn] Feuerwache OT 2
firefighter [ˈfaɪəfaɪtə] Feuerwehrmann / -frau OT 2
firefighting [ˌfaɪəˈfaɪtɪŋ] Brandbekämpfung OT 2
fireplace [ˈfaɪəpleɪs] Kamin OT 1
   firewood [ˈfaɪəwʊd] Brennholz OT 4
fireworks [ˈfaɪəwɜːks] Feuerwerk OT 3
   firework display [ˈfaɪəwɜːk dɪˈspleɪ] Feuerwerk OT 4
firm [fɜːm] Firma; Kanzlei WS 2, 52
first [fɜːst] erste(r,-s) OT 1
first aid [ˌfɜːst ˈeɪd] Erste Hilfe OT 2
first aid kit [ˌfɜːst ˈeɪd kɪt] Verbandkasten; Erstehilfekasten OT 2
fish [fɪʃ] Fisch OT 1
fish finger [ˌfɪʃ ˈfɪŋɡə] Fischstäbchen OT 1
fishing [ˈfɪʃɪŋ] Angeln OT 2
fist [fɪst] Faust WS 1, 21
to fit [fɪt] passen OT 1
fit [fɪt] in Form; geeignet OT 2
fitness [ˈfɪtnəs] Fitness OT 2
five [faɪv] fünf OT 1
to fix [fɪks] korrigieren OT 2
fizzy [ˈfɪzi] kohlensäurehaltig OT 2
flag [flæɡ] Fahne OT 1
flagship [ˈflæɡʃɪp] Flaggschiff OT 3
flamingo [fləˈmɪŋɡəʊ] Flamingo OT 2
flammable [ˈflæməbl] brennbar OT 2
flashlight [ˈflæʃlaɪt] Taschenlampe OT 2
flask [flɑːsk] Thermosflasche OT 3
flat [flæt] Wohnung OT 1
flavour [ˈfleɪvə] Geschmack OT 2
flea market [fliː ˈmɑːkɪt] Flohmarkt; Trödelmarkt WS 3, 95
flesh [fleʃ] Fleisch OT 2
flexibility [ˌfleksəˈbɪləti] Flexibilität WS 4, 144
flexible [ˈfleksəbl] anpassungsfähig; flexibel OT 4
flight [flaɪt] Flug OT 2
flight crew [ˈflaɪt kruː] Flugpersonal OT 2
to flip [flɪp] umdrehen OT 4
float [fləʊt] Umzugswagen; Parade-Wagen OT 4
to float [fləʊt] treiben; schweben OT 3
flood [flʌd] Hochwasser; Flut OT 2

Appendix

VOCABULARY

flooding [ˈflʌdɪŋ] Fluten; Überflutung OT 4
floor [flɔː] Boden; Stockwerk OT 1
flour [ˈflaʊə] Mehl OT 3
flower [ˈflaʊə] Blume OT 1
flowing [ˈfləʊɪŋ] fließend WS 2, 57
fluency [ˈfluːənsi] Sprachbeherrschung WW, 11
fluent [ˈfluːənt] fließend OT 3
fluffy [ˈflʌfi] flauschig OT 2
flute [fluːt] Querflöte OT 2
to **fly** [flaɪ] fliegen OT 1
flyer [ˈflaɪə] Flyer OT 4
flying [ˈflaɪɪŋ] Fliegen OT 1
focus [ˈfəʊkəs] Fokus OT 1
to **focus** [ˈfəʊkəs] fokussieren OT 4
focused [ˈfəʊkəst] fokussiert OT 4
to **fold** [fəʊld] falten OT 2
folk [fəʊk] Volks… OT 2
    folk hero [ˈfəʊk hɪərəʊ] Volksheld OT 4
folklore [ˈfəʊklɔːr] Folklore WS 1, 24
folks [fəʊks] Leute OT 2
to **follow** [ˈfɒləʊ] folgen OT 2
    to **follow a journey** [ˈfɒləʊ ə ˌdʒɜːni] eine Reise verfolgen OT 2
follower [ˈfɒləʊə] Anhänger(in) OT 3
fond: to **be fond of** [bi fɒnd] etw. mögen OT 4
food [fuːd] Essen OT 1
    food poisoning [ˈfuːd ˌpɔɪzənɪŋ] Lebensmittelvergiftung OT 2
foolish [ˈfuːlɪʃ] unklug; blöd WS 3, 100
foot [fʊt] Fuß OT 1
    square foot [skweə fʊt] Quadratfuß OT 2
football [ˈfʊtbɔːl] Fußball OT 1
footpath [ˈfʊtpɑːθ] Fußpfad OT 1
footprint [ˈfʊtprɪnt] Fußabdruck OT 3
for [fər] für OT 1
force [fɔːs] Kraft OT 1
to **force** [fɔːs] zwingen OT 2
forecast [ˈfɔːkɑːst] Prognose OT 3
foreground [ˈfɔːɡraʊnd] Vordergrund OT 3
forehand [ˈfɔːhænd] Vorhand OT 3
foreign [ˈfɒrən] ausländisch; fremd OT 1
foreigner [ˈfɒrənə] Fremde(r) OT 3
foremost [ˈfɔːməʊst] zuvorderst WW, 11
forest [ˈfɒrɪst] Wald OT 1
forever [fərˈevə] für immer OT 2
to **forget** [fəˈɡet] vergessen OT 1
to **forgive** [fəˈɡɪv] vergeben OT 2
fork [fɔːk] Gabel OT 2
forklift [ˌfɔːklɪft] Gabelstapler WS 2, 70

form [fɔːm] Form OT 1
to **form** [fɔːm] gründen; bilden OT 4
formal [ˈfɔːml] förmlich; formell WS 1, 19
    formally [ˈfɔːməli] formell WS 2, 57
format [ˈfɔːmæt] Format WS 2, 56
formation [fɔːˈmeɪʃn] Formation WS 1, 21
former [ˈfɔːmə] ehemalig OT 4
to **formulate** [ˈfɔːmjuleɪt] formulieren OT 4
fort [fɔːt] Festung OT 2
fortnight [ˈfɔːtnaɪt] zwei Wochen OT 2
fortress [ˈfɔːtrəs] Zitadelle; Festung OT 3
fortunately [ˈfɔːtʃənətli] glücklicherweise WS 2, 57
fortune [ˈfɔːtʃuːn] Glück; Reichtum OT 3
forty [ˈfɔːti] vierzig OT 1
forum [ˈfɔːrəm] Forum WS 2, 62
fossil [ˈfɒsl] fossil OT 3
to **foul** [faʊl] foulen OT 3
to **found** [faʊnd] begründen; gründen OT 4
foundation [faʊnˈdeɪʃn] Grundlage; Fundament WS 1, 21
founder [ˈfaʊndər] Gründer(in) WS 2, 69
fountain [ˈfaʊntən] Springbrunnen OT 1
four [fɔː] vier OT 1
fourteen [ˌfɔːˈtiːn] vierzehn OT 1
fox [fɒks] Fuchs OT 1
to **frack** [fræk] fracken WS 1, 27
fracking [ˈfrækɪŋ] Fracking WS 1, 26
frame [freɪm] Rahmen OT 4
frantic [ˈfræntɪk] hektisch; aufgeregt OT 3
freak [friːk] Begeisterte(r); Freak OT 4
freckle [ˈfrekl] Sommersprose OT 2
free [friː] frei; kostenlos OT 1
freed [friːd] befreit OT 4
freedom [ˈfriːdəm] Freiheit OT 3
freelance [ˈfriːlɑːns] freiberuflich WS 2, 79
freelancer [ˈfriːlɑːnsə] Freiberufler(in) WS 2, 63
freeze-dried [ˈfriːz draɪd] gefriergetrocknet OT 4
freezer [ˈfriːzə] Gefrierschrank OT 3
freezing [ˈfriːzɪŋ] kalt OT 2
French [frentʃ] französisch; Französisch OT 1
    French fries [ˌfrentʃ ˈfraɪz] Pommes frites OT 2
    French horn [ˌfrentʃ ˈhɔːn] Waldhorn OT 1

frequency [ˈfriːkwənsi] Häufigkeit OT 1
to **frequent** [friːˈkwənt] aufsuchen WW, 11
frequent [ˈfriːkwənt] häufig WS 1, 26
    frequently [ˈfriːkwəntli] häufig OT 3
fresh [freʃ] frisch OT 1
freshman [ˈfreʃmən] Student im ersten Jahr; Studienanfänger(in) OT 4
Friday [ˈfraɪdeɪ] Freitag OT 1
fridge [frɪdʒ] Kühlschrank OT 1
friend [frend] Freund(in) OT 1
    to **make friends** [meɪk ˈfrendz] (sich) anfreunden OT 2
friendly [ˈfrendli] freundlich OT 1
friendship [ˈfrendʃɪp] Freundschaft OT 3
fries [fraɪz] Pommes frites OT 2
to **frighten** [ˈfraɪtn] erschrecken OT 3
frightened [ˈfraɪtnd] verängstigt OT 1
frightening [ˈfraɪtnɪŋ] erschreckend OT 1
frisbee [ˈfrɪzbi] Frisbee OT 1
frizzy [ˈfrɪzi] kraus OT 3
frog [frɒɡ] Frosch WS 4, 143
from [frəm] von; aus OT 1
    from around the world [frəm əˌraʊnd ði ˈwɜːld] aus aller Welt OT 1
front [frʌnt] Vorderseite; Vorderteil OT 1
    in front of [ɪn frʌnt əv] vor OT 1
frontier [ˈfrʌntɪə] Grenzland OT 4
frozen [ˈfrəʊzn] gefroren OT 4
fruit [fruːt] Obst OT 1
frustrated [frʌˈstreɪtɪd] frustriert OT 3
frustrating [frʌˈstreɪtɪŋ] frustrierend WS 3, 92
to **fry** [fraɪ] braten; frittieren OT 2
fuel [ˈfjuːəl] Brennstoff OT 2
to **fulfil** [fʊlˈfɪl] verwirklichen; erfüllen OT 4
full [fʊl] voll OT 1
fun [fʌn] Spaß OT 1
    good fun [ɡʊd ˈfʌn] ziemlich spaßig OT 2
function [ˈfʌŋkʃn] Funktion OT 4
to **fund** [fʌnd] finanzieren OT 3
fundraiser [ˈfʌndreɪzə] Spendensammler(in) OT 2
fundraising [ˈfʌndreɪzɪŋ] Spendensammlung OT 2
funeral [ˈfjuːnərəl] Beerdigung WS 2, 64
funny [ˈfʌni] lustig; merkwürdig OT 1
furniture [ˈfɜːnɪtʃə] Möbel OT 1
further [ˈfɜːðə] weiter OT 4
furthermore [ˌfɜːðəˈmɔːr] außerdem; weiterhin WS 2, 68
fuss [fʌs] Aufregung OT 4

Appendix

VOCABULARY

fussy [ˈfʌsi] pingelig; wählerisch OT 2
future [ˈfjuːtʃə] Zukunft OT 2
fuzz [fʌz] Fussel; Belag OT 4

G

gadget [ˈgædʒɪt] Gerät; technische Spielerei OT 4
to gain [geɪn] erlangen OT 1
galaxy [ˈgæləksi] Galaxie OT 1
gallery [ˈgæləri] Galerie OT 1
gallon [ˈgælən] Gallone OT 3
game [geɪm] Spiel OT 1
game console [ˈgeɪm kənsəʊl] Spielekonsole OT 4
gaming [ˈgeɪmɪŋ] Spielen OT 4
gamer [ˈgeɪmə] Gamer(in); Spieler(in) OT 4
gang [gæŋ] Bande; Gang WS 2, 64
gap [gæp] Lücke OT 3
garage [ˈgærɑːʒ] Garage; Werkstatt OT 4
garbage [ˈgɑːbɪdʒ] Abfall OT 2
garbage collector [ˈgɑːbɪdʒ kəˈlektə] Müllarbeiter(in) OT 4
garden [ˈgɑːdn] Garten OT 1
gardener [ˈgɑːdnə] Gärtner(in) OT 4
gardening [ˈgɑːdnɪŋ] Gartenarbeit OT 1
gas [gæs] Gas; Benzin OT 3
to gasp [gɑːsp] keuchen OT 2
gate [geɪt] Tor OT 1
to gather [ˈgæðə] sammeln OT 4
gatherer [ˈgæðərər] Sammler(in) WS 1, 22
gay [geɪ] schwul; früher: fröhlich WS 3, 89
geek [giːk] Geek; Spezialist(in) WS 3, 104
gel [dʒel] Gel OT 1
gelateria [ˈdʒelæˈtɪərɪə] italienisches Eiscafé WS 2, 69
gender [ˈdʒendə] Geschlecht; Gender OT 4
gendered [ˈdʒendəd] geschlechtsspezifisch WS 3, 93
genderless [ˈdʒendələs] geschlechtslos WS 3, 92
general [ˈdʒenrəl] allgemein OT 3
  generally [ˈdʒenrəli] im Allgemeinen; hauptsächlich OT 4
to generate [ˈdʒenəreɪt] erzeugen OT 4
generation [ˌdʒenəˈreɪʃn] Generation OT 4
generous [ˈdʒenərəs] großzügig OT 3
genre [ˈʒɒrə] Genre OT 4
gentleman [ˈdʒentlmən] Herr; Gentleman OT 3

gently [ˈdʒentli] sanft OT 3
genuinely [ˈdʒenjuɪnli] echt WS 2, 67
geocache [ˈdʒiːəʊkæʃ] Geocache OT 2
geocaching [ˈdʒiːəʊkæʃɪŋ] Geocaching OT 2
geographical [ˌdʒiːəˈgræfɪkl] geografisch OT 4
geography [dʒiˈɒgrəfi] Erdkunde; Geografie OT 1
geology [dʒiˈɒlədʒi] Geologie OT 2
German [ˈdʒɜːmən] deutsch OT 1
gesture [ˈdʒestʃə] Geste OT 4
to get [get] bekommen OT 1
  to get down [get daʊn] hinunterkommen OT 2
  to get hit [get hɪt] getroffen sein; geschlagen sein OT 4
  to get off [getˈɒf] aussteigen OT 2
  to get on [getˈɒn] zusteigen OT 2
  to get ready [get ˈredi] vorbereiten OT 1
  to get rid of [get rɪd əv] loswerden OT 3
  to get up [get ʌp] aufstehen OT 1
ghost [gəʊst] Geist OT 2
giant [ˈdʒaɪənt] riesig OT 2
gift [gɪft] Geschenk OT 1
gift voucher [ˈgɪft vaʊtʃə] Geschenkgutschein OT 1
gig [gɪg] Gig; Auftritt WS 2, 62
ginormous [dʒaɪˈnɔːməs] gigantisch OT 2
giraffe [dʒəˈrɑːf] Giraffe OT 1
girl [gɜːl] Mädchen OT 1
to give [gɪv] geben OT 1
  to give a talk [gɪv əˈtɔːk] einen Vortrag / Referat halten OT 2
  to give up [gɪvˈʌp] aufgeben OT 2
glad [glæd] froh OT 1
gladiator [ˈglædieɪtə] Gladiator(in) OT 3
glamorous [ˈglæmərəs] glamourös OT 4
gland [glænd] Drüse WS 4, 143
glass [glɑːs] Glas OT 1
glasses [ˈglɑːsɪz] Brille OT 1
glimpse [glɪmps] flüchtiger Blick WS 4, 126
to glitter [ˈglɪtə] glitzern OT 2
global [ˈgləʊbl] global; weltweit OT 4
global warming [ˌgləʊbl ˈwɔːmɪŋ] Klimaerwärmung; Erderwärmung OT 3
globe [gləʊb] Globus; Erdkugel WS 1, 13
glove [glʌv] Handschuh OT 1
glue [gluː] Klebstoff OT 1
to gnaw [nɔː] abnagen OT 2
go: a go [ə gəʊ] ein Versuch OT 2

to go [gəʊ] gehen; fahren OT 1
  to go ahead [ˌgəʊ əˈhed] weitermachen OT 4
  to go to sleep [ˌgəʊ təˈsliːp] einschlafen OT 1
  to go out [gəʊ aʊt] ausgehen OT 1
goal [gəʊl] Tor OT 1
goalkeeper [ˈgəʊlkiːpə] Torwart(in) OT 3
goat [gəʊt] Ziege OT 4
God [gɒd] Gott OT 4
godmother [ˈgɒdmʌðər] Patentante WS 1, 15
gold [gəʊld] Gold OT 2
golden [ˈgəʊldən] golden OT 3
gold rush [ˈgəʊld rʌʃ] Goldrausch OT 4
to gongoozle [gɒŋˈguːzl] gaffen OT 3
gongoozler [gɒŋˈguːzlə] Gaffer OT 3
good [gʊd] gut OT 1
goodbye [gʊdˈbaɪ] Auf Wiedersehen! OT 1
goodies [ˈgʊdiz] tolle Kleinigkeiten OT 2
goods [gʊdz] Güter OT 4
goose [guːs] Gans OT 4
gospel [ˈgɒspl] Gospel OT 2
to govern [ˈgʌvn] regieren OT 3
government [ˈgʌvənmənt] Regierung OT 3
GPS (global positioning system) [ˌdʒiː piː ˈes] Navigationssystem; Globales Positionsbestimmungssystem OT 2
to grab [græb] greifen OT 3
grade [greɪd] Klassenstufe OT 2
to graduate [ˈgrædʒuət] einen akademischen Grad erlangen OT 3
graffiti [grəˈfiːti] Graffiti WS 3, 121
grain [greɪn] Korn WS 3, 102
gram [græm] Gramm OT 2
grammar [ˈgræmə] Grammatik OT 1
gramophone [ˈgræməfəʊn] Grammofon OT 4
grand [grænd] grandios; großartig WS 3, 89
grandchild [ˈgræntʃaɪld] Enkel(in); Enkelkind OT 3
granddad [ˈgrændæd] Opa OT 1
grandfather [ˈgrænfɑːðə] Großvater OT 2
grandma [ˈgrænmɑː] Oma OT 1
grandmother [ˈgrænmʌðə] Großmutter OT 1
grandpa [ˈgrænpɑː] Opa OT 1
grandparents [ˈgrænpeərənts] Großeltern OT 1
grandson [ˈgrænsʌn] Enkel OT 1

Appendix

VOCABULARY

grant [grɑːnt] Förderung; Zuschuss **WS 2**, 64
graph [grɑːf] Graph; Diagramm **WS 3**, 89
graphic ['græfɪk] Grafik OT 3
grass [grɑːs] Gras OT 1
grateful ['greɪtfl] dankbar **WS 1**, 20
grave [greɪv] Grab **WS 1**, 38
gravity ['grævəti] Erdanziehungskraft; Schwerkraft OT 4
gravy ['greɪvi] Bratensoße OT 1
great [greɪt] groß; toll OT 1
Greek [griːk] griechisch OT 2
green [griːn] grün OT 1
greenhouse ['griːnhaʊs] Treibhaus OT 1
to greet [griːt] grüßen **WS 2**, 57
greeting ['griːtɪŋ] Gruß **WS 1**, 29
grey [greɪ] grau OT 1
grid: off the grid [ɒf ðə grɪd] vom Netz OT 4
grief [griːf] Trauer **WS 1**, 21
grill [grɪl] Grill **WS 1**, 40
to grin [grɪn] grinsen OT 2
groceries ['grəʊsəriz] Lebensmittel OT 4
grocery ['grəʊsəri] Lebensmittel **WS 3**, 103
grocery store ['grəʊsəri stɔː] Lebensmittelladen OT 4
gross [grəʊs] ätzend; ekelhaft OT 3
ground [graʊnd] Boden; Erde; Platz OT 1
    ground control ['graʊnd kəntrəʊl] Bodenstation OT 4
to ground [graʊnd] Hausarrest erteilen **WS 3**, 121
    group [gruːp] Gruppe OT 1
to grow [grəʊ] wachsen; anbauen OT 1
growth [grəʊθ] Wachstum **WS 3**, 102
grubby ['grʌbi] dreckig OT 2
to grumble ['grʌmbl] mosern; murren; schimpfen OT 2
to guarantee [ˌgærən'tiː] garantieren **WS 3**, 100
guardian ['gɑːdiən] Betreuer(in) OT 2
to guess [ges] schätzen OT 1
guessing game ['gesɪŋ geɪm] Rätselraten OT 1
guest [gest] Gast OT 2
guide [gaɪd] Führer(in) OT 1
guidebook ['gaɪdbʊk] Reiseführer OT 1
guideline ['gaɪdlaɪn] Richtlinie; Regel OT 3
guilty ['gɪlti] schuldig **WS 3**, 100
guitar [gɪ'tɑː] Gitarre OT 1
guitarist [gɪ'tɑːrɪst] Gitarrist(in) OT 1

gun [gʌn] Schusswaffe OT 4
gunman ['gʌnmən] Schütze OT 4
gurning ['gɜːnɪŋ] Grimassieren OT 2
guy [gaɪ] Kerl; Typ OT 2
    guys [gaɪz] Leute OT 2
gym [dʒɪm] Fitnesscenter; Turnhalle OT 3
gymnasium [dʒɪm'neɪziəm] Sporthalle; Turnhalle OT 4
gymnastics [dʒɪm'næstɪks] Gymnastik OT 1

H

habit ['hæbɪt] Gewohnheit OT 4
habitat ['hæbɪtæt] Habitat; Lebensraum OT 4
habitation [ˌhæbɪ'teɪʃn] Bewohnbarkeit OT 4
hair [heə] Haare OT 1
haircut ['heəkʌt] Haarschnitt OT 2
hairstyle ['heəstaɪl] Frisur **WS 3**, 92
halal [hə'læl] halal OT 3
half [hɑːf] halbe(r,-s); halb OT 1
    half past ['hɑːf pɑːst] eine halbe Stunde nach OT 1
half-time ['hɑːfˌtaɪm] Halbzeit OT 2
halfway [ˌhɑːf'weɪ] halb; halbwegs OT 3
hall [hɔːl] Diele; Halle OT 1
Halloween [ˌhæləʊ'iːn] Halloween OT 2
halt [hɔːlt] Haltestelle OT 2
ham [hæm] Schinken OT 3
hamburger ['hæmbɜːgə] Hamburger OT 2
hamster ['hæmstə] Hamster OT 1
hand [hænd] Hand OT 1
to hand [hænd] reichen **WS 3**, 97
    to hand in [hænd' ɪn] einreichen OT 2
handbag ['hændbæg] Handtasche OT 3
handbook ['hændbʊk] Handbuch OT 3
handle ['hændl] Griff OT 2
handout ['hændaʊt] Handout; Flugblatt OT 4
handset ['hændset] Mobilteil OT 2
handsome ['hænsəm] gut aussehend OT 1
to handwrite ['hændraɪt] mit der Hand schreiben **WS 2**, 63
handwriting ['hændraɪtɪŋ] Handschrift OT 2
handwritten [ˌhænd'rɪtn] handschriftlich **WS 4**, 144
handy ['hændi] praktisch; nützlich OT 2
to hang out [hæŋ aʊt] herumhängen OT 1; rumhängen; abhängen **WS 1**, 17
to hang on [ˌhæŋ'ɒn] warten OT 2

to happen ['hæpən] geschehen; passieren OT 1
    to happen upon ['hæpən ə'pɒn] zufällig entdecken OT 4
happy ['hæpi] glücklich OT 1
    happily ['hæpɪli] glücklich; glücklicherweise OT 2
harbour ['hɑːbə] Hafen OT 2
hard [hɑːd] hart OT 1
hardly ['hɑːdli] kaum OT 3
to harm [hɑːm] verletzen; schaden OT 2
harmful ['hɑːmfl] schädlich OT 3
harmless ['hɑːmləs] harmlos; unbedenklich **WS 3**, 94
harness ['hɑːnɪs] Sicherheitsgurt; Gurt OT 1
harp [hɑːp] Harfe OT 1
harpist ['hɑːpɪst] Harfenist(in) OT 3
harsh [hɑːʃ] rau **WS 1**, 19
harvest ['hɑːvɪst] Ernte OT 4
to harvest ['hɑːvɪst] ernten OT 4
hash browns [ˌhæʃ'braʊnz] kleine gebratene Kartoffelwürfel, wie Rösti OT 3
hashtag ['hæʃtæg] Hashtag **WS 2**, 65
hat [hæt] Hut; Mütze OT 1
to hate [heɪt] hassen OT 1
to have [həv] haben OT 1
    to have a son [həv ə 'sʌn] einen Sohn bekommen OT 1
    to have got ['hæv gɒt] haben OT 1
    to have to ['hæv tə] müssen OT 1
hazard ['hæzəd] Gefahr; Risiko OT 2
he [hiː] er OT 1
head [hed] Kopf OT 1
to head out [hed aʊt] aufbrechen; losfahren OT 4
to head back [hed bæk] gehen zurück; zurückkehren **WS 1**, 19
headache ['hedeɪk] Kopfschmerzen OT 1
headband ['hedbænd] Stirnband; Kopfband OT 3
heading ['hedɪŋ] Überschrift OT 1
headline ['hedlaɪn] Schlagzeile OT 2
headquarter ['hed'kwɔːtə] Headquarter; Hauptsitz OT 4
headset ['hedset] Headset OT 4
headshot ['hedʃɒt] Portraitfoto **WS 2**, 56
    head teacher [ˌhed 'tiːtʃə] Schulleiter(in) OT 1
headword ['hedwɜːd] Stichwort OT 2
healing ['hiːlɪŋ] Heilung **WS 1**, 21
health [helθ] Gesundheit OT 2

Appendix

VOCABULARY

healthcare [ˈhelθkeə] Gesundheitswesen OT 4
healthy [ˈhelθi] gesund OT 2
heap [hi:p] Haufen OT 4
to hear [hɪə] hören OT 1
heart [hɑ:t] Herz OT 2
  by heart [baɪ hɑ:t] auswendig OT 2
heartland [ˈhɑ:tlænd] Kernland; Herzland OT 4
hearty [ˈhɑ:ti] herzhaft OT 2
to heat [hi:t] heizen OT 3
heater [ˈhi:tə] Heizung OT 2
heating [ˈhi:tɪŋ] Heizung OT 3
heatwave [ˈhi:tweɪv] Hitzewelle WS 1, 26
heaven [ˈhevn] Himmel WS 2, 64
heavy [ˈhevi] schwer OT 1
hectare [ˈhekteər] Hektar WS 1, 27
hectic [ˈhektɪk] hektisch OT 4
hedge [hedʒ] Hecke WS 2, 59
hedgehog [ˈhedʒhɒg] Igel OT 1
height [haɪt] Höhe OT 1
heir [eər] Erbe / Erbin WS 2, 64
helicopter [ˈhelɪkɒptə] Hubschrauber OT 2
hell [hel] Hölle WS 2, 64
hello [həˈləʊ] hallo OT 1
helmet [ˈhelmɪt] Helm OT 1
to help [help] helfen OT 1
helper [ˈhelpə] Helfer(in) OT 3
helpful [ˈhelpfl] hilfreich OT 1
helpless [ˈhelpləs] hilflos OT 4
helpline [ˈhelplaɪn] Hotline OT 2
hemisphere [ˈhemɪsfɪər] Hemisphäre WS 1, 13
hen [hen] Henne OT 2
heptathlon [hepˈtæθlən] Siebenkampf OT 2
her [hə] sie; ihr OT 1
herb [hɜ:b] Kraut OT 3
herd [hɜ:d] Herd OT 4
to herd [hɜ:d] treiben OT 2
here [hɪə] hier OT 1
heritage [ˈherɪtɪdʒ] Erbe; Tradition WS 1, 21
hero [ˈhɪərəʊ] Held(in) OT 3
hers [hɜ:z] ihre(r, -s) OT 2
herself [hɜːˈself] sich (selbst) OT 3
to hesitate [ˈhezɪteɪt] zögern OT 3
hesitation [ˌhezɪˈteɪʃn] Zögern OT 3
heterosexual [ˌhetərəˈsekʃuəl] heterosexuell WS 3, 93
Hey! [heɪ] He! OT 1
hi [haɪ] hallo OT 1
hiccup [ˈhɪkʌp] Schluckauf OT 2
to hide [haɪd] sich verstecken OT 3

high [haɪ] hoch OT 1
to highlight [ˈhaɪlaɪt] hervorheben OT 3
highway [ˈhaɪweɪ] Highway; Landstrasse OT 3
hike [haɪk] Wanderung OT 2
to hike [haɪk] wandern OT 1
hiker [ˈhaɪkə] Wanderer / Wanderin OT 2
hiking [ˈhaɪkɪŋ] Wandern OT 1
hiking boot [ˈhaɪkɪŋ bu:t] Wanderstiefel OT 2
hill [hɪl] Hügel OT 1
hilly [ˈhɪli] hügelig OT 2
him [hɪm] ihn / ihm OT 1
himself [hɪmˈself] (sich) selbst OT 1
Hindu [ˈhɪndu:] hinduistisch OT 1
hip [hɪp] Hüfte OT 3
hip hop [ˈhɪp hɒp] Hip-Hop OT 1
hippopotamus [ˌhɪpəˈpɒtəməs] Nilpferd OT 2
to hire [haɪə] mieten OT 3
his [hɪz] seine(r,-s) OT 1
Hispanic [hɪˈspænɪk] hispanisch OT 3
historian [hɪˈstɔ:riən] Historiker(in) OT 3
historic [hɪˈstɒrɪk] historisch OT 3
historical [hɪˈstɒrɪkl] geschichtlich OT 2
history [ˈhɪstri] Geschichte OT 1
to hit [hɪt] schlagen OT 1
hob [hɒb] Kochfeld OT 3
hobby [ˈhɒbi] Hobby OT 1
hockey [ˈhɒki] Hockey OT 1
to hold [həʊld] halten OT 1
holder [ˈhəʊldə] Halter WS 2, 70
hole [həʊl] Loch OT 1
hole punch [həʊl pʌntʃ] Locher WS 2, 70
holiday [ˈhɒlədeɪ] Urlaub OT 1
holidaymaker [ˈhɒlədeɪmeɪkə] Urlauber(in) OT 3
home [həʊm] Zuhause OT 1
homecoming [ˈhəʊmkʌmɪŋ] Absolvententreffen an Schulen oder Universitäten OT 4
homeland [ˈhəʊmlænd] Heimat OT 4
homeless [ˈhəʊmləs] heimatlos; obdachlos OT 3
homelessness [ˈhəʊmləsnəs] Obdachlosigkeit OT 4
homemade [ˈhəʊmmeɪd] selbst gemacht; selbst zubereitet OT 3
homepage [ˈhəʊmpeɪdʒ] Startseite OT 1
homeschooled [ˌhəʊmˈsku:ld] zu Hause unterrichtet OT 4
homesick [ˈhəʊmsɪk] voll Heimweh OT 2

homesickness [ˈhəʊmsɪknəs] Heimweh OT 4
hometown [ˈhəʊmtaʊn] Heimatstadt OT 4
homework [ˈhəʊmwɜ:k] Hausaufgaben OT 1
honest [ˈɒnɪst] ehrlich OT 3
honey [ˈhʌni] Honig; Schatz (als Kosename) OT 2
to honour [ˈɒnə] ehren WS 1, 21
hoodie [ˈhʊdi] Kapuzenpullover OT 1
to hook [hʊk] haken OT 4
to hope [həʊp] hoffen OT 1
hopeful [ˈhəʊpfl] hoffnungsvoll WS 1, 27
hopefully [ˈhəʊpfəli] hoffentlich OT 4
hopeless [ˈhəʊpləs] hoffnungslos; hilflos OT 4
horizon [həˈraɪzn] Horizont WS 1, 20
horizontal [ˌhɒrɪˈzɒntl] horizontal OT 4
hormone [ˈhɔ:məʊn] Hormon WS 3, 93
horn [hɔ:n] Horn OT 2
horrible [ˈhɒrəbl] furchtbar OT 2
horror [ˈhɒrə] Horror; Grauen OT 2
horse [hɔ:s] Pferd OT 1
horse-drawn [ˈhɔ:s drɔ:n] pferdebespannt OT 1
horse riding [ˈraɪdɪŋ] Reiten OT 1
hospital [ˈhɒspɪtl] Krankenhaus OT 1
hospitality [ˌhɒspɪˈtæləti] Gastfreundschaft OT 2
to host [həʊst] ausrichten OT 3
hostel [ˈhɒstl] Hostel OT 2
hot [hɒt] heiß; scharf OT 1
hotel [həʊˈtel] Hotel OT 1
hound [haʊnd] Spürhund OT 2
hour [ˈaʊə] Stunde OT 1
hourly [ˈaʊəli] stündlich; Stunden- WS 2, 82
house [haʊs] Haus OT 1
houseboat [ˈhaʊsbəʊt] Hausboot OT 3
household [ˈhaʊshəʊld] häuslich; Haushalts- OT 4
housekeeper [ˈhaʊski:pə] Haushälter(in) OT 3
housewife [ˈhaʊswaɪf] Hausfrau WS 2, 63
housework [ˈhaʊswɜ:k] Hausarbeit OT 1
housing [ˈhaʊzɪŋ] Wohnraum; Unterkunft OT 3
how [haʊ] wie OT 1
however [haʊˈevə] jedoch OT 2
howl [haʊl] Geheul WS 1, 23
hug [hʌg] Umarmung OT 1
to hug [hʌg] sich umarmen OT 4
huge [hju:dʒ] riesig OT 2

Appendix

VOCABULARY

human [ˈhju:mən] menschlich OT 3; Mensch WS 1, 27
humanitarian [hju:ˌmænɪˈteəriən] humanitär WS 2, 61
humorous [ˈhju:mərəs] humorvoll WS 4, 145
humour [ˈhju:mə] Humor OT 3
hundred [ˈhʌndrəd] hundert OT 1
Hungarian [hʌŋˈgeəriən] ungarisch OT 2
hunger [ˈhʌŋgə] Hunger OT 4
hungry [ˈhʌŋgri] hungrig OT 1
to **hunt** [hʌnt] jagen OT 2
hunter [ˈhʌntə] Jäger(in) WS 1, 20
hurricane [ˈhʌrɪkən] Hurrikan; Orkan WS 1, 26
to **hurry** [ˈhʌri] (sich) beeilen OT 1
to **hurt** [hɜ:t] schmerzen; wehtun OT 1
hurt [hɜ:t] verletzt OT 1
husband [ˈhʌzbənd] Ehemann; Mann OT 2
to **hydrate** [haɪˈdreɪt] hydratisieren OT 4
hygiene [ˈhaɪdʒi:n] Hygiene OT 4
hype [haɪp] Hype WS 2, 67
hyper-connected [ˈhaɪpə kəˈnektɪd] angeschlossen OT 4
hyperlink [ˈhaɪpəlɪŋk] Hyperlink OT 3
hypothermia [ˌhaɪpəˈθɜ:miə] Unterkühlung OT 2

I

I [aɪ] ich OT 1
ice [aɪs] Eis OT 1
iceberg [ˈaɪsbɜ:g] Eisberg OT 3
ice cream [ˌaɪsˈkri:m] Eis; Eiscreme OT 1
ice lolly [aɪs ˈlɒli] Eis am Stiel OT 1
icon [ˈaɪkɒn] Symbol; Ikone WW, 11
iconic [aɪˈkɒnɪk] ikonisch; Kult... OT 3
ICT (information and communications technology) [ˌaɪ si:ˈti:] Informations- und Kommunikationstechnologie OT 1
icy [ˈaɪsi] eisig WS 3, 100
idea [aɪˈdɪə] Idee OT 1
ideal [aɪˈdi:əl] ideal OT 2
  ideally [aɪˈdi:əli] idealerweise WS 2, 57
identical [aɪˈdentɪkl] identisch WS 4, 145
to **identify** [aɪˈdentɪfaɪ] identifizieren OT 3
identity [aɪˈdentəti] Identität OT 3
idol [ˈaɪdl] Idol WS 3, 102
if [ɪf] falls OT 1
ignition [ɪgˈnɪʃn] Zündung OT 4
to **ignore** [ɪgˈnɔ:] ignorieren OT 4

ill [ɪl] krank OT 2
illegal [ɪˈli:gl] illegal OT 3
illiterate [ɪˈlɪtərət] analphabetisch OT 4
illness [ˈɪlnəs] Krankheit OT 2
to **illustrate** [ˈɪrɪtəbl] darstellen; illustrieren OT 3
illustration [ˌɪləˈstreɪʃn] Illustration OT 2
image [ˈɪmɪdʒ] Bild OT 1
imaginary [ɪˈmædʒɪnəri] imaginär; fiktiv OT 4
imagination [ɪˌmædʒɪˈneɪʃn] Vorstellung; Fantasie OT 4
imaginative [ɪˈmædʒɪnətɪv] fantasievoll OT 4
to **imagine** [ɪˈmædʒɪn] sich etw. vorstellen; sich einbilden; glauben OT 1
immediate [ɪˈmi:diət] unmittelbar; umgehend WS 1, 22
immediately [ɪˈmi:diətli] sofort OT 1
immigrant [ˈɪmɪgrənt] Einwanderer / Einwanderin OT 3
to **immigrate** [ˈɪmɪgreɪt] einwandern WS 1, 18
immigration [ˌɪmɪˈgreɪʃn] Einwanderungscontrolle OT 2
impact [ˈɪmpækt] Auswirkung OT 3
to **impart** [ɪmˈpɑ:t] vermitteln OT 4
impatient [ɪmˈpeɪʃnt] ungeduldig OT 3
imperative [ɪmˈperətɪv] Imperativ; Befehlsform OT 1
to **import** [ˈɪmpɔ:t] importieren; einführen OT 3
importance [ɪmˈpɔ:təns] Bedeutung; Wichtigkeit OT 2
important [ɪmˈpɔ:tnt] wichtig OT 1
impossible [ɪmˈpɒsəbl] unmöglich OT 2
impractical [ɪmˈpræktɪkl] unpraktisch OT 4
to **impress** [ɪmˈpres] beeindrucken WS 3, 100
impressed [ɪmˈprest] beindruckt OT 4
impression [ɪmˈpreʃn] Eindruck WS 1, 16
to **improve** [ɪmˈpru:v] verbessern OT 2
improvement [ɪmˈpru:vmənt] Verbesserung OT 3
improvisation [ˌɪmprəvaɪˈzeɪʃn] Improvisation OT 2
to **improvise** [ˈɪmprəvaɪz] improvisieren OT 2
in [ɪn] im OT 1
inaccessible [ˌɪnækˈsesəbl] unzugänglich OT 3

inappropriate [ˌɪnəˈprəʊpriət] unpassend WS 4, 144
inch [ɪntʃ] Zoll (2,54 cm) OT 2
incident [ˈɪnsɪdənt] Vorfall; Ereignis WS 3, 101
to **include** [ɪnˈklu:d] einschließen OT 1
included [ɪnˈklu:dɪd] inklusive OT 1
including [ɪnˈklu:dɪŋ] inklusive OT 1
inclusion [ɪnˈklu:ʒn] Inklusion WS 3, 88
inclusive [ɪnˈklu:sɪv] integrativ OT 4
income [ˈɪnkʌm] Einkommen OT 4
incorrectly [ˌɪnkəˈrektli] falsch; fehlerhaft WS 3, 102
increase [ˈɪnkri:s] Zunahme OT 3
to **increase** [ɪnˈkri:s] anwachsen; erhöhen OT 3
increasingly [ɪnˈkri:sɪŋli] zunehmend WS 1, 27
incredible [ɪnˈkredəbl] unglaublich OT 2
  incredibly [ɪnˈkredəbli] unglaublich OT 3
incubator [ˈɪŋkjubeɪtər] Inkubator; Unterstützer von Start-ups WS 2, 52
indecision [ˌɪndɪˈsɪʒn] Unentschlossenheit WS 1, 38
indefinite [ɪnˈdefɪnət] unbestimmt OT 1
independence [ˌɪndɪˈpendəns] Unabhängigkeit OT 2
independent [ˌɪndɪˈpendənt] selbstständig OT 3
  independently [ˌɪndɪˈpendəntli] selbstständig; unabhängig WS 2, 66
index [ˈɪndeks] Index; Register OT 4
indexer [ˈɪndeksə] Indexer OT 4
Indian [ˈɪndiən] indisch OT 2
to **indicate** [ˈɪndɪkeɪt] angeben; zeigen WS 2, 68
indigenous [ɪnˈdɪdʒənəs] einheimisch WS 1, 20
indignity [ɪnˈdɪgnəti] Demütigung WS 1, 21
individual [ˌɪndɪˈvɪdʒuəl] Einzelne(r) OT 4
individual [ˌɪndɪˈvɪdʒuəl] individuell OT 3
  individually [ˌɪndɪˈvɪdʒuəli] einzeln OT 4
indoor [ˈɪndɔ:] Innen... OT 2
indoors [ˌɪnˈdɔ:z] drinnen OT 3
induction [ɪnˈdʌkʃn] Einführung WS 2, 70
industrial [ɪnˈdʌstriəl] Industrie... OT 2
industry [ˈɪndəstri] Industrie OT 2
inexpensive [ˌɪnɪkˈspensɪv] billig; preiswert OT 4

Appendix

VOCABULARY

inexperienced [ˌɪnɪkˈspɪəriənst] unerfahren **WS 2**, 83
infection [ɪnˈfekʃn] Entzündung OT 2
infinite [ˈɪnfɪnət] unendlich OT 4
infinitive [ɪnˈfɪnətɪv] Infinitiv OT 2
to inflict [ɪnˈflɪkt] aufdrängen **WS 1**, 21
influence [ˈɪnfluəns] Einfluss OT 4
to influence [ˈɪnfluəns] beeinflussen OT 4
influencer [ˈɪnfluənsə] Influencer(in) **WS 3**, 105
influenza [ˌɪnfluˈenzə] Grippe; Influenza **WS 1**, 22
infographic [ˌɪnfəʊˈɡræfɪk] Infografik OT 3
informal [ɪnˈfɔːml] informell **WS 1**, 16
information [ˌɪnfəˈmeɪʃn] Information OT 1
informative [ɪnˈfɔːmətɪv] informativ; instruktiv OT 3
to inform [ɪnˈfɔːm] informieren OT 4
ingredient [ɪnˈɡriːdiənt] Zutat OT 2
to inhabit [ɪnˈhæbɪt] bewohnen **WS 1**, 20
inhumane [ˌɪnhjuːˈmeɪn] inhuman; menschenunwürdig OT 4
initially [ɪˈnɪʃəli] zunächst; anfangs **WS 1**, 41
initiative [ɪˈnɪʃətɪv] Initiative; Kampagne OT 4
to injure [ˈɪndʒə] verletzen OT 2
injury [ˈɪndʒəri] Verletzung OT 2
injustice [ɪnˈdʒʌstɪs] Ungerechtigkeit OT 4
inn [ɪn] Gasthaus OT 2
inner [ˈɪnər] innerer **WS 2**, 53
innocent [ˈɪnəsnt] unschuldig **WS 4**, 144
innovation [ˌɪnəˈveɪʃn] Innovation; Neuheit OT 4
innovative [ˈɪnəveɪtɪv] innovativ OT 4
innovator [ˈɪnəveɪtə] Innovator(in) OT 4
input [ˈɪnpʊt] Beitrag OT 4
insane [ɪnˈseɪn] verrückt; wahnsinnig **WS 3**, 92
insect [ˈɪnsekt] Insekt OT 1
inside [ˌɪnˈsaɪd] in; innerhalb OT 1
insides [ˌɪnˈsaɪdz] Innereien OT 3
insight [ˈɪnsaɪt] Einsicht **WS 2**, 66
inspiration [ˌɪnspəˈreɪʃn] Inspiration; Eingebung OT 4
to inspire [ɪnˈspaɪə] inspirieren; anregen OT 3
  to get inspired [ɡet ɪnˈspaɪəd] inspiriert sein OT 4
to install [ɪnˈstɔːl] installieren OT 4

instance: for instance [fəˈɪnstəns] beispielsweise; zum Beispiel **WS 4**, 141
instead [ɪnˈsted] stattdessen OT 2
institution [ˌɪnstɪˈtjuːʃn] Einrichtung OT 4
to instruct [ɪnˈstrʌkt] einweisen **WS 2**, 71
instruction [ɪnˈstrʌkʃn] Anweisung OT 1
instructive [ɪnˈstrʌktɪv] instruktiv; lehrreich **WS 1**, 31
instructor [ɪnˈstrʌktə] Lehrer(in) OT 3
instrument [ˈɪnstrəmənt] Instrument OT 1
insulted [ˈɪnsʌltɪd] beleidigt **WS 1**, 24
integrated [ˈɪntɪɡreɪtɪd] integriert **WS 3**, 118
intelligent [ɪnˈtelɪdʒənt] intelligent OT 2
to intend [ɪnˈtend] beabsichtigen **WS 3**, 105
intense [ɪnˈtens] stark; ernsthaft **WS 1**, 30
to interact [ˌɪntərˈækt] interagieren OT 4
interaction [ˌɪntərˈækʃn] Interaktion OT 4
interactive [ˌɪntərˈæktɪv] interaktiv **WS 4**, 141
intercultural [ˌɪntəˈkʌltʃərəl] interkulturell **WS 4**, 144
interest [ˈɪntrəst] Interesse OT 1
interested [ˈɪntrəstɪd] interessiert OT 1
interesting [ˈɪntrəstɪŋ] interessant OT 1
interior [ɪnˈtɪəriər] Binnenland; das Innere **WS 1**, 13
intern [ɪnˈtɜːn] Praktikant(in); Volontär(in) OT 4
internal [ɪnˈtɜːnl] intern **WS 3**, 115
internal combustion [ɪnˈtɜːnl kəmˈbʌstʃən] Verbrennungs- OT 4
international [ˌɪntəˈnæʃnəl] international OT 1
internet [ˈɪntənet] Internet OT 1
internship [ˈɪntɜːnʃɪp] Praktikum OT 4
to interpret [ɪnˈtɜːprət] interpretieren OT 4
interpretation [ɪnˌtɜːprəˈteɪʃn] Interpretation **WS 4**, 146
interpreter [ɪnˈtɜːprɪtə] Dolmetscher(in) OT 4
to interrupt [ˌɪntəˈrʌpt] unterbrechen OT 2
intersex [ˈɪntəseks] Intersex **WS 3**, 93
interview [ˈɪntəvjuː] Vorstellungsgespräch; Interview OT 1

to interview [ˈɪntəvjuː] ein Vorstellungsgespräch führen mit; interviewen OT 1
interviewer [ˈɪntəvjuːə] Interviewer(in) OT 1
into [ˈɪntuː] in OT 1
intonation [ˌɪntəˈneɪʃn] Intonation OT 4
to introduce [ˌɪntrəˈdjuːs] vorstellen OT 2
introduction [ˌɪntrəˈdʌkʃn] Vorstellung; Einführung OT 2
introductory [ˌɪntrəˈdʌktəri] Anfangs-; Einführungs- **WS 3**, 103
to invade [ɪnˈveɪd] einmarschieren OT 3
invasion [ɪnˈveɪʒn] Invasion; Eingriff **WS 1**, 21
invasive [ɪnˈveɪsɪv] invasiv **WS 1**, 23
to invent [ɪnˈvent] erfinden OT 2
invention [ɪnˈvenʃn] Erfindung OT 4
inventor [ɪnˈventə] Erfinder(in) OT 2
inversion [ɪnˈvɜːʃn] Inversion **WS 3**, 118
to invert [ɪnˈvɜːt] umkehren; umstellen **WS 1**, 29
to invest [ɪnˈvest] investieren OT 3
investigator [ɪnˈvestɪɡeɪtə] Ermittler(in) OT 4
investment [ɪnˈvestmənt] Investition OT 3
investor [ɪnˈvestə] Investor(in); Geldgeber(in) OT 4
invitation [ˌɪnvɪˈteɪʃn] Einladung; Aufforderung OT 1
to invite [ɪnˈvaɪt] einladen OT 2
  to invite along [ɪnˈvaɪt əˈlɒŋ] mit einladen OT 2
to involve [ɪnˈvɒlv] einbeziehen; umfassen OT 4
involved [ɪnˈvɒlvd] involviert; teilnehmend OT 3
Iranian [ɪˈreɪniən] iranisch OT 4
Irish [ˈaɪrɪʃ] irisch OT 1
irony [ˈaɪrəni] Ironie **WS 4**, 145
irregular [ɪˈreɡjələ] unregelmäßig OT 1
irritable [ˈɪrɪtəbl] reizbar OT 3
irritated [ˈɪrɪteɪtɪd] verärgert OT 2
Islamic [ɪzˈlæmɪk] islamisch **WS 3**, 88
island [ˈaɪlənd] Insel OT 2
islander [ˈaɪləndə] Insulaner(in) **WS 1**, 12
isle [aɪl] Eiland; kleine Insel **WS 1**, 30
Israeli [ɪzˈreɪli] israelisch OT 2
issue [ˈɪsjuː] Thema; Angelegenheit; Ausgabe OT 2
it [ɪt] es / ihm OT 1
Italian [ɪˈtæliən] italienisch OT 2

Appendix

VOCABULARY

itchy [ˈɪtʃi] juckend OT 2
item [ˈaɪtəm] Gegenstand OT 2
its [ɪts] sein; ihr OT 1
itself [ɪtˈself] sich (selbst) OT 3
ivory [ˈaɪvəri] Elfenbein OT 3

J

jacket [ˈdʒækɪt] Jacke OT 1
jack-o-lantern [ˌdʒæk ə ˈlæntən] Kürbislaterne OT 2
jail [dʒeɪl] Gefängnis WS 3, 100
jam [dʒæm] Marmelade OT 2
Jamaican [dʒəˈmeɪkən] jamaikanisch OT 1
January [ˈdʒænjuəri] Januar OT 1
Japanese [ˌdʒæpəˈniːz] japanisch OT 1
jar [dʒɑː] Einweckglas OT 2
jazz [dʒæz] Jazz OT 2
jeans [dʒiːnz] Jeanshose OT 1
jewelry [ˈdʒuːəlri] Schmuck OT 2
jewel [ˈdʒuːəl] Juwel OT 1
job [dʒɒb] Stelle; Job; Aufgabe OT 1
  to **do a good / great job** [duː ə gʊd / greɪtˈ dʒɒb] gute Arbeit leisten OT 2
  job hopping [ˈdʒɒb hɒpɪŋ] wiederholter Stellenwechsel WS 2, 62
jobless [ˈdʒɒbləs] arbeitslos WS 2, 65
to **jog** [dʒɒg] traben; joggen OT 2
to **join** [dʒɔɪn] Mitglied werden in; eintreten in OT 1
joke [dʒəʊk] Witz OT 2
to **joke** [dʒəʊk] Witze machen OT 2
journal [ˈdʒɜːnl] Journal; Fachzeitschrift WW, 11
journalism [ˈdʒɜːnəlɪzəm] Journalismus WS 2, 79
journalist [ˈdʒɜːnəlɪst] Journalist(in) OT 2
journey [ˈdʒɜːni] Reise; Fahrt OT 1
joyride [ˈdʒɔɪraɪd] Spritztour (mit einem gestohlenen Auto) WS 3, 100
joyriding [ˈdʒɔɪraɪdɪŋ] Spritztour (mit einem gestohlenen Auto) WS 3, 101
judge [dʒʌdʒ] Richter(in); Preisrichter(in) OT 2
to **judge** [dʒʌdʒ] einschätzen; beurteilen OT 2
Judgement Day [ˈdʒʌdʒmənt deɪ] jüngste Gericht OT 4
judging [ˈdʒʌdʒɪŋ] Beurteilung OT 2
judo [ˈdʒuːdəʊ] Judo OT 1
juice [dʒuːs] Saft OT 1
July [dʒuˈlaɪ] Juli OT 1
jumbled [ˈdʒʌmbld] durcheinander OT 2
to **jump** [dʒʌmp] springen OT 2
jumper [ˈdʒʌmpə] Pullover OT 1
June [dʒuːn] Juni OT 1
jungle [ˈdʒʌŋgl] Dschungel OT 4
junior [ˈdʒuːniə] Junior(in) OT 2
junk food [ˈdʒʌŋk fuːd] ungesundes Essen WS 3, 102
junky [ˈdʒʌŋki] schlecht; mangelhaft OT 4
just [dʒʌst] genau; nur OT 1
justice [ˈdʒʌstɪs] Gerechtigkeit OT 4
to **justify** [ˈdʒʌstɪfaɪ] rechtfertigen WS 1, 38

K

kangaroo [ˌkæŋgəˈruː] Känguru WS 1, 12
karate [kəˈrɑːti] Karate OT 1
kart racing [kɑːt reɪsɪŋ] Kartrennen OT 3
kayaking [ˈkaɪækɪŋ] Kajakfahren OT 2
keen: to be keen [tə bi kiː] auf etw. scharf sein; auf etw. Lust haben OT 4
to **keep** [kiːp] bleiben; behalten; aufbewahren OT 2
  to **keep away** [kiːp əˈweɪ] fernbleiben; fernhalten OT 2
  to **keep in touch** [ˌkiːp ɪn ˈtʌtʃ] in Kontakt bleiben OT 2
keeper [ˈkiːpə] Hüter(in) OT 4
ketchup [ˈketʃəp] Ketchup OT 1
kettle [ˈketl] Kessel; Wasserkocher OT 2
key [kiː] Schlüssel OT 1
to **key (in)** [kiː ɪn] tippen; eintippen OT 2
keyboard [ˈkiːbɔːd] Tastatur; Keyboard OT 1
keyword [ˈkiːwɜːd] Stichwort OT 4
to **kick** [kɪk] treten OT 1
kickball [ˈkɪkbɔːl] Kickball OT 4
kid [kɪd] Kind OT 1
kidnapper [ˈkɪdnæpə] Entführer(in) OT 2
kidney bean [ˈkɪdni biːn] Kidneybohne OT 2
to **kill** [kɪl] töten OT 1
kilometre [ˈkɪləmiːtə] Kilometer OT 1
kimchi [ˈkɪmtʃi] Kimchi OT 1
kin [kɪn] Verwandtschaft; Familie WS 1, 21
kind [kaɪnd] Art OT 1
kind [kaɪnd] freundlich; nett OT 1
  kindly [ˈkaɪndli] netterweise OT 2
king [kɪŋ] König OT 1
kingdom [ˈkɪŋdəm] Königreich OT 4
kiss [kɪs] Kuss OT 3
kit [kɪt] Ausrüstung OT 2
kitchen [ˈkɪtʃɪn] Küche OT 1
kite-surfing [kaɪt ˈsɜːfɪŋ] Kitesurfen WS 1, 43
kiwi [ˈkiːwiː] Kiwi OT 1
knee [niː] Knie OT 1
to **kneel** [niːl] knien OT 1
knife [naɪf] Messer OT 2
to **knight** [naɪt] zum Ritter schlagen OT 3
knock [nɒk] Klopfen OT 2
  to **knock over** [nɒkˈ əʊvə] umstoßen OT 2
to **know** [nəʊ] wissen OT 1
  well known [ˌwel ˈnəʊn] bekannt OT 2
knowledge [ˈnɒlɪdʒ] Wissen OT 4
knowledgeable [ˈnɒlɪdʒəbl] kenntnisreich OT 3
koala [kəʊˈɑːlə] Koala WS 1, 13
kookaburra [ˈkʊkəbʌrə] Kookaburra; Lachender Hans WS 1, 13
Korean [kəˈriən] koreanisch OT 1

L

lab [læb] Labor OT 2
label [ˈleɪbl] Etikett OT 1
labor [ˈleɪbə] Arbeitskraft; Arbeit OT 4
laboratory [ləˈbɒrətri] Labor OT 4
lack [læk] Mangel OT 3
ladder [ˈlædə] Leiter OT 2
lady [ˈleɪdi] Dame OT 1
laid-back [ˌleɪd ˈbæk] locker; entspannt OT 4
lake [leɪk] See OT 1
lakefront [ˈleɪkfrʌnt] Seeufer OT 4
lakeside [ˈleɪksaɪd] Seeufer OT 4
lamb [læm] Lamm OT 1
lamp [læmp] Lampe OT 1
to **land** [lænd] landen OT 1
landfill [ˈlændfɪl] Mülldeponie OT 3
landline [ˈlændlaɪn] Festnetz OT 4
landmark [ˈlændmɑːk] Wahrzeichen OT 4
landscape [ˈlændskeɪp] Landschaft OT 2
lane [leɪn] Fahrspur; Gasse OT 2
laneway [leɪnweɪ] Sträßchen WS 1, 17
language [ˈlæŋgwɪdʒ] Sprache OT 1
lantern [ˈlæntən] Laterne OT 2
lanyard [ˈlænjɑːd] Umhängeband; Kordel WS 2, 70
laptop [ˈlæptɒp] Laptop OT 1
large [lɑːdʒ] groß OT 2
lasagna [ləˈzænjə] Lasagne OT 1
laser [ˈleɪzə] Laser OT 3
to **last** [lɑːst] andauern OT 2

Appendix
VOCABULARY

last [lɑːst] letzte(r,-s) OT 1
late [leɪt] spät OT 1
later [ˈleɪtə] später OT 1
Latin [ˈlætɪn] Latein OT 1
Latino [læˈtiːnəʊ] lateinamerikanisch OT 2
to **laugh** [lɑːf] lachen OT 1
to **launch** [lɔːntʃ] starten; auf den Markt bringen OT 4
laundry [ˈlɔːndri] Wäsche OT 4
lava [ˈlɑːvə] Lava WS 1, 24
law [lɔː] Gesetz OT 3
lawn [lɔːn] Rasen WS 2, 59
lawyer [ˈlɔɪə] Rechtsanwalt / -anwältin OT 4
to **lead** [liːd] führen OT 3
leading [ˈliːdɪŋ] führend OT 2
leader [ˈliːdə] Leiter(in) OT 1
leadership [ˈliːdəʃɪp] Führung OT 4
leaf [liːf] Blatt OT 4
leaflet [ˈliːflət] Reklamezettel OT 2
league [liːg] Liga OT 2
to **lean** [liːn] lehnen OT 3
leap [liːp] Sprung WS 4, 146
to **learn** [lɜːn] lernen OT 1
learner [ˈlɜːnə] Lernende(r); Fahranfänger(in) OT 3
to **lease** [liːs] leasen; mieten OT 4
least [liːst] wenigste(r, -s) OT 2
leather [ˈleðə] Leder OT 3
to **leave** [liːv] verlassen OT 1
 to **leave behind** [ˌliːv bɪˈhaɪnd] hinterlassen OT 2
left [left] linke(r, -s) OT 1
leg [leg] Bein OT 1
legal [ˈliːgl] rechtlich; legal OT 4
legal aid [ˌliːgl ˈeɪd] Rechtshilfe WS 2, 58
to **legalize** [ˈliːgəlaɪz] legalisieren WS 3, 90
legend [ˈledʒənd] Legende OT 2
legislation [ˌledʒɪsˈleɪʃn] Rechtsvorschriften WS 1, 21
leisure [ˈleʒə] Freizeit OT 3
lemonade [ˌleməˈneɪd] Zitronenlimonade OT 1
to **lend** [lend] leihen OT 2
length [leŋθ] Länge OT 2
lens [lenz] Linse OT 4
leopard [ˈlepəd] Leopard OT 2
lesbian [ˈlezbiən] lesbisch WS 3, 93
less [les] weniger OT 2
lesson [ˈlesn] Unterricht OT 1
to **let** [let] lassen OT 1
 let's [lets] lass / lasst uns OT 4
letter [ˈletə] Brief; Buchstabe OT 1

introductory letter [ˌɪntrəˈdʌktəri ˈletə] Einführungsbrief OT 4
lettuce [ˈletɪs] Kopfsalat OT 2
level [ˈlevl] Niveau; Stufe; Standard OT 2
to **level off** [ˈlevl ɒf] einpendeln WS 3, 98
liberty [ˈlɪbəti] Freiheit OT 1
librarian [laɪˈbreəriən] Bibliothekar(in) OT 4
library [ˈlaɪbrəri] Bibliothek OT 1
licence [ˈlaɪsns] Erlaubnis OT 3
to **lick** [lɪk] lecken OT 3
lid [lɪd] Deckel OT 2
to **lie** [laɪ] liegen OT 1
life [laɪf] Leben OT 1
lifeguard [ˈlaɪfgɑːd] Rettungsschwimmer(in) OT 4
lifestyle [ˈlaɪfstaɪl] Lebensstil; Lifestyle OT 4
life-threatening [ˈlaɪf ˌθretnɪŋ] lebensbedrohlich OT 2
lifetime [ˈlaɪftaɪm] Lebenszeit; Leben OT 2
to **lift** [lɪft] anheben; hochheben; heben OT 3
light [laɪt] Licht OT 1; leicht OT 3
to **light** [laɪt] anzünden WS 1, 40
 lightbulb [ˈlaɪtbʌlb] Glühbirne OT 3
lighting [ˈlaɪtɪŋ] Beleuchtung OT 4
like [laɪk] irgendwie; also; wie; als ob OT 1
to **like** [laɪk] gernhaben; mögen OT 1
 would like / love [wʊd laɪk / lʌv] hätte(n) gern; möchte(n) OT 1
likely [ˈlaɪkli] wahrscheinlich OT 3
to **limit** [ˈlɪmɪt] einschränken; begrenzen OT 3
limp [lɪmp] schlaff OT 4
line [laɪn] Linie; Text (eines Schauspielers); Seil OT 1
linguist [ˈlɪŋgwɪst] Sprachwissenschaftler(in); Linguist(in) WS 3, 106
link [lɪŋk] Verbindung OT 2
 linking verb [ˈlɪŋkɪŋ vɜːb] Kopula OT 2
 linking word [ˈlɪŋkɪŋ wɜːd] Verbindungswort OT 4
linked [lɪŋkt] verbunden OT 2
lion [ˈlaɪən] Löwe / Löwin OT 1
lip [lɪp] Lippe OT 2
liquid [ˈlɪkwɪd] flüssig OT 2
list [lɪst] Liste OT 1
to **list** [lɪst] auflisten OT 3
to **listen** [ˈlɪsn] hören; zuhören OT 1

listener [ˈlɪsnə] Hörer(in); Zuhörer(in) OT 4
liter [ˈliːtə] Liter OT 4
literal [ˈlɪtərəl] wörtlich WS 4, 146
literary [ˈlɪtərəri] literarisch WS 3, 115
literature [ˈlɪtrətʃə] Literatur OT 4
litre [ˈliːtə] Liter WS 1, 15
litter [ˈlɪtə] herumliegende Abfälle OT 2
little [ˈlɪtl] klein OT 1
livable [ˈlɪvəbl] bewohnbar WS 3, 116
to **live** [lɪv] leben; wohnen OT 1
liveable [ˈlɪvəbl] bewohnbar OT 4
lively [ˈlaɪvli] lebhaft WS 1, 43
liver [ˈlɪvər] Leber WS 3, 102
livestock [ˈlaɪvstɒk] Vieh; Viehbestand WS 3, 103
living room [ˈlɪvɪŋ ruːm] Wohnzimmer OT 1
to **load up** [ləʊd ʌp] aufladen WS 3, 102
load [ləʊd] Ladung WS 1, 13
 loads of [ˈləʊdz əv] eine Menge OT 3
loan [ləʊn] Darlehen; Leihgabe WS 2, 64
to **loathe** [ləʊð] nicht ausstehen können; hassen WS 1, 23
local [ˈləʊkl] Einheimische(r); einheimisch OT 2
 locally [ˈləʊkəli] hier; am Ort OT 3
located [ləʊˈkeɪtɪd] gelegen WS 1, 24
location [ləʊˈkeɪʃn] Standort OT 2
loch [lɒx] See OT 1
lock [lɒk] Schloss OT 2
to **lock** [lɒk] abschließen OT 2
locker [ˈlɒkə] Spind; Schließfach OT 2
lodge [lɒdʒ] Gasthaus OT 2
log [lɒg] Holzscheit OT 3
to **log on** [ˈlɒgɒn] sich einloggen OT 3
logical [ˈlɒdʒɪkl] logisch; folgerichtig WS 1, 32
logo [ˈləʊgəʊ] Logo OT 1
lonely [ˈləʊnli] einsam OT 3
long [lɒŋ] lang OT 1
loo [luː] Klo OT 2
loo break [ˈluː breɪk] Klopause OT 2
to **look** [lʊk] sehen OT 1
 to **look after** [lʊk ˈɑːftə] aufpassen auf OT 1
 to **look at** [lʊk æt] anschauen; ansehen OT 1
 to **look forward to** [ˌlʊk ˈfɔːwəd tə] (sich) auf etw. freuen OT 1
 to **look lost** [lʊk lɒst] verloren aussehen OT 4
to **lose** [luːz] verlieren OT 1
loser [ˈluːzər] Verlierer(in) WS 2, 62
loss [lɒs] Verlust WS 1, 21

Appendix

VOCABULARY

lot: a lot [ə lɒt] viel; sehr OT 1
   lots [lɒts] viel OT 1
lottery [ˈlɒtəri] Lotterie OT 3
loud [laʊd] laut OT 1
loudspeaker [ˈlaʊdˌspiːkə] Lautsprecher OT 2
to love [lʌv] lieben OT 1
lovely [ˈlʌvli] hübsch; schön OT 1
lover [ˈlʌvə] Liebhaber(in) OT 3
low [ləʊ] tief OT 1
   low-income [ləʊ ˈɪnkʌm] einkommensschwach OT 4
loyal [ˈlɔɪəl] treu WS 3, 95
luck [lʌk] Glück OT 1
   good luck [gʊd ˈlʌk] Alles Gute! OT 2
lucky [ˈlʌki] glücklich; glückbringend OT 2
   luckily [ˈlʌkɪli] glücklicherweise OT 4
luggage [ˈlʌgɪdʒ] Gepäck OT 4
lunch [lʌntʃ] Mittagessen OT 1
lunch break [ˈlʌntʃ breɪk] Mittagspause OT 1
lunchtime [ˈlʌntʃtaɪm] Mittagszeit OT 1
lung [lʌŋ] Lunge OT 3
lust [lʌst] Lust WS 3, 96
luxurious [lʌgˈʒʊəriəs] luxuriös OT 2
luxury [ˈlʌkʃəri] Luxus WS 2, 64
lynx [lɪŋks] Luchs OT 2
lyrics [ˈlɪrɪks] Songtext; Liedtext OT 2

M

ma'am [mæm] gnädige Frau OT 2
machine [məˈʃiːn] Maschine OT 1
machinery [məˈʃiːnəri] Maschinen OT 2
mad [mæd] verrückt; böse OT 2
madam [ˈmædəm] gnädige Frau OT 1
made of [meɪd əv] gemacht aus OT 2
madman [ˈmædmən] Irrer; Verrückter OT 4
magazine [ˌmægəˈziːn] Zeitschrift OT 1
magic [ˈmædʒɪk] Zauber OT 1
magical [ˈmædʒɪkl] magisch OT 2
magician [məˈdʒɪʃn] Zauberer / Zauberin OT 1
magnetic [mægˈnetɪk] magnetisch OT 2
magnet [ˈmægnət] Magnet OT 1
mail [meɪl] Post OT 1
   snail mail [ˈsneɪl meɪl] Schneckenpost; traditioneller Brief OT 4
mailbox [ˈmeɪlbɒks] Briefkasten; Mailbox OT 4
mail carrier [ˈmeɪl kæriə] Postbote / -botin OT 4
main [meɪn] Haupt... OT 1

main course [ˈmeɪn kɔːs] Hauptgang OT 1
mainland [ˈmeɪnlænd] Festland OT 3
mainly [ˈmeɪnli] hauptsächlich OT 2
to maintain [meɪnˈteɪn] warten; pflegen OT 4
maintenance [ˈmeɪntənəns] Wartung OT 3
major [ˈmeɪdʒə] bedeutend OT 2
majority [məˈdʒɒrəti] Mehrheit OT 4
to make [meɪk] kochen; machen OT 1
   to make a mess [meɪk ə ˈmes] ein Chaos anrichten OT 2
maker [ˈmeɪkə] Macher(in) OT 3
malamute [ˈmæləˌmjuːt] Malamut OT 2
male [meɪl] männlich OT 2
mall [mɔːl] Einkaufszentrum OT 3
malware [ˈmælweə] Malware OT 3
mammal [ˈmæml] Säugetier OT 2
man [mæn] Mann OT 1
to manage [ˈmænɪdʒ] leiten; managen OT 1
management [ˈmænɪdʒmənt] Management; Geschäftsführung WS 2, 51
manager [ˈmænɪdʒə] Geschäftsführer(in); Manager(in); Leiter(in) OT 1
to mandate [ˈmændeɪt] anordnen WW, 11
man-made [ˌmæn ˈmeɪd] menschengemacht; künstlich OT 1
manner [ˈmænə] Weise OT 2
manufacture [ˌmænjuˈfæktʃə] Herstellung; Produktion OT 4
manufacturer [ˌmænjuˈfæktʃərə] Hersteller(in) OT 4
manufacturing [ˌmænjuˈfæktʃərɪŋ] Produktion; Herstellung WS 2, 63
manure [məˈnjʊə] Dung OT 3
many [ˈmeni] viele OT 1
   many times [ˈmeni taɪmz] häufig; oftmals OT 4
Maori [ˈmaʊri] Maori OT 1
map [mæp] Landkarte OT 1
maple [ˈmeɪpl] Ahorn OT 3
marathon [ˈmærəθən] Marathon OT 2
   half marathon [ˈhɑːf ˌmærəθən] Halbmarathon OT 2
marbles [ˈmɑːblz] Murmelspiel OT 4
March [mɑːtʃ] März OT 1
march [mɑːtʃ] Marsch OT 3
marching band [ˈmɑːtʃɪŋ bænd] Blaskapelle OT 4
margin [ˈmɑːdʒɪn] Rand WS 3, 107
marine [məˈriːn] Meeres... OT 4

maritime [ˈmærɪtaɪm] Marine... OT 3
to mark [mɑːk] korrigieren OT 2
marker [ˈmɑːkə] Markierung; Filzstift OT 1
market [ˈmɑːkɪt] Markt OT 1
marketable [ˈmɑːkɪtəbl] vermarktbar OT 4
marketing [ˈmɑːkɪtɪŋ] Marketing; Vermarktung OT 4
marketplace [ˈmɑːkɪtpleɪs] Markt WW, 11
market segment [ˌmɑːkɪt ˌsegment] Marktsegment WS 3, 104
marquee [mɑːˈkiː] Markise; Zelt OT 2
marriage [ˈmærɪdʒ] Ehe WS 2, 64
to marry [ˈmæri] heiraten OT 1
mask [mɑːsk] Maske OT 3
mass [mæs] Massen- OT 4
mass sport [mæs spɔːt] Massensport OT 3
massacre [ˈmæsəkə] Massaker OT 3
massive [ˈmæsɪv] riesig OT 3
master [ˈmɑːstə] Meister(in) OT 4
match [mætʃ] Spiel; Wettkampf OT 1
mate [meɪt] Kumpel WS 1, 14
material [məˈtɪəriəl] Material; Stoff OT 3
math [mæθ] Mathematik / Mathe OT 1
mathematician [ˌmæθəməˈtɪʃn] Mathematiker(in) OT 3
mathematics [ˌmæθəˈmætɪks] Mathematik / Mathe OT 1
maths [mæθs] Mathematik / Mathe OT 1
matter [ˈmætə] Angelegenheit; Problem OT 2
   What's the matter? [wɒts ðə ˈmætə] Was ist los? OT 2
mature [məˈtʃʊə] reif; mündig WS 3, 96
maximum [ˈmæksɪməm] Maximum OT 2
May [meɪ] Mai OT 1
may [meɪ] könnte(n) OT 1
maybe [ˈmeɪbi] vielleicht OT 1
mayonnaise [ˌmeɪəˈneɪz] Mayonnaise OT 1
mayor [meə] Bürgermeister(in) OT 3
me [miː] mich; mir OT 1
meadow [ˈmedəʊ] Wiese OT 2
meal [miːl] Mahlzeit OT 1
to mean [miːn] bedeuten OT 1
mean [miːn] gemein OT 2
meaning [ˈmiːnɪŋ] Sinn; Bedeutung OT 1
meaningful [ˈmiːnɪŋfl] sinnvoll WS 3, 96

Appendix

VOCABULARY

meanwhile [ˈmiːnwaɪl] inzwischen; mittlerweile **WS 4**, 126
measles [ˈmiːzlz] Masern **WS 1**, 22
to measure [ˈmeʒə] messen; ausmessen; abschätzen OT 4
measurement [ˈmeʒəmənt] Maß; Maßeinheit OT 2
meat [miːt] Fleisch OT 1
meatball [ˈmiːtbɔːl] Fleischklößchen; Hackfleischbällchen OT 1
meatloaf [ˈmiːt ləʊf] Hackbraten OT 3
meaty [ˈmiːti] Fleisch... OT 3
mechanical [məˈkænɪkl] mechanisch **WS 2**, 81
medal [ˈmedl] Medaille OT 2
media [ˈmiːdiə] Medien OT 2
  social media [ˌsəʊʃl ˈmiːdiə] soziale Medien OT 2
mediation [ˌmiːdiˈeɪʃn] Mediation; Vermittlung OT 1
medical [ˈmedɪkl] ärztliche Untersuchung; medizinisch OT 1
  medical science [ˈmedɪkl ˈsaɪəns] Heilkunde; Medizin OT 4
medication [ˌmedɪˈkeɪʃn] Medikation **WS 3**, 93
medicine [ˈmedsn] Medikament; Medizin OT 2
medium [ˈmiːdiəm] mittelgroß OT 1
medium-sized [ˈmiːdiəm saɪzd] mittelgroß OT 2
to meet [miːt] treffen OT 1
meeting [ˈmiːtɪŋ] Besprechung; Treffen OT 1
meetinghouse [ˈmiːtɪŋhaʊs] Andachtshaus; Gebetshaus OT 4
melody [ˈmelədi] Melodie OT 2
to melt [melt] schmelzen OT 4
member [ˈmembə] Mitglied OT 1
memoir [ˈmemwɑː] Memoiren; Erinnerung **WS 4**, 126
memorable [ˈmemərəbl] unvergesslich OT 3
to memorize [ˈmeməraɪz] auswendig lernen; merken OT 4
memory [ˈmeməri] Gedächtnis OT 1
mental [ˈmentl] geistig; mental OT 4
to mention [ˈmenʃn] erwähnen OT 3
mentor [ˈmentɔː] Lehrmeister(in); Mentor(in) OT 4
menu [ˈmenjuː] Speisekarte OT 1
mess [mes] Unordnung OT 3
to mess up [ˌmesˈʌp] in Unordnung bringen; vergeigen OT 2
message [ˈmesɪdʒ] Nachricht OT 1
to message [ˈmesɪdʒɪŋ] texten OT 3

messy [ˈmesi] unordentlich; chaotisch OT 2
metal [ˈmetl] Metall OT 1
metaphor [ˈmetəfər] Metapher **WS 4**, 145
method [ˈmeθəd] Methode OT 1
metre [ˈmiːtə] Meter OT 1
metro [ˈmetrəʊ] U-Bahn OT 1
Mexican [ˈmeksɪkən] mexikanisch OT 4
microbe [ˈmaɪkrəʊb] Mikrobe OT 4
microphone [ˈmaɪkrəfəʊn] Mikrofon OT 4
microscope [ˈmaɪkrəskəʊp] Mikroskop OT 4
microwave [ˈmaɪkrəweɪv] Mikrowelle **WS 2**, 70
mid [mɪd] in der Mitte; mittel OT 4
midday [ˌmɪdˈdeɪ] Mittag OT 4
middle [ˈmɪdl] Mitte OT 1
  middle school [ˈmɪdl skuːl] Mittelschule OT 2
midfielder [ˌmɪdˈfiːldə] Mittelfeldspieler(in) OT 3
midge [mɪdʒ] Mücke OT 3
midnight [ˈmɪdnaɪt] Mitternacht OT 1
midwest [ˌmɪdˈwest] mittlerer Westen OT 4
midwestern [ˌmɪdˈwestən] mittlerer Westen OT 4
might [maɪt] könnte(n) OT 1
mighty [ˈmaɪti] sehr; mächtig OT 3
migrant [ˈmaɪɡrənt] Migrant(in); herumziehend OT 4
to migrate [maɪˈɡreɪt] migrieren OT 3
migration [maɪˈɡreɪʃn] Migration OT 3
mile [maɪl] Meile OT 1
military [ˈmɪlətri] Militär OT 4
milk [mɪlk] Milch OT 1
millennial [mɪˈleniəl] die Generation der Jahrtausendwende OT 4
million [ˈmɪljən] Million OT 1
to mime [maɪm] pantomimisch darstellen OT 2
mind [maɪnd] Verstand OT 1
mind-expanding [maɪnd ɪkˈspænd] sinneserweiternd OT 2
mind map [ˈmaɪnd mæp] Gedankenkarte; Mindmap OT 1
to mind [maɪnd] etw. macht jmdm. etw. aus OT 4
mine [maɪn] meine(r, -s); Bergwerk; Mine OT 2
miner [ˈmaɪnə] Bergarbeiter OT 4
mini [ˈmɪni] klein OT 2
miniature [ˈmɪnətʃə] sehr klein OT 3
minibus [ˈmɪnibʌs] Kleinbus OT 2

minimum [ˈmɪnɪməm] Mindest... OT 1
mining [ˈmaɪnɪŋ] Bergbau... OT 3
minor [ˈmaɪnər] gering; klein **WS 1**, 21
minority [maɪˈnɒrəti] Minderheit **WS 3**, 98
mint [mɪnt] Minze OT 2
minute [ˈmɪnɪt] Minute OT 1
mirror [ˈmɪrə] Spiegel OT 1
miserable [ˈmɪzrəbl] unglücklich OT 2
misfit [ˈmɪsfɪt] Außenseiter(in) OT 4
misleading [ˌmɪsˈliːdɪŋ] irreführend OT 3
mismatched [ˌmɪsˈmætʃ] nicht zusammenpassend OT 4
to miss [mɪs] vermissen OT 2
missing [ˈmɪsɪŋ] fehlend OT 1
mission [ˈmɪʃn] Mission OT 4
mistake [mɪˈsteɪk] Fehler OT 2
  by mistake [baɪ mɪˈsteɪk] versehentlich OT 2
mistakenly [mɪˈsteɪkənli] fälschlich; irrtümlicherweise **WS 3**, 118
mistreatment [ˌmɪsˈtriːtmənt] Misshandlung **WS 1**, 21
to misunderstand [ˌmɪsʌndəˈstænd] missverstehen **WS 1**, 21
misunderstanding [ˌmɪsʌndəˈstændɪŋ] Missverständnis OT 4
misunderstood [ˌmɪsʌndəˈstʊd] verkannt; missverstanden OT 4
to mix [mɪks] mischen OT 2
  to mix up [mɪks ʌp] vermischen; durcheinanderbringen OT 2
  mixed up [ˌmɪkst ˈʌp] durcheinander OT 2
mixture [ˈmɪkstʃə] Mischung OT 3
mob [mɒb] Meute **WS 1**, 21
mobile [ˈməʊbaɪl] mobil OT 1
mobile phone [ˈməʊbaɪl] Handy OT 1
modal [ˈməʊdl] Modalverb OT 2
model [ˈmɒdl] Modell OT 1
modern [ˈmɒdn] modern OT 1
module [ˈmɒdjuːl] Modul OT 4
mom [mɒm] Mama OT 1
moment [ˈməʊmənt] Moment OT 1
monarch [ˈmɒnək] Monarch(in); Herrscher(in) **WS 2**, 64
monastery [ˈmɒnəstri] Kloster OT 3
Monday [ˈmʌndeɪ] Montag OT 1
money [ˈmʌni] Geld OT 1
monk [mʌŋk] Mönch OT 3
monkey [ˈmʌŋki] Affe OT 2
monolingual [ˌmɒnəˈlɪŋɡwəl] einsprachig **WS 1**, 22
monologue [ˈmɒnəlɒɡ] Monolog **WS 3**, 115

two hundred and fifty-three **253**

Appendix

VOCABULARY

monotone [ˈmɒnətəʊn] monoton OT 4
monster [ˈmɒnstə] Monster OT 1
month [mʌnθ] Monat OT 1
monument [ˈmɒnjumənt] Denkmal OT 1
mood [muːd] Stimmung WS 3, 97
moon [muːn] Mond OT 4
to **moor** [mɔː] vertäuen; anlegen OT 3
mooring [ˈmɔːrɪŋ] Anlegeplatz OT 3
more [mɔː] mehr OT 1
moreover [mɔːrˈəʊvə] außerdem WW, 11
morning [ˈmɔːnɪŋ] Morgen OT 1
mosque [mɒsk] Moschee OT 1
mosquito [məˈskiːtəʊ] Stechmücke OT 2
most [məʊst] der / die / das meiste; die meisten OT 1
motel [məʊˈtel] Motel OT 3
mother [ˈmʌðə] Mutter OT 1
motif [məʊˈtiːf] Motiv WS 4, 146
motion picture [ˌməʊʃn ˈpɪktʃə] Film; Spielfilm OT 4
to **motivate** [ˈməʊtɪveɪt] motivieren OT 4
motivated [ˈməʊtɪveɪtɪd] motiviert WS 2, 59
motivating [ˈməʊtɪveɪtɪŋ] motivierend; anregend WS 3, 108
motivation [ˌməʊtɪˈveɪʃn] Motivation; Begründung WS 2, 55
to **motor** [ˈməʊtə] fahren OT 3
mountain [ˈmaʊntən] Berg OT 1
mountain range [ˈmaʊntən reɪndʒ] Bergkette; Gebirgszug OT 4
mouse [maʊs] Maus OT 2
mouth [maʊθ] Mund OT 1
mouthguard [ˈmaʊθɡɑːd] Mundschutz OT 2
mouthwash [ˈmaʊθwɒʃ] Mundwasser OT 4
to **move** [muːv] bewegen; umziehen OT 1
to **move on** [muːv ɒn] weitergehen OT 4
movement [ˈmuːvmənt] Bewegung WS 1, 27
movie [ˈmuːvi] Film OT 1
moving van [ˈmuːvɪŋ ˌvæn] Umzugswagen OT 2
to **mow** [məʊ] mähen WS 3, 93
MP (Members of Parliament) [ˌem ˈpiː] Abgeordnete WS 1, 44
Mr [ˈmɪstə] Herr OT 1
Mrs [ˈmɪsɪz] Frau OT 1
much [mʌtʃ] viel OT 1

to **muck around** [mʌk əˈraʊnd] Herumblödeln WS 3, 93
muffin [ˈmʌfɪn] Muffin OT 1
mug [mʌɡ] Becher; Tasse OT 3
mule [mjuːl] Maultier OT 3
multi [mʌlti] multi… OT 3
multicultural [ˌmʌltiˈkʌltʃərəl] multikulturell WS 1, 31
multilogue [ˈmʌltilɒɡ] Multilog WS 4, 143
multiple choice [ˌmʌltɪpl ˈtʃɔɪs] Multiple-Choice OT 2
mum [mʌm] Mutti OT 1
mummy [ˈmʌmi] Mumie OT 2
mural [ˈmjʊərəl] Wandgemälde OT 2
to **murder** [ˈmɜːdə] ermorden OT 4
murky [ˈmɜːki] trübe OT 4
muscle [ˈmʌsl] Muskel OT 4
museum [mjuːˈziːəm] Museum OT 1
mushroom [ˈmʌʃrʊm] Pilz; Champignon OT 1
music [ˈmjuːzɪk] Musik… OT 1
musical [ˈmjuːzɪkl] Musik-; musikalisch OT 2
musical instrument [ˌmjuːzɪkl ˈɪnstrəmənt] Musikinstrument OT 2
musician [mjuːˈzɪʃn] Musiker(in) OT 2
Muslim [ˈmʊzlɪm] Muslim OT 3
mussel [ˈmʌsl] Muschel OT 4
must [mʌst] müssen OT 1
mustard [ˈmʌstəd] Senf OT 2
my [maɪ] mein OT 1
myself [maɪˈself] ich (selbst) OT 3
mystery [ˈmɪstri] Rätsel; Mysterium OT 2
myth [mɪθ] Mythos; Legende WS 1, 20

N

to **nag** [næɡ] meckern; nörgeln WS 4, 144
nail [neɪl] Nagel; Fingernagel WS 2, 64
name [neɪm] Name OT 1
   first name [ˈfɜːst neɪm] Vorname OT 2
   last name [ˈlɑːst neɪm] Nachname OT 2
to **name** [neɪm] benennen OT 4
nap [næp] Nickerchen WS 1, 38
nappy [ˈnæpi] Windel OT 3
narrator [nəˈreɪtə] Erzähler(in) WS 1, 38
narrow [ˈnærəʊ] eng OT 2
narrowboat [ˈnærəʊbəʊt] schmales Kanalboot; Hausboot OT 3
nasty [ˈnɑːsti] unangenehm OT 2
nation [ˈneɪʃn] Nation OT 2
national [ˈnæʃnəl] national OT 1

nationality [ˌnæʃəˈnæləti] Staatsangehörigkeit OT 2
native [ˈneɪtɪv] einheimisch OT 3
natural [ˈnætʃrəl] natürlich OT 1
nature [ˈneɪtʃə] Natur OT 2
navigating [ˈnævɪɡeɪt] Navigation OT 4
navy [ˈneɪvi] Marine OT 3
near [nɪə] nah / nahe; in der Nähe von OT 1
nearby [ˌnɪəˈbaɪ] in der Nähe OT 3
nearly [ˈnɪəli] fast OT 1
neat [niːt] ordentlich OT 4
necessary [ˈnesəsəri] notwendig OT 3
necessity [nəˈsesəti] Notwendigkeit WW, 11
neck [nek] Hals OT 1
to **need** [niːd] brauchen OT 1
negative [ˈneɡətɪv] Verneinung; Negativ OT 1
neighbourhood [ˈneɪbəhʊd] Nachbarschaft OT 4
neighbour [ˈneɪbə] Nachbar(in) OT 2
neither [ˈnaɪðə] auch nicht; weder OT 2
nerve [nɜːv] Nerv OT 3
nervous [ˈnɜːvəs] nervös OT 2
nervously [ˈnɜːvəsli] nervös OT 2
nest [nest] Nest OT 3
net [net] Netz OT 3
netball [ˈnetbɔːl] Netzball OT 1
netbook [ˈnetbʊk] Netbook OT 4
network [ˈnetwɜːk] Netzwerk WS 1, 27
neutral [ˈnjuːtrəl] neutral OT 3
never [ˈnevə] nie OT 1
new [njuː] neu OT 1
news [njuːz] Neuigkeit(en) OT 1
newsletter [ˈnjuːzletə] Mitteilungsblatt; Newsletter OT 4
newspaper [ˈnjuːzpeɪpə] Zeitung OT 1
next [nekst] nächste(r, -s) OT 1
   next to [ˈnekst tuː] neben OT 1
nice [naɪs] schön; nett OT 1
to **nickname** [ˈnɪkneɪm] Spitzname geben WS 1, 13
nickname [ˈnɪkneɪm] Spitzname OT 4
night [naɪt] Nacht OT 1
nightmare [ˈnaɪtmeə] Albtraum OT 4
nine [naɪn] neun OT 1
nineteen [ˌnaɪnˈtiːn] neunzehn OT 1
ninety [ˈnaɪnti] neunzig OT 1
no [nəʊ] nein OT 1
nobody [ˈnəʊbədi] niemand OT 1
to **nod** [nɒd] nicken OT 2
noise [nɔɪz] Geräusch; Lärm OT 1
noisy [ˈnɔɪzi] laut OT 1
nomadic [nəʊˈmædɪk] nomadisch WS 1, 22

Appendix

VOCABULARY

to **nominate** [ˈnɒmɪneɪt] nominieren OT 4
nomination [ˌnɒmɪˈneɪʃn] Nominierung; Ernennung OT 4
none [nʌn] keine(r, -s) OT 2
non-profit [ˌnɒnˈprɒfɪt] gemeinnützig OT 4
non-verbal [ˌnɒn ˈvɜːbl] nonverbal OT 4
noon [nuːn] Mittag OT 4
nor [nɔː] noch; weder noch OT 4
norm [nɔːm] Regel; Standard WS 2, 62
normal [ˈnɔːml] normal OT 1
   normally [ˈnɔːməli] gewöhnlich; normalerweise OT 1
north [nɔːθ] Nord- OT 1
northern [nɔːðən] nördlich OT 2
nose [nəʊz] Nase OT 2
nosebleed [ˈnəʊzbliːd] Nasenbluten WS 3, 97
not [nɒt] nicht OT 1
note [nəʊt] Notiz; Schein OT 1
notebook [ˈnəʊtbʊk] Notizbuch OT 2
nothing [ˈnʌθɪŋ] nichts OT 1
to **notice** [ˈnəʊtɪs] bemerken OT 1
noticeboard [ˈnəʊtɪsbɔːd] Anschlagbrett OT 1
noun [naʊn] Substantiv; Nomen; Hauptwort OT 1
novel [ˈnɒvl] Roman OT 2
November [nəʊˈvembə] November OT 1
now [naʊ] jetzt OT 1
nowadays [ˈnaʊədeɪz] heutzutage OT 3
nowhere [ˈnəʊweə] nirgendwo OT 2
nuclear [ˈnjuːklɪə] Atom...; Nuklear... OT 3
number [ˈnʌmbə] Zahl; Nummer OT 1
numerous [ˈnjuːmərəs] zahlreich; viele WS 4, 141
nun [nʌn] Nonne OT 4
nurse [nɜːs] Krankenschwester / -pfleger OT 1
nut [nʌt] Nuss OT 4
nutrition [njuˈtrɪʃn] Ernährung WS 3, 108
nutritious [njuˈtrɪʃəs] nahrhaft OT 4
NVQs (national vocational qualifications) [en viː kjuː] nationale berufliche Abschlüsse WS 2, 51

O

oats [əʊts] Haferflocken OT 3
object [ˈɒbdʒɪkt] Gegenstand; Objekt OT 1
   object pronoun [ˌɒbdʒekt ˈprəʊnaʊn] Objektpronomen OT 1

objection [əbˈdʒekʃn] Einwand OT 3
objective [əbˈdʒektɪv] Ziel OT 4
obligation [ˌɒblɪˈɡeɪʃn] Verpflichtung OT 2
obliged [əˈblaɪdʒd] verpflichtet WS 2, 56
observation [ˌɒbzəˈveɪʃn] Beobachtung OT 3
to **observe** [əbˈzɜːv] beobachten OT 4
observer [əbˈzɜːvə] Beobachter(in) WS 2, 61
obvious [ˈɒbvɪəs] offensichtlich OT 3
   obviously [ˈɒbvɪəsli] offenbar; offensichtlich OT 1
occasionally [əˈkeɪʒnəli] gelegentlich OT 2
occupation [ˌɒkjuˈpeɪʃn] Tätigkeit; Beschäftigung OT 4
ocean [ˈəʊʃn] Ozean OT 3
October [ɒkˈtəʊbə] Oktober OT 1
octopus [ˈɒktəpəs] Krake; Oktopus OT 1
odd [ɒd] eigenartig OT 2
   odd one out [ɒd wʌn aʊt] Außenseiter(in); etwas, was nicht in die Reihe passt OT 2
oddity [ˈɒdəti] Kuriosität OT 4
of [əv] von OT 1
   of course [əv ˈkɔːs] natürlich OT 1
off [ɒf] von; aus; weg OT 1
offence [əˈfens] Straftat WS 1, 21
to **offend** [əˈfend] beleidigen OT 3
offender [əˈfendə] Täter(in) WS 3, 100
offer [ˈɒfə] Angebot OT 1
to **offer** [ˈɒfə] anbieten OT 2
office [ˈɒfɪs] Büro OT 1
office park [ˈɒfɪs pɑːk] Büropark OT 2
officer [ˈɒfɪsə] Offizier(in) OT 2
official [əˈfɪʃl] Amtsperson OT 3; offiziell OT 4
offstage [ˈɒfˌsteɪdʒ] aus dem Off OT 2
often [ˈɒfn] oft OT 1
oil [ɔɪl] Öl OT 1
OK [əʊˈkeɪ] in Ordnung OT 1
old [əʊld] alt OT 1
old-fashioned [ˌəʊldˈfæʃnd] altmodisch OT 4
Olympic [əˈlɪmpɪk] olympisch OT 1
omelette [ˈɒmlət] Omelett OT 2
on [ɒn] auf; an; in OT 1
once [wʌns] einmal OT 2
   Once upon a time... [ˈwʌns əpɒn ə ˈtaɪm] Es war einmal... OT 1
one [wʌn] eins OT 1
onion [ˈʌnjən] Zwiebel OT 2
onion ring [ˈʌnjən rɪŋ] Zwiebelring OT 2
online [ˌɒnˈlaɪn] online OT 1

online forum [ˌɒnˈlaɪn ˈfɔːrəm] Online-Forum OT 4
only [ˈəʊnli] nur OT 1
onscreen [ˌɒnˈskriːn] auf dem Bildschirm; auf der Leinwand OT 2
onto [ˈɒntuː] auf OT 1
open [ˈəʊpən] offen OT 1
opening times [ˈəʊpnɪŋ ˌtaɪmz] Öffnungszeiten OT 1
to **open** [ˈəʊpən] aufmachen; öffnen OT 1
to **operate** [ˈɒpəreɪt] bedienen; operieren WS 2, 61
operation [ˌɒpəˈreɪʃn] Operation OT 3
operator [ˈɒpəreɪtə] Leitstellendisponent(in); Telefonist(in) OT 2
opinion [əˈpɪnjən] Meinung OT 3
opponent [əˈpəʊnənt] Gegner(in) OT 2
opportunity [ˌɒpəˈtjuːnəti] Gelegenheit OT 2
opposing [əˈpəʊzɪŋ] gegnerisch OT 3
opposite [ˈɒpəzɪt] Gegenteil OT 1
opposition [ˌɒpəˈzɪʃn] Opposition; Gegner WS 1, 21
oppression [əˈpreʃn] Unterdrückung WS 4, 126
optimistic [ˌɒptɪˈmɪstɪk] optimistisch OT 2
to **optimize** [ˈɒptɪmaɪz] optimieren WS 2, 60
option [ˈɒpʃn] Wahl OT 2
optional [ˈɒpʃənl] optional OT 2
or [ɔː] oder OT 1
orange [ˈɒrɪndʒ] orange OT 1
orangejuice [ˈɒrɪndʒ dʒuːs] Orangensaft OT 1
orbit [ˈɔːbɪt] Orbit; Umlaufbahn OT 4
orchestra [ˈɔːkɪstrə] Orchester OT 1
order [ˈɔːdə] Bestellung; Reihenfolge OT 1
to **order** [ˈɔːdə] bestellen; befehlen OT 1
ordinary [ˈɔːdnri] normal OT 2
organ [ˈɔːɡən] Orgel; Organ OT 3
organic [ɔːˈɡænɪk] biologisch (angebaut) OT 2
organization [ˌɔːɡənaɪˈzeɪʃn] Organisation OT 2
organizational [ˌɔːɡənaɪˈzeɪʃənl] organisatorisch OT 4
to **organize** [ˈɔːɡənaɪz] organisieren OT 1
organizer [ˈɔːɡənaɪzə] Organisator(in) OT 3
oriental [ˌɔːriˈentl] orientalisch OT 1

Appendix

VOCABULARY

orientation [ˌɔːriənˈteɪʃn] Orientierung OT 4
origin [ˈɒrɪdʒɪn] Ursprung OT 3
original [əˈrɪdʒənl] ursprünglich; Original... OT 3
   originally [əˈrɪdʒənəli] ursprünglich OT 2
to originate [əˈrɪdʒɪneɪt] entstehen WS 1, 16
other [ˈʌðə] andere(r,-s) OT 1
otherwise [ˈʌðəwaɪz] sonst; ansonsten WS 2, 54
Ouch! [aʊtʃ] Aua! OT 1
ought to [ˈɔːt tə] sollte etw. tun WS 2, 57
our [ˈaʊə] unser OT 1
ours [ɑːz] unsere(r, -s) OT 2
ourselves [ɑːˈselvz, ˌaʊəˈselvz] uns OT 3
out [aʊt] heraus; aus OT 1
outback [ˈaʊtbæk] Hinterland OT 4
outcome [ˈaʊtkʌm] Ergebnis; Resultat WS 1, 38
outdated [ˌaʊtˈdeɪtɪd] veraltet WS 2, 64
outdoor [ˈaʊtdɔː] draußen OT 3
outdoors [ˈaʊtdɔːz] draußen OT 2
outer [ˈaʊtər] Außen... WS 2, 53
outfit [ˈaʊtfɪt] Kleider; Outfit WS 2, 64
to outline [ˈaʊtlaɪn] skizzieren OT 3
outside [ˌaʊtˈsaɪd] draußen OT 1
outstanding [aʊtˈstændɪŋ] herausragend OT 3
outward [ˈaʊtwəd] äußerlich; äußere (r, -s) WS 4, 145
outward journey [ˈaʊtwəd ˈdʒɜːni] Hinfahrt OT 3
oven [ˈʌvn] Ofen OT 4
over [ˈəʊvə] über OT 1
overboard [ˈəʊvəbɔːd] über Bord OT 3
to overdo [ˌəʊvəˈduː] übertreiben WS 3, 102
overgrown [ˌəʊvəˈɡrəʊn] überwuchert; überwachsen OT 4
to overhear [ˌəʊvəˈhɪə] hören; mithören OT 3
to overlook [ˌəʊvəˈlʊk] übersehen WS 2, 55
overly [ˈəʊvəli] übermäßig WS 2, 57
overnight [ˌəʊvəˈnaɪt] über Nacht OT 2
overseas [ˌəʊvəˈsiːz] ausländisch OT 2
to oversee [ˌəʊvəˈsiː] überwachen; beaufsichtigen OT 4
to overuse [ˌəʊvəˈjuːs] zu oft verwenden OT 2
overview [ˈəʊvəvjuː] Überblick; Übersicht OT 4

overweight [ˌəʊvəˈweɪt] übergewichtig WS 3, 103
Ow! [aʊ] Au! OT 1
own [əʊn] eigene(r,-s) OT 1
   on one's own [ɒn wʌnz ˈəʊn] allein OT 2
to own [əʊn] besitzen OT 4
owner [ˈəʊnə] Besitzer(in) OT 2

P

PA (public address) system [piː ˈeɪ ˌsɪstəm] Lautsprecheranlage OT 2
to pack [pæk] packen OT 2
package [ˈpækɪdʒ] Paket OT 3
packaged food [ˈpækɪdʒd fuːd] verpacktes Essen OT 4
packaging [ˈpækɪdʒɪŋ] Verpackung OT 3
packet [ˈpækɪt] Paket OT 2
pad [pæd] Notizblock WS 2, 71
paddle [ˈpædl] Paddel OT 3
paddle-boarding [ˈpædlbɔːdɪŋ] Paddle-Boarding OT 1
paddling [ˈpædlɪŋ] Paddeln OT 4
page [peɪdʒ] Seite OT 1
pain [peɪn] Schmerz OT 2
painful [ˈpeɪnfl] schmerzhaft OT 2
   painfully [ˈpeɪnfəli] schmerzhaft OT 2
painkiller [ˈpeɪnkɪlə] Schmerzmittel OT 2
paint [peɪnt] Farbe OT 2
to paint [peɪnt] malen OT 1
painted [ˈpeɪntɪd] gestrichen OT 1
painting [ˈpeɪntɪŋ] Malen; Gemälde OT 1
pair [peə] Paar OT 1
pajamas [pəˈdʒɑːməz] Schlafanzug; Pyjama OT 4
Pakistani [ˌpækɪˈstɑːni] Pakistaner(in); pakistanisch OT 4
palace [ˈpæləs] Palast OT 1
pan [pæn] Pfanne OT 2
pancake [ˈpænkeɪk] Pfannkuchen OT 4
panda [ˈpændə] Pandabär OT 1
pandemic [pænˈdemɪk] Pandemie WS 2, 62
panel [ˈpænl] Paneel; Platte WS 2, 78
to panic [ˈpænɪk] in Panik geraten OT 2
panoramic [ˌpænəˈræmɪk] Panorama... OT 3
panther [ˈpænθə] Panther OT 2
paper [ˈpeɪpə] Papier OT 1
paperwork [ˈpeɪpəwɜːk] Schreibarbeit WS 2, 69
parade [pəˈreɪd] Umzug; Parade OT 2

paradise [ˈpærədaɪs] Paradies OT 4
paragliding [ˈpærəɡlaɪdɪŋ] Gleitschirmfliegen WS 2, 67
paragraph [ˈpærəɡrɑːf] Absatz OT 1
parallelism [ˈpærəlelɪzəm] Parallelismus WS 4, 145
Paralympics [ˌpærəˈlɪmpɪks] paralympische Spiele OT 3
paramedic [ˌpærəˈmedɪk] Rettungssanitäter(in) OT 1
to paraphrase [ˈpærəfreɪz] umschreiben WS 2, 71
parcel [ˈpɑːsl] Paket OT 4
pardon [ˈpɑːdn] Verzeihung; Entschuldigung WS 2, 70
parent [ˈpeərənt] Elternteil OT 1
park [pɑːk] Park OT 1
park ranger [ˈpɑːk ˌreɪndʒə] Forstbeamter / -beamtin OT 2
to park [pɑːk] parken OT 1
parking ticket [ˈpɑːkɪŋ tɪkɪt] Parkzettel OT 1
parliament [ˈpɑːləmənt] Parlament OT 1
part [pɑːt] Teil OT 1
   part of speech [ˌpɑːt əv ˈspiːtʃ] Wortart OT 2
to participate [pɑːˈtɪsɪpeɪt] teilnehmen WS 4, 143
participation [pɑːˌtɪsɪˈpeɪʃn] Beteiligung WS 3, 99
participle [pɑːˈtɪsɪpl] Partizip OT 2
particular [pəˈtɪkjələ] besondere(r,-s) OT 4
   in particular [ɪn pəˈtɪkjələr] insbesondere WS 1, 21
   particularly [pəˈtɪkjələli] besonders WS 4, 144
partly [ˈpɑːtli] teilweise OT 3
partner [ˈpɑːtnə] Partner(in) OT 1
partnership [ˈpɑːtnəʃɪp] Partnerschaft; Kooperation OT 4
part-time [ˌpɑːt ˈtaɪm] Teilzeit...; nebenberuflich OT 4
party [ˈpɑːti] Party; Feier OT 1
to pass [pɑːs] zuspielen; an etw. vorbeifahren OT 3
   to pass an exam [ˌpɑːs ən ɪɡˈzæm] eine Prüfung bestehen OT 2
passenger [ˈpæsɪndʒə] Passagier(in); Fahrgast OT 2
passionate [ˈpæʃənət] leidenschaftlich OT 4
   passionately [ˈpæʃənətli] leidenschaftlich WS 2, 64
passport [ˈpɑːspɔːt] Pass OT 2

Appendix

VOCABULARY

passport control [ˈpɑːspɔːt kənˌtrəʊl] Passkontrolle OT 2
password [ˈpɑːswɜːd] Kennwort; Passwort OT 4
past [pɑːst] nach OT 1
past participle [ˌpɑːst pɑːˈtɪsɪpl] Partizip Perfekt OT 2
past progressive [pɑːst prəˈgresɪv] Verlaufsform der Vergangenheit OT 2
pasta [ˈpæstə] Nudeln OT 1
to **paste** [peɪst] kleben; einfügen OT 2
pastor [ˈpɑːstə] Pfarrer(in) OT 2
pat [pæt] Klaps OT 3
pâté [ˈpæteɪ] Pastete OT 1
patent [ˈpætnt] Patent OT 4
to **patent** [ˈpætnt] patentieren OT 4
path [pɑːθ] Weg OT 1
patient [ˈpeɪʃnt] Patient(in) OT 1
patriot [ˈpeɪtrɪət] Patriot(in) OT 2
patron [ˈpeɪtrən] Schirmherr(in) WS 2, 64
pattern [ˈpætn] Muster OT 1
pause [pɔːz] Pause OT 3
to **pause** [pɔːz] eine Pause machen OT 3
pavement [ˈpeɪvmənt] Gehweg; Bürgersteig OT 1
to **pay** [peɪ] bezahlen OT 1
payday [ˈpeɪdeɪ] Zahltag WS 2, 83
payment [ˈpeɪmənt] Bezahlung OT 2
PE (physical education) [ˌpiːˈiː] Sportunterricht OT 1
pea [piː] Erbse OT 1
peace [piːs] Frieden WS 3, 93
peaceful [ˈpiːsfl] friedlich; einträchtig OT 2
peak [piːk] Gipfel; Spitzen… WS 3, 98
pear [peə] Birne OT 1
pedal [ˈpedl] Pedal OT 4
to **pedal** [ˈpedl] in die Pedale treten OT 4
pedigree [ˈpedɪɡriː] Rasse… OT 3
peer [pɪə] Peer WS 1, 21
pen [pen] Stift OT 1
penal [ˈpiːnl] strafrechtlich WS 1, 18
penalty [ˈpenəlti] Strafe; Strafstoß OT 3
pencil [ˈpensl] Bleistift OT 1
pencil case [ˈpensl ˌkeɪs] Federtasche OT 1
pencil sharpener [ˈpensl ˌʃɑːpnə] Anspitzer OT 1
penguin [ˈpeŋɡwɪn] Pinguin OT 1
penicillin [ˌpenɪˈsɪlɪn] Penizillin OT 2
penny [ˈpeni] Penny OT 1
people [ˈpiːpl] Leute OT 1
pepper [ˈpepə] Paprika; Pfeffer OT 2

to **perceive** [pəˈsiːv] empfinden; erkennen WS 1, 38
percent [pəˈsent] Prozent OT 4
percentage [pəˈsentɪdʒ] Prozent OT 3
perfect [ˈpɜːfɪkt] perfekt OT 1
to **perfect** [ˈpɜːfɪkt] perfektionieren OT 4
to **perform** [pəˈfɔːm] auftreten OT 2
performance [pəˈfɔːməns] Aufführung OT 2
performer [pəˈfɔːmə] Künstler(in); Darsteller(in); Interpret(in) OT 2
perhaps [pəˈhæps] vielleicht OT 3
period [ˈpɪərɪəd] Zeit; Epoche OT 3
permanent [ˈpɜːmənənt] permanent; dauerhaft WS 2, 51
permission [pəˈmɪʃn] Erlaubnis OT 2
permit [pəˈmɪt] Erlaubnis OT 3
to **permit** [pəˈmɪt] erlauben WS 2, 64
persecution [ˌpɜːsɪˈkjuːʃn] Verfolgung OT 4
person [ˈpɜːsn] Person; Mensch OT 1
personal [ˈpɜːsənl] persönlich OT 2
personality [ˌpɜːsəˈnæləti] Persönlichkeit OT 4
to **personalize** [ˈpɜːsənəlaɪz] personalisieren WS 3, 104
personification [pəˌsɒnɪfɪˈkeɪʃn] Personifikation; Verkörperung WS 4, 145
personnel [ˌpɜːsəˈnel] Personal; Mitarbeiter WS 4, 144
perspective [pəˈspektɪv] Ansicht; Perspektive OT 4
to **persuade** [pəˈsweɪd] überreden; überzeugen OT 3
persuasive [pəˈsweɪsɪv] überzeugend WS 1, 13
pessimistic [ˌpesɪˈmɪstɪk] pessimistisch OT 4
pest [pest] Schädling; Plage; Plagegeist OT 2
pesticide [ˈpestɪsaɪd] Pestizid OT 4
pet [pet] Haustier OT 1
petition [pəˈtɪʃn] Antrag OT 3
petrol [ˈpetrəl] Benzin OT 4
pharmacist [ˈfɑːməsɪst] Apotheker(in) OT 2
pharmacy [ˈfɑːməsi] Apotheke OT 2
PhD (Doctor of Philosophy) [ˌpiː eɪtʃ ˈdiː] Doktortitel; Doktor der Philosophie WS 2, 69
phenomenon [fəˈnɒmɪnən] Phänomen WS 1, 30
philosophy [fəˈlɒsəfi] Philosophie OT 4
phone [fəʊn] Telefon OT 1

to **phone** [fəʊn] telefonieren OT 2
phone call [ˈfəʊn kɔːl] Telefonat OT 2
phonograph [ˈfəʊnəɡrɑːf] Phonograph OT 4
photo [ˈfəʊtəʊ] Foto OT 1
to **photocopy** [ˈfəʊtəʊkɒpi] fotokopieren OT 4
photograph [ˈfəʊtəɡrɑːf] Foto OT 1
photographer [fəˈtɒɡrəfə] Fotograf(in) OT 3
photography [fəˈtɒɡrəfi] Fotografie OT 4
phrase [freɪz] Wendung OT 1
physical [ˈfɪzɪkl] körperlich OT 2
physics [ˈfɪzɪks] Physik OT 4
pianist [ˈpɪənɪst] Pianist(in) OT 2
piano [piˈænəʊ] Klavier OT 1
to **pick** [pɪk] pflücken; auswählen OT 1
to **pick up** [pɪk ʌp] aufheben OT 2
picker [ˈpɪkə] Sammler(in) OT 3
pickle [ˈpɪkl] Gurke; Gewürzgurke OT 1
pickpocket [ˈpɪkpɒkɪt] Taschendieb(in) OT 4
picnic [ˈpɪknɪk] Picknick OT 1
picture [ˈpɪktʃə] Bild OT 1
pie [paɪ] (gedeckter) Obstkuchen OT 1
piece [piːs] Stück; Teil OT 1
in one piece [ɪn ˌwʌn ˈpiːs] heil OT 2
pier [pɪər] Kai WS 3, 121
pierced [pɪəst] durchstochen OT 3
pig [pɪɡ] Schwein OT 1
pile [paɪl] Haufen; Stapel WS 1, 27
pilgrimage [ˈpɪlɡrɪmɪdʒ] Pilgerfahrt OT 3
pill [pɪl] Pille OT 1
pillow [ˈpɪləʊ] Kopfkissen OT 2
pilot [ˈpaɪlət] Pilot(in) OT 3
to **pilot** [ˈpaɪlət] steuern OT 4
pin [pɪn] Stecknadel OT 1
to **pin** [pɪn] heften OT 1
pineapple [ˈpaɪnæpl] Ananas OT 3
ping-pong [ˈpɪŋ pɒŋ] Tischtennis OT 1
pink [pɪŋk] rosa OT 1
pioneer [ˌpaɪəˈnɪə] Pionier(in) OT 4
pipeline [ˈpaɪplaɪn] Pipeline OT 4
pirate [ˈpaɪrət] Pirat(in) OT 3
pitch [pɪtʃ] Spielfeld OT 3
pizza [ˈpiːtsə] Pizza OT 1
pizza deliverer [ˈpiːtsə dɪˈlɪvərə] Pizzalieferant(in) OT 4
place [pleɪs] Ort OT 1
place mat [ˈpleɪs mæt] Platzdeckchen OT 2
plagiarism [ˈpleɪdʒərɪzəm] Plagiat OT 2
to **plagiarize** [ˈpleɪdʒəraɪz] plagiieren OT 2

Appendix

VOCABULARY

plain [pleɪn] nicht Besonders; gutbürgerlich OT 4
plains [pleɪnz] Prärie; Flachland WS 1, 21
to **plan** [plæn] planen OT 1
plane [pleɪn] Flugzeug OT 1
planet ['plænɪt] Planet OT 2
planetarium [ˌplænɪ'teəriəm] Planetarium OT 1
planetary science ['plænətri 'saɪəns] planetarische Wissenschaft; Planetenforschung OT 4
planner ['plænə] Planer(in) OT 3
plant [plɑːnt] Pflanze OT 2
plaster ['plɑːstə] Verputz; Gips; Pflaster OT 1
plastic ['plæstɪk] Kunststoff OT 2
plate [pleɪt] Teller OT 1
platform ['plætfɔːm] Bahnsteig OT 1
platypus ['plætɪpəs] Schnabeltier WS 1, 13
play [pleɪ] Theaterstück OT 1
to **play** [pleɪ] spielen OT 1
player ['pleɪə] Spieler(in) OT 1
playground ['pleɪɡraʊnd] Spielplatz; Schulhof OT 1
playlist ['pleɪlɪst] Playlist; Wiedergabeliste OT 4
playwright ['pleɪraɪt] Dramatiker(in) WS 4, 145
to **plead** [pliːd] sich bekennen; plädieren WS 3, 101
pleasant ['pleznt] angenehm WS 1, 13
please [pliːz] bitte OT 1
pleased [pliːzd] zufrieden OT 1
pleasure ['pleʒə] Freude OT 1
plenty ['plenti] reichlich; viel OT 2
plot [plɒt] Handlung OT 4
plum [plʌm] Pflaume OT 1
plural ['plʊərəl] Plural; Mehrzahl OT 1
poacher ['pəʊtʃə] Wilderer / Wilderin OT 3
poaching ['pəʊtʃɪŋ] Wilderei OT 3
pocket ['pɒkɪt] Tasche OT 2
pocketknife ['pɒkɪtnaɪf] Taschenmesser OT 2
pocket money ['pɒkɪt mʌni] Taschengeld OT 2
podcast ['pɒdkɑːst] Podcast OT 1
podium ['pəʊdiəm] Podium OT 3
poem ['pəʊɪm] Gedicht OT 1
poet ['pəʊɪt] Dichter(in) OT 3
poetry ['pəʊətri] Poesie; Dichtung OT 1
point [pɔɪnt] Punkt OT 1
to **point** [pɔɪnt] zeigen OT 1

pointless ['pɔɪntləs] sinnlos; zwecklos OT 4
poison ['pɔɪzən] Gift OT 1
poisonous ['pɔɪzənəs] giftig WS 4, 143
pole [pəʊl] Stange; Pol OT 3
police [pə'liːs] Polizei OT 1
police officer [pə'liːs ɒfɪsə] Polizist(in) OT 1
policy ['pɒləsi] Politik; Regel OT 3
Polish ['pəʊlɪʃ] polnisch OT 2
polite [pə'laɪt] höflich OT 1
political [pə'lɪtɪkl] politisch OT 4
politician [ˌpɒlə'tɪʃn] Politiker(in) OT 3
poll [pəʊl] Umfrage WS 3, 92
to **pollute** [pə'luːt] verschmutzen; verseuchen WS 1, 23
pollution [pə'luːʃn] Umweltverschmutzung OT 2
polo ['pəʊləʊ] Polo OT 3
polyp ['pɒlɪp] Polyp WS 1, 26
polyurethane [ˌpɒli'jʊərəθeɪn] Polyurethan (Kunststoff) OT 4
pond [pɒnd] Teich OT 4
pony ['pəʊni] Pony OT 3
pool [puːl] Lache; Schwimmbecken OT 1
poor [pʊə] arm OT 1
pop [pɒp] Pop OT 2
popcorn ['pɒpkɔːn] Popcorn OT 2
Pope [pəʊp] Papst OT 3
popular ['pɒpjələ] beliebt OT 1
population [ˌpɒpjə'leɪʃn] Bevölkerung OT 3
porch [pɔːtʃ] Veranda OT 4
pork [pɔːk] Schweinefleisch OT 2
porridge ['pɒrɪdʒ] Haferbrei OT 3
port [pɔːt] Hafen OT 2
portable ['pɔːtəbl] tragbar OT 4
portal ['pɔːtl] Portalseite WS 3, 106
portfolio [pɔːt'fəʊliəʊ] Mappe; Portfolio OT 4
portion ['pɔːʃn] Portion; Menge OT 4
to **pose a threat** [pəʊz ə θret] eine Bedrohung darstellen WS 1, 44
position [pə'zɪʃn] Position OT 3
positive ['pɒzətɪv] Positiv OT 1
possession [pə'zeʃn] Besitz WS 3, 89
possessive [pə'zesɪv] besitzanzeigend; Possessiv... OT 1
possessive determiner [pəˌzesɪv dɪ'tɜːmɪnə] Possessivbegleiter OT 1
possibility [ˌpɒsə'bɪləti] Möglichkeit OT 2
possible ['pɒsəbl] möglich OT 2
post [pəʊst] Post OT 1
to **post** [pəʊst] posten OT 3

post box ['pəʊst bɒks] Briefkasten OT 1
postcard ['pəʊstkɑːd] Postkarte OT 1
postcode ['pəʊstkəʊd] Postleitzahl OT 1
poster ['pəʊstə] Plakat OT 1
potato [pə'teɪtəʊ] Kartoffel OT 1
  jacket potato [ˌdʒækɪt pə'teɪtəʊ] Ofenkartoffel OT 1
  mashed potato [ˌmæʃt pə'teɪtəʊ] Kartoffelbrei OT 1
  sweet potato [ˌswiːt pə'teɪtəʊ] Süßkartoffel OT 4
potential [pə'tenʃl] Potenzial WS 2, 69
poultry ['pəʊltri] Geflügel OT 2
pound [paʊnd] Pfund OT 1
to **pour** [pɔː] gießen OT 1
poverty ['pɒvəti] Armut OT 3
power ['paʊə] Kraft; Macht WS 1, 27
powered ['paʊəd] angetrieben OT 4
powerful ['paʊəfl] mächtig; kräftig WS 1, 20
powerless ['paʊələs] kraftlos; machtlos OT 4
practical ['præktɪkl] praktisch OT 3
practice ['præktɪs] Praxis; Übung OT 2
to **practise** ['præktɪs] üben OT 1
to **pray** [preɪ] beten WS 1, 39
prayer [preə] Gebet OT 4
precise [prɪ'saɪs] genau; konkret WS 4, 140
predator ['predətər] Raubtier; Räuber WS 1, 23
to **predict** [prɪ'dɪkt] vorhersagen OT 4
predictable [prɪ'dɪktəbl] vorhersehbar WS 1, 22
prediction [prɪ'dɪkʃn] Vorhersage OT 2
to **prefer** [prɪ'fɜː] vorziehen OT 1
preference ['prefrəns] Vorliebe OT 3
pregnant ['pregnənt] schwanger OT 4
prejudice ['predʒədɪs] Nachteil; Vorurteil WS 1, 39
premier ['premiə] erste OT 2
preparation [ˌprepə'reɪʃn] Vorbereitung OT 2
to **prepare** [prɪ'peə] vorbereiten OT 1
preposition [ˌprepə'zɪʃn] Präposition; Verhältniswort OT 2
preschool ['priːskuːl] Kindergarten; Vorschule WS 3, 99
present ['preznt] Geschenk; Gegenwart OT 1
  present perfect [ˌpreznt 'pɜːfɪkt] vollendete Gegenwart OT 2
  present progressive ['preznt prəˌɡresɪv] Verlaufsform des Präsens OT 1

Appendix

VOCABULARY

to **present** [prɪˈzent] präsentieren; vorstellen OT 1
presentation [ˌpreznˈteɪʃn] Präsentation OT 1
presenter [prɪˈzentə] Moderator(in) WS 3, 91
to **preserve** [prɪˈzɜːv] erhalten OT 3
president [ˈprezɪdənt] Präsident(in) OT 4
to **press** [pres] drücken OT 1
pressure [ˈpreʃə] Druck OT 3
pressured [ˈpreʃəd] unter Druck gesetzt WS 3, 94
to **pretend** [prɪˈtend] vorgeben; so tun, als ob OT 2
pretty [ˈprɪti] hübsch OT 1
to **prevent** [prɪˈvent] verhindern; abhalten OT 4
preventable [prɪˈventəbl] vermeidbar WS 1, 21
prevention [prɪˈvenʃn] Vermeidung OT 2
previous [ˈpriːviəs] bisherig; vorherig OT 4
previously [ˈpriːviəsli] früher OT 3
price [praɪs] Preis OT 1
pride [praɪd] Stolz OT 4
primary [ˈpraɪməri] Haupt…; Grund… OT 1
prince [prɪns] Prinz OT 1
principal [ˈprɪnsəpl] Rektor(in) OT 2
to **print** [prɪnt] (aus)drucken OT 2
printer [ˈprɪntər] Drucker WS 2, 71
prison [ˈprɪzn] Gefängnis OT 1
prisoner [ˈprɪznər] Gefangene; Häftling WS 1, 18
privacy [ˈprɪvəsi] Privatsphäre OT 3
private [ˈpraɪvət] privat OT 3
privateer [ˌpraɪvəˈtɪə] Freibeuter OT 3
privilege [ˈprɪvəlɪdʒ] Privileg; Recht WS 2, 64
privileged [ˈprɪvəlɪdʒd] privilegiert WS 2, 65
prize [praɪz] Preis; Gewinn OT 1
probably [ˈprɒbəbli] wahrscheinlich OT 2
probation [prəˈbeɪʃn] Bewährung WS 3, 100
problem [ˈprɒbləm] Problem OT 1
problem-solver [ˈprɒbləm sɒlvə] Problemlöser(in) OT 4
problem-solving [ˈprɒbləm sɒlvɪŋ] problemlösend OT 4
pro bono [ˌprəʊ ˈbəʊnəʊ] ehrenamtlich; kostenlos WS 2, 61

procedure [prəˈsiːdʒə] Prozedur; Verfahren WS 4, 146
process [ˈprəʊses] Prozess OT 4
to **process** [ˈprəʊses] verarbeiten OT 4
procession [prəˈseʃn] Umzug OT 2
to **produce** [prəˈdjuːs] erzeugen OT 3
producer [prəˈdjuːsər] Erzeuger; Hersteller WS 1, 18
product [ˈprɒdʌkt] Produkt OT 2
production [prəˈdʌkʃn] Produktion; Herstellung OT 4
product placement [ˌprɒdʌkt ˈpleɪsmənt] Produktplatzierung WS 3, 104
profession [prəˈfeʃn] Beruf; Profession WS 1, 18
professional [prəˈfeʃənl] professionell OT 2
professor [prəˈfesə] Professor(in) OT 4
profile [ˈprəʊfaɪl] Steckbrief; Profil OT 3
profit [ˈprɒfɪt] Profit; Gewinn OT 4
profound [prəˈfaʊnd] profund; tief WS 1, 21
program [ˈprəʊɡræm] Programm; Kurs OT 3
programme [ˈprəʊɡræm] Programm; Sendung OT 2
to **programme** [ˈprəʊɡræm] programmieren OT 2
programmer [ˈprəʊɡræmə] Programmierer(in) OT 3
programming [ˈprəʊɡræmɪŋ] Programmieren OT 1
progress [ˈprəʊɡres] Fortschritt OT 4
progressive [prəˈɡresɪv] fortschrittlich; progressiv OT 1
project [ˈprɒdʒekt] Projekt OT 1
projector [prəˈdʒektə] Projektor; Beamer OT 1
prolonged [prəˈlɒŋd] anhaltend; verlängert WS 1, 23
prom [prɒm] Schulball OT 3
promise [ˈprɒmɪs] Versprechen OT 2
to **promise** [ˈprɒmɪs] versprechen OT 2
to **promote** [prəˈməʊt] fördern WS 1, 41
prompt [prɒmpt] Stichwort; Aufforderung OT 4
pronoun [ˈprəʊnaʊn] Pronomen; Fürwort OT 1
to **pronounce** [prəˈnaʊns] aussprechen OT 3
pronunciation [prəˌnʌnsiˈeɪʃn] Aussprache OT 2
proof [pruːf] Beweis OT 4
prop [prɒp] Stütze; Requisite OT 1
proper [ˈprɒpə] richtig; anständig OT 3

properly [ˈprɒpəli] ordentlich; in richtiger Art und Weise OT 2
property [ˈprɒpəti] Eigentum; Immobilie WS 1, 23
proportion [prəˈpɔːʃn] Anteil WS 2, 64
to **propose** [prəˈpəʊz] einen Heiratsantrag machen WS 2, 64
pro [prəʊ] Vorteil OT 2
to **prosecute** [ˈprɒsɪkjuːt] bestrafen; verfolgen WS 4, 144
prosecutor [ˈprɒsɪkjuːtə] Staatsanwalt / -anwältin WS 3, 100
protagonist [prəˈtæɡənɪst] Protagonist(in) WS 3, 115
to **protect** [prəˈtekt] schützen OT 2
protein [ˈprəʊtiːn] Protein; Eiweiß OT 4
protest [ˈprəʊtest] Protest OT 3
to **protest** [prəʊˈtest] protestieren OT 3
protester [prəˈtestə] Demonstrant(in); Protestierer(in) WS 1, 33
protocol [ˈprəʊtəkɒl] Protokoll WS 2, 64
prototype [ˈprəʊtətaɪp] Prototyp OT 4
proud [praʊd] stolz OT 2
to **prove** [pruːv] beweisen OT 3
proverb [ˈprɒvɜːb] Sprichwort WS 3, 88
to **provide** [prəˈvaɪd] zur Verfügung stellen; versorgen (mit) OT 4
province [ˈprɒvɪns] Provinz WS 3, 101
to **provoke** [prəˈvəʊk] verursachen; hervorrufen WS 4, 145
psycho [ˈsaɪkəʊ] Psychopath(in) OT 4
psychologist [saɪˈkɒlədʒɪst] Psychologe / -login WS 2, 67
psychology [saɪˈkɒlədʒi] Psychologie WS 2, 67
pub [pʌb] Kneipe OT 2
puberty [ˈpjuːbəti] Pubertät WS 3, 93
public transport [ˌpʌblɪk ˈtrænspɔːt] öffentliche Verkehrsmittel OT 2
public [ˈpʌblɪk] öffentlich OT 2
publication [ˌpʌblɪˈkeɪʃn] Veröffentlichung WW, 11
publicity [pʌbˈlɪsəti] Publizität WS 2, 64
to **publish** [ˈpʌblɪʃ] veröffentlichen OT 2
publisher [ˈpʌblɪʃə] Verleger(in) WS 2, 55
pueblo [ˈpwebləʊ] Pueblo OT 3
to **pull** [pʊl] ziehen OT 1
pulse [pʌls] Hülsenfrucht OT 4
to **pump** [pʌmp] pumpen OT 4
pumpkin [ˈpʌmpkɪn] Kürbis OT 2
punctual [ˈpʌŋktʃuəl] pünktlich OT 4
to **punctuate** [ˈpʌŋktʃueɪt] mit Satzzeichen versehen OT 3
punctuation [ˌpʌŋktʃuˈeɪʃn] Zeichensetzung OT 1

two hundred and fifty-nine **259**

Appendix

VOCABULARY

to **punish** [ˈpʌnɪʃ] bestrafen OT 3
punishment [ˈpʌnɪʃmənt] Strafe **WS 3**, 117
puppy [ˈpʌpi] Welpe OT 2
purchase [ˈpɜːtʃəs] Kauf; Ankauf OT 4
purple [ˈpɜːpl] lila OT 1
purpose [ˈpɜːpəs] Zweck OT 4
to **pursue** [pəˈsjuː] verfolgen OT 4
to **push** [pʊʃ] stoßen OT 2
pushy [ˈpʊʃi] aufdringlich; penetrant OT 4
to **put** [pʊt ʌp] tun; stellen OT 1
   to **put away** [pʊtˈəweɪ] wegräumen OT 2
   to **put on** [ˈpʊt ɒn] aufführen; veranstalten OT 2
   to **put out** [pʊt aʊt] löschen OT 2
   to **put up** [pʊt] heben; errichten OT 1
puzzle [ˈpʌzl] Puzzle; Rätsel OT 2
pyjamas [pəˈdʒɑːməz] Schlafanzug OT 3

Q

quack! [kwæk] Quak! (Ente) OT 2
quad biking [kwɒd ˈbaɪkɪŋ] Vierradfahrzeug fahren OT 2
qualification [ˌkwɒlɪfɪˈkeɪʃn] Qualifikation; Eignung **WS 1**, 21
qualified [ˈkwɒlɪfaɪd] qualifiziert **WS 2**, 51
quality [ˈkwɒləti] Eigenschaft; Qualität OT 3
quantity [ˈkwɒləti] Anzahl; Menge OT 4
quarry [ˈkwɒri] Steinbruch OT 1
quarter [ˈkwɔːtə] Viertel; Quartier OT 1
   quarter to [ˈkwɔːtə tə] viertel vor OT 1
quarterback [ˈkwɔːtəbæk] Quarterback OT 2
queen [kwiːn] Königin OT 1
queer [kwɪər] schwul; queer **WS 3**, 93
quesadilla [ˌkeɪsəˈdiːə] Quesadilla OT 4
question [ˈkwestʃən] Frage OT 1
questionnaire [ˌkwestʃəˈneə] Fragebogen OT 1
queue [kjuː] Schlange; Warteschlange OT 1
to **queue** [kjuː] anstehen; Schlange stehen OT 4
quick [kwɪk] schnell OT 2
   quickly [ˈkwɪkli] schnell OT 2
quiet [ˈkwaɪət] still; ruhig OT 1
quilt [kwɪlt] Steppdecke OT 4
to **quit** [kwɪt] kündigen; verlassen OT 4
quite [kwaɪt] ziemlich OT 2
quiz [kwɪz] Quiz OT 2
quotation mark [kwəʊˈteɪʃn mɑːk] Anführungszeichen OT 2

to **quote** [kwəʊt] zitieren OT 2

R

rabbit [ˈræbɪt] Kaninchen OT 1
race [reɪs] Rennen OT 2
racing [ˈreɪsɪŋ] Rennsport OT 2
racism [ˈreɪsɪzəm] Rassismus **WS 3**, 89
racist [ˈreɪsɪst] rassistisch OT 4
racket [ˈrækɪt] Schläger OT 2
radical [ˈrædɪkl] radikal; grundlegend OT 4
radio [ˈreɪdiəʊ] Radio OT 1
radio station [ˈreɪdiəʊ ˌsteɪʃn] Radiosender OT 2
radius [ˈreɪdiəs] Radius OT 2
rafting: white water rafting [waɪt ˈwɔːtə ˈrɑːftɪŋ] Wildwasser fahren OT 3
to **rage** [reɪdʒ] wüten **WS 1**, 38
raid [reɪd] Razzia **WS 4**, 135
rail [reɪl] Schiene; Eisenbahn OT 2
railway [ˈreɪlweɪ] Bahn; Eisenbahn OT 1
railway line [ˈreɪlweɪ laɪn] Eisenbahnlinie OT 2
to **rain** [reɪn] regnen OT 1
rainbow [ˈreɪnbəʊ] Regenbogen OT 1
raincoat [ˈreɪnkəʊt] Regenmantel OT 3
rainfall [ˈreɪnfɔːl] Regen; Niederschlag **WS 1**, 27
rainforest [ˈreɪnfɒrɪst] Regenwald OT 2
rainstorm [ˈreɪnstɔːm] Regenschauer; Gewitter **WS 1**, 20
rainwater [ˈreɪnwɔːtə] Regenwasser OT 4
to **raise** [reɪz] heben; erheben OT 2
rally [ˈræli] Treffen; Kundgebung OT 4
ramp [ræmp] Rampe OT 2
random [ˈrændəm] zufällig; willkürlich **WS 1**, 22
to **range** [reɪndʒ] umfassen; reichen von … bis OT 4
ranger [ˈreɪndʒə] Aufseher(in); Förster(in) OT 3
to **rank** [ˈræŋk] in eine Rangfolge bringen OT 4
ranking [ˈræŋkɪŋ] Rangfolge OT 4
rap [ræp] Rap OT 1
rapping [ˈræpɪŋ] Rappen OT 1
rare [reə] selten OT 2
raspberry [ˈrɑːzbəri] Himbeere OT 1
to **rate** [reɪt] bewerten OT 2
rather [ˈrɑːðə] ziemlich OT 3
raw [rɔː] roh OT 3
to **reach** [riːtʃ] erreichen OT 3
to **react** [riˈækt] reagieren OT 3
reaction [riˈækʃn] Reaktion OT 4
to **read** [riːd] lesen OT 1

reader [ˈriːdə] Leser(in) OT 3
reading [ˈriːdɪŋ] Lesen OT 1
ready [ˈredi] bereit OT 1
real [rɪəl] echt OT 1
realistic [ˌrɪəˈlɪstɪk] realistisch OT 4
   realistically [ˌrɪəˈlɪstɪkli] realistisch **WW**, 11
reality [riˈæləti] Realität OT 4
to **realize** [ˈrɪəlaɪz] erkennen OT 2
really [ˈrɪəli] wirklich; sehr OT 1
reason [ˈriːzn] Grund OT 1
to **reassess** [ˌriːəˈses] einschätzen **WS 2**, 62
to **rebel** [ˈrebl] rebellieren OT 4
rebellion [rɪˈbeljən] Aufstand OT 4
to **recall** [rɪˈkɔːl] erinnern an **WS 4**, 140
to **receive** [rɪˈsiːv] erhalten OT 2
recent [ˈriːsnt] neueste(r); jüngst OT 4
   recently [ˈriːsntli] neulich OT 3
reception [rɪˈsepʃn] Rezeption; Empfang OT 1
receptionist [rɪˈsepʃənɪst] Empfangschef(in); Rezeptionist(in) OT 1
recipe [ˈresəpi] Rezept OT 2
to **recite** [rɪˈsaɪt] rezitieren; auswendig aufsagen OT 4
recognition [ˌrekəɡˈnɪʃn] Anerkennung **WS 1**, 38
to **recognize** [ˈrekəɡnaɪz] erkennen OT 2
to **recommend** [ˌrekəˈmend] empfehlen OT 2
recommendation [ˌrekəmenˈdeɪʃn] Empfehlung **WS 3**, 101
reconciliation [ˌrekənsɪliˈeɪʃn] Versöhnung **WS 1**, 38
to **record** [rɪˈkɔːd] aufnehmen OT 1
to **recover** [rɪˈkʌvə] sich erholen OT 4
re-creation [ˌriːkriˈeɪʃn] Nachstellung; Neugestaltung OT 4
recreational [ˌrekriˈeɪʃənl] Freizeit… OT 3
rectangular [rekˈtæŋɡjələ] rechteckig OT 2
to **recycle** [ˌriːˈsaɪkl] wiederverwerten OT 2
recycler [ˌriːˈsaɪklə] Wiederverwerter(in) OT 3
recycling [ˌriːˈsaɪklɪŋ] Recycling OT 2
red [red] rot OT 1
to **reduce** [rɪˈdjuːs] reduzieren; verringern OT 2
reef [riːf] Riff **WS 1**, 24
re-enactment [ˌriːɪˈnæktmənt] Nachstellung OT 4

Appendix
VOCABULARY

to **refer** [rɪˈfɜː] sich beziehen OT 3
referee [ˌrefəˈriː] Schiedsrichter(in) OT 3
reference [ˈrefrəns] Orientierung; Verweis OT 4
to **refine** [rɪˈfaɪn] verfeinern OT 4
to **reflect** [rɪˈflekt] spiegeln WS 1, 21
reformation [ˌrefəˈmeɪʃn] Reformation OT 4
refreshment [rɪˈfreʃmənt] Erfrischungsgetränk OT 2
refrigerator [rɪˈfrɪdʒəreɪtə] Kühlschrank OT 4
refugee [ˌrefjuˈdʒiː] Flüchtling OT 4
refugee camp [ˌrefjuˈdʒiː kæmp] Flüchtlingslager OT 4
refuse [ˈrefjuːs] Müll OT 2
to **refuse** [rɪˈfjuːz] sich weigern OT 4
refuse collector [ˈrefjuːs kəlektə] Müllmann / -frau OT 2
regarding [rɪˈɡɑːdɪŋ] bezüglich WS 4, 140
reggae [ˈreɡeɪ] Reggae OT 2
region [ˈriːdʒən] Region OT 4
regional [ˈriːdʒənl] regional WS 1, 30
to **register** [ˈredʒɪstə] (sich) anmelden; registrieren OT 4
to **regret** [rɪˈɡret] bereuen OT 2
regular [ˈreɡjələ] regelmäßig OT 1
regularly [ˈreɡjələli] regelmäßig OT 2
regulation [ˌreɡjuˈleɪʃn] Vorschrift; Regulation WS 2, 62
rehearsal [rɪˈhɜːsl] Probe OT 2
to **rehearse** [rɪˈhɜːs] proben OT 3
reign [reɪn] Herrschaft OT 3
to **reign** [reɪn] herrschen OT 3
reindeer [ˈreɪndɪə] Rentier OT 2
to **reinforce** [ˌriːɪnˈfɔːs] verstärken; bekräftigen WS 3, 92
to **reinvent** [ˌriːɪnˈvent] wieder erfinden OT 4
to **relate** [rɪˈleɪt] sich beziehen auf OT 3
related to [rɪˈleɪtɪd tə] in Bezug auf OT 4
relation [rɪˈleɪʃn] Verwandte(r) OT 2
relationship [rɪˈleɪʃnʃɪp] Beziehung OT 3
relative [ˈrelətɪv] Verwandte; Angehörige OT 1; relativ OT 2
relative pronoun [ˌrelətɪv ˈprəʊnaʊn] Relativpronomen OT 2
relatively [ˈrelətɪvli] relativ; ziemlich WS 3, 120
to **relax** [rɪˈlæks] sich entspannen; loslassen OT 2
relaxation [ˌriːlækˈseɪʃn] Erholung OT 3
relaxing [rɪˈlæksɪŋ] erholsam OT 2

to **release** [rɪˈliːs] veröffentlichen; auf den Markt bringen OT 4
relevant [ˈreləvənt] wichtig; relevant OT 4
reliable [rɪˈlaɪəbl] verlässlich OT 4
relief [rɪˈliːf] Erleichterung; Hilfe OT 4
to **relieve** [rɪˈliːv] erleichtern; entlasten WS 4, 145
relieved [rɪˈliːvd] erleichtert OT 2
religion [rɪˈlɪdʒən] Religion OT 3
religious [rɪˈlɪdʒəs] religiös OT 1
religious studies [rɪˈlɪdʒəs ˈstʌdiz] Religionsunterricht OT 1
to **relive** [riːˈlɪv] wieder erleben OT 4
to **rely** [rɪˈlaɪ] sich verlassen auf WW, 11
to **remain** [rɪˈmeɪn] bleiben OT 4
remaining [rɪˈmeɪnɪŋ] restlich; übrig WS 1, 41
remains [rɪˈmeɪnz] Überreste OT 3
remark [rɪˈmɑːk] Bemerkung WS 4, 145
remarriage [ˌriːˈmærɪdʒ] Wiederverheiratung WS 3, 98
to **remarry** [ˌriːˈmæri] wieder heiraten WS 3, 119
to **remember** [rɪˈmembə] (sich) erinnern an OT 1
to **remind** [rɪˈmaɪnd] erinnern OT 2
remorse [rɪˈmɔːs] Reue WS 3, 100
remote [rɪˈməʊt] entfernt; abgelegen WS 1, 13
remotely [rɪˈməʊtli] aus der Ferne OT 4
remote control [rɪˌməʊt kənˈtrəʊl] Fernbedienung OT 4
remotely [rɪˈməʊtli] aus der Ferne WS 2, 63
removal [rɪˈmuːvl] Entfernung WS 1, 21
removal van [rɪˈmuːvəl væn] Umzugswagen OT 2
to **remove** [rɪˈmuːv] entfernen OT 2
renewable [rɪˈnjuːəbl] erneuerbar WS 1, 26
to **rent** [rent] mieten OT 4
rental [ˈrentl] Miet... OT 4
to **repaint** [ˌriːˈpeɪnt] übermalen OT 4
to **repair** [rɪˈpeə] reparieren OT 2
to **repay** [rɪˈpeɪ] vergüten; zurückzahlen WS 3, 121
to **repeat** [rɪˈpiːt] wiederholen OT 1
repetition [ˌrepəˈtɪʃn] Wiederholung OT 4
to **rephrase** [ˌriːˈfreɪz] neu formulieren; umformulieren OT 4
to **replace** [rɪˈpleɪs] ersetzen OT 3
replica [ˈreplɪkə] Kopie OT 4
to **reply** [rɪˈplaɪ] antworten OT 1
report [rɪˈpɔːt] Bericht OT 2

to **report** [rɪˈpɔːt] berichten OT 1
reporter [rɪˈpɔːtə] Reporter(in) OT 1
reptile [ˈreptaɪl] Reptil OT 2
republic [rɪˈpʌblɪk] Republik OT 4
request [rɪˈkwest] Bitte OT 2
to **require** [rɪˈkwaɪə] verlangen; fordern OT 4
requirement [rɪˈkwaɪəmənt] Voraussetzung WS 1, 33
rescue [ˈreskjuː] Rettung OT 2
to **rescue** [ˈreskjuː] retten OT 4
research [rɪˈsɜːtʃ] Forschung OT 2
to **research** [rɪˈsɜːtʃ] forschen OT 2
researcher [rɪˈsɜːtʃə] Forscher(in) OT 2
reservation [ˌrezəˈveɪʃn] Reservierung; Reservat OT 1
to **reserve** [rɪˈzɜːv] reservieren OT 3
reserved [rɪˈzɜːvd] reserviert OT 2
resettlement [ˌriːˈsetlmənt] Umsiedlung OT 4
resident [ˈrezɪdənt] Bewohner(in) OT 3
to **resign** [rɪˈzaɪn] zurücktreten WS 1, 43
to **resist** [rɪˈzɪst] widerstehen WS 3, 94
resistance [rɪˈzɪstəns] Widerstand; hier: Resistenz WS 1, 22
resistant [rɪˈzɪstənt] widerstandsfähig; resistent WS 3, 103
to **resolve** [rɪˈzɒlv] entscheiden WS 1, 21
resort [rɪˈzɔːt] Urlaubsort; Zuflucht OT 2
resource [rɪˈsɔːs] Ressource; Mittel OT 4
resourceful [rɪˈsɔːsfl] erfinderisch OT 4
to **respect** [rɪˈspekt] achten OT 3
respectful [rɪˈspektfl] respektvoll OT 3
to **respond** [rɪˈspɒnd] reagieren; antworten OT 3
respondent [rɪˈspɒndənt] Befragte(r) WS 3, 107
response [rɪˈspɒns] Reaktion; Antwort WS 3, 118
responsibility [rɪˌspɒnsəˈbɪləti] Verantwortung OT 3
responsible [rɪˈspɒnsəbl] verantwortlich OT 3
rest [rest] übrige; restliche OT 1
to **rest** [rest] ausruhen OT 1
restaurant [ˈrestrɒnt] Restaurant OT 1
to **restore** [rɪˈstɔː] wiederherstellen OT 4
restriction [rɪˈstrɪkʃn] Einschränkung WS 1, 19
result [rɪˈzʌlt] Ergebnis OT 2
to **resume** [rɪˈzjuːm] übernehmen; wieder annehmen WS 1, 24

Appendix

VOCABULARY

retailer [ˈriːteɪlə] Händler; Einzelhändler OT 4
to retell [ˌriːˈtel] nacherzählen OT 4
retirement home [rɪˈtaɪəmənt həʊm] Seniorenheim OT 3
to return [rɪˈtɜːn] zurückkehren OT 2
reusable [ˌriːˈjuːzəbl] wiederverwendbar OT 3
to reuse [ˌriːˈjuːs] wiederverwenden OT 2
to reveal [rɪˈviːl] verraten WS 3, 115
review [rɪˈvjuː] Rückblick OT 1
to revise [rɪˈvaɪz] revidieren; überarbeiten OT 2
revolting [rɪˈvəʊltɪŋ] abstoßend OT 2
revolution [ˌrevəˈluːʃn] Revolution OT 2
to revolutionize [ˌrevəˈluːʃənaɪz] revolutionieren OT 4
rewarding [rɪˈwɔːdɪŋ] lohnend OT 4
to rewrite [ˌriːˈraɪt] neu schreiben; umschreiben OT 1
rhetorical [rɪˈtɒrɪkl] rhetorisch WS 4, 143
rhinoceros [raɪˈnɒsərəs] Nashorn OT 2
rhyme [raɪm] Reim OT 1
rice [raɪs] Reis OT 1
rich [rɪtʃ] reich OT 1
ride [raɪd] Fahrt OT 1
to ride [raɪd] fahren; reiten OT 1
rider [ˈraɪdə] Fahrer(in); Reiter(in) OT 1
rifle [ˈraɪfl] Gewehr OT 4
to right [raɪt] aufrichten WS 1, 21
right [raɪt] rechte(r,-s); richtig OT 1
rights [raɪt] Rechte OT 3
rim [rɪm] Rand OT 3
to ring [rɪŋ] klingeln OT 1
ripe [raɪp] reif OT 4
ripped [rɪpt] gerissen OT 4
to rise [raɪz] aufsteigen OT 3
risk [rɪsk] Risiko; Gefahr OT 3
risky [ˈrɪski] gefährlich OT 3
ritual [ˈrɪtʃuəl] Ritual WS 1, 30
rivalry [ˈraɪvlri] Konkurrenz WS 1, 28
river [ˈrɪvə] Fluss OT 1
road [rəʊd] Straße OT 1
to roam around [rəʊm əˈraʊnd] durch stromern; herumwandern WS 1, 23
roast [rəʊst] gebraten OT 1
robot [ˈrəʊbɒt] Roboter OT 4
rock [rɒk] Stein; Rockmusik OT 2
  rock and roll [ˌrɒk ən ˈrəʊl] Rock and Roll OT 2
to rock [rɒk] schaukeln OT 3
rock climbing [ˈrɒk klaɪmɪŋ] Felsklettern OT 2
rocket [ˈrɒkɪt] Rakete OT 4

role [rəʊl] Rolle OT 1
roll [rəʊl] Rolle; Filmrolle OT 2
roller skate [ˈrəʊlə skeɪt] Rollschuh OT 4
Roman [ˈrəʊmən] römisch OT 2
roof [ˈruːf] Dach OT 1
room [ˈruːm] Raum OT 1
roommate [ˈrumˌmeɪt] Mitbewohner(in) WS 2, 67
root [ruːt] Wurzel OT 3
rope [rəʊp] Seil OT 1
rose [rəʊz] Rose OT 4
to rot [ˈrəʊt] verfaulen WS 1, 23
rough [rʌf] rau OT 4
round [raʊnd] rund; um ... herum OT 1
route [ruːt] Strecke OT 2
routine [ruːˈtiːn] Routine; Tagesablauf OT 4
rover [ˈrəʊvə] Forschungsfahrzeug OT 4
row [rəʊ] Reihe OT 1
rowing boat [ˈrəʊɪŋ bəʊt] Ruderboot OT 1
royal [ˈrɔɪəl] königlich OT 1
to rub [rʌb] reiben OT 3
rubber [ˈrʌbə] Gummi; Radiergummi OT 1
rubbish [ˈrʌbɪʃ] Müll OT 2
rubbish bin [ˈrʌbɪʃ ˌbɪn] Mülleimer OT 2
rubbish collection [ˈrʌbɪʃ kəˌlekʃn] Müllabfuhr OT 2
rucksack [ˈrʌksæk] Rucksack OT 1
rude [ruːd] unhöflich OT 1
rugby [ˈrʌgbi] Rugby OT 1
ruin [ˈruːɪn] Ruine OT 2
rule [ruːl] Regel OT 1
rulebook [ˈruːl bʊk] Regelwerk OT 2
ruler [ˈruːlə] Lineal OT 1
rummy [ˈrʌmi] Rommee OT 2
rumour [ˈruːmər] Gerücht WS 3, 109
run [rʌn] Punkte OT 1
to run [rʌn] laufen; rennen OT 1
  to run out [rʌn ˈaʊt] zur Neige gehen; zu Ende gehen OT 2
runaway [ˈrʌnəweɪ] Ausreißer(in) WS 4, 134
runner [ˈrʌnə] Läufer(in) OT 2
rural [ˈrʊərəl] ländlich OT 4
to rush [rʌʃ] eilen OT 2
  to rush off [rʌʃ ɒf] losstürzen; wegrennen OT 2
rush hour [ˈrʌʃ aʊə] Hauptverkehrszeit OT 1
Russian [ˈrʌʃn] russisch OT 2

S

sack [sæk] Sack OT 2

sacred [ˈseɪkrɪd] heilig OT 4
sad [sæd] traurig OT 1
saddened [ˈsædnd] betrübt WS 1, 24
saddle [ˈsædl] Sattel OT 3
safari [səˈfɑːri] Safari OT 2
safe [seɪf] sicher OT 1
safety [ˈseɪfti] Sicherheit OT 2
safety equipment [ˌseɪfti ɪˈkwɪpmənt] Sicherheitsausrüstung OT 2
to sail [seɪl] mit dem Schiff fahren; segeln OT 2
sailing [ˈseɪlɪŋ] Segeln OT 1
sailor [ˈseɪlə] Matrose OT 1
salad [ˈsæləd] Salat OT 1
salary [ˈsæləri] Gehalt; Lohn WS 2, 57
sale [seɪl] Sale; Ausverkauf OT 4
salmon [ˈsæmən] Lachs OT 1
salt [sɔːlt] Salz OT 3
same [seɪm] gleich OT 1
sample [ˈsɑːmpl] Probe OT 4
sand [sænd] Sand OT 1
sandal [ˈsændl] Sandale OT 4
sandwich [ˈsænwɪtʃ] Sandwich OT 1
sandy [ˈsændi] sandig OT 1
sassafras [ˈsæsəfræs] Sassafras OT 3
satellite [ˈsætəlaɪt] Satellit OT 4
satellite connection [ˈsætəlaɪt kəˈnekʃn] Satellitenverbindung OT 4
satisfying [ˈsætɪsfaɪɪŋ] zufriedenstellend; befriedigend WS 4, 146
Saturday [ˈsætədeɪ] Samstag OT 1
sauce [sɔːs] Soße OT 1
sausage [ˈsɒsɪdʒ] Wurst OT 1
sauté [ˈsəʊteɪ] geröstet OT 3
to save [seɪv] retten; sparen OT 2
savings [ˈseɪvɪŋz] Erspartes OT 3
savoury [ˈseɪvəri] pikant OT 3
savvy [ˈsævi] klug; schlau WS 3, 104
saxophone [ˈsæksəfəʊn] Saxofon OT 2
to say [seɪ] sagen OT 1
to scan [skæn] überfliegen; scannen OT 3
to scare [skeə] Angst machen OT 2
scared [skeəd] verängstigt OT 1
scarf [skɑːf] Schal OT 2
scary [ˈskeəri] unheimlich OT 1
to scavenge [ˈskævɪndʒ] nach etw. suchen WS 4, 130
scene [siːn] Szene OT 2
scenery [ˈsiːnəri] Landschaft OT 2
scenic [ˈsiːnɪk] malerisch WS 1, 17
schedule [ˈʃedjuːl] Stundenplan OT 2
to schedule [ˈʃedjuːl] festlegen; vereinbaren WS 2, 59
scheme [skiːm] Schema WS 4, 146

Appendix

VOCABULARY

school [skuːl] Schule OT 1
school bag [ˈskuːl bæɡ] Schultasche OT 1
school day [skuːl deɪ] Schultag OT 1
schooling [ˈskuːlɪŋ] Schulausbildung OT 4
school leaver [ˈskuːl liːvər] Schulabgänger(in) WS 2, 55
schoolmate [ˈskuːlmeɪt] Schulkamerad(in) OT 4
science [ˈsaɪəns] Wissen; Naturwissenschaften OT 1
science fiction [ˌsaɪəns ˈfɪkʃn] Science-Fiction OT 2
scientific [ˌsaɪənˈtɪfɪk] wissenschaftlich OT 3
scientist [ˈsaɪəntɪst] Naturwissenschaftler(in) OT 1
scissors [ˈsɪzəz] Schere OT 1
scone [skəʊn] brötchenartiges, süßes Gebäck OT 3
to score [skɔː] punkten OT 1
scoring [ˈskɔːrɪŋ] Treffen; Erzielen OT 1
Scottish [ˈskɒtɪʃ] schottisch OT 3
scout [skaʊt] Pfadfinder(in) OT 3
scrap [skræp] Abfall OT 4
scrapple [skræpl] Scrapple OT 3
to scratch [skrætʃ] kratzen OT 2
to scream [skriːm] schreien; kreischen OT 3
screen [skriːn] Bildschirm; Leinwand OT 1
script [skrɪpt] Drehbuch OT 1
sculpture [ˈskʌlptʃə] Skulptur OT 2
sea [siː] Meer OT 1
seabed [ˈsiːbed] Meeresboden OT 3
seabird [ˈsiːbɜːd] Seevogel WS 1, 24
seafood [ˈsiːfuːd] Meeresfrüchte OT 3
seal [siːl] Robbe OT 1
search [sɜːtʃ] Suche OT 2
to search [sɜːtʃ] suchen OT 2
seaside [ˈsiːsaɪd] Küste OT 1
season [ˈsiːzn] Jahreszeit OT 3
seasoning [ˈsiːzənɪŋ] Gewürz OT 2
seat [siːt] Sitzplatz OT 1
seating [ˈsiːtɪŋ] Sitzplätze OT 2
second [ˈsekənd] Sekunde; zweite(r, -s) OT 1
secondary [ˈsekəndri] weiterführend; sekundär OT 1
secondary school [ˈsekəndri ˌskuːl] Sekundarschule; weiterführende Schule OT 1
secondly [ˈsekəndli] zweitens OT 2
secret [ˈsiːkrət] Geheimnis OT 2
secretary [ˈsekrətri] Sekretär(in) OT 1

section [ˈsekʃn] Teil OT 2
secure [sɪˈkjʊə] sicher WS 2, 64
security [sɪˈkjʊərəti] Sicherheit OT 3
to see [siː] sehen OT 1
to seek [siːk] suchen WS 1, 16
to seem [siːm] scheinen OT 2
segment [ˈseɡmənt] Segment; Abschnitt WS 1, 30
seldom [ˈseldəm] selten WS 3, 106
to select [sɪˈlekt] wählen; auswählen OT 4
self: by one's self [baɪ wʌnz ˈself] allein OT 2
self-catering [ˌself ˈkeɪtərɪŋ] mit Selbstversorgung OT 3
self-checkout [ˌself ˈtʃekaʊt] Selbstzahlerkasse OT 4
self-employed [ˌself ɪmˈplɔɪd] selbständig WS 2, 63
selfie [ˈselfiː] Selfie OT 1
selfish [ˈselfɪʃ] egoistisch OT 3
self-motivated [ˌself ˈməʊtɪveɪtɪd] motiviert OT 4
self-sufficient [ˌself səˈfɪʃnt] unabhängig; autark OT 4
to sell [sel] verkaufen OT 1
semester [sɪˈmestə] Halbjahr; Semester OT 3
semi- [ˈsemi] halb- WS 1, 22
to send [send] schicken OT 1
sender [ˈsendə] Absender(in) OT 3
senior [ˈsiːniə] Oberstufenschüler(in); Senior(in) OT 4
senior citizen [ˌsiːniə ˈsɪtɪzn] Senior(in) OT 3
sensation [senˈseɪʃn] Gefühl OT 4
sense [sens] Sinn OT 2
sensible [ˈsensəbl] vernünftig OT 3
sensor [ˈsensə] Sensor OT 4
sentence [ˈsentəns] Satz OT 1
to sentence [ˈsentəns] verurteilen WS 3, 108
sentencing [ˈsentənsɪŋ] Verurteilung WS 3, 100
to separate [ˈseprət] (sich) trennen OT 4
separate [ˈseprət] getrennt OT 2
September [sepˈtembə] September OT 1
sequence [ˈsiːkwəns] Ablauf; Folge OT 4
to sequence [ˈsiːkwəns] in eine Reihenfolge bringen OT 3
sequencing [ˈsiːkwənsɪŋ] Sequenzierung; Reihenfolge OT 3
sequentially [sɪˈkwenʃəli] folgend; nacheinander OT 4

series [ˈsɪəriːz] Serie OT 1
serious [ˈsɪəriəs] ernst OT 2
seriously [ˈsɪəriəsli] ernst; im Ernst OT 2
seriousness [ˈsɪəriəsnəs] Ernsthaftigkeit WS 1, 44
serpent [ˈsɜːpənt] Schlange WS 1, 13
to serve [sɜːv] servieren; bedienen OT 1
server [ˈsɜːvə] Kellner(in) OT 4
service [ˈsɜːvɪs] Dienst OT 2
session [ˈseʃn] Sitzung; Session; Einheit OT 2
set [set] Satz OT 3
to set the stage [set ðə steɪdʒ] die Bühne vorbereiten OT 2
setting [ˈsetɪŋ] Einstellung OT 3
to settle [ˈsetl] sich ansiedeln OT 4
to settle down [ˌsetl ˈdaʊn] (sich) beruhigen OT 2
settlement [ˈsetlmənt] Siedlung OT 4
settler [ˈsetlə] Siedler(in) OT 3
seven [ˈsevn] sieben OT 1
seventeen [ˌsevnˈtiːn] siebzehn OT 1
seventy [ˈsevnti] siebzig OT 1
several [ˈsevrəl] mehrere; einige OT 2
severe [sɪˈvɪə] schwer; stark WS 1, 26
sewing machine [ˈsəʊɪŋ məʃiːn] Nähmaschine OT 3
sex [seks] Geschlecht; Sex WS 3, 90
shade [ʃeɪd] Schatten WS 1, 16
to shadow [ˈʃædəʊ] auf Schritt und Tritt begleiten; beschatten WS 2, 66
to shake [ʃeɪk] schütteln OT 2
to shake hands [ʃeɪk ˈhændz] jmdm. die Hand geben OT 2
shaky [ˈʃeɪki] wackelig OT 3
shall [ʃæl] werden OT 2
shame: That's a shame. [ðæts ə ˈʃeɪm] Das ist schade. OT 2
shampoo [ʃæmˈpuː] Shampoo OT 3
shape [ʃeɪp] Form OT 1
to shape [ʃeɪp] formen OT 3
shaped [ʃeɪpt] geformt OT 4
to share [ʃeə] teilen OT 1
shark [ʃɑːk] Hai WS 1, 24
she [ʃi] sie OT 1
shed [ʃed] Schuppen OT 1
sheep [ʃiːp] Schaf OT 1
sheepdog [ˈʃiːpdɒɡ] Hütehund OT 2
sheet [ʃiːt] Blatt OT 1
shelf [ʃelf] Regal OT 1
shelter [ˈʃeltə] Unterschlupf OT 2
shepherd [ˈʃepəd] Schäfer(in) OT 2
shift [ʃɪft] Schicht OT 4
to shine [ʃaɪn] scheinen OT 1
ship [ʃɪp] Schiff OT 2

two hundred and sixty-three **263**

Appendix

VOCABULARY

tall ship [ˌtɔːl ˈʃɪp] Großsegler OT 2
shipbuilding [ˈʃɪpbɪldɪŋ] Schiffbau OT 3
shirt [ʃɜːt] Hemd OT 1
shock [ʃɒk] Überraschung WS 3, 107
shocked [ʃɒkt] schockiert OT 4
shoe [ʃuː] Schuh OT 1
shoebox [ˈʃuːbɒks] Schuhschachtel OT 3
to shoot [ʃuːt] schießen OT 3
shop [ʃɒp] Laden OT 1
to shop [ʃɒp] kaufen; einkaufen OT 1
shoplifting [ˈʃɒplɪftɪŋ] Ladendiebstahl WS 3, 121
shopper [ˈʃɒpə] Käufer(in) OT 4
shopping [ˈʃɒpɪŋ] Einkaufen OT 1
shopping rota [ˈʃɒpɪŋ ˈrəʊtə] Einkaufsdienst WS 2, 70
shore [ʃɔː] Küste OT 2
short [ʃɔːt] kurz OT 1
shortage [ˈʃɔːtɪdʒ] Mangel WS 1, 18
to shorten [ˈʃɔːtn] kürzen; abkürzen WS 2, 67
shortlist [ˈʃɔːtlɪst] Auswahlliste OT 2
shorts [ʃɔːts] kurze Hose; Shorts OT 1
shot [ʃɒt] Schuss; Schnappschuss OT 4
should [ʃəd] sollte(n) OT 1
shoulder [ˈʃəʊldə] Schulter OT 1
shoulder pad [ˈʃəʊldə pæd] Schulterpolster OT 2
to shout [ʃaʊt] laut rufen OT 1
shovel [ˈʃʌvl] Schaufel OT 2
show [ʃəʊ] Vorstellung; Ausstellung OT 1
to show [ʃəʊ] zeigen OT 1
show-and-tell [ˌʃəʊ ən ˈtel] Kurzvortrag über einen mitgebrachten Gegenstand OT 1
shower [ˈʃaʊə] Dusche OT 2
showground [ˈʃəʊɡraʊnd] Ausstellungsgelände OT 2
showtime [ˈʃəʊtaɪm] Vorstellungsbeginn OT 4
shredded [ˈʃredɪd] gerieben; geschnetzelt OT 2
to shrug [ʃrʌɡ] Achseln zucken WS 3, 97
to shut [ʃʌt] zumachen; schließen OT 2
shy [ʃaɪ] schüchtern OT 2
sibling [ˈsɪblɪŋ] Geschwister(kind); Bruder WS 1, 28
sick [sɪk] krank OT 1
side [saɪd] Seite OT 1
sidewalk [ˈsaɪdwɔːk] Bürgersteig OT 4
sigh [saɪ] Seufzer OT 2
to sigh [saɪ] seufzen OT 3
sight [saɪt] Sehvermögen; Sehenswürdigkeit OT 1

sightseeing [ˈsaɪtsiːɪŋ] Besichtigungen OT 1
sign [saɪn] Schild OT 1
to sign [saɪn] unterschreiben OT 2
signal [ˈsɪɡnəl] Signal OT 2
significance [sɪɡˈnɪfɪkəns] Bedeutung; Wichtigkeit WS 1, 30
signpost [ˈsaɪnpəʊst] Wegweiser; Schild WS 2, 50
signposting [ˈsaɪnpəʊstɪŋ] Beschilderung; Wegweisung WS 4, 143
sign-up sheet [ˈsaɪn ʌp ˌʃiːt] Anmeldeliste OT 2
silence [ˈsaɪləns] Stille OT 2
silly [ˈsɪli] dumm; albern OT 1
silver [ˈsɪlvə] Silber...; silbern OT 1
similar [ˈsɪmələ] ähnlich OT 2
similarity [ˌsɪməˈlærəti] Ähnlichkeit OT 3
to simmer [ˈsɪmə] köcheln OT 2
simple [ˈsɪmpl] einfach OT 1
simple present [ˌsɪmpl ˈpreznt] einfaches Präsens; einfache Gegenwart OT 1
simplified [ˈsɪmplɪfaɪ] vereinfacht WS 4, 144
since [sɪns] seit OT 3
sincerely [sɪnˈsɪəli] aufrichtig; mit freundlichen Grüßen OT 4
to sing [sɪŋ] singen OT 1
singer [ˈsɪŋə] Sänger(in) OT 1
single [ˈsɪŋɡl] Einzel... OT 3
singular [ˈsɪŋɡjələ] Einzahl; Singular OT 1
sink [sɪŋk] Spülbecken OT 3
to sink [sɪŋk] sinken OT 3
sir [sɜː] Herr OT 1
siren [ˈsaɪrən] Sirene OT 3
sister [ˈsɪstə] Schwester OT 1
to sit [sɪt] sitzen OT 1
to sit down [sɪt daʊn] hinsetzen OT 1
site [saɪt] Platz OT 2
situation [ˌsɪtʃuˈeɪʃn] Lage; Situation OT 1
six [sɪks] sechs OT 1
sixteen [ˌsɪksˈtiːn] sechzehn OT 1
sixty [ˈsɪksti] sechzig OT 1
size [saɪz] Größe OT 1
to sizzle [ˈsɪzl] knistern WS 1, 40
to skate [skeɪt] Schlittschuh laufen OT 2
skateboard [ˈskeɪtbɔːd] Skateboard OT 4
to skateboard [ˈskeɪtbɔːd] Skateboardfahren gehen OT 4
skeleton [ˈskelɪtn] Skelett OT 1

sketch [sketʃ] Skizze; Sketch OT 4
to sketch [sketʃ] skizzieren; zeichnen OT 4
to ski [skiː] Ski laufen OT 1
skier [ˈskiːə] Skiläufer(in) OT 3
skiing [ˈskiːɪŋ] Skifahren OT 2
skilful [ˈskɪlfl] geschickt OT 3
skill [skɪl] Geschick; Fähigkeit OT 2
skilled [skɪld] geschickt; ausgebildet OT 4
to skim [skɪm] querlesen; überfliegen OT 3
skin [skɪn] Haut OT 2
skirt [skɜːt] Rock OT 1
skit [skɪt] Sketch OT 2
sky [skaɪ] Himmel OT 1
skyline [ˈskaɪlaɪn] Skyline WS 2, 67
skyscraper [ˈskaɪskreɪpə] Wolkenkratzer OT 3
slang [slæŋ] Slang WS 1, 28
to slap on [slæp ɒn] aufsetzen WS 1, 16
slave [sleɪv] Sklave / Sklavin OT 4
slavery [ˈsleɪvəri] Sklaverei OT 4
to sleep [sliːp] schlafen OT 1
sleeping bag [ˈsliːpɪŋ bæɡ] Schlafsack OT 2
sleepover [ˈsliːpəʊvə] Pyjama-Party OT 1
sleeve [sliːv] Ärmel OT 3
sleeveless [ˈsliːvləs] ärmellos OT 4
slice [slaɪs] Scheibe OT 1
slide [slaɪd] Folie OT 1
slideshow [ˈslaɪdʃəʊ] Präsentation; Diashow OT 3
slight [slaɪt] gering; leicht WS 3, 98
to slip on [slɪp] rasch anziehen WS 1, 16
slogan [ˈsləʊɡən] Slogan OT 2
to slop on [slɒp ɒn] auftragen WS 1, 16
slope [sləʊp] Piste OT 3
slow [sləʊ] langsam OT 2
slowly [ˈsləʊli] langsam OT 2
to slow down [sləʊ ˈdaʊn] (sich) verlangsamen OT 4
slum [slʌm] Slum OT 3
to slump [slʌmp] zusammensacken OT 4
small [smɔːl] klein OT 1
smallpox [ˈsmɔːlpɒks] Pocken OT 4
smart [smɑːt] intelligent; schlau OT 4
smartphone [ˈsmɑːtfəʊn] Smartphone OT 3
to smell [smel] riechen OT 1
to smile [smaɪl] lächeln OT 1
smoke [sməʊk] Rauch OT 2
smooth [smuːð] glatt OT 3
smoothly [ˈsmuːðli] glatt OT 3

Appendix

VOCABULARY

snack [snæk] Snack OT 1
snake [sneɪk] Schlange OT 1
   snakes and ladders [ˌsneɪks ən ˈlædəz] Leiterspiel OT 2
sneaker [ˈsniːkə] Turnschuh OT 4
sneaky [ˈsniːki] heimtückisch; hinterhältig WS 3, 118
snitch [snɪtʃ] Verräter(in) WS 3, 94
snore [snɔː] Schnarcher OT 1
snow [snəʊ] Schnee OT 1
snowboarding [ˈsnəʊbɔːdɪŋ] Snowboard fahren OT 3
snowy [ˈsnəʊi] verschneit OT 3
so [səʊ] also OT 1
soaked [səʊkd] durchnässt OT 3
soap [səʊp] Seife OT 2
to soar [sɔː] schweben OT 3
soccer [ˈsɒkə] Fußball OT 2
social [ˈsəʊʃl] sozial OT 2
to socialize [ˈsəʊʃəlaɪz] Kontakte pflegen; unter die Leute kommen OT 4
society [səˈsaɪəti] Gesellschaft OT 4
sociology [ˌsəʊsiˈɒlədʒi] Soziologie WS 2, 58
sock [sɒk] Socke OT 2
soda [ˈsəʊdə] Limo; Sprudel WS 3, 102
sofa [ˈsəʊfə] Sofa OT 1
soft [sɒft] weich OT 3
software [ˈsɒftweə] Software OT 1
soil [sɔɪl] Erdboden; Erde; Erdreich OT 2
solar [ˈsəʊlə] Sonnen… OT 3
   solar panel [ˌsəʊlə ˈpænl] Sonnenkollektor OT 3
   solar power [ˌsəʊlə ˈpaʊə] Solarenergie; Sonnenenergie OT 4
   solar system [ˈsəʊlə sɪstəm] Sonnensystem OT 1
soldier [ˈsəʊldʒə] Soldat(in) OT 1
soliloquy [səˈlɪləkwi] Monolog; Soliloquium WS 4, 145
solo [ˈsəʊləʊ] solo OT 2; Solo OT 4
solution [səˈluːʃn] Lösung OT 2
to solve [sɒlv] lösen OT 3
some [sʌm] etwas; einige OT 1
somebody [ˈsʌmbədi] jemand OT 1
somehow [ˈsʌmhaʊ] irgendwie WS 1, 41
someone [ˈsʌmwʌn] jemand OT 1
something [ˈsʌmθɪŋ] etwas OT 1
sometimes [ˈsʌmtaɪmz] manchmal OT 1
somewhere [ˈsʌmweər] irgendwo OT 1
son [sʌn] Sohn OT 1
song [sɒŋ] Lied OT 1
songwriter [ˈsɒŋraɪtə] Songwriter(in) OT 2
soon [suːn] bald OT 1

sore [sɔː] schmerzend OT 2
sorrow [ˈsɒrəʊ] Trauer; Kummer WS 4, 145
sorry [ˈsɒri] Entschuldigung OT 1
sort [sɔːt] Art OT 2
sound [saʊnd] Geräusch OT 1
to sound [saʊnd] klingen; ertönen OT 2
soup [suːp] Suppe OT 1
source [sɔːs] Quelle OT 2
south [saʊθ] Süd- OT 1
southern [ˈsʌðən] südlich OT 3
southwest [ˌsaʊθˈwest] Südwesten OT 3
souvenir [suːvəˈnɪə] Reiseandenken OT 1
spa [spɑː] Heilbad OT 3
space [speɪs] Platz; Feld; Weltraum OT 2
spacecraft [ˈspeɪskrɑːft] Raumfahrzeug OT 4
space exploration [ˈspeɪsˌekspləˈreɪʃn] Weltraumforschung OT 4
spaceship [ˈspeɪsʃɪp] Raumschiff OT 4
spacesuit [ˈspeɪssuːt] Raumanzug OT 4
spaghetti [spəˈɡeti] Spaghetti OT 1
spaniel [ˈspænjəl] Spaniel OT 2
Spanish [ˈspænɪʃ] spanisch OT 1
spark [spɑːk] Funke OT 2
to spark [spɑːk] entzünden OT 4
sparkling [ˈspɑːklɪŋ] sprudelnd OT 1
to speak [spiːk] sprechen OT 1
speaker [ˈspiːkə] Sprecher(in) OT 1
speaking [ˈspiːkɪŋ] Sprechen OT 1
to spear [spɪər] aufspießen WS 1, 24
special [ˈspeʃl] Tagesgericht; besondere(r, -s) OT 1
specialist [ˈspeʃəlɪst] speziell WS 3, 100
to specialize [ˈspeʃəlaɪz] sich spezialisieren OT 4
species [ˈspiːʃiːz] Spezies; Art WS 1, 23
specific [spəˈsɪfɪk] bestimmt; konkret; spezifisch OT 3
spectacular [spekˈtækjələ] spektakulär OT 2
spectator [spekˈteɪtə] Zuschauer(in) OT 3
to speculate [ˈspekjuleɪt] spekulieren; nachdenken OT 4
speech [spiːtʃ] Rede OT 1
speech bubble [ˈspiːtʃ bʌbl] Sprechblase OT 2
speed [spiːd] Geschwindigkeit OT 2
to spell [spel] buchstabieren OT 1
spelling [ˈspelɪŋ] Rechtschreibung; Schreibweise OT 1
to spend [spend] ausgeben; verbringen OT 1

spice [spaɪs] Gewürz OT 3
spiced [spaɪst] gewürzt OT 4
spider [ˈspaɪdə] Spinne OT 1
spiky [ˈspaɪki] stachelig; spitz WS 2, 63
to spill [spɪl] verschütten OT 2
spiral [ˈspaɪrəl] Spirale; Wendel WS 1, 21
spirit [ˈspɪrɪt] Geist OT 2
to spit [spɪt] spucken OT 4
spite: in spite of [ɪn spaɪt əv] trotz WS 1, 23
split [splɪt] Riss OT 3
to split up [ˌsplɪtˈʌp] sich trennen WS 3, 90
to spoil [spɔɪl] verderben OT 2
spoilage [ˈspɔɪlɪdʒ] Verderben; Abfall OT 4
spokeswoman [ˈspəʊkswʊmən] Sprecherin OT 2
sponsor [ˈspɒnsə] Sponsor(in); Geldgeber(in) OT 2
to sponsor [ˈspɒnsə] finanziell unterstützen OT 2
sponsored [ˈspɒnsəd] gesponsert; gestiftet OT 2
sponsorship [ˈspɒnsəʃɪp] finanzielle Unterstützung OT 2
spontaneous [spɒnˈteɪniəs] spontan WS 4, 143
spoon [spuːn] Löffel OT 2
spoonful [ˈspuːnfʊl] Löffel (Maßangabe) OT 2
sport [spɔːt] Sport OT 1
   to be a good sport [bi ə ɡʊd spɔːt] kein(e) Spielverderber(in) sein OT 2
sporting [ˈspɔːtɪŋ] sportlich; Sport… WS 1, 15
sportsman [ˈspɔːtsmən] Sportler OT 3
sportspeople [ˈspɔːts piːpl] Sportler(innen) OT 3
sportswoman [ˈspɔːtswʊmən] Sportlerin OT 2
to spot [spɒt] erspähen OT 1
spotlight [ˈspɒtlaɪt] Mittelpunkt des Interesses OT 4
to sprain [spreɪn] verstauchen OT 2
to spray [spreɪ] sprühen WS 3, 121
to spread (out) [spred] verbreiten OT 4
spring [sprɪŋ] Frühling; Quelle OT 2
   hot spring [ˈhɒt sprɪŋ] Thermalquelle OT 2
spring clean [ˌsprɪŋ ˈkliːn] Frühjahrsputz OT 2
to sprinkle [ˈsprɪŋkl] streuen OT 2
sprint [sprɪnt] Sprint OT 3
sprinter [ˈsprɪntə] Sprinter(in) OT 3

Appendix

VOCABULARY

square [skweə] Quadrat; Feld; Platz OT 1
squash [skwɒʃ] Kürbis OT 4
squirrel [ˈskwɪrəl] Eichhörnchen OT 1
stability [stəˈbɪləti] Stabilität **WS 2**, 64
stable [ˈsteɪbl] stabil; sicher **WS 2**, 63
to **stack** [stæk] stapeln OT 4
stadium [ˈsteɪdiəm] Stadion OT 1
staff [stɑːf] Personal OT 3
stage [steɪdʒ] Phase; Bühne OT 2
stage directions [ˈsteɪdʒ dərekʃnz] Bühnenanweisungen OT 2
stairs [ˈsteəz] Treppe / Treppenstufen OT 1
stalactite [ˈstæləktaɪt] Stalaktit OT 1
stalagmite [ˈstæləgmaɪt] Stalagmit OT 1
stall [stɔːl] Bude; Stall OT 2
to **stand** [stænd] stehen OT 1
   to **stand up** [ˈstænd ʌp] aufstehen OT 1
standard [ˈstændəd] normal; Standard... OT 3
stanza [ˈstænzə] Stanze; Strophe **WS 4**, 146
stapler [ˈsteɪplə] Tacker OT 2
star [stɑː] Stern; Star OT 1
to **stare** [steə] starren OT 2
start [stɑːt] Anfang OT 1
to **start** [stɑːt] anfangen; beginnen OT 1
starter [ˈstɑːtə] Vorspeise OT 1
to **starve** [stɑːv] hungern (lassen); verhungern (lassen) OT 1
state [steɪt] Staat OT 1
to **state** [steɪt] erklären; festlegen **WS 3**, 108
statement [ˈsteɪtmənt] Aussage OT 1
station [ˈsteɪʃn] Station; Bahnhof OT 1
stationery [ˈsteɪʃənri] Schreibwaren **WS 2**, 69
statistic [stəˈtɪstɪk] Statistik OT 3
statue [ˈstætʃuː] Statue OT 1
status [ˈsteɪtəs] Status; Stand OT 4
to **stay** [steɪ] bleiben OT 1
steady [ˈstedi] ruhig; stabil OT 3
steak [steɪk] Steak OT 1
to **steal** [stiːl] klauen OT 2
steam [stiːm] Dampf OT 2
   steam train [ˈstiːm treɪn] Dampfzug OT 2
steel [stiːl] Stahl OT 2
steep [stiːp] steil OT 2
to **steer** [stɪə] steuern OT 3
stegosaurus [ˌstegəˈsɔːrəs] Stegosaurus OT 1
STEM (science, technology, engineering, mathematics) [stem]

MINT (Mathematik, Informatik, Naturwissenschaft und Technik) **WS 2**, 68
step [step] Schritt; Stufe OT 1
to **step** [step] treten OT 4
   to **step in** [step ˈɪn] eintreten OT 4
stereotype [ˈsteriətaɪp] Stereotype; Klischee **WS 1**, 39
to **stereotype** [ˈsteriətaɪp] stereotypisieren **WS 2**, 68
stereotypical [ˌsteriəˈtɪpɪkl] stereotypisch **WS 3**, 93
steroid [ˈsterɔɪd] Steroid **WS 3**, 102
stew [stjuː] Eintopf OT 2
steward [ˈstjuːəd] Verwalter OT 4
to **stick** [stɪk] kleben OT 1
sticky [ˈstɪki] klebrig; selbstklebend OT 1
stigma [ˈstɪgmə] Stigma **WS 2**, 65
still [stɪl] immer noch OT 1; ruhig OT 4
sting [stɪŋ] Stich OT 2
to **sting** [stɪŋ] stechen OT 2
stingray [ˈstɪŋreɪ] Stachelrochen **WS 1**, 44
to **stir** [stɜː] rühren OT 2
stock [stɒk] Viehbestand; Bestand OT 2
stockroom [ˈstɒkruːm] Lagerraum **WS 2**, 59
stomach [ˈstʌmək] Magen OT 2
stone [stəʊn] Stein OT 1
stop [stɒp] Halt; Haltestelle OT 2
to **stop** [stɒp] anhalten; aufhören OT 1
storage [ˈstɔːrɪdʒ] Lagerung; Aufbewahrung OT 3
store [stɔː] Laden OT 1
storeroom [ˈstɔːruːm] Lagerraum; Abstellraum **WS 3**, 121
storm [stɔːm] Sturm OT 2
story [ˈstɔːri] Geschichte OT 1
storyboard [ˈstɔːrɪbɔːd] Storyboard; Szenenbuch OT 4
storybook [ˈstɔːrɪbʊk] Geschichtenbuch OT 2
stove [stəʊv] Ofen OT 3
straight [streɪt] gerade; direkt OT 3
   straight away [streɪt əˈweɪ] sofort; gleich OT 2
strange [streɪndʒ] seltsam OT 1
strategic [strəˈtiːdʒɪk] strategisch OT 4
strategy [ˈstrætədʒi] Strategie OT 4
straw [strɔː] Trinkhalm; Strohhalm; Stroh OT 4
strawberry [ˈstrɔːbəri] Erdbeere OT 1
stream [striːm] Bach OT 2
streamer [ˈstriːmə] Luftschlangen OT 4
street [striːt] Straße OT 1

street collection [ˈstriːt kəlekʃn] Straßensammlung OT 2
strength [streŋθ] Stärke OT 2
to **strengthen** [ˈstreŋkθn] stärker werden; stärker machen **WS 3**, 99
stress [stres] Stress; Betonung OT 1
stressed [strest] gestresst; angestrengt OT 2
stressful [ˈstresfl] stressig OT 4
to **stretch** [stretʃ] dehnen OT 2
strict [strɪkt] streng OT 2
strike [straɪk] Streik OT 4
to **strike** [straɪk] schlagen; zuschlagen; streiken OT 1
striker [ˈstraɪkə] Stürmer(in) OT 3
string [strɪŋ] Schnur; Saite OT 2
strip [strɪp] Band; Streifen **WS 2**, 70
stroke [strəʊk] Schlag OT 3
strong [strɒŋ] stark OT 2
to **structure** [ˈstrʌktʃə] strukturieren; aufbauen **WS 1**, 31
structure [ˈstrʌktʃə] Struktur OT 1
to **struggle** [ˈstrʌgl] sich anstrengen; sich bemühen **WS 2**, 64
student [ˈstjuːdnt] Student(in); Schüler(in) OT 1
student council [ˈstjuːdnt ˈkaʊnsl] Schülerrat OT 2
studies [stʌdiz] Studium; Wissenschaft OT 1
studio [ˈstjuːdiəʊ] Studio **WS 1**, 30
to **study** [ˈstʌdi] studieren OT 1
stuff [stʌf] Zeug OT 2
stunning [ˈstʌnɪŋ] toll; atemberaubend **WS 1**, 26
stupid [ˈstjuːpɪd] dumm OT 2
   stupidly [ˈstjuːpɪdli] dumm OT 2
style [staɪl] Stil OT 2
stylish [ˈstaɪlɪʃ] schick OT 4
stylistic [staɪˈlɪstɪk] stilistisch **WS 4**, 145
sub-heading [ˈsʌb ˌhedɪŋ] Unterüberschrift OT 2
subject [ˈsʌbdʒɪkt] Thema; Fach; Subjekt OT 1
   subject pronoun [ˌsʌbdʒekt ˈprəʊnaʊn] Subjektpronomen OT 1
to **subject** [ˈsʌbdʒɪkt] unterwerfen OT 4
   submarine [ˌsʌbməˈriːn] U-Boot OT 3
to **subscribe** [səbˈskraɪb] abonnieren **WW**, 11
substitute [ˈsʌbstɪtjuːt] Ersatz OT 3
substitution [ˌsʌbstɪˈtjuːʃn] Ersatz OT 3
subway [ˈsʌbweɪ] U-Bahn OT 1
to **succeed** [səkˈsiːd] erfolgreich sein OT 2
success [səkˈses] Erfolg OT 3

Appendix

VOCABULARY

successful [səkˈsesfl] erfolgreich OT 2
successive [səkˈsesɪv] aufeinanderfolgend; fortlaufend **WS 1**, 21
such [sʌtʃ] so OT 2
sudden [ˈsʌdn] plötzlich OT 2
   suddenly [ˈsʌdənli] plötzlich OT 1
to **suffer** [ˈsʌfə] leiden **WS 1**, 20
sufficient [səˈfɪʃnt] ausreichend; genug **WW**, 11
sugar [ˈʃʊgə] Zucker OT 3
to **suggest** [səˈdʒest] vorschlagen OT 1
suggestion [səˈdʒestʃən] Vorschlag OT 1
suicide [ˈsuːɪsaɪd] Selbstmord **WS 1**, 21
suit [suːt] Anzug OT 1
to **suit** [suːt] jmdm. stehen OT 1
suitable [ˈsuːtəbl] geeignet OT 4
suitcase [ˈsuːtkeɪs] Koffer OT 2
to **sulk** [sʌlk] schmollen OT 3
to **sum up** [sʌm ʌp] zusammenfassen OT 4
to **summarize** [ˈsʌməraɪz] zusammenfassen OT 2
summary [ˈsʌməri] Zusammenfassung OT 3
summer [ˈsʌmə] Sommer OT 1
sun [sʌn] Sonne OT 1
sunburn [ˈsʌnbɜːn] Sonnenbrand OT 2
sunburnt [ˈsʌnbɜːnt] sonnenverbrannt **WS 1**, 40
Sunday [ˈsʌndeɪ] Sonntag OT 1
sunglasses [ˈsʌnglɑːsɪz] Sonnenbrille OT 2
sunny [ˈsʌni] sonnig OT 1
sunscreen [ˈsʌnskriːn] Sonnenschutzmittel OT 2
sunset [ˈsʌnset] Sonnenuntergang OT 3
sunshine [ˈsʌnʃaɪn] Sonnenschein OT 3
sunstroke [ˈsʌnstrəʊk] Sonnenstich OT 2
superhero [ˈsuːpəhɪərəʊ] Superheld **WS 3**, 102
superlative [suˈpɜːlətɪv] Superlativ OT 2
supermarket [ˈsuːpəmɑːkɪt] Supermarkt OT 1
to **supervise** [ˈsuːpəvaɪz] beaufsichtigen OT 3
supervision [ˌsuːpəˈvɪʒn] Überwachung; Aufsicht **WS 3**, 101
supervisor [ˈsuːpəvaɪzə] Leiter(in) OT 4
supplement [ˈsʌplɪmənt] Nahrungsergänzung **WS 3**, 102
supply [səˈplaɪ] Vorrat OT 3
to **support** [səˈpɔːt] unterstützen OT 1

supporter [səˈpɔːtə] Befürworter(in); Fan OT 2
supportive [səˈpɔːtɪv] unterstützend **WS 1**, 14
to **suppose** [səˈpəʊz] vermuten; annehmen OT 1
sure [ʃʊə] sicher OT 1
   to **make sure** [meɪk ˈʃʊə] sichergehen; sicherstellen OT 2
surely [ˈʃʊəli] sicherlich OT 4
surface [ˈsɜːfɪs] Oberfläche OT 3
surfer [ˈsɜːfə] Surfer OT 4
surfing [ˈsɜːfɪŋ] Surfen OT 1
surgeon [ˈsɜːdʒən] Chirurg(in) OT 3
surgery [ˈsɜːdʒəri] Sprechstunde; Praxis **WS 2**, 66
surprise [səˈpraɪz] Überraschung OT 1
surprised [səˈpraɪzd] überrascht OT 1
surprising [səˈpraɪzɪŋ] überraschend OT 2
survey [ˈsɜːveɪ] Umfrage OT 1
to **survey** [ˈsɜːveɪ] befragen **WS 3**, 98
survival [səˈvaɪvl] Überleben OT 2
to **survive** [səˈvaɪv] überleben OT 3
sushi [ˈsuːʃi] Sushi OT 1
sustainability [səˌsteɪnəˈbɪləti] Nachhaltigkeit OT 3
sustainable [səˈsteɪnəbl] nachhaltig OT 4
to **swallow** [ˈswɒləʊ] schlucken; hinunterschlucken OT 4
swamp [swɒmp] Sumpf OT 2
to **swap** [swɒp] tauschen OT 1
to **swear** [sweə] schwören OT 4
to **sweat** [swet] schwitzen OT 2
sweatshirt [ˈswetʃɜːt] Sweatshirt OT 1
sweaty [ˈsweti] verschwitzt **WS 3**, 95
Swedish [ˈswiːdɪʃ] schwedisch OT 4
to **sweep** [swiːp] fegen OT 4
sweet [swiːt] Bonbon OT 2
sweet corn [ˈswiːt kɔːn] Zuckermais OT 1
sweetheart [ˈswiːthɑːt] Liebste(r); Liebes **WS 3**, 95
swelling [ˈswelɪŋ] Schwellung OT 2
to **swim** [swɪm] schwimmen OT 1
swimmer [ˈswɪmə] Schwimmer(in) OT 2
swimming [ˈswɪmɪŋ] Schwimmen OT 1
switch [swɪtʃ] Schalter OT 3
to **switch on** [swɪtʃ ɒn] anschalten OT 1
swollen [ˈswəʊln] geschwollen OT 2
sword [sɔːd] Schwert OT 1
syllable [ˈsɪləbəl] Silbe OT 2
symbol [ˈsɪmbl] Symbol OT 1
sympathetic [ˌsɪmpəˈθetɪk] mitfühlend OT 3

to **sympathize** [ˈsɪmpəθaɪz] mit jmdm. mitleiden; mitfühlen **WS 4**, 138
synaesthesia [ˌsɪnəsˈθiːziə] Synästhesie OT 2
synagogue [ˈsɪnəgɒg] Synagoge OT 1
synonym [ˈsɪnənɪm] Synonym OT 2
synthetic [sɪnˈθetɪk] synthetisch OT 4
syrup [ˈsɪrəp] Sirup OT 3
system [ˈsɪstəm] System OT 1
systematically [ˌsɪstəˈmætɪkli] systematisch **WS 1**, 22

T

tab [tæb] Tab OT 3
table [ˈteɪbl] Tisch OT 1
tablespoon [ˈteɪblspuːn] Esslöffel OT 2
tablet [ˈtæblət] Tablette OT 2
to **tackle** [ˈtækl] angreifen OT 3
taco [ˈtækəʊ] Taco OT 1
tactic [ˈtæktɪk] Taktik OT 2
tag [tæg] Etikett; kurze Schnur, die gelochte Blätter zusammenhält OT 2
tail [teɪl] Schwanz OT 2
Taiwanese [taɪwɑːˈniːz] taiwanisch OT 4
to **take into account** [teɪk ˈɪntə əˈkaʊnt] berücksichtigen; beachten **WS 3**, 101
to **take** [teɪk] nehmen OT 1
   to **take a joke** [teɪk ə dʒəʊk] Spaß verstehen OT 2
   to **take a photo** [ˌteɪk ə ˈfəʊtəʊ] ein Foto machen OT 1
   to **take charge** [teɪk tʃɑːdʒ] die Leitung übernehmen OT 2
   to **take for granted** [teɪk fə ˈgrɑːntɪd] für selbstverständlich halten OT 4
   to **take out** [ˈteɪk aʊt] rausbringen OT 4
   to **take part** [teɪk ˈpɑːt] teilnehmen OT 2
   to **take turns** [teɪk tɜːnz] (sich) abwechseln OT 1
   to **take up** [teɪk ʌp] mit etw. anfangen; aufnehmen OT 1
takeout [ˈteɪkaʊt] Essen zum Mitnehmen OT 4
tale [teɪl] Geschichte OT 2
talent [ˈtælənt] Talent; Begabung OT 2
talented [ˈtæləntɪd] talentiert OT 3
talk [tɔːk] Vortrag; Rede OT 2
to **talk** [tɔːk] reden OT 1
tall [tɔːl] groß; hoch OT 1
tally [ˈtæli] Gesamtliste OT 4
tank [tæŋk] Tank OT 3
to **tap** [tæp] tippen; klopfen OT 2
tape [teɪp] Klebeband OT 1

Appendix

VOCABULARY

target [ˈtɑːɡɪt] Ziel OT 2
to **target** [ˈtɑːɡɪt] zielen auf WS 3, 118
task [tɑːsk] Aufgabe OT 1
taste [teɪst] Geschmack OT 4
to **taste** [teɪst] schmecken OT 1
tasty [ˈteɪsti] schmackhaft OT 2
tattoo [təˈtuː] Tätowierung OT 3
tax [tæks] Steuer OT 4
  tax-payer [ˈtækspeɪər] Steuerzahler(in) WS 2, 64
taxi [ˈtæksi] Taxi OT 1
tea [tiː] Tee OT 1
  tea light [ˈtiː laɪt] Teelicht OT 2
to **teach** [tiːtʃ] unterrichten OT 1
teacher [ˈtiːtʃə] Lehrer(in) OT 1
team [tiːm] Mannschaft OT 1
teammate [ˈtiːmmeɪt] Mitspieler(in) OT 2
teamwork [ˈtiːmwɜːk] Teamwork; Gruppenarbeit OT 4
tear [tɪə] Träne OT 2
to **tear** [teə] reißen OT 2
to **tease** [tiːz] ärgern OT 1
tech [tek] technisch OT 2
tech-orientated [tekɔːrientɪd] techorientiert WS 2, 63
technical [ˈteknɪkl] technisch OT 4
technique [tekˈniːk] Technik; Methode OT 4
technological [ˌteknəˈlɒdʒɪkl] technisch; technologisch OT 4
technology [tekˈnɒlədʒi] Technologie OT 1
teen [tiːn] Teenager OT 2
teenage [ˈtiːneɪdʒ] Teenager… OT 4
teenager [ˈtiːneɪdʒə] Teenager; Jugendliche(r) OT 2
tooth [tuːθ] Zahn OT 2
teleconference [ˈtelikɒnfrəns] Telefonkonferenz OT 3
telegraph [ˈtelɪɡrɑːf] Telegraf OT 4
television [ˈtelɪvɪʒn] Fernseher OT 2
to **tell** [tel] erzählen OT 1
temperature [ˈtemprətʃə] Temperatur OT 2
template [ˈtempleɪt] Vorlage OT 4
temple [ˈtempl] Tempel OT 1
to **tempt** [tempt] versuchen; locken WS 2, 57
ten [ten] zehn OT 1
to **tend to** [tend] zu etw. neigen; zu etw. tendieren WS 2, 68
tennis [ˈtenɪs] Tennis OT 1
tense [tens] Zeitform; Tempus OT 1
tension [ˈtenʃn] Anspannung OT 4
tent [tent] Zelt OT 1

term [tɜːm] Semester OT 2
terrible [ˈterəbl] schrecklich OT 1
terrier [ˈteriə] Terrier OT 2
terrified [ˈterɪfaɪd] verängstigt OT 3
territory [ˈterətri] Gebiet WS 1, 12
test [test] Test OT 1
text [tekst] SMS; Text OT 1
to **text** [tekst] texten OT 1
than [ðən] als OT 1
to **thank** [θæŋk] danken OT 1
thanks [θæŋks] danke OT 1
Thanksgiving [ˌθæŋksˈɡɪvɪŋ] amerikanisches Erntedankfest OT 2
that [ðæt] diese(r, -s); jene(r, -s) OT 1
  That'll be … [ðætl bi] Das macht… OT 2
the [ðiː] der; die; das OT 1
theatre [ˈθɪətə] Theater OT 1
theft [θeft] Diebstahl WS 3, 94
their [ðeə] ihr OT 1
theirs [ðeəz] ihre(r, -s) OT 2
them [ðem] sie; ihnen OT 1
theme [θiːm] Thema OT 4
themselves [ðəmˈselvz] sich (selbst) OT 3
then [ðen] dann OT 1
theoretical [ˌθɪəˈretɪkl] theoretisch OT 4
  theoretically [ˌθɪəˈretɪkli] theoretisch WS 2, 57
theory [ˈθɪəri] Theorie OT 1
there [ðeə] da; dort OT 1
  there is / are [ðeə ɪz / ɑ] es gibt OT 1
therefore [ˈðeəfɔː] deshalb OT 3
thermostat [ˈθɜːməstæt] Thermostat; Temperaturregler WS 2, 70
these [ðiːz] diese OT 1
they [ðeɪ] sie OT 1
thick [θɪk] dick OT 1
thigh [θaɪ] Oberschenkel OT 1
thin [θɪn] dünn OT 1
thing [θɪŋ] Ding OT 1
to **think** [θɪŋk] denken OT 1
  to **think about** [ˈθɪŋk əbaʊt] denken an; nachdenken über OT 1
  to **think of** [ˈθɪŋk əv] denken an; sich erinnern an OT 1
third [θɜːd] Dritte(r,-s) OT 1
thirsty [ˈθɜːsti] durstig OT 1
thirteen [ˌθɜːˈtiːn] dreizehn OT 1
thirty [ˈθɜːti] dreißig OT 1
this [ðɪs] diese(r,-s) OT 1
thorn [θɔːn] Stachel OT 2
thoroughly [ˈθʌrəli] völlig; durchaus WS 2, 67
those [ðəʊz] diese; jene dort OT 1

though [ðəʊ] obwohl; jedoch OT 2
thought [θɔːt] Gedanke OT 4
thoughtful [ˈθɔːtfl] nachdenklich; rücksichtsvoll OT 3
thoughtless [ˈθɔːtləs] gedankenlos; rücksichtslos OT 2
thought-provoking [ˈθɔːt prəvəʊkɪŋ] zum Nachdenken anregend WS 4, 139
thousand [ˈθaʊznd] Tausend OT 1
threat [θret] Gefahr WS 1, 27
to **threaten** [ˈθretn] gefährden WS 1, 18
three [θriː] drei OT 1
thrifting [ˈθrɪftɪŋ] Secondhand shoppen OT 4
thrift store [ˈθrɪft stɔː] Secondhandladen OT 4
throat [θrəʊt] Hals OT 2
throne [θrəʊn] Thron WS 2, 64
throng [θrɒŋ] Menschenmenge OT 2
through [θruː] durch OT 1
throughout [θruːˈaʊt] während; durchweg OT 3
to **throw** [θrəʊ] werfen OT 1
  to **throw away** [ˌθrəʊ əˈweɪ] wegwerfen OT 2
  to **throw up** [θrəʊ ʌp] (sich) übergeben OT 2
thumb [θʌm] Daumen OT 4
thunderstorm [ˈθʌndəstɔːm] Gewitter OT 2
Thursday [ˈθɜːzdeɪ] Donnerstag OT 1
thus [ðʌs] dadurch; daher WS 1, 21
tick [tɪk] Haken; Häkchen OT 2
ticket [ˈtɪkɪt] Eintrittskarte; Fahrkarte OT 1
ticket office [ˈtɪkɪt ˌɒfɪs] Fahrkartenschalter OT 2
to **tidy** [ˈtaɪdi] aufräumen OT 1
tidy [ˈtaɪdi] aufgeräumt OT 2
tie [taɪ] Krawatte OT 1
to **tie** [taɪ] binden; anbinden OT 2
tiger [ˈtaɪɡə] Tiger OT 1
till [tɪl] bis OT 2
to **tilt** [tɪlt] sich neigen OT 3
time [taɪm] Zeit OT 1
  all the time [ɔːl ði: taɪm] die ganze Zeit OT 2
timeline [ˈtaɪmlaɪn] Zeitachse OT 2
timely [ˈtaɪmli] rechtzeitig; passend OT 3
timer [ˈtaɪmər] Timer; Zeituhr WS 2, 70
timetable [ˈtaɪmteɪbl] Fahrplan; Stundenplan OT 1
timing [ˈtaɪmɪŋ] Zeitpunkt OT 3
tin [tɪn] Zinn; Dose OT 2
tinder [ˈtɪndə] Zunder OT 2

Appendix

VOCABULARY

tinned [tɪnd] in Dosen OT 2
tiny [ˈtaɪni] winzig OT 1
tip [tɪp] Spitze; Hinweis OT 1
to **tip over** [tɪp ˈəʊvə] umkippen WS 1, 29
tipping point [ˈtɪpɪŋ pɔɪnt] Kipppunkt; Trendwende WS 1, 27
tired [ˈtaɪəd] müde OT 1
tissue [ˈtɪʃuː] Taschentuch WS 3, 97
title [ˈtaɪtl] Titel OT 1
to [tuː] zu OT 1
toad [təʊd] Kröte OT 2
toast [təʊst] Toast OT 2
tobacco [təˈbækəʊ] Tabak OT 3
today [təˈdeɪ] heute OT 1
toe [təʊ] Zeh OT 1
together [təˈgeðə] zusammen OT 1
toilet [ˈtɔɪlət] Toilette OT 2
   composting toilet [ˈkɒmpɒstɪŋ ˈtɔɪlət] Biotoilette OT 3
token [ˈtəʊkən] Zeichen; Geste WS 1, 38
tolerance [ˈtɒlərəns] Toleranz WS 3, 89
tolerant [ˈtɒlərənt] tolerant OT 4
tomato [təˈmɑːtəʊ] Tomate OT 1
tomboy [ˈtɒmbɔɪ] burschikoses Mädchen; Wildfang WS 3, 93
tomorrow [təˈmɒrəʊ] morgen OT 1
ton [tʌn] Tonne OT 2
tone [təʊn] Ton WS 1, 39
toner cartridge [ˈtəʊnə ˈkɑːtrɪdʒ] Tonerkartusche WS 2, 71
tongue [tʌŋ] Zunge OT 3
tonight [təˈnaɪt] heute Abend OT 1
too [tuː] zu; auch OT 1
tool [tuːl] Werkzeug OT 2
toothbrush [ˈtuːθbrʌʃ] Zahnbürste OT 4
toothpaste [ˈtuːθpeɪst] Zahnpasta OT 4
top [tɒp] obere(r, -s); Spitze OT 1
to **top** [tɒp] belegen OT 3
topic [ˈtɒpɪk] Thema OT 1
torch [tɔːtʃ] Taschenlampe OT 1
torchlight [ˈtɔːtʃlaɪt] Licht der Taschenlampe OT 1
tortoise [ˈtɔːtəs] Schildkröte OT 1
to **toss** [tɒs] werfen OT 3
total [ˈtəʊtl] gesamt OT 1
to **touch** [tʌtʃ] berühren; anfassen OT 1
touchdown [ˈtʌtʃdaʊn] Touchdown OT 2
touchscreen [ˈtʌtʃskriːn] Berührungsbildschirm OT 4
tough [tʌf] hart OT 4
tour [tʊə] Reise; Rundgang OT 1
to **tour** [tʊə] besuchen; besichten WS 1, 29
tourism [ˈtʊərɪzəm] Tourismus OT 2

tourist [ˈtʊərɪst] Tourist(in) OT 1
tournament [ˈtɔːnəmənt] Turnier OT 3
towards [təˈwɔːdz] in Richtung OT 2
towel [ˈtaʊəl] Handtuch OT 2
tower [ˈtaʊə] Turm OT 1
town [taʊn] Stadt OT 1
township [ˈtaʊnʃɪp] Gemeinde OT 4
townspeople [ˈtaʊnzpiːpl] Stadtbewohner(innen) OT 4
towpath [ˈtəʊpɑːθ] Treidelpfad OT 3
toxic [ˈtɒksɪk] toxisch; giftig OT 4
toy [tɔɪ] Spielzeug OT 2
track [træk] Weg OT 1
tractor [ˈtræktə] Traktor OT 2
trade [treɪd] Handel; Geschäft WW, 11
tradition [trəˈdɪʃn] Tradition OT 2
traditional [trəˈdɪʃənl] traditionell OT 1
traffic [ˈtræfɪk] Verkehr OT 1
traffic jam [ˈtræfɪk dʒæm] Stau OT 2
to **traffic** [ˈtræfɪkt] verschleppen; illegalen Handel treiben OT 4
trafficker [ˈtræfɪktə] Schlepper OT 4
tragedy [ˈtrædʒədi] Tragödie WS 4, 145
trail [treɪl] Pfad; Spur OT 2
trailer [ˈtreɪlə] Trailer OT 4
train [treɪn] Zug OT 1
to **train** [treɪn] trainieren OT 2
trainer [ˈtreɪnər] Turnschuh; Trainer(in) OT 4
training [ˈtreɪnɪŋ] Ausbildung OT 2
training course [ˈtreɪnɪŋ kɔːs] Ausbildungslehrgang; Weiterbildungslehrgang OT 2
tram [træm] Straßenbahn OT 1
trans [trænz] trans... WS 3, 93
transatlantic [ˌtrænzətˈlæntɪk] transatlantisch OT 3
to **transcribe** [trænˈskraɪb] abschreiben; transkribieren WS 2, 58
transcriber [trænˈskraɪbə] Transkribierer(in) WS 2, 58
transcript [ˈtrænskrɪpt] Abschrift; Niederschrift WS 1, 21
to **transfer** [trænsˈfɜː] transferieren; übertragen OT 4
to **transform** [trænsˈfɔːm] verändern OT 4
transformation [ˌtrænsfəˈmeɪʃn] Veränderung; Verwandlung OT 4
transgender [trænzˈdʒendər] transsexuell WS 3, 93
transition [trænˈzɪʃn] Wechsel; Übergang WS 2, 67
to **translate** [trænsˈleɪt] übersetzen OT 1

transplant [trænsˈplɑːnt] Transplantation OT 3
transport [ˈtrænspɔːt] Verkehr; Verkehrsmittel OT 2
to **trap** [træp] fangen WS 3, 93
trash [træʃ] Abfall OT 2
   trash can [ˈtræʃ kæn] Mülleimer OT 2
trauma [ˈtrɔːmə] Trauma WS 1, 38
travel [ˈtrævl] Reisen OT 1
to **travel** [ˈtrævl] reisen OT 1
travel agent [ˈtrævl eɪdʒənt] Reisekauffrau / -mann OT 3
traveller [ˈtrævələ] Reisende(r) OT 3
tray [treɪ] Tablett OT 2
treadmill [ˈtredmɪl] Laufband OT 4
treasure [ˈtreʒə] Schatz OT 3
to **treat** [triːt] behandeln OT 4
treatment [ˈtriːtmənt] Behandlung WS 1, 38
tree [triː] Baum OT 1
to **trek** [trek] trecken OT 2
to **tremble** [ˈtrembl] zittern OT 2
trend [trend] Trend OT 4
trespasser [ˈtrespəsər] Unbefugte(r) WS 4, 144
trial [ˈtraɪəl] Prozess OT 2
triangle [ˈtraɪæŋgl] Dreieck; Triangel OT 2
triangular [traɪˈæŋgjələ] dreieckig OT 3
tribal [ˈtraɪbl] Stammes... OT 3
tribe [traɪb] Stamm OT 3
trick [trɪk] Trick WS 3, 104
tricky [ˈtrɪki] kompliziert OT 4
trilogy [ˈtrɪlədʒi] Trilogie WS 1, 29
trip [trɪp] Reise; Ausflug OT 1
to **trip** [trɪp] stolpern OT 2
trolley [ˈtrɒli] Wagen OT 1
trophy [ˈtrəʊfi] Pokal OT 2
tropical [ˈtrɒpɪkl] tropisch OT 4
to **trot** [trɒt] traben OT 2
trouble [ˈtrʌbl] Schwierigkeit; Ärger OT 2
trousers [ˈtraʊzəz] Hose OT 1
truck [trʌk] Laster; Lastkraftwagen OT 1
true [truː] wahr; richtig OT 1
truly [ˈtruːli] wirklich WS 1, 43
trumpet [ˈtrʌmpɪt] Trompete OT 2
trunk [trʌŋk] Kofferraum OT 2
to **trust** [trʌst] vertrauen OT 3
truth [truːθ] Wahrheit OT 3
to **try** [traɪ] versuchen OT 1
   to **try out** [traɪ aʊt] ausprobieren OT 2
tube [tjuːb] Schlauch; Londoner U-Bahn OT 1

Appendix

VOCABULARY

Tuesday [ˈtjuːzdeɪ] Dienstag OT 1
tuition [tjuˈɪʃn] Studiengebühr(en) **WS 2**, 64
tuna [ˈtjuːnə] Thunfisch OT 1
tunnel [ˈtʌnl] Tunnel OT 3
turbine [ˈtɜːbaɪn] Turbine OT 4
turkey [ˈtɜːki] Truthahn OT 1
turn: It's your turn. [ˌɪts ˈjɔː tɜːn] Du bist dran. OT 1
to **turn** [tɜːn] drehen OT 2
  to **turn off** [tɜːn ˈɒf] ausschalten OT 2
turntable [ˈtɜːnteɪbl] Drehscheibe OT 2
turtle [ˈtɜːtl] Schildkröte OT 2
  leatherback turtle [ˈleðəbæk ˌtɜːtl] Lederrückenschildkröte OT 2
tusk [tʌsk] Stoßzahn OT 3
tutor [ˈtjuːtə] Tutor(in) OT 4
to **tutor** [ˈtjuːtə] Nachhilfeunterricht geben OT 4
TV [ˌtiːˈviː] Fernsehen OT 1
tweezers [ˈtwiːzəz] Pinzette OT 2
twelve [twelv] zwölf OT 1
twenty [ˈtwenti] zwanzig OT 1
twice [twaɪs] zweimal OT 2
twig [twɪɡ] Zweig OT 2
twin [twɪn] Zwilling OT 1
to **twinkle** [ˈtwɪŋkl] glitzern OT 4
twisted [ˈtwɪstɪd] verdreht OT 1
two [tuː] zwei OT 1
type [taɪp] Art OT 2
typewriter [ˈtaɪpraɪtə] Schreibmaschine **WS 2**, 82
typical [ˈtɪpɪkl] typisch OT 2
typist [ˈtaɪpɪst] Schreibkraft **WS 2**, 58
tyrannosaurus rex [tɪˌrænəˈsɔːrəs ˈreks] Tyrannosaurus rex OT 1

U

ugly [ˈʌɡli] hässlich OT 1
umbrella [ʌmˈbrelə] Regenschirm OT 1
unacceptable [ˌʌnəkˈseptəbl] inakzeptabel **WS 1**, 25
unaccompanied minor [ˌʌnəkʌmpənid ˈmaɪnə] alleinreisendes Kind OT 2
unaware [ˌʌnəˈweər] in Unkenntnis; unwissend **WS 4**, 145
unbelievable [ˌʌnbɪˈliːvəbl] unglaublich OT 2
uncle [ˈʌŋkl] Onkel OT 1
uncomfortable [ʌnˈkʌmftəbl] unbequem OT 3
uncountable [ʌnˈkaʊntəbl] unzählbar OT 1
to **uncover** [ʌnˈkʌvə] freilegen OT 3

undecided [ˌʌndɪˈsaɪdɪd] unentschieden; unentschlossen **WS 1**, 19
under [ˈʌndə] unter OT 1
underdog [ˈʌndədɒɡ] Außenseiter(in); Underdog **WS 1**, 21
to **undergo** [ˌʌndəˈɡəʊ] durchmachen **WS 4**, 145
underground [ˈʌndəɡraʊnd] U-Bahn OT 1
to **underline** [ˌʌndəˈlaɪn] unterstreichen OT 1
underneath [ˌʌndəˈniːθ] darunter OT 3
to **understand** [ˌʌndəˈstænd] verstehen OT 1
to **understate** [ˌʌndəˈsteɪt] unterbewerten; untertreiben **WW**, 11
underwater [ˌʌndəˈwɔːtə] Unterwasser-; unter Wasser OT 2
underworld [ˈʌndəwɜːld] Unterwelt **WS 4**, 126
undocumented [ʌnˈdɒkjumentɪd] nicht erfasst OT 4
undrained [ʌnˈdreɪnd] nicht abgetropft OT 2
undrinkable [ʌnˈdrɪŋkəbl] untrinkbar **WS 1**, 23
unemployed [ˌʌnɪmˈplɔɪd] arbeitslos **WS 2**, 65
unemployment [ˌʌnɪmˈplɔɪmənt] Arbeitslosigkeit OT 3
unexpected [ˌʌnɪkˈspektɪd] unerwartet **WS 3**, 107
  unexpectedly [ˌʌnɪkˈspektɪdli] unerwarteterweise OT 3
unfair [ˌʌnˈfeə] nicht fair OT 2
unfairness [ˌʌnˈfeənəs] Ungerechtigkeit; Unfairness OT 4
unforgettable [ˌʌnfəˈɡetəbl] unvergesslich **WS 4**, 126
unfortunately [ʌnˈfɔːtʃənətli] leider OT 3
unfriendly [ʌnˈfrendli] unfreundlich OT 4
unhappy [ʌnˈhæpi] unglücklich OT 1
unhealthy [ʌnˈhelθi] ungesund OT 1
uni [ˈjuːni] Uni OT 3
uniform [ˈjuːnɪfɔːm] Uniform OT 1
to **unify** [ˈjuːnɪfaɪ] vereinigen **WS 3**, 115
union [ˈjuːniən] Union; Bund **WS 3**, 91
unique [juˈniːk] einzigartig OT 2
unisex [ˈjuːnɪseks] Unisex-; nicht geschlechtsspezifisch **WS 3**, 93
unit [ˈjuːnɪt] Einheit **WS 3**, 90
to **unite** [juˈnaɪt] sich vereinigen **WS 1**, 13

unity [ˈjuːnəti] Einheit **WS 1**, 30
universal [ˌjuːnɪˈvɜːsl] allgemein; universal **WS 2**, 58
university [ˌjuːnɪˈvɜːsəti] Universität OT 1
unknown [ˌʌnˈnəʊn] unbekannt OT 3
unless [ənˈles] außer wenn OT 4
unlike [ˌʌnˈlaɪk] anders als OT 3
  unlikely [ʌnˈlaɪkli] unwahrscheinlich OT 4
to **unlock** [ˌʌnˈlɒk] aufschließen; entriegeln OT 1
unlucky [ʌnˈlʌki] glücklos OT 2
unnecessary [ʌnˈnesəsəri] unnötig; überflüssig OT 4
to **unpack** [ˌʌnˈpæk] auspacken OT 2
unpaid [ˌʌnˈpeɪd] unbezahlt **WS 2**, 54
unpredictability [ˌʌnprɪˌdɪktəˈbɪləti] Unberechenbarkeit OT 2
unsafe [ʌnˈseɪf] gefährlich OT 3
unspoilt [ˌʌnˈspɔɪlt] unberührt OT 3
unsurprisingly [ˌʌnsəˈpraɪzɪŋli] erwartungsgemäß OT 3
until [ʌnˈtɪl] bis OT 3
unusual [ʌnˈjuːʒuəl] ungewöhnlich OT 2
unwell [ʌnˈwel] krank OT 2
up [ʌp] hinauf; nach oben OT 1
upbringing [ˈʌpbrɪŋɪŋ] Erziehung **WS 2**, 68
to **update** [ˈʌpdeɪt] aktualisieren OT 3
to **upload** [ˈʌpləʊd] hochladen OT 3
upset [ʌpˈset] verärgert; traurig OT 2
upside [ˈʌpsaɪd] Vorteil OT 4
upstairs [ˌʌpˈsteəz] oben; im oberen Stockwerk OT 1
uptight [ˌʌpˈtaɪt] verklemmt **WS 3**, 90
upwards [ˈʊpwədz] aufwärts; nach oben OT 3
urban [ˈɜːbən] städtisch; urban OT 4
to **urge** [ɜːdʒ] dringend bitten; drängen OT 4
urgently [ˈɜːdʒəntli] dringend **WS 1**, 26
us [ʌs] uns OT 1
to **use** [juːz] benutzen OT 1
useful [ˈjuːsfl] nützlich OT 1
user [ˈjuːzə] Benutzer(in) OT 2
usher [ˈʌʃə] Platzanweiser(in) OT 4
usual [ˈjuːʒuəl] üblich OT 2
  usually [ˈjuːʒuəli] normalerweise OT 1

V

vacation [veɪˈkeɪʃn] Urlaub OT 2
to **vacuum** [ˈvækjuːm] staubsaugen OT 4

270 two hundred and seventy

Appendix

VOCABULARY

vacuum cleaner [ˈvækjuːm kliːnə] Staubsauger OT 4
vague [veɪg] unbestimmt; vage WS 1, 24
valley [ˈvæli] Tal OT 1
valuable [ˈvæljuəbl] wertvoll OT 2
value [ˈvæljuː] Wert OT 4
vampire [ˈvæmpaɪə] Vampir(in) OT 2
van [væn] Transporter; Lieferwagen OT 4
to **vandalize** [ˈvændəlaɪz] zerstören; verwüsten WS 4, 128
vanilla [vəˈnɪlə] Vanille OT 1
variation [ˌveəriˈeɪʃn] Variante; Variation WS 1, 31
variety [vəˈraɪəti] Vielfalt; Auswahl WS 1, 24
various [ˈveəriəs] verschiedene WS 1, 22
varnish [ˈvɑːnɪʃ] Lack WS 2, 64
to **vary** [ˈveəri] variieren WS 3, 109
vast [vɑːst] enorm; groß WS 3, 106
vegan [ˈviːgən] Veganer(in); vegan OT 1
vegetable [ˈvedʒtəbl] Gemüse OT 1
vegetarian [ˌvedʒəˈteəriən] Vegetarier(in); vegetarisch OT 1
veggie [ˈvedʒi] vegetarisch OT 2
vehicle [ˌviːəkl] Fahrzeug OT 1
  off-road vehicle [ˈɒf rəʊd ˌviːəkl] Geländefahrzeug OT 1
vein [veɪn] Vene; Ader WS 1, 21
velvety [ˈvelvəti] samtartig OT 2
vending machine [ˈvendɪŋ məʃiːn] Automat OT 1
venom [ˈvenəm] Gift WS 1, 38
venue [ˈvenjuː] Veranstaltungsort OT 3
verb [vɜːb] Verb; Zeitwort OT 1
verbal [ˈvɜːbl] verbal; mündlich WS 2, 61
versatile [ˈvɜːsətaɪl] vielseitig OT 3
verse [vɜːs] Strophe OT 1
version [ˈvɜːʒn] Version OT 3
versus [ˈvɜːsəs] versus OT 4
vertical [ˈvɜːtɪkl] senkrecht; vertikal OT 4
very [ˈveri] sehr OT 1
vest [vest] Weste; Unterhemd OT 2
vet [vet] Tierarzt / -ärztin OT 4
veterinarian [ˌvetərɪˈneəriən] Tierarzt / -ärztin OT 4
via [ˈviːə] über OT 2
vibrant [ˈvaɪbrənt] dynamisch; lebhaft WS 1, 19
to **vibrate** [vaɪˈbreɪt] vibrieren; pulsieren OT 4
victim [ˈvɪktɪm] Opfer OT 4

video [ˈvɪdiəʊ] Videokassette; Video OT 1
video clip [ˈvɪdiəʊ klɪp] Videoclip OT 2
video game [ˈvɪdiəʊ geɪm] Videospiel OT 2
view [vjuː] Sicht; Aussicht OT 1
viewer [ˈvjuːə] Zuschauer(in) OT 3
viewing gallery [ˈvjuːɪŋ gæləri] Aussichtsgalerie OT 1
viewpoint [ˈvjuːpɔɪnt] Aussichtspunkt OT 3
village [ˈvɪlɪdʒ] Dorf OT 1
villager [ˈvɪlɪdʒə] Dorfbewohner(in) OT 4
vintage [ˈvɪntɪdʒ] alt; klassisch WS 2, 52
violence [ˈvaɪələns] Gewalt OT 4
  non-violence [ˌnɒn ˈvaɪələns] Gewaltlosigkeit OT 3
violent [ˈvaɪələnt] gewalttätig WS 1, 27
violet [ˈvaɪələt] violett OT 1
violin [ˌvaɪəˈlɪn] Geige OT 1
virtual [ˈvɜːtʃuəl] virtuell OT 4
visa [ˈviːzə] Visum OT 4
vision [ˈvɪʒn] Vision OT 4
to **visit** [ˈvɪzɪt] besuchen OT 1
visitor [ˈvɪzɪtə] Besucher(in) OT 1
visual [ˈvɪʒuəl] Bildmaterial OT 4
visual [ˈvɪʒuəl] visuell OT 2
  visually [ˈvɪʒuəli] optisch; visuell WS 2, 60
visual aid [ˌvɪʒuəl ˈeɪd] Anschauungsmaterial OT 4
visual art [ˈvɪʒuəl ˈɑːt] bildende Kunst OT 2
visualization [ˌvɪʒuəlaɪˈzeɪʃn] Visualisierung OT 3
vital [ˈvaɪtl] lebenswichtig OT 4
vlog [vlɒg] Vlog; Video-Blog OT 3
vlogger [ˈvlɒgə] Vlogger(in) OT 3
vocals [ˈvəʊklz] Gesang OT 2
vocational [vəʊˈkeɪʃənl] beruflich WS 2, 50
voice [vɔɪs] Stimme OT 2
  tone of voice [təʊn əv vɔɪs] Tonfall; Artikulierung OT 4
to **voice** [vɔɪs] äußern; zum Ausdruck bringen OT 4
volleyball [ˈvɒlibɔːl] Volleyball OT 3
volunteer [ˌvɒlənˈtɪə] Freiwillige(r); Ehrenamtliche(r) OT 2
to **volunteer** [ˌvɒlənˈtɪə] (sich) freiwillig melden; ein Ehrenamt haben OT 2
to **vote** [vəʊt] wählen OT 1
vowel [ˈvaʊəl] Vokal; Selbstlaut OT 1
voyage [ˈvɔɪɪdʒ] Reise OT 3

W
wacky [ˈwæki] verrückt; verdreht OT 4
waffle [ˈwɒfl] Waffel OT 3
wage [weɪdʒ] Gehalt OT 4
wagon [ˈwægən] Wagen OT 4
wagon train [ˈwægən treɪn] Treck; Wagenzug OT 4
to **wait** [weɪt] warten OT 1
waiter [ˈweɪtə] Kellner(in) OT 1
to **wake up** [ˈweɪk ʌp] aufwachen OT 1
walk [wɔːk] Spaziergang; Wanderung OT 2
to **walk** [wɔːk] laufen; gehen (zu Fuß) OT 1
walker [ˈwɔːkə] Wanderer / Wanderin OT 3
wall [wɔːl] Wand OT 1
wall display [ˈwɔːl dɪˈspleɪ] Wandzeitung OT 2
wallet [ˈwɒlɪt] Brieftasche OT 1
to **want** [wɒnt] wollen OT 1
war [wɔː] Krieg OT 2
wardrobe [ˈwɔːdrəʊb] Kleiderschrank OT 1
warm [wɔːm] warm OT 2
warm-up [ˈwɔːm ʌp] Aufwärmübung OT 2
to **warm up** [ˈwɔːm ʌp] aufwärmen OT 2
to **warn** [wɔːn] warnen OT 3
warrior [ˈwɒriə] Krieger(in) OT 2
warship [ˈwɔːʃɪp] Kriegsschiff OT 3
to **wash** [wɒʃ] waschen OT 2
washing up [ˌwɒʃɪŋ ˈʌp] Geschirrspülen OT 2
wasp [wɒsp] Wespe OT 3
waste [weɪst] Abfall OT 3
to **waste** [weɪst] verschwenden OT 3
to **watch** [wɒtʃ] beobachten OT 1
watchman [ˈwɒtʃmən] Wächter WS 4, 126
water [ˈwɔːtə] Wasser OT 1
waterbus [ˈwɔːtə bʌs] Wasserbus OT 3
waterfall [ˈwɔːtəfɔːl] Wasserfall OT 1
waterhole [ˈwɔːtəhəʊl] Wasserloch WS 1, 20
watering hole [ˈwɔːtərɪŋ həʊl] Wasserstelle WS 1, 23
waterproof [ˈwɔːtəpruːf] wasserdicht OT 2
waterproofs [ˈwɔːtəpruːfs] wasserdichte Kleidung OT 3
wave [weɪv] Welle OT 1
to **wave** [weɪv] winken OT 2
way [weɪ] Weg OT 1

Appendix

VOCABULARY

waypoint [ˈweɪpɔɪnt] Zwischenstation OT 2
we [wi] wir OT 1
weak [wiːk] schwach OT 3
weakness [ˈwiːknəs] Schwäche OT 4
wealth [welθ] Reichtum; Vermögen OT 4
weapon [ˈwepən] Waffe OT 3
to wear [weə] tragen OT 1
weather [ˈweðə] Wetter OT 1
webinar [ˈwebɪnɑː] Webinar OT 4
website [ˈwebsaɪt] Webseite OT 1
to wed [wedɪd] heiraten OT 3
wedding [ˈwedɪŋ] Hochzeit OT 3
Wednesday [ˈwenzdeɪ] Mittwoch OT 1
weed [wiːd] Unkraut WS 1, 28
week [wiːk] Woche OT 1
weekday [ˈwiːkdeɪ] Wochentag OT 3
weekend [ˈwiːkend] Wochenende OT 1
weekly [ˈwiːkli] wöchentlich OT 3
to weigh [weɪ] wiegen OT 3
weight [weɪt] Gewicht OT 4
weightlessness [ˈweɪtləsnəs] Schwerelosigkeit OT 4
weightlifting [ˈweɪtlɪftɪŋ] Gewichtheben OT 4
weird [wɪəd] seltsam OT 1
welcome [ˈwelkəm] willkommen OT 1
well [wel] also OT 1
   well done [wel ˈdʌn] gut gemacht OT 1
wellness [ˈwelnəs] Wellness; Wohlbefinden OT 4
Welsh [welʃ] walisisch OT 1
west [west] West- OT 1
westward [ˈwestwəd] westwärts OT 4
wet [wet] nass OT 2
wetsuit [ˈwetsuːt] Taucheranzug; Neoprenanzug OT 1
whale [weɪl] Wal OT 1
whaling [ˈweɪlɪŋ] Walfang OT 2
what [wɒt] was OT 1
whatever [wɒˈtevə] was auch immer; egal welche OT 3
wheat [wiːt] Weizen WS 1, 27
wheel [wiːl] Rad OT 1
wheelchair [ˈwiːltʃeə] Rollstuhl OT 2
wheelchair user [ˈwiːltʃeə ˌjuːzə] Rollstuhlfahrer(in) OT 2
when [wen] wann OT 1
whenever [wenˈevə] wann auch immer OT 4
where [weə] wo OT 1
whereas [ˌweərˈæz] während WS 2, 68
wherever [weərˈevə] wo (auch) immer OT 3

whether [ˈweðə] ob; falls; wann OT 1
which [wɪtʃ] welche(r, -s) OT 1
while [waɪl] während OT 1
whistle [ˈwɪsl] Pfeife OT 2
to whistle [ˈwɪsl] pfeifen OT 2
white [waɪt] weiß OT 1
to whizz [wɪz] zischen OT 2
who [huː] wer / wen / wem OT 1
whoever [huːˈevə] wer auch immer OT 4
whole [həʊl] ganz OT 1
whose [huːz] wessen; dessen / deren OT 2
why [waɪ] warum OT 1
wicket [ˈwɪkɪt] Wicket; Törchen OT 1
wide [waɪd] weit OT 2
wife [waɪf] Frau; Ehefrau OT 1
wild [waɪld] wild OT 2
wilderness [ˈwɪldənəs] Wildnis OT 2
wildfire [ˈwaɪldfaɪə] Waldbrand OT 2
wildlife [ˈwaɪldlaɪf] Tierwelt; Pflanzenwelt OT 2
willing: to be willing [bi ˈwɪlɪŋ] bereit sein OT 4
wimp [wɪmp] Feigling; Schwachmat WS 3, 94
to win [wɪn] gewinnen OT 1
wind [wɪnd] Wind OT 2
to wind [ˈwaɪnd] sich schlängeln; winden WS 1, 20
windlass [ˈwɪndləs] Winsch OT 3
window [ˈwɪndəʊ] Fenster OT 1
to windsurf [ˈwɪndsɜːf] windsurfen OT 1
windsurfer [ˈwɪndsɜːfə] Windsurfer(in) OT 1
windsurfing [ˈwɪndsɜːfɪŋ] Windsurfen OT 1
windy [ˈwɪndi] windig OT 2
wine [waɪn] Wein OT 1
wing [wɪŋ] Flügel OT 1
winner [ˈwɪnə] Gewinner(in); Sieger(in) OT 1
winning [ˈwɪnɪŋ] gewinnend WS 2, 56
winter [ˈwɪntə] Winter OT 1
wipe [waɪp] Wischtuch OT 4
wisdom tooth [ˈwɪzdəm] Weisheitszahn WS 2, 63
to wish [wɪʃ] wünschen OT 3
witch [wɪtʃ] Hexe OT 2
with [wɪð] mit OT 1
within [wɪˈðɪn] innerhalb OT 4
without [wɪˈðaʊt] ohne OT 2
to witness [ˈwɪtnəs] Zeuge einer Sache sein; beobachten WS 3, 107
woman [ˈwʊmən] Frau OT 1
wombat [ˈwɒmbæt] Wombat WS 1, 26

to wonder [ˈwʌndə] sich fragen OT 3
wonderful [ˈwʌndəfl] wunderbar OT 1
wood [wʊd] Holz OT 2
wood-burning [ˈwʊdˈbɜːnɪŋ] holzverbrennend OT 4
wooden [ˈwʊdn] hölzern OT 1
wool [wʊl] Wolle OT 2
woolly [ˈwʊli] wollig; aus Wolle OT 2
word [wɜːd] Wort OT 1
to work [wɜːk] arbeiten OT 1
   to work out [wɜːk aʊt] herausfinden OT 2
workbook [ˈwɜːkbʊk] Arbeitsheft OT 1
worker [ˈwɜːkə] Arbeiter(in) OT 2
workforce [ˈwɜːkfɔːs] Arbeitskräfte WW, 11
workload [ˈwɜːkləʊd] Arbeitsbelastung; Arbeitslast WS 2, 69
workman [ˈwɜːkmən] Arbeiter OT 3
workout [ˈwɜːkaʊt] Fitnesstraining WS 1, 14
workplace [ˈwɜːkpleɪs] Arbeitsplatz OT 2
work placement [ˈwɜːk pleɪsmənt] Praktikum WS 2, 50
workshop [ˈwɜːkʃɒp] Werkstatt OT 1
workspace [ˈwɜːkspeɪs] Arbeitsbereich WS 2, 70
world [wɜːld] Welt OT 1
worldwide [ˌwɜːldˈwaɪd] weltweit OT 3
worm [wɜːm] Wurm OT 1
worried [ˈwʌrid] besorgt OT 1
to worry [ˈwʌri] (sich) Sorgen machen OT 1
   No worries. [nəʊ ˈwʌriz] Keine Sorge. OT 2
to worsen [ˈwɜːsn] verschlechtern; verschlimmern WS 1, 27
to worship [ˈwɜːʃɪp] eine Religion ausüben; anbeten OT 4
worth [wɜːθ] lohnenswert OT 4
   to be worth it [wɜːθ ɪt] (sich) lohnen OT 1
worthwhile [ˌwɜːθˈwaɪl] lohnend OT 2
Wow! [waʊ] Toll! OT 1
wowed [waʊd] entzückt; begeistert OT 4
to wrap [ræp] einwickeln OT 2
wreath [riːθ] Kranz OT 3
wreck [rek] Wrack OT 3
wrestling [ˈreslɪŋ] Ringen OT 2
to wriggle [ˈrɪgl] schlängeln OT 2
wrist [rɪst] Handgelenk OT 1
wristband [ˈrɪstbænd] Armband OT 4
to write [raɪt] schreiben OT 1

Appendix
VOCABULARY

to **write down** [ˌraɪt ˈdaʊn] aufschreiben OT 2
writer [ˈraɪtə] Autor(in); Schriftsteller(in) OT 2
writing [ˈraɪtɪŋ] Schreiben OT 1
wrong [rɒŋ] falsch OT 1
  What's wrong? [wɒts ˈrɒŋ] Was ist los? OT 2

X
X-ray [ˈeks reɪ] Röntgen OT 1

Y
yacht [jɒt] Jacht OT 2
yard [jɑːd] Garten OT 2
yeah [jeə] ja OT 1
year [jɪə] Jahr OT 1
yellow [ˈjeləʊ] gelb OT 1
yes [jes] ja OT 1
yesterday [ˈjestədeɪ] gestern OT 1
yet [jet] noch; schon OT 2
yoga [ˈjəʊɡə] Yoga **WS 2**, 71
yoghurt [ˈjɒɡət] Joghurt OT 1
you [juː] du / Sie; man OT 1
young [jʌŋ] jung OT 1
your [jɔː] dein / Ihr; euer / Ihr OT 1
yours [jɔːz] deine(r, -s); eure(r, -s); ihre(r, -s) OT 2
yourself [jəˈself] dich / sich; dich / sich (selbst) OT 1
youth [juːθ] Jugend OT 1
youth hostel [ˈjuːθ hɒstl] Jugendherberge OT 2
yuck [jʌk] Igitt! OT 3

Z
zebra [ˈzebrə] Zebra OT 1
zebra crossing [ˌzebrə ˈkrɒsɪŋ] Zebrastreifen OT 1
zero [ˈzɪərəʊ] null OT 1
zip [zɪp] Reißverschluss OT 1
zip line [ˈzɪp laɪn] Seilrutsche OT 1
zombie [ˈzɒmbi] Zombie OT 2
zone [zəʊn] Zone OT 2
zoo [zuː] Zoo OT 1
zucchini [zuˈkiːni] Zucchini OT 3

Dictionary: German – English

3
3D-Druck 3D printing OT 1

A
Aal eel OT 4
abdecken to cover OT 2
Abdeckung cover OT 1
Abend evening OT 1
Abendessen dinner OT 1
Abenteuer adventure OT 1
abenteuerlustig adventurous OT 2
aber but OT 1
Abfahrt exit; departure OT 2
Abfall garbage; trash OT 2; waste OT 3; spoilage; scrap OT 4
    herumliegende Abfälle litter OT 2
Abflug departure OT 2
Abfluggate departure gate OT 2
Abflugschalter check-in desk OT 2
abgefüllt bottled OT 3
abgelegen remote WS 1, 13
Abgeordnete MP (Members of Parliament) WS 1, 44
abgetropft drained OT 2
    nicht abgetropft undrained OT 2
abgießen to drain OT 2
abhalten to prevent OT 4
abhängen to hang out OT 1
    abhängen (von) to depend OT 2
abhängig addicted OT 3
abholen to fetch OT 4
Abholzung deforestation WS 1, 41
Abklärung clarification OT 4
abkürzen to shorten WS 2, 67
Abkürzung abbreviation WS 3, 106
Ablauf sequence OT 4
Abmessung dimension OT 2
abnagen to gnaw OT 2
abonnieren to subscribe WW, 11
abreißen to demolish WS 1, 23
absagen to cancel OT 4
Absatz paragraph OT 1
abschätzen to measure OT 4
abschließen to finish OT 1; to lock OT 2; to finalize WS 3, 109
Abschluss degree OT 4
Abschnitt segment WS 1, 30
abschreiben to transcribe WS 2, 58
Abschrift transcript WS 1, 21
abseilen to abseil OT 2
Absender(in) sender OT 3
Absicht aim OT 4

absichtlich deliberately WS 4, 145
absolut absolute OT 3
Absolvent(in) alumnus OT 4
absprengen to blast WS 3, 104
abstammen von to descend from WS 3, 91
Abstammung descent WS 1, 31
abstauben to dust off WS 1, 21
absteigend downward WS 1, 21
Abstellraum storeroom WS 3, 121
abstoßend revolting OT 2
abstrakt abstract WS 4, 145
Abteilung department WS 2, 55
abwärts downward WS 1, 21
Abwasch: den Abwasch machen to do the dishes OT 2
abwechseln to take turns OT 1
abweichen to differ WS 4, 144
abwischen to dust off WS 1, 21
Abzeichen badge OT 1
Achse axis OT 4
Achseln zucken to shrug WS 3, 97
acht eight OT 1
achten to respect OT 3
achtzehn eighteen OT 1
achtzig eighty OT 1
Ackerland farmland OT 4
Ader vein WS 1, 21
Adjektiv adjective OT 1
Adler eagle OT 2
Adrenalinstoß adrenaline rush OT 1
Adresse address OT 1
Adverb adverb OT 1
Affe monkey OT 2
afrikanisch African OT 2
Agakröte cane toad WS 4, 143
Agentur agency OT 4
aggressiv aggressive OT 3
ähnlich similar OT 2
Ähnlichkeit similarity OT 3
Ahorn maple OT 3
akademisch academic WW, 11
    einen akademischen Grad erlangen to graduate OT 3
Akkordeon accordion OT 2
Akrostichon acrostic WS 1, 20
Aktion action OT 1; campaign OT 3
aktiv energetic OT 2; active OT 4
aktivieren to activate OT 4
Aktivismus activism OT 4
Aktivist(in) activist WS 2, 52
Aktivität activity OT 1

aktualisieren to update OT 3
aktuell current OT 4
akustisch acoustic OT 2
Akzent accent OT 1
akzeptabel acceptable WS 3, 116
Alarm alarm OT 2
alarmieren to alert OT 2
alaskisch Alaskan OT 2
albern silly OT 1
Albtraum nightmare OT 4
Album album OT 3
Algorithmus algorithm WS 2, 69
Alkohol alcohol OT 3
alkoholisch alcoholic OT 3
alle all; everybody OT 1
Allee avenue OT 1
allein on one's own OT 2
    alleinreisendes Kind unaccompanied minor OT 2
Allergie allergy OT 1
allergisch allergic OT 2
alles all; everything OT 1
allgemein general OT 3; universal WS 2, 58
    im Allgemeinen generally OT 4
Alliteration alliteration WS 4, 145
alltäglich everyday OT 3
Alpaka alpaca OT 2
Alphabet alphabet OT 1
alphabetisch alphabetical OT 2
als as; than OT 1
also like; so; well OT 1
alt old OT 1; vintage WS 2, 52
Alter age OT 1
    im Alter von aged OT 1
älter elderly OT 4
Alternative alternative OT 2
Älteste(r) elder WS 1, 21
altmodisch old-fashioned OT 4
Ambition ambition OT 4
amerikanisch American OT 1
Amphitheater amphitheatre OT 3
Amtsperson official OT 3
amüsant entertaining OT 3; amusing WS 2, 80
amüsiert amused OT 3
an at; on OT 1
analphabetisch illiterate OT 4
Analyse analysis WS 3, 108
analysieren to analyse OT 3
Ananas pineapple OT 3
anbauen to grow OT 1; to cultivate OT 4

Appendix

VOCABULARY

anbeten to worship OT 4
anbieten to offer OT 2
anbinden to tie OT 2
Andachtshaus meetinghouse OT 4
andauern to continue OT 1; to last OT 2
andere(r, -s) other OT 1
ändern to change OT 1
anders als unlike OT 3
Änderung change OT 1
Aneignung appropriation WS 1, 38
Anekdote anecdote OT 4
anerkannt certified WS 4, 139
anerkennen to acknowledge WS 1, 21; to appreciate WS 2, 67
Anerkennung recognition WS 1, 38
Anfang start OT 1
anfangen to start; to take up; to begin OT 1; to commence OT 4
anfangs initially WS 1, 41
Anfangs… introductory WS 3, 103
anfassen to feel; to touch OT 1
anfreunden to make friends OT 2
anführen to cite OT 2
Anführung (einer Quelle) citation OT 2
Anführungszeichen quotation mark OT 2
angeben to indicate WS 2, 68
Angebot offer OT 1
Angehörige relative OT 1
Angelegenheit issue; matter OT 2
Angeln fishing OT 2
angemessen appropriately OT 3; appropriate OT 4; adequate WS 4, 146
angenehm enjoyable OT 2; pleasant WS 1, 13
anschalten to switch on OT 1
angeschlossen hyper-connected OT 4
Angestellte(r) employee OT 4
angestrengt stressed OT 2
angetrieben powered OT 4
angreifen to attack; to tackle OT 3
angrenzend adjoining OT 3
Angriff assault WS 3, 100
Angst fear OT 3
 Angst machen to scare OT 2
ängstlich afraid OT 2
anhalten to stop OT 1
anhaltend prolonged WS 1, 23
Anhänger(in) follower OT 3
anheben to lift OT 3
Ankauf purchase OT 4
ankern to anchor OT 4
anklagen to charge WS 3, 100
anklicken to click on OT 3
ankommen to arrive OT 1
Ankunft arrival OT 2

geschätzte Ankunftszeit ETA (estimated time of arrival) OT 2
Anlage facility OT 4
anlegen to moor OT 3
Anlegeplatz mooring OT 3
Anliegen cause OT 2
Anmeldeliste sign-up sheet OT 2
anmelden to register OT 4
annehmen to suppose OT 1; to accept OT 3; to adopt WS 1, 30
 wieder annehmen to resume WS 1, 24
anordnen to mandate WW, 11
anpassen to conform WS 3, 93
Anpassung assimilation OT 4
anpassungsfähig flexible; adaptable OT 4
anregend motivating WS 3, 108
Anruf call OT 1
 einen Anruf entgegennehmen to take a call OT 2
anrufen to call OT 1
Anrufer(in) caller OT 2
Ansage announcement OT 2
ansagen to announce OT 2
anschauen to look at OT 1
Anschauungsmaterial visual aid OT 4
anscheinend apparently OT 4
Anschlagbrett noticeboard OT 1
Anschlagtafel bulletin board OT 4
anschließen to fasten OT 1
ansehen to look at OT 1
Ansicht attitude OT 3
ansiedeln to settle OT 4
Ansiedler(in) colonizer WS 1, 20
ansonsten otherwise WS 2, 54
Anspannung tension OT 4
Anspitzer pencil sharpener OT 1
anständig proper OT 3
anstehen to queue OT 4
anstoßen to bump into OT 2
anstrengen: sich anstrengen to struggle WS 2, 64
Anstrengung effort WW, 11
Anteil proportion WS 2, 64
Antenne antenna OT 2
antibiotisch antibiotic WS 3, 103
antik ancient OT 2
antiseptisch antiseptic OT 2
Antrag petition OT 3; application OT 4
Antwort answer OT 1; response WS 3, 118
antworten to reply OT 1
anwachsen to increase OT 3
Anwalt / Anwältin counsel WS 3, 101
Anweisung instruction OT 1; direction OT 3

Anzahl quantity OT 4
anziehen to attract OT 4
 anziehend attractive OT 4
 rasch anziehen to slip on WS 1, 16
Anzug suit OT 1
anzünden to light WS 1, 40
Apfel apple OT 1
Apotheke chemist's shop; drugstore; pharmacy OT 2
Apotheker(in) chemist; pharmacist OT 2
App app OT 4
appetitlich appetizing OT 3
applaudieren to applaud OT 2
Applaus applause OT 2
April April OT 1
Aquädukt aqueduct OT 3
aquatisch aquatic OT 4
Äquator equator WS 1, 13
Ära era OT 4
Arbeit labour OT 4; employment WS 2, 50
 gute Arbeit leisten to do a good / great job OT 2
arbeiten to work OT 1
Arbeiter workman OT 3
Arbeiter(in) worker OT 2
Arbeitgeber(in) employer OT 3
Arbeitsbelastung workload WS 2, 69
Arbeitsbereich workspace WS 2, 70
Arbeitsheft workbook OT 1
Arbeitskraft labor OT 4
 Arbeitskräfte workforce WW, 11
Arbeitslast workload WS 2, 69
arbeitslos jobless WS 2, 65; unemployed WS 2, 65
Arbeitslosigkeit unemployment OT 3
Arbeitsplatz workplace OT 2
Archäologe / Archäologin archeologist OT 4
Architekt(in) architect WS 1, 28
Architektur architecture OT 2
archivieren to archive OT 4
Arena arena OT 1; amphitheatre OT 3
Ärger trouble OT 2; anger OT 3
 Ärger bekommen to be in trouble OT 2
ärgerlich annoying; angrily OT 2
ärgern to tease OT 1; to annoy OT 3
argumentativ argumentative WS 2, 68
argumentieren to argue OT 2
Arktis Arctic OT 4
arktisch Arctic OT 4
Arm arm OT 1
arm poor OT 1
Armband wristband OT 4

VOCABULARY

Armee army OT 3
Ärmel sleeve OT 3
ärmellos sleeveless OT 4
Armut poverty OT 3
Art kind OT 1; type; sort OT 2; species WS 1, 23
Artikel article OT 1
Artikulierung tone of voice OT 4
Artwork artwork WS 3, 107
Arzt / Ärztin doctor OT 1
asexuell asexual WS 3, 93
asiatisch Asian OT 4
Aspekt aspect OT 4
Assimilation assimilation OT 4
Assistent assistant OT 1
Assistenzhund service dog OT 2
assoziieren to associate OT 4
Ast branch OT 2
Asterisk asterisk OT 4
Astronaut(in) astronaut OT 4
Astronomie astronomy OT 1
Asylbewerber(in) asylum seeker OT 4
Atem(zug) breath OT 2
   außer Atem out of breath OT 2
atemberaubend breathtaking OT 3; stunning WS 1, 26
atemlos breathless OT 3
athletisch athletic OT 4
atmen to breathe OT 2
Atmosphäre atmosphere OT 3
Atom... nuclear OT 3
attraktiv attractive OT 4
ätzend gross OT 3
Au-pair au pair WS 2, 53
Au! Ow! OT 1
   Aua! Ouch! OT 1
Aubergine eggplant OT 2
auch too; also; as well OT 1
   auch nicht either OT 1; neither OT 2
Audiodatei audio file OT 2
Audiotagebuch audio diary OT 2
auf on; onto OT 1
aufbauen to structure WS 1, 31
aufbewahren to keep OT 2
Aufbewahrung storage OT 3
aufbrechen to head out OT 4
aufdrängen to inflict WS 1, 21
aufdringlich pushy OT 4
aufeinanderfolgend successive WS 1, 21
Aufenthaltsraum breakout area WS 2, 70
Aufforderung invitation OT 1; prompt OT 4
aufführen to put on OT 2
Aufführung performance OT 2
Aufgabe task; job OT 1; assignment OT 4

aufgeben to give up OT 2
aufgeräumt tidy OT 2
aufgeregt excited OT 1; frantic OT 3
aufgrund von due to WW, 11
aufheben to pick up OT 2
aufhören to finish; to stop OT 1
aufladen to charge OT 4; to load up WS 3, 102
auflisten to list OT 3
aufmachen to open OT 1
Aufmerksamkeit attention OT 2
aufmuntern cheer up OT 1
Aufmunterung encouragement WS 4, 140
aufnehmen to take up; to record OT 1
aufpassen to pay attention OT 2
   aufpassen auf to look after OT 1
aufräumen to tidy OT 1
aufregend exciting OT 1
Aufregung excitement OT 3; fuss OT 4
aufrichten to right WS 1, 21
aufrichtig sincerely OT 4
Aufruf appeal OT 2
Aufsatz essay OT 2
Aufschläger(in) server OT 3
aufschließen to unlock OT 1
aufschreiben to write down OT 2
Aufseher(in) attendant; ranger OT 3
aufsetzen to slap on WS 1, 16
Aufsicht supervision WS 3, 101
aufspießen to spear WS 1, 24
Aufstand rebellion OT 4
aufstehen to stand up; to get up OT 1
aufsteigen to rise OT 3
aufsuchen to frequent WW, 11
auftauchen to appear OT 3
auftragen to slop on WS 1, 16
Auftragnehmer(in) contractor WS 2, 62
auftreten to perform OT 2
Auftritt gig WS 2, 62
aufwachen to wake up OT 1
aufwärmen to warm up OT 2
Aufwärmübung warm-up OT 2
aufwärts upwards OT 3
Auge eye OT 1
Augenbraue eyebrow OT 4
Augenlid eyelid OT 2
August August OT 1
Aula assembly hall OT 1
aus from; out; off OT 1
ausbeuten to exploit OT 3
Ausbeutung exploitation OT 4
Ausbildung training OT 2; education OT 3; appenticeship WS 2, 50
Ausbildungslehrgang training course OT 2

Ausdruck expression OT 1
   zum Ausdruck bringen to voice OT 4
ausdrucken to print OT 2
ausdrücken to express OT 3
auseinanderfallen to fall apart OT 4
Auseinandersetzung argument OT 1
Ausflug trip OT 1
Ausführung delivery OT 3
Ausgabe issue OT 2
Ausgang exit OT 2
Ausgangssperre curfew OT 3
ausgeben to spend OT 1
ausgebildet skilled OT 4
ausgeglichen evenly OT 4
ausgehen to go out OT 1
   mit jmdm. ausgehen to date WS 3, 96
ausgeprägt distinctive WS 1, 30
ausgestorben extinct OT 2
ausgezeichnet excellent OT 3
Ausgrenzung discrimination WS 1, 39
Ausland abroad OT 4
ausländisch foreign OT 1; overseas OT 2
ausmachen to determine WS 3, 93
   etw. macht jmdm. etw. aus to mind OT 4
Ausmaß extent WS 1, 39
ausmerzen to eradicate OT 4
ausmessen to measure OT 4
auspacken to unpack OT 2
ausprobieren to try out OT 2
ausreichend sufficient WW, 11
ausreichend adequate WS 4, 146
Ausreißer(in) runaway WS 4, 134
ausrichten to host OT 3
ausrotten to eradicate OT 4
ausrufen to declare OT 4
ausruhen to rest OT 1
Ausrüstung kit; equipment OT 2
Aussage statement OT 1
ausschalten to turn off OT 2
ausschließen to exclude WS 3, 109
ausschließlich exclusively WW, 11
Ausschnitt clip OT 1; excerpt WS 3, 115
Ausschuss committee OT 2
Aussehen appearance OT 3
Außen... outer WS 2, 53
Außenseiter(in) underdog WS 1, 21
Außenseiter(in) odd one out OT 2; misfit OT 4
außer except OT 2; apart from OT 3
   außer wenn unless OT 4
außerdem moreover WW, 11; besides WS 2, 60; furthermore WS 3, 68; in addition WS 4, 141
äußere (r, -s) outward WS 4, 145
Außerirdische(r) alien OT 2

Appendix
VOCABULARY

äußerlich outward **WS 4**, 145
außermusikalisch extra-musical OT 2
äußern to voice OT 4
Aussicht view OT 1; perspective OT 4
Aussichtsgalerie viewing gallery OT 1
Aussichtspunkt viewpoint OT 3
Aussprache pronunciation OT 2
aussprechen to pronounce OT 3
ausstehen: nicht ausstehen können to loathe **WS 1**, 23
aussteigen to get off OT 2
ausstellen to exhibit OT 2
Ausstellung show; exhibition OT 1; display OT 3
Ausstellungsgelände showground OT 2
Aussterben extinction **WS 1**, 27
Ausstoss emission OT 3
ausstreichen to cross out OT 1
Austausch exchange OT 1
Ausverkauf sale OT 4
Auswahl variety **WS 1**, 24
auswählen to choose OT 1
Auswahlfach elective OT 4
Auswahlliste shortlist OT 2
Auswanderer / Auswanderin emigrant OT 3
auswandern to emigrate OT 4
ausweisen to deport OT 4
auswendig by heart OT 2
   auswendig aufsagen to recite OT 4
auswirken: sich auswirken auf to affect OT 3
Auswirkung impact OT 3
Auszeichnung award OT 2
Auszubildende(r) apprentice **WS 2**, 52
Auszug extract OT 4; excerpt **WS 1**, 32
autark self-sufficient OT 4
authentisch authentic **WS 3**, 104
Auto car OT 1
autokrank carsick OT 2
Automat vending machine OT 1
automatisieren to automate OT 4
Automobil automobile OT 4
autonom autonomous OT 4
Autor(in) author OT 1; writer OT 2
autorisiert authorized **WS 4**, 144
Autorität authority OT 3
Avatar avatar OT 3

B
Baby baby OT 1
babysitten to babysit OT 4
Babysitter(in) babysitter OT 4
Bach stream OT 2; creek OT 3
backen to bake OT 1
Bäcker(in) baker OT 3

Bäckerei bakery OT 4
Backup backup OT 4
Bad bath OT 2
Badewanne bath OT 2
Badezimmer bathroom OT 1
Badminton badminton OT 1
Bagel bagel OT 1
Bahn railway OT 1
Bahnhof station OT 1
Bahnsteig platform OT 1
Bakterie bacteria **WS 3**, 103
bald soon OT 1
Balken beam OT 3
Balkendiagramm bar chart OT 4
Ball ball OT 1
Ballett ballet OT 3
Ballon balloon OT 3
Banane banana OT 1
Band band OT 1; strip **WS 2**, 70
Bande gang **WS 2**, 64
Bank bench; bank OT 3
Banking banking **WS 2**, 63
Bankwesen banking **WS 2**, 63
Bar bar OT 1
Bär bear OT 1
Bargeld cash OT 1
Barriere barrier OT 3
barrierefrei accessible OT 2
Baseball baseball OT 1
basieren to base on OT 4
Basis base OT 4; basis **WS 2**, 61
Basketball basketball OT 1
Batterie battery OT 2
Bau construction OT 4
Bauarbeiter(in) builder OT 2
bauen to build OT 1
Bauer / Bäuerin farmer OT 2
Bauernhaus farmhouse OT 3
Bauernhof farm OT 1
Baum tree OT 1
Baumstamm caber OT 3
Baumwolle cotton OT 4
bayerisch Bavarian OT 2
beabsichtigen to aim OT 4; to intend **WS 3**, 105
beachten to take into account **WS 3**, 101
Beamer projector OT 1
beanspruchen to claim **WS 1**, 18
beantworten to answer OT 1
beaufsichtigen to supervise OT 3; to oversee OT 4
beauftragen to delegate OT 4
bebauen to cultivate OT 4
Becher mug OT 3
Becken basin OT 3
Bedenken concern **WS 1**, 33

bedeuten to mean OT 1
bedeutend major OT 2
Bedeutung meaning OT 1; importance OT 2; significance **WS 1**, 30
bedienen to operate **WS 2**, 61
bedienen to serve OT 1
Bedingung condition OT 3
Bedrohung threat **WS 1**, 44
   eine Bedrohung darstellen to pose a threat **WS 1**, 44
beeilen: sich beeilen to hurry OT 1
beeindrucken to impress **WS 3**, 100
beeinflussen to influence OT 4
beenden to conclude OT 4
beengt cramped OT 3
Beerdigung funeral **WS 2**, 64
Beere berry OT 4
Beet bed OT 1
befehlen to order OT 1
Befehlsform imperative OT 1
befehlshabend commanding OT 2
befestigen to attach OT 4
befragen to survey **WS 3**, 98
Befragte(r) respondent **WS 3**, 107
Befragung census **WS 3**, 90
befreit freed OT 4
befriedigend satisfying **WS 4**, 146
Befund finding OT 4
Befürworter(in) supporter OT 2
Begabung talent OT 2
begegnen to face OT 4
begehen to commit OT 4
begeistert excited OT 1; enthusiastic OT 3; wowed OT 4
Beginn advent **WS 1**, 23
beginnen to start; to begin OT 1
beglaubigt certified **WS 4**, 139
Begleiter(in) escort OT 3
begleitet accompanied OT 3
begrenzen to limit OT 3
Begriff concept OT 4
begründen to found; to establish OT 4
Begründung motivation **WS 2**, 55
behalten to keep OT 2
Behälter bin; container OT 2
behandeln to treat OT 4
Behandlung treatment **WS 1**, 38
behaupten to claim **WS 1**, 18
Behinderung disability OT 2
bei at; by OT 1
beide both OT 1
Bein leg OT 1
   wieder auf die Beine kommen to bounce back **WS 1**, 21
beindruckt impressed OT 4
beinhalten to contain OT 3

two hundred and seventy-seven **277**

Appendix
VOCABULARY

Beispiel example OT 1
    zum Beispiel for instance **WS 4**, 141
beispielsweise or instance **WS 4**, 141
Beitrag contribution; input OT 4
bekannt well known; familiar OT 2
    bekannt geben to announce OT 2
Bekanntgabe announcement OT 2
bekennen: sich bekennen to plead **WS 3**, 101
bekommen to get OT 1
bekräftigen to reinforce **WS 3**, 92
Belag fuzz OT 4
belegen to top OT 3
beleidigen to offend OT 3
beleidigt insulted **WS 1**, 24
Beleuchtung lighting OT 4
beliebt popular OT 1
bellen to bark OT 2
bemannt crewed OT 4
bemerken to notice OT 1
Bemerkung remark **WS 4**, 145
bemühen: sich bemühen to struggle **WS 2**, 64
benachteiligt disadvantaged **WS 2**, 61; discriminated **WS 2**, 89
Benehmen behaviour OT 2
benehmen: sich benehmen to behave OT 2
beneiden to envy **WS 3**, 91
benennen to name OT 4
benutzen to use OT 1
Benutzer(in) user OT 2
Benutzeroberfläche desktop OT 4
Benzin gas OT 3; petrol OT 4
beobachten to watch OT 1; to observe OT 4; to witness **WS 3**, 107
Beobachter(in) observer **WS 2**, 61
Beobachtung observation OT 3
bequem comfortable OT 1
Bequemlichkeit convenience OT 4
Berater(in) counsellor OT 2; advisor **WS 2**, 51; consultant **WS 2**, 62
Beratung counselling **WS 3**, 100
berechtigt authorized **WS 4**, 144
bereit ready OT 1; all set OT 2
    bereit sein to be willing OT 4
bereits already OT 2
bereuen to regret OT 2
Berg mountain OT 1
bergab downhill **WS 1**, 13
Bergarbeiter(in) miner OT 4
Bergbau... mining OT 3
Bergkette mountain range OT 4
Bergsteigen climbing OT 1
Bergwerk mine OT 2
Bericht report OT 2

berichten to report OT 1
berücksichtigen to take into account **WS 3**, 101
Beruf profession **WS 1**, 18
beruflich vocational **WS 2**, 50
beruhigen to settle down OT 2
berühmt famous OT 1
berühren to touch OT 1
beschädigen to damage OT 2
beschäftigen to engage OT 4
    beschäftigt busy OT 1
Beschäftigung occupation OT 4; employment **WS 2**, 50
beschämt ashamed OT 3
beschatten to shadow **WS 2**, 66
Beschilderung signposting **WS 4**, 143
beschreiben to describe OT 1
beschreibend descriptive **WS 3**, 115
Beschreibung description OT 2
Beschwerde complaint OT 2
beschweren to complain OT 3
besichten to tour **WS 1**, 29
Besichtigungen sightseeing OT 1
besiegen to beat OT 2
Besitz possession **WS 3**, 89
besitzanzeigend possessive OT 1
besitzen to own OT 4
Besitzer(in) owner OT 2
besondere(r, -s) special OT 1
besonders especially OT 2; in particular OT 4; particularly **WS 4**, 144
besorgt worried OT 1; anxious OT 2; concerned **WS 1**, 26
    besorgt sein to care OT 1
besprechen to discuss OT 1
Besprechung discussion; meeting OT 1
besser better OT 1
Bestand stock OT 2
Bestandteil element OT 2
bestätigen to confirm OT 4; to acknowledge **WS 1**, 21
beste(r, -s) best OT 1
Besteck cutlery OT 3
bestehen: aus etw. bestehen to consist of **WS 1**, 32
Bestellung order OT 1
Bestie beast **WS 4**, 132
bestimmen to define OT 4; to dictate **WS 3**, 93; to determine **WS 3**, 93
bestimmt definite OT 1; assertive; specific OT 3
    bestimmter Artikel definite article OT 1
Bestimmungswort determiner OT 1
bestrafen to punish OT 3; to prosecute **WS 4**, 144

besuchen to attend; to visit OT 2; to tour **WS 1**, 29
Besucher(in) visitor OT 1
Bete: Rote Bete beetroot OT 4
Beteiligung participation **WS 3**, 99
beten to pray **WS 1**, 39
betonen to emphasize **WS 3**, 105
Betonung stress OT 1; emphasis **WS 3**, 95
Betreuer(in) guardian OT 2; carer **WS 3**, 93
betrübt saddened **WS 1**, 24
Bett bed OT 1
betteln to beg **WS 4**, 138
beunruhigt alarmed OT 3
beurteilen to judge OT 2; to assess **WS 2**, 51
Beurteilung judging OT 2
Bevölkerung population OT 3
Bevölkerungszählung census **WS 3**, 90
bewaffnet armed **WS 3**, 93
Bewährung probation **WS 3**, 100
bewegen to move OT 1
beweglich agile OT 3
Bewegung movement **WS 1**, 27
Beweis proof OT 4
beweisen to prove OT 3
bewerben to apply OT 3
Bewerber(in) applicant OT 4
Bewerbung application OT 4
bewerten to rate OT 2; to evaluate OT 4
Bewertung evaluation **WS 2**, 61
bewohnbar liveable OT 4
Bewohnbarkeit habitation OT 4
bewohnen to inhabit **WS 1**, 20
Bewohner(in) resident OT 3; dweller OT 4
bewölkt cloudy OT 4
bewusst aware **WS 2**, 64; deliberately **WS 4**, 46
Bewusstsein awareness **WS 2**, 64
bezahlbar affordable OT 4
bezahlen to pay OT 1
Bezahlung payment OT 2
beziehen to refer OT 3
    sich auf etw. beziehen to relate to OT 3; to centre around **WS 4**, 145
Beziehung relationship OT 3
Bezirk district OT 1
Bezug: in Bezug auf related to OT 4
bezüglich regarding **WS 4**, 140
Bibliothek library OT 1
Bibliothekar(in) librarian OT 4
Biene bee OT 1
Bier beer OT 3
Bild picture; image OT 1

Appendix

VOCABULARY

bilden to form OT 4
Bildmaterial visual OT 4
Bildschirm screen OT 1
Bildtext caption OT 1
Bildungs- educational OT 3
Bildunterschrift caption OT 1
bilingual bilingual OT 2
billig cheap OT 2; inexpensive OT 4
binden to tie OT 2
Bingo bingo OT 1
Binnenland interior WS 1, 13
Biodiversität biodiversity OT 4
Biografie biography OT 4
biografisch biographical WS 1, 39
Biologe / Biologin biologist OT 4
Biologie biology OT 2
biologisch biological WS 1, 30
   biologisch angebaut organic OT 2
Biotoilette composting toilet OT 3
Birne pear OT 1
bis till OT 2; until OT 3
bisexuell bisexual WS 3, 93
bisher so far OT 2
bisherig previous OT 4
Biss bite OT 2
Bitte request OT 2
bitte please OT 1
bitten to ask OT 1; urge OT 4
bitterlich bitterly WS 1, 24
Blase bubble OT 1; blister OT 2
blasen to blow OT 2
Blaskapelle marching band OT 4
Blatt sheet OT 1; leaf OT 4
blau blue OT 1
Blazer blazer OT 1
bleiben to stay OT 1; to keep OT 2; to remain OT 4
Bleistift pencil OT 1
Blick glimpse WS 4, 126
Blickwinkel angle WS 4, 141
blind blind OT 2
Blindenführhund guide dog OT 2
Blocker blocker WS 3, 93
blockieren to block OT 3
blöd dumb WS 3, 94; foolish WS 3, 100
Blog blog OT 1
Blogeintrag blogpost OT 4
Blogger(in) blogger OT 3
blond blonde OT 1
Blues blues OT 1
Blume flower OT 1
Blut blood OT 2
Blutvergießen bloodshed WS 1, 24
BMX-Rad fahren BMXing WS 3, 93
Boden: am Boden zerstört devastated WS 3, 117

Boden ground; bottom; floor OT 1
Bodenstation ground control OT 4
Bogen bow OT 2
Bohne bean OT 1
   Bohnen in Tomatensoße baked beans OT 1
bohren to drill OT 4
Bonbon sweet OT 2
Bonus bonus WS 2, 82
Boot boat OT 1
   Boot fahren to cruise OT 3
Bord aboard OT 4
   an Bord gehen to board OT 4
Bordstein curb WS 3, 100
Böse evil WS 4, 126
böse angry OT 1; mad OT 2
Bouquet bouquet OT 3
Boygroup boyband OT 2
brainstormen to brainstorm OT 2
Brandbekämpfung firefighting OT 2
brandneu brand-new OT 2
brasilianisch Brazilian OT 2
braten to fry OT 2
Bratensoße gravy OT 1
brauchen to need OT 1
braun brown OT 1
brechen to break OT 1
brennbar flammable OT 2
brennen to burn OT 2
brennend blazing WS 1, 40
Brennholz firewood OT 4
Brennstoff fuel OT 2
Brett board OT 1
Brief letter OT 1
Briefkasten post box OT 1; mailbox OT 4
Brieftasche wallet OT 1
Briefumschlag envelope OT 2
Brille glasses OT 1
bringen to bring OT 1
Brise breeze OT 3
britisch British OT 1
Broccoli broccoli OT 1
Brombeere blackberry OT 1
Broschüre brochure OT 1; booklet OT 2
Brot bread OT 1
Brotkrumen breadcrumbs OT 3
Brotverdiener(in) breadwinner WS 2, 63
Browser browser OT 4
Brücke bridge OT 1
Bruder brother OT 1
brutal brutal WS 1, 21
Brutalität brutality WS 1, 20
Buch book OT 1
buchen to book OT 2
Bücherregal bookcase OT 1

Buchstabe letter OT 1
buchstabieren to spell OT 1
Bucht bay OT 1
Buchung booking OT 2
Bude stall OT 2
Büffel buffalo OT 4
Buffet buffet OT 3
Bühne stage OT 2
Bühnenanweisungen stage directions OT 2
Bund federation WS 1, 18
Bundesregierung federal government WS 1, 27
Bungee-Jumping bungee jumping OT 3
bunt coloured OT 1
Burg castle OT 1
Bürgermeister(in) mayor OT 3
Bürgersteig pavement OT 1; sidewalk OT 4
Büro office OT 1
Büropark office park OT 2
Bürste brush OT 2
Bus bus OT 1
Busch bush OT 2
Buschfeuer bushfire WS 1, 26
Buschland bushland WS 1, 27
Bushaltestelle bus stop OT 1
Busladung busload WS 1, 25
Bussard buzzard OT 2

C

Café café OT 1
Cafeteria cafeteria OT 2
Camp camp OT 1
Camper(in) camper OT 2
Camping camping OT 1
Campingplatz campsite OT 1
Campus campus OT 2
Canyon canyon OT 3
Cartoon cartoon OT 4
Cellist(in) cellist OT 2
Cello cello OT 2
Celsius centigrade OT 4
Cent cent OT 1
Champignon mushroom OT 1
Chaos: ein Chaos anrichten to make a mess OT 2
chaotisch disorganized; messy OT 2; chaotic WS 2, 55
Charakter character OT 1
Charakterisierung characterization WS 3, 115
charmant charming OT 3
Chart chart OT 4
Checkliste checklist OT 1
Cheerleader(in) cheerleader OT 3

Appendix

VOCABULARY

Chef(in) boss OT 2
Chemikalie chemical OT 3
Chemiker(in) chemist OT 2
Chili chili OT 2
chillen to chill **WS 3**, 95
chinesisch Chinese OT 1
Chip crisp OT 1
Chirurg(in) surgeon OT 3
Cholera cholera OT 4
Chor choir OT 1
Chorizo chorizo OT 2
Coaching coaching OT 4
Cola cola OT 1
Comicheft comic OT 1
Commonwealth commonwealth **WS 1**, 21
Computer computer OT 1
computerbasiert computerized OT 4
computergesteuert computerized OT 4
Computerraum computer lab OT 2
Computing computing **WS 2**, 51
Container container OT 2
cool cool OT 1
Cornflakes cereal OT 1
Countdown countdown OT 4
Cousin(e) cousin OT 1
Cracker cracker OT 3
Cranberry cranberry OT 4
Curry(gericht) curry OT 1
    mit Curry gewürzt curried OT 1
cybermobben to cyberbully **WS 3**, 107
Cybermobbing cyber bullying OT 4
Cybersicherheit cyber security OT 4

D

da there OT 1
Dach roof OT 1
Dachboden attic OT 3
dadurch thus **WS 1**, 21
daher thus **WS 1**, 21
Dame lady OT 1
Damespiel checkers; draughts OT 1
Dämon demon **WS 1**, 38
Dampf steam OT 2
Dampfzug steam train OT 2
danach afterwards OT 3
dankbar grateful **WS 1**, 20
danke thanks OT 1
danken to thank OT 1
dann then OT 1
Darlehen loan **WS 2**, 64
darstellen to illustrate OT 3
Darsteller(in) performer OT 2
darunter underneath OT 3; beneath **WS 1**, 21

das the OT 1
Datei file OT 3
Daten data OT 3
Datum date OT 2
dauerhaft permanent **WS 2**, 51
Daumen thumb OT 4
    Daumen gedrückt fingers crossed OT 1
Deal deal OT 4
Debatte debate OT 3
Debattierklub debating club OT 4
Decke blanket OT 2; ceiling OT 4
Deckel lid OT 2
defekt faulty OT 2
definieren to define OT 4
Definition definition OT 1
definitiv definitely OT 1
Degradierung degradation **WS 1**, 21
dehnen to stretch OT 2
dehydriert dehydrated OT 2
dein your OT 1
    deine(r, -s) yours OT 2
Dekade decade **WS 3**, 93
Dekorateur(in) decorator OT 3
dekorieren to decorate OT 4
delegieren to delegate OT 4
Delfin dolphin OT 1
Delikatesse delicacy OT 3
demokratisch democratic OT 4
Demonstrant(in) protester **WS 1**, 33
Demonstration demonstration OT 4
Demonstrativbegleiter demonstrative OT 1
Demütigung indignity **WS 1**, 21
Denim denim OT 4
denken to think OT 1
    denken an to think about; to think of OT 1
Denkmal monument OT 1
deportieren to deport OT 4
Depression depression OT 4
deprimierend depressing OT 4
deprimiert depressed OT 4
der the OT 1
derzeit currently **WS 3**, 93
deshalb therefore OT 3
Design design OT 1
Designer(in) designer OT 3
designieren to designate **WS 1**, 24
Desktop desktop OT 4
dessen / deren whose OT 2
Detail detail OT 2
detailliert detailed OT 3
deutlich clearly OT 3; considerably **WS 3**, 98

deutsch German OT 1
Dezember December OT 1
Diabetes diabetes **WS 2**, 65
diagnostizieren to diagnose OT 4
Diagramm diagram OT 3; chart OT 4; graph **WS 3**, 89
Dialekt dialect **WS 1**, 22
Dialog dialogue OT 1
Diashow slideshow OT 3
Diät diet OT 3
Diäten dieting **WS 3**, 102
diätetisch dietary **WS 3**, 103
dich / sich yourself OT 1
Dichte density OT 4; closeness **WS 3**, 115
Dichter(in) poet OT 3
Dichtung poetry OT 1
dick thick OT 1
die the OT 1
Diebstahl theft **WS 3**, 94
Diele hall OT 1
Diener(in) attendant OT 3
Dienst service OT 2
Dienstag Tuesday OT 1
diese these; those OT 1
diese(r, -s) this; that OT 1
Diesel diesel OT 3
digital digital OT 3
Digitalisierung digitalization **WS 3**, 106
Dilemma dilemma OT 4
Ding thing OT 1
Dingo dingo **WS 1**, 23
Dinosaurier dinosaur OT 1
Diplom diploma **WS 2**, 58
direkt straight; direct OT 3
diskriminieren to discriminate **WS 2**, 56
Diskriminierung discrimination **WS 1**, 39
Diskussion discussion OT 1
ditto ditto OT 4
Doktortitel PhD (Doctor of Philosophy) **WS 2**, 69
Dokument document OT 4
Dokumentation documentary OT 2
Dollar dollar OT 1
Dolmetscher(in) interpreter OT 4
Donnerstag Thursday OT 1
Doppel (Tennis) doubles OT 3
Doppel... double OT 1
doppelt double OT 1
Dorf village OT 1
Dorfbewohner(in) villager OT 4
dort there OT 1
Dose can; tin OT 2
    in Dosen tinned; canned OT 2
Drache dragon OT 1

Appendix

VOCABULARY

Drama drama OT 1
Dramatiker(in) playwright WS 4, 145
dramatisch dramatic WS 3, 98
drängen to urge OT 4
drastisch drastic WS 1, 22
draußen outside OT 1; outdoor(s) OT 2
Dreck dirt OT 4
dreckig grubby OT 2; filthy OT 4
Drehbuch script OT 1
drehen to turn OT 2
Drehscheibe turntable OT 2
drei three OT 1
Dreieck triangle OT 2
dreieckig triangular OT 3
dreißig thirty OT 1
dreiundzwanzig twenty-three OT 1
dreizehn thirteen OT 1
Dresscode dress code OT 4
dringend urgently WS 1, 26
drinnen indoors OT 3
Dritte(r, -s) third OT 1
Droge drug OT 3
Drogerie drugstore OT 2
Drohne drone OT 3
Druck pressure OT 3
    unter Druck setzen to pressure WS 3, 94
drücken to press OT 1
Drucker printer WS 2, 71
Drüse gland WS 4, 143
Dschungel jungle OT 4
du / Sie you OT 1
Dudelsack bagpipe OT 3
dumm silly OT 1; stupid OT 2; dumb WS 3, 94
Dung manure OT 3
Dünger fertilizer OT 3
dunkel dark OT 1
Dunkelheit darkness WS 4, 126
dünn thin OT 1
durch through OT 1
durchaus absolutely OT 2
durcheinander jumbled; mixed up OT 2
durcheinanderbringen to mix up OT 2
durchführen to conduct OT 3
durchmachen to undergo WS 4, 145
durchnässt soaked OT 3
durchschnittlich average OT 4
durchsetzen to enforce OT 4
durchstochen pierced OT 3
durchstromern to roam around WS 1, 23
durchweg throughout OT 3
dürfen to be allowed to OT 2
dürr arid WS 1, 23
Dürre drought WS 1, 23
durstig thirsty OT 1
Dusche shower OT 2
Dutzend dozen OT 4
Dynamik dynamic WS 3, 106
dynamisch vibrant WS 1, 19
dystopisch dystopian WS 4, 126

E

E-Roller e-scooter WS 2, 71
ebenfalls ditto OT 4
ebenso alike WS 3, 94
echt real OT 1; genuine WS 2, 67; authentic WS 3, 104
Ecke corner OT 1
E-Commerce e-commerce OT 4
effizient efficient OT 4
egal welche whatever OT 3
egoistisch selfish OT 3
Ehe marriage WS 2, 64
Ehefrau wife OT 1
ehemalig former OT 4
Ehemalige(r) alumnus OT 4
Ehemann husband OT 2
ehren to honour WS 1, 21
Ehrenamt: ein Ehrenamt haben to volunteer OT 2
ehrenamtlich pro bono WS 2, 61
Ehrenamtliche(r) volunteer OT 2
ehrgeizig ambitious OT 4
ehrlich honest OT 3
Ei egg OT 1
Eichhörnchen squirrel OT 1
eifrig eager OT 2
eigenartig odd OT 2
eigene(r, -s) own OT 1
Eigenschaft feature OT 1; quality OT 3
eigenständig distinct WS 1, 22
eigentlich actually OT 2
Eigentum property WS 1, 23
Eignung qualification WS 1, 21
Eiland isle WS 1, 30
eilen to rush OT 2
Eimer bin OT 2
ein(e) a; an OT 1
    ein(e) andere(r, -s) another OT 1
einbeziehen to involve OT 4
Einbildung imagination OT 4
eindeutig definite OT 1; distinct WS 1, 22
Eindruck impression WS 1, 16
einfach easy OT 1
einfallsreich fancy OT 2
einfangen to capture OT 4
Einfluss influence OT 4
    politischer Einfluss political clout OT 4
einfügen to paste OT 2

einführen to import OT 3
Einführung introduction OT 2; advent WS 1, 23; induction WS 2, 54
Einführungs... introductory OT 4
Eingang entrance OT 1
Eingangsbereich entrance hall OT 1
Eingangshalle entrance hall OT 1
Eingebung inspiration OT 4
eingravieren to engrave OT 4
Eingriff invasion WS 1, 21
einheimisch local OT 2; native OT 3; indigenous WS 1, 20
Einheimische(r) local OT 2
Einheit session OT 2
einig: sich einig sein to agree OT 1
einige some OT 1; several OT 2
Einkaufen shopping OT 1
einkaufen to shop OT 1
Einkaufsdienst shopping rota WS 2, 70
Einkaufszentrum mall OT 3
Einkommen income OT 4
einkommensschwach low-income OT 4
einladen to invite OT 2
    mit einladen to invite along OT 2
Einladung invitation OT 1
einloggen to log on OT 3
einmal once OT 2
    Es war einmal... Once upon a time ... OT 1
einmarschieren to invade OT 3
einpendeln to level off WS 3, 98
einreichen to hand in OT 2
Einrichtung institution OT 4
eins one OT 1
einsam lonely OT 3
Einsatz in action OT 2
einschätzen to judge OT 2; to reassess WS 2, 62
einschlafen to go to sleep OT 1; to fall asleep OT 2
einschließen to include OT 1
einschränken to limit OT 3
    sich einschränken to downsize OT 3
Einschränkung restriction WS 1, 19
Einsendung entry OT 2
Einsicht insight WS 2, 66
einsprachig monolingual WS 1, 22
Einstand deuce OT 3
Einstellung setting; attitude OT 3
eintippen to key in OT 2
Eintopf stew OT 2
einträchtig peaceful OT 2
Eintrag entry OT 2
eintragen to enter OT 2
eintreten to enter OT 2; to step in OT 4
    eintreten in to join OT 1

Appendix
VOCABULARY

Eintritt admission **WS 1**, 38
Eintrittskarte ticket OT 1
einundzwanzig twenty-one OT 1
Einwand objection OT 3
Einwanderer / Einwanderin immigrant OT 3
einwandern to immigrate **WS 1**, 18
Einwanderungskontrolle immigration OT 2
Einweckglas jar OT 2
einweisen to instruct **WS 2**, 71
einwickeln to wrap OT 2
Einwohner(in) citizen OT 3
Einzahl singular OT 1
Einzel… single OT 3
Einzelhändler retailer OT 4
einzeln individually OT 4
Einzelne(r) individual OT 4
einzigartig unique OT 2
Eis ice; ice cream OT 1
    Eis am Stiel ice lolly OT 1
Eisberg iceberg OT 3
Eiscreme ice cream OT 1
Eisenbahn rail OT 2
Eisenbahn railway OT 1
Eisenbahnlinie railway line OT 2
eisig icy **WS 3**, 100
Eiweiß protein OT 4
ekelhaft disgusting; gross OT 3
ekeln to disgust **WS 3**, 93
Elefant elephant OT 1
elektrisch electric OT 1; electrical OT 4
Elektronik electronics OT 2
elektronisch electronical OT 4; electronic **WS 1**, 16
elementar elementary OT 2
elf eleven OT 1
Elfenbein ivory OT 3
Ellbogen elbow OT 1
Elternteil parent OT 1
E-Mail email OT 1
    E-Mail schreiben to email OT 2
Emission emission OT 3
Emoji emoji OT 3
Emoticon emoticon **WS 4**, 141
emotional emotional **WS 1**, 17
Empfang reception OT 1
Empfangschef(in) receptionist OT 1
empfehlen to recommend OT 2
Empfehlung recommendation **WS 3**, 101
empfinden to perceive **WS 1**, 38
empören to disgust **WS 3**, 93
Ende end OT 1; ending OT 2
enden to end OT 1
endgültig final OT 1
endlos endless OT 4

Endung ending OT 2
Endzone end zone OT 2
Energie energy OT 2
energisch energetic OT 2
eng narrow OT 2; close OT 3
engagiert dedicated **WS 2**, 83
Engel angel OT 3
englisch English OT 1
Enkel grandson OT 1
Enkelin granddaughter OT 3
Enkelkind grandchild OT 3
enorm vast **WS 3**, 106
entdecken to discover OT 3; to happen upon OT 4
Entdeckung discovery OT 4
Ente duck OT 2
Entfärbung bleaching **WS 1**, 26
entfernen to remove OT 2
entfernt remote **WS 1**, 13
Entfernung distance OT 2; removal **WS 1**, 21
entführen to abduct OT 4
Entführer(in) kidnapper OT 2
enthalten to contain OT 3
enthaupten to behead OT 3
entkommen to escape OT 2
entlang along OT 1
entlassen to dismiss **WS 2**, 70; to fire **WS 2**, 70
entlasten to relieve **WS 4**, 145
entleeren to empty OT 4
entmutigen to discourage **WS 2**, 68
entriegeln to unlock OT 1
entschädigen to make amends **WS 3**, 100
Entschädigung compensation **WS 1**, 38
entscheiden to decide; to resolve OT 1
entscheidend decisive **WS 3**, 115
Entscheidung decision OT 1
entschlossen determined OT 3
Entschlossenheit determination **WS 1**, 21
entschuldigen to excuse OT 1; to apologize OT 2
Entschuldigung apology OT 2; pardon **WS 2**, 70
    Entschuldigung! sorry OT 1
entspannen: (sich) entspannen to relax OT 2; to chill (out) OT 4
entspannt relaxed; laid-back OT 4
entsprechend equivalent OT 4; corresponding **WS 3**, 106
entstehen to originate **WS 1**, 16
enttäuschend disappointingly OT 3
enttäuscht disappointed OT 2
Enttäuschung disappointment **WS 1**, 45

entwerfen to design OT 3; to draft **WS 3**, 107
entwickeln to develop OT 2
    sich entwickeln to evolve OT 4
Entwickler(in) developer **WS 2**, 52
Entwicklung development OT 4; evolution **WS 3**, 106
Entwurf design OT 1; draft OT 2
entzückt delighted OT 3; wowed OT 4
Entzugsprogramm detox OT 2
entzünden to spark OT 4
Entzündung infection OT 2
Epidemie epidemic OT 4
Epoche period OT 3
er he OT 1
Erbe heritage **WS 1**, 21
Erbe / Erbin heir **WS 2**, 64
Erbse pea OT 1
Erdanziehungskraft gravity OT 4
Erdbeben earthquake OT 2
Erdbeere strawberry OT 1
Erdboden soil OT 2
Erde ground OT 1; earth OT 2
Erderwärmung global warming OT 3
Erdkugel globe **WS 1**, 13
Erdkunde geography OT 1
Ereignis event OT 1; incident **WS 3**, 101
erfahren experienced OT 3
Erfahrung experience OT 2
erfasst: nicht erfasst undocumented OT 4
erfinden to invent OT 2
Erfinder(in) inventor OT 2
erfinderisch resourceful OT 4
Erfindung invention OT 4
Erfolg success OT 3
erfolgreich successful OT 2
    erfolgreich sein to succeed OT 2
erforderlich to require OT 4
erforschen to explore OT 1
erfreut delighted OT 3
Erfrischungsgetränk refreshment OT 2
erfüllen to fulfil OT 4
erfunden fictional OT 2
Ergebnis result OT 2; finding OT 4; outcome **WS 1**, 38
erhalten to receive OT 2; to preserve OT 3
erhältlich available OT 3
Erhaltung conservation OT 2
erheben to raise OT 2
erhöhen to raise OT 2; to increase OT 3
erholen to recover OT 4
erholsam relaxing OT 2
Erholung relaxation OT 3
erinnern to remind OT 2

Appendix

VOCABULARY

erinnern an to recall **WS 4**, 140
sich erinnern an to remember; to think of OT 1
Erinnerung memoir **WS 4**, 126
Erkältung cold **WS 2**, 65
erkennen to realize; to recognize OT 2; to perceive **WS 1**, 38
erklären to explain OT 1; to state **WS 3**, 108
Erklärung explanation OT 1; declaration OT 4
erkunden to explore OT 1
erlangen to gain OT 1
erlauben to allow OT 3; to permit **WS 2**, 64
Erlaubnis permission OT 2; permit; licence OT 3
erlaubt allowed OT 3
erleben to relive OT 4
erleichtern to relieve **WS 4**, 145
Erleichterung relief OT 4
ermächtigen to empower **WS 2**, 69
Ermittler(in) investigator OT 4
ermorden to murder OT 4
ermutigen to encourage OT 2
Ernährer(in) breadwinner **WS 2**, 63
Ernährung nutrition **WS 3**, 108
Ernährung nutrition OT 4
ernennen to designate **WS 1**, 24; to appoint **WS 1**, 41
Ernennung nomination OT 4
erneuerbar renewable **WS 1**, 26
ernst serious OT 2
ernsthaft intense **WS 1**, 30
Ernsthaftigkeit seriousness **WS 1**, 44
Ernte crop; harvest OT 4
Erntedankfest Thanksgiving OT 2
Erntehelfer(in) farmhand OT 4
ernten to harvest OT 4
erreichen to reach OT 3; to achieve OT 4
errichten to put up OT 1
Ersatz substitution; substitute OT 3
erscheinen to appear OT 3
erschöpft exhausted OT 2
erschrecken to frighten OT 3
erschreckend frightening OT 1
erschüttert devastated **WS 3**, 117
ersetzen to replace OT 3
erspähen to spot OT 1
Erspartes savings OT 3
erstaunen to amaze **WS 3**, 121
erstaunlich amazing OT 1; astonishing **WS 1**, 27
erstaunlicherweise astonishingly OT 3
erstaunt amazed OT 3
erste(r, -s) first OT 1; premier OT 2

Erste Hilfe first aid OT 2
ertönen to sound OT 2
ertrinken to drown OT 3
Erwachsene(r) adult OT 1
erwähnen to mention OT 3
erwarten to expect OT 2
Erwartung expectation **WS 3**, 92
erwartungsgemäß unsurprisingly OT 3
erweitern to expand OT 4
erweitert extended **WS 3**, 91
erzählen to tell OT 1
Erzähler(in) narrator **WS 1**, 38
erzeugen to produce OT 3; to generate OT 4
Erzeuger producer **WS 1**, 18
erziehen to educate **WS 1**, 20
Erziehung upbringing **WS 2**, 68
Erzielen scoring OT 1
es it OT 1
  es gibt there is / are OT 1
Essen food OT 1
  Essen zum Mitnehmen takeout OT 4
Esslöffel tablespoon OT 2
Essstäbchen chopstick OT 1
Esszimmer dining room OT 1
Etagenbett bunk bed OT 3
ethisch ethical OT 3
ethnisch ethnically **WS 1**, 18
ethnisch ethnic **WS 1**, 31
Etikett label OT 1; tag OT 2
Etikette etiquette OT 3
etwa approximately **WS 1**, 13
etwas some; something OT 1
euch (selbst) yourselves OT 3
euer / Ihr your OT 1
eure(r, -s) yours OT 2
Evolution evolution **WS 3**, 106
ewig eternal OT 4
exekutieren to execute OT 3
Existenz existence **WS 1**, 44
existieren to exist OT 3
exotisch exotic OT 2
expandieren to expand OT 4
Expedition expedition OT 2
Experiment experiment OT 1
experimentieren to experiment OT 4
Experte / Expertin expert OT 3
explizit explicitly **WS 4**, 141
explodieren to explode **WS 1**, 23
Exporteur(in) exporter **WS 1**, 27
exportieren export **WS 1**, 44
Extra... extra OT 1
Extrem extreme **WS 3**, 102
extrem extreme OT 3; drastic **WS 1**, 22
extrovertiert extroverted **WS 2**, 55

F
fabelhaft fabulous OT 2
Fabrik factory OT 4
Fach subject OT 1
Fachzeitschrift journal **WW**, 11
fähig capable OT 4; competent **WS 2**, 58
Fähigkeit skill; ability OT 2
Fahne flag OT 1
Fahranfänger(in) learner OT 3
Fähre ferry OT 2
fahren to go; to drive; to ride OT 1; to motor OT 3
Fahrer(in) rider; driver OT 1
Fahrerkabine cab OT 4
Fahrerlaubnis driver's license OT 4
Fahrgast passenger OT 2
Fahrkarte ticket OT 1
Fahrkartenschalter booking office; ticket office OT 2
Fahrplan timetable OT 1
Fahrpreis fare **WS 1**, 18
Fahrrad bike OT 1; bicycle OT 2
  Fahrrad fahren to cycle OT 1
Fahrspur lane OT 2
Fahrt journey; ride OT 1
Fahrzeug vehicle OT 1
fair unfair OT 2
Fakt fact OT 1
Faktor factor **WS 1**, 26
fallen to fall OT 1; to decrease **WS 3**, 98
  fallen lassen to drop OT 1
falls whether; if OT 1
falsch false; wrong OT 1; fake **WS 3**, 95
  falscher Freund false friend OT 2
fälschlich mistakenly **WS 3**, 118
falten to fold OT 2
Familie family OT 1; kin **WS 1**, 21
Fan fan OT 1; supporter OT 2
fangen to catch OT 1; to trap **WS 3**, 93
Fantasie fantasy OT 2; imagination OT 4
fantasievoll imaginative OT 4
fantastisch fantastic OT 1
Fantasy fantasy OT 2
Farbe colour OT 1; paint OT 2; dye OT 4
Färbemittel dye OT 4
farbenfroh colourful OT 3
farbig coloured OT 1
Farmarbeiter(in) farmworker OT 4
fast nearly OT 1; almost OT 2
Faszination fascination OT 4
faszinierend fascinating OT 3
Faust fist **WS 1**, 21
Februar February OT 1
Feder feather OT 2
Federtasche pencil case OT 1
Fee fairy OT 2

two hundred and eighty-three **283**

Appendix

VOCABULARY

Feedback feedback OT 1
fegen to sweep OT 4
fehlend missing OT 1
Fehler fault; mistake OT 2
fehlerhaft blemished **WS 1**, 21
Feier party OT 1; celebration; ceremony OT 2
feierlich ceremonial OT 3
feiern to celebrate OT 1; to feast OT 4
Feigling wimp **WS 3**, 94
Feind enemy OT 1
Feinkostladen deli **WS 1**, 15
Feld field; square OT 1; space OT 2
Fels rock OT 2
Felsen cliff **WS 1**, 22
Fenster window OT 1
Ferienlager camp OT 1
fern far-off OT 2; faraway OT 4
Fernbedienung remote control OT 4
fernbleiben to keep away OT 2
Ferne: aus der Ferne remotely OT 4
Fernglas binoculars OT 2
fernhalten to keep away OT 2
Fernsehen TV OT 1; television OT 2
fertigstellen to finalize **WS 3**, 109
Fest festival OT 1; feast OT 4
festhalten: an etw. festhalten to cling to OT 2
Festival festival OT 1
Festland mainland OT 3
festlegen to schedule **WS 2**, 59; to state **WS 3**, 108
Festlichkeit festivity OT 4
festmachen to fasten OT 1
Festmahl feast OT 4
festnehmen to capture OT 4
Festnetz landline OT 4
Festung fort OT 2; fortress OT 3
Fett fat OT 2
fettgedruckt bold OT 1
Feuer fire OT 2
Feuerwache fire station OT 2
Feuerwehrmann / -frau firefighter OT 2
Feuerwerk fireworks OT 3; firework display OT 4
Figur figure OT 3
figurativ figurative **WS 4**, 146
Fiktion fiction OT 2
fiktiv imaginary OT 4
Film film; movie OT 1; motion picture OT 4
Filmemacher(in) filmmaker **WS 1**, 30
Filmrolle roll OT 2
Filzstift marker OT 1
Finalist(in) finalist **WS 2**, 69
finanziell financial **WS 2**, 63

finanziell unterstützen to sponsor OT 2
finanzieren to fund OT 3
Finanzwirtschaft finance **WS 2**, 81
finden to find OT 1
Finger finger OT 1
Fingernagel fingernail OT 2
Firma company OT 1; firm **WS 2**, 52
Fisch fish OT 1
Fischstäbchen fish finger OT 1
Fischsuppe chowder OT 3
Fitness fitness OT 2
Fitnesscenter gym OT 3
Fitnesstraining workout **WS 1**, 14
Flachland plains **WS 1**, 21
Flaggschiff flagship OT 3
Flamingo flamingo OT 2
Flasche bottle OT 1
flauschig fluffy OT 2
Fleisch meat OT 1; flesh OT 2
Fleischer(in) butcher OT 4
Fleischklößchen meatball OT 1
flexibel flexible OT 4
Flexibilität flexibility **WS 4**, 144
Fliege bow-tie OT 2
fliegen to fly OT 1
fließend fluent OT 3; flowing **WS 2**, 57
Flohmarkt flea market **WS 3**, 95
Flüchtling refugee OT 4
Flüchtlingslager refugee camp OT 4
Flug flight OT 2
Flugblatt handout OT 4
Flügel wing OT 1
Flughafen airport OT 1
Flugpersonal flight crew OT 2
Flugzeug plane OT 1; airplane; aeroplane OT 4
Fluss river OT 1
flüssig liquid OT 2
Flut flood OT 2
Fluten flooding OT 4
Flyer flyer OT 4
Fokus focus OT 1
fokussieren to focus OT 4
Folge consequence; sequence OT 4; episode **WS 3**, 95
folgen to follow OT 2
folgend sequentially OT 4
folgerichtig logical **WS 1**, 32
Folie slide OT 1
Folklore folklore **WS 1**, 24
fordern to require; to demand OT 4
fördern to promote **WS 1**, 41
Förderung grant **WS 2**, 64
Form form; shape OT 1
  in Form fit OT 2

Format format **WS 2**, 56
Formation formation **WS 1**, 21
formell formal **WS 1**, 19
formen to shape OT 3
förmlich formal **WS 1**, 19
formulieren to formulate OT 4
  neu formulieren to rephrase OT 4
forschen to research OT 2
Forscher(in) researcher OT 2; explorer OT 3
Forschung research OT 2
Forstbeamter / -beamtin park ranger OT 2
Förster(in) ranger OT 3
fortgeschritten advanced OT 4
fortlaufend successive **WS 1**, 21
Fortschritt advance; progress OT 4
fortschrittlich progressive OT 1
Forum forum **WS 2**, 62
fossil fossil OT 3
Foto photo; photograph OT 1
  ein Foto machen to take a photo OT 1
Fotoapparat camera OT 1
Fotograf(in) photographer OT 3
Fotografie photography OT 4
fotokopieren to photocopy OT 4
foulen to foul OT 3
fracken to frack **WS 1**, 27
Fracking fracking **WS 1**, 26
Frage question OT 1
Fragebogen questionnaire OT 1
fragen to ask OT 1
  sich fragen to wonder OT 3
französisch French OT 1
Frau Mrs; woman; wife OT 1
Freak freak OT 4
frech cheeky OT 1
frei free OT 1
Freiberufler(in) freelancer **WS 2**, 63
freiberuflich freelance **WS 2**, 79
Freibeuter privateer OT 3
Freiheit liberty OT 1; freedom OT 3
freilegen to uncover OT 3
Freitag Friday OT 1
freiwillig: sich freiwillig melden to volunteer OT 2
Freiwillige(r) volunteer OT 2
Freizeit leisure OT 3
  Freizeit... recreational OT 3
fremd foreign OT 1
Fremde(r) foreigner OT 3
Freude pleasure OT 1
freuen to look forward to OT 1
Freund(in) friend OT 1
freundlich friendly; kind OT 1
Freundschaft friendship OT 3

Appendix
VOCABULARY

Frieden peace **WS 3**, 93
friedlich peaceful OT 2
Frisbee frisbee OT 1
frisch fresh OT 2
Frisur hairstyle **WS 3**, 92
Fritte chip OT 1
frittieren to fry OT 2
froh glad OT 1
fröhlich cheerful **WS 2**, 57; gay **WS 3**, 89
Frosch frog **WS 4**, 143
früh early OT 1
früher previously OT 3
Frühling spring OT 2
Frühjahrsputz spring clean OT 2
Frühstück breakfast OT 1
Frühstücksflocken cereal OT 1
frustrierend frustrating **WS 3**, 92
frustriert frustrated OT 3
Fuchs fox OT 1
fühlen to feel OT 1
führen to lead OT 3
Führer(in) guide OT 1
Führerhaus cab OT 4
führerlos driverless OT 4
Führerschein driving licence OT 2; driver's license OT 4
Führung leadership OT 4
Führungskraft executive **WS 3**, 88
füllen to fill OT 2
Fundament foundation **WS 1**, 21
fünf five OT 1
fünfte(r, -s) fifth OT 1
fünfzehn fifteen OT 1
fünfzig fifty OT 1
Funke spark OT 2
Funktion function OT 4
für for OT 1
Furcht fear OT 3
furchtbar horrible OT 2
fürchterlich awful OT 1
Fürwort pronoun OT 1
Fuß foot OT 1
Fußabdruck footprint OT 3
Fußball football OT 1; soccer OT 2
Fussel fuzz OT 4
Fußknöchel ankle OT 1
Fußpfad footpath OT 1
Füttern feeding OT 2
füttern to feed OT 2

G

Gabel fork OT 2
Gabelstapler forklift **WS 2**, 70
gaffen to gongoozle OT 3
Gaffer gongoozler OT 3
Galaxie galaxy OT 1
Galerie gallery OT 1
Gallone gallon OT 3
Gamer(in) gamer OT 4
Gang course OT 1
Gans goose OT 4
ganz whole OT 1; completely OT 2
ganze(r, -s) entire OT 3
Garage garage OT 4
Garten garden OT 1; yard OT 2
    Garten hinterm Haus backyard OT 2
Gartenarbeit gardening OT 1
Gärtner(in) gardener OT 4
Gas gas OT 3
Gasse lane OT 2
Gast guest OT 2
Gastfreundschaft hospitality OT 2
Gasthaus lodge; inn OT 2
Gebäude building OT 1
geben to give OT 1
Gebet prayer OT 4
Gebetshaus meetinghouse OT 4
Gebiet area OT 1; territory **WS 1**, 12
gebildet cultured OT 4
Gebirgszug mountain range OT 4
geboren sein to be born OT 2
gebraten roast OT 1
gebrochen broken OT 1
Gebühr fee OT 3
Geburt birth OT 2
Geburtsdatum date of birth OT 2
Geburtsort birthplace OT 4
Geburtstag birthday OT 1
Gedächtnis memory OT 1
Gedanke thought OT 4
gedankenlos thoughtless OT 2
Gedicht poem OT 1
geeignet fit OT 2; suitable OT 4
Geek geek **WS 3**, 104
Gefahr danger; hazard OT 2; risk OT 3; threat **WS 1**, 24
gefährden to threaten **WS 1**, 18; to endanger **WS 1**, 26
gefährdet endangered OT 2
gefährlich dangerous OT 1; risky; unsafe OT 3
gefangen nehmen to arrest **WS 1**, 21
Gefangene(r) prisoner **WS 1**, 18
Gefängnis prison OT 1; jail **WS 3**, 100
Geflügel poultry OT 2
geformt shaped OT 4
gefriergetrocknet freeze-dried OT 4
Gefrierschrank freezer OT 3
gefroren frozen OT 4
Gefühl feeling OT 2; emotion OT 3; sensation OT 4

gegen against OT 1
    etw. gegen etw. tun to do sth. about sth. OT 2
Gegend area; district OT 1
gegensätzlich contrasting OT 4
Gegenstand object OT 1; item OT 2
Gegenteil opposite OT 1; contrast OT 3
Gegenwart present OT 1
Gegner(in) opponent OT 2; opposition **WS 1**, 21
gegnerisch opposing OT 3
gegrillt barbecued OT 4
gehackt chopped OT 2
Gehalt wage OT 4; salary **WS 2**, 57
Geheimnis secret OT 2
gehen to go OT 1
    zu Fuß gehen to walk OT 1
Geheul howl **WS 1**, 23
Gehirn brain OT 2
Gehirnwäsche: einer Gehirnwäsche unterziehen to brainwash **WS 1**, 38
gehorchen: nicht gehorchen to disobey **WS 1**, 24
gehören to belong OT 2
Gehörlose deaf **WS 2**, 65
Gehweg pavement OT 1
Geige violin OT 1
Geist spirit; ghost OT 2
geistig mental OT 4
gekocht boiled OT 1
Gel gel OT 1
Geländearbeit fieldwork OT 4
Geländefahrzeug off-road vehicle OT 1
gelangweilt bored OT 1
gelb yellow OT 1
Geld money OT 1
Geldgeber(in) sponsor OT 2; investor OT 4
gelegen located **WS 1**, 24
Gelegenheit opportunity OT 2
gelegentlich occasionally OT 2
gelockt curly OT 3
Gemälde painting OT 1
gemäß according to OT 3
gemein mean OT 2
Gemeinde township OT 4
gemeinnützig non-profit OT 4
Gemeinschaft community OT 2
gemischt blended **WS 3**, 90
gemischtgeschlechtlich co-ed; co-educational OT 2
Gemüse vegetable OT 1
gemütlich cozy OT 3; comfy OT 4
genau just OT 1; exact OT 2; detailed OT 3; accurate OT 4; precise **WS 4**, 140
genehmigen to approve OT 3

two hundred and eighty-five **285**

Appendix

VOCABULARY

Generation generation OT 4
    die Generation der Jahrtausendwende millennial OT 4
genervt annoyed OT 2
genial brilliant OT 1
genießen to enjoy OT 1
Genre genre OT 4
Gentleman gentleman OT 3
genug enough OT 1; sufficient WW, 11
Geocache geocache OT 2
Geografie geography OT 1
geografisch geographical OT 4
Geologie geology OT 2
Gepäck baggage OT 2; luggage OT 4
Gepäckausgabe baggage claim OT 2
gerade straight OT 3; currently WS 3, 93
Gerät appliance; device OT 3; gadget OT 4
Geräusch sound; noise OT 1
gerecht fair OT 2
Gerechtigkeit justice OT 4
Gericht dish OT 2; court WS 1, 43
    jüngstes Gericht Judgement Day OT 4
gering minor WS 1, 21; slight WS 3, 98
gerissen ripped OT 4
gernhaben to like OT 1; to care about OT 2
    hätte(n) gern would like / love OT 1
geröstet sauté OT 3
Gerücht rumour WS 3, 109
gesamt total OT 1
Gesamtliste tally OT 4
Gesang vocals OT 2
Geschäft business OT 3; deal OT 4; trade WW, 11
Geschäftsfrau businesswoman OT 4
Geschäftsführer(in) manager OT 1
Geschäftsführung management WS 2, 51
Geschäftsmann businessman OT 4
geschehen to happen OT 1
Geschenk present; gift OT 1
Geschenkgutschein gift voucher OT 1
Geschichte history; story OT 1; tale OT 2
Geschichtenbuch storybook OT 2
geschichtlich historical OT 2
Geschick skill OT 2
geschickt skilful OT 3; skilled OT 4
Geschirr dishes OT 2
Geschirrspülen washing up OT 2
Geschirrspülmaschine dishwasher OT 4
Geschlecht gender OT 4; sex WS 3, 90
geschlechtslos genderless WS 3, 92
geschlechtsspezifisch gendered WS 3, 93

Geschlechtswort article OT 1
geschlossen closed OT 1
Geschmack flavour OT 2; taste OT 4
geschnetzelt shredded OT 2
Geschwindigkeit speed OT 2
Geschwister(kind) sibling WS 1, 28
geschwollen swollen OT 2
Gesellschaft society OT 4
Gesetz law OT 3; act WS 1, 19
Gesicht face OT 1
Gesichtsausdruck facial expression OT 4
gespannt curious OT 4
gesponsert sponsored OT 2
Gespräch conversation OT 1
gesprächig chatty OT 3
Gesprächs… conversational WS 1, 31
Geste gesture OT 4; token WS 1, 38
gestern yesterday OT 1
gestiftet sponsored OT 2
gestresst stressed OT 2
gestrichen painted OT 1
gesund healthy OT 2
Gesundheit health OT 2
Gesundheitswesen healthcare OT 4
Getränk drink OT 1
Getreide crop OT 4
getrennt divided; separate OT 2
Gewalt violence OT 4
Gewaltlosigkeit non-violence OT 3
gewalttätig violent WS 1, 27
Gewehr rifle OT 4
Gewicht weight OT 4
Gewichtheben weightlifting OT 4
Gewinn prize OT 1; profit OT 4
gewinnen to win OT 1
Gewinner(in) winner OT 1
Gewitter thunderstorm OT 2; rainstorm WS 4, 108
Gewohnheit habit OT 4
gewöhnlich normally OT 1; common OT 4
gewollt künstlerisch arty WS 2, 60
Gewürz seasoning OT 2; spice OT 3
Gewürzgurke pickle OT 1
gewürzt spiced OT 4
gießen to pour OT 1
Gift poison OT 1; venom WS 1, 38
giftig toxic OT 4; poisonous WS 4, 52
Gig gig WS 2, 62
gigantisch ginormous OT 2
Gipfel peak WS 3, 98
Gips plaster OT 1
Giraffe giraffe OT 1
Gitarre guitar OT 1
Gitarrist(in) guitarist OT 1

Gladiator(in) gladiator OT 3
glamourös glamorous OT 4
Glas glass OT 1
glatt smooth OT 3
Glaube belief OT 4
glauben to believe OT 2
gleich same OT 1
gleichartig fellow WS 1, 21
gleichberechtigt equal OT 4
Gleichberechtigung equality WS 1, 39
Gleichgewicht balance OT 3
Gleitschirmfliegen paragliding WS 2, 67
glitzern to glitter OT 2; to twinkle OT 4
global global OT 4
Globus globe WS 1, 13
Glocke bell OT 1
Glück luck OT 1; fortune OT 3
glückbringend lucky OT 2
glücklich happy OT 1; lucky OT 2
glücklicherweise fortunately WS 2, 57
glücklos unlucky OT 2
Glückwünsche congratulations OT 2
Glühbirne lightbulb OT 3
Gold gold OT 2
golden golden OT 3
Goldrausch gold rush OT 4
Gospel gospel OT 2
Gott God OT 4
Grab grave WS 1, 38
graben to dig OT 1
Grad degree OT 4
Graffiti graffiti WS 3, 121
Grafik graphic OT 3
Gramm gram OT 2
Grammatik grammar OT 1
Grammofon gramophone OT 4
grandios grand WS 3, 89
Graph graph WS 3, 89
Gras grass OT 1
gratulieren to congratulate OT 2
grau grey OT 1
Grauen horror OT 2
Grausamkeit cruelty WS 3, 103
gravieren to engrave OT 4
greifen to grab OT 3
Grenze border OT 3; boundary WS 2, 62
Grenzland frontier OT 4
griechisch Greek OT 2
Griff handle OT 2
Grill grill WS 1, 40
Grillen barbecue OT 2
grinsen to grin OT 2
Grippe influenza WS 1, 22
groß tall; big; great OT 1; large OT 2; vast WS 3, 106

Appendix

VOCABULARY

großartig awesome OT 2; grand WS 3, 89
Großaufnahme close-up OT 4
Großbuchstabe capital letter OT 1
Größe size OT 1
Großeltern grandparents OT 1
Großmutter grandmother OT 1
Großsegler tall ship OT 2
Großvater grandfather OT 2
großzügig generous OT 3
grün green OT 1
Grund reason OT 1; cause OT 2
Grund... primary OT 1; elementary OT 2; basic OT 4
gründen to found; to form OT 4
Gründer(in) founder WS 2, 69
Grundlage foundation WS 1, 21; basis WS 2, 61
grundlegend radical OT 4
grundsätzlich basic OT 4
Grundschule elementary school OT 2
Gruppe group OT 1
Gruppenarbeit teamwork OT 4
gruselig creepy WS 1, 13
Gruß greeting WS 1, 29
  mit freundlichen Grüßen sincerely OT 4
grüßen to greet WS 2, 57
günstig convenient OT 4
Gurke pickle OT 1
Gurt harness OT 1
Gürtel belt OT 2
gut fine; good; all right OT 1
  gut aussehend handsome OT 1
Gutacher(in) assessor WS 2, 51
gutbürgerlich plain OT 4
Güter goods OT 4
Gutschein coupon OT 2
guttun to benefit OT 2
Gymnastik gymnastics OT 1

H

Haare hair OT 1
Haarschnitt haircut OT 2
Habe belongings OT 3
haben feature OT 1
Habitat habitat OT 4
Hackbraten meatloaf OT 3
Hackfleischbällchen meatball OT 1
Hafen port; harbour OT 2
Haferbrei porridge OT 3
Haferflocken oats OT 3
Häftling prisoner WS 1, 18
Hähnchen chicken OT 1
Hai shark WS 1, 24
Häkchen tick OT 2

haken to hook OT 4
Haken tick OT 2
halal halal OT 3
halb half OT 1; halfway OT 3
  eine halbe Stunde nach half past OT 1
halb... semi- WS 1, 22
Halbjahr semester OT 3
Halbmarathon half marathon OT 2
halbwegs halfway OT 3
Halbzeit half-time OT 2
Halle hall OT 1
hallo hello; hi OT 1
Halloween Halloween OT 2
Hals neck OT 1; throat OT 2
Halsband collar OT 2
Halt stop OT 2
halten to hold OT 1
Halter holder WS 2, 70
Haltestelle stop; halt OT 2
Haltung attitude OT 3
Hamburger burger OT 1; hamburger OT 2
Hamster hamster OT 1
Hand hand OT 1
  jmdm. die Hand geben to shake hands OT 2
  mit der Hand schreiben to handwrite WS 2, 63
Handbuch handbook OT 3
Handel trade WW, 11; commerce WS 2, 50
  illegalen Handel treiben to traffic OT 4
Handgelenk wrist OT 1
Händler(in) retailer OT 4
Handlung plot OT 4
Handout handout OT 4
Handschrift handwriting OT 2
handschriftlich handwritten WS 4, 144
Handschuh glove OT 1
Handtasche handbag OT 3
Handtuch towel OT 2
Handy mobile phone OT 1; cell phone OT 2
Harfe harp OT 1
Harfenist(in) harpist OT 3
harmlos harmless WS 3, 94
hart hard OT 1; tough OT 4
Hashtag hashtag WS 2, 65
hassen to hate OT 1; to loathe WS 1, 23
hässlich ugly OT 1
Haufen heap OT 4; pile WS 1, 27
häufig frequently OT 3; many times OT 4; frequent WS 1, 26
Häufigkeit frequency OT 1

Haupt... primary; main OT 1; core OT 4
Hauptgang main course OT 1
hauptsächlich mainly OT 2; generally OT 4
Hauptsitz headquarter OT 4
Hauptstadt capital OT 1
Hauptverkehrszeit rush hour OT 1
Hauptwort noun OT 1
Haus house OT 1
Hausarbeit housework OT 1; chore OT 4
Hausarrest erteilen to ground WS 3, 121
Hausaufgaben homework OT 1
Hausboot narrowboat; houseboat OT 3
Häuschen cottage OT 3
Hausfrau housewife WS 2, 63
Haushälter(in) housekeeper OT 3
Haushalts... household OT 4
Haushaltsgerät appliance OT 3
häuslich household OT 4
Hausmeister(in) caretaker OT 1
Haustier pet OT 1
Haut skin OT 2
Headquarter headquarter OT 4
Headset headset OT 4
heben to raise OT 2; to lift OT 3
Hecke hedge WS 2, 59
heften to pin OT 1
heil in one piece OT 2
Heilbad spa OT 3
heilen to cure OT 4
heilig sacred OT 4
Heilkunde medical science OT 4
Heilung healing WS 1, 21
Heimat homeland OT 4
heimatlos homeless OT 3
Heimatstadt hometown OT 4
heimtückisch sneaky WS 3, 118
Heimweh homesickness OT 4
heiraten to marry OT 1; to wed OT 3
Heiratsantrag: einen Heiratsantrag machen to propose WS 2, 64
heiß hot OT 1
heizen to heat OT 3
Heizung heater OT 2; heating OT 3
Hektar hectare WS 1, 27
hektisch frantic OT 3; hectic OT 4
Held(in) hero OT 3
helfen to help OT 1
Helfer(in) helper OT 3
Helm helmet OT 1
Hemd shirt OT 1
Hemisphäre hemisphere WS 1, 13
Henne hen OT 2
heraus out OT 1
herausfinden to find out OT 1; to work out OT 2

Appendix
VOCABULARY

herausfordern to challenge **WS 3**, 92
Herausforderung challenge OT 2
Herausgeber(in) editor OT 2
herausragend outstanding OT 3
Herbst autumn OT 2
Herd cooker OT 3
Herde herd OT 4
Herr Mr; Sir OT 1; gentleman OT 3
herrisch bossy OT 2
Herrschaft reign OT 3
herrschen to reign OT 3
Herrscher(in) monarch **WS 2**, 64
Hersteller(in) manufacturer OT 4; producer **WS 1**, 18
Herstellung production; manufacture OT 4; manufacturing **WS 2**, 63
Herumblödeln to muck around **WS 3**, 93
herumhängen to hang out OT 1
herumwandern to roam around **WS 1**, 23
herumziehend migrant OT 4
hervorheben to highlight OT 3
hervorrufen to provoke **WS 4**, 145
Herz heart OT 2
herzhaft hearty OT 2
heterosexuell heterosexual **WS 3**, 93
Heureka-Erlebnis eureka moment OT 4
heute today OT 1
    heute Abend tonight OT 1
heutzutage nowadays OT 3
Hexe witch OT 2
hier here OT 1; locally OT 3
Highway highway OT 3
Hilfe relief OT 4
hilflos helpless; hopeless OT 4
hilfreich helpful OT 1
Himbeere raspberry OT 1
Himmel sky OT 1; heaven **WS 2**, 64
hinauf up OT 1
hindeuten: auf etw. hindeuten to denote **WS 4**, 144
hinduistisch Hindu OT 1
Hinfahrt outward journey OT 3
hinfallen to fall over OT 2
hinsetzen to sit down OT 1
hinter behind OT 1
Hintergrund background OT 3
hinterhältig sneaky **WS 3**, 118
Hinterland outback OT 4
hinterlassen to leave behind OT 2
hinüber across OT 1
hinunter down OT 1
hinunterkommen to get down OT 2
hinunterschlucken to swallow OT 4
Hinweis tip; clue OT 1

hinzufügen to add OT 1
Hip-Hop hip hop OT 1
hispanisch Hispanic OT 3
Historiker(in) historian OT 3
historisch historic OT 3
Hitzewelle heatwave **WS 1**, 26
Hobby hobby OT 1
hoch high; tall OT 1
hochheben to lift OT 3
hochladen to upload OT 3
Hochschule college OT 2
Hochwasser flood OT 2
Hochzeit wedding OT 3
Hockey hockey OT 1
Hof court; courtyard OT 3
hoffen to hope OT 1
hoffentlich hopefully OT 4
hoffnungslos hopeless OT 4
hoffnungsvoll hopeful **WS 1**, 27
höflich polite OT 1
Höhe height OT 1
Höhepunkt climax **WS 4**, 145
Höhle cave OT 1
holen to fetch OT 4
Hölle hell **WS 2**, 64
holprig bumpy OT 4
Holz wood OT 2
hölzern wooden OT 1
Holzscheit log OT 3
Honig honey OT 2
hören to hear OT 1
Hörer(in) listener OT 1
Horizont horizon **WS 1**, 20
horizontal horizontal OT 4
Hormon hormone **WS 3**, 93
Horn horn OT 2
Horror horror OT 2
Hose trousers OT 1
    kurze Hose shorts OT 1
Hostel hostel OT 2
Hotdog hot dog OT 2
Hotel hotel OT 1
Hotline helpline OT 2
hübsch lovely; pretty OT 1
Hubschrauber helicopter OT 2
Hüfte hip OT 3
Hügel hill OT 1
hügelig hilly OT 2
Huhn chicken OT 1
Hühnerstall coop OT 4
Hülle cover OT 1
Hülsenfrucht pulse OT 4
humanitär humanitarian **WS 2**, 61
Humor humour OT 3
humorvoll humorous **WS 4**, 145
Hund dog OT 1

Hundedreck dog mess OT 2
hundert hundred OT 1
Hunger hunger OT 4
hungern (lassen) to starve OT 1
Hungersnot famine OT 4
hungrig hungry OT 1
Hurrikan hurricane **WS 1**, 26
husten to cough OT 2
Hut hat OT 1
Hütehund sheepdog OT 2
Hüter(in) keeper OT 4
hydratisieren to hydrate OT 4
Hygiene hygiene OT 4
Hymne anthem **WS 1**, 31
Hype hype **WS 2**, 67
Hyperlink hyperlink OT 3

I
ich I OT 1
    ich selbst myself OT 3
ideal ideal OT 2
idealerweise ideally **WS 2**, 57
Idee idea OT 1
identifizieren to identify OT 3
identisch identical **WS 4**, 145
Identität identity OT 3
Idol idol **WS 3**, 102
Igel hedgehog OT 1
Igitt! yuck OT 3
ignorieren to ignore OT 4
ihm / ihn him OT 1
ihnen them OT 1
ihr their; her OT 1
ihre(r, -s) hers; theirs; yours OT 2
Ikone icon WW, 11
ikonisch iconic OT 3
illegal illegal OT 3
Illustration illustration OT 2
illustrieren to illustrate OT 3
imaginär imaginary OT 4
immer always OT 1
    für immer forever OT 2
    immer noch still OT 1
Immobilie property **WS 1**, 23
Imperativ imperative OT 1
importieren to import OT 3
Improvisation improvisation OT 2
improvisieren to improvise OT 2
in at; on; into; inside OT 1
inakzeptabel unacceptable **WS 1**, 25
Index index OT 4
Indexer(in) indexer OT 4
indisch Indian OT 2
individuell individual OT 3
Industrie industry OT 2
Industrie... industrial OT 2

VOCABULARY

Infinitiv infinitive OT 2
Influencer(in) influencer WS 3, 105
Influenza influenza WS 1, 22
Infografik infographic OT 3
Information information OT 1
informativ informative OT 3
informell informal WS 1, 16
informieren to inform OT 4
Ingenieur(in) engineer OT 3
Ingenieurwesen engineering OT 1
Inhalt content OT 2
inhuman inhumane OT 4
Initiative initiative OT 4
Inklusion inclusion WS 3, 88
inklusive including; include OT 1
Inkubator incubator WS 2, 52
innen indoor(s) OT 2
Innenhof courtyard OT 3
Innenstadt downtown; inner city OT 4
Innere: das Innere interior WS 1, 13
Innereien insides OT 3
innerer inner WS 2, 53
innerhalb inside OT 1; within OT 4
Innovation innovation OT 4
innovativ innovative OT 4
Innovator(in) innovator OT 4
insbesondere in particular WS 1, 21
Insekt insect OT 1
Insektenhaus bughouse OT 1
Insel island OT 2
    kleine Insel isle WS 1, 30
Inserat advert OT 1
Inspiration inspiration OT 4
inspirieren to inspire OT 3
installieren to install OT 4
instruktiv informative OT 3; instructive WS 1, 31
Instrument instrument OT 1
Insulaner(in) islander WS 1, 12
integrativ inclusive OT 4
integriert integrated WS 3, 118
intelligent clever OT 1; intelligent OT 2; smart OT 4
Intelligenz: künstliche Intelligenz
    AI (artificial intelligence) WS 2, 69
interagieren to interact OT 4
Interaktion interaction OT 4
interaktiv interactive WS 4, 141
interessant interesting OT 1
Interesse interest OT 1
    im Interesse von on behalf of WS 1, 21
interessieren: sich interessieren to care about OT 2
interessiert interested OT 1
interkulturell intercultural WS 4, 144
intern internal WS 3, 115

international international OT 1
Internet internet OT 1
Internethandel e-commerce OT 4
Interpret(in) performer OT 2
Interpretation interpretation WS 4, 146
interpretieren to interpret OT 4
Intersex intersex WS 3, 93
Interview interview OT 1
interviewen to interview OT 1
Interviewer(in) interviewer OT 1
Intonation intonation OT 4
Invasion invasion WS 1, 21
invasiv invasive WS 1, 23
Inversion inversion WS 3, 118
investieren to invest OT 3
Investition investment OT 3
Investor(in) investor OT 4
involviert involved OT 3
inzwischen meanwhile WS 4, 126
iranisch Iranian OT 4
irgendein(e) any OT 1
irgendetwas anything OT 1
irgendjemand anybody OT 1; anyone OT 2
irgendwie like OT 1; somehow WS 1, 41
irgendwo somewhere OT 1; anywhere OT 2
irisch Irish OT 1
Ironie irony WS 4, 145
Irre madman OT 4
irreführend misleading OT 3
irrtümlicherweise mistakenly WS 3, 118
islamisch Islamic WS 3, 88
israelisch Israeli OT 2
italienisch Italian OT 2
    italienisches Eiscafé gelateria WS 2, 69

J

ja yes; yeah OT 1
Jacht yacht OT 2
Jacke jacket OT 1
jagen to chase OT 1; to hunt OT 2
Jäger(in) hunter WS 1, 20
Jahr year OT 1
Jahreszeit season OT 3
Jahrhundert century OT 2
jährlich annual WS 2, 65
Jahrmarkt fairground OT 2; fair OT 4
Jahrzehnt decade WS 3, 93
jamaikanisch Jamaican OT 1
Januar January OT 1
japanisch Japanese OT 1
Jazz jazz OT 2
je ever OT 1
Jeanshose jeans OT 1

Jeansstoff denim OT 4
jede(r, -s) everybody; every; each; everyone OT 1
jederzeit anytime OT 3
jedoch though; however OT 2
jemand someone; somebody OT 1
jene(r, -s) that OT 1
    jene dort those OT 1
jenseits beyond WS 1, 30
jetzt now OT 1
Job job OT 1
joggen to jog OT 2
Joghurt yoghurt OT 1
Journal journal WW, 11
Journalismus journalism WS 2, 79
Journalist(in) journalist OT 2
jubeln to cheer OT 2
juckend itchy OT 2
Judo judo OT 1
Jugend youth OT 1
Jugendbetreuer(in) counsellor OT 2
Jugendherberge youth hostel OT 2
Jugendliche(r) teenager OT 2
Juli July OT 1
jung young OT 1
Junge boy OT 1
jüngst recent OT 4
Juni June OT 1
Junior(in) junior OT 2
Juwel jewel OT 1

K

Kabel cable WS 1, 44
Kabine cabin OT 2
Kabinett cabinet WS 2, 71
Kaffee coffee OT 1
Käfig cage OT 4
Kai pier WS 3, 121
Kajakfahren kayaking OT 2
Kalender calendar OT 1
Kalorie calorie WS 3, 102
kalt cold OT 1; freezing OT 2
Kamel camel WS 1, 23
Kamera camera OT 1
Kameramann cameraman WS 4, 138
Kamin fireplace OT 1
Kamm comb OT 2
Kammer chamber OT 2
    kleine Kammer closet OT 2
Kampagne campaign OT 3; initiative OT 4
Kampf fight OT 1
kämpfen to fight OT 1
Kanal canal OT 3
Kanalboot narrowboat OT 3
Kandidat(in) candidate OT 4

Appendix

VOCABULARY

Känguru kangaroo **WS 1**, 12
Kaninchen rabbit OT 1
Kantine canteen OT 1
Kanu canoe OT 1
Kanufahren canoeing OT 1
Kanzlei firm **WS 2**, 52
Kapitel chapter OT 1
Kapsel capsule OT 4
Kapuzenpullover hoodie OT 1
Karamelle caramel OT 3
Karate karate OT 1
Karbon carbon OT 3
Karotte carrot OT 1
Karriere career OT 3
Karte card OT 1
Karteikarte cue card OT 4
Kartoffel potato OT 1
Kartoffelbrei mashed potato OT 1
Karton carton OT 2
Kartrennen kart racing OT 3
Käse cheese OT 1
Kasse cash register OT 2; check-out OT 4
Kassierer(in) cashier; bank teller OT 4
Kästchen box OT 1
katastrophal catastrophic OT 4
Katastrophe disaster OT 2
Katastrophengebiet disaster area OT 2
Kategorie category OT 3
Kathedrale cathedral OT 1
Katholik(in) Catholic OT 3
Katze cat OT 1
Kauf purchase OT 4
kaufen to buy; to shop OT 1
Käufer(in) shopper OT 4
kaum hardly OT 3
keimtötend antiseptic OT 2
keine(r, -s) none OT 2
Keks biscuit OT 1; cookie OT 3
Keller cellar OT 4
Kellner(in) waiter OT 1
kenntnisreich knowledgeable OT 3
Kennwort password OT 4
Kerl guy OT 2
Kern core OT 4
Kernland heartland OT 4
Kerze candle OT 2
Kerzenlicht candlelight OT 4
Kessel kettle OT 2
Ketchup ketchup OT 1
Kette chain OT 2
keuchen to gasp OT 2
Keulen cull **WS 1**, 23
keulen to cull **WS 1**, 23
Keyboard keyboard OT 1
Kickball kickball OT 4
Kidneybohne kidney bean OT 2

Kilometer kilometre OT 1
Kind child; kid OT 1
Kindergarten preschool **WS 3**, 99
Kindheit childhood OT 3
Kino cinema OT 1
kippen to dump **WS 4**, 144
Kipppunkt tipping point **WS 1**, 27
Kirche church OT 1
Kissen cushion OT 1
Kiste box OT 1; crate OT 4
Kitesurfen kite-surfing **WS 1**, 43
Kiwi kiwi OT 1
Klammer clip OT 1; bracket OT 2
klammern to cling OT 2
Klan clan OT 3
Klang (einer Glocke) bong OT 1
Klaps pat OT 3
klar clear OT 2; evident **WS 4**, 141
klären to clarify OT 4
Klarinette clarinet OT 2
Klasse class OT 1
Klassenkamerad(in) classmate OT 3
Klassenstufe grade OT 2
Klassenzimmer classroom OT 1
klassisch classic; classical OT 2; vintage **WS 2**, 52
klatschen to clap OT 1
klauen to steal OT 2
Klavier piano OT 1
Klebeband tape OT 1
kleben to stick OT 1; to paste OT 2
klebend sticky OT 4
klebrig sticky OT 1
Klebstoff glue OT 1
Kleid dress OT 3
   Kleider clothes OT 1; outfit **WS 2**, 64
Kleiderordnung dress code OT 4
Kleiderschrank wardrobe OT 1
Kleidung clothes OT 1; clothing OT 3
klein small; little OT 1; minor **WS 1**, 21
   sehr klein miniature OT 3
Kleinbus minibus OT 2
Kleingeld cash OT 1
Kletterer(in) climber OT 2
klettern to climb OT 1
klicken to click **WS 3**, 104
Klima climate OT 2
Klimaerwärmung global warming OT 3
Klingel doorbell OT 2
klingeln to ring OT 1
klingen to sound OT 2
Klinik clinic **WS 2**, 66
klinisch clinical **WS 3**, 108
Klippe cliff **WS 1**, 22
klirren to clash OT 2
Klischee stereotype **WS 1**, 39

Klo loo OT 2
Klopfen knock OT 2
klopfen to tap OT 2
Kloß dumpling OT 4
Kloster monastery OT 3
Klub club OT 1
klug savvy **WS 3**, 104
Kneipe pub OT 2
Knete dough OT 2
Knie knee OT 1
knien to kneel OT 1
knistern to sizzle **WS 1**, 40
Knochen bone OT 1
Knödel dumpling OT 4
Knopf button OT 1
knuddelig cuddly OT 1
Koala koala **WS 1**, 13
Koch / Köchin chef OT 1
köcheln to simmer OT 2
kochen to make; to cook OT 1; to boil OT 2
   kochend heiß boiling OT 1
Kochfeld hob OT 3
Koffein caffeine **WS 3**, 102
Koffer case OT 1; suitcase OT 2
Kofferraum trunk OT 2
Kohl cabbage OT 1
Kohle coal OT 2
   glühende Kohle ember **WS 4**, 126
Kohlendioxid carbon dioxide **WS 1**, 26
Kohlenhydrat carbohydrate **WS 3**, 102; carb **WS 3**, 103
kohlensäurehaltig fizzy OT 2
Kojote coyote **WS 4**, 127
Kollege(-in) colleague OT 4
kolonial colonial OT 4
Kolonialisierung colonization **WS 1**, 22
Kolonie colony OT 4
kolonisieren to colonize **WS 3**, 91
Kolonist(in) colonist OT 3
Kombination combination OT 3
kombinieren to combine OT 4
Komitee committee OT 2
Komma comma OT 3
Kommandant(in) captain; commander OT 4
kommen to come OT 1
   näher kommen to approach OT 4
Kommentar comment OT 1
kommentieren to comment OT 3
Kommerz commerce **WS 2**, 50
kommerziell commercial OT 4
kommunizieren to communicate OT 4
Komödie comedy **WS 4**, 145
Komparativ comparative OT 2
Kompass compass OT 2

Appendix

VOCABULARY

kompetent competent **WS 2**, 58
Kompetenz competence **WS 4**, 144
komplex complex **WS 1**, 32
Kompliment compliment **WS 4**, 140
kompliziert complicated OT 2; tricky OT 4
komponieren to compose OT 3
Komponist(in) composer OT 2
Kompost compost OT 3
Kompromiss compromise **WS 3**, 92
Kondor condor OT 3
Konferenz conference OT 4
Konflikt conflict OT 2
Kongress convention OT 4
König king OT 1
Königin queen OT 1
königlich royal OT 1
Königreich kingdom OT 4
konkret specific OT 3; precise **WS 4**, 118
Konkurrent(in) competitor OT 4
Konkurrenz competition OT 1; rivalry **WS 1**, 28
konkurrenzorientiert competitive OT 3
konkurrieren to compete OT 2
Können ability OT 2
können can OT 1; to be able to; to be allowed to OT 2
    könnte might; may OT 1
Konsequenz consequence OT 4
Konstellation constellation **WS 3**, 115
konstruktiv constructive **WS 4**, 140
Kontakt contact OT 1
    in Kontakt bleiben to keep in touch OT 2
    Kontakte pflegen to socialize OT 4
Kontext context OT 4
Kontinent continent OT 3
Kontrabass double bass OT 2
Kontrast contrast OT 3
Kontrolle control OT 3
kontrollieren to control OT 4
Konvention convention OT 4
Konzentration concentration OT 4
konzentrieren to concentrate OT 3
    sich auf etw. konzentrieren to centre around **WS 4**, 145
Konzept concept OT 4
Konzert concert OT 1
Kookaburra kookaburra **WS 1**, 13
Kooperation partnership OT 4
Kopf head OT 1
    Kopf hoch! cheer up OT 1
Kopfband headband OT 3
Kopfkissen pillow OT 2
Kopfsalat lettuce OT 2
Kopfschmerzen headache OT 1

Kopie replica OT 4
kopieren to copy OT 1
Koralle coral **WS 1**, 26
Korb basket OT 3
Kordel lanyard **WS 2**, 70
koreanisch Korean OT 1
Korn grain **WS 3**, 102
Körper body OT 1
körperlich physical OT 2
Korporations... corporate **WW**, 11
Korrektur correction OT 4
Korridor corridor OT 2
korrigieren to correct OT 1; to fix; to mark OT 2
kosmopolitisch cosmopolitan **WS 1**, 19
Kosten cost OT 1
kosten to cost OT 1
kostenlos free OT 1; pro bono **WS 2**, 61
Kostüm costume; fancy dress OT 2
krabbeln to crawl **WS 1**, 20
Krabbeltier creepy-crawly OT 2
krachen to crash OT 3
Kraft force OT 1; power **WS 1**, 27
kräftig powerful **WS 1**, 20
kraftlos powerless OT 4
Krake octopus OT 1
Krampf cramp OT 2
Kran crane OT 4
krank sick OT 1; unwell; ill OT 2
Krankenhaus hospital OT 1
Krankenschwester / -pfleger nurse OT 1
Krankenwagen ambulance OT 1
Krankheit disease; illness OT 2
Kranz wreath OT 3
Krapfen doughnut OT 2
kratzen to scratch OT 2
kraus frizzy OT 3
Kraut herb OT 3
Krawatte tie OT 1
kreativ creative OT 2
Kreativität creativity OT 4
Krebs cancer OT 4
Kreditkarte credit card OT 1
kreieren to create OT 2
Kreis circle OT 1
kreischen to scream OT 3
Kreisdiagramm pie chart OT 4
kreuzen to cross OT 1
Kreuzfahrt cruise OT 2
    eine Kreuzfahrt machen to cruise OT 3
Kreuzung crossroads OT 1
Kricket cricket OT 1
kriechen to crawl **WS 1**, 20
Krieg war OT 2
Krieger(in) warrior OT 2

Kriegsschiff warship OT 3
Kriminelle(r) criminal OT 3
Krise crisis OT 3
Kritik criticism **WS 4**, 140
kritisch critical **WS 1**, 23
kritisieren to criticize OT 3
Krokodil crocodile **WS 1**, 44
Krone crown OT 1
krönen to crown OT 1
Kröte toad OT 2
Krücke crutch OT 2
Küche kitchen OT 1; cuisine OT 3
Kuchen cake OT 1
Küchenchef(in) chef OT 1
Kugelschreiber ballpoint pen OT 1
Kuh cow OT 1
kühl cool OT 1
kühlen to cool OT 3
Kühlschrank fridge OT 1; refrigerator OT 4
Kult... iconic OT 3
kultiviert cultured OT 4
Kultur culture OT 1
kulturell cultural OT 3
Kummer sorrow **WS 4**, 145
Kumpel mate **WS 1**, 14
Kumpel buddy OT 2
Kunde / Kundin customer OT 3; client **WS 2**, 70
Kundgebung rally OT 4
kündigen to quit OT 4
Kunst art OT 1
    bildende Kunst visual art OT 2
Künstler(in) performer OT 2; entertainer; artist OT 3
künstlich man-made OT 1; artifical OT 3
    künstliche Intelligenz artificial intelligence OT 4
Kunststoff plastic OT 2
Kunstwerk artwork **WS 3**, 107
Kunstwissenschaft fine art OT 2
Kupfer copper OT 1
Kuppel cupola OT 4
Kürbis pumpkin OT 2; squash OT 4
Kürbislaterne jack-o-lantern OT 2
Kuriosität oddity OT 4
Kurs course OT 1; program OT 3
kursieren to circulate OT 4
kurz short OT 1; brief **WS 2**, 56
kürzen to shorten **WS 2**, 67
kuschelig cuddly OT 1
Kuss kiss OT 3
Küste seaside; coast OT 1; shore OT 2; coastline **WS 1**, 32
Küsten... coastal OT 1
Küstenlinie coastline **WS 1**, 32

two hundred and ninety-one **291**

Küstenwache coastguard OT 2
Kutsche buggy OT 4
Kutschfahrten carriage driving OT 2

L

Labor lab OT 2; laboratory OT 4
Lache pool OT 1
lächeln to smile OT 1
lachen to laugh OT 1
    Lachender Hans kookaburra **WS 1**, 13
Lachs salmon OT 1
Lack varnish **WS 2**, 64
Laden shop; store OT 1
Ladendiebstahl shoplifting **WS 3**, 121
Ladung cargo OT 3; load **WS 1**, 13
Lage situation OT 1; circumstance **WS 3**, 100
Lagerfeuer campfire OT 2
Lagerraum stockroom **WS 2**, 59; storeroom **WS 3**, 121
Lagerung storage OT 3
Lamm lamb OT 1
Lampe lamp OT 1
Land countryside OT 1
    an Land ashore OT 4
Landarbeiter(in) farmhand; farmworker OT 4
landen to land OT 1
Landkarte map OT 1
ländlich rural OT 4
Landschaft landscape; scenery OT 2
Landstrasse highway OT 3
Landwirtschaft farming; agriculture OT 2
landwirtschaftlich agricultural OT 4; agrarian **WS 1**, 22
lang long OT 1
Länge length OT 2
langsam slow OT 2
langweilig boring OT 1; dull **WS 3**, 88
Lappen cloth OT 2
Laptop laptop OT 1
Lärm noise OT 1
Lasagne lasagna OT 1
Laser laser OT 3
lassen to let OT 1
lässig casual **WS 3**, 104
Laster truck OT 1
Lastkraftwagen truck OT 1
Latein Latin OT 1
lateinamerikanisch Latino OT 2
Laterne lantern OT 2
Laufband treadmill OT 4
laufen to walk; to run OT 1
Läufer(in) runner OT 2
laut loud; noisy OT 1; aloud OT 2

Lautsprecher loudspeaker OT 2
Lautsprecheranlage PA (public address) system OT 2
Lava lava **WS 1**, 24
leasen to lease OT 4
Leben life OT 1; lifetime OT 2
    Leben nach dem Tod afterlife **WS 4**, 126
leben to live OT 1
lebendig alive OT 4
lebensbedrohlich life-threatening OT 2
Lebenslauf Curriculum Vitae **WS 2**, 56
Lebensmittel groceries OT 4
Lebensmittelladen grocery store OT 4
Lebensmittelverarbeitung food processing OT 4
Lebensmittelvergiftung food poisoning OT 2
Lebensraum habitat OT 4
Lebensstil lifestyle OT 4
lebenswichtig vital OT 4
Lebenszeit lifetime OT 2
Leber liver **WS 3**, 102
Lebewesen creature OT 4
lebhaft lively **WS 1**, 43; vibrant **WS 1**, 19
lecken to lick OT 3
lecker delicious OT 1
LED Birne LED bulb OT 3
Leder leather OT 3
leer empty OT 1; blank OT 4
leeren to empty OT 4
legal legal OT 4
legalisieren to legalize **WS 3**, 90
Legende legend OT 2; myth **WS 1**, 20
lehnen to lean OT 3
Lehrer(in) teacher OT 1; instructor OT 3
Lehrling apprentice **WS 2**, 52
Lehrmeister(in) mentor OT 4
lehrreich instructive **WS 1**, 31
Lehrstelle apprenticeship **WS 2**, 50
Leiche corpse **WS 1**, 38
leicht easy OT 2; light OT 3; slight **WS 3**, 98
Leichtathletik athletics OT 1
leichtsinnig carelessly OT 2
leiden to suffer **WS 1**, 20
leidenschaftlich passionate OT 4
leider unfortunately OT 3
leihen to lend; to borrow OT 2
Leihgabe loan **WS 2**, 64
Leinwand screen OT 1
    auf der Leinwand onscreen OT 2
leisten to afford OT 2
Leistung achievement OT 2
leiten to manage OT 1
Leiter ladder OT 2

Leitung: die Leitung übernehmen to take charge OT 2
Leopard leopard OT 2
lernen to learn OT 1
    auswendig lernen to memorize OT 4
Lernende(r) learner OT 3
lesbisch lesbian **WS 3**, 93
Lesen reading OT 1
lesen to read OT 1
Leser(in) reader OT 3
Lesezeichen marker OT 1
letzte(r, -s) last OT 1
leuchtend bright OT 1
leugnen to deny **WS 3**, 89
Leute people OT 1; folks; guys OT 2
    unter die Leute kommen to socialize OT 4
Licht light OT 1
liebe(r, -s) dear OT 1
lieben to love OT 1
Liebes sweetheart **WS 3**, 95
Liebhaber(in) lover OT 3
Lieblings... favourite OT 1
Liebste(r) sweetheart **WS 3**, 95
Lied song OT 1
Liedtext lyrics OT 2
liefern to deliver OT 4
Lieferung delivery OT 3
Lieferwagen van OT 4
liegen to lie OT 1
Lifestyle lifestyle OT 4
Liga league OT 2
lila purple OT 1
Limo soda **WS 3**, 102
Lineal ruler OT 1
Linguist(in) linguist **WS 3**, 106
Linie line OT 1
linke(r, -s) left OT 1
Linse lens OT 4
Lippe lip OT 2
Liste list OT 1
Liter litre; liter OT 4
literarisch literary **WS 3**, 115
Literatur literature OT 4
Loch hole OT 1
Locher hole punch **WS 2**, 70
locken to tempt **WS 2**, 57
locker laid-back OT 4; casual **WS 3**, 104
Löffel spoon OT 2
logisch logical **WS 1**, 32
Logo logo OT 1
Lohn salary **WS 2**, 57
lohnen to be worth it OT 1
lohnend worthwhile OT 2; rewarding OT 4
lohnenswert worth OT 4

Appendix

VOCABULARY

Lokführer(in) engineer OT 3
Lokomotive engine OT 2
löschen to put out OT 2; to delete OT 4
Löscher extinguisher **WS 2**, 71
lösen to solve OT 3
losfahren to head out OT 4
loslassen to relax OT 2
losstürzen to rush off OT 2
Lösung solution OT 2
loswerden to get rid of OT 3
Lotterie lottery OT 3
Löwe / Löwin lion OT 1
Luchs lynx OT 2
Lücke gap OT 3
Luft air OT 1
Luftschlangen streamer OT 4
Lunge lung OT 3
Lust lust **WS 3**, 96
    auf etw. Lust haben to be keen on sth. OT 4
lustig funny OT 1; amusing **WS 2**, 80
luxuriös luxurious OT 2
Luxus luxury **WS 2**, 64

M
machen to make; to do OT 1
    Das macht... That'll be ... OT 2
Macher(in) maker OT 3
Macht power **WS 1**, 27
mächtig mighty OT 3; powerful **WS 1**, 20
machtlos powerless OT 4
    burschikoses Mädchen tomboy **WS 3**, 93
Mädchen girl OT 1
Magen stomach OT 2
magisch magical OT 2
Magnet magnet OT 1
magnetisch magnetic OT 2
mähen to mow **WS 3**, 93
Mahlzeit meal OT 1
Mai May OT 1
Mailbox mailbox OT 4
Mais corn OT 3
Maisbrot cornbread OT 4
malen to paint OT 1
malerisch scenic **WS 1**, 17
Mama mum OT 1
man you OT 1
Management management **WS 2**, 51
managen to manage OT 1
Manager(in) manager OT 1
manchmal sometimes OT 1
Mandant(in) client **WS 2**, 70
Mangel lack OT 3; shortage **WS 1**, 18
mangelhaft junky OT 4
Mann man OT 1; husband OT 2

männlich male OT 2
Mannschaft team OT 1; crew OT 2
Mantel coat OT 1
Mappe portfolio OT 4
Marathon marathon OT 2
Märchen fairy tale OT 1
Marine navy OT 3
    Marine... maritime OT 3
Marke brand OT 4
Marketing marketing OT 4
markieren to bookmark OT 4
Markise marquee OT 2
Markt market OT 1; marketplace **WW**, 11
    auf den Markt bringen to launch; to release OT 4
Marktsegment market segment **WS 3**, 104
Marmelade jam OT 2
Marsch march OT 3
März March OT 1
Maschine machine OT 1
    Maschinen machinery OT 2
Masern measles **WS 1**, 22
Maske mask OT 3
Maß measurement OT 2
Massaker massacre OT 3
Masse zusetzen to bulk up **WS 3**, 102
Maßeinheit measurement OT 2
Massen... mass OT 4
Massensport mass sport OT 3
Material material OT 3
Mathematik / Mathe maths; math OT 1; mathematics OT 3
Mathematiker(in) mathematician OT 3
Matrose sailor OT 1
Maultier mule OT 3
Maus mouse OT 2
Mauszeiger cursor OT 3
Maximum maximum OT 2
Mayonnaise mayonnaise OT 1
mechanisch mechanical **WS 2**, 81
meckern to nag **WS 4**, 144
Medaille medal OT 2
Mediation mediation OT 1
Medien media OT 2
Medikament medicine OT 2
Medikation medication **WS 3**, 93
Medizin medicine OT 2; medical science OT 4
medizinisch medical OT 1
Meer sea OT 1
Meeres... marine OT 4
Meeresboden seabed OT 3
Meeresfrüchte seafood OT 3
Mehl flour OT 3
mehr more OT 1; anymore OT 2

mehrere several OT 2
Mehrheit majority OT 4
Mehrzahl plural OT 1
Meile mile OT 1
mein my OT 1
    meine(r, -s) mine OT 2
Meinung opinion OT 3
    anderer Meinung sein to disagree OT 2
Meinungsverschiedenheit disagreement OT 2
meiste most OT 1
Meister(in) master OT 4
Melodie melody OT 2
Memoiren memoir **WS 4**, 126
Menchenmenge throng OT 2
Menge crowd OT 1; amount OT 2; portion; quantity OT 4
    eine Menge loads of OT 3
Mensch person OT 1; human **WS 1**, 27
menschengemacht man-made OT 1
Menschenmenge crowd OT 1
menschenunwürdig inhumane OT 4
menschlich human OT 3
mental mental OT 4
Mentor(in) mentor OT 4
merken: sich merken to memorize OT 4
Merkmal feature OT 1
merkwürdig funny OT 1
messen to measure OT 4
Messer knife OT 2
Metall metal OT 1
Metapher metaphor **WS 4**, 145
Meter metre OT 1
Methode method OT 1; technique OT 4
Metzger(in) butcher OT 4
Meute mob **WS 1**, 21
mexikanisch Mexican OT 4
mich me OT 1
Miet... rental OT 4
mieten to hire OT 3; to rent OT 4
Migrant(in) migrant OT 4
Migration migration OT 3
migrieren to migrate OT 3
Mikrobe microbe OT 4
Mikrofon microphone OT 4
Mikroskop microscope OT 4
Mikrowelle microwave **WS 2**, 70
Milch milk OT 1
Militär military OT 4
Milliarde billion OT 2
Million million OT 1
Minderheit minority **WS 3**, 98
Mindest... minimum OT 1
Mindmap mind map OT 1
Mine mine OT 2

VOCABULARY

MINT (Mathematik, Informatik, Naturwissenschaft und Technik) STEM (science, technology, engineering, mathematics) **WS 2**, 68
Minute minute OT 1
Minze mint OT 2
mir me OT 1
mischen to mix OT 2; to combine OT 4
Mischung mixture OT 3
Missbrauch abuse OT 4
Misserfolg failure OT 4
Misshandlung mistreatment **WS 1**, 21
Mission mission OT 4
Missverständnis misunderstanding OT 4
missverstehen to misunderstand **WS 1**, 21
mit with OT 1
Mitarbeiter personnel **WS 4**, 144
Mitarbeiter(in) colleague OT 4
mitbegründen to co-found OT 4
Mitbewerber(in) competitor OT 4
Mitbewohner(in) roommate **WS 2**, 67
mitfühlen to sympathize **WS 4**, 138
mitfühlend sympathetic OT 3
Mitglied member OT 1
   Mitglied werden in to join OT 1
mithören to overhear OT 3
mitleiden to sympathize **WS 4**, 138
Mitspieler(in) teammate OT 2
Mittag noon; midday OT 4
Mittagessen lunch OT 1
Mittagspause lunch break OT 1
Mittagszeit lunchtime OT 1
Mitte centre; middle OT 1
   in der Mitte mid OT 4
Mitteilungsblatt newsletter OT 4
Mittel resource OT 4
Mittelfeldspieler(in) midfielder OT 3
mittelgroß medium OT 1; medium-sized OT 2
Mittelschule middle school OT 2
Mitternacht midnight OT 1
mittlerweile meanwhile **WS 4**, 126
Mittwoch Wednesday OT 1
mitwirken to contribute OT 4
Mitwirkung contribution OT 4
mobben to bully **WS 3**, 90
Mobbing bullying OT 2
Möbel furniture OT 1
mobil mobile OT 1
Mobilteil handset OT 2
möchte(n) would like / love OT 1
Modalverb modal OT 2
Mode fashion OT 1
Modell model OT 1

Moderator(in) presenter **WS 3**, 91
modern modern OT 1
Modul module OT 4
mögen to like OT 1; to be fond of OT 4
   nicht mögen to dislike OT 3
möglich possible OT 2
Möglichkeit chance; possibility OT 2
Moment moment OT 1
momentan at the moment OT 2
Monarch(in) monarch **WS 2**, 64
Monat month OT 1
Mönch monk OT 3
Mond moon OT 4
Monolog monologue **WS 3**, 115; soliloquy **WS 4**, 145
monoton monotone OT 4
Monster monster OT 1
Montag Monday OT 1
Moosberre cranberry OT 4
moralisch ethical OT 3
Morgen morning OT 1; acre OT 4
morgen tomorrow OT 1
Morgendämmerung dawn OT 4
Moschee mosque OT 1
mosern to grumble OT 2
Motel motel OT 3
Motiv motif **WS 4**, 146
Motivation motivation **WS 2**, 55
motivieren to motivate OT 4
motiviert self-motivated OT 4; motivated **WS 2**, 59
Motor engine OT 2
Mountainbiken mountain biking OT 2
Mücke midge OT 3
müde tired OT 1
Muffin muffin OT 1
Mühe effort **WW**, 11
Müll rubbish; refuse OT 2
Müllabfuhr rubbish collection OT 2
Müllarbeiter(in) garbage collector OT 4
Mülldeponie landfill OT 3
Mülleimer rubbish bin; trash can OT 2
Müllmann / -frau refuse collector OT 2
multikulturell multicultural **WS 1**, 31
Multilog multilogue **WS 4**, 143
Mumie mummy OT 2
Mund mouth OT 1
mündig mature **WS 3**, 96
mündlich verbal **WS 2**, 61
Mundschutz mouthguard OT 2
Mundwasser mouthwash OT 4
Münze coin OT 1
Murmelspiel marbles OT 4
murren to grumble OT 2
mürrisch crossly OT 3
Muschel mussel OT 4

Museum museum OT 1
Musik music OT 1
musikalisch musical OT 2
Musiker(in) musician OT 2
Musikinstrument musical instrument OT 2
Muskel muscle OT 4
   Muskeln aufbauen to bulk up **WS 3**, 102
Muslim Muslim OT 3
müssen must; to have to OT 1
Muster pattern OT 1
mutig bold OT 1
Mutter mother OT 1
Mutti mum OT 1
Mütze hat; cap OT 1
Mysterium mystery OT 2
Mythos myth **WS 1**, 20

N

nach after; past OT 1; according to OT 3
   nach hinten backwards OT 3
   nach oben up OT 1; upwards OT 3
   nach Christus AD (Anno Domini) OT 2
Nachbar(in) neighbour OT 2
Nachbarschaft neighbourhood OT 4
nachdenken to speculate OT 4; to consider **WW**, 11
   zum Nachdenken anregend thought-provoking **WS 4**, 139
   nachdenken über to think about OT 1
nachdenklich thoughtful OT 3
nacheinander sequentially OT 4
nacherzählen to retell OT 4
Nachfrage demand OT 4
nachhallen to echo **WS 1**, 14
nachhaltig sustainable OT 4
Nachhaltigkeit sustainability OT 3
nachher afterwards OT 3
Nachhile geben to tutor OT 4
nachklingen to echo **WS 1**, 14
Nachkomme descendant OT 4
Nachmittag afternoon OT 1
Nachname last name OT 2
Nachricht message OT 1
nächste(r, -s) next OT 1
Nachstellung re-creation; re-enactment OT 4
Nacht night OT 1
Nachteil con OT 2; disadvantage; downside OT 3; drawback **WS 3**, 100
Nachtisch dessert OT 1
Nagel nail **WS 2**, 64
nah / nahe near OT 1; close OT 4
Nähe closeness **WS 3**, 115
   in der Nähe nearby OT 3

VOCABULARY

nähern to approach OT 4
Nähmaschine sewing machine OT 3
nahrhaft nutritious OT 4
Nahrungsergänzung supplement WS 3, 102
Name name OT 1
   mit dem Namen called OT 1
namens called OT 1
Nase nose OT 2
Nasenbluten nosebleed WS 3, 97
Nashorn rhinoceros OT 2
nass wet OT 2
Nation nation OT 2
national national OT 1
Nationalhymne anthem WS 1, 31
Natur nature OT 2
natürlich of course; natural OT 1
Naturwissenschaften science OT 1
Naturwissenschaftler(in) scientist OT 1
Navigation navigating OT 4
neben by; next to OT 1; beside OT 2; in addition to OT 4
nebenberuflich part-time OT 4
Negativ negative OT 1
nehmen to take OT 1
Neige: zur Neige gehen to run out OT 2
neigen to tilt OT 3
   zu etw. neigen to tend to WS 2, 68
nein no OT 1
nennen to call OT 1
Neoprenanzug wetsuit OT 1
Nerv nerve OT 3
nervig annoying OT 2
nervös nervous OT 2
Nest nest OT 3
Netbook netbook OT 4
nett nice; kind OT 1
Netz net OT 3
   vom Netz off the grid OT 4
Netzball netball OT 1
Netzsicherheit cyber security OT 4
Netzwerk network WS 1, 27
neu new OT 1
neueste(r) recent OT 4
Neugestaltung re-creation OT 4
Neugier curiosity OT 4
neugierig curious OT 4
Neuheit innovation OT 4
Neuigkeit(en) news OT 1
neulich recently OT 3
neun nine OT 1
neunzehn nineteen OT 1
neunzig ninety OT 1
neutral neutral OT 3
Neutronenbombe nuclear bomb OT 3
Newsletter newsletter OT 4

nicht not OT 1
nichts nothing OT 1
nicken to nod OT 2
Nickerchen nap WS 1, 38
nie never OT 1
Niederschlag rainfall WS 1, 27
Niederschrift transcript WS 1, 21
niedlich cute OT 1
niemand nobody OT 1
Nilpferd hippopotamus OT 2
nirgendwo nowhere OT 2
Niveau level OT 2
noch yet OT 2; nor OT 4
   noch ein(e) another OT 1
nomadisch nomadic WS 1, 22
Nomen noun OT 1
nominieren to nominate OT 4
Nominierung nomination OT 4
Nonne nun OT 4
nonverbal non-verbal OT 4
Nord- north OT 1
nördlich northern OT 2
nörgeln to nag WS 4, 144
normal normal OT 1; ordinary OT 2; standard OT 3; common OT 4
Notaufnahme Accident and Emergency OT 1
Notfall emergency OT 1
Notiz note OT 1
Notizblock pad WS 2, 71
Notizbuch notebook OT 2
notwendig necessary OT 3
Notwendigkeit necessity WW, 11
November November OT 1
Nudeln pasta OT 1
Nuklear... nuclear OT 3
null zero OT 1
Nummer number OT 1
nur just; only OT 1
Nuss nut OT 4
Nutzen benefit OT 2
nützlich useful OT 1; beneficial; handy OT 2

O

ob whether OT 1
obdachlos homeless OT 3
Obdachlosigkeit homelessness OT 4
oben upstairs OT 1; above OT 3
obere(r, -s) top OT 1
   im oberen Stockwerk upstairs OT 1
Oberfläche surface OT 3
oberhalb above OT 3
Oberschenkel thigh OT 1
Oberstufenschüler(in) senior OT 4
Objekt object OT 1

Obst fruit OT 1
Obstkuchen pie OT 1
obwohl although; though OT 2
oder or OT 1
Ofen stove OT 3; oven OT 4
Ofenkartoffel jacket potato OT 1
Off: aus dem Off offstage OT 2
offen open OT 1
offenbar obviously OT 1
offensichtlich evident WS 4, 141
offensichtlich obvious OT 1
öffentlich public OT 2
   öffentliche Verkehrsmittel public transport OT 2
offiziell official OT 4
Offizier(in) officer OT 2
öffnen to open OT 1
Öffnungszeiten opening times OT 1
oft often OT 1
oftmals many times OT 4
ohne without OT 2
ohnmächtig werden to faint OT 2
Ohr ear OT 1
ökologisch environmental OT 2; eco-friendly OT 3; ecological WS 1, 23
Ökonomie economy OT 3
Ökotourismus ecotourism OT 3
Oktober October OT 1
Oktopus octopus OT 1
Öl oil OT 1
olympisch Olympic OT 1
Oma grandma OT 1
Omelett omelette OT 2
Onkel uncle OT 1
online online OT 1
Opa grandpa; granddad OT 1
Operation operation OT 3
operieren to operate WS 2, 61
Opfer victim OT 4
Opposition opposition WS 1, 21
optimieren to optimize WS 2, 60
optimistisch optimistic OT 2
optional optional OT 2
optisch visually WS 2, 60
orange orange OT 1
Orangensaft orange juice OT 1
Orbit orbit OT 4
Orchester orchestra OT 1
ordentlich properly OT 2; neat OT 4
Ordnung: in Ordnung OK; all right OT 1
Organ organ OT 3
Organisation organization OT 2; agency OT 4
Organisator(in) organizer OT 3
organisatorisch organizational OT 4
organisieren to organize OT 1

two hundred and ninety-five **295**

Appendix

VOCABULARY

Orgel organ OT 3
orientalisch oriental OT 1
Orientierung reference; orientation OT 4
Original original OT 3
Orkan hurricane WS 1, 26
Ort place OT 1
    am Ort locally OT 3
    direkt vor Ort on the doorstep OT 4
Osten east OT 1
Ostern Easter OT 1
Österreicher(in) Austrian OT 4
östlich eastern OT 2
Outfit outfit WS 2, 64
Ozean ocean OT 3

P
Paar pair OT 1; couple OT 2
packen to pack OT 2
Pädagoge / Pädagogin educator OT 4
Paddel paddle OT 3
Paddle-Boarding paddle-boarding OT 1
paddeln to paddle OT 4
Paket packet OT 2; package OT 3; parcel OT 4
pakistanisch Pakistani OT 4
Palast palace OT 1
Pandabär panda OT 1
Pandemie pandemic WS 2, 62
Paneel panel WS 2, 78
Paniermehl breadcrumbs OT 3
Panik: in Panik geraten to panic OT 2
Panorama... panoramic OT 3
Panther panther OT 2
pantomimisch darstellen to mime OT 2
Papa dad OT 1
Papier paper OT 1
Paprika pepper OT 2
Papst Pope OT 3
Parade parade OT 2
    Parade-Wagen float OT 4
Paradies paradise OT 4
Parallelismus parallelism WS 4, 145
paralympische Spiele Paralympics OT 3
Park park OT 1
parken to park OT 1
Parkplatz car park OT 1
Parkzettel parking ticket OT 1
Parlament parliament OT 1
parteiisch biased OT 4
Partizip participle OT 2
    Partizip Perfekt past participle OT 2
Partner(in) partner OT 1
Partnerschaft partnership OT 4
Party party OT 1
Pass passport OT 2

Passagier(in) passenger OT 2
passen to fit OT 1
passend timely; appropriately OT 3
passieren to happen OT 1
Passkontrolle passport control OT 2
Passwort password OT 4
Pastete pâté OT 1
Patent patent OT 4
Patentante godmother WS 1, 15
patentieren to patent OT 4
Patient(in) patient OT 1
Patriot(in) patriot OT 2
Pause break OT 1; pause OT 3
    Pause machen to pause OT 3
Pedal pedal OT 4
    Pedale treten to pedal OT 4
Peer peer WS 1, 21
peinlich embarrassing OT 2
pendeln to commute WS 2, 63
Pendler(in) commuter OT 2
penetrant pushy OT 4
Penizillin penicillin OT 2
Penny penny OT 1
perfekt perfect OT 1
perfektionieren to perfect OT 4
permanent permanent WS 2, 51
Personal crew OT 2; staff OT 3; personnel WS 4, 144
personalisieren to personalize WS 3, 104
Personifikation personification WS 4, 145
persönlich personal OT 2
    persönliche Sachen belongings OT 3
Persönlichkeit personality OT 4
Perspektive perspective OT 4
pessimistisch pessimistic OT 4
Pestizid pesticide OT 4
Pfad trail OT 2
Pfadfinder(in) scout OT 3
Pfanne pan OT 2
Pfannkuchen pancake OT 4
Pfarrer(in) pastor OT 2
Pfeffer pepper OT 2
Pfeife whistle OT 2
pfeifen to blow; to whistle OT 2
Pfeil arrow OT 3
Pferd horse OT 1
pferdebespannt horse-drawn OT 1
Pferdewagen buggy OT 4
Pflanze plant OT 2
Pflanzenwelt wildlife OT 2
Pflaster plaster OT 1
Pflaume plum OT 1
pflegen to maintain OT 4
Pflicht duty WS 3, 91

pflücken to pick OT 1
Pfund pound OT 1
Phänomen phenomenon WS 1, 30
Phase stage OT 2
Philosophie philosophy OT 4
Phonograph phonograph OT 4
Physik physics OT 4
Pianist(in) pianist OT 2
Picknick picnic OT 1
pikant savoury OT 3
Pilgerfahrt pilgrimage OT 3
Pille pill OT 1
Pilot(in) pilot OT 3
Pilz mushroom OT 1
pingelig fussy OT 2
Pinguin penguin OT 1
Pinsel brush OT 2
Pinwand bulletin board OT 4
Pinzette tweezers OT 2
Pionier(in) pioneer OT 4
Pipeline pipeline OT 4
Pirat(in) pirate OT 3
Piste slope OT 3
Pizza pizza OT 1
plädieren to plead WS 3, 101
Plage pest OT 2
Plagegeist pest OT 2
Plagiat plagiarism OT 2
plagiieren to plagiarize OT 2
Plakat poster OT 1
planen to plan OT 1; to arrange OT 2; to design WS 2, 60
Planer(in) planner OT 3
Planet planet OT 2
planetarisch planetary OT 4
Planetarium planetarium OT 1
Planetenforschung planetary science OT 4
planieren to bulldoze WS 1, 27
Platte panel WS 2, 78
Platz square; ground OT 1; site; space OT 2; court OT 3
    auf die Plätze, fertig, los! Ready, set, go! OT 1
    einen ... Platz belegen to come ... OT 2
Platzanweiser(in) usher OT 4
Platzdeckchen place mat OT 2
plaudern to chatter OT 2
Playlist playlist OT 4
plötzlich suddenly OT 1; sudden OT 2
Plural plural OT 1
Pocken smallpox OT 4
Podcast podcast OT 1
Podium podium OT 3
Poesie poetry OT 1

VOCABULARY

Pokal trophy OT 2
Pol pole OT 3
Politik policy OT 3
Politiker(in) politician OT 3
politisch political OT 4
Polizei police OT 1
Polizist(in) police officer OT 1
polnisch Polish OT 2
Polo polo OT 3
Polyp polyp WS 1, 26
Polyurethan (Kunststoff) polyurethane OT 4
Pommes frites (French) fries OT 2
Pony pony OT 3
Pop pop OT 2
Popcorn popcorn OT 2
Portalseite portal WS 3, 106
Portfolio portfolio OT 4
Portion portion OT 4
Portraitfoto headshot WS 2, 56
Position position OT 3
Possessivbegleiter possessive determiner OT 1
Post post; mail OT 1
Postbote / -botin mail carrier OT 4
posten to post OT 3
Postkarte postcard OT 1
Postleitzahl postcode OT 1
Potenzial potential WS 2, 69
Praktikant(in) intern OT 4
Praktikum work placement WS 2, 50
Praktikum internship OT 4
praktisch handy OT 2; practical OT 3; convenient OT 4
Präposition preposition OT 2
Prärie plains WS 1, 21
Präsentation presentation OT 1; slideshow OT 3
präsentieren to present OT 1; to feature OT 4
Präsident(in) president OT 4
Praxis practice OT 2; surgery WS 2, 66
präzise accurate OT 4
Preis prize; price OT 1
preisgekrönt award-winning OT 4
Preisrichter(in) judge OT 2
preiswert inexpensive OT 4
prima fine OT 1
Prinz prince OT 1
privat private OT 3
Privatsphäre privacy OT 3
Privileg privilege WS 2, 64
privilegiert privileged WS 2, 65
Probe rehearsal OT 2; sample OT 4
proben to rehearse OT 3
Problem problem OT 1; matter OT 2

Problemlöser(in) problem-solver OT 4
Produkt product OT 2
Produktion production; manufacture OT 4; manufacturing WS 2, 63
Produktplatzierung product placement WS 3, 104
Profession profession WS 1, 18
professionell professional OT 2
Professor(in) professor OT 4
Profil profile OT 3
Profit profit OT 4
profitieren to benefit OT 2
profund profound WS 1, 21
Prognose forecast OT 3
Programm programme; channel OT 2; program OT 3
programmieren to programme OT 2
Programmierer(in) programmer OT 3
progressiv progressive OT 1
Projekt project OT 1
Projektor projector OT 1
Prominente(r) celebrity OT 3
Pronomen pronoun OT 1
Protagonist(in) protagonist WS 3, 115
Protein protein OT 4
Protest protest OT 3
protestieren to protest OT 3
Protestierer(in) protester WS 1, 33
Protokoll protocol WS 2, 64
Prototyp prototype OT 4
Provinz province WS 3, 101
Prozedur procedure WS 4, 146
Prozent percentage OT 3; percent OT 4
Prozess trial OT 2; process OT 4
Prüfer(in) checker OT 3
Prüfung exam OT 1
Psychologe / -login psychologist WS 2, 67
Psychologie psychology WS 2, 67
psychologische(r) Betreuer(in) counsellor OT 2
Psychopath(in) psycho OT 4
Pubertät puberty WS 3, 93
Publikum audience OT 2
Publizität publicity WS 2, 64
Pullover jumper OT 1
pulsieren to vibrate OT 4
pumpen to pump OT 4
Punkt point OT 1
punkten to score OT 1
pünktlich punctual OT 4
Puppe doll OT 3
putzen to brush OT 4; to clean WS 1, 40
Puzzle puzzle OT 2
Pyjama pajamas OT 4

Pyjama-Party sleepover OT 1

Q
Quadrat square OT 1
Quadratfuß square foot OT 2
Quälerei cruelty WS 3, 103
Qualifikation qualification WS 1, 21
qualifiziert qualified WS 2, 51
Qualität quality OT 3
Quarterback quarterback OT 2
Quartier quarter OT 1
queer queer WS 3, 93
Quelle spring; source OT 2
querfeldein cross-country OT 2
Querflöte flute OT 2
querlesen to skim OT 3
Quiz quiz OT 2

R
Rad wheel OT 1
  Rad fahren to bike OT 3
Radfahrer(in) cyclist OT 3
Radiergummi rubber OT 1
radikal radical OT 4
Radio radio OT 1
Radiosender radio station OT 2
Radius radius OT 2
Radweg bike lane OT 4
Rahmen frame OT 4
Rakete rocket OT 4
Rampe ramp OT 2
Rand edge; rim OT 3; margin WS 3, 107
Rangfolge ranking OT 4
  in eine Rangfolge bringen to rank OT 4
Rap rap OT 1
Rasen lawn WS 2, 59
Rasse... pedigree OT 3
Rassismus racism WS 3, 89
rassistisch racist OT 4
Rat advice OT 1; council OT 3
raten to advise OT 4
Rätsel puzzle; mystery OT 2
Rätselraten guessing game OT 1
rau rough OT 4; harsh WS 1, 19
Räuber predator WS 1, 23
Raubtier predator WS 1, 23
Rauch smoke OT 2
Raum room OT 1
Raumanzug spacesuit OT 4
räumen to clear OT 4
Raumfahrzeug spacecraft OT 4
Raumkapsel capsule OT 4
Raumschiff spaceship OT 4
rausbringen to take out OT 4
Razzia raid WS 4, 135

Appendix

VOCABULARY

reagieren to react; to respond OT 3
Reaktion reaction OT 4; response WS 3, 118
realistisch realistic OT 4
Realität reality OT 4
rebellieren to rebell OT 4
Rechenschaft: zur Rechenschaft ziehen to hold accountable WS 3, 100
Rechner computer OT 1
Rechnung bill OT 3
Recht privilege WS 2, 64
Rechte rights OT 3
rechte(r, -s) right OT 1
rechteckig rectangular OT 2
rechtfertigen to justify WS 1, 38
rechtlich legal OT 4
Rechtsanwalt / -anwältin lawyer OT 4; barrister WS 1, 43
Rechtschreibung spelling OT 1
Rechtshilfe legal aid WS 2, 58
Rechtsvorschriften legislation WS 1, 21
rechtzeitig timely OT 3
Recycling recycling OT 2
Redakteur(in) editor OT 2
Rede speech OT 1; talk OT 2
reden to talk OT 1
redigieren to edit OT 3
reduzieren to reduce OT 2; to downsize OT 3
Reformation reformation OT 4
Regal shelf OT 1
Regel rule OT 1; guideline; policy OT 3; norm WS 2, 82
regelmäßig regular OT 1
Regelung arrangement OT 3
Regelwerk rulebook OT 2
Regen rainfall WS 1, 27
Regenbogen rainbow OT 1
Regenmantel raincoat OT 3
Regenschauer rainstorm WS 1, 20
Regenschirm umbrella OT 1
Regenwald rainforest OT 2
Regenwasser rainwater OT 4
Reggae reggae OT 2
regieren to govern OT 3
Regierung government OT 3
Region region OT 4
regional regional WS 1, 30
Regisseur(in) film director OT 2
Register index OT 4
regnen to rain OT 1
Regulation regulation WS 2, 62
reiben to rub OT 3
reich rich OT 1
reichen to range OT 4; to hand WS 3, 97
reichlich plenty OT 2
Reichtum fortune OT 3; wealth OT 4
reif ripe OT 4; mature WS 3, 96
Reihe row OT 1
Reihenfolge order OT 1; sequencing OT 3
    in eine Reihenfolge bringen to sequence OT 3
Reim rhyme OT 1
reinigen to clean WS 1, 40
Reinigungsmittel cleaner OT 3
Reinigungstuch cleaning wipe OT 2
Reis rice OT 1
Reise journey; trip; tour OT 1; voyage OT 3
Reiseandenken souvenir OT 1
Reisebus coach OT 1
Reiseführer guidebook OT 1
Reisekauffrau / -mann travel agent OT 3
reisen to travel OT 1
Reisende(r) traveller OT 3
Reiseziel destination OT 4
reißen to tear OT 2
Reißverschluss zip OT 1
reiten to ride OT 1
Reiter(in) rider OT 1
reizbar irritable OT 3
reizvoll attractive OT 4
Reklamezettel leaflet OT 2
Rektor(in) principal OT 2
relativ relatively WS 3, 120
Relativpronomen relative pronoun OT 2
Relativsatz relative clause OT 2
relevant relevant OT 4
Religion religion OT 3
    eine Religion ausüben to worship OT 4
Religionsunterricht religious studies OT 1
religiös religious OT 1
Rennen race OT 2
rennen to run OT 1
Rennsport racing OT 2
Rentier reindeer OT 2
reparieren to repair OT 2
Reporter(in) reporter OT 1
Reptil reptile OT 2
Republik republic OT 4
Requisite prop OT 1
Reservat reservation OT 1
reservieren to reserve OT 3
Reservierung reservation OT 1
resistent resistant WS 3, 103
Resistenz resistance WS 1, 22
respektlos disrespectful OT 3
respektvoll respectful OT 3
Ressource resource OT 4
Restaurant restaurant OT 1
restlich remaining WS 1, 41
restliche rest OT 1
Resultat outcome WS 1, 38
retten to save OT 2; to rescue OT 4
Rettung rescue OT 2
Rettungsdienste emergency services OT 2
Rettungssanitäter(in) paramedic OT 1
Rettungsschwimmer(in) lifeguard OT 4
Reue remorse WS 3, 100
revidieren to revise OT 2
Revolution revolution OT 2
revolutionieren to revolutionize OT 4
Rezept recipe OT 2
Rezeption reception OT 1
Rezeptionist(in) receptionist OT 1
rezitieren to recite OT 4
rhetorisch rhetorical WS 4, 143
Richter(in) judge OT 2
richtig correct; right; true OT 1; proper OT 3; actual WS 2, 56
Richtlinie guideline OT 3
Richtung direction OT 3
    in Richtung towards OT 2
riechen to smell OT 1
Riesenrad ferris wheel OT 4
riesig enormous OT 1; huge; giant OT 2; massive OT 3
Riff reef WS 1, 24
Rinder cattle WS 1, 16
Rinderbrust beef brisket OT 4
Rindfleisch beef OT 2
Ringen wrestling OT 2
Risiko hazard OT 2; risk OT 3
Riss split OT 3
Ritual ritual WS 1, 30
Robbe seal OT 1
Roboter robot OT 4
Rock skirt OT 1
Rockmusik rock OT 2
roh raw OT 3
Rolle role OT 1; roll OT 2
Rollschuh roller skate OT 4
Rollstuhl wheelchair OT 2
Rollstuhlfahrer(in) wheelchair user OT 2
Roman novel OT 2
römisch Roman OT 2
Rommee rummy OT 2
Röntgen X-ray OT 1
rosa pink OT 1
Rose rose OT 4
rot red OT 1

Appendix
VOCABULARY

Routine routine OT 4
Routinearbeit chore **WS 1**, 16
Rückblick review OT 1
Rücken back OT 1
Rückgang decline **WS 1**, 22
Rückgrat backbone OT 2
Rückhand backhand OT 3
Rucksack rucksack OT 1; backpack OT 2
    mit Rucksack reisen to backpack OT 3
Rücksicht consideration **WS 4**, 140
rücksichtslos thoughtless OT 2
rücksichtsvoll thoughtful OT 3
rückwärts backwards OT 3
Ruderboot rowing boat OT 1
Ruf fame OT 3
rufen to shout OT 1
Rugby rugby OT 1
ruhig quiet OT 1; calm OT 2; steady OT 3; still OT 4
Ruhm fame OT 3
rühren to stir OT 2
Ruine ruin OT 2
rumhängen to hang out OT 1
rund round OT 1
Rundgang tour OT 1
russisch Russian OT 2

S
sachlich factual OT 4
Sack sack OT 2
Safari safari OT 2
Saft juice OT 1
sagen to say OT 1
Sahne cream OT 1
Saite string OT 2
Salat salad OT 1
Salz salt OT 3
sammeln to collect OT 1
Sammler(in) picker OT 3; gatherer **WS 1**, 22
Sammlung collection OT 2
Samstag Saturday OT 1
samtig velvety OT 2
Sand sand OT 1
Sandale sandal OT 4
sandig sandy OT 1
Sandwich sandwich OT 1
sanft gently OT 3
Sänger(in) singer OT 1
Satellit satellite OT 4
Sattel saddle OT 3
Satz sentence OT 1; set OT 3
Satzteil clause OT 2
sauber clean OT 1
sauer acidic **WS 1**, 26

Säugetier mammal OT 2
Säugling baby OT 1
Säule column OT 1
Saxofon saxophone OT 2
scannen to scan OT 3
Schach chess OT 1
Schachbrett chessboard OT 1
schade: das ist schade That's a shame. OT 2
schaden to harm; to damage OT 2
schädlich harmful OT 3; destructive **WS 1**, 41
Schädling pest OT 2
Schaf sheep OT 1
Schäfer(in) shepherd OT 2
schaffen to create OT 2; to achieve OT 4
Schal scarf OT 2
Schale dish OT 2
Schalter switch OT 3
Schaltkreis circuit OT 4
scharf hot OT 1
    auf etw. scharf sein to be keen on sth. OT 4
Schatten shade **WS 1**, 16
Schatz treasure OT 3
    Schatz (als Kosename) honey OT 2
schätzen to guess OT 1; to estimate **WS 1**, 22; to appreciate **WS 2**, 67
Schaubild diagram OT 3
Schaufel shovel OT 2
schaukeln to rock OT 3
Schauspieler(in) actor OT 1
Scheibe slice OT 1
scheiden: sich scheiden lassen to divorce OT 3
Scheidung divorce OT 3
Schein note OT 1
scheinen to shine OT 1; to seem OT 2; to appear OT 3
scheitern to fail OT 2
Schema scheme **WS 4**, 146
Schere scissors OT 1
Scheune barn OT 2
Schicht shift OT 4
schick fancy OT 2; stylish OT 4
schicken to send OT 1
Schiedsrichter(in) referee OT 3
Schiene rail OT 2
schießen to shoot OT 3
Schiff ship OT 2
    mit dem Schiff fahren to sail OT 2
Schiffbau shipbuilding OT 3
Schild sign OT 1; signpost **WS 2**, 50
Schildkröte tortoise OT 1; turtle OT 2
schimpfen to grumble OT 2
Schinken ham OT 3

Schirmherr(in) patron **WS 2**, 64
Schlacht battle OT 1
Schlachten cull **WS 1**, 23
schlachten to cull **WS 1**, 23
Schlafanzug pyjamas OT 3; pajamas OT 4
schlafen to sleep OT 1
schlaff limp OT 4
Schlafsack sleeping bag OT 2
Schlafzimmer bedroom OT 1
Schlag stroke OT 3
Schläger bat OT 1; racket OT 2
Schlagwort catchphrase **WS 1**, 44
Schlagzeile headline OT 2
Schlagzeug drums OT 1
Schlange queue; snake OT 1; serpent **WS 1**, 13
    Schlange stehen to queue OT 4
schlängeln: sich schlängeln to wriggle OT 2; to wind **WS 1**, 20
Schlankheitskuren dieting **WS 3**, 102
schlau smart OT 4; savvy **WS 3**, 104
Schlauch tube OT 1
schlecht bad OT 1; junky OT 4
schlemmen to feast OT 4
Schlepper(in) trafficker OT 4; coyote **WS 4**, 127
schließen to close OT 1; to shut OT 2
    schließen (aus etw.) to conclude OT 4
Schließfach locker OT 2
schließlich finally OT 1; eventually OT 3
Schlittschuh laufen to skate OT 2
Schloss lock OT 2
Schlucht canyon OT 3
Schluckauf hiccup OT 2
schlucken to swallow OT 4
Schluss conclusion OT 3
Schlüssel key OT 1
schmackhaft tasty OT 2
schmecken to taste OT 1
schmelzen to melt OT 4
Schmerz pain OT 2
schmerzen to hurt OT 1; to ache OT 3
schmerzend sore OT 2
schmerzhaft painful OT 2
Schmerzmittel painkiller OT 2
Schmetterling butterfly OT 2
Schminke face paint OT 2
schmollen to sulk OT 3
Schmuck jewelry OT 2
schmücken to decorate OT 4
Schmutz dirt OT 4
schmutzig dirty OT 1
Schnabeltier platypus **WS 1**, 13
Schnäppchen bargain OT 4
Schnappschuss shot OT 4

VOCABULARY

Schneckenpost snail mail OT 4
Schnee snow OT 1
schneiden to cut OT 2; to chop OT 3
schnell fast OT 1; quick OT 2
schnitzen to carve OT 2
schockiert shocked OT 4
Schokolade chocolate OT 1
schon already; yet OT 2
schön beautiful; nice; lovely OT 1
Schönheit beauty OT 3
schottisch Scottish OT 3
Schrank cupboard OT 1; cabinet WS 2, 71
schrecklich terrible; awful OT 1
Schreibarbeit paperwork WS 2, 69
schreiben to write OT 1
   neu schreiben to rewrite OT 1
Schreiben writing OT 1
Schreibkraft typist WS 2, 58
Schreibmaschine typewriter WS 2, 82
Schreibtisch desk OT 1
Schreibwaren stationery WS 2, 69
Schreibweise spelling OT 1
schreien to scream OT 3
Schriftsteller(in) writer OT 2
Schriftverkehr correspondence OT 4
Schritt step OT 1
   auf Schritt und Tritt begleiten to shadow WS 2, 66
Schublade drawer OT 3
schüchtern shy OT 2
Schuh shoe OT 1
Schuhschachtel shoebox OT 3
Schulabgänger(in) school leaver WS 2, 55
Schulausbildung schooling OT 4
Schulball prom OT 3
Schuld debt OT 4
schuldig guilty WS 3, 100
Schuldknecht bonded laborer OT 4
Schule school OT 1
Schüler(in) student OT 1
Schülerrat student council OT 2
Schulhof playground OT 1
Schulkamerad(in) schoolmate OT 4
Schulleiter(in) head teacher OT 1
Schultag school day OT 1
Schultasche school bag OT 1
Schulter shoulder OT 1
Schulterpolster shoulder pad OT 2
Schuppen shed OT 1
Schuss shot OT 4
Schüssel bowl OT 1
Schusswaffe gun OT 4
schütteln to shake OT 2

Schutz conservation OT 2; custody WS 3, 100
Schütze gunman OT 4
schützen to protect OT 2
schwach weak OT 3; dim OT 4
Schwäche weakness OT 4
schwanger pregnant OT 4
Schwanz tail OT 2
schwarz black OT 1
schweben to float; to soar OT 3
schwedisch Swedish OT 4
Schwein pig OT 1
Schweinefleisch pork OT 2
Schwellung swelling OT 2
schwer difficult; heavy OT 1; severe WS 1, 26
Schwerelosigkeit weightlessness OT 4
Schwerkraft gravity OT 4
Schwert sword OT 1
Schwester sister OT 1
schwierig difficult; challenging OT 1
Schwierigkeit trouble OT 2; difficulty OT 4
Schwimmbecken pool OT 1
schwimmen to swim OT 1
Schwimmer(in) swimmer OT 2
schwindlig faint OT 2
schwitzen to sweat OT 2
schwören to swear OT 4
schwul gay WS 3, 89; queer WS 3, 93
Science-Fiction science fiction OT 2
sechs six OT 1
sechzehn sixteen OT 1
sechzig sixty OT 1
Secondhandladen thrift store OT 4
See lake; loch OT 1
Seeufer lakefront; lakeside OT 4
Seevogel seabird WS 1, 24
segeln to sail OT 2
Segment segment WS 1, 30
sehen to look; to see OT 1
Sehenswürdigkeit sight OT 1; attraction OT 2
sehr very; really; a lot OT 1; mighty OT 3
   sehr gut brill OT 1
Sehvermögen sight OT 1
Seife soap OT 2
Seil line; rope OT 1
Seilrutsche zip line OT 1
seine(r, -s) his; its OT 1
sein to be OT 1
seit since OT 3
Seite page; side OT 1
   auf der anderen Seite across OT 1
Sekretär(in) secretary OT 1
sekundär secondary OT 1

Sekundarschule secondary school OT 1
Sekunde second OT 1
selbst: (sich) selbst himself OT 1; themselves; herself; itself OT 3
   selbst gemacht homemade OT 3
selbständig self-employed WS 2, 63
selbstbewusst confident OT 2
Selbstlaut vowel OT 1
Selbstmord suicide WS 1, 21
selbstständig independent OT 3
Selbstversorgung self-catering OT 3
selbstverständlich: für selbstverständlich halten to take for granted OT 4
Selbstvertrauen confidence WS 1, 21
Selbstzahlerkasse self-checkout OT 4
Selfie selfie OT 1
selten rare OT 2; seldom WS 3, 106
seltsam strange; weird OT 1
Semester term OT 2; semester OT 3
Sendung programme OT 2
Senf mustard OT 2
Senior(in) senior citizen OT 3; senior OT 4
Seniorenheim retirement home OT 3
senkrecht vertical OT 4
Sensor sensor OT 4
September September OT 1
Sequenzierung sequencing OT 3
Serie series OT 1
servieren to serve OT 1
Sessel armchair OT 1
Session session OT 2
seufzen to sigh OT 3
Seufzer sigh OT 2
Sex sex WS 3, 90
Shampoo shampoo OT 3
Shorts shorts OT 1
Sichel crescent OT 2
sicher sure; safe; certainly OT 1; certain OT 3; stable WS 2, 63; secure WS 2, 64
sichergehen to make sure OT 2
Sicherheit safety OT 2; security OT 3
Sicherheitsausrüstung safety equipment OT 2
Sicherheitsgurt harness OT 1
sicherlich certainly OT 1; surely OT 4
sicherstellen to make sure OT 2; to ensure OT 4
Sicht view OT 1
sie they; her; them; she OT 1
sieben seven OT 1
Siebenkampf heptathlon OT 2
siebzehn seventeen OT 1
siebzig seventy OT 1
Siedler(in) settler OT 3

Appendix

VOCABULARY

Siedlung settlement OT 4
Sieger(in) winner OT 1
Signal signal OT 2
Silbe syllable OT 2
Silber... silver OT 1
singen to sing OT 1
Singular singular OT 1
sinken to sink OT 3
Sinn meaning OT 1; sense OT 2
sinneserweiternd mind-expanding OT 2
sinnlos pointless OT 4
sinnvoll meaningful **WS 3**, 96
Sirene siren OT 3
Sirup syrup OT 3
Situation situation OT 1
sitzen to sit OT 1
Sitzplatz seat OT 1
Sitzung session OT 2
Skateboard skateboard OT 4
Skelett skeleton OT 1
Sketch skit OT 2; sketch OT 4
Ski laufen to ski OT 3
Skiläufer(in) skier OT 3
Skizze sketch OT 4
skizzieren to outline OT 3; to sketch OT 4
Sklave / Sklavin slave OT 4
Sklaverei slavery OT 4
Skulptur sculpture OT 2
Skyline skyline **WS 2**, 67
Slang slang **WS 1**, 28
Slogan slogan OT 2
Slum slum OT 3
Smartphone smartphone OT 3
SMS text OT 1
Snack snack OT 1
Snowboard fahren snowboarding OT 3
so such OT 2
Socke sock OT 2
Sofa sofa OT 1
sofort immediately OT 1; straight away OT 2
Software software OT 1
sogar even OT 1; actually OT 2
Sohn son OT 1
Solarenergie solar power OT 4
Soldat(in) soldier OT 1
sollte(n) should OT 1; ought to **WS 2**, 57
Solo solo OT 4
solo solo OT 2
Sommer summer OT 1
Sommersprosse freckle OT 2
Songtext lyrics OT 2
Songwriter(in) songwriter OT 2
Sonne sun OT 1
Sonnen... solar OT 3

Sonnenbrand sunburn OT 2
Sonnenbrille sunglasses OT 2
Sonnenenergie solar power OT 4
Sonnenkollektor solar panel OT 3
Sonnenschein sunshine OT 3
Sonnenschutzmittel sunscreen OT 2
Sonnenstich sunstroke OT 2
Sonnensystem solar system OT 1
Sonnenuntergang sunset OT 3
sonnenverbrannt sunburnt **WS 1**, 40
sonnig sunny OT 1
Sonntag Sunday OT 1
sonst otherwise **WS 2**, 54
   sonst noch else OT 1
Sorge concern **WS 1**, 33
Sorge: keine Sorge no worries OT 2
   sich Sorgen machen to worry OT 1
sorgfältig careful OT 1
sorglos careless OT 2
Soße sauce OT 1
sozial social OT 2
Soziologie sociology **WS 2**, 58
Spaghetti spaghetti OT 1
Spalte column OT 1
Spaniel spaniel OT 2
spanisch Spanish OT 1
sparen to save OT 2
Spaß fun OT 1
   Spaß verstehen to take a joke OT 2
spät late OT 1
Spaziergang walk OT 2
Speck bacon OT 1
Speisekarte menu OT 1
spektakulär spectacular OT 2
spekulieren to speculate OT 4
Spende donation OT 2
spenden to make a donation; to donate OT 2
Spendensammler(in) fundraiser OT 2
Spendensammlung fundraising OT 2
Spender dispenser **WS 2**, 70
spezialisieren to specialize OT 4
Spezialist(in) geek **WS 3**, 104
speziell specialist **WS 3**, 100
Spezies species **WS 1**, 23
spezifisch specific OT 3
Spiegel mirror OT 1
spiegeln to reflect **WS 1**, 21
Spiel game; match OT 1
Spielekonsole game console OT 4
spielen to play OT 1
Spieler(in) player OT 1; gamer OT 4
Spielfeld pitch OT 3
Spielfilm motion picture OT 4
Spielführer(in) captain OT 4
Spielplatz playground OT 1

Spielverderber: kein Spielverderber sein to be a good sport OT 2
Spielzeug toy OT 2
Spind locker OT 2
Spinne spider OT 1
Spirale spiral **WS 1**, 21
spitz spiky **WS 2**, 63
Spitze tip; top OT 1
Spitzen... peak **WS 3**, 98
Spitzensport elite sports OT 3
Spitzname nickname OT 4
   Spitzname geben to nickname **WS 1**, 13
Sponsor(in) sponsor OT 2
spontan spontaneous **WS 4**, 143
Sport sport; athletics OT 1
Sport... sporting **WS 1**, 15
Sporthalle gymnasium OT 4
Sportjacke blazer OT 1
Sportler(in) sportsman, sportswoman OT 3
   Sportler(innen) sportspeople OT 3
sportlich athletic OT 4; sporting **WS 1**, 15
Sportunterricht PE (physical education) OT 1
Sprachbeherrschung fluency **WW**, 11
Sprache language OT 1
Sprachwissenschaftler(in) linguist **WS 3**, 106
Sprechblase speech bubble OT 2
Sprechen speaking OT 1
sprechen to speak OT 1
Sprecher(in) speaker OT 1; spokesman; spokeswoman OT 2
Sprechstunde surgery **WS 2**, 66
Sprichwort proverb **WS 3**, 88
Springbrunnen fountain OT 1
springen to jump OT 2
Sprint sprint OT 3
Sprinter(in) sprinter OT 3
Spritztour (mit einem gestohlenen Auto) joyride **WS 3**, 100
Sprudel soda **WS 3**, 102
sprudelnd sparkling OT 1
sprühen to spray **WS 3**, 121
Sprung leap **WS 4**, 146
spucken to spit OT 4
Spülbecken sink OT 3
Spur trail OT 2
Spürhund hound OT 2
Staat state OT 1
Staatsangehörigkeit nationality OT 2
Staatsanwalt / -anwältin prosecutor **WS 3**, 100
stabil steady OT 3; stable **WS 2**, 63
Stabilität stability **WS 2**, 64

three hundred and one **301**

Appendix

VOCABULARY

Stachel thorn OT 2
stachelig spiky WS 2, 63
Stachelrochen stingray WS 1, 44
Stadion stadium OT 1
Stadt town; city OT 1
Stadtbewohner(innen) townspeople OT 4
städtisch urban OT 4
Stahl steel OT 2
Stalagmit stalagmite OT 1
Stalaktit stalactite OT 1
Stall stall OT 2
Stamm tribe OT 3
Stammes... tribal OT 3
Stand status OT 4
Standard level OT 2; default OT 3; norm WS 2, 62
Standort location OT 2
Stange pole OT 3
Stanze stanza WS 4, 146
Stapel pile WS 1, 27
stapeln to stack OT 4
Star star OT 1
stark strong OT 2; intense WS 1, 30; severe WS 1, 26
    stärker machen to strengthen WS 3, 99
    stärker werden to strengthen WS 3, 99
Stärke strength OT 2
stärken to empower WS 2, 69
starren to stare OT 2
starten to launch OT 4
Startseite homepage OT 1
Station station OT 1
Statistik statistic OT 3
stattdessen instead OT 2
Statue statue OT 1
Status status OT 4
Stau traffic jam OT 2
staubsaugen to vacuum OT 4
Staubsauger vacuum cleaner OT 4
Steak steak OT 1
stechen to sting OT 2
Stechmücke mosquito OT 2
Steckbrief profile OT 3
Stecknadel pin OT 1
Stegosaurus stegosaurus OT 1
stehen to stand OT 1
    jmdm. stehen to suit sb. OT 1
steigen to climb OT 1
steil steep OT 2
Stein stone OT 1; rock OT 2
Steinbruch quarry OT 1
Stelle job OT 1
stellen to put OT 1

stellvertretend deputy WS 1, 41
Steppdecke quilt OT 4
sterben to die OT 1
Stereotype stereotype WS 1, 39
stereotypisch stereotypical WS 3, 93
stereotypisieren to stereotype WS 2, 68
Stern star OT 1
Sternchen asterisk OT 4
Steroid steroid WS 3, 102
Steuer tax OT 4
steuern to steer OT 3; to pilot OT 4
Steuerzahler(in) tax-payer WS 2, 64
Stich sting OT 2
Stichwort headword OT 2; keyword; prompt OT 4
Stiefel boot OT 1
Stift pen OT 1
Stigma stigma WS 2, 65
Stil style OT 2
stilistisch stylistic WS 4, 145
still quiet OT 1
Stille silence OT 2
Stimme voice OT 2
    mit lauter Stimme aloud OT 2
Stimmung mood WS 3, 97
Stirnband headband OT 3
Stockbett bunk bed OT 3
Stockwerk floor OT 1
    im unteren Stockwerk downstairs OT 1
Stoff material OT 3
stolpern to trip OT 2
Stolz pride OT 4
stolz proud OT 2
stören to bother OT 4; to disturb WS 1, 20
Storyboard storyboard OT 4
stoßen to bump; to push OT 2
Stoßzahn tusk OT 3
Strafe penalty OT 3; punishment WS 3, 117
strafrechtlich penal WS 1, 18
Strafstoß penalty OT 3
Straftat offence WS 1, 21
Strand beach OT 1
Strandsegeln land yachting OT 3
Sträßchen laneway WS 1, 17
Straße road; street OT 1
Straßenbahn tram OT 1
Straßenmusiker(in) busker WS 1, 17
Straßensammlung street collection OT 2
Strategie strategy OT 4
strategisch strategic OT 4
Strauß bouquet OT 3
Strecke route OT 2

Streifen strip WS 2, 70
Streik strike OT 4
streiken to strike OT 4
Streit argument OT 1
streiten to argue OT 2
streng strict OT 2
Stress stress OT 1
stressig stressful OT 4
streuen to sprinkle OT 2
Stroh straw OT 4
Strohhalm straw OT 4
Strom electricity OT 2
Strophe verse OT 1; stanza WS 4, 146
Struktur structure OT 1
strukturieren to structure WS 1, 31
Stück piece; bit OT 1
Student(in) student OT 1
    Student im ersten Jahr freshman OT 4
Studienanfänger(in) freshman OT 4
Studiengebühr(en) tuition WS 2, 64
studieren to study OT 1
Studio studio WS 1, 30
Studium studies OT 1
Stufe step OT 1; level OT 2
Stuhl chair OT 1
Stunde hour OT 1
Stunden... hourly WS 2, 82
Stundenplan timetable OT 1; schedule OT 2
stündlich hourly WS 2, 82
Sturm storm OT 2
Stürmer(in) striker OT 3
stürzen to fall OT 1
Stütze prop OT 1
Subjekt subject OT 1
Subjektpronomen subject pronoun OT 1
Substantiv noun OT 1
Suche search OT 2
suchen to search OT 2; to seek WS 1, 16
    nach etw. suchen to scavenge for WS 4, 130
süchtig addicted OT 3
Süd... south OT 1
südlich southern OT 3
Südwesten southwest OT 3
Sumpf swamp OT 2
Superheld superhero WS 3, 102
Superlativ superlative OT 2
Supermarkt supermarket OT 1
Suppe soup OT 1
Surfen surfing OT 1
Surfer(in) surfer OT 4
Sushi sushi OT 1
Süßigkeit candy OT 4

Appendix

VOCABULARY

Süßkartoffel sweet potato OT 4
Sweatshirt sweatshirt OT 1
Symbol symbol OT 1; icon WW, 11
Synagoge synagogue OT 1
Synästhesie synaesthesia OT 2
Synonym synonym OT 2
synthetisch synthetic OT 4
System system OT 1
systematisch systematically WS 1, 22
Szene scene OT 2
Szenenbuch storyboard OT 4

T
Tab tab OT 3
Tabak tobacco OT 3
Tablett tray OT 2
Tablette tablet OT 2
Tacker stapler OT 2
Tafel board OT 1
Tag day OT 1
Tagebuch diary OT 1
Tagesablauf routine OT 4
Tagesausflug day trip; day out OT 2
Tagesgericht special OT 1
Tagesordnung agenda OT 3
Tageszeit daytime OT 1
täglich daily OT 2
taiwanisch Taiwanese OT 4
Takt beat OT 1
Taktik tactic OT 2
Tal valley OT 1
Talent talent OT 2
talentiert talented OT 3
Tank tank OT 3
Tante aunt OT 1
Tanz dance OT 1
tanzen to dance OT 1
Tänzer(in) dancer OT 3
tapfer brave OT 1
Tasche case; bag OT 1; pocket OT 2
Taschendieb(in) pickpocket OT 4
Taschengeld pocket money OT 2; allowance OT 3
Taschenlampe torch OT 1; flashlight OT 2
Taschenmesser pocketknife OT 2
Taschentuch tissue WS 3, 97
Tasse cup OT 1; mug OT 3
Tastatur keyboard OT 1
Tat deed WS 4, 126
Täter(in) offender WS 3, 100
Tätigkeit occupation OT 4
Tätowierung tattoo OT 3
Tatsache fact OT 1
tatsächlich actually OT 2
tauchen to dive OT 1; to dip OT 4

Taucheranzug wetsuit OT 1
tauschen to swap OT 1
Tausend thousand OT 1
Taxi taxi OT 1; cab OT 4
Teamwork teamwork OT 4
Technik technique OT 4
technisch tech OT 2; technological; technical OT 4
 technische Spielerei gadget OT 4
Technologie technology OT 1
technologisch technological OT 4
techorientiert tech-orientated WS 2, 63
Tee tea OT 1
Teelicht tea light OT 2
Teenager teenager; teen OT 2
Teich pond OT 4
Teig dough OT 2
Teil piece; part OT 1; section OT 2
teilen to share OT 1; to divide OT 2
teilnehmen to take part OT 2; to participate WS 4, 143
Teilung division WS 2, 62
teilweise partly OT 3
Teilzeit... part-time OT 4
Telefon phone OT 1
Telefonat phone call OT 2
telefonieren to phone OT 2
Telefonist(in) operator OT 2
Telefonkonferenz teleconference OT 3
Telegraf telegraph OT 4
Teller plate OT 1
Tempel temple OT 1
Temperatur temperature OT 2
Temperaturregler thermostat WS 2, 70
Tempus tense OT 1
tendieren zu to tend to WS 2, 68
Tennis tennis OT 1
Teppich carpet OT 4
Terminkalender diary OT 1
Terrier terrier OT 2
Test test OT 1
teuer expensive OT 1
Teufel devil WS 1, 39
Text text OT 1
 Text (eines Schauspielers) line OT 1
texten to message OT 3
Theater theatre OT 1
 Theater spielen to act OT 1
Theaterstück play OT 1
Theke counter OT 3
Thema subject OT 1
theoretisch theoretical OT 4
Theorie theory OT 1
Thermalquelle hot spring OT 2
Thermosflasche flask OT 3
Thermostat thermostat WS 2, 70

Thron throne WS 2, 64
Thunfisch tuna OT 1
tief low; deep OT 1; profound WS 1, 21
tief profound WS 1, 21
Tier animal OT 1; beast WS 4, 132
Tierarzt / -ärztin veterinarian; vet OT 4
Tierwelt wildlife OT 2
Tiger tiger OT 1
Timer timer WS 2, 70
tippen to tap OT 2
Tisch table OT 1
Tischtennis ping-pong OT 1
Titel title OT 1
Toast toast OT 2
Tochter daughter OT 1
Tod death OT 2
Todesdatum date of death OT 2
Toilette toilet OT 2
tolerant tolerant OT 4
Toleranz tolerance WS 3, 89
toll great OT 1; awesome OT 2; stunning WS 1, 26
 Toll! Wow! OT 1
Tomate tomato OT 1
Ton clay OT 4; tone WS 1, 39
Tonerkartusche toner cartridge WS 2, 71
Tonne ton OT 2
Tor goal; gate OT 1
Tortendiagramm pie chart OT 4
Torwart(in) goalkeeper OT 3
tot dead OT 1
total absolutely OT 2
töten to kill OT 1; to execute OT 3
Touchdown touchdown OT 2
Tourismus tourism OT 2
Tourist(in) tourist OT 1
toxisch toxic OT 4
traben to trot OT 2
Tradition tradition OT 2; heritage WS 1, 21
traditionell traditional OT 1
tragbar portable OT 4
tragen to wear; to carry OT 1
Tragetasche carrier bag OT 2
Tragödie tragedy WS 4, 145
Trailer trailer OT 4
Trainer(in) coach OT 1
trainieren to train OT 2
Traktor tractor OT 2
Träne tear OT 2
trans... trans WS 3, 93
transatlantisch transatlantic OT 3
transferieren to transfer OT 4
transkribieren to transcribe WS 2, 58
Transkribierer(in) transcriber WS 2, 58

three hundred and three **303**

Appendix
VOCABULARY

Transplantation transplant OT 3
transsexuell transgender WS 3, 93
trauen: sich trauen to dare OT 2
Trauer grief WS 1, 21; sorrow WS 4, 145
Traum dream OT 1
Trauma trauma WS 1, 38
träumen to dream OT 4
Träumer(in) dreamer OT 2
Traumzeit dreamtime WS 1, 20
traurig sad OT 1; upset OT 2
Treck wagon train OT 4
trecken to trek OT 2
Treffen meeting; scoring OT 1; rally OT 4
treffen to meet OT 1
treiben to herd OT 2; to float OT 3
Treibhaus greenhouse OT 1
Treidelpfad towpath OT 3
Trend fashion OT 1; trend OT 4
Trendwende tipping point WS 1, 27
trennen to separate OT 4; to split up WS 3, 90
Trennung division WS 2, 62
Treppe / Treppenstufen stairs OT 1
treten to kick OT 1; to step OT 4
treu loyal WS 3, 95
Triangel triangle OT 2
Trick trick WS 3, 104
Trilogie trilogy WS 1, 29
trinken to drink OT 1
Trinkhalm straw OT 4
trocken dry OT 2; arid WS 1, 23
Trödelmarkt flea market WS 3, 95
Trompete trumpet OT 2
tropisch tropical OT 4
tropfen to drip OT 3
trösten to comfort WS 3, 94
trotz in spite of WS 1, 23
trotzdem anyway OT 1
trüb cloudy; murky; dim OT 4
Truthahn turkey OT 1
Tschüss! bye OT 1
tun to put; to do OT 1
   so tun, als ob to pretend OT 2
Tunnel tunnel OT 3
Tür door OT 1
Turbine turbine OT 4
Turm tower OT 1
Turnhalle gym OT 3
Turnier tournament OT 3
Turnschuh trainer OT 1
Tüte bag OT 1
Tutor(in) tutor OT 4
typisch typical OT 2
Tyrannosaurus rex tyrannosaurus rex OT 1

U
U-Bahn metro; subway; underground OT 1
Übel evil WS 4, 126
üben to practise OT 1
über about; over OT 1; via OT 2
   über Bord overboard OT 3
   über Nacht overnight OT 2
überall everywhere OT 1; all over OT 2
überarbeiten to revise OT 2; to edit OT 3
Überblick overview OT 4
Überfall assault WS 3, 100
überfliegen to scan OT 3
überflüssig unnecessary OT 4
Überflutung flooding OT 4
überfüllt crowded OT 2
Übergang transition WS 2, 67
übergeben to throw up OT 2
übergenau fussy OT 2
übergewichtig overweight WS 3, 103
Überleben survival OT 2
überleben to survive OT 3
übermalen to repaint OT 4
übermäßig overly WS 2, 57
übernehmen to resume WS 1, 24
überprüfen to check OT 1
überqueren to cross OT 1
überraschend surprising OT 2
überrascht surprised OT 1; amazed OT 3
Überraschung surprise OT 1; shock WS 3, 107
überreden to persuade OT 3; to convince OT 4
Überreste remains OT 3
Überschrift heading OT 1
übersehen to overlook WS 2, 55
übersetzen to translate OT 1
Übersetzungsfalle false friend OT 2
Übersicht overview OT 4
übertragen to transfer OT 4
übertreiben to exaggerate OT 4; to overdo WS 3, 102
überwachen to oversee OT 4
überwachsen overgrown OT 4
Überwachung supervision WS 3, 101
überwiegend dominant WW, 11
überwuchert overgrown OT 4
überzeugen to persuade OT 3; to convince OT 4
überzeugend persuasive WS 1, 13
üblich usual OT 2
U-Boot submarine OT 3
übrig remaining WS 1, 41
übrige rest OT 1
Übung exercise OT 1; practice OT 2
Übungsheft exercise book OT 1

Ufer bank OT 3
Uhr clock OT 1
   um … Uhr at … o'clock OT 1
um around OT 1
   um … herum about; round OT 1
umarmen to hug OT 4; to embrace WS 1, 21
Umarmung hug OT 1
umdrehen to flip OT 4
umfallen to fall over OT 2
umfangreich considerably WS 3, 98
umfassen to involve; to range OT 4
Umfeld environment OT 2
umformulieren to rephrase OT 4
Umfrage survey OT 1; poll WS 3, 92
umgehen to deal with OT 2
umgehend immediate WS 1, 22
Umhang cloak OT 1
Umhängeband lanyard WS 2, 70
umkehren to invert WS 1, 29
umkippen to tip over WS 1, 29
Umkleide changing room OT 1
Umlaufbahn orbit OT 4
umschreiben to rewrite OT 1; to paraphrase WS 2, 71
Umsiedlung resettlement OT 4
Umstand circumstance WS 3, 100
Umstandswort adverb OT 1
umstellen to invert WS 1, 29
umstoßen to knock over OT 2
umstritten controversial WS 1, 23
Umwelt environment OT 2
Umwelt… environmental OT 2
Umweltschützer(in) environmentalist OT 3
Umweltverschmutzung pollution OT 2
umziehen to move OT 1
Umzug procession; parade OT 2
Umzugswagen moving van; removal van OT 2
unabhängig autonomous OT 4
Unabhängigkeit independence OT 2
unangenehm nasty OT 2
unbedenklich harmless WS 3, 94
Unbefugte(r) trespasser WS 4, 144
unbeholfen awkward WS 3, 94
unbekannt unknown OT 3
unbequem uncomfortable OT 3
Unberechenbarkeit unpredictability OT 2
unberührt unspoilt OT 3
unbestimmt indefinite OT 1; vague WS 1, 24
unbezahlt unpaid WS 2, 54
und and OT 1
   und so weiter etc. (et cetera) OT 1

Appendix

VOCABULARY

Underdog underdog **WS 1**, 21
uneben bumpy OT 4
unecht fake **WS 3**, 95
unendlich endless; infinite OT 4
unentschieden undecided **WS 1**, 19
unentschlossen undecided **WS 1**, 19
Unentschlossenheit indecision **WS 1**, 38
unerfahren inexperienced **WS 2**, 83
unerwartet unexpected **WS 3**, 107
unerwarteterweise unexpectedly OT 3
Unfairness unfairness OT 4
Unfall accident OT 1
unfreundlich unfriendly OT 4
ungarisch Hungarian OT 2
ungeduldig impatient OT 3
ungefähr about OT 1; approximately **WS 1**, 13
Ungerechtigkeit injustice; unfairness OT 4
ungeschickt clumsy OT 2; awkward **WS 3**, 94
ungesund unhealthy OT 1
   ungesundes Essen junk food **WS 3**, 102
ungewöhnlich unusual OT 2
unglaublich incredible; unbelievable OT 2
unglücklich unhappy OT 1
unheimlich scary OT 1
unhöflich rude OT 1
Uni uni OT 3
Uniform uniform OT 1
uninteressant dull **WS 3**, 88
Union union **WS 3**, 91
Unisex- unisex **WS 3**, 93
universal universal **WS 2**, 58
Universität university OT 1
Unkenntnis: in Unkenntnis unaware **WS 4**, 145
unklug foolish **WS 3**, 100
Unkraut weed **WS 1**, 28
unmittelbar immediate **WS 1**, 22
unmöglich impossible OT 2
unnötig unnecessary OT 4
unordentlich messy OT 2
Unordnung mess OT 3
unpassend inappropriate **WS 4**, 144
unpraktisch impractical OT 4
unregelmäßig irregular OT 1
uns us OT 1; ourselves OT 3
unsere(r, -s) our OT 1; ours OT 2
unschuldig innocent **WS 4**, 144
unter under OT 1; below OT 2; among OT 3
unterbewerten to understate **WW**, 11
unterbrechen to interrupt OT 2

Unterdrückung oppression **WS 4**, 126
unterhalten to entertain OT 4
Unterhalter(in) entertainer OT 3
unterhaltsam entertaining OT 3
Unterhaltung chat OT 1; entertainment OT 3
Unterhemd vest OT 2
Unterkühlung hypothermia OT 2
Unterkunft housing OT 3
Unternehmen company OT 1; corporation OT 4
unternehmensweit corporate **WW**, 11
Unternehmer(in) businessman; businesswoman OT 4; entrepreneur **WS 2**, 69
Unterricht class; lesson OT 1
unterrichten to teach OT 1
unterscheiden to differentiate **WS 3**, 115
   zwischen etw. unterscheiden to distinguish between **WS 4**, 143
Unterschied difference OT 1
unterschiedlich different OT 1
   unterschiedlich behandeln to discriminate **WS 2**, 56
Unterschlupf shelter OT 2
unterschreiben to sign OT 2
unterstreichen to underline OT 1
unterstützen to support OT 1; to assist **WS 2**, 59
unterstützend supportive **WS 1**, 14
Unterstützer von Start-ups incubator **WS 2**, 52
Unterstützung backup OT 4
   finanzielle Unterstützung sponsorship OT 2
Untersuchung analysis **WS 3**, 108
unterteilt divided OT 2
Untertitel caption OT 1
untertreiben to understate **WW**, 11
Unterüberschrift sub-heading OT 2
Unterwelt underworld **WS 4**, 126
unterwerfen to subject OT 4
untrinkbar undrinkable **WS 1**, 23
unvergesslich memorable OT 3; unforgettable **WS 4**, 126
unverwechselbar distinctive **WS 1**, 30
unvorsichtig carelessly OT 2
unwahrscheinlich unlikely OT 4
unwissend unaware **WS 4**, 145
unzählbar uncountable OT 1
unzugänglich inaccessible OT 3
uralt ancient OT 2
urban urban OT 4
Urkunde diploma **WS 2**, 58
Urlaub holiday OT 1; vacation OT 2
Urlauber(in) holidaymaker OT 3

Urlaubsort resort OT 2
Ursprung origin OT 3
ursprünglich originally OT 2; original OT 3
usw. etc. (et cetera) OT 1

V

vage vague **WS 1**, 24
Vampir(in) vampire OT 2
Vanille vanilla OT 1
Vanillesoße custard OT 1
Variante variation **WS 1**, 31
Variation variation **WS 1**, 31
variieren to vary **WS 3**, 109
Vater father OT 1
vegan vegan OT 1
Veganer(in) vegan OT 1
Vegetarier(in) vegetarian OT 1
vegetarisch vegetarian OT 1; veggie OT 2
Vene vein **WS 1**, 21
veraltet outdated **WS 2**, 64
Veranda porch OT 4
verändern to transform OT 4
Veränderung transformation OT 4
verängstigt scared; frightened OT 1; terrified OT 3
veranstalten to put on OT 2
Veranstaltungsort venue OT 3
verantwortlich responsible OT 3
   verantwortlich sein to be in charge of OT 3
Verantwortung responsibility OT 3
verärgert upset; irritated OT 2
Verb verb OT 1
verbal verbal **WS 2**, 61
Verband association; bandage OT 2
Verbandkasten first aid kit OT 2
verbergen to conceal **WS 3**, 93
verbessern to improve OT 2
Verbesserung improvement OT 3
verbieten to ban OT 3
verbinden to connect OT 2
Verbindung connection; link OT 2; combination OT 3
Verbindungswort linking word OT 4
verblassen to fade OT 2
Verbraucher(in) consumer **WS 3**, 104
Verbrechen crime OT 4
verbreiten to spread (out) OT 4
Verbrennungs… internal combustion OT 4
verbringen to spend OT 1
verbunden connected OT 1
Verderben spoilage OT 4
verderben to spoil OT 2
verdienen to deserve OT 2; to earn OT 3

Appendix

VOCABULARY

verdreht twisted OT 1; wacky OT 4
Verein club OT 1; association OT 2
vereinbaren to arrange OT 2; to schedule **WS 2**, 59
Vereinbarung arrangement; agreement OT 3
vereinfacht simplified **WS 4**, 144
vereinigen to unite **WS 1**, 13; to unify **WS 3**, 115
Verfahren procedure **WS 4**, 146
verfallen to decline **WS 3**, 98
Verfassung constitution **WS 1**, 39
verfaulen to rot **WS 1**, 23
verfeinern to refine OT 4
verfolgen to pursue OT 4
Verfolgung persecution OT 4
verfügbar available OT 3
Verfügung: zur Verfügung stellen to provide OT 4
vergeben to forgive OT 2; to award OT 4
vergeigen to mess up OT 2
vergessen to forget OT 1
Vergleich comparison OT 2
vergleichen to compare OT 1
vergüten to repay **WS 3**, 121
verhaften to arrest **WS 1**, 21
verhalten to act OT 1
Verhaltensregeln code of conduct **WS 4**, 140
Verhältniswort preposition OT 2
verhindern to prevent OT 4
verhungern (lassen) to starve OT 1
verkannt misunderstood OT 4
verkaufen to sell OT 1
Verkehr traffic OT 1; transport OT 2
Verkehrsmittel transport OT 2
verkleiden to dress up OT 2
verklemmt uptight **WS 3**, 90
verknallt: in jmdm. verknallt sein to have a crush on OT 4
Verkörperung personification **WS 4**, 145
verkünden to declare OT 4
verlangen to demand OT 4
verlängert prolonged **WS 1**, 23
verlangsamen to slow down OT 4
verlassen to leave OT 1
  sich verlassen auf to depend on OT 2; to rely on **WW**, 11
verlässlich reliable OT 4
verlegen embarrassed OT 3
Verleger(in) publisher **WS 2**, 55
verleihen to award OT 4
verletzen to harm OT 2
Verletzung injury OT 2
verlieren to lose OT 1
Verlierer(in) loser **WS 2**, 62

Verlust loss **WS 1**, 21
vermarktbar marketable OT 4
Vermarktung marketing OT 4
vermeidbar preventable **WS 1**, 21
vermeiden to avoid OT 4
Vermeidung prevention OT 2
vermischen to mix up OT 2
vermissen to miss OT 2
vermitteln: etwas vermitteln to impart; to communicate OT 4; to convey **WS 4**, 141
Vermittlung mediation OT 1
Vermögen wealth OT 4
vermuten to suppose OT 1
Verneinung negative OT 1
vernünftig sensible OT 3
veröffentlichen to publish OT 2; to release OT 4
Veröffentlichung publication **WW**, 11
Verordnung act **WS 1**, 19
Verpackung packaging OT 3
Verpflegungsservice catering service OT 4
verpflichtet obliged **WS 2**, 56
Verpflichtung obligation OT 2
Verputz plaster OT 1
verraten to reveal **WS 3**, 115
Verräter(in) snitch **WS 3**, 94
verringern to reduce OT 2
verrückt crazy OT 2; wacky OT 4; insane **WS 3**, 92
Verrückter madman OT 4
Versammlung assembly OT 1
verschieden diverse OT 4
verschiedene various **WS 1**, 22
verschlechtern to worsen **WS 1**, 27
verschlimmern to worsen **WS 1**, 27
Verschlüsselung code OT 1
verschmutzen to pollute **WS 1**, 23
verschneit snowy OT 3
verschütten to spill OT 2
verschwenden to waste OT 3
verschwimmen to blur **WS 2**, 62
verschwinden to disappear OT 3
verschwitzt sweaty **WS 3**, 95
versehentlich by accident; by mistake OT 2; accidentally OT 3
verseuchen to pollute **WS 1**, 23
Version version OT 3
Versöhnung reconciliation **WS 1**, 38
versorgen (mit) to provide OT 4
Versprechen promise OT 2
versprechen to promise OT 2
Verstand mind OT 1
verstärken to reinforce **WS 3**, 92
Verstärker amplifier OT 2

verstauchen to sprain OT 2
verstecken to hide OT 3
verstehen to understand OT 1
Versuch attempt; a go OT 2
  einen Versuch machen to have a go OT 2
versuchen to try OT 1
  jmdn. versuchen to tempt **WS 2**, 57
versus versus OT 4
vertäuen to moor OT 3
verteidigen to defend OT 3
Verteidiger(in) defender OT 3
Verteidigung defence **WS 2**, 61
verteilen to distribute OT 4
vertikal vertical OT 4
vertrauen to trust OT 3
vertraut familiar OT 2
verursachen to cause OT 2
verurteilen to sentence **WS 3**, 108; to convict **WS 3**, 108
Verurteilte(r) convict **WS 1**, 18
Verurteilung sentencing **WS 3**, 100
vervollständigen to complete OT 1
Verwahrung custody **WS 3**, 100
Verwalter(in) steward OT 4
Verwandlung transformation OT 4
Verwandte(r) relative OT 1; relation OT 2
Verwandtschaft kin **WS 1**, 21
Verweis reference OT 4
verwelken to fade OT 2
verwirklichen to fulfil OT 4
verwirrend confusing OT 2
verwirrt confused OT 2
verwundern to amaze **WS 3**, 121
verwüsten to vandalize **WS 4**, 128
Verzeihung pardon **WS 2**, 70
verzweifelt desperate OT 3
vibrieren to vibrate OT 4
Video video OT 1
Video-Blog vlog OT 3
Videoclip video clip OT 2
Videokassette video OT 1
Videokonferenztechnik video conferencing OT 4
Videospiel video game OT 2
Vieh livestock **WS 3**, 103
Viehbestand stock OT 2; livestock **WS 2**, 52
Viehhaltung cattle ranching **WS 3**, 103
viel lots; a lot; much OT 1; plenty OT 2
  viele many OT 1; numerous **WS 4**, 141
Vielfalt variety **WS 1**, 24
vielfältig diverse OT 4
Vielfältigkeit diversity OT 4
vielleicht maybe OT 1; perhaps OT 3
vielseitig versatile OT 3

Appendix

VOCABULARY

vier four OT 1
Viertel quarter OT 1
   viertel vor quarter to OT 1
vierundzwanzig twenty-four OT 1
vierzehn fourteen OT 1
vierzig forty OT 1
violett violet OT 1
virtuell virtual OT 4
Vision vision OT 4
Visualisierung visualization OT 3
visuell visual OT 2
Visum visa OT 4
Vita Curriculum Vitae **WS 2**, 56
Vlog vlog OT 3
Vlogger(in) vlogger OT 3
Vogel bird OT 1
Vokal vowel OT 1
Volks… folk OT 2
Volksheld folk hero OT 4
Volkstanz country dancing OT 1
voll full OT 1
Volleyball volleyball OT 3
völlig thoroughly **WS 2**, 67
Vollstreckung enforcement **WS 4**, 127
Volontär(in) intern OT 4
von of; from; by; off OT 1
vor ago; before; in front of OT 1
voraus ahead OT 3
Voraus: im Voraus beforehand **WS 4**, 143
Voraussetzung requirement **WS 1**, 33
vorbeifahren to pass OT 3
vorbereiten to prepare; to get ready OT 1
   die Bühne vorbereiten to set the stage OT 2
Vorbereitung preparation OT 2
Vordergrund foreground OT 3
Vorderseite front OT 1
Vorderteil front OT 1
Voreingenommenheit bias **WS 3**, 92
Vorfahr(in) ancestor OT 3
Vorfall incident **WS 3**, 101
vorführen to act out OT 1; to demonstrate OT 4
vorgeben to pretend OT 2
Vorhand forehand OT 3
Vorhang curtain OT 2
vorherig previous OT 4
Vorhersage prediction OT 2
vorhersagen to predict OT 4
vorhersehbar predictable **WS 1**, 22
Vorlage template OT 4
Vorliebe preference OT 3
vormundschaftlich custodial **WS 3**, 101
Vorname first name OT 2

Vorrat supply OT 3
Vorschlag suggestion OT 1
vorschlagen to suggest OT 1
Vorschrift regulation **WS 2**, 62
Vorschule preschool **WS 3**, 99
vorsichtig careful OT 1
Vorspeise starter OT 1
vorstellen to imagine; to present OT 1; to introduce OT 2
Vorstellung show OT 1; introduction OT 2
Vorstellungsbeginn showtime OT 4
Vorstellungsgespräch interview OT 1
   ein Vorstellungsgespräch führen to interview OT 1
Vorteil benefit; pro OT 2; advantage OT 3
Vortrag talk OT 2
Vorurteil prejudice **WS 1**, 39
Vorwurf: jmdm. Vorwürfe machen to blame **WS 3**, 92
vorziehen to prefer OT 1

W

wach awake OT 2
wachsen to grow OT 1
Wachstum growth **WS 3**, 102
Wächter watchman **WS 4**, 126
wackelig shaky OT 3
Waffe weapon OT 3
Waffel waffle OT 3
Wagen trolley; carriage OT 1; wagon OT 4
wagen to dare OT 2
Wagenzug wagon train OT 4
Wahl choice OT 1; option OT 2; election OT 3
wählen to vote OT 1; to dial OT 2; to select; to elect OT 4
wählerisch fussy OT 2
wahnsinnig insane **WS 3**, 92
wahr true OT 1
während while OT 1; during OT 2; throughout OT 3; whereas **WS 2**, 68
Wahrheit truth OT 3
wahrscheinlich probably OT 2; likely OT 3
Wahrzeichen landmark OT 4
Wal whale OT 1
Wald forest OT 1
Waldbrand wildfire OT 2
Waldhorn French horn OT 1
Walfang whaling OT 2
walisisch Welsh OT 1
Walspeck blubber OT 2
Wand wall OT 1

Wanderer / Wanderin hiker OT 2; walker OT 3
Wandern hiking OT 1
wandern to hike OT 1
Wanderstiefel hiking boot OT 2
Wanderung walk; hike OT 2
Wandgemälde mural OT 2
Wandschrank closet OT 2
Wandzeitung wall display OT 2
wann when OT 1
   wann auch immer whenever OT 4
warm warm OT 2
warnen to warn OT 3
warten to wait OT 1; to hang on OT 2
Warteschlange queue OT 1
Wartung maintenance OT 3
warum why OT 1
was what OT 1
   was auch immer whatever OT 3
Wäsche laundry OT 4
waschen to wash OT 2
Wasser water OT 1
   unter Wasser underwater OT 2
Wasser… aquatic OT 4
Wasserbus waterbus OT 3
wasserdicht waterproof OT 2
Wasserfall falls; waterfall OT 1
Wasserhahn faucet OT 4
Wasserkocher kettle OT 2
Wasserloch waterhole **WS 1**, 20
Wasserstelle watering hole **WS 1**, 23
Webinar webinar OT 4
Webkonferenz web conference OT 4
Webseite website OT 1
Wechsel transition **WS 2**, 67
Wechselgeld change OT 1
wechseln to change OT 1
Wecker alarm; alarm clock OT 2
weder neither OT 2
   weder noch nor OT 4
Weg track; way; path OT 1
weg off; away OT 1
wegen due to **WW**, 11
wegräumen to put away OT 2
wegrennen to rush off OT 2
wegschicken to dismiss **WS 2**, 70
Wegweiser signpost **WS 2**, 50
Wegweisung signposting **WS 4**, 143
wegwerfen to throw away OT 2
wehen to blow OT 2
wehtun to hurt OT 1; to ache OT 3
weiblich female OT 2
weich soft OT 3
weigern: sich weigern to refuse OT 4
Weihnachten Christmas OT 1

Appendix

VOCABULARY

Weihnachtsmarkt Christmas market OT 2
weil because OT 1
Wein wine OT 1
weinen to cry OT 1
Weise manner OT 2
Weisheitszahn wisdom tooth WS 2, 63
weiß white OT 1
weit far OT 1; wide OT 2
weiter anymore OT 2; further OT 4
Weiterbildungslehrgang training course OT 2
weiterführende Schule secondary school OT 1
weitergehen to move on OT 4
weiterhin furthermore WS 2, 68
weitermachen to continue OT 1; to go ahead OT 4
Weizen wheat WS 1, 27
welche(r, -s) which OT 1
Welle wave OT 1
Wellensittich budgie OT 1
Wellness wellness OT 4
Welpe puppy OT 2
Welt world OT 1
    aus aller Welt from around the world OT 1
weltoffen cosmopolitan WS 1, 19
Weltraum space OT 2
Weltraumforschung space exploration OT 4
weltweit worldwide OT 3; global OT 4
Wendel spiral WS 1, 21
Wendung phrase OT 1
wenige few OT 1
wer who OT 1
    wer auch immer whoever OT 4
Werbeagentur advertiser OT 3
Werbebanner banner ad WS 3, 105
Werber advertiser OT 3
Werbung advertisement OT 1; ad; advertising OT 2
    Werbung machen für to advertise OT 2
werden to become; shall, will OT 2
werfen to throw OT 1; to toss OT 3
Werft dockyard OT 3
Werkstatt workshop OT 1; garage OT 4
Werkzeug tool OT 2
Wert value OT 4
wertvoll valuable OT 2
Wesen creature OT 4
wesentlich essential OT 4
Wespe wasp OT 3
wessen whose OT 2

Weste vest OT 2
Westen west OT 1
    mittlerer Westen midwest; midwestern OT 4
westwärts westward OT 4
Wettbewerb competition OT 1
wetteifernd competitively OT 4
wetten to bet OT 1
Wetter weather OT 1
Wettkampf match OT 1
wichtig important OT 1; relevant; essential OT 4; critical WS 1, 23; dominant WW, 11
Wichtigkeit importance OT 2; significance WS 1, 30
Widerstand resistance WS 1, 22
widerstandsfähig resistant WS 3, 103
widerstehen to resist WS 3, 94
wie how; as OT 1
wieder again OT 1
Wiedergabeliste playlist OT 4
Wiedergutmachung leisten to make amends WS 3, 100
wiederherstellen to restore OT 4
wiederholen to repeat OT 1
    wiederholter Stellenwechsel job hopping WS 2, 62
Wiederholung repetition OT 4
Wiedersehen! goodbye OT 1
Wiederverheiratung remarriage WS 3, 98
wiederverwendbar reusable OT 3
wiederverwenden to reuse OT 2
wiederverwerten to recycle OT 2
Wiederverwerter(in) recycler OT 3
wiegen to weigh OT 3
Wiese meadow OT 2
wild wild OT 2; feral WS 1, 23
Wilderei poaching OT 3
Wilderer / Wilderin poacher OT 3
Wildfang tomboy WS 3, 93
Wildnis wilderness OT 2
Wildwasser fahren white water rafting OT 3
willkommen welcome OT 1
willkürlich random WS 1, 22
Wind wind OT 2
Windel nappy OT 3
winden to wind WS 1, 20
windig windy OT 2
windsurfen to windsurf OT 1
Windsurfer(in) windsurfer OT 1
winken to wave OT 2
Winsch windlass OT 3
Winter winter OT 1
winzig tiny OT 1

wir we OT 1
wirklich actual WS 2, 56
wirklich really OT 1; truly WS 1, 43
wirksam effective OT 4
Wirksamkeit effectiveness WS 4, 144
Wirkung effect OT 3
Wirtschaft economy OT 3
wirtschaftlich economic OT 4
Wirtschaftswissenschaften economics WS 2, 78
Wischtuch wipe OT 4
Wissen science OT 1; knowledge OT 4
wissen to know OT 1
Wissenschaft studies OT 1
wissenschaftlich scientific OT 3
Witz joke OT 2
wo where OT 1
    wo (auch) immer wherever OT 3
woanders elsewhere WS 3, 88
Woche week OT 1
Wochenende weekend OT 1
Wochentag weekday OT 3
wöchentlich weekly OT 3
Wohlbefinden wellness OT 4
Wohlfahrtsorganisation charity OT 2
wohnen to live OT 1
Wohnmobil camper van OT 4
Wohnraum housing OT 3
Wohnung flat; apartment OT 1
Wohnwagen caravan OT 1
Wohnzimmer living room OT 1
Wolke cloud OT 1
Wolkenkratzer skyscraper OT 3
wolkig cloudy OT 4
Wolle wool OT 2
    aus Wolle woolly OT 2
wollen to want OT 1
wollig woolly OT 2
Wombat wombat WS 1, 26
Wort word OT 1
Wortart part of speech OT 2
Wörterbuch dictionary OT 1
wörtlich literal WS 4, 146
Wrack wreck OT 3
wunderbar wonderful OT 1
wünschen to wish OT 3
Wurm worm OT 1
Wurst sausage OT 1
Wurzel root OT 3
Wüste desert OT 3
Wut anger OT 3
wüten to rage WS 1, 38

Y

Yoga yoga WS 2, 71

VOCABULARY

Z
Zahl number OT 1; figure OT 3
zählbar countable OT 1
zählen to count OT 1
zahlreich numerous **WS 4**, 141
Zahltag payday **WS 2**, 83
Zahn tooth OT 2
Zahnarzt / -ärztin dentist **WS 2**, 63
Zahnbürste toothbrush OT 4
Zahnpasta toothpaste OT 4
Zauber magic OT 1
Zauberer / Zauberin magician OT 1
Zaun fence **WS 1**, 12
Zebra zebra OT 1
Zebrastreifen zebra crossing OT 1
Zeh toe OT 1
zehn ten OT 1
Zeichen token **WS 1**, 38
Zeichen drawing OT 1
Zeichensetzung punctuation OT 1
Zeichentrickfilm cartoon OT 4
zeichnen to draw OT 1; to sketch OT 4
Zeichnung drawing OT 1
zeigen to indicate **WS 2**, 68
zeigen to show OT 1
Zeit time OT 1; period OT 3
Zeitachse timeline OT 2
Zeitform tense OT 1
zeitgenössisch contemporary OT 3
Zeitpunkt timing OT 3
Zeitrechnung: unserer Zeitrechnung AD (Anno Domini) OT 2
Zeitschrift magazine OT 1
Zeituhr timer **WS 2**, 70
Zeitung newspaper OT 1
Zeitwort verb OT 1
Zelle cell OT 1; booth OT 4
Zelt tent OT 1; marquee OT 2
zelten to camp OT 1
Zeltplatz campsite OT 1; campground OT 2
Zentimeter centimetre (cm) OT 2
Zentral- central OT 1
Zentrum centre OT 1
zeremoniell ceremonial OT 3
zerkleinert shredded OT 2
zerstören to vandalize **WS 4**, 128
zerstören to destroy OT 2
zerstörend destructive **WS 1**, 41
Zertifikat certificate OT 1
Zeug stuff OT 2
Zeuge(-in) sein to witness **WS 3**, 107
Zeugnis certificate OT 1

Ziege goat OT 4
ziehen to draw; to pull OT 1
Ziel target OT 2; aim; ambition; objective OT 4
zielen to aim OT 4
  zielen auf to target **WS 3**, 118
ziemlich quite OT 2; rather OT 3; relatively **WS 3**, 120
Ziffer digit OT 2
Zinn tin OT 2
zirkulieren to circulate OT 4
zischen to whizz OT 2
Zitadelle fortress OT 3
zitieren to quote; to cite OT 2
Zitronenlimonade lemonade OT 1
zittern to tremble OT 2
zögern to hesitate OT 3
Zoll customs OT 2
  Zoll (2,54 cm) inch OT 2
zollfrei duty free OT 2
Zombie zombie OT 2
Zone zone OT 2
Zoo zoo OT 1
zornig angrily OT 2
zu too; to OT 1
Zubehör accessory OT 3
Zucchini zucchini OT 3
Zucker sugar OT 3
Zuckermais sweet corn OT 1
Zufall chance OT 2
zufällig accidentally OT 3; random **WS 1**, 22
Zuflucht resort OT 2
zufrieden pleased OT 1
zufriedenstellend satisfying **WS 4**, 146
Zug train OT 1
Zugang access OT 4
zugänglich accessible OT 2
zugeben to admit OT 4
zugreifen auf to access OT 4
Zugriff access OT 4
Zuhause home OT 1
zuhören to listen OT 1
Zuhörer(in) listener OT 1
Zukunft future OT 2
zumachen to shut OT 2
zunächst initially **WS 1**, 41
Zunahme increase OT 3
Zunder tinder OT 2
Zündung ignition OT 4
zunehmend increasingly **WS 1**, 27
Zuneigung affection **WS 2**, 64

Zunge tongue OT 3
zurechtkommen to cope **WS 3**, 120
zurück back OT 1
zurückgehen to decrease **WS 3**, 98
zurückkehren to return OT 2; to head back **WS 1**, 19
zurücktreten to resign **WS 1**, 43
zurückzahlen to repay **WS 3**, 121
zusammen together OT 1
zusammenfassen to summarize OT 2; to sum up OT 4
Zusammenfassung summary OT 3
Zusammenhang context OT 4
zusammenpassen: nicht zusammenpassen to clash OT 2
zusammenpassend: nicht zusammenpassend mismatched OT 4
zusammensacken to slump OT 4
zusammenstoßen to bump into OT 2
zusätzlich in addition to OT 4
Zuschauer(in) spectator; viewer OT 3
zuschlagen to strike OT 1
Zuschuss grant **WS 2**, 64
zuspielen to pass OT 3
zuständig in charge OT 1
zusteigen to get on OT 2
zustimmen to approve OT 3
Zutat ingredient OT 2
zuversichtlich confident OT 2
zuvorderst foremost **WW**, 11
Zwangsarbeiter(in) bonded laborer OT 4
zwanzig twenty OT 1
Zweck purpose OT 4
zwecklos pointless OT 4
zweckmäßig: zweckmäßiges Gerät convenience OT 4
zwei two OT 1
  zwei Wochen fortnight OT 2
Zweifel doubt OT 4
Zweig twig OT 2
zweimal twice OT 2
zweisprachig bilingual OT 2
zweite(r, -s) second OT 1
zweitens secondly OT 2
zweiundzwanzig twenty-two OT 1
Zwiebel onion OT 2
Zwiebelring onion ring OT 2
Zwilling twin OT 1
zwingen to force OT 2
zwischen between OT 1; among OT 3
Zwischenstation waypoint OT 2
zwölf twelve OT 1

Dictionary: Names

A

Aborigine [ˌæbəˈrɪdʒɪni] indigenous people of Australia **WS 1**, 20
Adam [ˈædəm] boy's name **WS 2**, 79
Aesha [aɪˈiːʃə] girl's name **WS 2**, 82
Alan Moore [ælən mʊər] English comics writer **WS 4**, 126
Alcott [ˈɔːlkət] surname **WS 1**, 30
Amanda [əˈmændə] girl's name **WS 1**, 30
Amazon [ˈæməzən] a river in South America **WS 3**, 103
Amber [ˈæmbə] girl's name **WS 3**, 95
Amir [eˈmɪə] boy's name **WS 2**, 52
Amy [ˈeɪmi] girl's name **WW**, 11
Anangu [ˈaŋaŋʊ] a name used by members of several Aboriginal Australian groups and tribes **WS 1**, 24
Angelina Jolie [ændʒɛˈlinə dʒoʊˈliː] American actress, filmmaker and humanitarian **WS 3**, 88
Auckland [ˈɔːklənd] city in the North Island of New Zealand **WS 1**, 13
Australia [ɒˈstreɪliə] a country and continent between the Indian Ocean and the southern Pacific Ocean **WW**, 10
Avery [ˈeɪvəri] girl's name **WS 3**, 93
Ayers Rock [eɪərs ˈrɒk] former colonial name of Uluru **WS 1**, 24

B

Barkindji [baˈkindʒiː] an Australian Aboriginal tribal group in New South Wales, Australia **WS 1**, 15
Bastian [ˈbæstʃɪn] boy's name **WS 4**, 134
Bates [ˈbeɪts] surname **WS 1**, 14
Ben Ockrent [ben ˈɔkrent] contemporary British writer and theatre director **WS 2**, 76
Bob [bɒb] boy's name **WS 1**, 19
Bondi Beach [ˌbɒndaɪ ˈbiːtʃ] a popular beach in Sydney, Australia **WS 1**, 13
Brad [bræd] boy's name **WS 2**, 78
Brisbane [ˈbrɪzbən] the capital city of the state of Queensland in the east of Australia **WS 1**, 13
Bruce [ˈbrus] boy's name **WS 1**, 44

C

California [ˌkæləˈfɔːniə] a state in the southwest of the US **WS 3**, 99
Cambridge [ˈkeɪmbrɪdʒ] a city in eastern England **WS 2**, 82
Canada [ˈkænədə] a country in North America **WW**, 10
Canberra [ˈkænbərə] capital of Australia **WS 1**, 13
Cape Town [ˈkeɪp ˌtaʊn] a large city in South Africa **WS 2**, 67
Cardiff [ˈkɑːdɪf] capital of Wales **WS 2**, 52
Carla [ˈkɑːlə] girl's name **WS 3**, 94
Carter [ˈkɑːtə] boy's name **WS 3**, 119
Cathy [ˈkæθɪ] girl's name **WS 3**, 116
Charles [ˈtʃɑrlz] boy's name **WS 3**, 89
Christchurch [ˈkraɪstʃɜːtʃ] largest city in the South Island of New Zealand **WS 1**, 13
Christine [ˈkrɪstiːn] girl's name **WS 1**, 28
Colin [ˈkəʊlɪn] boy's name **WS 2**, 70
Conny [ˈkɒni] girl's name **WS 1**, 16

D

Daimler Chrysler [ˈdeɪmlə ˈkraɪzlə] a large company that produces many differnt types of cars **WW**, 11
Dan [dæn] boy's name **WS 2**, 59
David Ignatow [ˈdeɪvɪd ˈɪgnatov] American poet (1914 – 1997) **Extra pages**, 146
Diane [daɪˈæn] girl's name **WS 2**, 70
Dublin [ˈdʌblɪn] the capital of the Republic of Ireland **WS 2**, 66
Duncan [ˈdʌŋkən] boy's name **WS 2**, 65

E

Eddie Murphy [ˌedi ˈmɜrfi] an American actor, comedian, writer, producer, and singer **WS 1**, 44
Edinburgh [ˈedənbərə] the capital of Scotland **WS 2**, 55
Edmund Barton [ˈedmənd ˈbɑːtn] an Australian politician and judge (1849 – 1920) **WS 1**, 43
Eleni [əˈleɪni] girl's name **WS 1**, 14
Emily [ˈeməli] girl's name **WS 1**, 17
Emma [ˈemə] girl's name **WS 3**, 101

F

Ferris [ˈferəs] surname **WS 3**, 96
Fisher [ˈfɪʃər] surname **WS 3**, 93
Fred [fred] boy's name **WS 1**, 19

G

Gabriel [ˈgeɪbriəl] boy's name **WS 3**, 92
Garcia [gɑːˌsiːə] surname **WS 3**, 91
Glasgow [ˈglɑːzgəʊ] the largest city in Scotland **WS 2**, 55
Grace [greɪs] girl's name **WS 3**, 94
Great Barrier Reef [greɪt ˈbæriə ˌriːf] the world's largest coral reef system, off the coast of Queensland, Australia **WS 1**, 24
Greece [griːs] a country in southeast Europe **WW**, 11
Guatemala [ˌgwɑːtəˈmɑːlə] country in Central America **WS 4**, 130

H

Haka [ˈhɑːkə] a traditional Maori war dance **WS 1**, 30
Hansen [ˈhænsən] surname **WS 1**, 14
Harris [ˈhɛrɪs] surname **WS 2**, 65
Henry [ˈhenrɪ] boy's name **WS 2**, 81
Hindi [ˈhɪndi] an official language in India **WW**, 11
Hosier Lane [ˌhəʊzɪə ˈleɪn] popular street and tourist attraction in Melbourne **WS 1**, 17

I

Iran [ɪˈrɑːn] a country in southwest Asia **WS 4**, 126

J

Jacinda Ardern [dʒəˈsɪndə ˈɑːdɜːn] Prime Minister of New Zealand, born 26th July 1980 **WS 1**, 31
Jack [dʒæk] boy's name **WS 1**, 44
Jackie [ˈdʒæki] girl's name **WS 2**, 70
Jake [dʒeɪk] boy's name **WS 3**, 100
Jameson [ˈdʒeɪməsən] surname **WS 2**, 79
Jason [ˈdʒeɪsn] boy's name **WS 1**, 14
Jenny [ˈdʒeni] girl's name **WS 2**, 76
Jermaine [dʒəˈmeɪn] boy's name **WS 2**, 67
Joe [dʒəʊ] boy's name **WS 3**, 101
John [dʒɒn] boy's name **WS 1**, 41
Judith [ˈdʒuːdɪθ] girl's name **WS 1**, 19
Justin Trudeau [ˈdʒʌstɪn truːˈdəʊ] Prime Minister of Canada **WS 3**, 88

K

Karen McManus [ˈkærən mækˈmenəs] contemporary American author **WS 3**, 114
Katy [ˈkeɪti] girl's name **WS 3**, 106
Keira [ˈkɪərə] girl's name **WS 1**, 19
Kevin [ˌkevɪn] boy's name **WS 3**, 103

Appendix

VOCABULARY

Kevin Rudd [ˌkevɪn ˈrʌd] Australian Prime Minister (2007 – 2010 and 2013) **WS 1**, 21
Koula [ˈkuːlə] girl's name **WS 1**, 15
Kourakis [kuˈrɑːkis] surname **WS 1**, 15
Kristen [ˈkrɪstən] girl's name **WS 3**, 90
Kyle [kaɪl] boy's name **WS 3**, 101

L

La Limonada [ˌla limoˈnada] the biggest urban slum in Central America **WS 4**, 130
Lancashire [ˈlæŋkəʃə] a county in northwest England **WS 2**, 65
Langston Hughes [ˌlæŋkstən ˈhjuːz] American poet and activist (1901 – 1967) **Extra pages**, 147
Lara [ˈlɑːrə] girl's name **WS 3**, 121
Lauren [ˈlɔːrən] girl's name **WS 2**, 53
Libby [ˈlɪˌbi] girl's name **WS 1**, 16
Lily [ˈlɪli] girl's name **WS 3**, 95
Liz [lɪz] girl's name **WS 2**, 54
Lucas [ˈluːkəs] boy's name **WS 2**, 51
Lucy [ˈluːsi] girl's name **WS 2**, 55
Lynn [ˈlɪn] girl's name **WS 3**, 95

M

Malawi [məˈlɑːwi] a country in East Africa **WS 2**, 78
Manchester [ˈmæntʃəstə] a large city in the northwest of England **WS 2**, 52
Mandarin [ˈmændərɪn] the official language of China **WW**, 11
Maria [məˈriːə] girl's name **WS 3**, 91
Mark Haddon [mɑːk ˈhædən] British novelist and poet, born 28th October, 1962 **Extra pages**, 147
Martin [ˈmɑːtɪn] boy's name **WS 2**, 79
Marvin [ˈmɑːvɪn] boy's name **WS 2**, 82
Mary Oliver [ˌmeəri ˈɒlɪvə] American poet (1935 – 2019) **Extra pages**, 147
Max [mæks] boy's name **WS 2**, 78
Melbourne [ˈmelbən] capital city of Victoria, Australia **WS 1**, 13
Mexico [ˈmeksəkəʊ] a country to the south of the US **WS 4**, 138
Midlands [ˈmɪdləndz] the central part of England **WS 2**, 65
Mike [maɪk] boy's name **WS 2**, 83
Milford Sound [ˌmɪlfəd ˈsaʊnd] fjord in the south west of New Zealand's South Island **WS 1**, 30
Mina [ˈmɪnə] girl's name **WS 2**, 70
Mira [ˈmɪrə] girl's name **WS 3**, 95
Montreal [ˌmɒntriˈɔːl] a city in southern Quebec, in East Canada **WS 3**, 94

N

Nancy [ˈnænsi] girl's name **WS 2**, 69
Nasir [nəzˈiə] boy's name **WS 2**, 57
Nathan [ˈneɪθən] boy's name **WS 2**, 69
New Delhi [ˌnjuː ˈdeli] the capital city of India **WW**, 11
New Holland [ˌnjuː ˈhɒlənd] historical name for mainland Australia in the 17th century **WS 1**, 13
New South Wales [ˌnjuː saʊθ ˈweɪlz] a state in southeast Australia **WS 1**, 13
New Zealand [njuː ˈziːlənd] a country consisting of two main islands, North Island and South Island, and several smaller ones, in the Pacific Ocean, southwest of Australia **WS 1**, 13
Nguyen [wɪn] surname **WS 1**, 30
Nick [nɪk] boy's name **WS 1**, 14
Nicole [nɪˈkəʊl] girl's name **WS 3**, 92
Nina [ˈninə] girl's name **WS 1**, 29
Nottingham [ˈnɒtɪŋəm] an industrial city in central England **WS 2**, 65

O

Original All Blacks [əˈrɪdʒɪnəl ɔːl blæks] the first New Zealand national rugby union team **WS 1**, 30

P

Paris [ˈpærɪs] the capital city of France **WS 2**, 57
Perth [pɜːθ] a city in southwest Australia and capital of the state of Western Australia **WS 1**, 13
Philippines [ˈfɪlɪpiːnz] a country made up of over 7000 islands off the southeast coast of Asia **WS 1**, 19

Q

Quebec [kwɪˈbek] a province in eastern Canada **WW**, 11
Queensland [ˈkwiːnzlənd] a state in northeast Australia, whose capital and largest city is Brisbane **WS 1**, 12
Queenstown [ˈkwiːnztaʊn] city in the South Island of New Zealand **WS 1**, 30

R

Rachel [ˈreɪtʃəl] girl's name **WS 3**, 119
Ralph [rælf] boy's name **WS 3**, 95
Ricky [ˈrɪki] boy's name **WS 1**, 14
Robert O'Hara Burke [ˈrɒbət əʊˈhɑːrə bɜːk] an Australian explorer of Irish heritage (1821 – 1861) **WS 1**, 41

S

Sadie [ˈseɪdi] girl's name **WS 3**, 90
Salma [ˈsælmə] girl's name **WS 2**, 57
Sanjay [ˈsændʒeɪ] boy's name **WW**, 11
Santa Muerte [ˈsanta ˈmwerte] the Saint of Death in Mexican religion **WS 4**, 134
Sarah [ˈseərə] girl's name **WS 2**, 67
Shakespeare [ˈʃeɪkspɪə] an English writer of plays and poems, who is generally regarded as the greatest of all English writers (1564 – 1616) **WS 4**, 145
Shanghai [ʃæŋˈhaɪ] a city in East China **WS 2**, 67
Sheffield [ˈʃefiːld] a city in South Yorkshire in the north of England **WS 2**, 55
Spain [speɪn] a country in southwest Europe **WS 2**, 78
Steve Irwin [stiːv ˈɜːwən] an Australian zookeeper, conservationist, television personality, wildlife expert and environmentalist (1962 – 2006) **WS 1**, 44
Surrey [ˈsʌri] a county in southeast England **WS 2**, 79
Susannah [suːˈzænə] girl's name **WS 3**, 92
Sweden [ˈswiːdn] a country in Scandinavia, northern Europe **WS 3**, 98
Switzerland [ˈswɪtsələnd] a country in western Europe **WS 1**, 13
Sydney [ˈsɪdni] capital city of New South Wales and most populous city in Australia **WS 1**, 13

T

Table Mountain [ˈteɪbəl ˌmaʊntɪn] a high mountain in South Africa, it stands behind the city of Cape Town **WS 2**, 67
Tai [taɪ] boy's name **WS 1**, 28
Tarek [taːriq] boy's name **WS 3**, 97
Tasman Sea [tæzˈmeɪn siː] a sea of the South Pacific Ocean, situated between Australia and New Zealand **WS 1**, 30
Tayler [ˈteɪlər] boy's and girl's name **WS 3**, 93
Tom [tɒm] boy's name **WS 3**, 117
Tony Medina [ˈtəʊni meˈdiːnə] a poet, scholar, and children's book author (died in 2011) **WS 4**, 126
Torres Strait Islander [ˌtɔːrəs streɪt ˈaɪləndə] inhabitant of a group of 274 small islands in the Torres Strait **WS 1**, 12
Turner [ˈtɜːnə] surname **WS 1**, 14

VOCABULARY

U

Ukraine [juːˈkreɪn] a country in eastern Europe **WS 2**, 63

Uluru [ˌuːləˈruː] a rock formation in the Northern Territory, Australia **WS 1**, 24

UNESCO (United Nations Educational, Scientific, and Cultural Organization) [jʊˈneskəʊ] a part of the UN, which is concerned especially with providing help for poorer countries with education and science **WS 1**, 24

V

Valerie [ˈvæləri] girl's name **WS3**, 91

Vancouver [vænˈkuːvə] a city in British Columbia, Canada **WS 3**, 94

W

Wayne [ˈweɪn] boy's name **WS 3**, 97

Wellington [ˈwelɪŋtən] capital of New Zealand **WS 1**, 30

William Wills [ˌwɪljəm ˈwɪlz] a British explorer **WS 1**, 41

Y

Yu Garden [ˈju ˈɡɑːdn] an extensive Chinese garden located beside the City God Temple in the northeast of the Old City of Shanghai **WS 2**, 67

Acknowledgements

Text credits

p. 34/35: André Leslie, „Bernhard Holtermann: Ein Leben mit vielen Kapiteln", Goethe-Institut e. V., München, https://www.goethe.de/ins/au/de/kul/sup/gas/21865525.html; **p. 72:** „100 Jahre Workcamps", ijgd Bundesverein e. V., Hannover o. D., https://www.workcamps.org/workcamps; **p. 73:** "Starting the journey", Internationale Jugendgemeinschaftsdienste (ijgd) – Bundesverein e. V., Hannover, o. D., https://archiv.ijgd.de/workcampsinternational/deutschland/erfahrungsberichte/natur-umwelt/rothenfels-2018-xiao-w-from-china; **p. 76/77:** Ben Ockrent, *Hacktivist*, Hrsg. Andreas Galle. Ditzingen: Reclam, 2020; **p. 107:** „Cyberbullying Statistics", © 2006 – 2021 ENOUGH IS ENOUGH, https://enough.org/stats_cyberbullying; **p. 110/111:** „Cybermobbing an der Schule: Bedeutung und Hilfe", sorger's GmbH, Mühlheim-Kärlich 25.11.2021, https://www.schulranzen.net/blog/schulalltag/cybermobbing-an-der-schule-bedeutung-und-hilfe; **p. 111:** „Cyberbullying is a real problem in today's society", 2021 © Broadband Search.net, https://www.broadbandsearch.net/blog/cyber-bullying-statistics#post-navigation-0; **p. 114:** Karen McManus, *One of us is lying* (English edition), Kindle, pp. 229 – 231; **p. 146:** David Ignatow, *Against the Evidence: Selected Poems 1934 – 1994*, Middleton: Wesleyan University Press, 1994, p. 84; **p. 147:** Langston Hughes, *The Collected Works of Langston Hughes*, Columbia: University of Missouri Press, 2001, p. 61; Mark Haddon, *Trees*, Poemhunter.com, San Francisco, 25 August 2016, https://www.poemhunter.com/poem/trees-115/; Mary Oliver, *Dream Work*, New York: The Atlantic Monthly Press, 1986

Picture credits

|Alamy Stock Photo, Abingdon/Oxfordshire: AFPhoto 155.1; ALAN OLIVER 15.1; Ammentorp Photography 96.2; Artem Medvediev 102.1; Boethling, Joerg 78.1; byswat 94.2; Christoph & Friends/Das Fotoarchiv 156.1; Craddock, Samantha 168.1; creativephototeam 164.1; Cultura Creative RF 117.2; Dack, Simon / Telephoto Images 15.2; Daemmrich, Bob 117.1; dave cooil 151.1; David Noton Photography 41.2; Dolgachov, Lev 162.1; Einsiedel, Andreas von 79.1; Federico Caputo 69.1; Forstmanis, Kerin 17.2; fullempty 27.2; GL Archive 43.1; Grosclaude, Alain 31.2; Holli 45.1; ibreakmedia 83.1, 96.1; imageBROKER 10.2; Khaetskii, Valerii 79.2; Kuprevich, Hanna 11.5; LightField Studios Inc. 94.3; Lusiyk, Vira 160.1; Maridav 152.1; MBI 97.1, 167.1; Melnyk, Volodymyr 11.1; Michael, Andrew 17.1; North Wind Picture Archives 18.2; Oeland, Ingo 25.2; Panther Media GmbH 171.1; Paul Christian Gordon 102.2; Paul Mayall Australia 25.1; Pearson, Myrleen 119.1; Phillips, Mark 107.1; PHOVOIR 97.2; Probst, Peter 10.9; public domain sourced / access rights from Historical image collection by Bildagentur-online 10.4; Ramos, Giuseppe 111.1, 118.1; Sermulis, Edgars 106.2; Siedler, Stephan 10.1, 10.3; SOTK2011 20.1; Sowersby, Richard 40.1; STEKLO_KRD 73.2; Tack, Jochen 154.1; TorontoNews 88.2; Universal Images Group North America LLC 10.8; vivacity.tv 10.10; volkerpreusser 73.1; Wall, David 42.1; Wavebreakmedia Ltd FUS1811 68.3; Werner, Jannis 65.1; Westend61 GmbH 97.3; Wheatley, Michael 88.1; Zoonar GmbH 10.6, 27.1, 158.1. |Alamy Stock Photo (RMB), Abingdon/Oxfordshire: agefotostock 29.5; Ben-Ari, Rafael 12.2; Bildagentur-online/Schoening 39.1; Black, Ruth 32.1; Cavoretto, Stefano 68.2; clivestock 144.2; Crossick, Matt 76.1; Cruciatti, Piero 54.1; Daemmrich, Bob 139.2; Demidova, Ekaterina 68.1; DPK-Photo 30.2; du Feu, Geoff 52.2; Ekstrand, Jim 56.1; eldar nurkovic 103.1; Gekko Studios 12.4; Gino's Premium Images 102.6; Hasenkopf, Juergen 23.1; Imagebroker 23.3; imageBROKER 32.2; Ison, Chris 23.2; Jeffrey Isaac Greenberg 17+ 7.1; Jon Arnold Images Ltd 13.4, 24.1; L.S. Sandiford 143.1; Maskot 68.4; Michael, Andrew 241.2; Neelon(misc),

Appendix

ACKNOWLEDGEMENTS

Michael 144.1; Oeland, Ingo 12.1; Outback Australia 26.2; parkerphotography 52.3; Pearsall, Chris 62.1; Prisma by Dukas Presseagentur GmbH 13.1; public domain sourced / access rights from History and Art Collection 35.1; public domain sourced / access rights from Lakeview Images 18.1; Quayle, Paul 50.3; robertharding 29.4; Tetra Images 53.1; travellinglight 30.1; uknip 100.2; Urban Napflin 32.3; Wall, David 29.1; Wiskerke, Wim 241.1; ZUMA Press, Inc. 31.1. |Buccellato, Steve, Los Angeles: 126.1, 126.2, 127.1, 129.1, 131.1, 132.1, 135.1, 137.1, 138.1, 139.1. |CartoonStock.com, Bath: 64.1; Agarwal, Sunil 99.1; www.CartoonStock.com/Hardin, Patrick 22.2. |Creative Listening, Newick: 52.1, 58.1, 58.2, 61.1, 61.2, 143.2. |DESERT PEA MEDIA, Bathurst, NSW: 21.2. |Domke, Franz-Josef, Wunstorf: 3.1, 30.3, 41.1, 258.1, 259.1. |Donnelly, Karen, Brighton: 14.1, 14.2, 16.1, 16.2, 16.3, 16.4, 28.1, 28.2, 28.3, 29.2, 29.3, 29.6, 42.2, 51.1, 51.2, 51.3, 51.4, 70.1, 70.2, 89.4, 92.1, 92.2, 92.3, 94.1, 102.5, 142.1, 314.1, 314.2, 314.3. |fotolia.com, New York: cevahir87 10.7; totajla 5.1, 38.1. |Getty Images, München: Maskot 63.1, 63.2, 74.1, 74.2. |Hoth, Katharina, Erfurt: 99.2, 109.1. |iStockphoto.com, Calgary: AzmanJaka 62.4; Carillet, Joel 68.5; Damocean 26.3; darenwoodward 92.4; davidf 11.3; duncan1890 22.1; FatCamera 10.13; fcscafeine 146.1; ferrantraite 88.4; HRAUN 10.11; Irina_Strelnikova 140.1; kate_sept2004 116.1; kokkai 13.2; mgkaya 77.1; Moore Media 90.3; MStudioImages 90.2; Patil, Nikhil 11.4; pawel.gaul 66.1; PhotoTalk 10.12; RoBeDeRo 52.4; SDI Productions 11.2; VectorStory 106.1; ViewApart 100.1; xavierarnau 33.2. |Oxford Designers and Illustrators, Oxford: 141.2, 145.1. |Picture-Alliance GmbH, Frankfurt a.M.: Alan_Porritt 21.1. |Shutterstock.com, New York: Apolinarias 20.2, 36.1; Bogdan, Serban 13.3; delcarmat 76.2; Dragon Images 102.4; Franzi 89.3; James, Alexander S 26.1; Le Moal, Olivier 55.1; marekuliasz 50.1; Miceking 10.5; nisargmediaproductions 89.1; pixelheadphoto digitalskillet 89.2; Ragelis, Girts 62.3; Rashad Ashur76 66.2; Rawpixel.com 89.5; Urbanek, Michal 88.3; Wildfoto 12.3; YAKOBCHUK VIACHESLAV 104.1. |stock.adobe.com, Dublin: Brivio, Marco 24.2; Daisy Daisy 110.1; Idanupong 102.3; LIGHTFIELD STUDIOS 90.1; moodboard 62.2; motortion 110.2; Palmer, Matt 33.1; Race, Dan 5.2; suwatwongkham 50.2; ©AntonioDiaz 141.1. |Williamson, Pete, Kent, Southorough, Tunbridge Wells: 46.1, 47.1, 47.2, 48.1, 48.2, 49.1, 49.2, 84.1, 85.1, 86.1, 86.2, 87.1, 87.2, 87.3, 122.1, 123.1, 123.2, 125.1.

Audio credits

Dialogues and words and phrases produced by Anne Rosenfeld for RBA Productions (rbaproductions.co.uk). Recording engineer Mark Smith.

Track 18: "First Nation". Text (OT): Hirst, Robert George / Tasman, Keith. © SFM Publishing Pty Ltd/Sony/ATV Music Publishing (Germany) GmbH, Berlin

Track 19: "Brown Girl". Text (OT): Silverman, Jeffrey Scott / d'Annunzio, Vincent John jr / Patel, Aaradhna Jayantilal. © Jeffrey Scott Productions LLC/Vincent John Music/Kobalt Music Publishing/Printrechte Hal Leonard Europe GmbH

Video credits

Video 2: produced by Anne Rosenfeld for RBA Productions, Brighton (rbaproductions.co.uk). Editor: David Rafique

Video 2 (picture credits): structuresxx / iStockphoto.com; Classic Image / Alamy Stock Photo; Rainbird, John / Alamy Stock Photo; Lake Erie Maps and Prints / Alamy Stock Photo; geogphotos / Alamy Stock Photo; Hellier, Chris / Alamy Stock Photo; Swanepoel, Johan / Alamy Stock Photo; simonbradfield / iStockphoto.com; zetter / iStockphoto.com; slowmotiongli / iStockphoto.com; Aristine / iStockphoto.com; Griffiths, Ken / Alamy Stock Photo; Fare, Andrew / Alamy Stock Photo; Totajla / iStockphoto.com; DoraDalton / iStockphoto.com; FiledIMAGE / iStockphoto.com; Crux, John / Alamy Stock Photo; DPK-Photo / Alamy Stock Photo

Video 6 – 11: produced by James Vyner and Luke Vyner for Creative Listening, London (www.creativelistening.co.uk)

Video 12: provided courtesy of My Genderation, www.mygenderation.com

Medienbildung

Folgende **Kompetenzen** werden in *On Track 5* abgedeckt:

1.	**Suchen, Verarbeiten und Aufbewahren**	
1.1	Suchen und Filtern	S. 15; S. 21; S. 22/23; S. 25; S. 27; S. 32/33; S. 69; S. 107; S. 139
1.2	Auswerten und Bewerten	S. 11; S. 17; S. 18/19; S. 21; S. 22/23; S. 27; S. 31; S. 32/33; S. 56/57; S. 67; S. 90/91; S. 94; S. 98/99; S. 102; S. 104 – 107; S. 108/109; S. 138/139
1.3	Speichern und Abrufen	S. 22/23; S. 27; S. 31; S. 32/33; S. 55; S. 61; S. 65; S: 98/99; S. 103; S. 108/109
2.	**Kommunizieren und Kooperieren**	
2.1	Interagieren	S. 27; S. 29; S. 31; S. 32/33; S. 60/61; S. 65; S. 70/71; S. 92; S. 97; S. 103; S. 105; S. 106/107
2.2	Teilen	S. 15; S. 19; S. 23; S. 27; S. 29; S. 65; S. 92; 106/107
2.3	Zusammenarbeiten	S. 15; S. 22/23; S. 27; S. 29; S. 32/33; S. 65; S. 69; S. 92; S. 106/107
2.4	Umgangsregeln kennen und einhalten (Netiquette)	S. 58/59; S. 60/61; S. 70/71; S. 106/107
2.5	An der Gesellschaft aktiv teilhaben	S. 10/11; S. 26/27; S. 56 – 59; S. 60/61; S. 62 – 69; S. 70/71; S. 96/97; S. 104 – 107
3.	**Produzieren und Präsentieren**	
3.1	Entwickeln und Produzieren	S. 22/23; S. 25; S. 27; S. 29; S. 32/33; S. 52; S. 65; S. 69; S. 92/93; S. 97; S. 103; S. 106/107
3.2	Weiterverarbeiten und Integrieren	S. 15; S. 22/23; S. 25; S. 27; S. 31; S. 32/33; S. 65; S. 69; S. 92; S. 97
3.3	Rechtliche Vorgaben beachten	S. 22/23; S. 32/33; S. 104 – 107
4.	**Schützen und sicher agieren**	
4.1	Sicher in digitalen Umgebungen agieren	S. 16; S. 31; S. 32/33; S. 97; S. 104 – 107
4.2	Persönliche Daten und Privatsphäre schützen	S. 16; S. 31; S. 32/33; S. 97; S. 104 – 107
4.3	Gesundheit schützen	S. 102 – 103
4.4	Natur und Umwelt schützen	S. 24 – 27; S. 103
5.	**Problemlösen und Handeln**	
5.1	Technische Probleme lösen	S. 16; S. 104 – 107
5.2	Werkzeuge bedarfsgerecht einsetzen	S. 15; S. 21; S. 22/23; S. 25; S. 29; S. 32/33; S. 65; S. 69; S. 92; S. 103; S. 106/107
5.3	Eigene Defizite ermitteln und nach Lösungen suchen	S. 104 – 107
5.4	Digitale Werkzeuge und Medien zum Lernen, Arbeiten und Problemlösen nutzen	S. 15; S. 21; S. 22/23; S. 25; S. 29; S. 32/33; S. 65; S. 69; S. 92; S 103; S. 106/107
5.5	Algorithmen erkennen und formulieren	S. 104 – 107
6.	**Analysieren und Reflektieren**	
6.1	Medien analysieren und bewerten	S. 22/23; S. 32/33; S. 98/99; S. 104 – 107; S. 108/109
6.2	Medien in der digitalen Welt verstehen und reflektieren	S. 22/23; S. 32/33; S. 98/99; S. 104 – 107; S. 108/109

Classroom phrases

What your teacher can say
Can anyone remember … from our last session?
Who would like to explain?
What did you find out?
Don't interrupt each other.
Remember the advice about …
Can you think of any other tips?
Check your spelling in the dictionary.
Read and comment on each other's texts.
Compare your answers / solutions with a partner.
Make some notes about key points.
Give reasons for your opinion.
Read the text about … and be ready to talk about it in the next lesson.
Practise your talk at home or in front of your friends.

What you can say
What page are we on?
Can you write it on the board, please?
What does … mean?
What do you mean by …?
What's this in German / English?
Can you spell it, please?
Can you repeat the task, please?
I haven't finished the task yet.
I've already finished the task.
I've got something different.
Are we allowed to use our phones?
Can we do research on the internet?
Can we work with a partner / group?

Working with a partner / in a group / in class
Would you like to join us?
Let's go through our notes.
I'd like to make a suggestion.
Do you have a spare pen?
Can I borrow your book for a second?
Is there anything you would like to add?
I disagree. / I don't agree.
I agree (but …).
I see what you mean, but …
How do you fel about …?
That's a good point.
It's my turn / your turn.
You have a point, but …
Could I just say …
Sorry to interrupt …
Go ahead.
I'm sorry, what did you say?
When you say …, what exactly do you mean?
So what you're saying is …
What I mean is …
Just let me explain …
Whose turn is it?

Giving feedback
You did a great job.
I liked the part where you …
I had a feeling you really knew …
The visual aids were helpful.
The sound quality of your video is really clear.
I like the way you added …
What I really liked about your talk was that …
My favourite part was … because …
I think your presentation is good / interesting / funny because …
I like the way you used …
It really impressed me when you …
Can you say more about …, please?
My tip for you is to …
It would be better if you …
How about …?
Next time you should speak more clearly / loudly / slowly …
One suggestion would be …
Perhaps you should add …
Maybe you could include more information about …
You could also talk about …
I would like more descriptions of … / more information about … / more conversations between …

Media use	
Let's make a new document / slide.	Type the website address into the browser.
Copy / Insert the photo / text …	We need to refine our search.
Mark the text and copy it …	Let's read the information on the website …
Delete / Save the file.	Can you scroll up / down?
Let's share / post our blog / vlog online.	Click on the link.
We can drag and drop the files …	Let's watch the video.
Let's search for information online.	We should check the terms and conditions.
Let's go to the website.	We should bookmark our sources.

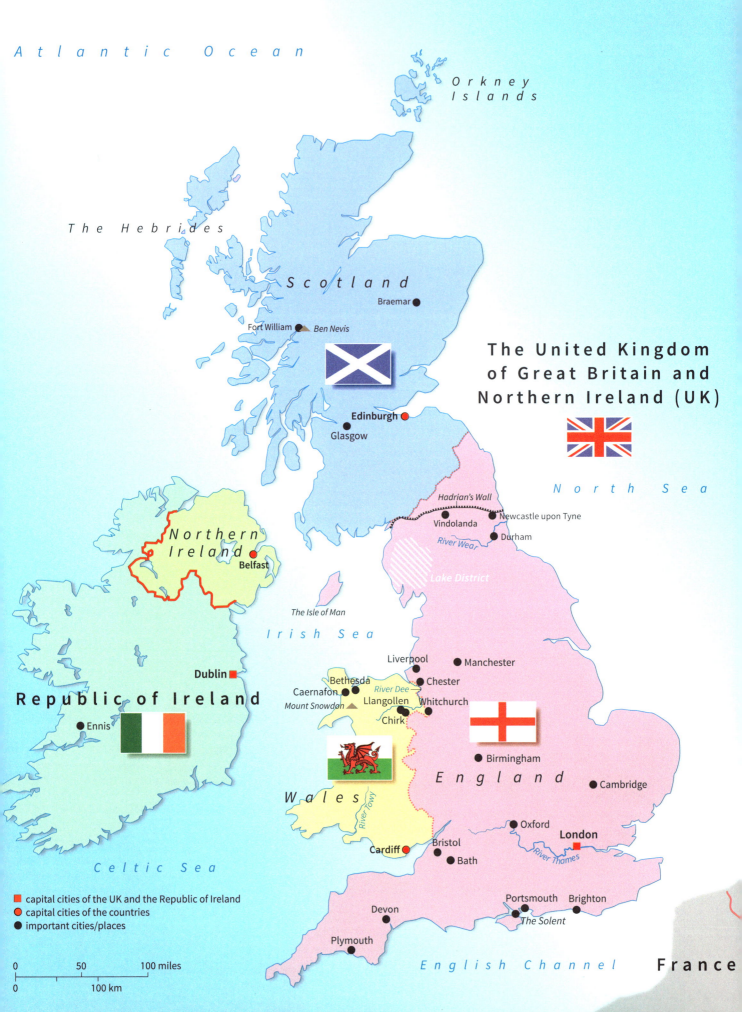